The Unabridged Journals of
SYLVIA PLATH

Sylvia Plath was born in 1932 in Massachusetts. She began
publishing poems and stories at a young age and by the
time she entered Smith College had won several poetry
prizes. She was a Fulbright Scholar in Cambridge,
England, and married British poet Ted Hughes in London
in 1956. The young couple moved to the States, where
Plath became an instructor at Smith College. Later, they
moved back to England, where Plath continued writing
poetry and wrote her novel, *The Bell Jar,* which was first
published under the pseudonym Victoria Lucas in England
in 1963. On February 11, 1963, Plath committed suicide.
Her *Collected Poems,* published posthumously in 1981,
won the Pulitzer Prize.

ABOUT THE EDITOR

Karen V. Kukil is Associate Curator of Rare Books at
Smith College, where she supervises scholarly use of the
Sylvia Plath Collection.

The Unabridged Journals of
SYLVIA PLATH
1950–1962

TRANSCRIBED

FROM THE ORIGINAL MANUSCRIPTS

AT SMITH COLLEGE

EDITED BY KAREN V. KUKIL

ANCHOR BOOKS

A Division of Random House, Inc.

New York

FIRST ANCHOR BOOKS EDITION, OCTOBER 2000

Library of Congress Cataloging-in-Publication Data
Plath, Sylvia.
[Journals of Sylvia Plath, 1950–1962]
The unabridged journals of Sylvia Plath, 1950–1962 / edited by
Karen V. Kukil.—1st Anchor Books ed.
p.   cm.
"Transcribed from the original manuscripts at Smith College."
Originally published: Journals of Sylvia Plath, 1950–1962. London :
Faber and Faber, 2000.
Include bibliographical references and index.
ISBN 0-385-72025-4
1. Plath, Sylvia—Diaries.   2. Poets, American—20th century—Diaries.
I. Kukil, Karen V.
II. Title.
PS3566.L27 Z469   2000
818'.5403—dc21
[B]

00-042024

www.anchorbooks.com

CONTENTS

APPENDICES

LIST OF ILLUSTRATIONS

PREFACE

Sylvia Plath speaks for herself in this unabridged edition of her journals. She began keeping diaries and journals at the age of eleven and continued this practice until her death at the age of thirty. It is her adult journals from 1950 to 1962 that comprise this edition. The text is an exact transcription of twenty-three original manuscripts in the Sylvia Plath Collection at Smith College in Northampton, Massachusetts. This collection of handwritten volumes and typed sheets documents Plath's student years at Smith College and Newnham College, Cambridge, her marriage to Ted Hughes, and two years of teaching and writing in New England. A few journal fragments from 1960 to 1962 complete the edition.

In 1981 when Smith College acquired all the manuscripts remaining in the possession of the Plath Estate in England, two of the journals in the archive were sealed by Ted Hughes until February 11, 2013. Plath's professional career as an instructor of English at Smith College, followed by a year as a writer in Boston, and her private therapy sessions with Ruth Beuscher are the focus of the two sealed journals written between August 1957 and November 1959. Both journals were unsealed by Ted Hughes shortly before his death in 1998 and are included in this edition.

The two bound journals that Plath wrote during the last three years of her life are not included in this publication. One of the journals 'disappeared', according to Ted Hughes in his foreword to Frances McCullough's edition of *The Journals of Sylvia Plath* (New York: Dial Press, 1982); it is still missing. The second 'maroon-backed ledger', which contained entries to within three days of Plath's suicide, was destroyed by Hughes.

The goal of this new edition of Sylvia Plath's journals is to present a complete and historically accurate text. The transcription of the manuscripts at Smith College is as faithful to the author's originals as possible. Plath's final revisions are preserved and her substantive deletions and corrections are discussed in the notes. Plath's spelling, capitalization, punctuation, and grammar, as well as her errors, have been carefully transcribed and are presented without editorial comment. Every nuance of the physical journals has been preserved, including Plath's practice of underlining certain words and passages in her journals. Original layout and page breaks, however, are not duplicated. Detailed descriptions of the physical features of the journals are contained in the notes.

The text is complete, except for a few names that have been shortened to initials and dashes to protect the privacy of living individuals. In two places, six sentences have been omitted (for a total of twelve omitted sentences). Ellipses that appear in the text were made by Sylvia Plath.

Eight main journals, written between 1950 and 1959, comprise the central narrative of this edition and are arranged separately in chronological order. Fifteen journal fragments and notebooks, written between 1951 and 1962, are arranged chronologically as appendices. Since a few journals and notebooks were kept simultaneously, there is some overlap. General biographical information is presented on the appropriate half-title for each of the eight principal journals. A few editorial notes, contained within square brackets and clearly marked 'ed.', direct the reader to relevant journal fragments in the appendices. These are the only extraneous notes that appear within the journals. Every effort has been made in this edition to give the reader direct access to Sylvia Plath's actual words without interruption or interpretation.

Factual notes have been provided at the end of the journals and appendices in order to preserve the flow of the text. Significant places, family, friends, and professional contacts are identified at their first mention. Annotations, textual variants, and specific physical characteristics of the journals are described, particularly when this information affects the meaning of the text. Marginalia such as exclamation points and tick marks are not recorded. The presence of a note is indicated by a superscript n after the term to be identified or described. Notes for each separate journal and appendix are keyed to appropriate page numbers. References to additional manuscript at Smith College and at other institutions are included in the notes when appropriate.

An extensive index completes the publication and serves as an additional reference guide.

Karen V. Kukil

PUBLISHER'S NOTE

In the years before his death, Ted Hughes was working towards the publication of Sylvia Plath's unabridged *Journals* both in Britain and America. In 1997 he passed the responsibility for the project to his children, Frieda and Nicholas, who had already held the copyright for some time. To this end, he authorized the opening of the journals that he had previously sealed.

Frieda and Nicholas entrusted the task of editing the book to Karen Kukil, Associate Curator of Rare Books at Smith College, Massachusetts. The project continued under the guidance of Ted Hughes until his death in October 1998, and was completed in December 1999.

These journals contain Sylvia Plath's opinions and not those of the publisher. Readers should keep in mind the colloquial meanings of words appropriate to the time period of the journals. For example, Plath used the word 'queer' to denote an eccentric or suspicious person, according to her annotated dictionary, and not a homosexual.

The Unabridged Journals of
SYLVIA PLATH

JOURNAL

July 1950 – July 1953

Sylvia Plath was born on 27 October 1932 at 2:10 p.m. in Boston, Massachusetts, to Otto and Aurelia Schober Plath. Her brother Warren was born on 27 April 1935. They lived at 24 Prince Street, Jamaica Plain, until 1936 when the family moved to 92 Johnson Avenue, Winthrop, Massachusetts, to be near Aurelia Plath's parents. Otto Plath died on 5 November 1940 from complications of diabetes. In 1942, Sylvia Plath moved to 26 Elmwood Road, Wellesley, Massachusetts, with her mother, brother, and maternal grandparents.

Sylvia Plath began writing the following journal during the summer of 1950 before leaving home for college in Northampton, Massachusetts. Some of the entries are excerpts from letters to friends. Plath matriculated with the class of 1954 at Smith College, but did not graduate until June 1955 because of the semester she missed during the fall of 1953.

THIS BOOK BELONGS TO

Sylvia Plath

Wellesley, Massachusetts

CLASS OF _1954_

SMITH COLLEGE

HARVARD COOPERATIVE SOCIETY
CAMBRIDGE, MASS.

legitimate cause + effect. Editor of SMITH
Review This morning; the one office on campus
I coveted; back to balance about psychology;
prospect of Harvard Summer School — holiday
tables under the trees. New York and Ray
(and neurology + brilliance) This weekend!
New Haven and Mike (sun, beach, strong good
love) The next.

Tonight, spring, plural, fertile, offering up
clean green leaf whorls to a soft moon
covered with fuzz-fractured clouds, and
god, The listening to auden read in Drew's
front livingroom, and Vind questioning,
darting scintillant wit. My Plato! pedestrian
I! And Drew, (exuberant exquisitely frail
intelligent Elizabeth) saying, "Now That is
really difficult."

Auden tossing his big head back with a
twist of wide ugly grinning lips, his sandy
hair, his coarse tweedy brown jacket, his
burlap-textured voice and The mackling
brilliant utterances — The naughty mischievous
boy genius, and The inconsistent white
hairless skin of his legs, and The short puffy
stubbed fingers — and The carpet slippers —
been to drink, and smoked lucky strikes in

Sylvia Plath

Aubade
by Louis Macneice

Having bitten on life like a sharp apple
Or, playing it like a fish, been happy,

Having felt with fingers that the sky is blue
What have we after that to look forward to?

Not the twilight of the gods but a precise dawn
Of sallow and grey bricks, and newsboys crying war.

"We only begin to live when we conceive life as tragedy . . ."
W. B. Yeats

"Hold to the now, the here, through which all future plunges to the past . . ."
James Joyce

1.

July 1950 – I may never be happy, but tonight I am content. Nothing more than an empty house, the warm hazy weariness from a day spent setting strawberry runners in the sun, a glass of cool sweet milk, and a shallow dish of blueberries bathed in cream. Now I know how people can live without books, without college. When one is so tired at the end of a day one must sleep, and at the next dawn there are more strawberry runners to set, and so one goes on living, near the earth. At times like this I'd call myself a fool to ask for more . . .

. . .

2.

Ilo″ asked me today in the strawberry field, "Do you like the Renaissance painters? Raphael and Michelangelo? I copied some of Michelangelo once. And what do you think of Picasso . . . These painters who make a circle and a little board going down for a leg?" We worked side by side in the rows, and he would be quiet for a while, then suddenly burst out with conversation, speaking with his thick German accent. He straightened up, his tan, intelligent face crinkling up with laughter. His chunky, muscular body was bronzed, and his blonde hair tucked up under a white handkerchief around his head. He said, "You like Frank Sinatra? So sendimental, so romandic, so moonlight night, Ja?"

. . .

3.

– A sudden slant of bluish light across the floor of a vacant room. And I knew it was not the streetlight, but the moon. What is more wonderful than to be a virgin, clean and sound and young, on such a night? . . . (being raped.)″

. . .

4.

– Tonight was awful. It was the combination of everything. Of the play "Goodbye My Fancy," of wanting, in a juvenile way, to be, like the heroine, a reporter in the trenches, to be loved by a man who admired me, who understood me as much as I understood myself. And then there was Jack, who tried so hard to be nice, who was hurt when I said all he wanted was to make out. There was the dinner at the country club, the affluence of money everywhere. And then there was the record . . . the one so good for dancing. I forgot that it was the one until Louie Armstrong began to sing in a voice husky with regret, "I've flown around the world in a plane, settled revolutions in Spain, the North pole I have charted . . . still I can't get started with

you." Jack said: "Ever heard it before?" So I smiled, "Oh, yes." It was Bob."
That settled things for me - - - a crazy record, and it was our long talks, his
listening and understanding. And I knew I loved him.

. . .

5.
– Tonight I saw Mary. Jack and I were pushing out of the theater in a current
of people, and she was edging the other way in a dark blue jacket. I hardly
recognized her with her eyes downcast, her face made up. But beautiful.
"I've been looking all over for you," I said. "Mary. Call me, write me." She
smiled, a little like the Mary I used to know, and she was gone. I knew I
would never have a friend quite like her. So I went out in a white dress, a
white coat, with a rich boy. And I hated myself for my hypocrasy. I love
Mary. Betsy is nothing but fun; hysterical fun. Mary is me . . . what I would
be if I had been born of Italian parents on Linden Street." She is something
vital, an artist's model, life. She can be rude, undependable, and she is more
to me than all the pretty, well-to-do, artificial girls I could ever meet. Maybe
it's my ego. Maybe I crave someone who will never be my rival. But with her
I can be honest. She could be a prostitute, and I would not give a damn; I'll
never deny her as a friend . . .

. . .

6.
– Today is the first of August. It is hot, steamy and wet. It is raining. I am
tempted to write a poem. But I remember what it said on one rejection slip:
After a heavy rainfall, poems titled RAIN pour in from across the nation.

7.
– I love people. Everybody. I love them, I think, as a stamp collector loves
his collection. Every story, every incident, every bit of conversation is raw
material for me. My love's not impersonal yet not wholly subjective either. I
would like to be everyone, a cripple, a dying man, a whore, and then come
back to write about my thoughts, my emotions, as that person. But I am not
omniscient. I have to live my life, and it is the only one I'll ever have. And
you cannot regard your own life with objective curiosity all the time . . .

. . .

8.
– With me, the present is forever, and forever is always shifting, flowing,
melting. This second is life. And when it is gone it is dead. But you can't
start over with each new second. You have to judge by what is dead. It's
like quicksand . . . hopeless from the start. A story, a picture, can renew

sensation a little, but not enough, not enough. Nothing is real except the present, and already, I feel the weight of centuries smothering me. Some girl a hundred years ago once lived as I do. And she is dead. I am the present, but I know I, too, will pass. The high moment, the burning flash, come and are gone, continuous quicksand. And I don't want to die.

. . .

9.

– Some things are hard to write about. After something happens to you, you go to write it down, and either you over dramatize it or underplay it, exaggerate the wrong parts or ignore the important ones. At any rate, you never write it quite the way you want to. I've just got to put down what happened to me this afternoon. I can't tell mother;" not yet, anyway. She was in my room when I came home, fussing with clothes, and she didn't even sense that something had happened. She just kept scolding and chattering on and on. So I couldn't stop her and tell her. No matter how it comes out, I have to write it.

It rained all afternoon at the farm," and I was cold and wet, my hair under a silk print kerchief, my red ski jacket over my sweatshirt. I had worked hard on beans all afternoon and picked over three bushels. Since it was five o'clock, people were leaving, and I was waiting beside the cars for my ride home. Kathy had just come up, and as she got on her bike she called, "Here comes Ilo."

I looked, and sure enough, there he was, coming up the road in his old khaki shirt with his familiar white handkerchief tied around his head. I was on conversational terms with him since that day we worked together in the strawberry field. He had given me a pen and ink sketch of the farm, drawn with detail and assurance. Now he was working on a sketch of one of the boys.

So I called, "Have you finished John's picture?"

"Oh, ya, ya," he smiled. "Come and see. Your last chance." He had promised to show it to me when he was done, so I ran out and got in step with him on his way to the barn. That's where he lives.

On the way, we passed Mary Coffee. I felt her looking at me rather strangely. Somehow I couldn't meet her eyes.

"Hullo, Mary," Ilo said.

"Hello, Ilo," Mary said in an oddly colorless voice.

We walked by Ginny, Sally, and a crowd of kids keeping dry in the tractor shed. A roar went up as we passed. A singsong, "Oh, Sylvia." My cheeks burned.

"Why do they have to tease me?" I asked. Ilo just laughed. He was walking very fast.

"We're going home in a little while," Milton yelled from the washroom.

I nodded and kept walking, looking at the ground. Then we were at the barn, a huge place, a giant high ceilinged room smelling of horses and damp hay. It was dim inside; I thought I saw the figure of a person on the other side of the stalls, but I couldn't be sure. Without saying a word, Ilo had begun to mount a narrow flight of wooden stairs.

"You live up there? All these stairs?"

He kept walking up, so I followed him, hesitating at the top.

"Come in, come in," he said, opening a door. The picture was there, in his room. I walked over the threshold. It was a narrow place with two windows, a table full of drawing things, and a cot, covered with a dark blanket. Oranges and milk were set out on a table with a radio.

"Here," he held out the picture. It was a fine pencil sketch of John's head.

"Why, how do you do it? With the side of the pencil?"

It seemed of no significance then, but now I remember how Ilo had shut the door, had turned on the radio so that music came out.

He talked very fast, showing me a pencil. "See, here the lead comes out, any size." I was very conscious of his nearness. His blue eyes were startlingly close, looking at me boldly, with flecks of laughter in them.

"I really have to go. They will be waiting. The picture was lovely."

Smiling, he was between me and the door. A motion. His hand closed around my arm. And suddenly his mouth was on mine, hard, vehement, his tongue darting between my lips, his arms like iron around me.

"Ilo, Ilo!" I don't know whether I screamed or whispered, struggling to break free, my hands striking wildly, futilely against his great strength. At last he let me go, and stood back. I held my hand against my mouth, warm and bruised from his kiss. He looked at me quizzically, with something like surprised amusement as he saw that I was crying, frightened. No one ever kissed me that way before, and I stood there, flooded with longing, electric, shivering.

"Why, why," he made sympathetic, depreciating little noises. "I get you some water."

He poured me out a glass, and I drank it. He opened the door, and I stumbled blindly downstairs, past Maybelle and Robert, the little colored children, who called my name in the corrupted way kids have of pronouncing things. Past Mary Lou, their mother, who stood there, a silent, dark presence.

And I was outdoors. A truck was going by. Coming from behind the barn. In it was Bernie - - - the horrible, short, muscular boy from the washroom. His eyes glittered with malicious delight, and he drove fast, so I could not catch up with him. Had he been in the barn? Had he seen Ilo shut the door, seen me come out? I think he must have.

I walked up past the washroom to the cars. Bernie yelled out, "Why are you crying?" I wasn't crying. Kenny and Freddy came by on the tractor. A group of boys, going home, looked at me with a light flickering somewhere in their eyes. "Did he kiss you?" one asked, with a knowing smile.

I felt sick. I couldn't have spoken if someone had talked to me. My voice was stuck in my throat, thick and furry.

Mr. Tompkins came up to the pump to watch Kenny and Freddy run the old stock car. They were nice, but they knew. They all must know.

"There's cutie pie," Kenny said.

"Cutie pie and angel face." Freddy said.

So I stood there, arms folded, staring at the whirring engine, smiling as if I was all right, as if nothing had happened.

Milton sat in the rumble seat with me going home. David drove, and Andy was in front. They all looked at me with that dancing light in their eyes. David said in a stiff, strained voice, "Everybody in the washroom was watching you go into the barn and making wisecracks."

Milton asked about the picture. We talked a little about art and drawing. They were all so nice. I think they may have been relieved at my narrow escape; they may have expected me to cry. They knew, though, they knew.

So I'm home. And tomorrow I have to face the whole damn farm. Good Lord, It might have happened in a dream. Now I can almost believe it did. But tomorrow my name will be on the tip of every tongue. I wish I could be smart, or flip, but I'm too scared. If only he hadn't kissed me. I'll have to lie and say he didn't. But they know. They all know. And what am I against so many . . .?

. . .

10.

– This morning I had my two left wisdom teeth out. At 9 A.M. I walked into the dentist's office. Quickly, with a heavy sense of impending doom, I sat in the chair after a rapid, furtive glance around the room for any obvious instruments of torture such as a pneumatic drill or a gas mask. No such thing. The doctor pinned the bib around my neck; I was just about prepared for him to stick an apple in my mouth and strew sprigs of parsley on my head. But no. All he did was ask, "Gas or novacaine?" (Gas or novacaine.

understand, and then this.) "You know," Emile looked at me, "we ought to sit down." I shook my head. "No?" he said. "How about some water, then. Feel all right?" (Feel all right. Oh, yes. Yes, thank you.) He steered me out to the kitchen, cool, smelling of linoleum, with the sound of the rain falling outside. I sat and sipped the water he brought me, while he stood looking down, his features strange in the half-light. I put the glass down. "That was quick," he said. "Should I have taken longer?" I stood up and his face moved in, his arms about me. After a while I pushed him away. "The rain's rather nice. It makes you feel good inside, elemental, just to listen." I was backed against the sink; Emile was close, warm, his eyes glittering, his mouth sensuous and lovely. "You," I said deliberately, "don't give a damn about me except physically." Any boy would deny that; any gallant boy; any gallant lier. But Emile shook me, his voice was urgent, "You know, you shouldn't have said that. You know? You know? The truth always hurts." (Even clichés can come in handy.) He grinned, "Don't be bitter; I'm not. Come away from the sink, and watch." He stepped back, drawing me toward him, slapping my stomach away, he kissed me long and sweetly. At last he let go. "There," he said with a quiet smile. "The truth doesn't always hurt, does it?" And so we left. It was pouring rain. In the car he put his arm around me, his head against mine, and we watched the streetlights coming at us, blurred and fluid in the watery dark. As we ran up the walk in the rain, as he came in and had a drink of water, as he kissed me goodnight, I knew that something in me wanted him, for what I'm not sure: He drinks, he smokes, he's Catholic, he runs around with one girl after another, and yet . . . I wanted him. "I don't have to tell you it's been nice," I said at the door. "It's been marvelous," he smiled. "I'll call you. Take care." And he was gone. So the rain comes down hard outside my room, and like Eddie Cohen,[n] I say, ". . . fifteen thousand years - - - of what? We're still nothing but animals." Somewhere, in his room, Emile lies, about to sleep, listening to the rain. God only knows what <u>he's</u> thinking.

12.

. . .

– There are times when a feeling of expectancy comes to me, as if something is there, beneath the surface of my understanding, waiting for me to grasp it. It is the same tantalizing sensation when you almost remember a name, but don't quite reach it. I can feel it when I think of human beings, of the hints of evolution suggested by the removal of wisdom teeth, the narrowing of the jaw no longer needed to chew such roughage as it was accustomed to; the gradual disappearance of hair from the human body; the adjustment of the human eye to the fine print, the swift, colored motion of the twentieth century. The feeling comes, vague and nebulous, when I consider the prolonged adolescence of our species; the rites of birth, marriage and death; all the primitive, barbaric ceremonies streamlined to modern times. Almost, I think, the unreasoning, bestial purity was best. Oh, something is there, waiting for me. Perhaps someday the revelation will burst in upon me and I will see the other side of this monumental grotesque joke. And then I'll laugh. And then I'll know what life is. –

. . .

13.

– Tonight I wanted to step outside for a few moments before going to bed; it was so snug and stale-aired in the house. I was in my pajamas, my freshly washed hair up on curlers. So I tried to open the front door. The lock snapped as I turned it; I tried the handle. The door wouldn't open. Annoyed, I turned the handle the other way. No response. I twisted the lock; there were only four possible combinations of handle and lock positions, and still the door stuck, white, blank and enigmatic. I glanced up. Through the glass square, high in the door, I saw a block of sky, pierced by the sharp black points of the pines across the street. And there was the moon, almost full, luminous and yellow, behind the trees. I felt suddenly breathless, stifled. I was trapped, with the tantalizing little square of night above me, and the warm, feminine atmosphere of the house enveloping me in its thick, feathery smothering embrace. –

. . .

14.

– This morning I am at low ebb. I did not sleep well last night, waking, tossing, and dreaming sordid, incoherent little dreams. I awoke, my head heavy, feeling as if I had just emerged from a swim in a pool of warm polluted water. My skin was greasy, my hair stiff, oily, and my hands as if I had touched something slimy and unclean. The thick August air does not help. I sit here lumpishly, an ache at the back of my neck. I feel that even if I washed myself all day in cold clear water, I could not rinse the sticky, untidy film away; nor could I rid my mouth of the furry unpleasant taste of unbrushed teeth. –

. . .

15.

– Tonight, for a moment, all was at peace inside. I came out of the house-across-the-street a little before twelve, sick with unfulfilled longing, alone, self-reviling. And there, miraculously was the August night. It had just rained, and the air was thick with warm damp and fog. The moon, full, pregnant with light, showed strangely from behind the small frequent clouds, poised like a picture puzzle that had been broken, with light in back, outlining each piece. There seemed to be no wind, but the leaves of the trees stirred, restless, and the water fell from them in great drops on the pavement, with a sound like that of people walking down the street. There was the peculiar smell of mould, dead leaves, decay, in the air. The two lights over the front steps were haloed with a hazy nimbus of mist, and strange insects fluttered up against the screen, fragile, wing-thin and blinded, dazed, numbed by the brilliance. Lightning, heat lightning flicked off and on, as if some stage hand were toying with the light switch. Two crickets, deep in the cracks in the granite steps, sang a sweet, haunting-thin trill. And because it was my home, I loved them. The air flowed about me like thick molasses, and the shadows from the moon and street lamp split like schizophrenic blue phantoms, grotesque and faintly repetitious. –

· · ·

16.

– Upstairs, in the bright, white, sterile cubicle of the bathroom, smelling of warm flesh and toothpaste, I bent over the washbowl in unthinking ritual, washing the proscribed areas, worshipping the glittering chromium, the light that clattered back and forth, brittle, blinding, from the faucets. Hot and cold; cleanliness coming in smooth scented green bars; hairs in thin, penciled lines, curving on the white enamel; the colored prescriptions, the hard, glassed-in jars, the bottles that can cure the symptoms of a cold or send you to sleep within an hour. And then to bed, in the same potentially fertile air, scented of lavendar, lace curtains and the warm feline odor like musk, waiting to assimilate you - - - everywhere the pallid waiting. And you are the moving epitome of all this. Of you, by you, for you. God, is this all it is, the ricocheting down the corridor of laughter and tears? Of self-worship and self-loathing? Of glory and disgust? –

· · ·

17.

– A little thing, like children putting flowers in my hair, can fill up the widening cracks in my self-assurance like soothing lanolin. I was sitting out on the steps today, uneasy with fear and discontent. Peter," (the little boy-across-the-street) with the pointed pale face, the grave blue eyes and the slow fragile smile came bringing his adorable sister Libby of the flaxen braids and

17

the firm, lyrically-formed child-body. They stood shyly for a little, and then Peter picked a white petunia and put it in my hair. Thus began an enchanting game, where I sat very still, while Libby ran to and fro gathering petunias, and Peter stood by my side, arranging the blossoms. I closed my eyes to feel more keenly the lovely delicate-child-hands, gently tucking flower after flower into my curls. "And now a white one," the lisp was soft and tender. Pink, crimson, scarlet, white . . . the faint pungent odor of the petunias was hushed and sweet. And all my hurts were smoothed away. Something about the frank, guileless blue eyes, the beautiful young bodies, the brief scent of the dying flowers smote me like the clean quick cut of a knife. And the blood of love welled up in my heart with a slow pain.

. . .

18.

– Now I'll never see him again, and maybe it's a good thing. He walked out of my life last night for once and for all. I know with sickening certainty that it's the end. There were just those two dates we had, and the time he came over with the boys, and tonight. Yet I liked him too much - - - way too much, and I ripped him out of my heart so it wouldn't get to hurt me more than it did. Oh, he's magnetic, he's charming; you could fall into his eyes. Let's face it: his sex appeal was unbearably strong. I wanted to know him - - - the thoughts, the ideas behind the handsome, confident, wise-cracking mask. "I've changed," he told me. "You would have liked me three years ago. Now I'm a wiseguy." We sat together for a few hours on the porch, talking, and staring at nothing. Then the friction increased, centered. His nearness was electric in itself. "Can't you see," he said. "I want to kiss you." So he kissed me, hungrily, his eyes shut, his hand warm, curved burning into my stom-ach. "I wish I hated you," I said. "Why did you come?" "Why? I wanted your company. Alby and Pete were going to the ball game, and I couldn't see that. Warrie and Jerry were going drinking; couldn't see that either." It was past eleven; I walked to the door with him and stepped outside into the cool August night. "Come here," he said. "I'll whisper something: I like you, but not too much. I don't want to like anybody too much." Then it hit me and I just blurted, "I like people too much or not at all. I've got to go down deep, to fall into people, to really know them." He was definite, "Nobody knows me." So that was it; the end. "Goodbye for good, then," I said. He looked hard at me, a smile twisting his mouth, "You lucky kid; you don't know how lucky you are." I was crying quietly, my face contorted. "Stop it!" The words came like knife thrusts, and then gentleness, "In case I don't see you, have a nice time at Smith." "Have a hell of a nice life," I said. And he walked off down the path with his jaunty, independent stride. And I stood there where he left me, tremulous with love and longing, weeping in the dark. That night it was hard to get to sleep.

. . .

19.

– Today the doorbell rang; it was little Peter. So I came out and sat on the front steps with him. I could sit by the hour listening to his prattling. He was jealous of Bob, asking in a small tight voice, "Who was that boy over your house? Who does he like best, Warren" or you?" And then, "He called me pipsqueak. If you had a baby would you call him pipsqueak?" "I'm not tan," he continued. "It's dirt. I don't like the looks of dirt, but I like the feel of it. Clean doesn't feel good because you're all wet." He played with Warren. I went up to my room, and I heard a commotion outside. Peter had climbed to the level of the window in the little maple tree and was shaking the leaves down. –

. . .

20.

From a letter to Ed – "Your letter came just now . . . The one about your walk in the city, about war. You don't know quite what it did to me. My mental fear, which can be at times forced into the background, reared up and caught me in the pit of my stomach; it became a physical nausea which wouldn't let me eat breakfast.

Let's face it: I'm scared, scared and frozen. First, I guess, I'm afraid for myself . . . the old primitive urge for survival. It's getting so I live every moment with terrible intensity. Last night, driving back from Boston, I lay back in the car and let the colored lights come at me, the music from the radio, the reflection of the guy driving. It all flowed over me with a screaming ache of pain . . . remember, remember, this is now, and now, and now. Live it, feel it, cling to it. I want to become acutely aware of all I've taken for granted. When you feel that this may be the good-bye, the last time, it hits you harder.

I've got to have something. I want to stop it all, the whole monumental grotesque joke, before it's too late. But writing poems and letters doesn't seem to do much good. The big men are all deaf; they don't want to hear the little squeaking as they walk across the street in cleated boots. Ed, I guess this all sounds a bit frantic. I guess I am. When you catch your mother, the childhood symbol of security and rightness, crying desolately in the kitchen; when you look at your tall, dreamy-eyed kid brother and think that all his potentialities in the line of science are going to be cut off before he gets a chance . . . it kind of gets you. –

19

...

21.

– Here I sit in the deep cushioned armchair, the crickets rasping, buzzing, chirring outside. It's the library, my favorite room, with the floor a medieval mosaic of flat square stones the color of old book-bindings . . . rust, copper, tawny orange, pepper-brown, maroon. And there are deep comfortable maroon leather chairs with the leather peeling off, revealing a marbled pattern of ridiculous pink. The books, all that you would fill your rainy days with, line the shelves; friendly, fingered volumes. So I sit here, smiling as I think in my fragmentary way: "Woman is but an engine of ecstasy, a mimic of the earth from the ends of her curled hair to her red-lacquered nails." Then I think, remembering the family of beautiful children that lie asleep upstairs, "Isn't it better to give in to the pleasant cycles of reproduction, the easy, comforting presence of a man around the house?" I remember Liz, her face white, delicate as an ash on the wind; her red lips staining the cigarette; her full breasts under the taut black jersey. She said to me, "But think how happy you can make a man someday." Yes, I'm thinking, and so far it's all right. But then I do a flipover and reach out in my mind to E., seeing a baseball game, maybe, perhaps watching television, or roaring with careless laughter at some dirty joke with the boys, beer cans lying about green and shiny gold, and ash trays. I spiral back to me, sitting here, swimming, drowning, sick with longing. I have too much conscience injected in me to break customs without disasterous effects; I can only lean enviously against the boundary and hate, hate, hate the boys who can dispel sexual hunger freely, without misgiving, and be whole, while I drag out from date to date in soggy desire, always unfulfilled. The whole thing sickens me. –

...

22.

– Yes, I was infatuated with you; I am still. No one has ever heightened such a keen capacity of physical sensation in me. I cut you out because I couldn't stand being a passing fancy. Before I give my body, I must give my thoughts, my mind, my dreams. And you weren't having any of those. –

...

23.

– There is so much hurt in this game of searching for a mate, of testing, trying. And you realize suddenly that you forgot it was a game, and turn away in tears. –

...

to my brain center. I let go. The pink, green, and yellow neons flashed on and off with a definite rhythm, each with its own particular tempo. Together they screamed out a syncopated color rhapsody. The faces; the cafés; the speed of light, steel cars. Swift; quick. Red; green. Flash; off. Stop; go. I let Bob lead me. I didn't look crossing streets. I stared at the people as we passed. Sometimes they stared back for an instant, but then flicked their gaze away, embarassed. The music jazzed out from the street cafés, and the sailors were like extras in a technicolor musical. The movie house itself had been a palace with tiers of glittering glass chandeliers, plush carpets and gleaming silver mirrors. So I walked along, loving, narcissus-like, my reflection in store windows, in the chromium on cars, superimposed on all we passed. There I was, tall, light-haired, in a kelly-green coat, a full black taffeta skirt. We passed through the Common to the public Gardens. The lights made the city bright with a strange, artificial dawn. We stopped on the stone bridge and leaned against the cold green metal railing. In the pond the lights were reflected against the feathery dark of the weeping willows. The empty swanboats drifted idly to and fro on the black glass of the water, and yellow leaves were strewn over the surface like confetti on a marble table-top after a party. I stood there, complete in myself: whole, we talked, and I said what I thought. He did not understand, but he listened, and liked me. "I love the people," I said. "I have room in me for love, and for ever so many little lives." I thought, a year ago I would have been thrilled with sheer amazement, sheer joy, if I knew I would stand here with Bob and have him love me. But now I smiled with impersonal tenderness. Eddie's bracelet was on my wrist. I held it up to the light. "See," I said, "I love it. It's me. It's individual." The silver caught the light and flashed out glinting white sparkles. The metal had absorbed the heat of my skin and was warm. Eddie, I thought. How ironic. You are a dream; I hope I never meet you. But your bracelet is the symbol of my composure . . . my division from the evening. I love you because you are me . . . my writing, my desire to be many lives. I will be a little god in my small way. At home on my desk is the best story" I've ever written. How can I tell Bob that my happiness streams from having wrenched a piece out of my life, a piece of hurt and beauty, and transformed it to typewritten words on paper? How can he know I am justifying my life, my keen emotion, my feeling, by turning it into print? We walked away, then, to a restaurant. I stared at one old man while I ate my hamburg. He was red-faced; sad. I concentrated hard. Man, I love you. I'm reaching out to you. I love you. Walking back to the car, the streets were wide, windswept and pale dark. I looked down an alley: beautiful blackness. Papers strewn in lowest ebb. Bill,[n] my one link with Saturday night life, is gone, and I have no one left. No one at all. I don't care about anyone, and the feeling is quite obviously mutual. What is it that makes one attract others? Last year I had several boys who wanted me for various reasons. I was sure of my looks, sure of my magnetism, and my ego was satiated. Now, after my three blind dates – two of which flopped utterly and completely, the third has also deflated. I wonder how I ever thought I was desirable. But inside, I know. I used to have sparkle, self-assurance. I didn't turn green and serious and grave eyed at first. Now I know what the girl meant in "Celia Amberley" when she said: "If he will kiss me, everything will be all right; I'll be pretty again." First I need some boy, any boy, to be captivated by my appearance – some boy like Emile. Then I need someone real, who will be right for me now, here, and soon. Until then I'm lost. I think I am mad at times. Tonight Bill and I were bored stiff with each other. First it was a long, dull rainy afternoon of sitting in his room listening to the radio & looking at pictures. Then it was supper at crowded Valentine's. Then that disgustingly puerile burlesque show which turns my stomach when I think of it. Then hamburg & coffee in a lonely diner, the lights too bright, the music too brassy, the silence too long. To top it off, we drove back at 11. I wanted to go in, and yet was afraid to face the girls who would wonder if another evening had gone stale or thought me queer. Ah, what the hell do I care what they think – (damn much.) Anyhow, he stopped the car and we hashed the mess out pretty futiley. I didn't want to say I didn't give a damn about him, but just wanted to be kissed good and hard, and that he wasn't capable of satisfying me even in that way. So I told him various lies about liking him, and he told me about his girl. From now on when a boy starts telling me about his lost loves I am going to run in the opposite direction screaming loudly. It is a bad sign. Somehow I bring out such confidences, and I'm pretty sick of hearing about Bobbé or Dorothy or P.K. or Liota. God damn them all. I will bury <u>my</u> Perry,[n] John, and Emile for good. The future is what matters – because one never reaches it, but always stays in the present – like the White Queen who had to run like the wind to remain in the same spot. Lord, what will I be? Where will the careless conglomeration of environment, heredity and stimulus lead me? Someday I may say: It was of great significance that I sat and laughed at myself in a convertible with the rain coming down in rattling sheets on the canvas roof. It influenced my life that I did not find content immediately and easily - - and now I am I because of that. It was inestimably important for me to look at the lights of Amherst[n] town in the rain, with the wet black tree-skeletons against the limpid streetlights and gray November mist, and then look at the boy beside me and feel all the hurting beauty go flat because he wasn't the right one – not at all. And I may say that my philosophy has been deeply affected by the fact that windshield wipers ticked off seconds too loudly and hopelessly, that my clock drips loud sharp clicks too monotonously on my hearing. I can hear it even through the pillow I muffle it with – the tyrannical drip drip drip drip of seconds along the night. And in the day, even when I'm not there, the seconds come out in little measured strips of time. And I wind the clock. And I look at the windshield wipers cutting an arch out of the sprinkled raindrops on the glass. Click-click. Clip-clip. Tick-tick. snip-snip. And it goes on and on. I could smash the measured clicking sound that haunts me – draining away life, and dreams, and idle reveries. Hard, sharp, ticks. I hate them. Measuring thought, infinite space, by cogs and wheels. Can you understand? Someone, somewhere, can you understand me a little, love me a little? For all my despair, for all my ideals, for all that – I love life. But it is hard, and I have so much – so very much to learn –

. . .

32.
— Click-click: tick-tick
Clock snips time in two
Lap of rain
In the drain pipe
Two o'clock
And never you.
Never you, down the evening,
I cannot"
Cry, or even smile
Acidly or bitter-sweetly
For never you and incompletely.
Things surround me;
I could touch
Soap or toothbrush
Desk or chair.
Never mind the three dimensions
All is flat, and you not there.
Letters, paper, stamps
And white. And black.
typewritten-you, and there

It is.
The trickle, liquid trickle
Of rain in drain-pipe
Is voice enough
For me tonight.
And the click-click
Hard quick click-click
Of the clock
Is pain enough,
enough heart-beat"
For me tonight.
The narrow cot,
The iron bed
Is space enough
And warmth enough . . . "
Enough, enough.
To bed and sleep
And tearless creep
The formless seconds
Minutes hours
And never you
The raindrops weep
And never you
And tick-tick,
    tick-tick
        pass the hours.

33.
– God, who am I? I sit in the library tonight, the lights glaring overhead, the fan whirring loudly. Girls, girls everywhere, reading books. Intent faces, flesh pink, white, yellow. And I sit here without identity: faceless. My head aches. There is history to read - - centuries to comprehend before I sleep, millions of lives to assimilate before breakfast tomorrow. Yet I know that back at the house there is my room, full of my presence. There is my date this weekend: someone believes I am a human being, not a name merely. And these are the only indications that I am a whole person, not merely a knot of nerves, without identity. I'm lost. Huxley would have laughed. What a conditioning center this is! Hundreds of faces, bending over books, fans whirring, beating time along the edge of thought. It is a nightmare. There

is no sun. There is only continual motion. If I rest, if I think inward, I go
mad. There is so much, and I am torn in different directions, pulled thin,
taut against horizons too distant for me to reach. To stop with the German
tribes and rest awhile: But no! On, on, on. Through ages of empires, of
decline and fall. Swift, ceaseless pace. Will I never rest in sunlight again –
slow, languid & golden with peace? –

. . .

34.
Gold leaves shiver
In this crack of time;
Yellow flickers
In the shrill clear sun;
Light pirouettes
In ballet dress,
While blue above
Leaps the sheer sky.

Gold leaves dangle
In the wind.
Gold threads snap.

In giddy whirls
And sweeps of fancy
Sunlit leaves plane down.
Lisping along the street
In dry and deathless dance
The leaves on slipshod feet
Advance.
  Breathless,
    Restless,
      Gold leaves twirl,
        Spiral,
          Circle,
            Curl.

Brief gold glitters
In the gutters;
Flares and flashes,
Husky rushes.

Brisk wind hushes
  hushes
    hushes.

And in that moment,
Silent, cold,
Across the lawn,
Dull pools of gold.

35·

– I can't resist writing about my date last Saturday night. It is now Monday, November the twentieth, eleven thirty p.m. I have just completed my third English theme: "Character is Fate." If I had to hazard three words to sum up my philosophy of life, I'd choose those. Friday afternoon I had no date. It was to be a big weekend over at Amherst, and there was no chance of my being called by any of the four boys I have met from over there. So I waited, almost hopeless. All my friends who had dates asked me where I was going. I decided to laugh at my grim fate and not conceal my shame: "I'm staying here unless a blind date turns up." Eventually my ignominy paid off. Anne Davidow[n] managed to secure me a blind date in a round-about way, and I was so overjoyed by the fact I would save my face (what a flabby character I am) by being out of the house with a male on Saturday night that I didn't care if he were five feet tall. I took the bus over with two other girls. It was a crisp frosty November night, with the lights dry and bright against the hard black edges of the dark. The bus driver turned the lights out, and we rolled along in our warm secure twilit world. Up across the soaring stone bridge over the Connecticut river, with the orange lights clear and strange in our eyes. And on, on to Amherst town. My mind soared in fancy and anticipation. Perhaps, perhaps this would be the one to pull me out of my plunge. I knew I looked nice – in my simply cut black velvet suit with the skirt full as a caress and the red jersey showing through the scooped neckline. Guy[n] and his friends were there to meet us. He was six-two, nice-looking and sweet in general. There was no spark, no sudden attraction, but that is as it should be. He was wholesome, and we both felt the warm glow of ending up with an attractive date. In reality, this chance evening tied up my life here so far in a neat knot as far as the social angle is concerned. The only person absent from my list was Austin[n] – he should have been there to see me in my glory! First, at dinner, as the six of us were walking into the hall, we saw Ted Powell and his mother. Ted was with his family and an adorable blonde of his choosing, no doubt. I saw his lips form the words, "There's Sylvia Plath," and I looked over and waved nonchalantly. That was two stars in my cap: one, Mrs. Powell could see me looking nice & happy with an attractive boy; two, Ted could do the same and thus jolt my image more clearly into his memory for possible future reference (God, what an ego I have.) That was only the beginning. At James Hall, where we played silly games, I saw Pat's" beau from Wellesley, Peter White, who is in my opinion flabby. I made a mental note that he noticed me, but probably did not know who I was. At the festive Mardi Gras I saw Corby Johnson," my adorable sophomore date of last Friday – who seemed to be dateless. He perked up his eyebrows and waved cheerily. In the process of going to the dance hall I saw Bob Blakesley, Jeanne Woods, too, both from home - - an added triumph. Perhaps best of all was seeing Bill on the dance floor as Guy and I swooped here and there. I noted with amusement that Liota was much on my type – tall, with light brown long hair. Bill noticed me with an imperceptible droop of one eyelid, while I gave him a slight friendly nod. I was so glad he saw me having a good time. The whole evening was made more enjoyable by renewing myself in the public eye of various strategic people by appearing in such a favorable light. To top things off, the first results, perhaps not <u>entirely</u> due to my presence at the Mardi Gras, came through today. Bill called very humbly and asked if I had had a good time. I gaily told him yes, whereupon he replied that he had not such a good time as a result of a cold (yuk, yuk!) He asked if I would like a ride home on Thanksgiving with two other boys and himself. What could frost my cake more? I accepted. I have started on the rise upward after bouncing around a little on rock bottom. I know I am capable of getting good marks: I know I am capable of attracting males. All I need to do is keep my judgment, sense of balance and philosophic sense of humor, and I'll be fine, no matter what happens. If character <u>is</u> fate, I sure am adjusting mine under my lucky star – * * *

. . .

36.
– Now I know what loneliness is, I think. Momentary loneliness, anyway. It comes from a vague core of the self - - like a disease of the blood, dispersed throughout the body so that one cannot locate the matrix, the spot of contagion. I am back in my room at Haven House" after the Thanksgiving Holidays. Homesick is the name they give to that sick feeling which dominates me now. I am alone in my room, between two worlds. Downstairs are the few girls who have come in – no freshman, no one I really know. I could go down with letter paper as an excuse for my presence, but I won't

yet - - - not yet. No, I won't try to escape myself by losing myself in artificial chatter "Did you have a nice vacation?" "Oh, yes, and you?" I'll stay here and try to pin that loneliness down. I hardly can remember those four days of Thanksgiving – a blur of home, smaller than when I left, with the spots on the darkened yellow wallpaper more visible; my old room, now no longer really mine, with all my things gone; Mother, Grammy," Clem" and Warren and Bob; my walk with the boys before the family reunion and dinner; my talk with Bob after we saw "The Red Shoes; " my date at the party Saturday, tall, blonde, and horribly popular, and then Sunday – numb, gray, and just as I had begun to accustom myself to familiar faces, the ride back. Oh yes, the ride back. When "Hump"" got in back beside me, Tooky" next to me, told him to get in front because his legs were too long. So my one clutch on the situation was gone. All the other three boys were short. Tooky could talk gaily to all about times they had in common. Oh, she had the situation well in hand, and I was jealous of her superior reserve of tactics – in other words, I grudgingly admired her. So there it was, two hours of driving through the dark, the warmth of the people on either side of me – animal warmth penetrates regardless of sensibilities and arbitrary mental barricades. I was there, yet not there. Part was back home, with love and security, and part was at Smith, the present necessity and hope. So here I am, In my room. I can't surround myself with friends and chatter and oblivion because my few comrades are not yet here. I can't deceive myself out of the bare stark realization that no matter how enthusiastic you are, no matter how sure that character is fate, nothing is real, past or future, when you are alone in your room with the clock ticking loudly into the false cheerful brilliance of the electric light. And if you have no past or future which, after all, is all that the present is made of, why then you may as well dispose of the empty shell of present and commit suicide. But the cold reasoning mass of gray entrail in my cranium which parrots "I think, therefore I am," whispers that there is always the turning, the upgrade, the new slant. And so I wait. What avail are good looks? To grab temporary security? What avail are brains? Merely to say "I have seen; I have comprehended?" Ah yes, I hate myself for not being able to go downstairs naturally and seek comfort in numbers. I hate myself for having to sit here and be torn between I know not what within me. Here I am, a bundle of past recollections and future dreams, knotted up in a reasonably attractive bundle of flesh. I remember what this flesh has gone through; I dream of what it may go through. I record here the actions of optical nerves, of taste buds, of sensory perception. And, I think: I am but one more drop in the great sea of matter, defined, with the ability to realize my existence. Of the millions, I, too, was potentially everything at birth. I, too, was stunted, narrowed, warped, by my environment, my outcroppings of heredity. I, too, will find a set of beliefs, of standards to live by, yet the very satisfaction of finding them will be marred by the fact that I have reached the ultimate in shallow, two-dimensional living – a set of values. This loneliness will blur and diminish, no doubt, when tomorrow I plunge again into classes, into the necessity of studying for exams. But now, that false purpose is lifted and I am spinning in a temporary vacuum. At home I rested and played, here, where I work, the routine is momentarily suspended and I am lost. There is no living being on earth at this moment except myself. I could walk down the halls, and empty rooms would yawn mockingly at me from every side. God, but life is loneliness, despite all the opiates, despite the shrill tinsel gaiety of "parties" with no purpose, despite the false grinning faces we all wear. And when at last you find someone to whom you feel you can pour out your soul, you stop in shock at the words you utter – they are so rusty, so ugly, so meaningless and feeble from being kept in the small cramped dark inside you so long. Yes, there is joy, fulfillment and companionship – but the loneliness of the soul in it's appalling self-consciousness, is horrible and overpowering –

. . .

37

– This is my first snow at Smith. It is like any other snow, but from a different window, and there lies the singular charm of it. Downstairs someone just exclaimed "Oh, look at it!" But I have been looking for quite some time now, ever since the first scatter-brained flakes began to circle down in aimless little swoops and spins. All I need is to hear sleighbells and the sound of "Silent Night" in the distance. Yes, it is like any snow, in any year, and although I have a Botany exam in two hours, I must stop a little, and look. The flakes are big and loosely put together, and the red and blue rooftops are muted and secretive. Girls bicycle by in brief spurts of color and motion, and the bare trees are that smoky-lavendar, gray and withdrawn. And just a little while ago it was summer time, and I was walking with Bob along the quiet, green, leaf-arched streets, looking up at my window, wondering how it would feel to be on the other, the inside. Well, I know now. I know a little more how much a simple thing like a snowfall can mean to a person. Because for all the theories about condensation and a temperature above 32°, for all that, it is pleasant for the optical nerves to register the impulse of floating, frozen ashes, of motion that enhances space behind. I can almost fancy that the house across the street is melting and crumbling into whiteness. Now there is a stippling of white caught on the edge of things, and I wonder what would happen to us all if the planes came, and the bombs. It's one thing to look at snow from a lighted, steam-heated room; it's one thing to walk out into it with lifted face and woolen clothes a few inches thick. But to live out in that white world, to scratch for a living from the withdrawn lavendar trees, the pale frozen ground. No, no. But the squirrels would still be there, and the birds. Long after, unless the smoke and the radioactivity (Oh, Marie Curie, if you could know!) got them. I can only hazard. In the back of my mind there are bombs falling, women & children screaming, but I can't describe it now. I don't know how it will be. But I do know that nothing will matter much – I mean whether or not I went to House Dance" or to a party at New Year's. It is amusing to wonder whether dreams would matter at all, or "freedom" or "democracy." I think not; I think there would only be the wondering what to eat and where to sleep and how to build out of the wreckage of life and mankind. Yet, while America dies like the great Roman Empire died, while the legions fail and the barbarians overrun our tender, steak-juicy, butter-creamy million-dollar-stupendous land, somewhere there will be the people that never mattered much in our scheme of things anyway. In India, perhaps, or Africa, they will rise. It will be long before everyone is wiped out. People live in war time, they always have. There was terror down through history – and the men who saw the Spanish Armada sail over the rim of the world, who saw the Black death wipe out half of Europe, those men were frightened, terrified. But though they lived and died in fear, I am here; we have built again. And so I will belong to a dark age, and historians will say "We have few documents to show how the common people lived at this time. Records lead us to believe that a majority were killed. But there were glorious men." And school children will sigh and learn the names of Truman and Senator McCarthy. Oh, it is hard for me to reconcile myself to this. But maybe this is why I am a girl - - - so I can live more safely than the boys I have known and envied, so I can bear children, and instill in them the biting eating desire to learn and love life which I will never quite fulfill, because there isn't time, because there isn't time at all, but instead the quick desperate fear, the ticking clock, and the snow which comes too suddenly upon the summer. Sure, I'm dramatic and sloppily semi-cynical and semi-sentimental. But in leisure years I could grow and choose my way. Now I am living on the edge. We all are on the brink, and it takes a lot of nerve, a lot of energy, to teeter on the edge, looking over, looking down into the windy blackness and not being quite able to make out, through the yellow, stinking mist, just what lies below in the slime, in the oozing, vomit-streaked slime; and so I could go on, into my thoughts, writing much, trying to find the core, the meaning for myself. Perhaps that would help, to synthesize my ideas into a philosophy for me, now, at the age of eighteen, but the clock ticks, ah yes, "At my back I hear, time's winged chariot hovering near." And I have too much conscience, too much habit to sit and stare at snow, thick now, and evenly white and muffling on the ground. I must learn the difference between alcoholic and acetic acid fermentation and much else that does not matter to me now. God, I scream for time to let go, to write, to think. But no. I have to exercise my memory in little feats just so I can stay in this damn wonderful place which I love and hate with all my heart. And so the snow slows and swirls, and melts along the edges. The first snow isn't good for much. It makes a few people write poetry, a few wonder if the Christmas shopping is done, a few make reservations at the skiing lodge. It's a sentimental prelude to the real thing. It's picturesque & quaint. And damn it to hell, if I don't be quiet I'll <u>never</u> get that Botany done! –

. . .

38.
– The reason that I haven't been writing in this book for so long is partly that I haven't had one decent coherent thought to put down. My mind is, to use a disgustingly obvious simile, like a wastebasket full of waste paper; bits of hair, and rotting apple cores. I am feeling depressed from being exposed to so many lives, so many of them exciting, new to my realm of experience. I pass by people, grazing them on the edges, and it bothers me. I've got to admire someone to really like them deeply – to value them as friends. It was that way with Ann: I admired her wit, her riding, her vivacious imagination – all the things that made her the way she was. I could lean on her as she leaned on me. Together the two of us could face anything – only not quite anything, or she would be back. And so she is gone, and I am bereft for awhile. But what do I know of sorrow? No one I love has ever died or been tortured. I have never wanted for food to eat, or a place to sleep. I have been gifted with five senses and an attractive exterior. So I can philosophize from my snug little cushioned seat. So I am going to one of the most outstanding colleges in America; I am living with two thousand of the most outstanding girls in the United States. What have I to complain about? Nothing much. The main way I can add to my self-respect is by saying that I'm on scholarship, and if I hadn't exercised my free will and studied through high school I never would be here. But when you come right down to it, how much of that

33

<u>was</u> free will? How much was the capacity to think that I got from my parents, the home urge to study and do well academically, the necessity to find an alternative for the social world of boys and girls to which I was forbidden acceptance? And does not my desire to write come from a tendency toward introversion begun when I was small, brought up as I was in the fairy-tale world of Mary Poppins and Winnie-the-Pooh? Did not that set me apart from most of my school mates? – the fact that I got all A's and was "different" from the rough-and-tumble Conways – <u>how</u> I am not quite sure, but "different" as the animal with the touch of human hands about him when he returns to the herd. All this may be a subtle way of egoistically separating myself from the common herd, but take it for what it's worth. As for free will, there is such a narrow crack of it for man to move in, crushed as he is from birth by environment, heredity, time and event and local convention. If I had been born of Italian parents in one of the caves in the hills I would be a prostitute at the age of 12 or so because I had to live (why?) and that was the only way open. If I was born into a wealthy New York family with pseudo-cultural leanings, I would have had my coming-out party along with the rest of them, and be equipped with fur coats, social contacts, and a blasé pout. How do I know? I don't; I can only guess. I wouldn't be I. But I am I now; and so many other millions are so irretrievably their own special variety of "I" that I can hardly bear to think of it. I: how firm a letter; how reassuring the three strokes: one vertical, proud and assertive, and then the two short horizontal lines in quick, smug succession. The pen scratches on the paper . . . I . . . I . . . I . . . I . . . I . . . I.

. . .

39.

– I am jealous of those who think more deeply, who write better, who draw better, who ski better, who look better, who live better, who love better than I. I am sitting at my desk looking out at a bright antiseptic January day, with an icy wind whipping the sky into a white-and-blue froth. I can see Hopkins House," and the hairy black trees; I can see a girl bicycling along the gray road. I can see the sun light slanting diagonally across the desk, catching on the iridescent filaments of nylon in the stockings I hung over the curtain rod to dry. I think I am worthwhile just because I have optical nerves and can try to put down what they perceive. What a fool!

. . .

40.

– Hopkins house is ugly. I see it when I get up every morning to shut the window, and whenever I write at my desk. It is all awkward corners, all gawky red chimneys, gables, blue tile roofs, red tile roofs worn to a purple, and yellow walls with white and blackened green woodwork. It is smeared with the year's grime, paint peeling, soiled window frames, and naked shrubs scrounging against the basement windows. I can almost hear their brittle bony branches squeaking hideously as the wind stirs them against the scabby wood of the house. Yet I love Hopkins House. Such is the resiliency of man that he can become fascinated by ugliness which surrounds him everywhere and wish to transform it by his art into something clinging and haunting in it's lovely desolation. I would paint the geometric shutters patterned against the oblongs of yellow wood, the trapezoids and slouching angles of the roof, the angled jutting of the drain pipes – I would paint in a bleak and geometric tension of color and form – what I see across the street . . . the ugliness which by man's sense of wishful thinking becomes a beauty touching us all. After being conditioned as a child to the lovely never-never land of magic, of fairy queens and virginal maidens, of little princes and their rose bushes, of poignant bears and Eyore-ish donkeys, of life personalized, as the pagans loved it, of the magic wand, and the faultless illustrations – the beautiful dark-haired child (who was you) winging through the midnight sky on a star-path in her mothers box of reels, - - of Griselda in her feather-cloak, walking barefoot with the Cuckoo in the lantern-lit world of nodding Mandarins, - - - of Delight in her flower-garden with the slim-limbed flower sprites, - - - of the Hobbit and the dwarves, gold-belted with blue and purple hoods, drinking ale and singing of dragons in the caverns of the valley - - - - all this I knew, and felt, and believed. All this was my life when I was young. To go from this to the world of "grown-up" reality. To feel the tender skin of sensitive child-fingers thicken; to feel the sex organs develop and call loud to the flesh; to become aware of school, exams (the very words as unlovely as the sound of chalk shrilling on the blackboard,) bread and butter, marriage, sex, compatibility, war, economics, death and self. What a pathetic blighting of the beauty and reality of childhood. Not to be sentimental, as I sound, but why the hell are we conditioned into the smooth strawberry-and-cream Mother-Goose-world, Alice-in-Wonderland fable, only to be broken on the wheel as we grow older and become aware of ourselves as individuals with a dull responsibility in life? ★ to learn snide and smutty meanings of words you once loved, like "fairy." ★ to go to college fraternity parties where a boy buries his face in your neck or tries to rape you if he isn't satisfied with burying his fingers in the flesh of your breast. ★ to learn that there are a million girls who are beautiful and each day that more leave behind the awkward teen-age stage, as you once did, and embark on the adventure of being loved and petted. ★ to be aware that you must compete somehow, and yet that wealth and beauty are not in your realm. ★ to learn that a boy will make a careless remark about "your side of town" as he drives you to a road house in his father's latest chromium-plated convertible. ★ to learn that you might-have-been more of an "artist" than you are if you had been born into a family of wealthy intellectuals. ★ to learn that you can never learn anything valid for truth, only momentary, transitory sayings that apply to you in your moment, your locality, and your present state of mind. ★ to learn that love can never come true, because the people you admire like Perry are unattainable since they want someone like P.K. ★ to learn that you only want them because you can't have them. ★ to learn that you can't be a revolutionary. ★ to learn that while you dream and believe in Utopia, you will scratch & scrabble for your daily bread in your home town and be damn glad if there's butter on it. ★ to learn that money makes life smooth in some ways, and to feel how tight and threadbare life is if you have too little. ★ to despise money, which is a farce, mere paper, and to hate what you have to do for it, and yet to long to have it in order to be free from slaving for it. ★ to yearn toward art, music, ballet and good books, and get them only in tantalizing snatches. ★ to yearn for an organism of the opposite sex to comprehend and heighten your thoughts and instincts, and to realize that most American males worship woman as a sex machine with rounded breasts and a convenient opening in the vagina, as a painted doll who shouldn't have a thought in her pretty head other than cooking a steak dinner and comforting him in bed after a hard 9–5 day at a routine business job. ★ to realize that there <u>are</u> some men who like a girl as a companion in mind as well as body, and want to take picnics in the sunlight instead of parking on a dark road at midnight after an evening of sexual stimulation while walking around a crowded dance floor and embracing breast to breast, stomach to stomach. ★ to realize that just as you will meet one of the few whom you could learn to be companionable with, the War of Double Hate will blow his guts out for the sake of shedding the light of freedom on the darkened half of the oppressed peoples of the world. ★ to study the futility of war, and read the UN charter, and then to hear the announcer on the radio blithely announce "The stars and stripes march" for our courageous fighting forces. ★ to know that there is a mental hospital on the hill in back of the college," and to have seen the little shoddy man walk out of the gate, his face a mongoloid study of slobbering foolishness, and to have seen him somberly drop an eyelid in a wink at you, while eyes and mouth remained wide open and fleshily ignorant of their existance in his face. ★ to have won $100 for writing a story and not believe that I am the one who wrote it. ★ to know that other girls read my biography in Seventeen and envy me as one of the chosen fortunates, as I envied others two years ago. ★ to know that for those qualities I covet in others, those same others covet qualities in still others. ★ to know a lot of people I love pieces of, and to want to synthesize those pieces in me somehow, be it by painting or writing. ★ to know that millions of others are unhappy and that life is a gentleman's agreement to grin and paint your face gay so others will feel they are silly to be unhappy, and try to catch the contagion of joy, while inside so many are dying of bitterness and unfulfillment ★ to take a walk with Marcia Brown" and love her for her exuberance, to catch some of it, because it's real, and once again love life day by day, color by color, touch by touch, because you've got a body & mind to exercise, and that is your lot, to exercise & use it as much as you can, never mind whose got a better or worse body & mind, but stretch yours as far as you can. ★ to know that it's four twenty-three o'clock by the watch you got for graduation and that in three days you have your first mid year exam and that you'd much rather read anything but what you have to, but you do have to, and you will, although you've already wasted two hours writing stream-of-consciousness stuff in here when your stream isn't even much to brag about, after all.

41.

... There comes a time when you walk downstairs to pick up a letter you forgot, and the low confidential voices of the little group of girls in the living room suddenly ravels into an incoherent mumble and their eyes slide slimily through you, around you, away from you in a snaky effort not to meet the tentative half-fear quivering in your own eyes. And you remember a lot of nasty little tag ends of conversation directed at you and around you, meant for you, to strangle you on the invisible noose of insinuation. You know it was meant for you; so do they who stab you. But the game is for both of you to pretend you don't know, you don't really mean, you don't understand. Sometimes you can get a shot back in the same way, and you and your antagonist rival each other with brave smiles while the poison darts quiver, maliciously, in your mutual wounds. More often you are too sickened to fight back, because you know the fear and the inadequacy will crawl out in your words as they crackle falsely on the air. So you hear her say to you "We'd rather flunk school and be sociable than stick in our rooms all the time," and very sweetly "I never see you. You're always studying in your rooom!" And you keep your mouth shut. And oh, how you smile!

. . .

42.

. . . She personifies the word cute. She's short and luscious. You notice her short "thumpable" nose, her long lashes, her green eyes, her long waist-length hair, her tiny waist. She is Cinderella and Wendy and Snow White. Her face is cute. She talks cute with white teeth under a bright lipsticked mouth. Her smile is cute, and she is perfectly coordinated. She can skate like Sonja Henie; ski like anyone-who-can-ski-well; swim like an Olympian; dance like some modern creature (I don't know much about dancing.) She is fluid. She smokes cutely. You are always aware of her insolent breasts which pout at you <u>very</u> cutely from their position as high and close to her shoulders as possible. They are versatile breasts, always clamoring for attention. Perhaps they are angry at her face which does not notice them, but smiled lashily and innocently above them. They are gay breasts, pushing out delightfully plump curves in her weak-willed sweaters. They are proud breasts, lifting their pointed nipples haughtily under the black, gold-buttoned taffeta or the shiny green satin. She is a breasty girl, and those two centers of emotion and nerve endings are shields, proud standards to lift to life and to the human race.

. . .

43.

. . . Linda is the sort of girl you don't remember when you meet her for the second time. She is rather homely, and nondescript as an art gum eraser. Her eyes are nervous and bright like neurotic goldfish. Her skin is muddy; maybe she has acne. Hair: straight, brown, oily. But she left some of her stories with you. And she can write. Better than you ever dreamed of writing. She tossed off conversation that breathed love and sex and fear and infatuation and yet was only a series of sharp, brief pistol-shot sentences. You took out your story - - the one that won third prize in SEVENTEEN. You felt sick as you reread the paragraphs of lyrical sentimentality that seemed so real and genuine a few months ago. You couldn't even say it was antiseptic and understated: it was hideously obvious. So you got rid of your astonishment that someone could write so much more dynamically than you. You stopped cherishing your aloneness and poetic differentness to your delicately flat little bosom. You said: she's too good to forget. How about making her a friend and competitor – you could learn alot from her. So you'll try. So maybe she'll laugh in your face. So maybe she'll beat you hollow in the end. So anyhow, you'll try, and maybe, possibly, she can stand you. Here's hoping!

. . .

44.

. . . She came back from the infirmary today:

"Good to see you back," you lied from your seat in the armchair where you were reading <u>The Morning Song from Senlin</u> and crying inside at the refrain.

She came in and sat down with her flashing toothy grin that you have learned to bear without flinching too obviously.

"ter-r-rific to be back," she said, rolling the r's the way she always does and raising her eyebrows and shoulders simultaneously in sort of a shrugging motion as if she were going to take off the ground. That's the way she lets you know she's happy. Only she can't let it go at that. Her tender ego needs more, so she tries a pneumatic drill:

"Got a ter-r-rific letter today!" she says. Your cue:

You ask who from.

"Oh, you tease," a coy, demure glance. The kitten won't purr before you pat it. Once you start the coffee-grinder going it won't stop:

"He said he missed me and that if I'd stayed around the Beta House I wouldn't get sick."

That was a subtle inference that she deserted her steady to go out with a Williams man last week.

"Got a letter from Bill, too, I see." (How nice and ego-building you can be if you grit your teeth and try hard enough.)

"Oooh, yes." (Another airy quivering of eyebrows-and-shoulder.) "And Tom, and Chuck, and Phil. I don't know what to do with all my men."

You don't say anything on purpose, so it falls a little flat. She waits a minute, then:

"Who did <u>you</u> go out with last weekend."

You toss off a thumbnail sketch of the guy whom you had a blind date with, noticing that when you say he's goodlooking she shuts her ears to the rest. There might be something nice about him. She couldn't stand to hear that. You go on about Bob from Rensselaer. You don't give a damn about him, so you pretend. She's really deaf now. Finally she goes. Maybe she knows she's made you jealous. Maybe she just wants to have you make her feel good the way you used to before you got sick of her. Anyhow, both of you feel worse for the encounter.

She's cute now, you admit, going back to <u>Senlin</u> and the dewdrops repeating three clear tones. She used to be scared, but when a woman knows a man's crazy for her she can flaunt all other women with a glow of confidence. Especially the ones who are more talented in superficial things, who don't happen to be in love; who read <u>Senlin</u>.

And you laugh at yourself for needing to retaliate in her own infantile way by a hollow totaling of your conquests. Conversation about boys between girls is so often a "gentleman's agreement" to keep quiet for a reasonable amount of time while you talk about yourselves, of yourselves, by yourselves, and for yourselves, not giving a damn about the other. And you're just as wrong as she. More so, since you are so small that you can't be magnanimous but have to fall to using her own weapons. Aren't your own security enough? Maybe not. –

· · ·

45.

... Another blind date. This one is older – partly bald, the girls said, and quiet-but-nice. You laugh nervously in the bedroom as Pat gets ready. She didn't know what she was getting you in for. You make some crack about going for the fatherly type. You own father" is dead. Pat looks worried, and you love her for it. She's so beautifully child-like and innocent as a Delicious apple.

You meet Bill in the car. It's his convertible. You get a side glance as he drives: not bad – hair receding on temples, but manly. Good blue eyes and a neat mouth. Neat features.

Conversation is bad from the beginning.

"Do you like football?" (This is like highschool: find out her interests.)

You don't, but you can't squelch him quite so soon. You parry: "Do you?" (The old double-switch.)

"Yes. Where do you come from?"

"Wellesley, Mass." You run off glibly.

"Don't give me a hard time."

"What?" You don't get it.

Traffic occupies his attention. Later there is a group of you sitting in the fraternity house. His room is a senior suite on the first floor. A fire is going, and the rugs and pine-panels are cosily collegiate. You are in a chair and he is on a foot-stool at your feet. Other couples are talking – most of them go steady. Anyhow, they're old hands. You've had all you can take of good-looking vacuums and shallow socialites. So you try to be basic. You are such a basic character yourself, anyway.

"You know," your voice is low, confidential, and you lean forward, elbows on knees, chin propped in hands, eyes level with his. You notice briefly that you can get lost in his eyes. An encouraging sign. They aren't lazy, they blaze at you. Heartened, you go on:

"You know, it's too bad you don't get to know people in a crowd, like this. So often you never do more than find out where your date lives."

He agrees.

O.K. "I'm willing to let you know me if you'll do the same. Then tonight won't be a total loss. You'll say: I know a little about a person that no one else knows very well."

He agrees, and you both lean forward, meaning business. He starts talking about political science. You ask questions, loving him for sharing a little of what matters with you. His father was a lawyer.

Then he asks if you want to dance. You dance in the dark living room. He holds you close, saying "Sylvy, oh, Sylvy. You know, we're an awful lot alike."

You like that. You've scored a beachhead. You've got security after a fashion.

"Let's take a walk," he says. "I want to talk. We can't talk here."

You get your coat. Out the back door through the pantry. There are tin cans, boots, and an old mat by the door. It bangs behind you. The night is still, dry, and cold. The air is dry ice.

"I take a walk here Sundays," he says. He has led you up behind a fraternity house to a clearing in the pines overlooking the city. The perfect place to discuss god & life. You sit down, leaning against a pine tree trunk.

"My father died two weeks ago," he says simply.

"Tell me." This is life; material; for sympathy.

"I was there before. He wanted me to be a lawyer. I was there when he died. I came back and didn't talk to anyone. I went out with girls who didn't give a damn . . . . He used to talk to me the way you did about my thesis."

His head has fallen on your shoulder; he is lying next to you as you sit, impulsively patting his shoulder maternally. There there baby.

"Tell me. About the war." (He's a veteran. Pat told you. He was disabled. You wonder if he has a wooden leg and think how noble you would be if he had one.)

"Where were you hurt?" you ask delicately.

"I got hit in the lungs by a shell. I was in the hospital two years."

"What's it like to fight? to kill someone?" (Your curiosity is aflame. Granted you can't be a man, but he can tell you how it was.)

He is nonchalant. "You go from one island to another, practicing. Then one day you start out again. 'This one isn't taken,' they say. You get out. You eat, sleep, joke. What do you do if you see an accident? You try to fix him up. That's all you do to your guys in war. It's not so different."

You want to be worldly. You remember Eddie's letters. You ask with impersonal gravity, "Have you had many women?"

"One in Hawaii. I cried the day we left; she was beautiful."

"How about that nurse you mentioned?"

"She left me."

"What was her name?"

"Emmy."

"Any others?"

"A girl in high school. She wasn't at all like you. She liked to drink alot."

"Oh."

"Sylvy?"

"Yes?"

"I want you to be mine, all mine."

(You think vaguely of a marriage proposal. How lovely – he has become captivated by your keen and sympathetic mind.)

"When?" You ask materialistically. (Maybe he'll say something about after four years . . .)

"Now." His leg lifts over yours. You feel reality, cold and icy, on your illusions.

"No." You sit up, indignant.

He fights you. He is strong.

"Lay, Sylvy. Lay."

You are sick. He is damn strong. His arms and hands are pushing you down. You roll in the pine needles. You are scared. You think: This is one time your innocence won't help you; you're done.

But then you're on top, shaking him, your hair falling in your face. He has relaxed. He's listening to the words pouring out.

"I hate you. Damn you. Just because you're a boy. Just because you're never worried about having babies!"

You trail off. You sound ridiculous. You are playing a part. You want him, yet you remember: "Once a woman has intercourse she isn't satisfied." "You need time and security for full pleasure." "You'll be finished at Smith."

So you stop, explaining weakly how it is.

He gets up, after you stop shaking him and you sit up yourself. He acts hurt, – petulant.

"All right," he goes off muttering into the shadows. "I'm a fool. Getting drunk and trusting a damn girl. All right."

It is too dark to see where he has gone.

"Bill!" You call softly, "come back."

No answer; no sound

All right, he's getting even by leaving you alone in the woods.

You get up and start walking to the path. The pine branches snap underfoot. It is black and strange. He is sitting over there on a stump, head in hands, muttering, or crying. You approach and kneel penitently before him.

"I'm sorry."

A lot of muttering and petulance.

"You're acting like a spoiled brat," you say.

"You don't know how it is," he says. "You can't, when you're all burning, on fire inside."

(O.K., so you don't.)

At last he forgives you. (What for? You should be forgiving him.)

Reconciled, he lies on his back, his head in your lap. You sit, cross-legged, cradling his head.

"Bend down. Kiss me."

(After what you've refused, it's a small favor, but you hold back.)

"Bend down." His arm pulls your head to his.

You kiss. He takes your hand, pulls it along. You touch soft, writhing flesh. You scream in a quick indrawn breath. So this is what it's like to have a boy want you to masturbate him. You pull away, disgusted, yet not disgusted. Lightening hasn't struck you. It's only . . . but you say "No no no no no no no."

He realizes now, maybe, that you are only a kid, only eighteen. So you go back to the fraternity house. You know that you won't go out with him again if he asks. But you will never take a walk. You will never be alone. And you hate him because he has deprived you of that: - - walks and aloneness. And you hate him because he is a boy. And you won't see him if he asks again."

. . .

46.

. . . What is my life for and what am I going to do with it? I don't know and I'm afraid. I can never read all the books I want; I can never be all the people I want and live all the lives I want. I can never train myself in all the skills I want. And why do I want? I want to live and feel all the shades, tones, and variations of mental and physical experience possible in my life. And I am horribly limited. Yet I am not a cretin: lame, blind and stupid. I am not a veteran, passing my legless, armless days in a wheelchair. I am not that mongoloidish old man shuffling out of the gates of the mental hospital. I have much to live for, yet unaccountably I am sick and sad. Perhaps you could trace my feeling back to my distaste at having to choose between alternatives. Perhaps that's why I want to be everyone – so no one can blame me for being I. So I won't have to take the responsibility for my own character development and philosophy. People are happy - - - if that means being content with your lot: feeling comfortable as the complacent round peg struggling in a round hole, with no awkward or painful edges – no space to wonder or question in. I am not content, because my lot is limiting, as are all others. People specialize; people become devoted to an idea; people "find themselves." But the very content that comes from finding yourself is over-shadowed by the knowledge that by doing so you are admitting you are not only a grotesque, but a special kind of grotesque.

. . .

47.

. . . Admittedly some people live more than others. The excitement curve of a telephone operator, white-haired, lumpy as a pallid pudding with knots of blue arthritic veins for raisins, would no doubt be shallow" = a slow undulation with a monotonous mechanical basis, heightened by a slight bump for a movie or dinner with the "girls." But the life of a Willa Cather, a Lillian Helman, a Virginia Woolf - - - would it not be a series of rapid ascents and probing descents into shades and meanings – into more people, ideas and conceptions? Would it not be in color, rather than black-and-white, or more gray? I think it would. And thus, I not being them, could try to be more like them: to listen, observe, and feel, and try to live most fully.

. . .

48.

. . . I don't believe in God as a kind father in the sky. I don't believe that the meek will inherit the earth: The meek get ignored and trampled. They decompose in the bloody soil of war, of business, of art, and they rot into the warm ground under the spring rains. It is the bold, the loud-mouthed, the cruel, the vital, the revolutionaries, the mighty in arms and will, who march over the soft patient flesh that lies beneath their cleated boots.

. . .

49.

. . . I don't believe there is life after death in the literal sense. I don't believe my individual ego or spirit is unique and important enough to wake up after burial and soar to bliss and pink clouds in heaven. If we leave the body behind as we must, we are nothing. All that makes me different from Betty Grable is my skin, my mind, my time and my environment. All that separates me from being Thomas Mann is that I was born in America, and not in his home town of Lubeck; that I am a girl, he a man; that he was inheritor of a particular set of glands and a lump of brain tissue which are tuned differently from mine. He is different now. But he will die. Sinclair Lewis died: the shriveled face leered from the newspaper picture, and I remembered Carol of Main Street, Martin Arrowsmith, and Doctor Gottlieb. Sinclair is now slowly decomposing in his tomb. The spark went out; the hand that wrote, the optical and auditory nerves that recorded, the brain folds that recreated - - - all are limp, flaccid, rotting now. Edna St. Vincent Millay is dead – and she will never push the dirt from her tomb and see the apple-scented rain in slanting silver lines, never. George Bernard Shaw is dead – and the wit has been snuffed out, the light is gone. Do vegetarians rot more rapidly than meat-eaters? But they left something – and other people will feel part of what they felt. But you can never recreate completely, and they are dead. The human mind is so limited it can only build an arbitrary heaven – and usually the physical comforts they endow it with are naively the kind that can be perceived as we humans perceive – nothing more. No: perhaps I will awake to find myself burning in hell. I think not. I think I will be snuffed out. Black is sleep; black is a fainting spell; and black is death, with no light, no waking. And how I bleed for all the individuals on the battle fields – who thought "I am I, and I know this, that there is dying with no one knowing." I know a little how it must be – to feel the waters close above you for the third time, and to feel the internal juice sapping away, leaving you empty. To have your mind broken, and the contents evaporated, gone. For with the record of images we have ingrained in our heads, all goes and is nothing. Antoine St. Exupery once mourned the loss of a man and the secret treasures that he held inside him. I loved Exupery; I will read him again, and he will talk to me, not being dead, or gone. Is that life after death – mind living on paper and flesh living in offspring? Maybe. I do not know.

. . .

50.

. . . Frustrated? Yes. Why? Because it is impossible for me to be God – or the universal woman-and-man – or anything much. I am what I feel and think and do. I want to express my being as fully as I can because I somewhere picked up the idea that I could justify my being alive that way. But if I am to express what I am, I must have a standard of life, a jumping-off place, a technique – to make arbitrary and temporary organization of my own personal and pathetic little chaos. I am just beginning to realize how false and provincial that standard, or jumping-off place, must be. That is what is so hard for me to face.

51.

... They're really going to mash the world up this time, the damn fools. When I read that description of the victims of Nagasaki I was sick: "And we saw what first looked like lizards crawling up the hill, croaking. It got lighter and we could see that it was humans, their skin burned off, and their bodies broken where they had been thrown against something." Sounds like something out of a horror story. God save us from doing that again. For the United States did that. Our guilt. My country. No, never again. And then one reads in the papers "Second bomb blast in Nevada bigger than the first!" What obsession do men have for destruction and murder? Why do we electrocute men for murdering an individual and then pin a purple heart on them for mass slaughter of someone arbitrarily labeled "enemy?" Weren't the Russians communists when they helped us slap down the Germans? And now. What could we do with the Russian nation if we bombed it to bits? How could we "rule" such a mass of foreign people - - - we, who don't even speak the Russian language? How could we control them under our "democratic" system, we, who even now are losing that precious commodity, freedom of speech? (Mr. Crockett," that dear man, was questioned by the town board. A supposedly "enlightened" community. All he is is a pacifist. That, it seems, is a crime.) Why do we send the pride of our young men overseas to be massacred for three dirty miles of nothing but earth? Korea was never divided into "North" and "South." They are one people; and our democracy is of no use to those who have not been educated to it. Freedom is not of use to those who do not know how to employ it. When I think of that little girl on the farm talking about her brother – "And he said all they can think of over there is killing those God-damn Koreans." What does she know of war? Of lizard-like humans crawling up a hillside? All she knows is movies and school room gossip. Oh, America's young, strong. So is Russia. And how they can think of atom-bombing each other, I don't know. What will be left? War will come some day now, with all the hothead leaders and articles "What If Women are Drafted?" Hell, I'd sooner be a citizen of Africa than see America mashed and bloody and making a fool of herself. This country has a lot, but we're not always right and pure. And what of the veterans of the first and second world wars? The maimed, the crippled. What good their lives? Nothing. They rot in the hospitals, and we forget them. I could love a Russian boy – and live with him. It's the living, the eating, the sleeping that everyone needs. Ideas don't matter so much after all. My three best friends are Catholic. I can't see their beliefs, but I can see the things they love to do on earth. When you come right down to it, I do believe in the freedom of the individual – but to kill off all the ones who could forge a strong nation? How foolish! Of what good – living and freedom without home, without family, without all that makes life?

. . .

52.

I believe that there are people who think as I do, who have thought as I do, who will think as I do. There are those who will live, unconscious of me, but continuing my attitude, so to speak, as I continue, unknowingly, the similar attitude of those before me. I could write and write. All it takes is a motion of the hand in response to a brain impulse, trained from childhood to record in our own American brand of hieroglyphics the translations of external stimuli. How much of my brain is wilfully my own? How much is not a rubber stamp of what I have read and heard and lived? Sure, I make a sort of synthesis of what I come across, but that is <u>all</u> that differentiates me from another person? - - - That I have banged into and assimilated various things? That my environment and a chance combination of genes got me where I am?

. . .

53.

. . . Can Smith help me? Yes: more than any other place within my means could. How? By opening more opportunities for aim and achievement than I could reach if I went anywhere else. Perhaps not <u>more</u> opportunities, but different sorts of opportunities, and, by hazard, more desirable ones. So what remains for me now? To throw up my hands at my inevitable narrowness? No: to meet Smith now and try to let the nagging questions ride; to get good grades, although I do not believe in them, but believe rather that man's brain is a poor recorder, forgetful and vague. Remember about the shadow of past knowledge. Write about your own experience. By that experience someone else may be a bit richer some day. Read widely of others experiences in thought and action – stretch to others <u>even though</u> <u>it</u> <u>hurts</u> <u>and</u> <u>strains</u> and would be more comfortable to snuggle back in the comforting cotton-wool of blissful ignorance! Hurl yourself at goals above your head and bear the lacerations that come when you slip and make a fool of yourself. Try always, as long as you have breath in your body, to take the hard way, the Spartan way – and work, work, work to build yourself into a rich, continually evolving entity!

. . .

54.

... tonight is Friday, <u>March 16, 1951.</u> It is about time to begin again to write here, firmly resolved (as I always am at each new attempt) to be as honest and neat as possible about the rather nebulous thinking processes I go through on paper.

I am again at a loss as to where to begin. But I think I shall tell you about Dick" for a little while. Because I sit here at my desk as usual. Someone shuffles in slippers down the hall, singing. Doors close. The kerchief around my head presses the hard knobs of rag curlers into my scalp. It is very hot, and the radiator breathes steam. So I open the window a little. Listen to me: There are a few times when out of the marble-and-mud that is life there is one layer of solid marble. There are a few times when the songs that are written, the poems that are written, the plays that are written, come alive. By accident you fall onto a stage-set put aside for a tragedy for the lesser gods, and you utter words that were in the script written in the leaves and in the grass for some heroic cast.

All boys and girls go to dances; We did. All boys and girls are lovely in youth and adolescence; we were. Dancing together was not low or degrading. There was something there in each of us, behind the immaculate black tux, behind the bare shouldered white gown - - - something that made the mutual electric, drowsy magnetism of yes and no, of plus and minus, of black and white, of he and she unutterably right. No explanations needed.

Walking back alone in the raw March wind, we passed the streets, full of taxis, waiting, waiting, empty, empty. Then the road was bare and wind-swept, and the air was like gulps of cold water as it blew across our mouths. Street lights chiseled out clear areas of light out of dark. My hair whipped back in the wind, and the white circle of net billowed and hushed and shushed about my silver feet. Stride and stride and stride and stride. Freely walking, hand in hand. No people; no parties; no warmth; no blur of lights, voices, flesh, wine. Two of us, strong and together along the streets. Stride and stride. Then stop. Heads tilted back to the stars. Words, now, about the legends, and lines ran around the sky drawing in Orion and The Big and Little Bear. Then quiet, growing loud and louder, more loudly than a roaring sea, pressing in, in, in. Dry leaves made a rattling against the gutter like dead peas in a pod. The wind rushed by and by and ever by. Words again. "This is like being in church."

Dissect your sentence, oh professors! Point out verb and noun and participial phrase. Dry, dry, the word; creaking dry; hissing dry and imperfectly low. Dissect the word "church", oh men with dictionnaries in hand. Tell how it means "a building for public worship, esp., Christian worship." Tell how it connotates a variety of things – white walls, song, childhood and Sunday chicken dinners. But no, I laugh at you all even as I listen.

A kiss, then. Kisses are given and received. There are kisses given by mothers to their children, by lovers to their sweethearts, by men on the street to their prostitutes. A meeting of the lips. That is all, animal as we are, that is our own particular generic peculiarity. And yet, without being vague and star-eyed, I may say that a kiss may be a physical symbol of a mental adoration. That, and a delight. For brought up as we are in the custom and moral conscience of our tribe and era, we think and talk about kisses. We are not blind spores or plus and minus strains of bread mold meeting. We have a cold gray lump of tissue beneath the cartilige in our cranium, and if a reaction is ingrained deeply enough, our nerve impulses are blocked in accordance with the nature of our conditioning. So when reason rebels not, harmony is reached between the brain impulse and the endocrine glands.

A kiss. Once new and sweetly. Then stairs, and I said nothing. Not "Goodbye-I-had-a-lovely-time." No words to grate along the final edges of an evening. I sat in a wicker chair under the lights, and he went down; the door clicked shut; the quiet was heavy with the sleep of people in the other rooms. I stared long at the stair railing, brown varnished and peeling. The light threw a barred shadow on the pale green wall. "Stair railings," I said, and laughed. "All this, all life, is reduced to stair railings."

I got up and went about the tedious business of undressing, of putting white cloth shapes in neat piles, of undoing filmy brown nylon, of letting stiff white net slip to the floor, of running water and putting soap on washcloth on face and arms and neck. The cat scratched claws on the chair. I patted the fur, holding the warm animal against my bare breast, where it purred for a little. Then bed, and again the luxury of dark. Still the blood and flesh of me were electric and singing quietly. But it ebbed and ebbed and dark and sleep and oblivion came and came, surging, surging, surging inward, lapping and drowning with no-name, no-identity, none at all. Just nothing, yet the seeds of awakening and life slumbered there in the dark

. . .

(55.)

... Some sleep is like a pile of garbage, with egg shells jagged, and vermin swarming over lurid orange peels, coffee grounds and sick wan lettuce leaves; that is the sleep of nightmare fragments, when the operation or the exam is coming the next day. Some sleep is bleak and gray, sparing with its calm and soothing treatment; that is the sleep of the worker, when each day is like the last and the next, and all time is present. But there are sleeps that are born of spring and of the slumbering hibernation of bears in leaf-hushed caves. My ears caught the twitter of birds, strange and early. My shut eyelids felt sun, and my nose smelled earth, and my skin felt warm wind. Eyes closed, body not yet mine, but still part of something – of air, of earth, of fire, of water. – And the sound of cars along the street and someone breathing in the next bed. I opened my eyes and pulled my body to me again. Leaning on an elbow, there was the window open, the curtains blowing in the Saturday wind, and the sunlight and shadow sharp and clear on the building across the street. To lie and regret the emergence from the womb as the umbilical cord is snipped, neatly, and the knot tied. To regret, regret, and know that the next move will be to arise, to walk to the toilet, one foot after another, to sit on the seat, sleepily, releasing the bright yellow stream of urine, yawning, and undoing rags from brown hair and curls. To get up, brush teeth, wash face, and begin again, in the merciless daylight, all the rituals of dressing that our culture subscribes to

. . .

(56.) A bikeride begins in afternoon sunlight on a Saturday. There is the familiar feeling of hands gripping handlebars, feet circling on pedals, thin tires turning over pavement with a humming that transfers itself in a tantalizing motion through the end of your spine along the marrow of your bones. You spin across a bridge, and the whir of tires takes on a lower more vibrant note as you ride on the grill-work, with green water staring at you from under the open places. The road knots up and around a hill or two and then there is the rock: destination one. So you hoist the bike over a fence, and walk it up the rutted mud path, flanked by stands of oak and pine. On the right: Lake Saltonstall," blue and flat in the sun. On the left: trees and hills of trees. Ahead: an eternity of rough path, dipping, and then climbing sharply. Sneakers, biting into treacherous cushions of last year's dead and pale brown leaves. Cold wind gnawing at the open spaces, and at the thin blue dungarees flapping about your legs. There was a time of sitting on a rock to rest, with the shadow of the night coming on from behind, and casting the hill-shadow on the lake, now muted to a dull secretive gray. Colder air, and a consciousness of lateness insinuated blades of ice into the mind and flesh. At last then, a paved road. Singing down on uncontrolled wheels; the first hill ricocheted to a stop and calmed down into even slopes of highway. We chased the sunset, a smoky pink flag ahead beyond the city. The night chased us in a carbon-colored tide spreading across the sky behind, with street lights stabbing periods of light like banners, beacons, following two fugitives. The streets were friendly then, and the web of home knit tighter about us as we wheeled to a stop before the dormitory. Feet frozen, aching against pavement. Eyes blurred with wind-tears. Cheeks burned red from cold air slashing at them. And there we were. The roller coaster of the afternoon ended just as you thought you'd never make it up the highest logo. Perchance to eat, perchance to sleep . . . perchance, perchance

. . .

(57.) No, you don't. It's a play now, and you don't have time to change to aqua dress, gold shoes and Reggie's fur coat. You walk down the aisles, among sleek black taffeta dresses, dangling crystal earrings, bare shoulders and high heels – only you have your old black jersey and red skirt on, and you carry his old khaki jacket. Do you shrink inward and want to melt into the plush floor carpet? Ah, no, not at all. You walk down proudly, laughing into all faces, laughter filling all the cracks in your self assurance like plaster. You are happy and proud to have him sit beside you, laugh with you, and hold your hand once. When you are young, what does it matter if you forget and leave your diamond tiara on the bureau back home? When you are old, there will be time enough to worry about that.

(58.) Now I am surely becoming an incurable romantic. But please, hear me out. After the play we walked out, breaking from the crowd that pushed out in knots of people up the aisles, raveling at the exit-signs. Another cold black March night. So I said to myself, unassuming creature that I am, "he-was-being-chivalrous-last-night-because-it-was-traditional-to-kiss-date-after-dance." I steeled myself to a cool goodbye at the head of the stairs. "I have something to show you," he said as we neared the house. He turned our steps across the street to the Chem Lab." There was a road on the hill behind the building, and a fence bordering the road, and a field of grass beyond the fence. I sat on a fence post, looking over the field to the road below and beyond. Lights blinked yellow white, and cars moved and scurried to and fro. I felt what the 19th century romantics must have felt: The extension of the soul into the realm of nature. I felt that my feet were growing into the hill, and that I was a jutting outgrowth of the elements . . . a humanized tree stump, or something equally improbable. He stood in back of me, hands on my shoulders, and the wind broke against him as I sat in the shelter of his upright body. Then we walked out to the crest of the field, wading through the grass, arm in arm. "You know," he said, "I was wondering how to be when you came – cool and casual – or friendly . . . and you make it so easy." So he put his arms around me and put his cheek against mine, kissing me, then, once. The wind blew my hair back and whipped tears into my eyes as the two of us stood facing each other. Walking back, we talked about ourselves – conversation not to be reproduced – but I remember laughing as he said he had been wary of asking me down and a bit bitter because of my "popularity." When we got to the house I couldn't bear to have him come up stairs and see me in the light – windblown hair and tearful eyes may be delightful on a dark hilltop under the stars – but under a 100° watt Edison bulb in a narrow hallway – God forbid! So we stood outside, and he was softspoken and touched his lips to mine once sweetly as Chuck came out the door. I said good night to the two boys, and went upstairs alone.

(59.) What is more tedious than boy-girl episodes? Nothing; yet there is no tedium that will be recorded so eternally. Eve baited Adam back in the dark ages, but it is the tragedy of man to die and be born again, and with each new birth the cycle begins all over again. Variations on a theme. Yet the other night I felt a preview of myself ten years hence breathe down my neck with a chilly whisper. The two of us were "babysitting" at his house this Friday, and younger brother" had been allowed to stay up till we came. The parents left, and we went upstairs to the bedroom where a small vociferous boy bounced eagerly during the reading of some A. A. Milne poems by older brother. Then the light was turned out, and in the quiet, older b. asked younger b. questions and listened respectfully for answers. Yours truly sat on the bottom of the bed, partly a stranger, wanting to be loved by the little one, touched when he asked her to stay and keep him company. Then it was time to leave him to sleep. The man got up and left. He had no identity, but as his back loomed dark in the light cracking in through the open door, he was the Man who would be the chosen one to father children and I was the Mate, bending last over the bed, whispering a little word into my son's ear as I closed the door. But in the light, downstairs, I was Sylvia and he was himself, and there was the sea between us again. (I said there was a "sea." No, I will chide myself. There was only a cushion, and a tray of icecream and cookies. But it served, it served.)

(60.) After this charming little bouquet of idyllic description I will be earthy and matter-of-fact. I will say that I hated bobby pins and buttons when I was little. I liked the clean quick flash of zippers, but despized the round, fingered little objects on shirts and sweaters. I ran away screaming when a woman bent cooingly over a baby-carriage and crooned "My, what a dear little button-nose your baby has!" I was nauseated at the sight of bobby pins. I would not touch them. Once, on the day I was going home from the hospital after having my tonsils out, a woman in my ward asked me to carry some bobby pins to the lady in the next bed. Revolted, I held out a stiff unwilling hand, flinching as the cold clammy little pins touched my skin. They were cold and shiny, as with grease, and sickeningly suggestive of warmth and disgusting, intimate contact with dirty hair.

(61.) March 29th – Thursday

Some people have to have silence and peace when they write. I am in a bad position, looking at writing from the point of view of celestial inspiration. My fat fleshy grandmother sits in the corner, breathing loudly, sewing on the coat I will wear tomorrow. The ice box clicks and whirrs. From the downstairs bathroom comes the bristly sound of my brother brushing his teeth. If I were going to be realistic, I would not say much more than "It looks like an add of the middle-middle class home." Yet somehow I don't give a damn about the srcaped place on the yellowed and finger spotted wallpaper. I don't care too much that the rug in the dining room is blueflowered and has the threads showing where the chairs are scraped across it, or that the chair seats, once shining maroon with satin stripe, are now darkened and greasy with food stains. I can almost ignore the room grammy loves so much – with its unbelievable color combination = pale blue wall paper with sprays of pink and white pussy-willows, dusty rose bedspreads, maroon rugs, and an off-blue and pink flowered chair. It's funny, but now I'm home, and no matter how many mansions I will see, I won't care about the shabbiness of this dear little house. For I feel a great equanimity about peoples opinions, now. I don't care any more about the handsome wealthy boys who come gingerly into the living room to take out the girl they thought would look nice in an evening cocktail dress . . . I said I wanted to go out with them to meet new people. I ask you, what logic is there in that? What guy you would like, would see the depths in a girl outwardly like all the other physical american queenies? So why go places with guys you can't talk to? You'll never meet a soul that way - - - not the sort you want to meet. Better to stay in your garret reading than to go from one party to another. Face it, kid: unless you can be yourself, you won't stay with anyone for long. You've got to be able to talk. That's tough. But spend your nights learning, so you'll have something to say. Something the "attractive intelligent man" will want to listen to.

All this preamble (above), and what I really wanted to get down before I head off to New York was more like this:

(62) ... An open letter: to you whom it concerns:

I won't call you darling; that would be cute. And I'm not being cute, not tonight. I wanted to tell you how you are beginning to be the one I can talk to. I have always talked: sometimes to Mary, sometimes to Eddie, sometimes to myself. More often to myself. But suddenly, with the need to take a concrete human being for a confidante, I build my framework of a world around you. I don't write this to you, because it is not time. I may never tell you, and, in years, I may not need to, because you might become part of my life - - - physically and mentally ... and there would be no need to verbalize, because you would understand.

Perry said today that his mother said "Girls look for infinite security; boys look for a mate. Both look for different things." I am at odds. I dislike being a girl, because as such I must come to realize that I cannot be a man. In other words, I must pour my energies through the direction and force of my mate. My only free act is choosing or refusing that mate. And yet, it is as I feared: I am becoming adjusted and accustomed to that idea. And if I could be your companion I would laugh at those previous fears. I like what you heighten in me. And I am amazed that I, so proud and distainful of custom, could consider marriage an honorable and vital estate. But under certain circumstances I do justly consider it that.

Tonight I went to a hen party. I will tell about that later. I want to talk about getting the bus home, and my walk down from Weston road, and what I talked about to myself on the way to this room, this chair, this instant, (which is gone, even as my pen scratches the first "i.")

(63) There is a certain unique and strange delight about walking down an empty street alone. There is an off-focus light cast by the moon, and the streetlights are part of the spotlight apparatus on a bare stage set up for you to walk through. You get a feeling of being listened to, so you talk aloud, softly, to see how it sounds:

I am walking down this street and I am being propelled by a force too powerful for me to break because eighteen years of walking down streets had chained me to the inevitable action of going from one place to another and always repeating the circle or line and returning home without stopping or wondering ... my feet move one after the other and I cannot stop them ... they are heading home and I know in my head that I must go home because tomorrow I must get up early to go to New York ... yet in all these blind box houses there is no one to listen to me or hear my feet clicking ... or perhaps behind one of those black gaping bedroom windows someone lies on the edge of oblivion and my footsteps are grinding mechanical anonymous sounds along the edges of sleep . . . footsteps without feet or legs or body . . . but I <u>have</u> a body . . . and I am curled up in its neat and miraculous network of muscles bones and nerves . . . I am woven into a snug automatic cocoon of flesh-and-blood . . . and I feel only a curious amusement as my feet move me on and as the world slips by and houses never stop but turn a side foreshortening to a front and lapsing to a side always moving as I move . . . but I can stop and to prove it I will . . . there . . . there . . . I am standing still and my feet have stopped clicking . . . they are waiting docilely in their snail like leather houses . . . but I could not turn and walk back . . . no . . . but some night I will break these eighteen years of walking home and walk all night, away from the magnet that pulls and attracts me like a scrap of metal . . . and now I am walking again . . . . but I will take this road instead of mine . . . I will assert myself feebly and approach from a less frequented path . . . so these houses have shadows strange across their faces, and I could not go up to the door and knock and say: Let me come in and suck your life and sorrow from you as a leech sucks blood; let me gorge myself on your sensations and ideas and dreams; let me crawl inside your guts and your cranium and live like a tapeworm for a while, draining your life substance into myself . . . no; the houses have strange leaf shadows on their faces . . . . they draw their tree leaves like a veil across their faces . . . and I walk in the middle of the road . . . can shadows clutch you, trip you? . . . I think I could be strangled by those shadows . . . so I walk and now I am at a corner . . . if a man should step from behind that mailbox . . . if a man should crawl out of that mailbox . . . if that mailbox should shudder, stretch, uncurl and become a man, I should ask him who he was and if he liked walking down streets at night . . . and he would be tall and lean because that is the animal dream of our age . . . and he would walk all night and all tomorrow with me . . . and I would talk and unrust the words and thoughts which stagnate in me from lack of verbal expression . . . but there I go . . . it is perhaps significant that I transformed the mailbox into a man and not a woman . . . I am part man, and I notice women's breasts and thighs with the calculation of a man choosing a mistress . . . but that is the artist and the analytical attitude toward the female body . . . for I am more a woman; even as I long for full breasts and a beautiful body, so do I abhor the sensuousness which they bring . . . I desire the things which will destroy me in the end . . . I wonder if art divorced from normal and conventional living is as vital as art combined with living: in a word, would marriage sap my creative energy and annihilate my desire for written and pictorial expression which increases with this depth of unsatisfied emotion . . . or would I achieve a fuller expression in art as well as in the creation of children? . . . . Am I strong enough to do both well? . . . That is the crux of the matter, and I hope to steel myself for the test . . . as frightened as I am . . . and now the houses are turning still, and there are a few rooms lit where I can see into a square of warm yellow light where people move and revolve in the little boxes which house them . . . . shell-less crabs . . . flesh caged in steel shells of cars and planes and trains . . . . and I would walk and talk aloud to myself all night . . . but I cannot because my feet have brought me to the door . . . the twentieth century is an age of popular fallacies, of scientism and of symbolism . . . so I pause before the door and I know that of all the houses turning after me as I passed, this house is the one where I was young and where I turned through time . . . and this doorstep is the one crowded with the ghosts of boys and all varieties of kisses . . . and I am surrounded by the friendly fingered familiar places of the brief whirl in color and motion and words and actions . . . which has been my life . . . so I know instinctively, like the rat in the maze, that this door opens . . . this of all the doors . . . my feet know this is the door . . . my eyes know . . . and there is no doubt whether it will be the lady or the tiger" . . . because here I snip off the thread of aloneness and enter into the ritual and rooms that are the family, that are the home . . . . and my umbilical cord never has been cut cleanly . . . so I press thumb-down-on-latch and step up into light, into tomorrow, into people I know by sight, by sound, by touch, by smell, by flavor . . . . and the door closes behind me, and I turn the lock with a click that shuts out the disturbing wasteland of sleeping streets and fenceless acres of night . . . .

(64) Notes on an experimental film:" scenario by Dali: a shock film: sex and sadism:

Opening: "Il y a une fois . . . " man idly whittles fingernail with razor . . . goes on porch outside . . . looks at sky . . . (switch to sky) . . . three thin clouds slice horizontally over a full moon . . . (girl's face on screen) . . . moon again . . . (girl's face again) . . . hand of man lifts eye and slits it neatly with razor . . . closeup of gore . . . .

Next scene: Man bicycling with box around neck . . . . female drapery . . . . (switch to woman looking out of window) . . . man seen from above . . . falls to sidewalk . . . she rushes down . . . kisses his motionless face . . . . . (back to room) . . . woman opens box . . . lays clothes on bed . . . . man materializes . . . . looks in curious absorbtion at his own hand . . . . (closeup of hand) . . . a red wound in center of palm and ants scurrying busily in and out . . .

<u>Next</u>: Man and woman watch from window . . . . (down in street) . . . .
sexless female pokes in tender and casual fascination with stick at object on
ground . . . . object is human hand . . . . police push crowds away . . . . she
clasps hand to her . . . puts it in box . . . . cars speed by as she stands meditatively in street . . . . (from widow again) . . . car approaches . . . crushes her
. . . man turns from window . . . approaches woman with lust . . . . traps her
. . . . hands reach and caress breasts and hips under print dress . . . . hands
feel breasts and dressed figure becomes nude . . . then clothed . . . breasts
become buttocks . . . . and the hands smooth the resilient contours . . .
(strong sense of lust awakened . . .) . . . woman escapes . . . . man
approaches dragging two grand pianos . . . weighted with deer, cannon balls,
priests . . . (superhuman force of lust?) . . . . woman escapes through door
. . . hand reaches after her (closeup of crawling ants in wound . . .)

<u>Next</u>: Woman enters room . . . . sees moth as speck on curtain . . . . moth
enlarges . . . (closeup . . . with skull on back) . . . skull becomes man . . . . he
wipes his mouth . . . . and it disappears . . . . she screams and rapidly puts
lipstick on her own lips . . . . hair grows from his lips . . . . she looks under
her arm . . . . hair is gone . . . . (sexual symbol of erotic zones?) . . . closes
door and runs to beach . . . . picks up handsome man . . . . laughs &
embraces . . . down the shore . . . pick up rags & remnants of box . . . . kick
them away . . . laugh & go on . . .

– End –

(65)

– And so it seems I must always write you letters here that I can never send.
And so I will write to you a few lines that came during class on Monday after
your visit, after I said things to you that I should not have said, and so, here
it is:

> The slime of all my yesterdays
> Rots in the hollow of my skull:
>
> And if my stomach would contract
> Because of some explicable phenomenon
> Such as pregnancy or constipation
> I would not remember you
>
> Or that because of sleep
> Infrequent as a moon of green cheese,
> That because of food

Nourishing as a violet petal
That because of these

And in a few fatal yards of grass,
In a few lengths of sky and treetops . . .

A future was lost yesterday
As easily and irretrievably
As a tennis ball at twilight.

(66) Outside it is warm and blue and April. And I have to digest Darwin, Marx, and Wagner. I'd like to rip out my brain and set it to assimilating the printed hieroglyphics in this book, and send my body down to the tennis courts in animal imbecility to jerk muscles in proper coordination and feel only the bestial and sensuous delight of sun on skin.

(67) Indecision and reveries are the anesthetics of constructive action.

(68) I seem to grow more acutely conscious of the swift passage of time as I grow older. When I was small, days and hours were long and spacious, and there was play and acres of leisure, and many children's books to read. I remember that as I was writing a poem on "Snow" when I was eight. I said aloud, "I wish I could have the ability to write down the feelings I have now while I'm still little, because when I grow up I will know how to write, but I will have forgotten what being little feels like." And so it is that childlike sensitivity to new experiences and sensations seems to diminish in an inverse proportion to the growth of technical ability. As we become polished, so do we become hardened and guilty of accepting eating, sleeping, seeing, and hearing too easily and lazily, without question. We become blunt and callous and blissfully passive as each day adds another drop to the stagnant well of our years.

(69) For future reference:
To be incorporated into a sarcastic poem about a fat, greasy, and imperfect grandmother:

"Laugh as you lift your eyes to the heavens
And think of her fat pink soul
Blundering among the logical five-pointed stars."

(70) I have the choice of being constantly active and happy or introspectively passive and sad. Or I can go mad by ricocheting in between.

(71) Written, as usual, in the tense and crucial interval when I should be studying for a Botany exam:

"Geography Lesson"

On the yellow part of the map,
On the flat yellow part of the map
Are a million microscopic men,
A million million microscopic men.
    Dry blow the little winds,
    Wet drop the little rains,
    All in a whisper,
    A minute whisper
On the yellow part of the map.

On the orange part of the map,
On the bright orange part of the map,
Are a million microscopic cars,
A million million microscopic cars.
    Red blink the little stop-signs,
    Green blink the little go-signs.
    All at the crossroads,
    The unseen crossroads
On the orange part of the map.

On the blue green part of the map,
The pale blue green part of the map,
Are a million microscopic towns,
A million million microscopic towns.
    Bright shine the little houses,
    Straight go the little Main Streets,
    All in the sunlight,
    The thin small sunlight,
On the blue green part of the map.

On the red-brown part of the map,
The rich red-brown part of the map,
Are a million microscopic trees

A million million microscopic trees.
    Green grow the little tree-leaves,
    Quick sway the little branches,
    All in the summer,
    The split-second summer
On the red brown part of the map.

On the lavendar part of the map
On the light lavendar part of the map
Are a million microscopic cannons,
A million million microscopic cannons.
    Shrill squeak the little bullets,
    Sharp bark the little shotguns,
    And now a river
    A bright red river
Stains the lavendar part of the map.

———

(72) Blue-painted and metallic animal,
    Where on the amorphic tree of evolution
    Did you arise?
    You wait patiently in the lavender rain
    And leaf-yellow April mist,
    Your thin silver windshield wipers
    Ticking mechanically
    Across the transparent glass cornea
    Of your cold and vacant eye.
    Your pistoned heart chugs and throbs
    And on your four round feet
    Slowly you roll away.

(73) They have made their cities
    Functional and swift.
    You cannot have your April
    Virginal and solitary
    Any more.
    She comes screaming
    And tittering
    In purple and red flowers
    Along the landscaped park;

She has blatant breasts
And the bright lipsticked mouth
Of a Broadway chorus girl.
She is featured lately
In a lownecked silk blouse
On the cover of Life magazine.

(74) Wet blows the wind
And wet the rain:

—

The shiny beetle-coated cars
Crawl through the watered streets
With waffle-patterned tires
Slithering slow along the pavement.

—

Down the hall comes Mary, bearing sheets
Crisp squares of folded linen
And, dressed in green, she greets me
With a toothless morning grin.

(75) The mindless April leaves heave sighs
And twirl in aimless sarabandes.
My fingers curl and clutch the skies;
Green blood flows in green-veined hands.

(76) Across the street carpenters hammer on roof:
Casual scaffolding and the sound of hammers
Ricocheting between the painted yellow walls
Of this house and that.
Down the backstairs a maid comes
To empty a pail of lettuce in the garbage bin.
A wooden plank sinks slowly through strata of air,
Falling from liver-purple roof to flat matter of fact earth.
The sound of the crash waits and then
Reverberates tardily.

Clank of hammer on steel pipe
Syncopates in my purple throat.
And the rigid rod of duty
Crumbles in me like weak plaster.

(77) Mental nausea of daily squash
flabby cauliflower
and grease dripping slick and sheepish
onto the placid plate of mind.

(78) Open windows in the art studio," and the mercuric twinkling April air flows in across the desks and laps about my ankles. Spring is in the pink and lavendar paint stains on the floor; in the pink and orange neck of the girl in front of me; in the crooked part in her yellow hair, drawn back into two uncombed blonde braids; in the easy stride of the thin blackhaired man in the light gray suit, walking down below on the pale pink sidewalk.

(79) April 1951
It is fortunate, fortunate indeed that this man called Cohen" stands on the lecture platform, and that his nasal voice crackles against my eardrums, and that his words and his astringent wit trickle down the cerebral creases of my understanding. It is fortunate, fortunate indeed, that pictures of old movie stills are flashed upon the twilit screen to lacquer the retina of my eye which notates, around the edge, the dim heads and the murmurs of these girls.

One girl looks around; the planes of her shaded face advance and recede again behind her hair. I am I, with all the individuality of an earthworm. After a rain, who knows the unique pink worm by the twist of its elastic segments. Only the guts of the worm know. And it is nothing to crush the yellow liquid intestines under a casual heel.

(80) Two hours, after that, of Botany," and the slow tedium of rusty scalpels scraping clumsily on moss and blindly twirling lenses and knitting in between the languid sight of protococcus, and the dry factual volley of information from the loose fleshy mouth of the instructor. When he bends over the microscope before you, you trace the purple clusters of capillaries under the coarse porousness of his skin, striped with short bristly hairs and rutted where loose creases swing flabbily from his neck and jowls. "Here at the end of the pointer is a protonema with buds on it." Here at the end of the pointer is a sick and squirming human intestine.

(81) June 15, 1951
The rain comes down again, on the indecently big green leaves, and there is the wet hiss of drops splashing and puckering the flat veined vegetable surfaces. Although the rain is neutral, although the rain is impersonal, it

becomes for me a haunting and nostalgic sound. The still air of the house smells of warm stagnant human flesh and of onions, and I sit, back to the radiator, the metal ribs of it pressing against my shoulders. I am in my old room once more, for a little, and I am caught in musing - - how life is a swift motion, a continuous flowing, changing, and how one is always saying goodbye and going places, seeing people, doing things. Only in the rain, sometimes, only when the rain comes, closing in your pitifully small radius of activity, only when you sit and listen by the window, as the cold wet air blows thinly by the back of your neck – only then do you think and feel sick. You feel the days slipping by, elusive as slippery pink worms, through your fingers, and you wonder what you have for your eighteen years, and you think about how, with difficulty and concentration, you could bring back a day, a day of sun, blue skies and watercoloring by the sea. You could remember the sensual observations that made that day reality, and you could delude yourself into thinking – almost – that you could return to the past, and relive the days and hours in a quick space of time. But no, the quest of time past is more difficult than you think, and time present is eaten up by such plaintive searchings. The film of your days and nights is wound up tight in you, never to be re-run – and the occasional flashbacks are faint, blurred, unreal, as if seen through falling snow. Now, you begin to get scared. You don't believe in God, or a life-after-death, so you can't hope for sugar plums when your non-existent soul rises. You believe that whatever there is has got to come from man, and man is pretty creative in his good moments – pretty mature, pretty perceptive for his age – how many years is it, now? How many thousands? Yet, yet in this era of specialization, of infinite variety and complexity and myriad choices, what do you pick for yourself out of the grab-bag? Cats have nine lives, the saying goes. You have one; and some-where along the thin, tenuous thread of your existence there is the black knot, the blood clot, the stopped heartbeat that spells the end of this particu-lar individual which is spelled "I" and "You" and "Sylvia." So you wonder how to act, and how to be – and you wonder about values and attitudes. In the relativism and despair, in the waiting for the bombs to begin, for the blood (now spurting in Korea, in Germany, in Russia) to flow and trickle before your own eyes, you wonder with a quick sick fear how to cling to earth, to the seeds of grass and life. You wonder about your eighteen years, ricocheting between a stubborn determination that you've done well for your own capabilities and opportunities . . . that you're competing now with girls from all over America, and not just from the hometown: and a fear that you <u>haven't</u> done well enough – You wonder if you've got what it takes to keep building up obstacle courses for your self, and to keep leaping through them, sprained ankle or not. Again the refrain, what <u>have</u> you for your eighteen years? And you know that whatever tangible things you <u>do</u> have, they cannot be held, but, too, will decompose and slip away through your coarse-skinned and death-rigid fingers. So you will rot in the ground, and so you say, what the hell? Who cares? But <u>you</u> care, and somehow you don't want to live just one life, which could be typed, which could be tossed off in a thumbnail sketch = "She was the sort of girl . . . . " And end in 25 words or less. You want to live as many lives as you can . . . you're a capitalist from way back . . . and because you're eighteen, because you're still vulnerable, because you still don't have faith in yourself, you talk a little fliply, a little too wisely, just to cover up so you won't be accused of sentimentality or emotionalism or feminine tactics. You cover up, so you can still laugh at yourself while there's time. And then you think of the flesh-and-blood people you know, and wonder guiltily where all this great little flood of confidence is getting you. (That's the pragmatic approach - - - <u>where</u> are you getting? <u>what</u> are you getting? Measure your precepts and their values by the tangible good you derive from their use.) Take the grandparents, now. What do you know about them? Sure, they were born in Austria, they say "cholly" for "jolly" and "ven" for "when". Grampy" is white-haired, terribly even-tempered, terribly old, terribly endearing in his mute and blind admiration of everything you do. (You take a bitter and rather self-righteous pride in the fact that he's a steward at a Country Club.) Grammy is spry, with a big fat bosom and spindly arthritic legs. She cooks good sour cream sauce and makes up her own recipes. She slurps her soup, and drops particles of food from her plate down the front of her dresses. She is getting hard of hearing, and her hair is just beginning to turn gray. There is your dead father who is somewhere in you, interwoven in the cellular system of your long body which sprouted from one of his sperm cells uniting with an egg cell in your mother's uterus. You remember that you were his favorite when your were little, and you used to make up dances to do for him as he lay on the living room couch after supper. You wonder if the absence of an older man in the house has anything to do with your intense craving for male company and the delight in the restful low sound of a group of boys, talking and laughing. You wish you had been made to know Botany, Zoology and Science when you were young. But with your father dead, you leaned abnormally to the "Humanities" personality of your mother. And you were frightened when you heard yourself stop talking and felt the echo of her voice, as if she had spoken in you, as if you weren't quite you, but were growing and continuing in her wake, and as if her expressions were growing and emanating from your face. (Here upon you ponder, and wonder if that's what happens to older people when they die contented - - - that they feel they have somehow transcended the wall of flesh which is crumbling fatally and forever around them and that their fire and protoplasm and pulse have leapt over bounds and will live on in off spring, continuing the chain of life . . .) Then there is your brother – 6 feet four inches tall, lovable and intelligent. You fought with him when you were little, threw tin soldiers at his head, gouged his neck with a careless flick of your iceskate . . . and then last summer, as you worked on the farm, you grew to love him, confide in him, and know him as a person . . . and you remember the white look of fear about his mouth that day they had all planned to throw you in the wash tub – and how he rallied to your defense. Yes, you can outline the people you've lived with these eighteen years in a few sentences . . . yet could you give an account of their lives, their hopes, their dreams? You could try, perhaps, but they would be much the same as yours . . . for you are all an inexplicable unity – this family group with its twisted tensions, unreasoning loves and solidarity and loyalty born and bred in blood. These people are the ones most basically responsible for what you are. Then there are the teachers – Miss Norris, the principle of grammar school; Miss Raguse, the tall, hideous 7th grade English teacher who loved poetry, and read it aloud to the class, even to the little boys destined to be garage mechanics; Mr. Crockett, the man through high school who fostered your intellectual life, along with that of your circle of class-mates who took the three year advanced English course; Mrs. Koffka," this year at Smith, who took up the torch and made you want to know, to think, to learn, to beat your head out against the knowledge of centuries. And there are the girls, who have come singly in a strange continuity to grow more and more intensely, to meet your growth, from the summers of camping and fern-hut building with Betsy Powley, to the tennis and talks with Mary Ventura and the pretty black-haired wit of Ruth Geisel, to the sweet senti-ment of Patsy O'Neil, to the synthesis of these in Marcia. And the boys, from Jimmy Beal, who drew you pictures of pretty girls in fifth grade, and roller-skated along the beach and planned to get married in a little white house with roses on a picket fence – (you remember, absurdly now, how his little sister was drowned on the beaches while walking on ice cakes, and how you didn't know just how to react to his white, drawn face when you saw him back at school. You wanted to say nice things and how sorry you were, and then you felt a sudden hardening and strange anger at him for his weakness which intensified yours. So you stuck out your tongue at him and made a face. And you never played with him again.) There was tall gawky John Stenberg who printed "Sylvia loves John" on his printing press and scattered little slips of paper all over the streets and in every desk at school. Mortified, yet secretly excited by such attention, you scorned his gifts of a rabbit's foot and a date to the carnival. (Later years would have found you infinitely grateful for any of his attentions whatever.) A blank of several awkward and ungainly and ugly adolescent years ended suddenly with a brief mental infatuation, and then a slow awakening of physical relationships with boys, from the first time, at the traditional age of sixteen, that you found that a kiss was not as distasteful as once imagined. And so you could list the thirty or forty boys you've gone out with in the last two years of your dating existence – and append a brief, if not astringent, note of gratitude to each one for an increased education in conversation, confidence and - - - so on. Till now you comb your hair with practiced casualness and go downstairs to greet the man of the hour with a careless sparkle in your eyes born of years of "faux pas" and blunders. Gone are the days where a date began in the afternoon, with an agony of nervousness prickling the back of the neck, making hands slippery and cold with sweat – sickening nausea that wouldn't let you eat supper – or do anything besides wait tensely, ready for at least half an hour before the boys came, and able only to check and re-check for slip-showing or hair-uncurled. And you look now at your reflection on the window and smile – for all your fat nose, you're quite a presentable long and lithe piece of tan flesh. And your mirth congeals on your full mouth as you think of yourself growing used to your reflection after year on year of mirror-glimpses. If you had a wen on either cheek, you'd get used to that, too. And the rain is still coming down, and it is getting later and later . . . and you aren't the sort of human being that can write till four in the morning and stay whole, so you trail off . . .

(82) And there was yesterday, the six of us on the Cape," in the beach wagon. A bright and laughing tension glittering dangerously between you and the one in the front seat who was your partner. (Have you a capacity for love of someone beside yourself? I wonder, sometimes.) You walked and you drove in the rain. You talked, taunted and teased, eating in the parked station wagon on a rise in the lonely wet black road that undulated along by the sea. Outside, beyond the cold thin glass of the rain blurred window you could see the ocean, remote and pale blue-gray, far out on the sand flats. The land was a warmer gray, with under washes of tawny yellow; soiled, and gloomy green underbrush cowered low along the dunes, and a cold tattoo of

metallic raindrops beat on the canvas beach wagon roof. Inside the windows steamed from breath and heat of six bodies, rain trickled from slickers down into dark wet puddles on the rubber floor matting, and there was the wet smell of tunafish and peeled oranges. Afterwards there was more driving through the rain, and the nebulous tunnels of green smudged a unique frosted green against the windows, seen through the film of steam collecting there. A dry stop at the "Sail Loft" – a barn of a place with fishnet curtains at the windows, full of expensive wool and cotton clothes and a sparkling blue-black haired girl name Pam. People – all young – came in, and there was talk, with boys especially. You wondered briefly if the Great God could stoop to jealously – and then you felt the lovely placating touch of hands on hair in a long light caress that could have been termed possessive. You felt very gay, very foolish, very cold and wet in the big chilly room with all the boys and girls. There was a visit at a new house – a meeting of a pert, wraith-slim red haired girl called Debby and a blonde baby boy who didn't talk, but who dimpled at his sister's laughter. A kitchen window – big and glassed in, overlooked a hill of scrub pine, and the sea, even more grayly blue and distant than ever. You stared out, and then watched the lovely broad-shouldered blonde boy across the room stare broodingly at nothing, and idly flexing his mouth in little grimaces – you felt a feeling of belonging to him curl cosily inside you and go to sleep like a kitten in front of a fire place. To leave him in the rain for a long while – that was next, next and unreal. Lightly he said he wanted to show you his room and told the rest you'd be right back. (Girls can be so careless with affection . . . you recalled a year ago, a barn, and steps leading upward, as these did.) Almost surprised you let yourself be enfolded in strong arms, in a last futile attempt to conserve and gather the lovely warmth and life pulse spilling from the fibers of the other. You saw blue eyes, light blue and keen, suddenly intent and was it, was it misting? Downstairs then, and good-bye, good-bye my love, good-bye. You felt no reality, no knife of sorrow cut your intestines to bits. Only a weariness, a longing for a shoulder to sleep on, a pair of arms to curl up in – and a lack of that now. Must you wait again, till some boy down the beach likes you, asks you out, kisses you - - - and you see the evening shrink to an artificial two-dimensional slice of time - - - - must you wait till then before you feel the full impact of your loneliness?

(83) July – 1951 – And so you sit on the porch outside your room, looking past the white patterned fence, like a stiff wooden ruffle, which stands up around the gray floorboards. You look across the long green lawn which

slopes to the street, where the cars flow by, red lights winking on in the twilight. You can see the ocean, gray, rustling with waves, and blending into the fainter gray of sky. You took a tall glass of milk upstairs with you, and two small ripe peaches. Strangely lovely, it was, to sit out on the porch, with the small cool rivers of night air lapping arms and legs; strangely pleasant to bite into the sweet rounded peach, letting the tongue-drenching juice fill your mouth. You walked over to the dishpan where they left the little turtle a few days ago. He was getting soft, they said, and the sun might do him good. But the turtle basked in sun for several days, forgotten, and the water dried up, and there was no food, no moist wet place for him to hide from the bright summer sun. So you found him, on his back, withered legs and head drawn into his shell, eyes sunken into his minute green head, and you let his frail shell body fall back on the dry stones. An Airplane sounds, far off in the gray sky, and the american flag languidly rides the eddies of wind above the Preston Hotel. Three weeks you have been here, and now that you suddenly have decided to leave, it seems quite a poor thing to do. The injustice and rebellion built up inside you, against the children's tantrums, against the daily chores, against the living always in the shadow of the lives of others – all the tired feelings and emotional disturbances burst forth today. And Marcia, in tears, and you, somber, agreed to leave. Definitely; positively, with no compromises. Your souls were going to be your own. Change of person. So Marcia called her father and told him she was coming home. I planned to call mother tomorrow. Outside, we stood together.

"Look at that ocean," she said. "Lovely, isn't it?"

"Yeah," I said.

"First time I've felt so good; first time I noticed the trees and the blue."

"Yeah. I feel terrific now," I said.

"We'll be nice - - oh, I'll even give the last few days free."

"Sure. Sure thing."

I went in. My feet hurt. I got Joey's blue bowl, poured Sugar Crisp in it, and filled her tin cup with milk. I heard her, then, walking up the cellar stars, bumping up, and todding into the kitchen to her high chair. I lifted her up, put on her bib, and she drank some milk.

"I-wanna-piece" . . . she pointed to a bag of peanuts.

You gave her one. She ate it gravely, and then stood up. One foot lifted. "Daddy," she said hope-fully, reaching out for you to lift her down. "No," you said, sitting her down. "Daddy" became a cry, then a wail. You lifted up the flailing bundle, thinking, oh brother, this is just about the last time. No more will I cart screaming children around, no more. I put her on the bed, crooning determinedly over the screaming. "Poor baby, you haven't had a nap today, no wonder you're tired. Does your arm hurt? Where's Joey's hand? Where's Joey's hand? There it is!" The last, repeated in a questioning, then a triumphant tone, usually intrigued her. Tonight she quieted momentarily, then began again. So you put her in the crib, sponge her hot dirty, chubby little face. She cries fretfully and tiredly. You start to sing in your tuneless monotone, "Bye-bye baby, remember you're my baby . . . " Eyes open wide. Thumb goes to mouth. A few convulsive sniffles. Translucent eyelids droop and lift, droop and slowly lift, and droop. You pull down the blinds. You shut the door after you, proud that you sang her to sleep, fond of her baby face and cuddly, firm little body.

That starts you feeling a little sorry. You won't ever see her again. She won't even remember you.

Pinny has been put to bed, Mrs. Mayo tells you in the kitchen. Two down, one to go. Freddy is in his pajamas, as the Mayos" leave for a cocktail party. You sit making faces at Freddy, and he laughs and laughs. As you dry the last dish, he says,

"I like being little and staying up."

"Why?" you ask.

"Because then big people have to wait on me. I like them to wait on me. I like to get up late in the morning, too."

"Why?" You are really fascinated.

"So they have to keep my food hot."

"What'll happen when you grow up?"

"Oh, then that will be bad. I'll have to wait on someone. No I won't either; Daddy doesn't."

There is something perversely and obstinately endearing about the back of Freddie's Head. You play songs on the piano for him, and he is strangely docile. Every few minutes he gives you a sip of iced tea, as if you were a girl dying of thirst. Sweetly he goes to bed. You sit out on the porch, to get a last look at the ocean. Really, if you can even have just a few minutes before bed, it isn't so bad. Then you wish Marcia hadn't called her father. They have all been so nice . . . you can't go through with it and leave. Somehow, you could never face yourself, quite. You would always feel that you might have done better, you might have at least finished it. So you are surprised to see that you really don't want to go home. You see how shut-in you would feel, in your little room. How closely the trees and houses and familiar paths would crowd upon you, stifling you, smothering you, enclosing you. Here, the house is big and spacious and luxuriously comfortable. The sink is big and clean. The stove is gradually becoming more of a friend. You are a prisoner of sorts, and yet you have made yourself so. You accepted this job for what you could make out of it. You didn't realize that for 14 hours a day you would be mentally and emotionally bound to children. But is it not worthwhile to accept it for the seven weeks more which remain – and to leave with a sense of accomplishment, if nothing else?

(84) From here to happiness is a road, flat, upright, distances in between blotted out by vision, yet realized by intelligence. From here to there is a road leading down blue pajamas to feet, to bed post, to screen door, to gray slatted porch roof, rain-puddled and drenched, to decorative white railing, to a road, to a line of sand, to a gray, rain beaten sea. Not yet to leave, not yet. For this road is a way to savor, a way back to living again as living is full. Not of bridge-playing, not of eating a frappe with two other girls, not even of talking with another. Aloneness and selfness are too important to betray for company.

(85) The most vital spot in the world for me was today in the rain, in an old gravel parking lot in Marblehead," where, beyond a rusty shack, was the harbor, and the neat upright forest of masts. Houses were close together, and yellow flowers were growing in the wild grass. Somehow, sitting there in the light blue Plymouth, your Grandmother beside you, your mother in back, you cried with love for them because they were your own people, your own kind. Yet not all your own kind, but you were of their blood and bone, and no barriers were between. You talked, and cried a little, as you sat, for the beauty of the wild, lanky yellow flowers, and the rain, trickling down the blurred and wavy windows, rushing in streams down the windows. This hour was yours, to steer through the narrow crooked streets, to sit and talk and watch the rain, to absorb the love of kin, of rain, of the masts of sloops and schooners. And when you swung the car into reverse, roaring out, back to your job, you felt whole and human once again. Someday you will find your way back to that parking spot by the gravel drive, and you will remember how it was, so forever you can carry it in you as it was, giving life and a new sight in the rainy space of an hour.

(86) Tonight each child went to bed after a bath. First Joey, who fussed and cried as you took the pants off her plump little body, and ran the water in the tub. Laughing, then, as you threw the soap into the water with a splash, she wriggled about in the water until you had rubbed her with soap and she was

as sweet smelling and slippery as any wet, freshly bathed baby. Her long white nightgown went on then, and clean diapers. Docilely she let you put her in the crib, where you bent over her for a while, letting her pinch your nose and cheeks, smile and gurgle as she made her suprised face, and watched for you to imitate her. Then you pulled down the blinds, saying "Good-night" as the room darkened. How to say how lovely her plump two year old body is, and her baby face, smooth skinned, fair, pink cheeked, green-eyed, with a fringe of silky yellow hair? How to say that her life is to be filled with love, admiration, Paris dresses, the cream of food and drink . . . all her life? But this is to be so, for now it is, and this baby is secure in love and in comfort.

Pinny was next, and you gave her a "front seat" up the stairs. In her pale blue party dress, white shoes and blonde hair, she was just a hard-living little girl, a bit unsure of herself because of the love lavished on the baby and because of the domineering mastery of talkative Freddie. Her big brown eyes, pointed face and husky voice softened under the special love and attention you gave her. You learned that by making her feel important, much could be gained. A cookie, a love pat and back rub ("Oh, that feels so good!) and a song, set her off to sleep, hugging her soft, worn, special pillow. You remember how she said the first night you came, "I like a pillowcase to hug. A soft little one."

Freddie was last, and by far the most interesting and amusing. A talkative Kewpie-doll faced boy of seven, with a Beau Brummel taste for socks and jerseys that match, and for shirts and bow ties – he appreciates more advanced stories, and is extremely clever. Tonight, after a tale about a crooked mouse, he responded to my ritual "Going to give me a goodnight hug?" with a kiss on one eyelid. "Now I have to kiss the other eye," he said. "Then mouth." His little mouth smacked softly. "I have to give your neck four, because it's so large." And so to bed.

Something maternal awakened, perhaps, by the physical contact with such lovely young babies? Something sensual aroused by young hands at breast, young cheeks against face, young warm child bodies under hands? Perhaps. And tonight was a good night, thus I feel correspondingly tender. There will be other bad nights, but remembering the versatile quicksilver shifting of children's moods, I smile with equanimity and do not cherish grudges, as most of us adults do, letting them fester like a cancer. But I let my emotions run on the same forgiving and transient track.

(87) "Wonder who's going to get drunk first?" Doctor Mayo made a face,

and I giggled, spreading the stiff orange cheese in little pats on the Ritz crackers. Mrs. Mayo was pouring sliced peaches and juice over a great plate of little white cakes. Macaroni and cheese sauce reposed in two great glazed brown crocks, while a huge wooden bowl waited to receive the salad. Cocktail glasses and a tray of icecubes and bottles rested on the sideboard. Twenty people for dinner, and I didn't know whether I was in the way or not.

"How are you at whipping cream?" Mrs. Mayo asked.

"Guess I could manage."

"I always whip it in the sink; it's steadier."

I tried to make the beater whir very quickly. A little muscle twitched in my arm, the cream whirled liquidly, thickening in white foam. What if it turned to butter? The time was getting close. Soon the People would come, and then it would be the usual thing: putting the children to bed, answering the last plaintive cries for a drink of water. And then would come the giddy sense of freedom. It would be past eight o'clock, and still light enough to read outside on the gray slatted porch. So you could sit there for a while until Marcia came to help you with the dishes – dishes of twenty people, twenty lovely crisp gay people.

From Freddie's window I peered with a delicious shiver as I pulled down the blind. By leaving just a crack between the blind and the windowsill, I could satisfy my curiosity. Down below, on the stone terrace with the white railing; down below, with the white and green painted chairs sat a group of men and women, some familiar, some not. One woman leaned against the railing, hands crossed in front of her, dressed in dark blue, with a red rose at the point of a low V-neckline. Mrs. Mayo sat and talked with a group of women, while Doctor Mayo merged into the tan, gray, beige line of men. What were they talking about? What was the subtle line that marked you from entering a group such as this?

"Get into bed, now, Freddie," I said to the small boy at the window.

"I just want to see Nancy. She just walked in. Just can I take one little peep?"

"Just one quick peep."

"She's so pretty in a purple dress. I bet she weighs more than you. I bet she weighs two hundred hundred pounds."

A glance at Nancy, Jack's girl. Oblivious of my calculating stare, she walked across the stage, smiled friendly at someone I couldn't quite see, and stood down below, in that strange, half-curious, half-comical world on the terrace.

Out on the porch, now, I can hear the voices coming up to me, laughter, raveled words. Up here, on the second floor porch, the air blurs the syllables and continuity of conversation like sky-writing, blown from a clear lucid penciled white line to a puffy amorphous mass of cloud.

Green of grass, gray of ocean, and a deepening shade of sky, faintly pink. Always a roaring of sound in my ears – wind heaving in the trees, waves rustling on the shore, cars whirring along the turnpike. The moon, now, over the green-black tufted tops of the pines, is getting more luminous with the dying day. From the anemic, faintly cloudy globe of daytime, it is becoming chalkily, shiningly white. Third quarter lunar phase. In your mind's eye you try to draw in the shaded part of the sphere. But it is invisible to you, amputated optically and neatly by thousands of miles of blue sky . . . atmosphere thickening like blue water.

Down below a thick burry voice rasps, "The moon's out." The reply ravels and threads on the tree leaves, and is lost to you.

(88) There is a sound that will always be strange and unique in your remembering. It is the sound made by you and Marcia, walking on the stony beach in Marblehead. Along the North shore coast there must be many such beaches, short, hewn out of the rock, sandless, clean. Great shelves of rounded stones slope down steeply, like steppes, into the sea. Worn smooth by the waves, and baked hot by the sun, the rocks and stones shifted and clattered under our feet, sounding like the rattle and clank of chains. It was to that sound of rocks, rolling and colliding under us, that we hiked along the beach in the hot July sunlight. Both of us were deeply tan and our hair was bleached from the sun. Our skin was stiff and caked with salt, dried and crusty from swimming in the icy lucid blue water. I licked my arm for the salt taste. Up the face of a rock cliff we climbed, finding footholds as we went along. The rock was yellow-orange, hot and jagged.

"God, look at the blue," I said.

"Wait till you get to the top," Marty said.

She was right. Atop the great rock formation you stood, and the whole ocean curled up bluely at your feet. Slowly, with a great, patient, unanimous motion, the huge bulk of tide water heaved up and back, up and back along the coast. Sails flicked in and out of the light far out in the bay. The horizon blurred into the sky. Far, far down, at your feet, the water was the strangely clear turquoise and clouded yellow-green where submerged strata of rock were close to the surface of the sea. Small, small, you were, two brown animals crawling, minute, microscopic, up the side of a great cliff, in the huge sunlight, by a blue gigantic sea.

"I want my children to be conceived by the sea," Marty said. And suddenly she was right. Naked bodies, two, on the rocks, under the big sky, the big stars, the big night wasteland. So much more frightening, so much more clean than if they lay, side by side, on a hot, narrow bed, in the small thick dark box of a man-made bedroom.

(89) Lying on my stomach on the flat warm rock, I let my arm hang over the side, and my hand caressed the rounded contours of the sun-hot stone, and felt the smooth undulations of it. Such a heat the rock had, such a rugged and comfortable warmth, that I felt it could be a human body. Burning through the material of my bathing suit, the great heat radiated through my body, and my breasts ached against the hard flat stone. A wind, salty and moist, blew damply in my hair; through a great glinting mass of it I could see the blue twinkle of the ocean. The sun seeped into every pore, satiating every querulous fiber of me into a great glowing golden peace. Stretching out on the rock, body taut, then relaxed, on the altar, I felt that I was being raped deliciously by the sun, filled full of heat from the impersonal and colossal god of nature. Warm and perverse was the body of my love under me, and the feeling of his carved flesh was like no other – not soft, not malleable, not wet with sweat, but dry, hard, smooth, clean and pure. High, bonewhite, I had been washed by the sea, cleansed, baptised, purified, and dried clean and crisp by the sun. Like seaweed, brittle, sharp, strong-smelling – like stone, rounded, curved, oval, clean – like wind, pungent, salty – like all these was the body of my love. An orgiastic sacrifice on the altar of rock and sun, and I arose shining from the centuries of love, clean and satiated from the consuming fire of his casual and timeless desire.

(90) I am tired, and the evening world beats dead, flat, numb. To sleep, no, never to wake and turn in thoughtless rest to sleep again. To wait, rather, while the dawn comes early, and wetly shining. To rise to the day, and to the crises and the indecisive lulls. And to wait, taut, smiling, till evening, and the time after eight o'clock, again, to the time you go to bed, which is yours, which is brief and private. To take, from the closet occasionally, your yellow dress, not yet worn, and hold it up against your dark tan, and smile, and say, "Oh, Dick, how wonderful to see you. Stop; don't move. Just let me look at you." Two days more of living, and then Dick.

(91) Variations on a theme:

Letter form: A strange time, indeed, to compose letters is five thirty in the morning. However, with the well-timed punctuality of an alarm clock I awoke in a gray dawn today, listening instinctively for the cry of the baby which never came, only the crescendo of sleepy musical chirpings of birds in neighboring trees.

Quiet, cool and green is the early morning world, after a violent rain last night, bright flickers of lightning and sharp cracks of thunder. It is with an odd and victorious sense of going home that I shall return to Swampscott to lose myself again in the fresh, wholesome and thoroughly theraputic company of children.

And so it is that with my leaning toward allegories, similes and meta-phors, I suddenly find a vehicle to express a few of the many disturbing thoughts which have been with me since yesterday. I mentioned that I would try to describe the feeling I had toward an anonomous part of the Mas-sachusetts coastline. Simple as this task may seem, I wanted to wait until I could do it even partial justice because it forms the core of my continually evolving philosophy of thought and action.

On a relatively unfrequented, stony beach there is a great rock which juts out over the sea. After a climb, an ascent from one jagged foothold to another, a natural shelf is reached where one person can stretch at length, and stare down into the tide rising and falling below, or beyond to the bay, where sails catch light, then shadow, then light, as they tack far out near the horizon. The sun has burned these rocks, and the great continuous ebb and flow of the tide has crumbled the boulders, battered them, worn them down to the smooth sun-scalded stones on the beach which rattle and shift under-foot as one walks over them. A serene sense of the slow inevitability of the gradual changes in the earth's crust comes over me; a consuming love, not of a god, but of the clean unbroken sense that the rocks, which are nameless, the waves which are nameless, the ragged grass, which is nameless, are all defined momentarily through the consciousness of the being who observes them. With the sun burning into rock and flesh, and the wind ruffling grass and hair, there is an awareness that the blind immense unconscious impersonal and neutral forces will endure, and that the fragile, miraculously knit organism which interprets them, endows them with meaning, will move about for a little, then falter, fail, and decompose at last into the anonomous soil, voiceless, faceless, without identity.

From this experience I emerged whole and clean, bitten to the bone by sun, washed pure by the icy sharpness of salt water, dried and bleached to the smooth tranquillity that comes from dwelling among primal things.

From this experience also, a faith arises to carry back to a human world of small lusts and deceitful pettiness. A faith, naïve and child like perhaps, born as it is from the infinite simplicity of nature. It is a feeling that no matter what the ideas or conduct of others, there is a unique rightness and beauty to life which can be shared in openness, in wind and sunlight, with a fellow human being who believes in the same basic principles.

Yet, when such implicit belief is placed in another person, it is indeed shattering to realize that a part of what to you was such a rich, intricate, whole conception of life has been tossed off carelessly, lightly – it is then that a stunned, inarticulate numbness paralyzes words, only to give way later to a deep hurt. It is hard for me to say on paper what I believe would best be reserved for a lucid vocal discussion. But somehow I did want you to know a little of what your surprising and perhaps injudiciously confidential information did to me yesterday. A feeling that there was no right to condemn, but that still somehow there was a crumbling of faith and trust. A feeling that there was a way to rationalize, to condone, if only by relegating a fellow human from the unique to the usual.

So there it is. The rock and the sun are waiting on the next day off – and solace.

(92.) It seems to me more than ever that I am a victim of introspection. If I have not the power to put myself in the place of other people, but must be continually burrowing inward, I shall never be the magnanimous creative person I wish to be. Yet I am hypnotized by the workings of the individual, alone, and am continually using myself as a specimen. I am possessive about time alone, more so now that my working hours are not spent studying for myself, but dancing attendance to a family. Here I am in the midst of a rich, versatile family, as close as I could get. I have made my wish come true – almost – and, as It were, picked up the roof of this lovely, spacious white house and walked in. True, in actuality I am relegated by my position to a circumscribed area of confidence, but even so, here I am. Yet so constantly am I moving, working, acting, that I do not often think "How strange this is . . . I am competently frying eggs for three children on Sunday morning while the parents sleep. I must learn more about these people – try to understand them, put myself in their place." No, instead I am so busy keeping my head above water that I scarcely know who I am, much less who anyone else is.

But I must discipline myself. I must be imaginative and create plots, knit motives, probe dialogue – rather than merely trying to record descriptions and sensations. The latter is pointless, without purpose, unless it is later to be synthesized into a story. The latter is also a rather pronounced symptom of an oversensitive and unproductive ego.

93. Now I am not sure about that letter I sent. Not sure at all. For was I not the one who acquiesced, mutely responsive and receptive? Was I not guilty of letting a boy be drawn to self-hatred? And yet does it not all come again to the fact that it is a man's world? For if a man chooses to be promiscuous, he may still aesthetically turn up his nose at promiscuity. He may still demand a woman be faithful to him, to save him from his own lust. But women have lust, too. Why should they be relegated to the position of custodian of emotions, watcher of the infants, feeder of soul, body and pride of man? Being born a woman is my awful tragedy. From the moment I was conceived I was doomed to sprout breasts and ovaries rather than penis and scrotum; to have my whole circle of action, thought and feeling rigidly circumscribed by my inescapable feminity. Yes, my consuming desire to mingle with road crews, sailors and soldiers, bar room regulars – to be a part of a scene, anonomous, listening, recording – all is spoiled by the fact that I am a girl, a female always in danger of assault and battery. My consuming interest in men and their lives is often misconstrued as a desire to seduce them, or as an invitation to intimacy. Yet, God, I want to talk to everybody I can as deeply as I can. I want to be able to sleep in an open field, to travel west, to walk freely at night . . .

94. July 19 – This morning I awoke into dampness, the windows white and vague with fog. This afternoon, while all the family was out the first big storm came. I had just washed my hair, and the rain began, big, wet drops from the great spread of sky. The house was darkened, and the lights burned weakly, it seemed, in face of the great noise of falling water outside. As excited as a child, I called to Marcia, who was playing the piano, and ran down the long carpeted hall to the front door, where I could look through the screen to the wildly heaving trees, the gray ocean, angry with white foam, the crackling blasts of sheet lightning and the immediate whip cracks and rattling, banging, earsplitting bursts of thunder. Water ran in rivers down the pavement, and suddenly I remembered to shut the windows. But even as I ran from room to room, trying to close the fourteen or fifteen windows on the side where the rain was coming in, it was too late, and the

sills were wet with puddles, and the water was collecting in streams along the floor.

(95) Tonight, after playing ping pong down in the Blodgett's" basement playroom I walked back into the house with a perceptible sense of proprietorship. If nothing else, in one month I have come to regard this place with an air of home. Upstairs, especially, I am complete sovereign. I still remember the day I drove up with Dick and stood in awestruck fear outside the gate, gazing at the great lawn, the long white house, the clump of huge copper beech trees spaced carefully on the grass. Never, I thought, could I walk with carefree equanimity on that carefully clipped lawn. But I do now. Yes, and tonight I felt the wetness heavy about me; leaves, pregnant with water, soaked the sleeve of my jersey as I brushed past the bush by the kitchen steps. Up the carpeted stairs to my room, lighted only by the moon, which shone across the porch and the wet window sill with a liquid luminosity. An inexplicable quiver of intense, almost contraband, excitement filled me as I pushed open the screen door, swollen shut by the rain, and walked out onto the porch. I sat down on the cold, slick tile roof and stared at the moon shadow of the porch railing, slanting across the floor. Somehow, I think, I have a delicious feeling of presumptuousness which comes perhaps from a secret enjoyment of living with rich people and listening to and observing them. It is like hearing a supposedly confidential conversation. You wonder only how you can ever bear to live anywhere else, away from the sea, the physical ease, the sun, the spaciousness. Seated on the porch, straight ahead was the ocean, above was the big sky, with a hazy, faintly orange-tinged moon. The moon and stars seemed very small for such a big sky. Down below stretched the lawn, the street, the beach, in a line of open view. How hard it will be to return home, where the little green pine trees grow in such a close square around the house, where you can't move freely in a room without bumping into the furniture, where mother serves cranberry juice in cream cheese glasses on an old white celluloid tray. Here the lawns swoop to the open sea, the rooms are lofty, with great picture windows, and sparkling green and golden cocktails are served on cracked ice and silver trays. How to return to the smallness, the imperfection, which is home?

(96) Under the greenshaded lights, Elaine, still in her white maid's uniform, was playing pool. Her face was red and shiny as she leaned over the table, trying for a long shot.

Marcia slouched over the piano, her tan a golden brown against her blue sweater, banging out a jazzy version of "Ja-Da."

Wicker chairs were scattered in profusion about the pine paneled game room. The spasmodic click-click . . . . click-click of the ping pong ball sounded as Cynthia and Joan banged out an irregular ralley, stopping to chase the round white ball under the intricate path of chair and table legs after wild shots.

"Sorry," Cynthia said, serving a high one too hard, so that it missed the proper green square.

"Heck," Joan chased it up to the fireplace, reached behind an andiron and extricated it.

The click-click . . . click-click started up again.

Elaine poised for another shot, slid the stick through her fingers and drove a yellow ball into the pocket. She put down the stick and went to sit on the bench beside Marcia, who had stopped to have a cigarette.

"Donald's out tonight," she said. "Some girl called, and I left a message on his pillow."

"Did you turn down the bed corners?" Marcia grinned.

"Yup. Almost decided to put in hot coals to warm the sheets." Elaine grinned back.

"You've got it rough. I'd be mad as anything if they made me wear a uniform."

"You've got it easy. You can just take care of the kids. That way you're part of the family. I'm lower; I'm only the maid."

"Hell, don't talk that way. You're just as good as they are. Besides, it's just for the summer."

"I know. But still."

"Sure. Don't you suppose I feel it? In the morning when I sit in the kitchen with the kids, drinking canned orange juice from a jelly glass, while Donald gets his tray on the porch, fresh squeezed juice in a goblet! Let me tell you, I wonder why he's the one to get waited on, instead of me."

Cynthia and Joan had stopped playing, and moved over to sit on the floor by the piano.

"This is a terrific set up you two have got here," Joan said to Marcia and Elaine. "Don't they ever use this game room? If I lived here, I'd use it every minute."

"Yeah, it's neat," said Cynthia. "All I do is file letters and write down numbers on big sheets all day."

79

"What's it like to work in a big insurance company?" Marcia asked, grinding out her cigarette in a grimy little snow of ashes.

"Oh, it's O.K. Every week there's some anniversary or somebody's leaving, so they have a shower, and you go up and see orchids all over the place. My section is mostly married women though."

"Tell us about it. Do you get to know them much?" Elaine wanted to know.

"Well, there's people like Harriet, the old maid. One of the women came back to work pregnant, after Harriet had kept telling her she'd never make a good mother. 'Well, don't you think I'll be a good mother now?' the woman asked Harriet. 'No, I don't' Harriet sniffed. 'You shouldn't of done it.' "

(97) I was out in the kitchen doing the dishes, scraping the soggy puddles of cereal and milk off the sticky plates, when Dr. Mayo walked in in his white jacket, hair slicked back from his thin face. He stood for a while, making cocktails. At last he said:

"Oh, to be young again . . . "

"What brought that on?" I asked, peering into the cupboard for some Bab-o.

"Oh, so I could enjoy these things more."

"You don't do too badly . . . "

I was suddenly struck by the comedy of the situation. Here was a young, tan eighteen year old girl perpetually doing dishes, while a husband and wife in the thirties went to one dinner and one dance and one cocktail party after another. Somehow, it seemed, the situation could well be reversed.

Mrs. Mayo rustled into the kitchen, tall, slender and darkly beautiful in a flowing nylon gown of aqua – three tones of light, medium and dark which blended and flowed into one another. She stood and made cheese crackers to go with the cocktails.

"Seems I always end up cooking in a formal," she said.

(98) The blonde girl stood in front of the mirror in the ladies Room of the eastern Yacht club. Her head thrown back, fringed by a copper scallop of short curls, her hips slanted boldly forward, she tossed her black and white stole from one shoulder to another, striking a seductive pose each time she did so.

"Ah could weah it lak this," she drawled, twisting the scarf of material about her narrow waist. "Or lak this," she wrapped it about her neck, the long fringed black ends trailing cape-like down her back. The girl seemed oblivious to all except her own reflection in the mirror before her. Would she never stop twisting the material about her body?

The fat woman who was her mother sat in a wicker chair, smiling, her carefully drawn red lips curved in a calculating grin. Her arms and hands moved slowly, plumply, like twining cobras. Little dangerous insinuating sparks lighted in her eyes, compelling, fascinating. One fleshily soft thigh crossed over the other under the rough textured linen of her dress.

Out on the porch, the young boy was very drunk. He grinned at his date, and turned to the plump, arch woman, letting his hand caress her thigh. On the porch railing the blonde girl kicked her leg high, drawling "Oh, chi-chi veree chi-chi." Gurgling, laughing, she kissed her husband on the nose.

The blonde girl's sister sat lustreless, her long silver hair drooping to her shoulders. "I am a peeg," she said over and over again, showing her waist and full, slenderly pointed breasts under the Indian print dress she wore.

"Come here," the young, drunk boy said to her. "Sit next to me. I can't hear you talk."

The Manhattan slithered from his hand and fell to the floor with a soprano tinkle. Clumsily he wiped the widening stain which darkened the dress of his date. The table, covered with a transparent cloth of plastic, held the pool of spilt liquor. The boy tried to drink from the glass, but the cup of the goblet was split, and he cut his lip.

(99) Gray fog shredded thin along the flatwashed duncolored beach. Small dullgreen waves folded over upon themselves in a slither of dirty white foam, spreading out in sheets of water, reflecting the soiled morning sky. The blue tendrils of mist drifting up from the shore bleached out color in a pale soapy haze. Over the continuous in rushing sound of the tide came the shrill screams of the children, puckering the moist air that blew in smokily from the sea.

Blinding and whitehot behind the little curdled clouds, the sun began to burn through the grayblue layers of fog. Light glittered fresh and creamy on the white frame walls of the Beach Club, where blue and orange striped umbrellas made round smudges of shade beside the pool. Tinfoil bright streaks of light flickered and trembled through clear, chlorine blue water.

In green and blue deck chairs the women sat, heads back, eyes shut into the lemon-prickling glare of sun, grease shining fatly on skin, sun raw and red. Bathing suits bulged over breasts and thighs. Legs and arms extended like soft sausage, broiling with a smell of olive oil in the hot July morning.

(100) Her smooth tan feet slapped wetly over the concrete by the pool. Steam rose from overflow puddles of sunwarmed water seeping down into the porous pavement. Squinting against the glittering light which trembled, liquid and iridescent, on the shivering, shattered glass of the water, and slid whitely along the slippery flashing limbs of the swimmers, she walked down the granite steps onto the beach, where the sand was cool and soft under her stone scalded feet.

PRIVATE, only guests of members admitted: no trespassing. The wire fence around the pool and outdoor terrace was high. It enclosed the sterile turquoise blue pool, the striped umbrellas, the tennis courts, and the parking lot, where sleek shiny cars crowded, rump after chromium-plated rump.

A boy in wrinkled khaki pants and a T-shirt was spearing up dried black snarls of seaweed with a pitchfork. He moved slowly along the beach, – picking up the litter left by the last high tide . . .

(101) The wet gray August morning oozed in upon her consciousness as she lay limp on the porch cot. The damp softness of the sheets was cool against her skin. In the dim half light she stretched wearily, yawned, and thought, "No, not another day beginning." There was still time yet; time to lie languidly on the cot in the thick, rainmoist air; time to let eyelids open, shut, open, shut in a gradually quickening cadance until eyes remained open, staring at the green leaves crowding against the screen, tiredly straining to make out the sleeping huddled form of Lane on the cot by her side. Lane stirred, rubbed her eyes, and grunted plaintively into her pillow. Her hair tumbled into her eyes as she hauled herself up on one elbow and stared back at the girl on the other cot. "God," she said, "I can't get up. I can't face it." She let herself fall back on to the bed and nuzzled into the covers, trying to shut out the paling dawn.

Inside the house, Mrs. Avery came downstairs. Through the stained and dirty glass of the porch door, the girl watched the dark form move about in the deep shadows of the livingroom. Dampness permeated everything. The girl sat up in bed and swung her feet to the floor. The twine rug was clammy under the calloused soles of her bare feet. Her seersucker pajamas fell in damp folds about her body, clinging to her skin which felt slick, greasy and unclean, polluted by contact with the foul air.

Shakily the girl stood up, shook her head, and padded across the porch, opened the door to the livingroom after much pushing, as it was swollen by the moist air and stuck stubbornly to its wooden frame, and proceeded to the bathroom.

In the small steamy room, the girl sat sleepily down on the toilet, releasing the bright stream of strong smelling urine, rubbing her hands meditatively along the flesh of her bare thighs. A smell of soap and toothpaste, of warm, wet facecloths and damp towels curled around her as she sat slumped on the toilet seat, head in hands, thinking, "No, please, God, not another day beginning."

(102) It is 11:30 p.m. on the evening of August first, nineteen hundred and fifty one John Blodgett is seventy years old, and I am very tired. I wonder why I don't go to bed and go to sleep. But then it would be tomorrow, so I decide that no matter how tired, no matter how incoherent I am, I can skip one hour more of sleep and live. If I did not have this time to be myself, to write here, to be alone, I would somehow, inexplicably, lose a part of my integrity. As it is, what I have written here so far is rather poor, rather unsatisfactory. It is the product of an unimaginative girl, pre-occupied with herself, and continually splashing about in the shallow waters of her own narrow psyche. As an excuse, she claims these are writing exercises, a means of practice at expressing herself, of note taking for future stories. Yet on the merry-go-round of time there is scarcely enough to spent pondering and attempting to recapture details. In fact, if one has not the imagination to create characters, to knit plots, it does no good to jot down fragments of life and conversation, for alone they are disjointed and meaningless. It is only when these bits are woven into an artistic whole, with a frame of reference, that they become meaning-ful and worthy of more than a cursory glance. Therefore, think and work, think and work.

(103) Pinny kicked and screamed as I carried her upstairs. With a strong sense of power I tossed her on the bed in her party dress. "Mummy, mummy!" she yelled, her small face contorted, her legs and arms flailing.

"Call Sylvia," Grandma had said as they served cocktails in the dining-room. "Sylvia, Pinny slapped me when I asked her to go upstairs."

So Sylvia carried a howling holocaust up to bed. Holding down the furi-ous, scarlet-faced child, I touched by accident, the correct lever, "Do you," I intoned between my teeth, "want me to spank you?" She gasped, gulped for breath. "No . . . . " "Then not one more sound." There was, at last, silence. I undressed her, put on cotton underpants, and asked her to hug me good-night. With the sweetness of a victim who knows she's beaten, she kissed me goodnight. Rancor left, not festering, but placid.

Lane came up to my room, in her white uniform, looking very mischievous and pixie-ish. Her hair crisped in little impromptu curls about her face.

"They're eating, now," she said by way of explaining her presence. "Helen will call me I guess when she wants help with the dishes."

"I'm going to bed early," I said. "Sitting on Pinny doesn't agree with my constitution."

Just then there was a cool green silken rustle on the stairs. "Will you help," Mrs. Mayo asked, "with the dishes."

In the kitchen, contagious laughter trickled from the dining room to where we stood, scraping plates thick with fat and scabrous remains of baked potato. Helen stood over the sink, her heavy bulk sweating profusely, making dark wet stains on her faded print housedress.

"Have some turkey," she offered, puffing at her cigarette. The gutted carcass of the turkey reposed on a huge silver platter which held cold white waxen puddles of fat in the scalloped flutings of the edge.

Lane took a handful of peanuts from the counter of rejected and superfluous hors d'oeuvres instead. She brushed the salt from her hands after eating them.

"Better bring in the ice cream," Mrs. Mayo and her sister were out in the kitchen, busily lighting the red and white candles of the enormous birthday cake. On a green and blue sugar sea with coconut whitecaps sailed a brown icing sloop, proudly flaunting red and white and blue yacht club flags. The small wax candles dipped and flared as one of the boys carried the sugar objet d'art into the glittering laughter and gleaming linen festivity of the dining room where twenty dinnerguests sucked the last masticated fragments of turkey from their teeth, wiped greasy lips on dry linen napkins, and glowed under the expansive sociable flood of liquor through their blood streams.

The door swung shut, and Lane and I charlestoned crazily around the kitchen table, as Helen clucked in mock dismay, and plunged another load of dirty glasses into the steamy soapy water.

Later the guests adjourned to the livingroom for after-dinner coffee. Lane and I walked jauntily into the empty dining room and sat at either end of the great white table with twenty dirty dessert plates and glasses ringed about it. Ladling some melting vanilla ice cream on fresh plates we pretended we were Alice and the White Rabbit at the Mad Hatter's tea Party.

(104) There comes a time when all your outlets are blocked, as with wax. You sit in your room, feeling the prickling ache in your body which constricts your throat, tightens dangerously in little tear pockets behind your eyes.

One word, one gesture, and all that is pent up in you – festered resentments, gangrenous jealousies, superfluous desires – unfulfilled – all that will burst out of you in angry impotent tears – in embarrassed sobbing and blubbering to no one in particular. No arms will enfold you, no voice will say, "There, There. Sleep and forget." No, in your new and horrible independence you feel the dangerous premonitory ache, arising from little sleep and taut strung nerves, and a feeling that the cards have been stacked high against you this once, and that they are still being heaped up. An outlet you need, and they are sealed. You live night and day in the dark cramped prison you have made for yourself. And so on this day, you feel you will burst, break, if you cannot let the great reservoir seething in you loose, surging through some leak in the dike. So you go downstairs and sit at the piano. All the children are out; the house is quiet. A sounding of sharp chords on the keyboard, and you begin to feel the relief of loosing some of the great weight on your shoulders.

Quick footsteps up cellar stairs. A sharp thin annoyed face around the bannister. "Sylvia, will you please not play the piano in the afternoon during office hours. It bangs right through downstairs."

Paralyzed, struck numb, branded by his cold voice you lie "Sorry. I had no idea you could hear."

So that too is gone. And you grit your teeth, despising yourself for your tremulous sensitivity, and wondering how human beings can suffer their individualities to be mercilessly crushed under a machine-like dictatorship – be it of industry, state or organization – all their lives long. And here you agonize for a mere ten weeks of your life, when you have only four more weeks to go anyway.

Liberty, self-integral freedom, await around the corner of the calendar. All of life is not lost, merely an eighteeth summer. And perhaps something good has been sprouting in the small numb darkness all this while.

(105) And times there are when you feel very wise and ageless. You are sunning on the rocks, the water splashing at your feet, when a small chubby frecklefaced girl of about ten approaches you, her hand holding something that is invisible, but evidently quite precious.

"Do you know," she asks earnestly, "do starfish like hot or cold water best?"

(106) Today I made a Devil's Food Cake for the first time. While I was making the frosting, Joanne, sitting happily on the floor, spilled a box of Ivory Snow.

After mopping that sticky soapy mess up, I followed her to the living room, where she had located a carton of cigarettes, and had just emptied one pack in a sifting of loose tobacco on the Oriental rug. Picking her up under one arm, I headed back to the kitchen, where my layer cakes reposed. I couldn't figure out how to turn them over so that the plates would hold the two cakes. I put the plates upside down on top of the layers as they sat on the rack and turned the racks over so that the plates would turn out rightside up, holding the layers. Lack of foresight was revealed when the heavy rack, turned over on top of the cakes, crushed deeply into them and crumbled large pieces from the edge. I had not made enough frosting to spread over the side of the cake to conceal the messy uneven edges, so I cut three pieces of the worst-looking part for our lunch. They crumbled into little shapeless brown masses on the plates. So I hid them in a cupboard in order that no one would see them. When it would be dessert time I would spirit them out and hope the children would devour them quickly.

(107) God, the days go by and by, and here is the night before the second day. Downstairs, whitely powdered with confectioners' sugar, reposing in a round blue tin, are the date-nut bars I made. On the kitchen windowsill, cooling, is the large pottery bowl full of applesauce I made from green apples I picked in the orchard this afternoon. In the newspaper, the dead lock over a Korean armistice is still going on; a widow Tabor's letter about saving face and squeezing out more than a stalemate of the Chinese forces is getting a big play; Anglo-Iranian crisis is still rampant; senate voting a cut in foreign aid . . . (bad sign?) and on page 14 Mrs. MacGonigle, age 103, tells how to live to a ripe maturity: "Eat lots of fish and keep away from busses and trains." Three children whom I have grown to love sleep in the empty house. I lie here, sprawled naked on the bed, all windows open, and the rustling salt air blowing in across my smooth brown body, and the iced evening odor of cold cut wet grass, and the shush of waves breaking at the end of the street. And god, for the spirits of ammonia to make the weary lethargic-spirited mind sneeze itself into acute and tremulous awareness – there is the flood, the great silver blue swatch, the oriental silver twinkle of moonlight on ocean water.

(108) "Your hair smells nice, Pinny." I said, sniffing her freshly washed blonde locks. "It smells like soap."

"Does my eye?" she asked, wriggling her warm, nightgowned body on my arms.

"Does your eye what?"

"Smell nice?"

"But why should your eye smell nice?"

"I got soap in it," she explained.

(109) Over the sound of the electric garbage disposal unit, roaring hoarsely and devouring orange peels, egg shells and coffee grounds, I could hear the doctor on the phone. He was following a case which I had already heard snatches about in a similar way.

"This trouble seemed to be explained when we diagnosed a duodenal ulcer. We thought that once we put her on the proper diet, milk every hour, and so forth, that the disturbance would clear up. However, this morning she vomited several cupfuls of liquid, like coffee, which was really old blood. At her age we don't want to take chances, and will keep looking for a tumor . . . "

What could this not be worked into? Not only medical details, fine as a basis, but who is She, and who is the one who keeps calling to find out about Her condition? I must make up something to fill in the great gaps in my knowledge . . . Yet have I the will, the experience, the imagination?

(110) The wind has blown a warm yellow moon up over the sea; a bulbous moon, which sprouts in the soiled indigo sky, and spills bright winking petals of light on the quivering black water.

(111) I am at my best in illogical, sensuous description. Witness the bit above. The wind could not possibly blow a moon up over the sea. Unconsciously, without words, the moon has been identified in my mind with a balloon, yellow, light, and bobbing about on the wind. The moon, according to my mood, is not slim, virginal and silver, but fat, yellow, fleshy and pregnant. Such is the distinction between April and August, my present physical state and my sometime-in-the-future physical state. Now the moon has undergone a rapid metamorphoses, made possible by the vague imprecise allusions in the first line, and become a tulip or crocus or aster bulb, whereupon comes the metaphor: the moon is "bulbous", which is an adjective meaning fat, but suggesting "bulb", since the visual image is a complex thing. The verb "sprouts" intensifies the first hint of a vegetable quality about the moon. A tension, capable of infinite variations with every combination of words, is created by the phrase "soiled indigo sky". Instead of saying blatantly "in the soil of the night sky", the adjective "soiled" has a double

focus: as a description of the smudged dark blue sky and again as a phantom noun "soil", which intensifies the metaphor of the moon being a bulb plant-ed in the earth of the sky. Every word can be analyzed minutely – from the point of view of vowel and consonant shades, values, coolnesses, warmths, assonances and dissonances. Technically, I suppose the visual appearance and sound of words, taken alone, may be much like the mechanics of music . . . or the color and texture in a painting. However, uneducated as I am in this field, I can only guess and experiment. But I do want to explain why I use words, each one chosen for a reason, perhaps not as yet the very best word for my purpose, but nevertheless, selected after much deliberation. For instance, the continuous motion of the waves makes the moonlight sparkle. To get a sense of fitful motion, the participleal adjectives "winking" (to suggest bright staccato sparks) and "quivering" (to convey a more legato and tremulous movement) have been used. "Bright" and "black" are obvi-ous contrasts of light & dark. My trouble? Not enough free thinking, fresh imagery. Too much subconscious clinging to clichés and downtrodden com-binations. Not enough originality. Too much blind worship of modern poets and not enough analysis and practice.

My purpose, which I mentioned quite nebulously a while back, is to draw certain attitudes, feelings and thoughts, into a psuedo-reality for the reader. ("Pseudo" of necessity.) Since my woman's world is perceived greatly through the emotions and the senses, I treat it that way in my writing – and am often overweighted with heavy descriptive passages and a kaleidoscope of similes.

I am closest to Amy Lowell, in actuality, I think. I love the lyric clarity and purity of Elinor Wylie, the whimsical, lyrical, typographically eccentric verse of e e cummings, and yearn toward T.S. Eliot, Archibald Macleish, Conrad Aiken . . . .

(112) And when I read, God, when I read the taut, spare, lucid prose of Louis Untermeyer, and the distilled intensities of poet after poet, I feel stifled, weak, pallid; mealy mouthed and utterly absurd. Some pale, hueless flicker of sensitivity is in me. God, must I lose it in cooking scrambled eggs for a man . . . hearing about life at second hand, feeding my body and letting my powers of perception and subsequent articulation grow fat and lethargic with disuse?

(113) Squinting into the bright sunlight, she stared at the flat rectangular expanse of water in the out door swimming pool. A frangible mosaic of

chlorineblue light, shot through with tinfoil sunstreaks, shattered, shivered, and again blended and remolded into a new quivering brittle pattern, only to break again into tremulous watery blue chaos with the splashing plunge of a diver from the ten foot tower.

(114) Slight revision: "And the wind has blown a warm yellow moon up over the sea: a bulbous moon which sprouts in the soiled indigo sky and spills winking white petals of light upon quivering black plains of ocean water.

(115) Helen sat at the kitchen table eating, her great soft doughy bulk leaning over her plate as she cut the fatty meat into small chunks and shoved them into her plump pink mouth, with her calloused fingers, like greasy white sausage.

"Och, I feel oily," she muttered through a mouthful of buttery mashed potato, "what with all them beets an butter an taters. I kin feel it; I'm getting fat. I'll have to stop eating next week."

Joanne was gurgling in her highchair. She had potato and butter in her hair, and her plump baby face was shining under stains of beet juice. "Budda. I wan budda . . . " she caroled, reaching a pink sticky hand toward the table.

"Watch this," Helen winked confidentially at me. She took a potato skin from her plate and folded it over a lump of butter. Joanne accepted the skin, slowly unfolded it, and with the expression of a two-year old Columbus discovering America, plucked forth the yellow blob of butter and devoured it.

"More budda . . . more budda . . . "

Helen chuckled and repeated the process of the folded potato skin. Joanne responded happily.

"Do you really think it's good for her to have all that butter?" I asked a bit anxiously, seeing a third greasy skin heading Joanne's way.

"It'll grease her cold, dont cha think?" Helen said. "Aspirin breaks it up, but butter'll grease it good."

(116) From the kitchen window, over the sink, she could see Fred, one of the gardeners, weeding the rows of lettuce. Beyond the algebraic green exactness of the rows were the apple trees, fully in leaf, with vermilion apples winking in the windy sunlight. The margins of the lawn were clipped in mathematical care, and the litter of the dying leaves and the fallen pinecones were scrupulously raked up in piles every morning and burned with the rubbish behind

the white shingled tool shed. Fred bent his creaking old back down over the ruffled pale green lettuce heads and tweaked the thin lanky weeds from the crumbled black soil. His faded blue shirt was open at the throat, showing a brown-stained neck, with the skin and muscles taut and wrinkled, like a walnut shell, or the gnarled dark surface of a peach stone. Soon he would come up to the back door with a large flat basket of baby beets, carrots and young milky tasseled corn.

"Does the missus want any vegetables," he would ask.

And the missus would come out into the kitchen, cool and slim in dark blue shantung shorts and shirt. "Why Fred," she would say with the gracious and accustomed familiarity she always used toward any of the family employees, "why Fred, fresh corn; how lovely."

The girl plunged another stack of egg-encrusted plates into the soapy dishwater. A wet slop on the plate with the rag. Rinse. Put in strainer. Slop. Rinse. Strainer. Slop. Rinse. Strainer.

And the missus left a pile of corn to be husked and cooked for dinner.

(117) August 30 – 1:45 p.m. Right about now I should start getting lyrical and extremely elated. I am just that, as a matter-of-fact, but my glorying in physical well-being is tempered by a touch of nostalgia of the "Sweet-Thames-Run-Softly-till-I-End-My-Song" variety. Only this time I will punctuate with my old "Never Again" refrain.

On the last day before the family comes home from their week's cruise, I sit in careless freedom on my large sunporch outside the guest room. In aqua haltar and blue shorts, wet hair drying, bleaching to streaked blond in the sun, sun tan oil splashed freshly on deepening brown flesh, my poetry books beside me. Ever since they went away, leaving Helen and me with the house and Pinny and Joanne I have felt the intangible steel cord of subservience loosened from my intestines. Never again will I linger in pure gastronomic liberty over a dinner of fresh corn and lambchops, or steak with fresh iced peaches and vanilla icecream for dessert. Never again will I dry myself after an invigorating swim in the blue salt ocean visible from this house on the hill, put on a clean cotton dress over a vivid, electric, cooly tingling body, and bike jauntily to market to buy "anything I want" to eat. Never again will I sit on the porch of this mansion, become so firmly and temporarily mine these past days, hearing the hoarse waves heaving, seeing the blue green water over the lawn, between the great pensive sighing trees. I could play my piano, if I wanted, or read, or sleep, or merely sit here, feet scalded by the burning gray-slatted floor, sun frying willing flesh, writing.

Today I got a post card – adorably and laboriously printed by my favorite Freddie. Pinny and Joey sleep dociley – beautiful lovable, spoiled babies – my children. Complete physical well-being, exalted environment, a sense of capability and self-integrality never before felt. God, for the sun, beating, beating, melting my body to gleaming warm bronze, bronze-thighed, bronze-breasted, ripe and full, glowing. And oh, for the thin copper threads of my hair, incandescent in the sun drenched wind. For the screams and squeals of children and gulls over the continuous splash of the waves. Blue, flashing white, space, heat, salt, bird twitters and chirps in the grieving, sighing trees, and at night, the dark, indigo sky, often the fog, and lights hanging in suspended blurred globes. Even wet laundry flapping in the grass-flavored wind. Even a childs' freshly-bathed body under my finger tips.

God, how I love it all. And who am I, God-whom-I-don't-believe-in? God-who-is-my-alter-ego? Suddenly the turn table switches to a higher speed, and in the whizzing that ensues I loose track of my identity. I act and react, and suddenly I wonder "Where is the girl that I was last year? . . . Two years ago? . . . What would she think of me now?" And I remember vaguely tolstoi's argument about fate and inevitability and free will. As an act recedes into the past and becomes imbedded in the network of one's individuality it seems more and more a product of fate - - inevitable. However, an act in the immediate present seems to be more a product of free will.

Is it not that a particular act becomes inevitable, while obviously so, since completed. Take the Smith business. I still can't remember just what put the idea of a double college application into my head, but apply I did. And a year ago last May, after having been accepted and even having gotten $850 scholarship from the college, I still didn't know whether or not I could go – because of complete lack of funds. Teetering then, as I did, I could not imagine myself in coming years – because I could not picture my environment – Wellesley, the old homestead – or Smith, the new untried independent field? Smith it became, and with it my horizons popped open – New Haven, New Jersey, New York – Dick, Marcia – and Mrs. Koffka – all the rest. Seems impossible now that anything else could have happened to me – such is the poverty of my imagination. This summer – aided by the agency of the Smith vocational office and Marcia, would hardly have come into being were it not for SMITH . . . Yet had I gone to Wellesley, I could only hazard about what might have appeared inevitable.

After incoherent rambling, I will say that I amuse my leisure hours by cultivating that stubborn unimaginative state of mind which refuses to dream, imagine or conjecture about any situation's reality except the present.

Events, as one grows older, first stand out in relief, and then start whizzing by like a deck of cards. Spoken words, felt emotions, actual situations – all lapse almost immediately into a dry, theoretical vacuum. For instance: Dick. All that occurred last spring - - - all that I thought and felt and said – and recorded as reality, has lapsed into that wooden mechanical world which can be wound up and set going in day dreams, ticking over like somebody else's movie film. But who is Dick? Who am I? My stubborn unimaginative self cannot conceive of him as a flesh-and-blood being any more, because in the last two-and-a-half months of my life he has only been a reality twice briefly and peculiarly. All tensions – mental and emotional, wound in those two encounters. Yet, not having had time to get used to the boy, I awoke after the real hours were gone – to find myself believing in him only in theory. Odd is the human complexity when examined and questioned. I wonder about all the roads not taken and am moved to quote Frost . . . but won't. It is sad to be able only to mouth other poets. I want someone to mouth me.

Dick is real only in that time was (which time is vaguely and dreamily recalled in dreams and in thoughtful seconds . . .) and in that time will be (a similiar vague and faceless conception of what will happen and where and with whom.) Time present is Non-Dick. And if I maintain that stubborn state where time present – made up only of temporary physical reality, sensual perceptions and spasmodic streams-of-consciousness – is the only reality, why then Dick is naught but an unsigned picture, a handful of letters and two carved wooden objects – a pickle fork & knife. But this state of mind is born of a renunciation of complexities. It is a negation of sorts. A return to the womb, Freud might have it. Overwhelmed by lack of time, race of time, speed of time, I retreat into non-thought – merely into Epicurean sensual observations and desires – momentary ephemeral flashes of well-being and ill-being. Do I think? After a fashion. Do I put myself in other people's minds and viscera? No. Not half enough. Do I listen? Yes. Tonight I listened for three solid hours to Ann Hunt[n] review her life, her background, and her vocations. Do I create? No, I reproduce. I have no imagination. I am submerged in circling ego. I listen, God knows why. I say I am interested in people. Am I rationalizing? God knows. Maybe he doesn't. If he lives in my head or under my left ventricle, maybe he's too uncomfortable to know much of anything.

Why am I obsessed with the idea I can justify myself by getting manuscripts published? Is it an escape – an excuse for any social failure – so I can say "No, I don't go out for many extra-curricular activities, but I spend alot of time writing." Or is it an excuse for wanting to be alone and meditate alone, not having to brave a group of women? (Women in numbers have always disturbed me.) Do I like to write? Why? About what? Will I give up and say "living and feeding a man's insatiable guts and begetting children occupies my whole life. Don't have time to write?" Or will I stick to the damn stuff and practice? Read and think and practice? I am worried about thinking. Mentally I have led a vegetable existence this summer.

However. After getting up at 6 am this morning, I am hardly in a lucid state at 1 am the next morning. Adieu.

(118.) Suddenly, I stopped dead. I had opened my calendar to the month of August as usual, to write in the neat white box labeled with day and date, a scant summary of the activities completed in the last 12 hours. Sickened, I saw that I had unwittingly completed the last day of August. Tomorrow would be September. God! All the quick futility of my days cascaded upon me, and I wanted to scream out in helpless fury at the hopeless inevitable going on of seconds, days and years. By the time I fill in this page, said I, I will have finished my job, gone home, spent four days at the Cape and either added to or detracted from my relationship with the one man-in-my-life at present, passed or failed my driving test, given my speech at the Smith Club tea, packed my things, and embarked on a merry-go-round among much jingling of bells and harnesses and neighing of horses, to whiz through another year of my life – becoming nineteen (where do they hide the young, tender years?) and beating out some sort of life at Smith . . . . . crisping into woollen autumn and into the darkening iron of November . . . and Christmas . . . vacation – grinding through an icy, mud-grimy January-February-March, and tentatively, unbelievingly, unfolding into another spring, when the damn world makes us think we are as young as we ever were and deceives us by pale lucid skies and the sudden opening of little leaves.

All this is a quick sketch of the scared naked fear and grief that congealed in me when I saw the vivid young living of my days boxed off and numbered in faceless white squares. Good bye, Freddie, Pinny, Joey – (my sweet, my love, who glanced in fragrant tilted-black lashed tenderness at me, cooing over supper cereal. God, how straight your two-year old back under the ankle-length white flannel night gown; how firm and clean your baby flesh.)

Good-bye Helen, and good-bye to your fat comforting Irish humor: "Lord, Sylvia, you should have seen that wave. It come in over her head and she was choking for breath when she come up. The water ran out of her for ten mintutes straight, streamin from her nose and mouth. An I said 'There goes the cold; salt water'll wash it out good . . . ' "

Good-bye, Katherine, with your thick glasses, and the one eye that looks at you sideways and the other that stares at you head on. Good-bye to your ugly, scaly arms, your gaunt crooked body in the dirty apron, your cracked, querulous voice and crabbed caviling which hides only, as I know, a deep and pathetic loneliness. Born of lack of your own kind, born of no one to talk to, no one who will wait and sympathize when you quaver plaintively: "I'm so ner-r-r-vous; so lonely; I can't sleep, and I'm so tired." Old, old, you are, with a cropped white head of stiff, greasy hair. Old, old you are, and Ireland and your girlhood are gone, as if they never were. Now you amble arthritically around the Blodgett kitchen, burning batches of toll-house cookies, and rattling among your bent aluminum saucepans on the ugly black stove.

Farewell, blonde, brown, adenoid-voiced Radcliffe senior Ann. For two months I lived next to you, and never spoke or knew you – really. And then, that night you came over when I was alone in the twilight in the kitchen, slicing peaches; I poured out a glass of milk for you, and scooped ice-cream on a plate, adding beside it grapes and a peach. I asked you about yourself, and you talked suddenly, on and on, until the planes of your face grew dark and the silver of your hair shone dully only, and still I could not move to turn on a light. Remember, I must, yet how can I, what you told me of your mother (Queen of the University of Oklahoma – descended from the woman who originated the palmer method of hand writing – who quit college in her first year to marry a handsome young man with insanity in his family. On the oil fields, the couple lived, and the woman taught in the day, worked in her husband's store in the evening, giving birth, at the age of 21, to a boy John, and at the age of 28, to a girl, Ann. During the depression, the father sent the mother to the store for medicine. When she returned with her two-year old daughter, he had shot himself to death in the garage. So she worked on, determined to send her children to college. She married again. A Mr. Matthews, who had also been married before, when young and spoiled, to a similiar woman who had left him. One-eighth an Indian, Matthews saved the funds from his "head-rights" from oil in Oklahoma, went to the University, and then on a fellowship to Europe and Geneva. On his return, he married. When his marriage failed he moved to a minute town in Oklahoma, settled in a one-room stone house with a few pots and pans and a typewriter, and wrote his first novel "Wannaka" which became a Book-of-the-Month. Ann was brought up in that one-room stone house. She never knew or played with anyone her own age. She and her brother never fought. Her mother sacrificed every thing for them. John went to Prép school and Harvard. He now is married and teaching English while writing a novel.

Ann went to Mary Burnham. In the summer she went back to Oklahoma and lay out in the grass in the sun by the stone house in the prairies. Her father never worked; he was too artistic to work for a living. Her parents borrowed money until no one would lend them anymore, because it never got paid back.

Ann got the south-western Regional to Radcliffe. She lived in a private home, cooking and taking care of children for board and room. While she was still at Mary Burnham, she thought that she would be completely happy if only she fell passionately in love. A friend of her brothers, whom she had seen only once at the awkward age of thirteen, suddenly and for no reason sent her a bottle of Chanel Number 5. They exchanged letters. He sent her a Bulova wristwatch. The next summer he drove up from texas in his Lincoln conertible with a bottle of Burbon, and they spent the evening at a road-house playing a jukebox that had classical music. He asked her to marry him. That was her first proposal.

Last summer, Ann worked at Melody Manor – an ancient and peculiar hotel on Lake George. Seems it was once a private mansion, built by a rich man who murdered his fiancée's lover. A young ambitious Polish boy, having begun a prosperous window-washing business in the United States, saved two-hundred thousand dollars and bought this great mansion, planning to turn it into a hotel.

Mr. Dombeck, however, did not have the funds needed, really to make a success of the place. There were hardly any guests. Ann worked seven days a week from seven am to pm as a secretary. She never saw the light of day. The first weeks she went to bed right after work, but then she started putting on a dress and going down to the bar after hours, playing poker with the guests, and often drinking there till after one in the morning.

The help was peculiar. There was the little old chamber maid, who always kept the light on in her room, lest she be molested. There was the dishwasher, who wore his hair long, dark, slicked back to the crown of his head, and who never changed his clothes all the time he was there. He followed Ann, always at a distance, and spoke strangely: his sole topic of conversation was that of ancient history – he talked continually of turkish leaders, of battles, of the Visigoths. Ann hazarded that he had once been confined in a prison or insane asylum where the only books he had been able to read were history books.

After an incident, absurd, involving Bernard, her boyfriend, she was asked to leave Melody Manor, on the pretense that they could no longer pay her $20 a week. By this time the place was $5000 dollars in debt. Ann knew; she kept the books.

Among the reasons for the failure of Melody Manor - - - the bar was a sunporch, with rugs and armchairs, and a place where a fountain used to play, with great glass doors overlooking the lake - - - "no one wants to drink in a front livingroom . . . especially at night"; then, too, the only entertainment was the electric organ. The man who played it was a small-time music teacher; he and his wife lived in the barn. The lake was there, lovely, to be sure, but with no place to swim – no beach, no boats.

And so Ann left . . . and so I leave Ann.

And so I leave the two streetlights at the end of Beach Bluff Avenue which shone in crosses of light through my open door every night. And the crickets chirping on the wind. And the blue of Preston Beach water, and the fat, gold-toothed, greasy-haired Jews sunning themselves, and oiling their plump, rutted flesh. Good-bye Castle Rock, where I swam with Marcia, with Lane, with Gordon, where I walked with Dick. And my quaint, crooked-streets of Marblehead, with hollyhocks springing tall from the narrow dooryards, and the cracked pavement.

I want to stay awake for the next three days and nights, drawing the threads of my summer cocoon neatly about me and snipping all the loose ends: to savor until the dying of the last wave, the last dawn, this place, the leaving of which means leaving a great space of living . . . and aging, aging. Heading back toward the close oppressive green of solid earth, of a corner lot in a little Suburb . . . of a closeness, a miscellaneous crowding of self and activities – and a brief nomadic existence before plunging onto the next great phase - - - my sophomore year.

So I perversely circle the late stars, drowsier and drowsier, sleepily longing for something - - - - - nothing – talking, working, eating, wondering always who am I? Who is this girl I hear talking?

September 1

(119) Here follows my first sonnet, written during the hours of 9 to 1 a.m. on a Saturday night, when in pregnant delight I conceived my baby. Luxuriating in the feel and music of the words, I chose and rechose, singling out the color, the assonance and dissonance and musical effects I wished – lulling myself by supple "l"'s and bland long "a's" and "o's." God, I am happy – It's the first thing I've written for a year that has tasted wholly good to my eyes, ears and intellect.

Sonnet: to Spring

you deceive us with the crinkled green
of juvenile stars, and you beguile us with
a bland vanilla moon of maple cream:
again you tame us with your april myth.

—

last year you tricked us by the childish jingle
of your tinsel rains; again you try,
and find us credulous once more. A single
diabolic shower, and we cry

—

to see the honey flavored morning tilt
clear light across the watergilded lawn.
although another of our years is spilt
on avaricious earth, you lure us on:

—

Again we are deluded and infer
That somehow we are younger than we were.

(120) And do your ears quite suddenly and without warning burn red? Or do you, washing dishes, with the same clothes you wore two years ago rotting under your armpits, still talk about the visigoths to your oh so pathetic self and divine nothing?

I put you in a book because a girl with pale blonde hair and an adenoidal and entirely charming nasal twang to her voice told me about you one night. The girl and I had been eating grapes in the twilight at the enamel kitchen table, and the planes of her face suddenly were growing darker, and I could hardly see her, but still we didn't move to turn on the light.

Two years ago you didn't change your clothes, and stood in the doorway of the old hotel, watching from afar a girl named Ann, with pale wet silver hair, walking alone in the night beside Lake George.

Acrid with the stench of dried sweat were your clothes, and your long slick oily black hair, and your hands were puffed and creased, soft and unhealthily white from the hot steaming dishwater.

Tell me (for I know you), do your ears burn red?

September – 1951

(121) I see it all now. Or at least I begin to see. I see in the boy who, because of necessity (lack of other contacts) has become the only answer to a need, the

germs of all I fear and would avoid. I see the equally blinding necessity of taking what is best for the time being, lest there be no such chance in the future.

Why am I so perturbed by what others rejoice in and take for granted? Why am I so obsessed? Why do I hate what I am being drawn into so inexorably? Why, instead of going to bed in the kindly, erotic dark, and smiling languidly to myself in the night, say "Some day I will be physically and mentally satiated, if I lead myself in the right path . . . " – why do I sit up later, until the physical fire grows cold, and lash my brains into cold calculating thought?

I do not love; I do not love anybody except myself. That is a rather shocking thing to admit. I have none of the selfless love of my mother. I have none of the plodding, practical love of Frank and Louise, Dot and Joe." I am, to be blunt and concise, in love only with myself, my puny being with it's small inadequate breasts and meagre, thin talents. I am capable of affection for those who reflect my own world. How much of my solicitude for other human beings is real and honest, how much is a feigned lacquer painted on by society, I do not know. I am afraid to face myself. Tonight I am trying to do so. I heartily wish that there were some absolute knowledge, some person whom I could trust to evaluate me and tell me the truth.

My greatest trouble, arising from my basic and egoistic self-love, is jealousy. I am jealous of men – a dangerous and subtle envy which can corrode, I imagine, any relationship. It is an envy born of the desire to be active and doing, not passive and listening. I envy the man his physical freedom to lead a double life – his career, and his sexual and family life. I can pretend to forget my envy; no matter, it is there, insidious, malignant, latent.

My enemies are those who care about me most. First: my mother. Her pitiful wish is that I "be happy." Happy! That is indefinable as far as states of being go. Or perhaps you can run it off glibly, as Eddie did, and say it means reconciling the life you lead with the life you wish to lead – (often, I think meaning the reverse.)

At any rate, I admit that I am not strong enough, or rich enough, or independent enough, to live up in actuality to my ideal standards. You ask me, what are those ideal standards? Good for you. The only escape (do I sound Freudian?) from the present set up as I see it, is in the exercise of a phase of life inviolate and separate from that of my future mate, and from all males with whom I might live. I am not only jealous; I am vain and proud. I will not submit to having my life fingered by my husband, enclosed in the larger circle of his activity, and nourished vicariously by tales of his actual exploits. I must have a legitimate field of my own, apart from his, which he must respect.

So I am led to one or two choices! Can I write? Will I write if I practice enough? How much should I sacrifice to writing anyway, before I find out if I'm any good? Above all, CAN A SELFISH EGOCENTRIC JEALOUS AND UNIMAGITIVE FEMALE WRITE A DAMN THING WORTH WHILE? Should I sublimate (my, how we throw words around!) my selfishness in serving other people – through social or other such work? Would I then become more sensitive to other people and their problems? Would I be able to write honestly, then, of other beings beside a tall, introspective adolescent girl? I must be in contact with a wide variety of lives if I am not to become submerged in the routine of my own economic strata and class. I will not have my range of acquaintance circumscribed by my mate's profession. Yet I see that this will happen if I do not have an outlet . . . of some sort.

Looking at myself, in the past years, I have come to the conclusion that I must, have a passionate physical relationship with someone – or combat the great sex urge in me by drastic means. I chose the former answer. I also admitted that I am obligated in a way to my family and to society (damn society anyway) to follow certain absurd and traditional customs – for my own security, they tell me. I must therefore, confine the major part of my life, to one human being of the opposite sex . . . that is a necessity because: ① I choose the physical relationship of intercourse as an animal and releasing part of life ② I can not gratify myself promiscuously and retain the respect and support of society, (which is my pet devil) – and because I am a woman: ergo: one root of envy for male freedom. ③ Still being a woman, I must be clever and obtain as full a measure of security for those approaching ineligible and aging years wherein I will not have the chance to capture a new mate – or in all probability. So, resolved: I shall proceed to obtain a mate through the customary procedure: namely, marriage.

That leaves innumerable problems. Since I have grown up enough to decide to marry, I now must be very careful. I have the aforementioned blots of selflove, jealousy and pride to battle with as intelligently as possible. (No, I can not delude myself).

The selflove I can hide or reweld by the Biblical saw of "losing myself and finding myself." For instance, I could hold my nose, close my eyes, and jump blindly into the waters of some man's insides, submerging my-self until his purpose becomes my purpose, his life, my life, and so on. One fine day I would float to the surface, quite drowned, and supremely happy with my newfound selfless self. Or I could devote myself to a Cause. (I think that is why there are so many women's clubs and organizations. They've got to feel emancipated and self important somehow. God Forbid that I become a Crusader. But I might surprise myself, and become a second Lucretia Mott or something equivalent.) Anyway, there are two tentative solutions for getting rid of selfishness – both involving a stoic casting-off of the thin tenuous little identity which I love and cherish so dearly – and being confident that, once on the other side, I shall never miss my own little ambitions for my conceited self, but shall be content in serving the ambitions of my mate, or of a society, or cause. (Yet I will not, I cannot accept any of those solutions. Why? Stubborn selfish pride. I will not make what is inevitable easier for my-self by the blinding ignorance-is-bliss "losing-and-finding" theory. Oh, no! I will go, eyes open, into my torture, and remain fully cognizant, unwinking, while they cut and stitch and lop off my cherished malignant organs.)

So much for selflove: I carry it with me like a dear cancerous relative – to be disposed of only when desperation sets in.

Now for jealousy. I can loop out of that one easily: by excelling in some field my mate cannot participate actively in, but can only stand back and admire. That's where writing comes in. It is as necessary for the survival of my haughty sanity as bread is to my flesh. I pay the penalty of the educated, emancipated woman: I am critical, particular, aristocratic in tastes. Perhaps my desire to write could be simplified to a basic fear of non-admiration and non-esteem. Suddenly I wonder: am I afraid that the sensuous haze of marriage will kill the desire to write? Of course – in past pages I have repeated and repeated that fear. Now I am beginning to see why! I am afraid that the physical sensuousness of marriage will lull and soothe to inactive lethargy my desire to work outside the realm of my mate – might make me "lose myself in him," as I said before, and thereby lose the need to write as I would lose the need to escape. Very simple.

If all my writing (once, I think, an outlet for an unfulfilled sensitivity – a reaction against unpopularity) is this ephemeral, what a frightening thing it is!

Let's take pride, now. Pride is mixed in with selflove and jealously. All are rooted in the same inarticulate center of me, I think. I feed myself on the food of pride. I cultivate physical appearance – Pride. I long to excell – to specialize in one field, one section of a field, no matter how minute, as long as I can be an authority there. Pride, ambition – what mean, selfish words!

Now back again to the present – the mating problem. What is best? Choice is frightening. I do not know: this is what I want. I only can hazard guesses on those poor fellows I meet by saying "This is what I do <u>not</u> want."

What profession would I choose, if I were a man? Is that a criterion? To choose the man I would be if I were a man? Pretty risky. Occupation? teacher, comes closest now – liesurely enough not to drive me to madness, intelligent of course – hell, I Don't Know! Why can't I try on different lives, like dresses, to see which fits best and is most becoming?

The fact remains, I have at best three years in which to meet eligible people. Few come as close as the one I now know. I would be betting on dark horses, not on a sure thing. Yet I am disturbed rather terribly by this sure thing. I am obsessed that it is this, or nothing, and that if I don't take this, it will be nothing, but if I do take this, I will be squeezed into a pretty stiff pattern, the rigor of which I do not like. Why not? Ah, I will tell you some of the seeds which will fester in me, sprouting dangerously under forseen conditions:

(1) He is drawn to attractive women – even if it is not to search for a mate: – all through life I would be subject to a physical, hence animal jealously of other attractive women – always afraid that a shorter girl, one with better breasts, better feet, better hair than I will be the subject of his lust, or love – and I would always be miserably aware that I had to live up to his expectations – or else, someone else would. – A woman, confined to the home, doesn't have the opportunity to feed her ego on attractive men.

(2) He regards a wife as a physical possession, to be proud of, like "a new car." Great! He is vain, proud, too. Score fault number one! He wants other people to be conscious of his valuable possession. What? You say "That's only normal?" Maybe it is only normal, but I resent the hint – of what? of material attitude. Okay, so I don't believe in spirit. I also don't believe in "owning" people – like a good whore or a pet canary.

(3) He wants, after he is dead, for a community to remember him – to admire him for a life he saved, a life he gave. No doubt that is why he wants to be a general practitioner in a small town – he could smugly and rightly consider himself the guardian of life & death and happiness of a large group of humans. (Perry would be a surgeon – so, I would have Dick be a surgeon. I am like Perry. Dick is gregarious; he loves life collectively. Perry is isolated; he loves life in the singular, not the plural.) I would have him specialize. He is not being selfless when he wants to be a country doctor – he is being proud, full of desire for self esteem and importance. He would of course need a wife (if only for physical and mental gratification, to cook meals and raise children – all purely pragmatic needs – save the mental one, which still is practical in that it involves pride again . . . and the satisfaction there of) – to

fit in to that environment. How good would I be at small town living? I haven't proved popular at school. My friends are a select few! How could I ever expect to be the town-minded, extroverted country doctor's wife! God knows. I don't. He needs the good solid homemaking type – with a little less fire, a little more practical devotion to her lord – i.e. Margaret Gordon.

Where does that leave me? In a position of awful responsibility. I can change, whittle my square edges to fit in a round hole. God, I hope I'm never going to massacre myself that way. (Oh, you say, I don't see life's big chance? Well maybe I just don't see all my limitations yet, let's leave it that way.) Or, I could tell the boy, before it is too late – warn him to set his sights on other prey – more domesticated prey, at that. Or I could just shut up and plunge – maybe making us both unhappy. Who knows? The most saddening thing is to admit that I am not in love. I can only love (if that means self denial – or does it mean self fulfillment? Or both?) by giving up my love of self and ambitions – why, why, why, can't I combine ambition for myself and another? I think I could, if only I chose a mate with a career demanding less of a wife in the way of town and social responsibility. But God, who is to say? You God, whom I invoke without belief, only I can choose, and only I am responsible. (Oh, the grimness of atheism!)

[Appendix 1 contains Sylvia Plath's 17–19 October 1951 journal fragment – ed.]

(122)
January 15 – 1952   Sonnet: Van Winkle's Village

Today, although the slant of sun reminds
Of other suns, although the rooks may call
The way they did long years ago, one finds
Van Winkle's village not the same at all . . .

The streets re-routed, and the citizens
Grown bland, incredulous, politely vague;
Agape, they marvel at the alien's
Archaic jargon; with mockery they plague

His puzzled queries. The woman at the door
Of his old house is young and strange; now where
Has Peter gone? And Dirck who sat of yore
To savor beer and meerschaum on the stair?

Perplexed, Van Winkle strokes (as doubts begin)
The century old beard that wreathes his chin.

(123)

February 25 – letter excerpt:

" . . . can you see, through the strange dark tunnel of cupped hands to the great cyclops eye, blurred, staring, flecked with one lightspot that grows and becomes a cloud, shifting, endowed with meaning, imposed upon it. Can you feel, listening with trained ear to heartbeat of the other, the wind shrieking and gasping and singing, as one listens to the vast humming inside the paradoxical cylinder of the telephone pole? Such uncharted, wild barrens there are behind the calm or mischievous shell that has learned its name but not its destiny.

There is still time to veer, to sally forth, knapsack on back, for unknown hills over which . . . only the wind knows what lies. Shall she, shall she veer? There will be time, she says, knowing somehow that in her beginning is her end and the seeds of destruction perhaps now dormant may even today begin sprouting malignantly within her. She turns away from action in one direction to that in another, knowing all the while that someday she must face, behind the door of her choosing, perhaps the lady, perhaps the tiger . . . "

(124)

May 15 – 1952 – Dust lies along the edges of my book, and my lusts and little ideas have gone spurting out in other ways – in sonnets, in stories, and in letters. And now that the rain beats (again) closing in wetly, splashing (again) liquidly on the full, smoothly thin green leaves, trickling like cool pure urine down the drain, now I can begin to talk (again) as I always do, before exams begin, before the heat gets turned on. I shall begin by saying that I am not the girl I was a year ago. Thank Time. No, I am now a sophomore at Smith College, and therein lies all the difference. All? By implication, yes: mentally I am active as before, more realistic perhaps. (Come now, what do you mean by "realistic"?) Well, I consider myself more aware of my limitations in a constructive way. I will still whip myself onward and upward (in this spinning world, who knows which is up?) toward Fulbright's, prizes, Europe, publication, males. Tangible, yes, after a fashion, as all weave into my physical experience – going, seeing, doing, thinking, feeling, desiring. With the eyes, the brain, the intestines, the vagina. From the inactive (collegiately), timid, introvertly-tended individual of last year, I have become altered. I have maintained my integrity by not being an office-seeker for the sake of publicity, yet I have directed my energies in channels which, although public, also perform the dual service of satisfying many of my creatives aims and needs. For example, I was elected Secretary of Honor Board" this spring – sent roses, flowers. And what do I do? I work with a stimulating group of the faculty – Dean Randall, et al. I learn the inside story about academic infringements – and get character material as well. Then, I am correspondent to the "Springfield Daily News" on Press Board" – which not only nets me about $10 per month, but gives me the strange thrill of feeling typewriter keys clatter under my fingers, of seeing my write-ups appear in inches in the daily Northampton column, of knowing everything that is going on in this great organic machine of a college. Also, I am going to be on the "Smith Review"" next year, and hope that I can whip it out of its tailspin of this year. All, all, involve time lovingly spent. And next year, next year I will honor in English – concentrating in Creative writing. At last I will be in small classes, doing independent research, becoming intimately acquainted with my instructors! This summer – ambitiously working seven days a week at the Belmont Hotel," waitressing. Thousands of people apply, and of them – I am accepted! Also, whether I kill myself in the attempt or not, I will pass my physical science requirement on my own – (never will I take it next year!) And previous to the summer, there will be days spent with my lovely mathematical Alison" in New York.

All, all, becomes profitable. Education is of the most satisfying and available nature. I am at Smith! Which two years ago was a doubtful dream – and that fortuitous change of dream to reality has led me to desire more, and to lash myself onward – onward. I dreamed of New York, I am going there. I dream of Europe – perhaps . . . perhaps.

Now there comes the physical part – and therein lies the problem. Victimized by sex is the human race. Animals, the fortunate lower beasts, go into heat. Then they are through with the thing, while we poor lustful humans, caged by mores, chained by circumstance, writhe and agonize with the apalling and demanding fire licking always at our loins.

I remember a cool river beach and a May night full of rain held in far clouds, moonly sparks raying on the water, and the close, dank, heavy wetness of green vegetation. The water was cold to my bare feet, and the mud oozed up between my toes. He ran then, on the sand, and I ran after him, my hair long and damp, blowing free across my mouth. I could feel the inevitable magnetic polar forces in us, and the tidal blood beat loud, Loud, roaring in my ears, slowing and rhythmic. He paused, then, I behind him, arms locked around the powerful ribs, fingers caressing him. To lie with him, to lie with him, burning forgetful in the delicious animal fire. Locked first upright, thighs ground together, shuddering, mouth to mouth, breast to breast, legs enmeshed, then lying full length, with the good heavy weight of body upon body, arching, undulating, blind, growing together, force fighting force: to kill? To drive into burning dark of oblivion? To lose identity? Not love, this, quite. But something else rather. A refined hedonism. Hedonism: because of the blind sucking mouthing fingering quest for physical gratification. Refined: because of the desire to stimulate another in return, not being quite only concerned for self alone, but mostly so. An easy end to arguments on the mouth: a warm meeting of mouths, tongues quivering, licking, tasting. An easy substitute for bad slashing with angry hating teeth and nails and voice: the curious musical tempo of hands lifting under breasts, caressing throat, shoulders, knees, thighs. And giving up to the corrosive black whirlpool of mutual necessary destruction. – Once there is the first kiss, then the cycle becomes inevitable. Training, conditioning, make a hunger burn in breasts and secrete fluid in vagina, driving blindly for destruction. What is it but destruction? Some mystic desire to beat to sensual annihilation – to snuff out one's identity on the identity of the other – a mingling and mangling of identities? A death of one? Or both? A devouring and subordination? No, no. A polarization rather – a balance of two integrities, changing, electrically, one with the other, yet with centers of coolness, like stars. || (And D. H. Lawrence did have something after all –). And there it is: when asked what role I will plan to fill, I say "What do you mean role? I plan not to step into a part on marrying – but to go on living as an intelligent mature human being, growing and learning as I always have. No shift, no radical change in life habits." Never will there be a circle, signifying me and my operations, confined solely to home, other womenfolk, and community service, enclosed in the larger worldly circle of my mate, who brings home from his periphery of contact with the world the tales only of vicarious experience to me, like so ⊙. No, rather, there will be two over-lapping circles, with a certain strong riveted center of common ground, but both with separate arcs jutting out in the world. A balanced tension; adaptible to circumstances, in which there is an elasticity of pull, tension, yet firm unity. Two stars, polarized: ⊘⊘ like so, in moments of communication that is complete, almost, like so, ⊘ almost fusing onto one. But fusion is an undesirable impossibility – and quite non-durable. So there will be no illusion of that.

So he accuses me of "struggling for dominance"? Sorry, wrong number.

Sure, I'm a little scared of being dominated. (Who isn't? Just the submissive, docile, milky type of individual. And that is Not he, Not me.) But that doesn't mean I, ipso facto, want to <u>dominate</u>. No, it is not a black-and-white choice or alternative like: "Either-I'm-victorious on-top-or-you-are." It is only <u>balance</u> that I ask for. Not the <u>continual</u> subordination of one persons desires and interests to the continual advancement of another's! That would be too grossly unfair

Let's get to the bottom of his question: <u>Why</u> is he so afraid of my being strong and assertive? Why has <u>he</u> found it necessary to be himself so aggressive and positive in planning and directing actions and events? Could it be because he has a "mother complex"? Just what is his relation toward his mother anyway? She has become a matriarch in the home – a sweet, subtle matriarch, to be sure, but nonetheless, a "Mom". (cf. Philip Wylie – "Generation of Vipers".) She has become ruler of finances, manager of the home, "<u>mother</u>" of her husband, who, even to my unschooled eye, has a striking amount of the characteristics of a small, childish, irresponsible <u>boy</u> – who can sulk, beg for service, attention, encouragement, and <u>get it</u>. (Handsome, somewhat vain, but still in the position very often of a schoolboy.) It is <u>she</u> who takes over the responsibility of facing reality. Not that this relationship, either, is so black-and-white, but that there <u>are</u> these elements in it, and they are important to illustrate my argument. Therefore, I accentuate them. She has, then, had a great influence over her sons. The one <u>I</u> am concerned with admits that he thinks he rebelled against the firm opinionated influence and made a tangible break by seducing a waitress, a Vassar girl, or what have you. Is there not a sort of duality, then, in him – a desire born of childhood, to be "mothered," to be a child, suckling at the breast (a transfer of eroticism from mother to girlfriend) – and yet to <u>escape</u> the subtle feminine snare and be free of the insidious feminine domination he has sensed in his home all these years: to assert his independent unattached virile vigor (and push his career to the utmost.) He does not seem to be particularly close to or admiring of his father. Is he subconsciously and consciously trying simultaneously to break out of a pattern that would imply following in his father's foot steps – and ricochet to the <u>opposite</u> end of the spectrum by imposing his own pattern on his wife. "I have my own career all marked out," he says somewhat defensively. It would seem so. It would seem he is building a protective wall around him to secure him from the matriarchal dominance which he is probably trying to escape from.

He would then be selfish – admitting also that he has never loved anybody. Why? Is he as afraid to give of himself, compromise, and sacrifice as I am? Quite possibly. He also, as I do to a certain extent, has a superiority complex . . . which often generates condescending and patronizing attitudes that I find extremely offensive. Also, in spite of the fact that he has tried with a vengeance to enter into my appreciation of art and my writing interests – to actually do and not just appreciate, (Is that a sign that he must compete and master me – symbolic, what?) he recently states that a poem "is so much inconsequential dust." With that attitude, how can he be so hypocritical as to pretend he likes poetry? Even some kinds of poetry? The fact remains that writing is a way of life to me: And writing not just from a pragmatic, money-earning point of view either. Granted, I consider publication a token of value and a confirmation of ability – but writing takes practice, continual practice. And if publication is not tangible immediately, if "success" is not forthcoming, would he force me into a defensive attitude about my passionate avocation? Would I be forced to give it up, cut it off? Undoubtedly, as the wife of such a medical man as he would like to be, I would have to. I do not believe, as he and his friends would seem to, that artistic creativity can best be indulged in masterful singleness rather than in marital cooperation. I think that a workable union should heighten the potentialities in both individuals. And so when he says "I am afraid the demands of wifehood and motherhood would preoccupy you too much to allow you to do the painting and writing you want . . . " The fear, the expectancy is planted. And so I start thinking, maybe he's right. Maybe all those scared and playful stream-of-consciousness letters were just touching again and again at this recurring string of doubt and premonition. As it stands now, he alternately denies and accepts me, as I silently do him. There is sometimes a great destructive, annihilating surge of negative fear and hate and recoiling: "I can't, I won't." And then there are long talks, patient, questioning, the physical attraction, soothing again, pacifying, lulling. "I love you." "Don't say that. You don't really. Remember what we said about the word Love." "I know, but I love this girl, here and now, I don't know who she is, but I love her." There is always coming again strongly the feeling as frantic in another way – really, what if I should deny this and never meet anyone as satisfying or, (as I have been hoping) better? To use a favorite metaphor: It is as if both of us, wary of oysters so rich and potent and at once digestively dangerous as they are, should agree to each swallow an oyster (our prospective mate) tied to a string (our reserve about committing ourselves. Then, if either or both of us found the oyster disagreeing with our respective digestive systems, we could yank up the oyster before it was too late, and completely assimilated in all its destructive portent (with marriage.) Sure, there might be a little nausea, a little regret, but the poisoning, corrosive, final, destructive, would not have had a chance to set in. And there we are: two scared, attractive, intelligent, dangerous, hedonistic, "clever" people.

So, weighing danger, I find it carries the balance. (He probably will, too.) Therefore I say "Je ne l'épouserai jamais! JAMAIS, JAMAIS!" And even there the doubts begin – if you find no one else as complete, as satisfying? If you spend the rest of your life bitterly regretting your choice? A choice you must make. And soon. Which will have the courage to be first? If I met someone I could love, it would be so painless. But I doubt if I will be that lucky again. Could I change my attitude & subordinate gladly to his life? Thousands of women would! It would depend on-fear-of-being-an-old-maid and sex-urge being strong enough. They aren't, at nineteen, (although the latter is pretty potent.) So there I am – if I could only say with faith: somewhere there is a man I could love and give of myself to with trust and without fear. If only. Then I wouldn't cling so desperately and strangely to this one beautiful intelligent, sensual human companion as I do. Or he to me. But desiring human flesh, companionship – "How we need that security! How we need another soul to cling to. Another body to keep us warm! To rest and trust . . . " I said so for Bob. I say it now again. How many men are left? How many more chances will I have? I don't know. But at nineteen I will take the risk and hope that I will have another chance or two!

(125) July 6 – 1952. Outwardly, all one could see on passing by is a tan, long-legged girl in a white lawn chair, drying her light brown hair in the late afternoon July sun, dressed in aqua shorts and a white-and-aqua halter. The sweat stands out in wet shining drops on her lean bare midriff, and trickles periodically in sticky streams down under her armpits and in back of her legs. To look at her, you couldn't tell much: how in one short month of being alive she has begun and loved and lost a job, made and foolishly and voluntarily cut herself off from several unique friends, met and captivated a Princeton boy," won one of two $500 prizes in a national College Fiction Contest" and received a delightful, encouraging letter from a well-known publisher" who someday "hopes to publish a novel she has written." There she sits, lazy, convalescent, sweating in the hot sun to maker her hair lighter, her skin darker. Tonight she will dress in the lovely white sharkskin hand-me-down dress of her last summer's employer and gaze winningly at her entranced Princeton escort over drinks and music, under a full moon. To look at her, you might not guess that inside she is laughing and crying, at her

own stupidities and luckinesses, and at the strange enigmatic ways of the world which she will spend a lifetime trying to learn and understand.

(126) Monday July 7 – Last night was good, not so good as the night before, because of the reversal, the balancing of roles. Saturday, after a try at a tennis rally in the hot July sun, with the saliva thickening in your mouth and the desperate and treacherous weakness of your limbs, he was stopping the car by the house and saying, "Well, are you going back to bed tonight after all this exertion?" "No," you say, getting out. "How about doing something tonight, then. A flick, maybe?" "Sure, love to." "I'll call." He drives off, and you run in, upstairs. Your eyelids are heavy, they dip, lift, dip again. You just about manage to strip and get into the shower and out and onto the bed. He does call, and you run downstairs, eager, in your thin blue cotton night gown, your bare feet feeling the slight film of dust and grit on the linoleum floor. He wants to see "Kind Hearts and Coronets" and Somerset Maughm's "Quartet." So do you. When he comes, you are fresh and apple-scented in the lovely shimmering tie-silk dress with the lavendar design on the silvery-beige background. He is protectively chivalrous, opening car doors, shutting them, and you think of Southern breeding. The drive is lovely, into Boston in the clear soft light of late sun still, and the leaves green and full, with the faint pink dust rising, layers of it looking liquid, drifting as through levels of clear champagne. Boston streets, Kenmore Square, and the carpeted, gilt-adorned palace interior of the theater, where in the darkness you find two seats, whisper a remark or two, and go lifting, speeding into the great moving magic of the silver screen which pulls all into itself, lulling with the magnetic other-worldliness all who sit in adoration before it. || The collection is taken discreetly at the door by the gaunt, gray-haired man in the scarlet uniform with the crust of gold braid, and the worshipers are ushered to their cushioned pews in reverent darkness. No matter if they are late; the service is continuous, and if the beginning of the first mass is missed, one may stay through the beginning of the second to achieve full continuity. In the democratic twilight, the clothes of the patrons are not in evidence. If Mrs. Allan's hat is out of taste, if Mac the cabdriver snores through the dull first lesson or the news reel, if Mamie and Joe nuzzle each other playfully, fondly in response to the sermon of a screen kiss, there is no one to be censorious, no one who really minds. For this is the altar at which more Americans spend their time and money, daily, nightly, than ever before. Here the mystic incense of the traditional popcorn, chewing gum and choc-olate, of mixed perfume and whiskey smells is neutralized and cooled by the

patented air-conditioning system. And here people can lose their identity in a splurge of altruism before the twentieth century god. His messengers, his missionaries are everywhere. Dark in the room above your heads, one runs the machine; reel after vibrating reel of divine life circles under his direction onto the mammoth screen, playing forth the drama, the life force, the Bible of the masses. Rave notices are circulated in the newspapers. Everybody reads them. Sex and slaughter are substituted for the sin and sulphur of the pulpits, now quite antiquated. Instead of watching a man dictate manners and morals, you watch the very workings of these manners and morals in an artificially constructed society which to you, is real. Which, to all the worshipers, is the most wonderful and temporary reality they could ever hope to know. The liquid, gleaming lips of movie actresses quiver in kiss after scintillating kiss; full breasts lift under lace, satin, low scallops: sex incarnate, (and the male worshiper feels his mouth go thick and sweat start, and the fire start burning in his loins. If he is with a girl, he puts his arm around her maybe, thinking of how her breasts would feel if maybe he could feed her a few too many beers – there's that place down by the river where the kids go parking and if he got started . . .) The male actor says "C'mere, baby," and his voice is rough, brash, intimate, and his strong arm bends behind her soft body, forcing her to him, against the muscular length of him, standing there, proud and virile . . . (and the female worshiper goes limp, thinking how good it would feel if only Johnny got tough, even if it was just playing, now and then, and pretended he was really going out for her in a big way – she could let her hair fall over one eye a little, and if she tucked in her blouse tighter, maybe pulled the neckline down a little lower, leaning toward him, maybe he would get started . . .)

So there it is, the Fire Sermon, and the choruses and responses, all to the music and the hymns, the superterrestrial, supercollosal paens to the good guy, the good girl, the sex organs of America . . . bigger & better marriages these days and more often please.

Sidetracking, that was. Now to the subject at hand which is not a lecture, nor yet, supposedly, an analogy between the church and the cinema, but rather a sketch of two people reacting together: a Princeton boy and a Smith girl.

At the movies, they laughed, long and delightedly together, for the films were British, intelligent, deft and mature – (no gorgeous women in WAVE uniforms doing variety can-cans on deck, or soft hatted men looking tough in plaid lumbershirts on a rearing horse –.)

His arm rested for a little on the back of her chair, and his hand, now and then, tightened appreciatively on her shoulder, and she wanted very badly for him to hold her in his arms because it was a long while since she had been made love to, and then it had been quite thoroughly and wonderfully. But she said no to herself, and again no. She would discipline her tender and desiring libido – but ah, how young and fair was his face, lean, boyish, with the full mouth and the strong, firm, young chin that could assert itself with an almost vegetable delicacy and resiliancy. His voice above all, clear, young, drawling southernly just now and then ... it was lights, dark, an attempt to find some place to go dancing ... a drive to his home and gin-gerale in a stylishly sunken pale blue livingroom, large, with all manner of divans, rugs, windowseats, patterned curtains. Going home at one o'clock, he did not put his glasses on, but drove with arm around girl, pulling her to him, her head upon his shoulder. He kissed her hand. "That was sweet of you to do," she said, quite charmed. "You are sweet, too. Sweet and nice. You know that, don't you?" She felt suddenly sweet and nice. "Sometimes I have to be told," she replied huskily. The car glided up before her house. A pale, jaundiced full moon shone in a clear yellow aura of light through the dark of pine trees. He pulled her to him, saying intensely, "I don't know, I don't know what it is. I've never felt this way before with any other girl . . . . more than anything else in the world," he whispered, his soft, young, boyish cheek against hers, "I want to love you." She let him kiss her once, pulled reluctantly away, thinking: The power, the power of the life force. Exulting inwardly, she walked to the door with him. || In her, beating loudly, strong-ly, was the neutral fact: the potent sex drive. It could be used for either her triumph or her downfall. It could be her most dynamic asset or her most tragic flaw. (Which? . . . the lady or the tigress? ten years should tell.)

Sunday, lately, at twilight, he called for her, driving again into the city in the lovely pale summer dusk, laced in colored neon with tiers of lights, blinking, syncopating in the dark, and the girl cool and brown, longlimbed, in a princess-styled white sharkskin dress, circular full skirt rustling like stiff cream over a starched crinoline, laughing delightedly inside herself at the wonder of being nineteen and going into town with a tall adorably opinion-ated Princetonian, cradled by the smooth plush rocking of a blue auto-mobile, and lulled by canned music sounding from the lighted arc of the radio face on the dashboard. (Remind her of all the times she scored material comforts as beastly and self-corrupting, and she would laugh throatily at you, and lean back to look down under her lashes as she has learned to do lately, and murmur: "And is not all of life material – based on the material – permeated by the material –? Should not one learn, gladly, to utilize the

THE JOURNALS OF SYLVIA PLATH

beauty of the fine material? I do not speak of the gross crudities of soporific television, of loud brash convertibles and vulgar display – but rather of grace and line and refinement – and there <u>are</u> wonderful and exciting things that only money can by, such as theater tickets, books, paintings, travel, lovely clothes, – and why deny them when one can have them? The only problem is to work, to stay awake mentally and physically – and **NEVER** to become mentally, physically, or spiritually flabby or over-complacent!") Disembarking in Copley Square they walk up in front of the Copley Plaza, under the brilliantly lighted awning, into the tall wide hallway where, to the left, there is a darkened room - - - he pushes the door open, peers into the dim carpeted interior. The girl follows, laughing softly and excitedly. There are empty chairs set helter-skelter about a smooth square polished floor where, he tells her, seizing her gaily by the waist and spinning her about in a waltz turn, they sometimes have dances. Laughing, hand in hand, they leave the unlighted room and cross over to the bar where there is more canned music coming, synthetic and formless, over loudspeakers concealed partially in the curtains along the wall. The bar itself is on the left wall as they come in, with the great mirrors reflecting all the glassy bottles, tall, thin, short, fat, holding, cradling clear fluids – ruby, garnet, gold, transparent, and the bartenders, whiteclad, red faced, slouched dozing behind the counter. The room is quiet, with only a few people sitting on the floor at tables with umbrellas over them, in a poor imitation of a Paris sidewalk cafe – and no one sitting on the slowly revolving raised platform in the center of the room with the strange plush couches (like an S, with the two seats in each curve, facing each other, and a slight swelling in the middle for a table, with a brass pole going up for the scalloped top of the merry-go-round) – all turning very quietly and sweetly, all well-oiled. And the girl clutches his arm, "Oh," she says, "Oh, we must sit up there. Where we can see all the people." So he smiles, and takes her by the hand, leading her up the steps of the merry-goround to one of the strange s-shaped divans, and they sit down facing each other, quite pleased with themselves, because they are both so young, so ambitious, so intelligent and attractive. The waiter comes up, subservient, bent over his pad solicitously. "What'll you have?" the boy asks the girl. She doesn't know; she is very ignorant about the names of drinks. "You order for me," she suggests sweetly, pleadingly. "Something I'll like." "Scotch-and-soda ... I mean water," he says "Do you want soda or water with yours?" he asks. She says soda, because it sounds better, more familiar, and the waiter goes off. They talk, then, (about life and how children are influenced and conditioned by their parents, how he went on camping trips, how he was elected Personnel Manager for the Nassau, Vice-President of Whig-Cliosophic Society – and postponed his history paper on Belgian neutrality, of how his grand-father bought rare antiques instead of storing money away because it was more secure that way, of how, of how she had gotten a favorable notice from a publisher who had read the proofs of one of her stories . . . and on and on, easily sliding in and out of a plethora of topics as college people do.) The drinks are brought, and the girl is inside herself frightened by the sight of what seems a trayful of glasses and bottles and colored plastic sticks. What to do with all of the glassy glitter and tinkle? Wait, she says to herself, and the waiter asks "Shall I mix them?" "Yes," the boy says, and the girl sits back, relieved, smiling to herself secretly as the waiter pours from a green glass bottle of what must be soda into a glass part full of an amber liquid which must be scotch. The waiter evaporates, then, quite neatly into thin air, and they talk and talk, and sip their drinks. When they are through, he orders another round, (and although suddenly behind her eyes there is a rising core of blur and once in a while the laugh comes out and chokes a word which wasn't quite pronounced the way it should have been, she is all right) and then it is later than they thought, so they step down from the very sweetly revolving well-oiled plush merry-go-round (after he has deftly paid the bill, expertly left an unobtrusive tip) and are out in the street once more . . . At the door, after he has driven her home, he takes her in his arms and kisses her on the mouth, (perhaps because he knows the blur is still there behind her dark eyes and that her mouth wants very badly to be kissed.) and she looks up as his mouth stays for a warm, wet moment on hers and can see his eyes are shut, the plane of his cheek hollowed, as if he were in a brief ecstatic world, drawing into himself a delicious and sweet sustenance. Then he let go and briskly, gaily, was off down the walk. The girl closed the door, and stood inside in the dark hall, her head against the cool smooth woodwork, listening to the car start outside, and drive away. She stood there motionless for a long while, her eyes shut, remembering hungrily the way his quivering young mouth had felt, and listening to the backsurging quiet of the night thickening, congealing around her in her loneliness and longing like an imprisoning envelope of gelatin . . .

(127)

July 10, Thursday: For three weeks I worked at the Belmont, waitressing in Side Hall, learning about people like Mrs. York and Mrs. Sanders; Ray, the coffeeman; the toast-man; Marietta, the housemother; Mr. & Mrs. Kinsley, the caretaker and the head of chambermaids; Oscar, the birdlike, picayune, humorous band leader, and Guy, and Ray, and Vulgar Charlie; August, the handsome, soft-shirted hairdresser who had been smoking against the rules for six years now; beautiful and faultless small dearly built Betsy Buck; dark-haired, spunky roommate Polly;" sharp, intelligent, mercenary, unscrupulous and dry-humored Gloria; brilliant, ebullient medical student Ray Wunderlich" of Columbia Medical School with his memory engrams; homely, intelligent lawstudent Art Kramer" with his $100 a week job at the Blossoms' millionaire homestead as night-attendant; handsome, garrulous Italian Gappy; stoic-faced Harvard law student and straight-backed busboy Clark Williams; handsome Bronx bastard ("legitimate") Lloyd Fisher from Dartmouth Med who told you some of the facts of life; Dave, the strange, fat red-faced Roast Cook; Ghris, the twinkly eyed second-cook; Mrs. Johnson, the tall, sharp Irish chef's wife with the acid brogue and the fiery temper – I could go on and on. And then there was the beach, and sun, and Dick and the late dates, and the heat and the black-uniforms – and the final fatal sinus infection.

Saturday night, the last one to be spent at the Belmont, in spite of a sore throat and sluggish apathy, I roused myself to have a final fling before I came down with whatever I was coming down with. (My Princetonian charming called quite wonderfully and unexpectedly, saying he was down for the week-end and would I like to go out.) So after waiting on at supper, I dashed back after 8, threw off my sweaty, longsleeved black uniform, my heavy shoes, ripped off my stockings, showered, shaved, perfumed and powdered, and donned my swish aqua strapless cotton with the little jacket. A pearl choker, white ballet shoes and white topper completed the ensemble, and very brown and very excited, I walked out to the parking lot to meet my escort.

The Mill Hill Club was big, commercialized, with a band, dance floor, and a continuous round of aggressive entertainment, so we sat, side by side, in a leatherette booth by an open window with a view of pines and a slice of lemon colored moon – listening to a birdlike man hammering hell out of a banjo, a great girl vocalist, and a splendid mimic. Singing, drinking, dancing, laughing (me in his arms, close, hot, banged into by people, crushed together, someone's heel prodding your calf, my elbow in a strangers ribs . . . his face, strange too in the light, looking down, laughing, smiling into mine, lips, seeking to kiss, laughter always, and knowing he liked the way I was, gay and tanned and glowing . . .) we passed the hours. Next day, (foolishly, I thought,) I made an afternoon date for tennis.

All that night, coughing, fevered, I couldn't sleep, but lay in the narrow bed, with the faint grit of sand I never could quite get off the sheets, and stared at the swatch of winking stars I could see over the roof of the boys' dorm. They shone, calm and mocking, through the thin filmy nylon stockings hung up in the window to dry. All the pros and cons and nasty, mealy-mouthed fears and dreads went swarming through my teeming, seething brain. The sickness I felt had reached a crisis; it was not turning back as I had hoped, but was, rather, advancing steadily. What to do? Whom to turn to? Where to go? What to tell Phil today? And so the morning came, and with it the verbal birth of an idea that had been sprouting in my subconscious all along at the sight of Wellesley-dwelling Princetonian. Why not, why not – go home with him and recuperate there? In peace and quiet!

A trip to the doctor's Sunday morning in the Belmont truck with tall, skinny blond Jack Harris, whose skin is always pink and peeling, and witty, big Pat Mutrie who can have you laughing just with a word, with a look. Bumping along, feeling hot and messy, over the country Cape roads, finally to come to the office of Doctor Norris Orchard who was frail, white-haired, like a kindly red faced bird. He hopped about, peering into my sinuses and down my throat, saying, "Well, dear, it may break your little heart, but I think you should go home for a few days to recuperate." Jubilant at his strategic and official confirmation of my plan, I drove back to the Belmont and threw all manner of clothes into my little black suit case – bathing suit, dirty pajamas, tennis shorts, and even a date dress and pearls just in case I should get well fast enough ... and Phil should chance to ask me out! I squared things away with Mr. Driscoll, who was questioning and curt, and ran out to the parking lot where Phil's car had just pulled in.

"Er ... Phil ... " I begin brightly, leaning on the windowsill and gazing in at him and the good-looking lean blond boy beside him, both of them dressed in tennis shorts ... "ah ... Phil, how would you like company on the way home?"

A queer look passes over his face, and the other boy (Rodger") starts laughing. "What happened?" Phil asks. "Did you get fired?"

"No. I just have got to go home to get some penicillin shots. Doctor's orders." That sounds official.

"Well, sure," he says.

"Can I get in now? I've got all my things?" So I run up and get the absurd little black suit case and, for some odd reason, my tennis racket. Fortunately for me it is starting to rain. No tennis, thank God.

I get in between the two boys and we drive off. Suddenly everything is very funny, very ridiculous. We are all laughing, and Rodger is looking over his glasses down his cute nose, pulling my hair, and being a hacker in general.

"We are going to pick up The Weasel," he says.

"The Weasel?" I ask. I look scared. He laughs.

So we drive into a driveway by a big white house with a lot of pillars. "It's all pillars," I observe brightly. That, it seems is the name of the place: The Pillars. It also seems this is where the millionaire lives. Art Kramer's millionaire. (Weasel, it develops, is the millionaire's Princetonian chauffeur.)

So Art comes out, in a suit, smiling in his endearing simian fashion, and leaning against the car. It is a small world. Then Weasel comes out, blond, blue-eyed, and in shirt sleeves. Not bad, but with a definite aura of weaselishness about him. He comes bearing gifts: beer cans. Full, too. He jumps into the back seat and we are off.

This time there is a great deal of laughing, and Rodge is trying to explain to Weasel how "This girl is the coolest thing I've seen yet; she comes up waving this pitiful little piece of paper, some doctor saying she should go home, and she goes home like she needs a vacation or something!" We stop for ice, and drive to a beach where there is a parking lot by sanddunes, and a view of witchgrass, and the rain coming down hard on a dirty, sodden, gray green sea.

The beer tastes good to my throat, cold and bitter, and the three boys and the beer and the queer freeness of the situation make me feel like laughing forever. So I laugh, and my lipstick leaves a red stain like a bloody crescent moon on the top of the beer can. I am looking very healthy and flushed and bright eyed, having both a good tan and a rather excellent fever.

We drop off the other two boys, then, and start the three-hour drive back to Wellesley through the pouring rain. It is comfortable, being with Phil, and there is a lot to talk about. The only trouble is that my voice is beginning to leave me. It must be the dampness or something, but the pitch is about an octave lower. So I decide philosophically to make the best of it and pretend I naturally have a very husky, sexy low voice: I've never had it so good.

We pick up Phil's dog, a spoiled big-eyed black cocker spaniel who sits with us in the front seat, looking very sad and very loving. Phil pats her, and so do I. Our hands meet, and he absently pats mine. I think all of a sudden maybe I could get very fond of this guy after all.

I get out of the car when it pulls up in front of the little white house I haven't seen for almost three weeks. I am suddenly very tired, very hungry. I say goodbye to Phil who asks if I want to go out that night. "No, Phil, thanks." He doesn't understand. I am going to be very sick. "Tennis tomorrow?" No, again.

Mother and Warren look up, startled, as I walk in. "Hello," I croak gaily. "I'm home for a visit." Mother smiles and says "Wait till I tell grammy! She dreamed you were coming home last night!" (As Frost said, Home is where when you go there, they have to take you in!")

(128.) July 11, Friday. A recuperation, tedious, with shots of penicillin, and now I have been breathing quite well for a week. The Belmont called up early one morning, and mother answered. They wanted to know definitely when I'd be coming back so they could hire another girl in the interim. (Some devilish split part in my personality had been whispering to me all week subconsciously: "Why go back? You're tired, fagged out, and the work is getting rough – no days off, pay not especially good. Then, too, only a few people who really like you. Why not stay home for the summer – rest, get your science done, write, go out with Phil, play tennis. You can afford to loaf. You deserve to, what with winning one of the two big prizes in Mademoiselle's College Fiction Contest with "Sunday at the Mintons'" so take a break for once. Sinusitis is such a beautiful excuse.") So the devil got into my vocal chords and I started prompting mother – "Say you don't know when I'll be well . . . that I'm still miserable . . . that I loved it there, but maybe it would be more convenient to get some one else." So mother said so, and they said they were sorry as everybody liked me, but they would get someone else. We looked at each other in dubious triumph.

Twenty-four hours later I got a letter from Polly and from Pat M. (saying how they missed me) from Art Kramer (saying how seeing me that day gave him just enough courage to want to ask me out) and from the Editor-in-Chief of Alfred Knopf, Publishers (saying how he liked the advance proofs of my story "Sunday at the Mintons'" which is coming out in Mlle and how he'd like to publish a novel [!] by me sometime in the future.) That little packet was IT: all I needed to start me raring to live again. In that brief interval I cursed myself for stupidly getting out of the Belmont job – for losing Ray, Art, Polly, Gloria – and all the might-have-beens: the wonderful-people-I-might-have-met-but didn't. And the beach 4 hours a day, and the swimming. And the tan & blond sunbleached hair. I was glum, morose, thinking: why didn't I tell them I'd be back in two weeks: then I could have rested completely and had a little social vacation in the bargain! (Fool. Fool. Damn Fool.)

And then I began to understand the difference between death-or-sickness-in-life as versus Life. When sick (both physically, as symptoms showed, and mentally, as I was trying to escape from something) I wanted to withdraw from all the painful reminders of vitality – to hide away alone in a peaceful stagnant pool, and not be like a crippled stick entangled near the bank of a jubilantly roaring river, torn at continually by the noisy current. So I went home, knowing that if I did so it would be hard to come back. The horrible exertion of forcing myself back into the current persisted all during the worst days of my depressing sinus infection – and the call came 24 hours too early. Then came the switch in attitude: Out of all the rationalizing, all the intellectual balancing of pros and cons, it comes down to the fact that when you are alive and vital, competition and striving with and among <u>people</u> overbalances everything else. No matter how logically I had reasoned out about the Belmont being dangerous for my health, unremunerative in proportion to the work performed, impossible as far as science study was concerned – <u>still</u> the magnetic whirlpool of slender, lovely young devils called and called to me above all. Life was not to be sitting in hot amorphic leisure in my backyard idly writing or not-writing, as the spirit moved me. It was, instead, running madly, in a crowded schedule, in a squirrel cage of busy people. Working, living, dancing, dreaming, talking, kissing – singing, laughing, learning. The responsibility, the awful responsibility of managing (profitably) 12 hours a day for 10 weeks is rather overwhelming when there is nothing, noone, to insert an exact routine into the large unfenced acres of time – which it is so easy to let drift by in soporific idling and luxurious relaxing. It is like lifting a bell jar off a securely clockwork-like functioning community, and seeing all the little busy people stop, gasp, blow up and float in the inrush, (or rather outrush,) of the rarified scheduled atmosphere – poor little frightened people, flailing impotent arms in the aimless air. That's what it feels like: getting shed of a routine. Even though one has rebelled terribly against it, even then, one feels uncomfortable when jounced out of the repetitive rut. And so with me. What to do? Where to turn? What ties, what roots? as I hang suspended in the strange thin air of back-home?

(129) <u>July 11</u> – Friday still. A willing, creative girl with a sense of humor, and three potential jobs, I am now, though. Thumbing desperately through Want Ads, I've considered becoming a painter of parchment lamp shades, a file clerk, a typist: Anything to give me that intangible-self-respect. Somehow I feel a great need for having a Job, no matter what, no matter how unremunerative. So I answered an add in the <u>Townsman</u> for "a highschool girl who likes to write" and ended up with Mrs. Williams, an aggressive and humerous widowed real-estate agent. (Never will I forget that amazing Wednesday with her which I started unsuspectingly enough with an inter-

view at 10:30 and ended, somewhat exhausted, at 4:30, after having met and talked with her other interviewees – the Court's (Janet and the unforgettable fat, wheezy brown-eyed doughy intellectual Mrs.), the professors wife; and met Crazy Grace, the scatterbrained housekeeper who talked to herself all the time and thought she could sell houses because she sold germicides once and "It takes a lot of personality, selling germicides." – there were the trips down town, the going through two houses – one with a busy mother and her babies, to sell for $18,900, and one with a clover-grown lawn that the fat, lethargic TV listening Raymond would never get around to mowing . . . for $20,500. There were the trips to new houses, the talking with builders and watching Mrs. Williams' aggressive, admirably unscrupulous methods of playing on every possible angle, no matter how shifty. All this, and a black-and-white float in Hopkins to cool our perspiring and sticky psyches. So I could be a Girl Friday for her all summer, maybe not earning anything, unless there should be a sale: seeing houses, wheedling builders, writing add copy, and even showing people houses if I got advanced enough. Veddy fascinating, if financially nebulous. Second is the possibility that Mrs. Williams herself will get me another job as waitress during the summer at the place where her daughter is working. That, however, is an off chance, in spite of the fact that she is best friends with the head of the Inn. The third and most promising job is one I read in the classified section of the <u>Christian Science Monitor</u> – a mother in Chatham (of all the strategic places – near Dick, Art, etc.!) wants a "neat, intelligent college-age girl of pleasing personality" to help with her two children. Sounds great. That's me. So I call, make an appointment for an interview this weekend, and it all sounds veddy promising – a quiet house evenings to study in, out of doors with the children, slower living, and just about as much pay as I'd make at the Belmont – we shall however, not yet count our chickens!

(130.)

<u>July 25</u> – Chickens being duly counted, hatched, and I at the Cantors'." Life: full, rich, long, part of the family, growing to know them and their quietnesses, their laughters, their convictions, and always subtly probing, questioning, the core – Christian Science. (And thinking how Catholics are indoctrinated, and how hard to argue with are these then also.) Not argue, but discuss. They start with one <u>major premise</u> – an omniscient, omnipresent, omnipotent God consisting of: Abstract qualities; perfect realities: Love, Life, Mind, Truth, Soul, Spirit, Principle. God is perfect and made man in his image, i.e.: perfect. God is not anthropomorphic – i.e. not like man,

corporeal. If god made man perfect, where did sickness, disease and death come from? From "mortal mind," from error, the figment of matter being myth, rising like "mist" (see Genesis) to cloud the truth, which is God. So Jesus came to heal man of sickness and sin & return him to Godliness, perfection, wholeness. If God is all and real and spirit, there can be no logical admission of error as real, as that would imply god is not omnipotent and everywhere, but had a rival, thus error is <u>unreal</u>. God is the only reality. Mind over matter, real over unreal, truth over error – and so on.

I would argue, or discuss, on <u>their</u> premise. More stimulating that way. A skeptic, I would ask for consistency first of all. If matter is unreal, if we are imprisoned in these clay carcasses, if disease is imaginary and unreal (Billy cries: "I hurt my elbow." She says: "Know the truth. You are God's child. Could God's child be hurt? Of course not. God has no elbows, no body. Know the truth and the truth will make you free.") if this is all so, then why pamper your "illness". <u>Some</u> devout Christian Scientists don't, and have let their wives or husbands die of cancer, for example. But these say "Error is trying to talk . . . " and let their children stay in bed if they "don't feel well." Also have their teeth filled. Now that, to me, seems illogical. It is all very well to say they don't have "enough understanding of the truth," and that Christian Science (C.S.) also stands for "common sense," but isn't that a tacit admission that matter, even if an illusion, is a pretty potent one? And that they are victims of it's tyranny? According to Mrs. C., any one, no matter how simple, can practice Christian Science by thinking about God first, and his divine unchanging spiritual qualities. And God gave man dominion over the fish of the sea and the fowl of the air. Hence man can vanquish the serpent of fear, turning it into a rod again, casting out fear, sickness, disease.

Now that I ponder over it, I do see a sudden neat edifice of logic, and I do agree with some of their generalizations in spite of the fact that I am philosophically at the other end of the pole, – a "matter worshiper."

First, I do believe that "thinking makes it so" and that "attitude is everything." This the Christian Scientists seem to use to illustrate the power of real mind (divine) over unreal mind (mortal). I believe that there is a realm (abstractly, hypothetically, of course) of absolute fact. Something IS. And that, in our poor human lingo, would be the "truth." (But as far as <u>I</u> am concerned, that truth is matter, not spirit.) However, to each individual man, viewing facets, slivers, fragments of this whole truth (which must be) through his own particular grotesque glass of distortion, the truth will be, for him, a mere magnification and personal fallible interpretation of the special facet, sliver or fragment he sees. No man can ever grasp the whole impersonal neutrality of a universe. That is hidden under the mists of subjectivity. We are merely variously constructed sounding boards for the noise of the pine tree falling (proverbially) in the forest. The sound is potential, even if no one is there to hear it. Just as radio programs are all around us, clogging the air, needing only a certain sensitive mechanism to make them a reality, a fact. So what is reality? The definition is so arbitrary. It could be the basic truth, the fact of matter, impersonal, neutral. Or it could be, for each individual, what that individual chooses to make of his corner of the world. Looking at the world through the distorted colored lens of the individual, one might see only a few objects clearly – a math problem, a clock, a jet plane. Even the neutral things seen would be colored by personal attitudes toward them. Reasoning deductively you would come to think, after picking up, squinting through, and putting down a number of these human lenses, that reality is relative, depending on what lens you look through. Each person, banging into the facts, neutral, impersonal in themselves (like the Death of someone) – interprets, alters, becomes obsessed with personal biases or attitutes, transmuting the objective reality into something quite personal (like the death of My Father = tears, sorrow, weeping, dolorous tints, numbing of certain areas of sensation and perception about the stream of life moving about one . . .) Hence, "Thinking makes it so." We all live in own dream-worlds and make and re-make our own personal realities with tender and loving care. And my dream-world – how much more valid, how much nearer to the truth is it than that of these people? Valid for me, perhaps – even though it is not metaphysical. Even if I do consider mucous and sinus real – and medical schools have been instituted to cure through medication such machinations of "error and mortal mind." If they believe in life-after-death in a heavenly spiritual realm, what a pleasant solace it is for them – and what individual strength it can give. Why quibble: "It is absurd. It isn't so." For me, it isn't so, and I turn to hide irreverent laughter when Susan, constipated, gets a lesson instead of a laxative. But for them, it is so, absolutely so. And thus individuals construct absolutely real dream Kingdoms – paradoxically all "true" although mutually exclusive at the same time. My dream-bubble of reality exists side by side with theirs, without breaking fragmentarily asunder. We live and move together in the realm of concrete experience, harmoniously, motivated and propelled by our own dream-realities. And even that idea of mine is no doubt itself an artificial dream-reality.

Man labors in laboratories to discover the truth, the unchanging fact. Yet what the head knows, the senses contradict. And who is to malign the senses, calling them false? Pick your winners, your own sides – concept (mind) says railroad tracks are parallel and never meet. Percept (sense: here, eyes) say railroad tracks meet at the distant point where one can plainly see that they converge. Which is true? <u>Both</u> concept and percept. Yes. And man can integrate the two as best he can, or choose one in preference of the other. He is "lord of the counter positions." He has been given dominion.

(131.) And as for myself, I perceive all through the senses – mind among them. I must read up on the neural theories, the complexities. Someday, they will be understood. I have that confidence in the mind and intellectual curiosity of man. "What is man that thou art mindful of him?" So paltry, and so colossal. So puny and so potential.

I wonder now, on August 6, lying here on my white bed, listening to the rain: slant long and hard on the roof outside my windows coming down liquidly, drippingly plural and generous from the low gray skies, fluently saying what I choose to make it say. Slanting down the screen in milky, translucent streams, prolific, uncaringly beneficent, it heals or annoys, (as we humans choose to translate it.) And I love it because of the sound, and the gray pluvial walls of it dropping down, closing in. Not knowing why. Not dissecting my liking or feeling, not being materialistic or matter-of-fact, but mystic – I will use vague elusive words like "rapport," "affinity," for the calm pleasure I feel welling up in me.

We perceive things through the concrete object and illustration. We see, we smell, we taste, we touch, we hear – and the abstract words are synthesized from the realms of concrete experience – from all the men kissing all the girls and all the mothers suckling all their babies, we get "love" – the abstract concept, and in turn apply it to the concrete individual percept: a particular individual man kisses a particular individual girl and says "I love you." They are "in love": in the abstract realm where their concrete acts harmonize with the atmosphere, synthetic-and man-made though it be. –

(132.) "Everything is the same but different."

Paradox again. Two mutually exclusive and contradictory adjectives are applied at the same time to the universe. And this phrase is again a unique insight into the repetitious and varied universe man has woken up in and begun to work at transforming into something he can call his own. We are all men, but as different as we are similar – as opposite as we are alike. We know a thing by its opposite corollary: hot by having experienced cold; good, by having decided what is bad; love by hate.

And yet Art says there are certain absolute moral standards in society approved of by all – that all is not relative as I would seem to imply. For instance, that nowhere is it "good" to do a friend dirt behind his back, kill him, for instance. All right – if a "friend" is defined as one with whom one has established a very close, personal attachment of love and understanding, it would be frowned on to injure him in anyway – but if he were going mad, this hypothetical friend, would you do what was requested by society and sent him to an asylum, or be true to his pitiful demented pleading and let him stay free as long as you could. Or, if he had defied the law, would your first loyalty be to him or to the welfare of the community? All questions being merely theoretical. And just for the record, consider all the potential "friends" we slaughter off in war, just because they are arbitrarily labeled "enemy."

Is everything we do an attempt to choose between the lesser of two evils? Is man, in this sense, born in original sin? Or perhaps just born into a world of "sin," sin being the tragic dilemma of making wrong or less wrong choices, with nothing to approve or condone the choice – nothing but the fruits of the choice and attendant action to decree whether the choice was good or bad. And even, then, always, the doubt.

(133.) August 8 – Friday – 9:45 p.m.
In bed, bathed, and the good rain coming down again – liquidly slopping down the shingled roof outside my window. All today it has come down, in its enclosing wetness, and at last I am in bed, propped up comfortably by pillows – listening to it spurting and drenching – and all the different timbers of tone – and syncopation. The rapping on the resonant gutters – hard, metallic. The rush of a stream down the drain pipe splattering flat on the earth, wearing away a small gully – the musical falling of itself, tinkling faintly on the tin garbage pails in a high pitched tattoo. And it seems that always in August I am more aware of the rain. A year ago it came down on my porch and the lawn and the flat gray sea beyond at the Mayos – closing me in the great house in the day, talking to me alone in my room in the evening as I sat alone in bed writing; surveying my kingdom from my throne: the lone streetlight on the corner, hanging solitary in a nimbus of light, and beyond it the gray indistinguishable fog and the rain sound blending with the wash of the sea. It shut me in a rock cave with Dick on Marblehead beach, drenching, soaking, and we threw rocks at a rusted tin can until it stopped coming down viciously and churning the sea to a flayed whiteness.

Two years ago August rain fell on me and Ilo, walking side by side, wordless, toward the barn. And it was raining when I came out from the loft, crying, my mouth bruised where he had kissed me. Rain closed about the windows of the car Emile and I rode home in, and fell outside the kitchen where we stood, in the dark, with the smell of linoleum, and the water always falling on the leaves outside the screen.

Three years ago, the hot, sticky August rain fell big and wet as I sat listlessly on my porch at home, crying over the way summer would not come again – never the same. The first story in print" came from that "never again" refrain beat out by the rain. August rain: the best of the summer gone, and the new fall not yet born. The odd uneven time.

(134.) August 9. Today I was alone with Joan, Sue and Bill. Mrs. Cantor gone. Car mine, and planning of meals and time allotment, it was good. Flowers – zinnias gold and rust and umber – pink and white and lavendar – bought in rash armfuls at a flower stand for guests this weekend. Four dozen eggs, beige, oval, full of protein – farm produce, where there was hay sweetly damp in a loft, a cow, and chickens. Three children chanting loudly in sing-song from the car window. Lunch then: good tunafish salad, tomatoes, crackers, cheese, and milk. So in the afternoon, late, with the rain still coming down, I left the children down with Joanie – and escaped in the Beachwagon to Chatham town. Inching the shiny green machine through the rainpuddled narrow streets to the town parking lot I felt an evil sense of victory and freedom. I was going to see Val Gendron" in the Bookmobile and I did.

I walked in the backdoor of "Lorania's Bookmobile", and my red slicker shed rivulets of water on the floor as I bent my head, scanning titles, while Val was talking to people up front. I sat on the floor then, looking at poetry books and the brightly covered, good clear-printed Modern Library editions. She was alone then, and remembered me.

So I asked her about a lot of things – how she got writing and where published, and where worked. She talked nicely to me - - - cynical, hardbitten, with a sneer, and then a quick look, a smile, soft fleetingly, that said she understood about how I was critical of my story, didn't like it now as much, and how it was best writing actually, the process, not the product. So she told me about the four page (1000 words a day) deal. No time limit – there's the catch. You don't have a time limit, it's the produce that counts. 365,000 words in a year is a hell of a lot of words. I start this fall. Four pages a day.

She is small, skinny, sallow, with black hair done up in back in a bun and braids under a visor khaki cap. A pointed face, glasses, and a dry, sarcastic drawl. Cats she has, in her shack, red-painted (she says) and no phone. Signs of loneliness? Of living too long with Val Gendron? Who to talk to? Who? I will find out. I will be no Val Gendron. But I will make a good part of Val Gendron part of me – someday. And the coffee grounds can be left out. For good. She has said I may visit her: a pilgrimage: — to my First Author.

135. August 10 – Always washed and bathed with the rain coming down. Thunder tonight. ("Lord, lord, though ridest.") Whistling over the mulberry trees thou goest. Lord, thy children are jaded, and their ears go flat with sound. Marveling in the thunder rumbling of thy voice no longer – they hear not, and the omens of the white gull and the flayed oak are as naught to their purblind sight. The prophecy in the thunder, the foreshadowings of the leaves quivering white, the dismay of the grass bent in the merciless wind are naught, lord.

Beat on the tin roofs with spears of rain, lord. Harry the steel cities with claps of thunder. Fling, fling thy light crackling across the face of the stone skytowers. They will hear not, they will see not, neither will they understand.

For they have built the walls of their citadels of steel, and their temples of rock, and they dwell within. Also have they lit the dark with colored neons, and the streets are lanced with shooting stars. More loudly knock, oh lord; with thy clarion blast flare aweful at the gates. Light, oh lord, sear white throbs and crack the skies; they will not hear.

Vain flash the proud lights in the city of man, red, blue, green and yellow and white. Color of apple, color of grape, of pear, of corn. Clear flash the proud lights, lord, and your far wheeling beacons pale, those far fixed stars, and the planets withered, shrunken, twirl in their forgotten orbits, pale, lord, in the light-bleached sky. In the white cold glare from the city of man.

Vain sound the proud horns in the city of man, sax, trombone, jazz, blues. Color of love, color of mourning, color of hot, color of crying. And all your noisy rains and thunders can not quench his inwardness. Down bangs the window where rain rattles in, and in the steamy haze within, loudly brazen the bands begin.

Ride in the sun crashing light victorious or hold back your rain. Cry in anger or in sorrow at the lost world, the mistaken ones. They are working. They will have you yet in harness.

136. August 12″ – Outside, in the wet low fog there was the low little car,

suave sleek red M-G, waiting. "Oh, no," the girl said. She had never ridden in an M-G before. And red was her favorite color.

"Oh, yes," he said, opening the door. She got in, tying the red silk scarf over her hair and settling low and comfortable beside him. It was strange, riding cradled so open, so near the ground.

Roaring through the fog they went careening along the shore highway, with the blur of fog closing them in, shredding in the light of far and few street lamps, Glow milky as of moonrise heralded coming cars, looming two yellow globes of light, coming, and then two red points of brightness dwindling behind.

Around corners the squeal of wheels. The car braces, leans, tilts back again. An Esso station looms light ahead. Lights marking out an area of brilliance by the roadside, and the red and black and white sign clear and printed saying gasoline suddenly and coherently in the lonely and spaceless dark. Slows by, then gone behind in a shriveling puddle of light.

They are laughing and he is singing loudly some dirty songs. He is in a glee club somewhere she thinks.

"You know," he looks down at her. "I don't even know your name." He is grinning, his face lean and boyish behind the glasses.

"What!" she laughs and tells him. After all, what has a name got to do with this night and fog? She would gladly be a Marcia or an Elaine or Doris being still she and riding still with this boy in an M-G.

So now he knows her name, and things are very conventional. He tells her he is a bastard. He is singing loudly, and he has just turned seventeen. Every other word he swears. He's old for seventeen, and he tells her she is cute.

She is feeling at this point, very maternal. It is occuring to her that she is almost three years older than he is, and she feels quite suddenly older, with a wealth of all kinds of life and experience behind her. The feeling grows big in her.

"I am very tired," he tells her. "You drive a while." He stops the car by the endless road, a hollowed out drive, and they trade seats. She gets used to the feel of the little car, good little red shiny MG. And her foot goes down on the accelerator.

By now his head is on her shoulder and his feet up on the door, knees bent, dangling over. He is drinking beer and sharing it with her, feeding her potato chips, and sleepily singing on her shoulder.

"You know," he is saying, "I used to raise hell with women. Petting and all that stuff. I've been out with some sluts, and ask any girl in Flushing about my reputation and she'll tell you . . . "

"So, now what?" the girl is asking, feeling her eyes straight on the road and on the tunnel of light carving out of the dark ahead as they go.

"So now it's different. Like you. First thing I saw, you were sweet and intelligent. Not every blonde has got brains, you know. It's your personality, I like. Not sex. You're no raving tearing beauty."

He doesn't know that last could hurt a little if she let it. But it doesn't because she doesn't.

She is thinking of how, even though she started late, there have been all the mouths and all the hands belonging to all the boys without faces and some with faces . . . some with blurred faces, indistinct now, far back.

"Have you ever liked two boys at once?" he is asking. "I mean both a lot at once for something. Like now I like Andy, she's as sweet as they come, and nice. But I like you. You're funny as hell, and cute. And there's that red head in the Dairy Bar. Wonder if she's working tonight . . . "

He is going on and on. God, the girl is thinking, absently letting her hand run through his hair, patting his head cradled in the hollow of her shoulder. He is drowsy, his head falls, grazing her breast. She would like to stop, to cradle his head. God, she is thinking, he is so terribly young, so terribly beginning.

Already she feels jaded. Weary, and gladly tired and old. Driving nowhere in the fog with his young head sleepily on her shoulder she feels the pulse of the motor beneath her foot, and the goodness of the speed, devouring the dark and the long lasting road. The time is going and she wants to keep it. Driving on around into the morning of the world with this beautiful-and-damned boy slumbering on her shoulder.

He is talking now. "You know," he says, "you have met a lot of boys like me and I have never before met any body like you. You've got it."

"What have I got?"

"I don't know. You've just got it." He is leaning his head over toward her, looking intense and baffled.

She feels like smiling at him, and her smile is tender. "You have such a long while ahead of you. It makes me quite dizzy to think of all the beautiful young girls now growing up that are ahead of you. And I will be growing older all the while they are growing up."

"I don't care." He leans over and kisses her hand on the steering wheel. Her voice had been, at that last remark, bright and edged with fear. "I don't care. I like you. You're sweet."

"No," she says, "it is all right now. But just for now. Because it is getting late. All the time it is getting late."

So they are near the house where she is living, and she drives up in the driveway.

"You can walk me to the door," she says. He is still groggy and sleepy, shaking his head. All at once he says oh and puts his arms around her.

She pushes him back, her hands against his chest, her mouth saying: no, not this as she looks at his mouth young and tender asking please, lips asking please. It is much better, she thinks, this way because of how now I am on the top directing both of us. Even the girl in me that would like to lead you into warm ways of love. Any girl, andy maybe, or any other little girl you can neck with or pet. But not me. It is much better, this way.

"All right," he says, "I am not hungry, though. I do not want you to think that I am hungry."

On the way to the door he staggers a little; she steadies him by the arm. "On two cans of that stuff only," he says bewildered. "Say, would like the rest of that case. Keep them in the icebox or something?"

"No," she says laughing. "They don't think I drink. You keep them. Don't let them go to waste."

"I can't," he says. "If mother found them she'd kill me. You know how mother's are," he finishes apologetically.

'Yeah," she says softly. "Sure, I know." You kid. You wonderful damn confused kid, she thinks. Me an old college woman, and you a prep school boy. God, the years, the years. I can count them now in two's and three's. Where have they gone so fast? Eaten by the raw swollen wind of time. Like the M-G ate up all that big nothingness of dark road. Don't go away, you passionate sweet swearing guy. Let me hold you, holding meanwhile the gone-far young tender sharp years.

"Good-night," he says, "but not good-bye."

"Good-night," she says, all at once grateful that it is not quite yet the almost goodbye she had been fearing.

—

(137.)

August 17 – Band Concert on Friday. Even from the house you can hear them playing, and the man's voice echoing across the lawn lots. There is first the rhythmic "tum-ta-tum-ta-tum-ta" beat of the drums, and then the band begins. Susan is quietly excited, her green eyes big and still with the wonder of all the colored balloons bobbing and dipping, and Billy squeals, skipping along in his little red-checked shirt and dungarees, pointing at the band stand that comes into view as we walk over the hill into the natural park amphitheater, into the area of light.

It is already twilight, and we spread our blanket on the hill side, settling down to listen. Behind the black outlines of the pines there is the fading afterglow, translucent, golden, of the setting sun, and the circle around the bandstand is dark with crowds of people on the grass. Children are always running, skipping, in and out of the grassy spot of brilliance surrounding the stand, trailing the large colored balloons, yellow, red, and blue. Somehow a green balloon gets loose, rising and turning on currents of air above the tops of the trees. There is a chorus of ohs and heads turn, watching the gleaming green balloon ascending, growing smaller and smaller, a fleck of green – lost at last against the darkening night sky. In the bushes, dark and wet with dew, the crickets are crying, shrill and sweet.

"I'm very glad ... " the band leader steps up to the microphone, a townsman, special tonight, master-of-ceremonies in his white suit and gold braid, smiling out at the crowds of summer folk, "I'm very happy to see so many here tonight, more even than last week, looks like. We've arranged a very special program tonight, and we'll start with a Gershwin medley ... " There is applause, and with an amiable grin the leader turns to face the band, his baton raised. A moment of silence, then the downbeat.

Seated on the circular white platform, gallant, all of them, in their red and blue uniforms and caps, the band breaks out into a jazzy version of "Liza". There is the flash of light, gold, silver, gleaming in darts and sparkles on the brass instrument. No one pays them, they are volunteers, from the town. But the boys love music, and tonight, in their bright uniforms, they are the crown princes of melody, seated in the circle of white-gold light, playing valiantly to the assembled crowds.

On the hill opposite an orange light flares as someone lights a match. There is the buttery salt smell of popcorn, and the children are sitting very still, moving a little, nodding in time to the beat of the music, unconsciously graceful. A little blonde girl toddles out in the arena of light where later the children will dance. She is dressed for best in a pink organdy skirt and top, a bonnet over her fair curls; she is balancing a large pink balloon, and sets a weaving course for the steps of the band stand. The dark figure of a man, her father, detaches itself from the shadow and steps forward to retrieve the little girl. There is a low undercurrent of friendly understanding laughter.

Lilting, swinging from one familiar Gershwin melody into another, the band plays on. For a mile around the cars are parked, and the people are all there in their summer suits and dresses – the old grayhaired couples, the old women in groups, like gentle lavender scented butterflies, softly, slowly talking. During the day you can see them rocking to and fro in green wicker chairs on all the wide verandas of all the tourist homes in town. Tonight is a big night for them, with the lights and crowds and the lilting melodies that remind them, wistfully, sweetly, of dances, of gay times years, who knows how many years ago? So they sit now, silent for a little, lost deep in reveries, entranced by the music, swinging now into a Strauss waltz. One small, fragile gray-haired lady is humming the melody softly to herself, her thin sweet voice quavering a little.

And the kids, all of them, will dance, keeping time to music, chorusing "Now We Go Looby-Loo" and then the teen-age couples will come out in the arena, and there will be waltzes, dark sky over, and the lights soft and the good big summer feeling inside you with the light gentle and the night cool and friendly. Always with the queer regret, blurring all the other summers into a fine nostalgic brew – distilling all the tart sweetnesses into this one, with the sea of music skipping over the time, and the feeling in you very warm and it is our town, we all together, very sweet, all summer light, sometimes almost tearful because it is so moving all the time. The fluid color the fluid sound, toward its ending. ("Into many a green valley, drifts the appalling snow./ Time breaks the threaded dances and the diver's brilliant bow.") And now I am sitting here crying almost because suddenly I am knowing in my head and feeling in my guts what those words mean when I did not know the full impact of them in the beginning, but merely their mystic beauty.

So it all moves in the pageant toward the ending, it's own ending. Everywhere, imperceptibly or otherwise, things are passing, ending, going. And there will be other summers, other band concerts, but never this one, never again, never as now. Next year I will not be the self of this year now. And that is why I laugh at the transient, the ephemeral; laugh, while clutching, holding, tenderly, like a fool his toy, cracked glass, water through fingers. For all the writing, for all the invention of engines to express & convey & capture life, it is the living of it that is the gimmick. It goes by, and whatever dream you use to dope up the pains and hurts, it goes. Delude yourself about printed islands of permanence. You've only got so long to live. You're getting your dream. Things are working, blind forces, no personal spiritual beneficent ones except your own intelligence and the good will of a few other fools and fellow humans. So hit it while it's hot.

(138.) August 19 – 1. a.m. Face it kid, you've had a hell of a lot of good breaks. No Elizabeth Taylor, maybe. No child Hemingway, but God, you are growing up. In other words, you've come a long way from the ugly introvert you were only five years ago. Pats on the back in order? O.K. Tan, tall, blondish, not half bad. And brains – "intuitiveness" in one direction at least. You get along with a great many different kinds of people. Under the same roof, close living, even. You have no real worries about snobbishness, pride, or a swelled head. You are willing to work. Hard, too. You have will-power and are getting to be practical about living – and also you are getting published. So you got a good right to write all you want. Four acceptances in 3 months – $500-<u>Mlle</u>, $25, $10-<u>Seventeen</u>, $3.50 <u>C.S.M.</u> (From caviar to peanuts, I like it all the way.)

(139.) Same time. After Val. God, the talk. First, her "shack" – red half-house with white trim, and her slouching thin and grubby in the doorway grinning. Plaid shirt, paint-stained levis. I walk in, feeling big and new and too clean. She is washing clothes in a basin. Dirty old clothes. Hot water gotten from kettle on stove.

I sit down in small kitchen. Wallpaper is brown background – colored Pennsylvania Dutch looking pattern. Dirty dishes on floor. Two cats: Prudence, a snooty black, sultry green-eyed Persian blood, and O'Hara. Ash-trays full of cigarettes. She smokes 2 cartons of <u>Wings</u> (cheap, non-advertised) a week. Can't taste, no palate left.

So I look around. She likes to cook – stews & ragouts especially. Things with wine. There is a shelf of cook-books over the refrigerator. Also a shelf of spices. She unscrews them and I smell each as she says, "Thyme, Basil, Marjoram . . . " and so on. There is also a preserving closet – jams, jellies, apple butter, beach plums. She picks and cans. Wild, sweet, tart, clear in glasses.

Outside is the garden. Neat grass lot reclaimed from pine woods. Flowers – some phlox, zinnias. Overgrown weeds in vegetables because of time Bookmobile job takes. There are strawberries, raspberries, peppers, beans, tomatoes, all in beds, squared off neat and clean-cut.

We take cake she has bought, a heap of green grapes, from the refrigerator. She grinds coffee, the smell is great, and we sit around waiting for the pot to boil. Meanwhile Prudence licks some frosting off the cake. Val cuts that part off, saves it for O'Hara. When the coffee is ready we climb the steep Cape Cod stairs to the workshop she has made herself.

It is all book shelves over the walls, Williamsburg blue-gray, and cream yellow. A rug she is braiding is on the floor, and balls of wool rag in a basket. A studio couch, a typewriter. Piles of manuscripts around, in boxes, on her desk. We sit cross legged on the floor, and start pouring ourselves cup after cup of coffee. I am a pig and have three hunks of cake. The four black kittens Prue is nursing come in and skitter around like black scritches of playful fluff. They are nosey, lean into my coffee cup, sneeze at the hot strong stuff and go skittering across the floor. One goes to sleep inside the edge of my skirt where it makes a comfortable fold on the floor.

I hear about agent's – Ann Elmo. Something-and-Otis. I read "Miss Henderson's Marriage." I like pace, tempo. I think it is a shade dull, characters don't come across human – oh, indefinable quality. But construction has poise, balance. Enviable by me at this stage. Also look through files of correspondence between her & agents. She's got "Haitian Holiday" on her mind. Novelette about bastard girl, too. So many stories! So much published.

"Bill" teaches C.W. at N.Y.U. Stories about him. Wm. Byron Mowery. Also about bank-job. Funny – hysterical. She pounds plush job out by publishing House Organ. Quits. Money too important. Not her own baby. House and garden are.

Knows Rachel Carson. Woods Hole. She has hit a jackpot, still goes around like Val, old jalop, old clothes, got a hit here and doesn't know what to do with this thing, people telling her how to write, but she is working on something now . . . . like good writer, enmeshed in present problem. Doesn't feed off leaf of laurel.

The kittens, the books all over, she has built and painted, the braided rug unfinished. A provider. The stories, and the winters. A ride back at midnight, talk about Evita Peron. (Whore or courtesan, she put on a great little show. Val likes skyrockets. Pretty, cute.)

Writing work. Writer builds illusion for man-on-street: shroud of mystery – no one wants to think their emotions can be played with, roused, by literary learned craft & intention. No one wants to think: this guy can reach inside & yank my heart because he wants to keep his pot boiling. So when they ask where the writer gets his ideas: "I lie on my couch; God speaks to me. Inspiration." That satisfies.

Yelling above the jalop motor. Home, coffee-drunk. Exhilarated. (Can't stop thinking I am just beginning. In 10 years I will be 30 and not ancient and maybe good. Hope. Prospects. Work, though, and I love it. Delivering babies. Maybe even both kinds. Val grinning at me in the faint light, face in shadow, tough talk, but good to me. I will write her from Smith. I will work, maybe drive down wintertime and visit. Maybe take Dick even. God, she has been great to me. Tonight best yet. All the boys, all the longing, then this perfection. Perfect love, whole living.)

She had a cricket in the wall and it creaked and chirped. She said build a good life. I wonder. I like her, yet not as blindly as could be – I can be critical. But she has lived, sold, produced. And how much she has already begun to teach me.

—

(140.)

August 20 – I am an outlet. The parents no longer understand their children. He is twenty-two and of voting age. Their ideas are brittle and too noble. (Al told me I would be a prude at 40. Let this be a warning unto me. And let me remember for the children I have.) They are too solicitous too late. Because he and she were virgins they are glad but afraid for the young ones. Afraid because suddenly of something. We do not know just what. But it is too late for one (and I can understand because in me too the fire of destruction flares blood hot and as for all the ideals I had, they are broken, malleable now, for compromise and rationalization. The ways to hell on earth are easy, and one can always cross out hell and scribble in heaven. So much sweeter that way.)

He is proud, strong, defiant. On the defensive. He will not speak. He could say: something is bothering you, but he will not. He is too proud. They pry; they go along when he takes a girl home from work. They ask: what kind of a girl is she? He says: she is free, white and twenty-two. He goes to bed immediately after. Before he falls asleep he hears his mother and brother whispering outside. He is proud in his impotent silent rage.

She said to me: I am worried about him: His brother says he is lonely. (She wants me to stay there after I get through work. I would like to but do not dare to.) Her husband has retreated from me. It is the story he takes to heart, stiffening in one reading all the reserve I had melted so carefully. Becoming all at once again cold and unresponsive. "For heavens sake," the wife says as he stands there impassive, "can't you kiss her!" So I throw myself in a bear hug quick at him and say "There." There.

Talking at the light with the young one I think how both struggles and pettinesses we iron out so somehow. Talking, kisses, warm hands and talk of breasts, soft and tender and hard strongness. Creative play and light laughter and warm richness, ineffable richness flooding where from? Not just sex, not just familiarity, but partly. Because there has been cold, sterile, desperate devouring, and not this warm, full, flowing over in loving laughter. Food and nourishment, replenishing the beaten blue and black mind and bodies, desiring more, yet somehow satisfying even without fulfilling. Each an outlet for the other. For him, a lighthouse sending out an

intermittent flash – centering desire on an attainable goal. For me – a growing cultivation of my body and the vague unobjectified hungers, aroused for
instance this afternoon in the boat with a boy two years younger than I,
blue-eyed, crewcut, lean, tan, beautifully built, muscles firm and neat and
body so tender young and lovely I must caress the neck unwisely, kiss the
lips once or twice. But one could not pull head to breast and keep the dream.
Always the dream. Loving two boys in one day differently for different
times. Kissing both and loving both. Honest, true, yet at least one would
become cynical, a little bitter, seeing me with the other. Not understanding
how a girl could be honest at one hour with one and at another place later
with another. But so it is for her. And so it will be.

(141.)
August 21 – 1:30 a.m. The boat sailed in the fresh wind out into the bay, and
the boy and girl were young and lovely. She riper, golden, older than he. But
he lean, tall, virile and unshaven. Laughing in wind and sunlight across the
blue of the bay. Reaching the long island beach they moor the boat, he
swimming out from it beautifully and cleanly, cleaving the water strong and
straight. God, how young he comes up from the sea: a Paris, lean and how
windbitten. Laughing, teeth white, they race over the dunes, the witchgrass
sharp under their bare feet. Over to where the blue of the Atlantic blinding
straight ahead. Towels on sand, picnic opened, they gorge young and hungry
on cheese and ham and mustard and coleslaw and tomatoes and peaches and
gingerale, filling full their stomachs, lying and eating the savory good food in
the sun, lying warm and curled after, drowsy. Head on her stomach he lies
back, she running long tenderly moving fingers through his hair, cut short,
soft. Carefully rapacious and hungry her fingers move along his cheek. They
read aloud then from "Science and Health" about marriage and spirit, she
wondering inside at the paradox of delusion: how he can deny matter and
flesh as real when one can make such healthful beauty out of them – how he
can be inconsistent and admire beauty of flesh, calling her cream and honey
because of her skin and white bathing suit. She cannot, she has decided,
undermine or take away his faith. She must somehow cultivate and work
through this which means so much to him. Because no matter what he labels
the highest good in him, spirit or otherwise, that is what she wants to bring
out.

So he tells her that she brings out the quality of love in him, and she says
he brings out strength and power. They caress each other companionably,
sunwarmed backs, and a quick kiss. Flesh, flesh, lovely warm young tender

real flesh. He would like to see her in 30 years – after he has made a lot of money. He will buy a beach buggy. A boat. He will take her for rides. They will live in a house overlooking the sea. They want, in a sudden splurge of altruism, to do things for each other. Perhaps, if she suddenly needs him, she will lift the phone receiver and will say: "Operator, this is very important, I must speak right away to Bob." And somewhere in the world Bob will lift the receiver and say "Operator, give me a girl named Sylvia." And the operator will say: "Sylvia is here, on the line."

Oh, how foolish, how pathetic. She is laughing on the way back, and he. He saying: I think we both found something we didn't expect to find, and she thinking: yes, you my vulnerable flesh, and me your tearing rending young strange idealism which I would tender and nourish to keep from all the pretty sexy girls that will wear your sharpness to a dull, flat, bored edge. Five years of college. What will they do to you? And all the while the water goes by, you so fleeting, the two of us so hopeless, and why do I love you so jealously? Wanting a promise, even though it must be broken, that you will remember me. Why? Because I suddenly grow old. And you so young. I want to remember, hold, and cherish for a little. No future in it. Soon the distance will be more apparent than the strange rapport. And I will not, as Al said (or rationalized) kill the illusion and the dream of our brief span of being together. No passion, and little pain. No more meetings and a clean quick death. Summer gone, you young darling, and I an older, wising woman. But God, your young lean face and body and reaching mind! Always I see you in the red low little M-G racing in the night, and against the blue sky on the bow standing proud in the sun – to leave you with an ideal of a girl – let me do that for you!

(142.)

Friday – August 22 – And so it will be. I come in around midnight, there's no telling with the wind blowing, and the wide night with the stars clear – and the lovely fleshly warmth and somehow close to tears because of giving him the ideal, the girl idea which he can always have with him. She is nonexistent, this girl he considers beautiful, soft, loving, intelligent perfection. She is a dream-vision I perhaps conjured up unwittingly, but "There is nothing good nor bad but thinking makes it so." For him, perfection with the name Sylvia exists. And so she is.

How to explain how I feel I owe him a great deal. He is so lean, intent, and young – and his mouth so sure and tender, closely moving over mine, he leaning back, looking tenderly and talking long, saying: If we can only learn together, study together these things, finding truth, unchanging. God, if only I could do something for you, anywhere, any time; reach out to me. I wouldn't care if you were pregnant, or had both legs amputated. I want so to help you.

And I, my throat thick and husky with awe and tenderness, loving terribly at once his young, dear, clean-cut idealistic faith: seeing in it the salvation of him from so much of the repetitive meaningless rot in the world – : I say: but you have done so much, Bobby, for me. Just being with you this little, learning with you. You have so much, so many potentials I can see. You are not the wiseguy in your best self, but so much more – fine and strong. No matter what the name of the girl will be, the one you go through life learning and living with – you know how love can be. (And I am listening to my voice go on – wondering how I can say these things: anything to keep whole his terrible dangerous precarious exquisite dream of perfection, of truth. We all in this world need something to cling to for a center of calm. I, to you, am lost in the gorgeous errors of flesh – you, to me, are blindly denying, in your spiritual monism, the antithetic dualisms of the universe which I see as real. But we both have our dreams. And it is how we live here that matters – not the motivating force which varies so radically.)

Bob, we say we may never meet again – no bathos here, no sentamentalism. Both of us strong, young, intelligent – separating to sure good lives, overcoming obstacles with power inherent in us, going on to good friendly warm circles. Good to be apart – with the strange and paradoxical separateness forever. Because we meet, and read aloud, and kiss sweetly, lips so right and wonderful I could cry to think I have made you love me. Oh, convert I can never be, but there is something here in your faith that gives you strength, I will give that faith impetus. I see, if I can plant with you the rightness of it all, you may believe always – in great trial more strongly.

And I, remembering your face in the dark, with the equal measured light from the Lighthouse shining, wheeling, catching in sharp light and shadow the terrible beauty of your lean cheek and slender jaw, and relinquishing you to the dark, only to catch you up again – I am full of a tender maternal, protecting love, warm and full, how full and rich. Your head, bending, nuzzling in the warm hollow of my shoulder, and I, with my fingers firm, tracing the strong line of your young neck. You say: God, if only I could tell you how much you mean to me. How I used to date girls and grab here and there and have a good selfish time. But it is so different with you. You are so sweet and gentle, the way I thought you would be. I love you. You are so beautiful and you bring out so much in me. You make me feel like a king."

So I kiss him, and there is the great dark sea ahead, and above the sheaves of yellow stars, shoals of cold bright pieces of light, and the great wind, blowing always cold gulps and gusts of air, big and soft in the tree leaves, hushing, miracles are happening, and I, strange and elated with a new wonder, child-like in my sudden power, look with eyes large in love and amazement at this intent lovely face so earnest, so close to mine.

I cannot bear to leave you, because you will forget, I will forget, except for perhaps once or twice a brief sharp sear of pain as a word, a laugh, a thought of truth, will cut like a knife at all that will have happened after now, bringing clear and wistful to mind the remembering of these few hours, night and day – and us so young, (even though older and apart I am from you – but somehow motherly and wising, seeing how by making you dream you love me in my beginning understanding – how thereby I can plant in you the seeds of your own brand of faith and strength. (I love you physically, dear guy, sweet one, your body and your keen quick mind – and mentally, and God knows why else. But it's true, what they say about turning from older guys, after learning from them, to the younger ones – and when, Bob my love, you are gone, there will be Phil to take your place – though he is not so well-versed in the art of love as you, nor yet so old for his chronological years.)

But of all the nights, rushing backward along the rocket-track of your experience and receding into the dark of your past subconsciousness, remember, remember how he trusting looked long and sweetly at you out of the dark at the door with all the wild wind in the dark grasses, and how love was there in his face – making you, miraculously, the dream girl and woman, sister and sweetheart, mother and spiritual mistress. You walked in, laughter, tears, welling confused, mingling in your throat. How can you be so many women to so many people, oh you strange girl?

All the young growing and testing and being once burned and twice shy and not knowing what to do, or where, or when to be how. And then this, the sudden intuitive flash, the sudden knowing when it is right to render up a dream, to speak so, to love so. It comes ripe in you suddenly and there is the taste of wisdom, aged full and mellow-flavored. You have gotten drunk and elated on the young firm tart green of early apples, and never wanted other. But the first ripened apple breaks open its fruit on the palate, and the sweet, savory juice floods in vindication into the hungry mouth, lyric lovely on the tongue.

Oh honey ancient gathered from the garden of rare weed and strange wild plant, years pass and you grow golden clear in the tree, shedding fragrance of wisdom upon the lovely summer air. (You have taken a drink from a wild fountain . . . "and all the wells of the valley / will never seem fresh or clear / all for that drink of mountain water / in the feathery green of the year." Not so, not so, for in parable the wells of the valley are sweet in their ripeness, and I will not cry forever, over the young wild spurting fountains – not forever.

(143.)

August 25 – "Look, honey," she said, very firm, very deliberate, "when I don't want to be kissed, I don't get myself kissed. I'm a big girl now; I can take care of myself."

The guy grinned. "You know," he said with a laugh, "I'm awfully glad to hear you can take care of yourself with me. Because I've been out with a lot of girls who sure as hell couldn't."

(144.)

– So you walked into the kitchen that saturday morning, (it being cold bright blue August,) lean, a little stooped, in a blue shirt, and Mrs. C. said, "Attila" this is Sylvia" while you said ignoring, "My name is Attila," with your trace of accent, the slight slur, the nasal inflection. Breakfast, then, with the toast and jam, bacon and coffee, all good-smelling and warm, with outside the sun-bright pieces of the day waiting. You talking with all, and I listening, thinking, oh, I want a lot to grow to know you.

And subsequently, during day and night and day again, talking, looking, exchanging laughter. Your hair long, black, combed back, and your eyes, the most wonderful part when flashing back a look of appreciative understanding, dark to blackness, blazing laughter. There is the indefinable alien air about you – not just your deep voice and uniquely lovely inflections, but an attitude toward life, a laughing wit, a comprehension of war, of escape, deep rooted – your graceful athletic build, strong, lean, resilient. The muscles in your thighs and calves are taut, powerful. Behind our playful beach wrestling there was the leashed iron fury of your potential strength.

You rode on the back of the beachwagon to Nauset with Joan and me, us asking about Hungary, your life, of how you got kicked out of the University by the Communists and got the five-year scholarship to Northeastern. At Nauset, you in tight blue trunks, eating hot pork chops, frankfurts, potato salad, playing with the children, your foreign accent pleasant and lyrical to the ear. Throwing ball, then, arm arcing back, sending the white ball unbelievably high, far, hard. A walk then, down the beach and back. Jogging home in the beachwagon, I now in back between Marvie and you, cold, legs dangling – You let me wear your sweater – the white cable-stitch one your mother made for you. It feels good on me, I warm and wearing something of yours.

Home, changed to dry clothes, I must go shopping. You come, I driving, and Susan with us for company. You come, carrying the bundles, I loaning you 10¢ to buy a comb at the Five & Ten. Going by the A & P there are a few boy clerks standing around outside by the stand. I go by not looking, and there is a moan. "That moan," say you, "was for your legs."

"How do you know?" I ask.

"I was looking," you say.

It is very good and quite wonderful walking with you down the bright Chatham streets with the sun bright, thick creamy light on the colored store-fronts, and all the summer people in their queer clothes – brown ladies in silk print dresses and ropes of white jewelry; girls in colored shorts – red, green, blue; bright tan faces, golden, bronze, pink, beige – all ripe with sun-color, moving easily and free in the summer sun. It is a very happy time for me with you walking there along beside me – a sort of "blutbrüderschaft" having been performed between we two – I wearing as mine your sweater and I buying you a comb, you carrying my bundles, I driving us both home in the long shiny green-and-gold-wood-crossed beach wagon. At home you are very gracious, very charming to everyone. After supper we put on records while we do dishes, and suddenly we are dancing, you and I, on the smooth shining linoleum. A strange look darkens murkily on Mrs. C's face. "You are holding her too close, Attila," she says. "She can't follow that way."

I look at you and murmer, laughing, "I learned your way. You know that." You laugh assent. There is the rhythmic leading of your legs with mine, my body against yours, suddenly very comfortable; we still being strangers; dancing gives us, in society, this strange prerogative of studiedly casual embrace.

(145.) "We have a lot in common. You just said two things I agree with," you say.

"What?" I ask.

"You are from the naturalist school of philosophy and you don't like women drivers."

(146.) You are a Calvinist. And a Hungarian. You laugh and say Hungarian officers have a much better reputation for love-making than even the French. Other countries win the wars; the Hungarian officers win the women.

147. I say: "I want to see you again sometime."

You say: "You are dis-inviting me."

I say: "I am not, what do you mean?"

You say: "When an American says: 'I want to see you sometime' it means the same as saying: 'I don't give a damn if I ever see you again at all.'"

148. <u>August 31</u> – 1:30 a.m. The clock has run down, stopped completely. I am glad. There is only the shrill irregular ticking of the crickets and the flowing, continuously, of the long, wide spacious wind outside. It is the last night, the last morning, and my light keeps burning longer than the rest. It will be dawn sometime, and I am far from tired, wanting to stay awake, greedily savoring this time of well-being, with two cups of scalding hot coffee in my stomach, and a warm good cheeseburger, and a light wit-barbed comedy, and the kisses of a boy who idealizes me warm still on my lips.

In the mirror, undressing, I look at the rather impish and mobile face that grins back at me, thinking: oh, growing to be a woman, to learn the art of subtle power! As long as men have ideals, as long as they are vulnerable, there is this power to create a dream for them.

Laughing, crying, I talk to Bobby. He would like me for a mother. I hold his head in my arms, looking down, tenderly, smiling, listening to his wild idealistic ravings, wondering at the miraculous youngness of him as he tells me how beautiful, how intelligent he finds me, how I have changed him, how we will someday live on a ranch or a desert island, and he will want me to write and be happy, and raise a hockey team.

Oh, God, what woman does not like to be told how wonderful she is, to see adoration naked in a young beautiful boy's eyes, to feel she can be young in her wisdom, in her intuitive feeling for the rightness of the situation. How powerful, how full of love I feel, honestly, for you, dear guy. And how they smiled at us in the Sou'wester – the cynical sweet little woman waitress, – thinking how crazy in love we were, holding hands over a cheeseburger, laughing, intense, serious, taking our empty cups of coffee back in the kitchen for more, and smiling at all the people, not caring what they thought, only us, being young, beautiful, and maybe not too damned.

Going out, I am warm, bubbling inside like a savory pot of coffee, down the stairs I skip, stretching my arms gladly to the stars. God, I have a long way to go before I am ready to say to one: it is you I will take and give to for the rest of my days. There are so many days, I think, and I have spent six weeks of days among how many men and boys: first of the summer: Lloyd

Fisher; Clark Williams (reading Eliot), Ray Wunderlich (philosophical-medical night walk); Phil Brawner (those lovely gay effervescent evenings); Jim McNealy" (the Esplanade and Louisberg Square at midnight); Art Kramer (plays, dinners, tea and pedantry;) Marvy Cantor (talk and a dance or two); Attila Kassay (dancing, swimming and a premature abortive attempt at a kiss – and a promise of a future); dear Bob Cochran (the M-G, sailing, theater, music circus, visits, readings); Chuck Dudley (motor picnic, long brotherly-sisterly talks.) And Dick, the recurring main theme. Always there, in the bass, or background, always if faintly, and then coming rich and sweet into strong melody again, the resolution of cacophony, and the ingenious weaving of all the rich and strange and exotic and erratic secondary themes into one rich full orchestration.

"I am a part of all that I have met." To you, all, whether or not you know, having wandered into the tissue of my life, and out again, you have left a momentary part of you which I will work into something. There is nothing but that it will suffer a sea change into something rich and strange. Through me transmuted.

Oh, I bite, I bite on life like a sharp apple. Playing it like a fish, I am happy. And what is happy? It is a going always on. There is something better to be done than I have done, and spurred by the fair delusion of progress, I will seek to progress, to whip myself on, to more and more – to learning. Always.

I have a well, deep, clear, and tartly sweet, of living. All the names, already, and the places. And I am nowhere near the ending. I feel, I must make a list, a diagram, a will, a tribute, to all of you who have fed my growing. Mrs. Morrill" ("You will have a happy life") Bob ("Be happy, I know you will, I know I don't have to worry about you"), Sue Slye" ("You'll get the greatest guy, and you'll have the cutest blonde kids"), and Mr. Cantor ("All I can say is the fellow who gets you will be a very fortunate guy" –) Oh, all of you, all of you with your faith in my potential: I love you all, I will give of myself, my joy, for I have so much, so terribly much.

And if I have learned nothing else, it is to listen and to love: everyone. A humanitarian, faith in man's potential for good. And a compassion for his weaknesses, his so-called original sins. World compounded of dualities, and man the compromising angelic devil.

In the car we laughed miracles of love and incredulous tenderness. Outside a woman wove down the street, her hair frizzed and bushy, her face ugly with hate, yelling at the man, who was faceless: "No more of your bull shit, why should I listen to your shitty talk . . . " I laugh, and say: stop, stop, you fools, or the sky will crumble and the forty-day rains begin, falling relentless from the angry heavens. And your car will not save you, nor your tardy repentance. Hush, hush your vile talk, he is being won from you.

And the world goes by creaking at the joints. You, dear, think you are in love with me. Yet you are not lost. There will be a million women. I am glad to be the first, tacking the gay standard as high as I can reach. You can match it, go beyond it someday, Bobby.

Hell, you deserve more than being in the Ladies' Home Journal. If only I could get you in the Atlantic: "The Kid Colossus." I will aim at the highest, too. A plot. Like "Knife-like, Flower-like," only different. To prove what. To begin where, to end where – from what point of view. Oh, I will brood this year to find the form for the content.

Val said: visualize, emotionalize, afterwards. Beginning writers work from the sense impressions, forget cold realistic organization. First get the cold objective plot scene set. Rigid. Then write the damn thing after lying on the couch and visualizing, whipping it to white heat, to life again, the life of the art, the form, not longer formless without frame of reference.

The wind continues by and by, and tomorrow there will be packing and tentative fare wells and Bob and Chuck and Dick – and rest and sleep. Packing, going, sad, glad, lonely for past: moving through so much continuous loveliness, proud to face present uprooting and stoic study program. Eager always still for the promising future which, even if twenty years are gone, is not the final word, nor the stiffening of old uncreative age. Always the promise, the hope, the dream, amid whatever poverty, war, disease and adversity – always persists the credulous human vision, of something better than that which is.

September 4 – 11:30 p.m. Science study program
(149.) The first day of rigor being over, I am torn between a multitude of conflicting emotions and insights. There is the grim pleasure that I managed to complete my page quota. There is the hysteric and persistent fear that I do not understand all I read, that my water-level of comprehension is a good deal lower than it would be if I were taking the course slowly, step by step, under the guidance of a competent instructor.

There is the urge to procrastinate, to escape from the rigid cage of study routine I have made for myself. It lures my by a multitude of enchanting distractions; it beckons in the form of magazines, gay colorful stories and pictures; it seeks to simulate hunger, calling me to lose myself in the rationalization of continuous and nervous eating; it comes over the telephone, through young male voices, asking me, (unknowingly) to come and do delightful things. Everywhere I turn, distraction beckons. It whispers: "How easy, to give up: excuses, you have good excuses. You were working, you were sick. Take a gut, plan to waste 6 hours per week next year. Forget about Phy. Sci. 193" and enjoy these last three weeks before the busy delightful whirl of college again begins."

To hell with you, I say. I have begun to work. My skin is broken out from subconscious anxiety and tension, self-induced. Nothing is more difficult than lashing a vagrant mind suddenly into long self-imposed stints of concentration. But I will learn a few things from this mass of material. I will read and ponder over my 70 page quota per day. That should take 10 days, approximately. I will then allow 5 days for writing, meditating and typing. It shouldn't be as hard as I make it seem, once I get accustomed to the discipline I myself invented. A few evenings a week I will allow myself a date, providing I get my quota done in due schedule

Today would be an absorbing study if I were good at stream-of-consciousness. My mind tried every trick to elude the prosaic task at hand. I got ideas for stories; the burning desire to revise recent poems and send them out flared bright; I suddenly decided in a spurt of clairvoyance that I would of course marry the other brother, and spent a good deal of time reasoning out pros and cons of one vs. the other. I picked up a magazine, hurtled into a story, rushed through, and came up for air feeling slightly sick and very naughty, getting an almost perverse pleasure when I realized 20 precious minutes were gone. The phone rang and I actually fell downstairs in my eagerness to answer it – symbolically running away from my duties – glad for any reasonably valid excuse.

And so, now, it is almost midnight of the first day, and I have broken my resolution to go to bed early – postponing sleep, and thereby the inevitable waking up in tomorrow. Another device of escape –. It seems that every year I wince and grovel through an obstacle course that looks quite formidable. Remember how tense I was last fall about the driver's license? The Smith Club tea speech? To be sure, I can always sneak out of this, but I won't let myself. It is an absorbing test of will-power – and of the conflicting wills that make up my psyche.

150. As for the husband: how cold, how material and objective I am. Also, how hypothetical! The hypothesis being that I could have either if I chose: and I actually believe I could convince either! I began with the youngest: a time of tender idealism, serious conversation. I believe I have kissed him

once. Perhaps twice. Strange, when one thinks of all the other boys, infinite experimental kisses, test tube infatuations, crushes, psuedo-loves. All through this physical separation, through the testing and the trying of the others, there has been this peculiar rapport, comradeship, of us two so alike, so similar, but for science-boy and humanities-girl – the introspection, self-examination, biannual deep summarizing conversations, and then the platonic parting. I broke the unspoken pact only once, and he also, when he kissed me slowly, quietly by the old mill in Brewster on a dark, star-blazing night a year ago this September. I accepted his kiss without emotion. It did nothing to me. I felt: "Here there is no worry, no fear of latent sexual fire. It is all a strange platonic passion. Serene, secure, lasting, never to be consumed by itself into ashes."

This fall, again, he asked me not to be too nice to him, because he would be susceptible. I acquiesed, laughing, telling him I was interested in boys as people, conquests in humanity, not in romance. A week ago we were reading on the double bed, and we fell asleep side-by-side. Drowsily half-wakened, I turned, warm and damp with sleep, and he was lying beside me, his face buried in the pillow, his arms tight around it, his skin a bronze tan, and the red of his hair like strands of copper. Suddenly tender, I thought, (remembering the way his face had been always young and understanding, shy, gentle, idealistic – and intelligent): "This is the one! After all the whirl and excitement and gay passionate flames, this is the one I will choose to come home to! The proverbial boy next door!"

Why? Why? Because he is a virgin? Because I want terribly to believe in pure idealism? Because I want, as all women do, to be loved devotedly, without fear of jealousy as I grow old, and the young pretty women continue to parade by? Because I believe we are both perfectionists? Because I see suddenly how he has grown, breaking the neat mold I made for him a while back? I would work hard – a home, children, and free lancing. I would work hard to preserve the idealism in him. And what a strange errand that is in today's world!

Why deny the other? I am taking him for granted. I am becoming patronizing, not seeing all that his keen mind contains. There is a barrier between. I see only the surface, thickened over now, with all the deep, passionate tensions and competative drives flickering ominously below. With him I would compete. Is it because I say subconsciously: "All right, I can't match you in sex experience, even though I would like to. But I'll show you I can beat you in other ways." Would not that horrible sickening jealousy and cynical relativism of last fall fester still in me – no matter how illogical or logical the cause of it? I can only guess. I think I have forgotten those women who sickened me so then. But I am not sure.

And so it is. I suddenly for no apparent reason think: I will marry the one with the red hair because I can leave the blond one alone better, and will not feel a little sad when there is his wife, the other woman. Whereas, the red-haired one always calls to me, and I am always wanting to be tender to him. Tall, lean, tweedy, I said. Here he is, only the red-hair is unique. And he does not smoke a pipe. Or read poetry. But there is the pleasant certitude of the familiar. And that is the security that is so tempting.

Will I ever fling myself into the multitudinous perils and uncertainties of life with a passionate Constantine;" a witty and sardonic and tempestuous Attila; a proud, wealthy aristocratic Philip? They enchant, they fascinate: I could carve myself to the new worlds they imply. But is it not the tragedy of man to be the reactionary, the conservative, and to always choose the certainty of daily bread above the light airy inconsistencies of foreign pastries?

September 20 – early toward young September 21 –

151 ("There are times," the young man told me softly, "when a man wishes a woman were a whore.") A vile dull evening. A horrible movie, both of us disgusted, staying in out of the rain, sleepy, critical. Driving in the roadster jaunty, bored through the Boston streets with the after-movie crowds thronging crosswalks, and the pink, green, blue, yellow neons all lighted blur in the streets, wet, smooth puddled black. Bored, cross, all wrong. Why do I not wear heels . . . because I look like such a bobby soxer in flat shoes? I am young, naive, childish, sixteen emotionally. My reactions are too obvious, too excitable easily. I gush over trivia, embroidering problematically on mere cold factual phenomena. I build too much him on a pedestal breathless with admiration ("Oh, really, yes, yes, go on . . . ") And I freeze at a touch. Ah, I am also twice fishing for compliments, and I would deny it with vehemence but for the fact that I am caught – subconscious though my line may be, and he is, damn him, too right. All that is wrong, it appears, is "that we have not gotten drunk together." There is a wall. We have inhibitions. And I force him into acting with my absurd overflowing enthusiasms. They are absurd, and I am acting – because I feel peculiar. He is foreign, alien, yet the different cultural and moral backgrounds we draw upon do not seem to matter too badly. Perhaps I am on the defensive, who knows. Over-reacting to the situation with a false burst of effusiveness. Because I want to conquer the cosmopolitan alien before I return to the rustic boy-next-door. (Feminine vanity?) Is not my first desperate rush of enthusiasm (remarked

upon formerly by Dick) <u>a vestige of my old fear of people running away, leaving me, forcing me to be alone?</u> Is it not a device subconsciously calculated to interest, to hold, to retain my partner, be it male or female? (I remember when Nancy Colson walked me home from Scouts in Winthrop with another girl. They would always run away giggling together when I started to tell them a story. I did not understand. Bewildered, breathless, I would run after them. And then I learned that they had arranged to run away so they wouldn't have to listen to my lengthy, dull rambling.) I will cultivate restraint. I will stop being a loud-mouthed puppy that falls all over people in a frantic effort to attract them. I want desperately to be liked. I have gone through a long period of awkward, self-conscious unpopularity. Although I could be called an extrovert now, there are still recurrent traces of my old inferiority complex. I put new people on a pedestal, worshipping them for their surprising kindness to me, for their benevolent notice. How many silver-plated statues have I erected, only to humanize them as I grew to know their vulnerable frailties – ? (John Hall," Bob Riedeman, Mr. Crockett, Marcia Brown, Constantine, Attila . . . The list could go on and on . . . Some stay remembered giants because not fully known: Mrs. Koffka, Doctor Booth," Miss Drew," Francesca Raccioppi" . . . yet even they have weaknesses, flaws, biases, blind spots.)

So I will prove to him I am not the shy respectable naive fool he thinks me. We park, and I, drowsing on his shoulder, am very glad to see the dark road and the leaves all around. I am sleepy and feel very sexy in my black velvet dress. So I just stay relaxed not saying anything, and he leans down and kisses me on the mouth for a long lovely while. I do not care, I will stop thinking. He kisses very nicely, and I will enjoy being kissed for what it is. I am growing quite warm and desiring, and his hands are good and strong behind my back, holding me to him, and I like to wait while his mouth kisses my neck, moving down to where my neckline goes deep, and my breasts hurt swollen a little, waiting for his hands to begin, and my hair is falling loose over my bare shoulders, and my mouth is soft and wet and wanting under his. For a long time no one says anything. Then he says: "Well, what do you know, a woman is being born."

"Are you surprised?"

"No." Simply.

"I didn't think you would be. I guess I am trying to prove something. We haven't gotten drunk."

"We didn't need to."

"But you said . . . "

"I know I said. It was a dirty thing to say, wasn't it?"

Stymied. I want to say: There is a purpose, a future. This is for some goal, some end. But it wasn't. The end was coition, physically. But I wasn't having any of that. I was being pragmatic. I felt like being kissed, petted, made love to. I would take it as far as I wanted to. To hell with him. I am not a tease, nor a whore – he could go home unsatisfied, rape a stranger, I didn't care. He had tried, chivalrously, (knowing a woman would be insulted if he didn't.) He is smart. He knows what he can expect from me. So he can take the consequences of associating with me.

To him I would perhaps be a dead end. No intercourse, just a halfway deal. But I am not yet the smart woman who can keep her reputation and be a highclass whore on the side. Not yet, anyway. Incredulous, (he wanted to know my address) I listened to him say: I am not just going to sit here and watch you disappear without knowing where to . . .

Everything but: What a pretty compromise between technical virginity and practical satisfaction!

152 Today was good. Mr. Crockett for two and one half hours in the afternoon, and after long talking in his green pine garden over sherry I got the flash of insight, the after-college objective. It is a frightening and wonderful thing: a year of graduate study in England. Cambridge or Oxford. It is as yet a vague move: money being the one great problem. But I have two years to work toward it; there are scholarships, fellowships; I am young, husky, and eager to work.

Problems it resolves and arouses: I will go to Paris, to Austria, during vacations. England will be the jumping-off place. I will bicycle all over England on weekends. No summer hosteling with the dull drudging miles, weariness, and inability to enjoy the heights of life – but perhaps a stay in the city at a cheap Inn – travel with a friend. Then back to England. I will write; stories, maybe even a novel. I think I will do graduate work in Philosophy. I am going to do it.

Main fear, nagging: men. I am in love with two brothers, embarrassingly so. I will leave. Unless I am lucky, both may give way to marrying while I am gone so I will come back to a big void. On the other hand, I may fall in love, have an affair with someone over "there." I need a year to get perspective, to free myself before I decide to be "of human bondage." And the danger is that in this move toward new horizons and far directions, that I may lose what I have now, and not find anything except loneliness. I want to eat my cake abroad and come home and find it securely on the doorstep if I still choose to accept it for the rest of my life. I am gambling. The workings of my destiny will be revealing the years hence.

Today a dream was planted: a name: England. A desire: study abroad. A course of action directed toward this end.

153 Dinner at Nortons, warm, glowing aqua candles, bright sudden pink-petaled yellow-centered asters. Swordfish and sour cream broiled (with Perry pink-faced bending over testing the taste.) Hollandaise and broccoli. Grape pie and icecream, rich, warm. And port, sharp, sweet, startling gulped with a sudden good sting behind the eyes and a relaxing into easy laughter. Good scalding black coffee. And Dick and I at home an evening, mutually warm, rich, seething with peace. "La Mer" often while dishes were done, and while sleepily relaxing by candle light. The music, going on, disturbing, haunting, ineffably strange and deeply moving, with all the great blind surging of the sea, and the thin flashes of sound, of light, of insight.

Sitting in the gray room, all blurred around the edges, candlelight shafting in, warmly in arms of him, placid, content, drowsy, yet alert and awake, the greatness of the day and the import of the time broke in upon me with a flash of joy and fear. I was going away to England out of the warm secure circle to prove something. There would be the going away and the coming back, and whatever would greet me on returning, I would take stoically, accepting the responsibility of my own will, be it free or predetermined by my nature and circumstances.

Outside the window it was dark, and the light from the kitchen was on the undersides of the tree leaves. It was all stark and unmoving, black, edged with the light. The tree was tall and filled the dark bigness of the window square. I had never felt so happy in that particular way. I was escaping, going away; from what? I had a semisecret aim, and I would extend the cycle of sterility and creation. Gathering forces into a tight tense ball for the artistic leap. Into what? The <u>Atlantic</u>? A novel? Dreams, private dreams. But if I work? And always work to think, and know, and practice technique always?

He fed me orange juice, half a cold peach, and kisses. Read from "The Sun Also Rises" and "The Enormous Room." Sleepy, candle light, and both feeling glad and warm and constructive . . . for once not mad cross-fire annihilation and destruction, willful and diabolic. Bourgeois. Middle-class. But life is long. And it is the long-run that balances the short flare of interest and passion. The long prosaic loaf of daily bread. But who to eat it with, and when to begin?

So much working, reading, thinking, living to do. A lifetime is not long enough. Nor youth to old age long enough. Immortality and permanence be damned. Sure I want them, but they are nonexistent, and won't matter when I rot underground. All I want to say is: I made the best of a mediocre job. It was a good fight while it lasted. And so life goes. (Mrs. McNab: "There was a force working.")

154

November 3 – God, if ever I have come close to wanting to commit suicide, it is now, with the groggy sleepless blood dragging through my veins, and the air thick and gray with rain and the damn little men across the street pounding on the roof with picks and axes and chisels, and the acrid hellish stench of tar. I fell into bed again this morning, begging for sleep, withdrawing into the dark, warm, fetid escape from action, from responsibility. No good. The mail bell rang and I jerked myself up to answer it. A letter from Dick. Sick with envy, I read it, thinking of him lying up there, rested, fed, taken care of, free to explore the books and thoughts at any whim. I thought of the myriad of physical duties I had to perform: write Prouty;" Life back to Cal;" write-up Press Board; call Marcia. The list mounted, obstacle after fiendish obstacle, they jarred, they leered, they fell apart in chaos, and the revulsion, the desire to end the pointless round of objects, of things, of actions, rose higher. To annihilate the world by annihilation of oneself is the deluded height of desperate egoism. The simple way out of all the little brick dead ends we scratch our nails against. Irony it is to see Dick raised, lifted to the pinnacles of irresponsibility to anything but care of his body – to feel his mind soaring, reaching, and mine caged, crying, impotent, self-reviling, an imposter. How to justify myself, my bold, brave humanitarian faith? My world falls apart, crumbles, "The center does not hold." There is no integrating force, only the naked fear, the urge of self-preservation.

I am afraid. I am not solid, but hollow. I feel behind my eyes a numb, paralyzed cavern, a pit of hell, a mimicking nothingness. I never thought, I never wrote, I never suffered. I want to kill myself, to escape from responsibility, to crawl back abjectly into the womb. I do not know who I am, where I am going – and I am the one who has to decide the answers to these hideous questions. I long for a noble escape from freedom – I am weak, tired, in revolt from the strong constructive humanitarian faith which presupposes a healthy, active intellect and will. There is no where to go – not home, where I would blubber and cry, a grotesque fool, into my mother's skirts – not to men where I want more than ever now the stern, final, paternal directive –

not to church which is liberal, free – no, I turn wearily to the totalitarian dictatorship where I am absolved of all personal responsibility and can sacrifice myself in a "splurge of altruism" on the altar of the Cause with a capital "C."

Now I sit here, crying almost, afraid, seeing the finger writing my hollow futility on the wall, damning me – god, where is the integrating force going to come from? My life up till now seems messy, inconclusive, disorganized: I arranged my courses wrong, played my strategy without unifying rules – got excited at my own potentialities, yet amputated some to serve others. I am drowning in negativism, self-hate, doubt, madness – and even I am not strong enough to deny the routine, the rote, to simplify. No, I go plodding on, afraid that the blank hell in back of my eyes will break through, spewing forth like a dark pestilence; afraid that the disease which eats away the pith of my body with merciless impersonality will break forth in obvious sores and warts, screaming "Traitor, sinner, imposter."

I can begin to see the compulsion for admitting original sin, for adoring Hitler, for taking opium. I have long wanted to read and explore the theories of philosophy, psychology, national, religious, & primitive consciousness, but it seems now too late for anything – I am a conglomerate garbage heap of loose ends – selfish, scared, contemplating devoting the rest of my life to a cause – going naked to send clothes to the needy, escaping to a convent, into hypochondria, into religious mysticism, into the waves – anywhere, anywhere, where the burden, the terrifying hellish weight of self-responsibility and ultimate self-judgment is lifted. I can see ahead only into dark, sordid alleys, where the dregs, the sludge, the filth of my life lies, unglorified, unchanged – transfigured by nothing: no nobility, not even the illusion of a dream.

Reality is what I make it. That is what I have said I believed. Then I look at the hell I am wallowing in, nerves paralyzed, action nullified – fear, envy, hate: all the corrosive emotions of insecurity biting away at my sensitive guts. Time, experience: the colossal wave, sweeping tidal over me, drowning, drowning. How can I ever find that permanence, that continuity with past and future, that communication with other human beings that I crave? Can I ever honestly accept an artificial imposed solution? How can I justify, how can I rationalize the rest of my life away?

The most terrifying realization is that so many millions in the world would like to be in my place: I am not ugly, not an imbecile, not poor, not crippled – I am, in fact, living in the free, spoiled, pampered country of America and going for hardly any money at all to one of the best colleges. I have earned $1000 in the last three years by writing. Hundreds of dreaming ambitious girls would like to be in my place. They write me letters, asking if they may correspond with me. Five years ago, if I could have seen myself now: at Smith (instead of Wellesley) with seven acceptances from <u>Seventeen</u> & one from <u>Mlle</u>, with a few lovely clothes, and one intelligent, handsome boy – I would have said: That is all I could ever ask!

And there is the fallacy of existence: the idea that one would be happy forever and aye with a given situation or series of accomplishments. Why did Virginia Woolf commit suicide? Or Sara Teasdale – or the other brilliant women – neurotic? Was their writing sublimation (oh horrible word) of deep, basic desires? If only I knew. If only I knew how high I could set my goals, my requirements for my life! I am in the position of a blind girl playing with a slide-ruler of values. I am now at the nadir of my calculating powers.

The future? God – will it get worse & worse? Will I never travel, never integrate my life, never have purpose, meaning? Never have time – long stretches, to investigate ideas, philosophy – to articulate the vague seething desires in me? Will I be a secretary – a self-rationalizing, uninspired house-wife, secretly jealous of my husband's ability to grow intellectually & pro-fessionally while I am impeded – will I submerge my embarrassing desires & aspirations, refuse to face myself, and go either mad or become neurotic?

Whom can I talk to? Get advice from? No one. A psychiatrist is the God of our age. But they cost money. And I won't take advice, even if I want it. I'll kill myself. I am beyond help. No one here has time to probe, to aid me in understanding myself . . . so many others are worse off than I. How can I selfishly demand help, solace, guidance? No, it is my own mess, and even if now I have lost my sense of perspective, thereby my creative sense of humor, I will not let myself get sick, go mad, or retreat like a child into blubbering on someone else's shoulder. Masks are the order of the day – and the least I can do is cultivate the illusion that I am gay, serene, not hollow and afraid. Someday, god knows when, I will stop this absurd, self-pitying, idle, futile despair. I will begin to think again, and to act according to the way I think. Attitude is a pitifully relative and capracious quality to base a faith on. Like the proverbial sand, it slides, founders, sucks me down to hell.

At present, the last thing I can do is be objective, self-critical, diagnostic – but I <u>do</u> know that my philosophy is too subjective, relative & personal to be strong and creative in all circumstances. It is fine in fair weather, but it dissolves when the forty day rains come. I must submerge it before a larger, transcending goal or craft. What that is I cannot not now imagine.

—

155

November 14 – All right, this is it. For the first time (since I heard about Dick) I have broken down and cried, and talked, and cried and talked again. I felt the mask crumple, the great poisonous store of corrosive ashes begin to spew out of my mouth. I have been needing, more than anything, to talk to somebody, to spill out all the tight, jealous, envious, apprehensive neurotic tensions in me: resentments at not being abroad; recriminations about missing the chance to get out of taking a routine science course; wish-dreams about the courses I could have taken instead – this year, last year, the year before; loneliness at having my two main outlets: Marcia and Dick, removed, distant, gone; jealousy, falling apart of my creative attitude toward life, emptiness, intensified by the pathetic, weak, nasal, negative, critical, inarticulate, fumbling approach – grotesque almost – of one who shall be nameless.

All right, tonight, after good pizza, chianti, hot coffee and laughter, I went upstairs to the green, white and red room which is light, and vitality and Marcia. There, on the bed, she touched the soft spot, the one vulnerable spot in the hard, frozen, acrid little core in me, and I could cry. God, it was good to let go, let the tight mask fall off, and the bewildered, chaotic fragments pour out. It was the purge, the catharsis. I talked, and began to remember how I was before, how integrated, how positive, how rich – rooming with Marcia last year was one of the most vital experiences of my life. I shall never forget the passionate discussions, the clear articulate arguments: what ecstasy compared to the shrill, whining, stumbling of this one who lies, breasts full and drooping, eyes drooping, mouth drooping. God!

I lay and cried, and began to feel again, to admit I was human, vulnerable, sensitive. I began to remember how it had been before; how there was that germ of positive creativeness. Character is fate; and damn, I'd better work on my character. I had been withdrawing into a retreat of numbness: it is so much safer <u>not</u> to feel, <u>not</u> to let the world touch one. But my honest self revolted at this, hated me for doing this. Sick with conflict, destructive negative emotions, frozen into disintegration I was, refusing to articulate, to spew forth these emotions – they festered in me, growing big, distorted, like pus-bloated sores. Small problems, mentions of someone else's felicity, evidence of someone else's talents, frightened me, making me react hollowly, fighting jealousy, envy, hate. Feeling myself fall apart, decay, rot, and the laurels wither and fall away, and my past sins and omissions strike me with full punishment and import. All this, all this foul, gangrenous, sludge ate away at my insides. Silent, insidious.

Until tonight, touching me, letting me be unproud and cry, she talked and listened, and the tightness relaxed that bound my ribs, that gripped my stomach. Escapist, cheater, I was, betraying a trust, a creative pledge to affirm life, hell and heaven, mud and marble.

It must be fatigue, lack of a sense of proportion, that makes me procrastinate and fear my science course. Damn, I can catch up and keep up in it. It may unduly emphasize details, I might be taking soc or Shakespeare or German, but hell, it was my mistake, and I've got to cut being a spoiled child about it. No mother is around to absolve me of my burdens, so I retreat in a numb womb of purposeless business with no integration whatsoever.

I rode home at 11:30 tonight, forcing great gulps of frosty air into my lungs, looking at the stars, up behind the black bare trees, and gasping at Orion. How long, how long since I noticed stars; no longer, now, mere inane pinpricks on a smothering sky of cheap cloth – but symbols, islands of light, soft, mysterious, hard, cold – all things, as much as I made them.

And Dick is recriminating himself, readjusting, trying to grow, too. And not living in the luxurious erotic Garden of Eden I imagined, either.

And so I rehabilitate myself – staying up late this Friday night in spite of vowing to go to bed early, because it is more important to capture moments like this, keen shifts in mood, sudden veering of direction – than to lose it in slumber. I had lost all perspective; I was wandering in a desperate purgatory (with a gray man in a gray boat in a gray river: an apathetic Charon dawdling upon a passionless phlegmatic River Styx . . . and a petulant Christ child bawling on the train . . .). The orange sun was a flat pasted disc on an smoky, acrid sky. Hell was the Grand Central subway on Sunday morning. And I was doomed to burn in ice, numb, cold, revolving in crystal, neutral, passive vacuums, void of sensation.

Tomorrow I will finish my science, start my creative writing story. It will be, I think about a weak, tense, nervous girl becoming the victim of the self-centered love of a man who is the spoiled pet of his mother. There will be an analogy, a symbol, perhaps, of a moth being consumed in the fire. I don't know, something. I will start slowly, for there must be sleep, and work, and more sleep, to rebuild again the higher towers. Remember: "People still live in houses." The word, quite lovely, "terminal." And the thought of all the books I must read this summer: The idea of fate, character, destiny, "free will."

You are twenty. You are not dead, although you were dead. The girl who died. And was resurrected. Children. Witches. Magic. Symbols. Remember the illogic of the fantasy. The strange tableau in the closet behind the bathroom: the feast, the beast, and the jelly-bean. Recall, remember: please do not die again. Let there be continuity at least – a core of consistency – even if your philosophy must be always a moving dynamic dialectic. The thesis is the easy time, the happy time. The antithesis threatens annihilation. The synthesis is the consummate problem.

How many futures – (how many different deaths I can die?) How am I a child? An adult? A woman? My fears, my loves, my lusts – vague, nebulous. And yet, think, think, think – and keep this of tonight, this holy, miraculous resuscitation of the creative integrating blind optimism which was dead, frozen, gone quite away.

To love, to be loved. By one; by humanity. I am afraid of love, of sacrifice on the altar. I am going to think, to grow, to sally forth, please, please, unafraid. Tonight, biking home toward midnight, talking to myself, sense of trap, of time, rolled the stone of inertia away from the tomb.

Tomorrow I will curse the dawn, but there will be other, earlier nights, and the dawns will be no longer hell laid out in alarms and raw bells and sirens. Now a love, a faith, an affirmation is conceived in me like an embryo. The gestation may be a while in producing, but the fertilization has come to pass.

Goodnight, oh Big Good Book.

156

Tuesday – November 18.

You are crucified by your own limitations. Your blind choices cannot be changed; they are now irrevocable. You have had chances; you have not taken them. You are wallowing in original sin; your limitations. You cannot even decide to take a walk in the country: you are not sure whether it is an escape or a refreshing cure from cooping yourself in your room all day. You have lost all delight in life. Ahead is a large array of blind alleys. You are half-deliberately, half-desperately, cutting off your grip on creative life. You are becoming a neuter machine. You cannot love, even if you knew how to begin to love. Every thought is a devil, a hell – if you could do a lot of things over again, ah, how differently you would do them! You want to go home, back to the womb. You watch the world bang door after door in your face, numbly, bitterly. You have forgotten the secret you knew, once, ah, once, of being joyous, of laughing, of opening doors.

157

January 10, 1953: Look at that ugly dead mask here and do not forget it. It is a chalk mask with dead dry poison behind it, like the death angel. It is what I was this fall, and what I never want to be again. The pouting disconsolate mouth, the flat, bored, numb, expressionless eyes: symptoms of the foul decay within. Eddie wrote me after my last honest letter saying I had better  go to get psychiatric treatment to root out the sources of my terrible problems. I smile, now, thinking: we all like to think we are important enough to need psychiatrists. But all I need is sleep, a constructive attitude, and a little good luck. So unbelievably much has happened since I last wrote in here:

Thanksgiving I met a man" I could want to see again and again. I spent three days with him up here at house dance. I got a sinus infection for a week. I saw Dick, went to Saranac" with him, and broke my leg skiing. I decided again that I could never live with him ever.

Now midyears approach. I haye exams to work for, papers to write. There is snow and ice and I have a broken leg to drag around for two hellish months.

Dick and I are doomed to <u>compete</u> always and never cooperate. I can't explain the qualities in us that aggravate our passionate jealousies, but I feel he wants to prove his virile dominance (e.g. In his writings, women have no personalities but are merely sex machines on which he displays his prowess in sexual technique; he grew a mustache and said if he shaved it off because I wanted him to it would be a sign of weakness and submission.) And, looking back on our relationship together I see now clearly the pattern of my continual desperate striving to measure up to what I thought were his standards of athletic ability, etc. Always I panted after him on a bicycle. Another thing, with him, although he always led and set the pace for sexual play, I never felt that I was <u>feminine</u> (implying a certain physical fragility – so a boy could masterfully pick up his girl and carry her, for instance.) Granted, I felt a seductive woman, but wearing flat heels always, feeling physically his equal in size, disturbed me. If I am going to be a woman, fine. But I want to experience my feminity to the utmost. Seeing him after two months, I no longer felt the desire flame up in me. I didn't particularly want him to touch me. For one thing, since he can't kiss me at all, I have the feeling (purely mental) that his mouth is a source of poisonous tuberculosis germs, and, therefore, unclean. I am, therefore, physically aloof. Also, I don't feel any emotion toward him – no longer the passionate, nervous, tense, sex-motivated hunger that I know was reciprocal. I don't love him, I never did. I don't think I deluded myself, except during that lovely Freshman spring when I made him into a golden god physically, morally, and mentally. Again I attribute my first attraction to a naive idealism. And now, I feel a new eagerness at the potential getting-to-know this new man: a different, more sensible, rational, realistic eagerness which is not cynical, but rather creative. I think I am ready to accept him right away as a human, fallible being. And to make myself always worthy of him as I can. Will I ever see him again? Will it work out? I don't know. I only know I feel about him the way I doubted I could feel about any man after Dick.

What do I see in him? Power, strength. Yes. I admire these qualities. Mentally and physically he is a giant. I looked at his face, heard him say my name, once, that Sunday, more lyrically than I could wish: he was a stranger, yet there was a flash of recognition, a sudden intuitive awareness: I would like to get to know this man; I could give a lot to him; I could perhaps learn what love was. I felt reserves of power, creative good, and strength in me that I had never been consciously aware of. I did much with him: talked over pizza, played in the stage props of alleyways, quoted poetry, drove into strange countries of snow, looked at pictures, ate ham and eggs in diners, walked about the mental hospital listening to the hoarse screaming before going to the cocktail party, danced, walked Sunday for a late breakfast downtown, and then out into the country, talking, my hand in his, and I went up in an airplane, shooting into the third dimension with the pilot we met, and he waited for me, walked back then together along the railroad tracks, spent hours drowsing by the fire in the livingroom. And then he went, and I went to the infirmary.

Objective account, what? But no mention of the glory, the joy, the exultation of being alive with him, to the fullest extent. I would like to see him much again, talk to him, see plays with him. Funny, but I'd like to go easy on the sexual part. I'm not impatient, the way I was two years, four years ago. I know we'd get along fine as far as sex is concerned; I just don't want to rush it ahead of the mental companionship. As far as I know, we are intellectually extremely compatible, or at least we are so potentially. God, I want to get to know him. If I could build an ideal and creative life with him, or someone like him, I would feel I had lived a testimony of constructive faith in a hell of a world. And our reality would be our heaven. Please: I dream of talking to him again, under apple trees at night in the hills of orchards; talking; quoting poetry; and making a good life. Please, I want so badly for the good things to happen.

—

[Appendix 2 contains Sylvia Plath's 'Back to School Commandments' – ed.]

158

January 12 – Again, I can not help muse upon the imprisonment of the individual in the cell of her own limitations. Now that I am condemned to a consistantly small radius of activity – mainly my room, I am aware more than ever of the fact that I <u>don't know</u> any of the girls in this house. Oh, I see them on the surface, gossip occasionally and friendly, but still, I have known none of them really – nor what ideas motivate them, drive them. I am as distant from the girls in my class as I could be. The few whom I feel I'd like to be close with hardly speak to me from force of habit. My circle of acquaintances has dwindled to a small faithful handful of people. The vast rich resources of Smith personalities lies untapped. Now I am resolved that this spring will be different. I will go to Haven, Albright, Wallace, Northrop, Gillett,[n] and begin to renew my acquaintances with the girls there. I will invite them to supper. I will bike to Browns[n] more often. I will try to get to know my faculty better. I will see Maria (I know <u>no one</u> in the quad!) Once again I will be the cheerful, gay, friendly person that I am really inside, and then, perhaps by some miracle, I will feel closer to my housemates. I am obsessed by my cast as a concrete symbol of my limitations and separation from others. I would like to write a symbolic allegory about a person who would not assert her will and communicate with others, but who always believed she was unaccepted, apart. Desperately, In an effort to be part of a certain group she breaks her leg skiing and has a morbid fear that her leg will not mend properly. When the cast is taken off, her leg has withered, and she shrivels up into dust, or something.

Anyhow, I shall chalk this first semester up as a nadir of every aspect of my life – scholastic, social, spiritual. I moved to a new house[n] (lost security, friends), catapulted into Chaucer unit[n] which took me all semester to adjust to, was forced by my own stupidity to take science, the first course I've hated; saw Dick get tuberculosis; lived with a girl who, compared to Marcia, appalled me – on all fronts, I foundered. And then the last straw broke my leg.

Now there is over one month left, just verging into the second semester, of this enforced seclusion (which has small delights – a clear winter sunset through the natural iron grillwork of black trees, a street lamp shining through ice-encased branches, blue sky glittering, and sun on ice-crusted snow. Loveliness, loveliness.)

Lights glimmer in faint perhapses on the dark doorsill. The eastern sky promises to lighten grayly: my cast <u>will</u> be off in a month, my exams <u>will</u> be over, <u>perhaps</u> I won't ever have to open my hated science book again; <u>perhaps</u> the man will want to see me again. That is all. But ah, how I long for the time to ripen fully, and the spring to come again after this long and appalling fall and winter. To come, and the bicycle be brought out, and the again-strong legs to pedal joyous and swiftly into the green, unfolding future! To dance along greening leaves into the sexual sunlight.

159

Sunday morning. January 18.

Awoke to look through blind chink into frozen wildernesses of ice-encased tree branches. Black iron twigs circled with cylinders of ice, exquisite, the frost-thickening of the world, glassed-in, and now later there is the universal dripping as a fuzz-blurred brilliant sun sears through gray layers of cloud, melting the world into liquid falling ice-drops.

The nadir is passed. I know that now. By a miracle of incident and attitude I am happier and more ecstatic at this particular moment than all this year ever (except for the actual ecstasy in time of House Dance weekend.) Again I am compelled to state how I believe that attitude is everything – how the blind, neutral dripping of the trees which I enjoyed intrinsically this early morning is now, suddenly, by mental magic, transmuted into something infinitely rich and ineffably strange, how the dismembered sound fragments integrate suddenly into a unity of music. And why all this sudden plunge upward of ecstasy? I was happier yesterday than ever before, so it is not as if one incident started me on the upgrade. But it certainly acted as a positive catalyst to accelerate the process. First let me tell you about the beginnings of my turning tide. Last time I talked to you, "lights were glimmering in faint perhapses." Now a few of the perhapses have come true. In every field of my endeavor, in every empty barren cubicle of myself: academic, social, artistic, inter-personal, (and on and on into subdivision after subdivision). There is the upswing, the turning, the sprouting of creative life again. I have gone through my winter solstice, and the dying god of life and fertility is reborn. In fact, my personal seasonal life is two months ahead of the spring equinox this year!

First of all, I have only one more science exam (midyear) – after which I need never ever to open the heavy hated puerile tome again! Yes, my petition went through, and I can audit the course (without credit) for the rest of the year: enjoying lectures per se, and doing none of the tedious memory work. This means that I can take the course in Milton next term," and concentrate on Modern poetry and creative writing for the rest of the year! Ah, bliss! Ah, joy! Academically, I plan to plunge whole-heartedly into the spring term. Honors gleams scintallant ahead of me!

Then, my vow to be cheerful and jolly about my legs, and gay with the girls in the house has worked wonders. Mirthful attitude is contagious, I find. I laugh they laugh. I feel so much closer to several girls now. Instead of a dastardly hindrance, my leg has become a passport, a revelation. Whole-heartedly I can say now, even with four weeks a head of me: I AM GLAD I BROKE IT! I have never been so shocked into awareness of the fortunate exquisite life I lead as when suddenly I was unable to walk. I realize now that I was really more crippled, mentally, all last fall, than I am, physically, now.

So that is the incipient beginning part of it. I am glad I wrote some of the sick naked hell I went through down in here. Otherwise, from my present vantage point, I could hardly believe it!

And now, the final crowning touch. For weeks I have been obsessed by the idea of him, recalling again and again the apparent intellectual companionship indicated by our one meeting, our few subsequent letters. I thought how hideous it would be if I never saw him again, never got to know him in reality, as I began to know him. I like talking about him, discussing him with other people: a rather obvious sublimation and substitution, that! And now suddenly, as if I conjured him up, the phone rang on the first floor this morning and a clear, silk, suave voice said: "How's the invalid." I don't know what I said. (I screamed inside, gasped, fell in an epileptic froth of ecstasy, mad, insane ecstasy, on the floor, all inside.) "I am in Northampton," he said. "Let me explain." He explained.

Up here for the weekend with a girl he met in Akron at a New Years party. He thought it would be nice to come see me this evening as she had to sing in Vespers. Nice, oh very nice. Inside I wondered: what is she like? Lovely? Brilliant? Oh, what?

"I got your letter Monday saying you were back here," he said. "Perry told me you would be home for about two weeks. I made this date quite a while back."

Oh, don't explain, you inconsistent boy. You have no obligations, no responsibility toward me at all, at all. Only except for the fact that you could very possibly be the first and last man I was willing to make myself vunerable for; to love, in the deepest, richest, intellectual and physical sense of the trite banal word! You made the date before you knew about my leg, no doubt. Perhaps Perry told you it would be noble to visit me. Perhaps you thought it would be a damn nice gesture since you didn't have anything better to do.

At any rate, I don't care. I am going to see you, maybe for once and all, thats up to you (damn, its always up to you) and that is all I ask. Sure, I'd like more. But this few houred-brief dropping from the clouds, from another girls plane, is a miracle to me in itself. I will remember mother's letter. If the French women can be bewitching reclining on a divan, so can I. I will be lovely, vivacious, witty, the very best me that I always want to be with you. Damn, oh damn. Every minute passing is all at once an unbelievable and doubtful century of agony and anticipation. I am not hungry. I am lean, taut, eager. God damn, I want to hoard the time with you like money. Now, ahead it lies. Seven hours hence. Each hour a savoring, an exquisite tasting of delight. The bell has rung for Pavlov's dogs, and the salivation has begun.

Never mind, dear Syl. He has proved, if nothing more, that beyond Dick there is another range of men. If this one goes, he will have served, to heighten me: "I am a part of all that I have met." I could orient myself about him. I have so much I want to give and share! God, I overflow with the vitality and ecstasy of being alive! Please, let me be casual and gay and right with him now. It will be gone too soon, and now there may be a never-nothing-no-hope-here-sign tacked up on the front-door of my left ventricle. God. I shall soon know.

160

Monday afternoon: January 19, 1953:

All right, the crisis is past. Miraculous, and quite unbelievably I have in my head now the certitude of a reality that will come to pass in a month and a half: a wonderful trade-in for a nightly ritual of dream fantasies! I am going to that magnificent event, the Yale Junior Prom with him: with the one boy in the whole college I give a damn about. And a very tender damn, at that! Anyway, it is not the fact of the Prom that delights (although it is a symbolic traditional weekend, in my own experience, too!) but mainly the idea of being with a stimulating, brilliant, magnificent male for three days of conventional and unconventional companionship! God, can I wait! Yes, damn it. I can! Think of seven weeks (instead of hours) of anticipation! (God, what a life – living in the future and the past and existing merely in the present.) I will work like a fanatical intellectual for the next month and a half. That is the benefit of having some definite occasion to look forward to in the sequence of time: you can orient your energies to work purposefully, knowing that, in the logic of the continual clock, the time of rejoicing will come around and you will live through it. (And then, damn it, it will of course be gone.) When there is no such future oasis in the desert of time, it is like living on a slide ruler of calculated dream fantasies. In my mind, for so long, now, I have kissed him, talked with him, and decided I am capable of love again, if I decide to make myself vulnerable again. Now I know that I will see him again. He didn't have to ask me to the prom. I honestly had inured myself to thinking I might never see him again. Then, yesterday, after the phone call, I was afraid: I thought: how terrible to renew again the physical image, to hurt myself on the edges of this resuscitated reality, only to fall back again into the futile never-never Land of Dreams.

He came early. I was in my bathrobe typing my dialogue paper when Debbie rushed into the room: "A man to see you." "O.K. I'll be down in ten minutes." "Ten?" "Five." Shaking I hurried to get dressed. I wanted to run down immediately to see him. I couldn't find my black velvet skirt. Damn. There it was. Aqua cashmere, pearls, hair back demure behind ears. God, how kindled, how incandescent a man can make a starved woman! It was fifteen minutes.

I came down the back stairs and walked up behind him in my cast, leaving my crutch in the hallway. "Hello, Myron." He was looking up the front stairs waiting for me. He looked eager and happy. He must have had a nice weekend with that other girl.

We sat on the couch in the livingroom and talked for an hour before supper. It was a little tense, and the silences were now and then a little jerky, but it was all right, and we teased and played. Suppertime he was quiet. After, the other boy called up: "tell Myron I'll be over in five minutes." "All right," I said, feeling sick. I hung up.

"He says he'll be over in five minutes. Myron, I can't bear it." I felt too vulnerable, too pleading, saying that.

We sat on a trunk in the side hall. He looked, clinically serious, down at my cast. "When will that be off?" he said determinedly. Hope flickered. "Oh, the first week in February, maybe the second." "I mean exactly when." "Well, by the middle of February." Still looking down: "Do you think you could dance, say by March 6?" A great champagne-colored bubble exploded inside me. "Sure, why?" How amazingly casual of me! "Yale Junior Prom. Would you like to dance then?" "Depends on who with?" "You could dance with Tommy Dorsey. He's playing." "He's not tall enough." "How about me, then." Hesitatingly: "Oh, I'd love to, really ... " "But what," he said quickly. "But I will!" The words bubbled out of me like colored lanterns. I actually hugged him impulsively. He seemed surprisingly glad: "I'll be proud

to have you." Then he talked of getting tickets to a play at the Schubert,"
and taking a bus to the ocean. I could hardly talk, I was so ecstatic. And then
the boy came. I saw Myron to the door. He was grinning: "I won't write to
ask you again, then. It's verbal, that's enough. It's better that way." "Fine."
"About letters . . . " "Oh, don't bother, if you've got exams coming up."
"No, it's not that. It's just that when I write you I want it to be my best, not
just conventional. I want it to say something." "Anything, as long as it's
you."

I put on his hat, back far on his head, so his hair showed, and he stood
there, boyish, grinning. "Goodbye." Goodbye, and that was that for a
month and a half. I wandered dazedly through the house and everybody
kept saying: "Sylvia, that's wonderful." "I'm so glad you're going!" One
nice thing about living with a hundred girls – excitement shared is multiplied
a hundred times!

<hr>

161

January 22 – Thursday – This simply has to stop! I am surely working myself
into an induced state of excitement and obsession. There are reasons for this,
obvious reasons. One, I have been deprived of sexual activity for long
unnatural months now and it is only normal that I transfer my daily and
nightly sex fantasies to the one male I have been seeing lately. Remember Al
Haverman" last house dance: that is a case history for you. That sudden
rapport, that sudden attraction and transference of physical adoration –
remember how you screamed ecstatically over Constantine, and shivered
over Attila, and talked heatedly with the handsome entomologist on the bus.
Remember all this, and think coolly: why do you react the way you are
reacting. Ask yourself coldly: am I rationalizing?

I have taken to retreating to bed in the long afternoons, pulling down the
blinds and filtering out the light, lying warm and soft and sexual under the
resilient light quilt and dreaming of him and talking to him. All right, I work
well and hard most of the time; I am probably at my peak of sexual desire,
and I should not wonder at my smouldering passion. So why not? Because,
you fool, he doesn't realize how you are transmuting him in your mind into
a strong, brilliant man who desires you mentally & physically. And being as
he will continue quite unaware of his role in your mind, you cannot expect
him to fulfil that role in life. You must not let yourself be disappointed.
Remember, you consider "love" a most intricate and complex word; and
among its manifold meanings is that of vulnerability arising from shared
weaknesses. There is a time for everything; and you must beware your predi-

lection for green apples. They may be sweet and tart and new and early, it's about time you learned to wait for the season of harvest. Take it slow, please. He is to be no engine for your ecstasy. Not yet, anyway.

Now why all this obsession with him; why this taking out and rereading a million times of letters? Well, it's like this. You weren't planning on seeing him for eight weeks, and now, suddenly and miraculously, all at once, he is writing that he would like to see you midsemester weekend, just a bit over a week away. The very suggestion of being with him so soon is almost unbearable in its intensity of gladness that you are overcome.

All right, you are intensely excited when you are with him. But it is, emphatically, not just sex or the prospect of sex that intrigues. You have gone out with handsomer, cavalierly boys – witness Phil, Attila, Constantine. You kissed them, laughed with them, and didn't mind leaving them. Why? Because they didn't offer a future? Maybe. But also because you know damn well that sex isn't ever enough for you. You want a brilliant mind that you can stimulate, but that you can also honestly look up to. And this one has it. He combines the loving gentleness of Bob with the athletic good cleanness of John Hall, and towers above the minds of them all, even Dick. Mentally he satisfies; physically he satisfies. Granted, there is a wide range of men in colleges all over the United States who would also satisfy, but this one you have met in actuality, and you are not going to waste your life in wishful thinking over the golden-man. You are no golden-woman yourself – just a rather vivacious human one!

It is rather blissful to share witty talk and intelligent letters with a man who is also three-dimensionally satisfactory as this one is. Eddie revolts me physically; I would vomit if he tried to kiss me. Dick is suddenly too stocky, too heavy, too short, making me always feel oxish. Not so this one. He even combines my favorite elements of Perry with a sort of clever observant worldliness that I enjoy infinitely.

What is he like? describe him to me, you say! I can not! He speaks slowly and soft, with a peculiar individual enunciation on each syllable, and his eyes are light-gray or green. His skin is not too good; he wears glasses. But he has deep-set eyes and a broad bone-structured forehead. I try to remember the turnings of his head, but I cannot. I have not studied his features long enough.

We have years of talking and acres of living to do yet before we even begin to know each other. Will we ever? I wonder. I wonder terribly. Am I afraid my life lacks organization? Am I scared to choose my path after college? Do I want to crawl into the gigantic paternal embrace of a mental colossus? A little, maybe. I'm not sure. But I think that I am much less a child than I was two, and oh yes four, years ago. I am learning how to compromise the wild dream ideals and the necessary realities without such screaming pain. My seventeen-year-old radical self would perhaps be horrified at this; but I am becoming wiser, I hope. I accept the idea of a creative marriage now as I never did before; I believe I could paint, write, and keep a home and husband too. Ambitious, wot? I also believe I probably wouldn't die at the act of "confining" myself to one man for fifty years. Oh, it is a great huge enormous decision, but the freeing of the self is part of this, too. I must stay aware of this: I could be more of a prisoner as an older, tense, cynical career girl than as a richly creative wife and mother who is always growing intellectually – who is committed to certain ideals and purposes shared with her mate. This could be heaven if we made it such. If choices must be made, they might as well be made gladly. So there.

And with him there would be a great, evolving, intellectual dignity to life. I am sure of it. I can walk tall and proud beside him in my body and in my mind. How will it work out? I don't know. In one year, two years, I will look back at the blind-alleys I wander in now and smile and think: My! how inevitable this past seems now that was once upon a time my very uncertain future!

162] January 24 . . . Saturday morning, and I am at the old game of catching time between my fingers as it is running, forever running, away. This last week has been a blissful relaxation: breakfast in bed, a slow, languid getting up, reading modern poetry, seeing an excellent play "Bell, Book and Candle" in Springfield, having leisure time to write witty letters – oh, all this. And now the sensuous delight of sitting warm and clear-eyed at my desk, looking out of the window into the thick, steamy, rain-lashed dripping air, and hearing the cars slithering by, and the persistent scritch of shovels on cement, scraping away the slush. All is muted and blurred with thaw, and there is the fresh wet pregnant smell of earth again that makes me long for spring (again.) And I have taken to reading the muscular packed verse of Gerard Manley Hopkins again: "The world is charged with the grandeur of God . . . " and then again: "How to keep – is there any, any, is there none such, nowhere known, some bow or brooch or braid or brace, lace, latch or catch or key to keep / Back beauty, keep it, beauty, beauty, beauty . . . from vanishing away?" Yes, obsessed, as always, with the vanishing of time!

163] January 25 – How to describe all the minute, exquisite, sensuous joys! I am becoming calmer in the core: I have <u>lived</u>, just <u>lived</u> in this college for a

week, and the experience has been delectable. Now the science exam lies ahead of me like a vile, inert monster – which I will master because I must.

(God, I am beginning to sound like Henley: "I am the master of my fate; I am the captain of my soul.") Well, yes, the leg has been an escape. All the pamperings given to the tuberculosis patient, and none of the eternities of loneliness. Very neat compromise: no jobs, no work but the scholastic minimum. Good food, sleep, company, and solitude. And best of all, after I go through the gruelling task of learning how to walk again, I'll be ready to assume the world: press board, smith review, classes et. al. Oh, it'll be a tough month first semester, but then it will be suddenly, miraculously, Junior Prom, and then bang! Spring vacation (which I shall spend wholly at home, writing, reading modern poetry and Milton! See Dick? Damned if I am! He can go rape and/or suavely seduce Anne. To hell.)

As for minute joys: I think this book ricochets between the feminine burbling I hate and the posed cynicism I would shun. One thing, I try to be honest. And what is revealed is often rather hideously unflattering. I want so obviously, so desperately to be loved, and to be capable of love. I am still so naive; I know pretty much what I like and dislike; but please, don't ask me who I am. "A passionate, fragmentary girl," maybe?

As for minute joys: as I was saying: do you realize the illicit sensuous delight I get from picking my nose? I always have, ever since I was a child – there are so many subtle variations of sensation. A delicate, pointed-nailed fifth finger can catch under dry scabs and flakes of mucous in the nostril and draw them out to be looked at, crumbled between fingers, and flicked to the floor in minute crusts. Or a heavier, determined forefinger can reach up and smear down-and-out the soft, resilient, elastic greenish-yellow smallish blobs of mucous, roll them round and jelly-like between thumb and fore finger, and spread them on the under surface of a desk or chair where they will harden into organic crusts. How many desks and chairs have I thus secretively befouled since childhood? Or sometimes there will be blood mingled with the mucous: in dry brown scabs, or bright sudden wet red on the finger that scraped too rudely the nasal membranes. God, what a sexual satisfaction! It is absorbing to look with new sudden eyes on the old worn habits: to see a sudden luxurious and pestilential "snot-green sea," and shiver with the shock of recognition.

164

January 26 – Monday morning: January dry, hard, glittering, cold, and the wicked naked beauty of the scraped blue skies and the sun sparks ricocheting jazzily off car rooftops. Last night it was cold, suddenly, the loud big wind riproaring down from some no-man's land of snow, and battering and blundering against windowframes, rocking them in their sockets, and barging into the flapping blinds, and shouldering through the brittle crackling trees: damned if I'm going to be raped by the North wind. I get up and close the window in the cold bare dark, and jump back desperately into bed, curling into a fetal position and warming my frigid hands between my thighs. This morning: I knew it would be this way: like before the old Botany exams when I got a sudden obsession to write in here: anything to put it off, studying. Oh, I was going to be a good girl and start studying yesterday, and go to the libe this morning. No soap; no sir. What do I do? Secretly try on dresses of one-who-shall-be-nameless to see if I can work up a new combination this weekend. Lovely! Damn you: procrastinator!

Lying in bed per usual this morning, under the big light resilient feather puff, I started worrying about how I should have taken all different courses here: 4 years of German, Psychology instead of Botany, Philosophy instead of Religion! God, I felt sick, or started to; life is so only-once, so single-chancish! It all depends on your arranging and synchronizing it so that when opportunity knocks you're right there waiting with your hand on the door knob. If I had known then what I do now, (i.e., that I would like to go to graduate school) I never would have concentrated so on English and Art. Koffka was right: college is no time for the would-be scholar to specialize. Graduate school is the place for that. And now I don't <u>want</u> to take grad study in English: I can carry English on myself after the specializing I have done in Honors here. Honors is fine if you can't go to graduate school and want to experience a microcosm of it. But now I would like to go on in either philosophy or psychology! Writing on the side (she says ambitiously.) But to write you have to live, don't you? Should I, then, get a job: in publishing company or factory or office? After all, I should be able to <u>observe</u> life intelligently and intuitively, and experience in living is something I'll <u>never</u> get in the idealized scholastic environment of graduate school where food and shelter are provided "gratis" if one is brilliant enough! As far as grad school goes, the most ideal sounds like Johns Hopkins where I could be taking elementary language and psych courses while doing intense work in English, or writing. I don't know of any other place where one could do that. Of course, there is always the ambitious project of trying for a Fulbright to England (only a million people want them; no competition, really.) This scheme would offer advantages yet nebulous, and equally vague disadvantages (one, most obvious, being the severing of American acquaintanceships for a dangerous year.) I would no doubt be able to travel during vacations, and learn to be quite independent. Who knows? It is all so uncertain. The two main other places I would consider are Radcliffe (near home, Harvard, but the program is nowhere as flexible as Johns Hopkins) or Columbia (New York, New Haven, and free culture, if men are around to take you to plays.) I have no desire to go west, even middle-west. For one thing, I might as well go "all the way" and head for England and Europe – or stay East, where education can't be beat. Really, I do want at least another year of education before I start living. Once I break the connection with school life it'll be hard getting back – on scholarship.

So that looks like it: Application (maybe) for a Fulbright, and if I don't get it, application for a scholarship to summer school in Britain and travel a bit after that, (maybe.) Johns Hopkins, or possibly Columbia as an alternate – and (maybe) I'll have to work my senior summer and plan to go abroad the next summer. After that: what? A job, obviously. Marriage, I hope, by the time I'm twenty-five, at least. Work in psychology, sociology, or bookishness.

I don't want to use higher education as an escape from responsibility, but I feel there is so much more awareness I should have before plunging onto the field of battle. This summer I must do gallons of reading in psych, philosophy – english: I have a colossal list of books. Why, oh why, in all those camp and social summers didn't I read more purposive lasting books instead of the young girl's novels? I suppose, though, that learning to get along with farm hands and Christian Scientists is at least, if not more, important than learning about Kant's categorical imperative. Still and all, I should like also in addition to be aware of the imperative!

Now that I talk this out with myself, the past doesn't look so deformed, nor the future so black. How much more hope I have now than my Mary Ventura (and how much less hope for freedom to wander than any casual glittering millionaire!) A philosophical attitude: a drinking and living of life to the lees: please don't let me stop thinking and start blindly frightendly accepting! I want to taste and glory in each day, and never be afraid to experience pain; and never shut myself up in a numb core of non-feeling, or stop questioning and criticising life and take the easy way out. To learn and think; to think and live; to live and learn: this always, with new insight, new understanding, and new love.

165

11 a.m. Still going on, ignoring science, peering out the window for mail. This morning also in bed I started dragging the still, stagnant, putridly and

potently rich sea of my subconscious. I want to work at putting together the complex mosaic of my childhood: to practice capturing feelings and experiences from the nebulous seething of memory and yank them out into black-and-white on the typewriter. Like in my attempt: "The Two Gods of Alice Denway."

Remember Florence-across-the-street, who had orange Japanese lanterns in her garden that used to crumple in your fingers with a dry crinkling sound? Remember how you used to lock the bathroom door (they told you not to because it might stick, and then the firemen would have to come in the window and get you,) and squat in fascinated discovery over the hand mirror on the floor and defecate? God, start remembering all the things; all the little things!

166

friday: january 29: 6 p.m. after science exam: everything is lovely lately. i am getting trite. a cliché coming true. a moonhappy night pouringlight on the dew. banalitybanalitybanality. hell damn bitch shit piss corruption: i have so many books i am perishing to read in my bookcase. hours-and-hours-and-hours-and hours. i could be caught in a bombastic blithering blizzard of rhetoric but no ... the lyric abstrusities of auden ring mystically down the circular canals of my ear and it begins to look like snow. the good gray conservative obliterating snow. smoothing (in one white lacy euphemism after another) out all the black bleak angular unangelic nauseous ugliness of the blasted sterile world: dry buds, shrunken stone houses, dead vertical moving people all all all go under the great white beguiling wave. and come out transformed. lose yourself in a numb dumb snowdaubed lattice of crystal and come out pure with the white virginal veneer you never had. god, the allusive illusions of the song of the cold: "If winter comes can spring be ... we're nearer to spring than we were in september i heard a bird sing in the dark of december", january, febmar, aprimay, apricots, beneath the bough. and thou, there has always furthermore in addition inescapably and forever got to be a thou. otherwise there is no i because i am what other people interpret me as being and am nothing if there were no people. (like the sound of the hack-neyed tree falling axed by old saws in the proverbial forest.)

i am reading "ulysses." god, it is unbelievably semantically big, great, mind cracking, and even webster's is a sterile impotent enuch as far as conceiving words goes . . . . " (excerpt from a letter) monday, february 2, 1953: all right, I now have a neat, tautskinned white baseball, red laced; that says my-name-and-his on it. he also, if it matters, likes breaded pork chops, prime ribs of roast beef, and good meats. (honestly, I am so disgusted with my mentality. I am not deep, I don't work, I revel and go lax with physical comforts. I am gone quite mad with the knowledge of accepting the overwhelming number of things I can never know, places I can never go, and people I can never be.) he knows what he wants, and how to get it and that he can get it. the main problem is to make him want and need me. only I don't even know if his is the life I want to put on. we sat and talked 24-hours split in half between two days. did I get to know him better? I think so. getting to know anybody is a hideous complex job. he, for all he says he is not deep, has strong powerful depths of motivation. from his telling me about his childhood environment, I can see the origin of his strong drives for success, security, power of intelligence, and financial independence. (He wants these things very hard). without the benefit of psychology courses I can intuitively and rationally understand his wanting these things. what could I be to him to fill in his needs: I could be a spontaneous, fertile, creative, motivating, encouraging force, and never let him go sterile or too discouraged. I could try to symbolize a vital creative beauty, a delight in life – god, who knows what? Does he need a woman? Seems offhand not, at least for four or five years. Eventually he seems to want a home and family. Beastly encouraging. If he did "love" some girl (he says he never has – has been only physically infatuated) I think his love would be more delightful and self-understanding than, say, Perry's. Perry wants to be loved and adored; a woman who reflects his glory lovingly he labels his "love," and endows her with all the wonderful qualities of his ideal. That is a euphemistic unrational egoistic love, in certain respects. Myron, I hope, and think, would more consciously question all the practical aspects of the relationship. I want to put down a few observations here about him so that later I can add to them and make a sort of pattern for his personality so I can understand him better, even if he is generally reticent.

He has come from simple stock: Austro-hungarian parents. He lives in Warren, Ohio, in a heterodox neighborhood of negroes, jews, germans, and other immigrants. He played baseball with the neighborhood kids all the time, all day, every day, stole things, built fires after dark and listened to the older guys tell stories. He doesn't know how to swim at all, because once when he was going swimming his uncle who was living with him told him he would be a laughing stock in his bathing suit because he was chubby. To this day he hates teasing, razzing, and "playing games". He says his father came over here, worked in the steel mines, saw no future in it, moved to Warren, Ohio, married at 28, and was a "Pool-playing bum." He says he doesn't know his father at all, and his mother not much better. Always his mother was inhibiting and fearful: no, don't do this; no you can't go out; no you can't ride your bike until such-and-such an age in the street. She cried always when he went away to school. Now she has a job and is happier with the "girls" in the shop. As for his brother Ted (who is 6' tall, a good build, good-looking, and a crack swimmer and almost 25) he says he dislikes him. Why? Because Ted has no self-discipline, drinks, smokes, and spends money "whoring around." He is always asking for money, and Myron and his father chipped in and bought him a car, and the only letter he wrote to Myron all year was one asking for money. Seems like he envies his kid brother who is going to Yale and also signing big baseball contracts. Myron says he has profited by every one of his brother's mistakes: Inside his brother must feel like a heel.

Now Myron, he never went out all during high school: didn't have a car, worked hard to earn money. First year at Yale he was afraid of flunking out, worked all the time, had only two dates, by accident or persuasion with a wealthy Vassar girl. Signed baseball contract with tigers, wrote prize-winning freshman English essay. Used to think girls could never learn the stuff he did at school. Never thought about marriage at all, until about this last year – even now the prospect seems amazingly far off in the future. Perry and Bob seem to have brought the subject closer to his thoughts. To him, his intellectual achievement is his first pride; baseball record the second. For these excellences he has gotten rewards. The reward-value makes them desirable. At Yale he has spent "minus $200" – his scholarship has more than taken care of everything. He paid $3000 income tax on his baseball earnings. For this he has received praise: this makes continuing to do well along these lines desirable. (Compare: my analogous success in school and in writing.) Above all, he wants to be a "man": independent and secure financially. He wants to be a good doctor, to plunge into life, to know about life, not to just sit back and philosophize. (Ironically, Dick now has swung to my way of thinking about literature, criticism, and writing – away from the mere science and calculation of living.) Doctoring would seem to combine prestige, financial well-being and intellectual stimulation. That is what he wants: power in those respects. Money: he had to grub for it when he was a kid. Intellectual life: his parents had no schooling: "Every step puts another barrier between him and his family." Does he need love, admiration, encouragement? Don't we all? He gets discouraged, too. He came up here saturday after lunch planning to go back that night – I persuaded him to stay over, and he did. (He isn't domineering at all, he says, and would never force his will on anyone. N.B.) Evidently he was in a self-depreciating mood, when he came. I like telling him nice true things about himself; I hope it makes him a little happy. I do not think he gets excited about things: he knows what he wants quite well and also how he can get it. Lovely.

Now enough factual background statement. He and I: sat in the living room, at Rahar's," at the coffee shop" and talked and did-not-talk as we pleased. He hates sitting: likes to talk walking. (N.B also) He sat next to me with his arm around me, warm and close and comfortable. Kissed me, too. Long and goodly saturday we stood on the porch in the rain, him pulling me against his body, and shutting his eyes and kissing me gently and for a long time, with his mouth moving softly on mine. I think I am a good deal more experienced in varieties of kisses than he is: I better be careful I don't shock him or make him think he needs more experience, because I like him this way, and perhaps subtly I can let him know how other ways I like to be kissed. He also carries me places in his arms, and I feel so feminine and light, even with my cast, it is so good to let the world black out quite and the equilibrium tilt inside my head: the carrying is a symbol of his virility: to me. Why do I like him so: more so than dick (so I don't even want to go up and see dick at the end of February)? He is like me in many ways: even the attitude about marriage, unromantic, practical, and reasonable, is like mine. In the long run, that is good, if difficult. I have a rather peculiar feeling that if I use my intelligence and pragmatism that I can become desirable and necessary to him. Maybe that is a damn illusion. Even though he says he is against the attitude that a woman is a prize possession, he likes them good-looking, and pretty intelligent. How do I like men? Hell, depends for what purpose. Everything from the worldly roué to the young innocent. But in the long run, I like not having to worry about what money can buy (sort of let's out teachers, even though they do live in academic circles & have summers off.) I like keen intelligence and intellectual curiosity: probably a professional man: doctor, lawyer, engineer, would do the trick. And a lot more. Giant, superman: mental and physical. He is these. Physically he meets all requirements (clearer skin is the only possible flaw.) Mentally, he is pretty great. The only terrible thing is: I am not sure I will ever know him really: I must see him in a lot of situations before I decide how he reacts, how he is inside. But somehow I am forcibly drawn to him. His lacks: no "family" prestige, etc., bother

me not a whit. After all, having none myself, that sort of thing isn't important. Hell, I guess I just like him quite alot!

168

February 12: snow again this morning, suddenly and deep. Myron's letter
and post card Tuesday: unbelievably heartening: picture of car, associated
with our possible future adventures together in faring forth into the world:
"to the lonely sea and the skies / to the fields and brooks and plains of
paradise." also a recognition of the amazing correlation and concordance of
our eclectic ideologies. and an expressed desire to see me again before prom:
all totaling a rather optimistic prognosis of the coming spring!

I was beginning to have to discipline my unrestrained thought-orientation
toward him. then the handsome intelligent newly unpinned gordon" came,
and there was a therapeutic amherst saturday with rain plastering the snow
outside, and the fire, and waxen candled champagne bottles and romberg-
and-musical records, and joyce-discussion, and chicken dinner at Valentine's, and the tentative and too-talked about kiss: and the hope of sometime
again maybe: all restored perspective. and just as I was congratulating
myself on no longer being a victim, the myronic reply – to encourage my
sense of victory over situations. at least now, magically transfigured by my
charming amherstian interlude, I may the better manage as I see fit the new
haven paragon.

oddly enough, myron is the first and only boy so far I would say "yes" to if
marriage were brought up! I don't think I ever really considered Bob, and
only considered dick and perry, although at one time I despaired of meeting
any boys excelling them, and so felt obliged to walk off with either one or
the other. and now, quite intellectually and coolly (I hope I don't deceive
myself here) I would consider judiciously the thought of living with him the
rest of my life: I guess I am "coming of age," or something.

dick is out because of innumerable reasons: cut-throat competitiveness,
pride, self-love and fear for ego, hereditary liabilities, lack of virginity, short
(for me) stockiness – all of which, although perhaps not obvious on a spot
appraisal, would increase the potential of corroding a creative felicitious
partnership. perry I know too well; we take each other forgranted; there
would be no discovery of personality there. perhaps, if I had met him as
shirley did, it might have worked. but he is a little too blindly idealistic for
me, I think.

myron, now, I do not know as earthly well as I do those two ergo, I am
blind to his faults and weaknesses so far. but I can generalize beyond my

own experience to a certain extent. why does he mostly appeal: because of the power of his promise and the promise of his power: he wants very hard what I want very hard: (and I am no longer the crackpot idealist who will eat red beans in a tenement all her life): I like theater, books, concerts, paintings, travel – all of which cost more than intangible dreams can buy. I like brilliance intellectually: he has that. and he likes the sun. and he thinks with me toward life.

power: he offers that. I am strong, in spite of being childish and weak now and then. but I am strong, individual thinking, for all that. I need a strong mate: I do not want to accidentally crush and subdue him like a steamroller as I would have Bob, certainly. I must find a strong potential powerful mate who can counter my vibrant dynamic self: sexual and intellectual. and while comradely, I must admire him: respect and admiration must equate with the object of my love (that is where the remnants of paternal, godlike qualities come in.) I do not want to be primarily a mother: mine cannot be a pitying and forgiving-black-sheep love: so out with the young handsome puppies: the phil McCurdy's," the Bob Cochran's – they are exquisite and lovely fun, but there is no future in them.

physically: myron is a hercules: carrying = symbolic: example of my tenderer femininity. more skilled than I, he excells in baseball, skating – and so on. while lean and lithe and athletic – appearing myself, I cannot stomach the fleshy, flabbiness of a male effete – myron is lean, hard and clean (no smoking, no drinking.) and I think he always will be.

mentally: he has a photographic memory, to all practical purposes – scientific to the core – a good balance – yet he appreciates and understands the most idealistic poetry – and is uniquely sensitive to literary beauty. (I have decided I cannot marry a writer or an artist – after gordon, I see how dangerous the conflict of egos would be – especially if the wife got all the acceptances!) so here we have a scientist, appreciative of the creative arts: lovely. my writing could proceed well, if it proceeds at all, in such a noncompetitive and benevolent frame. contrariwise, for him I would enjoy, I think, home-making and pleasing his taste in food – while continuing to serve as a life force – physically and mentally stimulating and sustaining.

ah, me – I sit here in the (cold) bluegreying of (cold) winter twilight calmly rationally pondering the wonder of this thing that has come upon me: hoping I do not want primarily to escape dick and "show" perry, to merely conquer the avowedly unconquerable. but rather marveling that my doubts are not more than they are, checking off in the squares of my tacit general and particular requirements one after the other, I find that in respect to the

<u>important</u> things (mind, philosophy of life, physical appeal and pureness) he lacks hardly anything, so cool, so rational, I add up the balance slate and the total decides that I just might let myself learn to love him: <u>if</u> I am capable of that much maligned emotion. at least I am <u>sure</u> that physical attraction was not the <u>root</u>, but rather the future flowering of this most lovely organically unified plant of ideas-and-emotions. because it would have to take a pretty potent sex-maniac to ween me from Dick's increasingly satisfying physical ritual – and the sexual attraction can start to grow, now that I know the intellectual attraction is well-begun.

and so I undertake my journeyings into the ways of vulnerability again, and of what <u>I</u> define as love . . .

—

169

February 18: "Oh, I would like to get in a car and be driven off into the mountains to a cabin on a wind-howling hill and be raped in a huge lust like a cave woman, fighting, screaming, biting in a ferocious ecstasy of orgasm . . . . " That sounds nice, doesn't it? Really delicate and feminine . . . . Do you think passionate people subconsciously consider a physical disability as an attack on sexual powers? I wonder at my morbid obsession with day-dreams this past month."

170 " Always him. Damn, what is the matter with me? Is it because I want somebody to orient myself about that I'm drawn to him, or am I drawn to him because he is exactly the sort of person I want to orient myself about? He is coming in a shiny new green car this weekend: the car is to him, I think, a symbol of power, manhood and independence and freedom from limita-tions. It is our means to travel, to see the world. And God, it is also a secure private room where I want very badly to tell him how I am entranced by his mind and his body. I want very much to hold the strength of his broad back to me and to shut my eyes and go away on the good slow black tide of his kisses. I could not want him so much if I did not become so stimulated by his brilliant thinking mind. Will Saturday ever ever come? The time <u>must</u> pass, but ah, how it drags, limps, loiters, stalls, procrastinates. Every minute tum-bles haphazardly along the obstacle course of day and night, and I am weary of counting them as they pass . . .

180 February 20: Reading critical books about Yeats all day today, meals in bed, and the good corn-thickened soup and tuna salad, lush with may-onnaise and pink succulent laced shreds of meat, and sliced quarters of

hardboiled egg, slick rubbery white crescents cradling the brilliant yellow powdery yolk, cool long gulps of milk, the savory brown resilience of ginger bread – and tonight the warm glutinous cheese-curded macaroni, green lima beans mealy and good on the tongue, and a sweet syrupy mash of peach slices. Somehow I am very thirsty, always, and the leg feels queer. Yesterday the Doctor Chrisman" cut it out of the cast and lifted the white plaster lid like a gravedigger opening a sealed coffin. The corpse of my leg lay there, horrible, dark with clotted curls of black hair, discolored yellow, wasted shapeless by a two month interment. I felt very cold and exposed and vulnerable, and the Xrays showed "it wasn't completely mended." Whirlpool bath at infirmary, and the skin flaking off raw and white and sore. Scraped at it with a razor at home gritting teeth at ugly thing: didn't want to claim it. Almost fell on stairs, stumbled on leg, felt sharp tingling pain. Not completely mended. Does that mean I don't walk on it for another month? Or do I bury the poor orphaned half-dead thing in another cast? Stepped on it today. Lightning didn't strike; didn't fall to floor. Queer: interim and rehabilitation is the worst, also indefiniteness. Classes missed, Myron called (voice and senses leave me when I talk to him suddenly on phone) car maybe not coming tomorrow, another falling of towers and toppling of masonry. I feel stuffy, as if there were not enough air to breathe – hot, and uneasy. Two months of no exercise have made me weak and plegmatic mentally and physically. On the short walk from here to the libe I drink the cold pure night air and the clear unbelievably delicate crescent-moonlight with a greedy reverence. Days are bizarre collections of hothouse languidities, mystical and poignant sensuous quotations (white thy fambles, red thy gan, and thy quarrons dainty is . . . " Dark, liquid loveliness of words half dimly understood.) Wrote first villanelle today and yesterday; another angle on the passage of time: tried to juxtapose the eternal paradox of ephemeral mortal beauty and eternal passage of time – a few puns: "plot" (course as well as with cunning) and "shemes" (patterns as well as treachery.) What I've been getting around to saying all this time is: want to quote from Yeats book something that struck me ★ : re Dryden's translation of Lucretius: "The tragedy of sexual intercourse is the perpetual virginity of the soul." "Sexual intercourse is an attempt to solve the eternal antinomy, doomed to failure because it takes place only on one side of the gulf." Swedenborg: "The sexual intercourse of angels is a conflagration of the whole being . . ."

181 – February 25. Yesterday the vindication of the dream fantasies began.

Tuesday, it was, and I dressed in white pleated wool skirt and stark black jersey, playing bridge, tense, excited, waiting. He didn't come and didn't come and didn't come. The last certitude, the last bulwark tumbled – his arrival in the new car was stalled in a malicious perpetual future. Upstairs, after four hours of waiting, frantic car-watching, typing, hot-and-cold tremors ("He is dead," I thought. "He has cracked up somewhere.") Every phone call was a surge of desperate hope, the falling of hope, – as always the wrong name was called – and then, after I had flung myself in futile aching rage on the bed, resolving sickly not to eat, not to look anymore down the road teaming with cars driven by the wrong people, I heard someone yell "Syl, a visitor." Unbelieving I rose, brushed away the scalding tears, and walked down to him. Outside: The Car: sleekly light blue, white-walled tires, dark blue top – inside, spacious and glassed. Driving then, trying for the mountains in the twilight, getting lost, turning, circling, finally to Look Park:" deserted, bleak, solitary, the black of frost hearted trees, bluesilver of moontissued snow, dark winding of road to a turnoff, water running black through icebanks, moon giddy, tinseling the world. Stop: and with the stop, the clock of the universe halted quite, and the breathing slowed easily rhythmic. Pulling me lightly to him, a kiss, experimental, tender, and then he circled me with his lean, ironsinewed arms until I ecstatically could not breathe, and always his mouth moving over mine more sweet and wetly and insistent than I could wish. all the words we said on letterpaper – religious, philosophical, physical ideas – and the complete concordance there, we said with our hungry mouths. Playfully wrestling we began then, and he twisting me rebelling to him, hurting good and hardly my arms, bending them behind me and pulling me fighting across him to lie helpless, laughing breathless, head cracked sudden down against windowsill, hard, stars springing out, and he kissing and kissing my mouth through my tumbled hair, turning me to him so I lay full upon him, along the length of his strong torso, breasts aching against the hard flatness of his fleshtaut ribs, stomach over the heat of his loins, and legs parted, alternating between his, down he pulled me, hand at/the small of my back, holding my head down to his continual kissing mouth. god, the ineluctable sweetness of the lean, firm flesh, and after, his head at my breast held, blindly leaning against the tender pointed slopes. all translated into the language of the limbs. I am obsessed by his sweet look, soft gentle-eyed at me, and his most endearing goodbye kiss. Now, always, the fading image rises in my head of the good full lying close to the strength and heat of him . . . god, let me make this powerful passion part of a rich, eclectic whole . . .

sunday, march 1 – sunlight raying ethereal through the white-net of the new formal bought splurgingly yesterday in a burst of ecstatic rightness, silver high heels are the next purchase – symbolizing my emancipation from walking flatfooted on the ground. silver-winged bodice of strapless floating-net gown: it is unbelievable that it could be so right! comparing the junior prom of this year with the junior prom of two years ago is grossly unfair – the white naive flatfooted puritanism of the innocent kiss then, and the ecstasy of idealism (to topple half a year hence:) against the rational exquisitely mature mental and physical heights of this promising event elude comparison. I want to be silverly beautiful for him: a sylvan goddess. honestly, life for me is certainly a gyre, spiraling up, comprehending and including the past, profiting by it, yet transcending it! I am going to make it my job to see that I never get caught revolving in one final repetitive circle of stagnation. anyhow, god knows when I've felt this blissful beaming euphoria, this ineluctable ecstasy! I can't stop effervescing: I have so many merry little pots bubbling away on the fire of my enthusiasm: myron, future trips, modern poetry, yeats, sitwell, tseliot, whauden, villanelles, maybe Mlle, maybe The New Yorker or the Atlantic (poems sent out make blind hope spring eternal – even if rejections are immanent) spring: biking, breathing, sunning, tanning. All so lovely and potential. yesterday: a case in point. at one o'clock he arrived, grinning widely, eager, appreciative, tall, tweedly jacketed, shoulders bulking broad. in the blindingly clear cut sun we set forth, driving jauntily along the curving country road to vermont: red sunflanked barns, spare fields, purplish blue mountains, ascetic white churchspires, greenblack fir trees, higher and higher: stopping by the side of the road to peer into maplesyrup buckets tapping trees, tasting the clear liquid, he carrying me back to the car: "How high shall I toss you?" "To the moon." god, the bliss of being lightly thrown in the air, caught, held. riding back then to mount tom, sun setting redly, moon suddenly rising unbelievably clatteringly clear and white through birch trees, he pulling me again to him ("let's face it, syl, you were just built for a tall man.") dark, strong undulating whirlpools of shuteyed warmth kisses lithe slender limbs mingling moonstriking he quoting shakespeare "If I profane this holy shrine whereon I touch" honest sadly plaintive, transient moment, and I now sit remembering how incredibly haunting it all was, faint from hunger, sleep, and crushed breathless to the thrust of his strong young lovely body. it has been so long – seven months at least, since I have felt the good black tides of lust drown and bathe me into relaxed slumbrous quiesence. lying the length of him, kissed and cherished in his arms: how can I come back to the necessary intellectual disciplines of the real world again? when the equally real world in my head sucks me jealously back into dreams, reconstructions and projections of being with him – reiterating "Ya know, syl, I <u>like</u> doing things with you, you're so appreciative." incredulous at the miracle of being so happy with him. and even when he says how tiresome it would be to settle down with one woman, and how he could envision only trading them in year after year for a new one like a car. since I superficially feel the same way about men, and since I am not scared of being undesirable physically or mentally, or unmarried, I can agree heartily and revel in the unentangling freedom of us both. laughingly I shall some time ask him when he will trade me in. oh, even if he does, the world will not end, and I am somehow irrationally sure he won't! god, girl, get to work: you've a milton exam to study for, a 20-page Drew paper to write, and hell knows what-all else. and you simply can't <u>wait</u> till next weekend: oh, you'll never be a junior phi bete" at this rate, cutie. ("I'm just a sentimentalist at heart," he said after singing "Overhead the moon is beaming . . . ") damn you, shut this book and stop thinking about him . . . I can't: I want want want to go back and live that hour over again. mike mike mike: I burnt my mouth on cheese and tomato pizza with you after 12 hours of no food, went sleepily sensibly to bed early to wake euphorically with the sun this morning, blissful and gay and rested and optimistic. (to work, thou crass sluggard!)

<u>183</u>

March 8 – letter excerpt:
"Firstly of all I was horrified to hear that the dear bearshooting imaginative adorable very lovable bright southernaccented sandy" I knew for such a little nice while is gone away. it is unjust, unnecessary, and difficult to comprehend. if it was god's will it is a very stupid arbitrary blood thirsty god, and I do not like him or believe in him or respect him because he is more foolish and mean than we are and has no sense of proportion of what people are good for living and what people are unfit. it is perhaps very good that there is another potential lynn coming to receive some of the love that sandy flourished in. the work and mind and food and love given to a child for growing, and then the sudden going away to where we don't know, we wish somewhere that would save the part we loved, but can't really believe that, and so say it was blind chance and rail against the arbitrariness of it. nothing being there to do but weep, or stand shocked silent by the sudden end, the shattered glass and toppling masonry, the ruin of all space, of a potential

universe, and put away the fragments left, and begin the cycle of growth over and over again, birth and death, birth and death. oh the tireless amazing unbelievably creative urge of we weary fallible battered humans. all this sorrow, injustice, war, blood lust, and still we persist in hopefully, faithfully, bringing forth children into the world. I loved that boy sandy, and all the sprouting of goodness and fineness in him. I love the lynns, and wish I could articulate my sorrow, or give them a microcosm of the great huge understanding and sympathy they deserve . . .

[Appendix 3 contains Sylvia Plath's three journal fragments, 24 March – 9 April 1953 – ed.]

184

April 9 – "If only something would happen?" Something being the revelation that transfigures existence; works a miraculous presto-chango upon the mundane mortal world – turning the toads and cockroaches back into handsome fairy princes, the Clark Kents into Superman – that calls unexpectedly up on the phone and says: "Your name has just been picked from a hat, like a rabbit, and we are giving you a million dollars", – or that announces in a sudden telegram: "Congratulations! Lady Rockefeller has just died and left you several estates and an enchanted source of continual private income". But instead, day after day, there are hardboiled eggs instead of frog legs for breakfast, and doubts and worries buzz and sting like the evil's in Pandora's box.

185 April 27 – Listen and shut up, oh, ye of little faith. On one certain evening in a certain year 1953 a certain complex of pitched tensions, physiological urges, and mental dragonflies combined to fill one mortal imperfect Eve with a fierce full rightness, force and determination corresponding to the ecstasy experienced by the starving saint on the desert who feels the crackling cool drops of God on his tongue and sees the green angels sprouting up like dandelion greens, prolific and infinitely unexpected.

Factors: something did happen. Russell Lynes on Harper's bought 3 poems ("Doomsday," "Go Get the Goodly Squab" and "To Eva Descending the Stair") for $100. Signifying what? first real professional acceptance, God, and all the possibilities: to keep cracking open my mind and my vocabulary breaking myself into larger more magnanimous orbits of understanding. Things have been happening like a chain of fire crackers, but every brilliant explosive fact must have a legitimate cause & effect.

Editor of <u>Smith Review</u> this morning: the one office on campus I coveted; back to balance about psychology; prospect of Harvard Summer School – holiday tables under the trees. New York and Ray (and neurology & brilliance) this weekend. New Haven and Mike (sun, beach, strong good love) the next.

Tonight, spring, plural, fertile, offering up clean green leaf whorls to a soft moon covered with fuzz-fractured clouds, and god, the listening to Auden" read in Drew's front living room, and vivid questioning, darting scintillant wit. My Plato! pedestrian I! And Drew, (exuberant exquisitely frail intelligent Elizabeth) saying, "Now that is really difficult."

Auden tossing his big head back with a twist of wide ugly grinning lips, his sandy hair, his coarse tweedy brown jacket, his burlap-textured voice and the crackling brilliant utterances – the naughty mischievous boy genius, and the inconsistent white hairless skin of his legs, and the short puffy stubbed fingers – and the carpet slippers – beer he drank, and smoked Lucky Strikes in a black holder, gesticulating with a white new cigarette in his hands, holding matches, talking in a gravelly incisive tone about how Caliban is the natural bestial projection, Ariel the creative imaginative, and all the intricate lyrical abstruosities of their love and cleavage, art and life, the mirror and the sea. God, god, the stature of the man. And next week, in trembling audacity, I approach him with a sheaf of the poems. Oh, god, if this is life, half heard, glimpsed, smelled, with beer and cheese sandwiches and the god-eyed tall-minded ones, let me never go blind, or get shut off from the agony of learning, the horrible pain of trying to understand.

Tonight: the unforgettable snatching of toothpicks and olive pits from the tables of the ambrosial gods!

186

May 5 – and what the hell do you think you can decide upon, act upon, or base your personal philosophy upon if at the sight of a tall reticent poetic genius named Gordon you feel sick, tense, excited, overthrown, eager, wanting to redeem horrible infirmary impression, hot and cold and desperately near tears. first you were almost going to condescend to marry M. <u>even if</u> he had bad skin, barbarian parents, cold calculating drives, male vanity and a rather unimaginative and rather prosaic way of making love while writing out chemistry formulas. then you heard about him making out with that empty-headed intense superficial childish and sexy bitch who cried and fought all one weekend with his roommate (whom she yelled at you that she loved desperately.) O.K., so he asked you first and you refused, so she is aggressive and flatters his male vanity, so you are most interested in his carrying-on as soon as you demur – maybe retaliation was his motive, maybe just plain hedonism? so you are disillusioned – why? because, you hypocrite, he is just as bad as you are! unscrupulous, vain, fickle, and hedonistic! so this weekend (coming) you are going to see him half a day later than planned, and how are you going to act? depends on what you want. but you aren't sure, and you aren't sure what he wants or needs either, so get down off your high horse and be fair. you know damn well that as soon as he confined himself to you, you'd be off with other dates, playing your damn sweet innocent song: "oh, but I don't want to confine myself to one person either! how well we'll get along!" so he makes out with her in the presence of your best friend – he'd be a dunce to think she wouldn't tell you. and he is no dunce, you do care. your vanity is hurt. that is superficial & negligible. what hurts most is your naive faith in his pureness, (which paradoxically you forgot in the surprising and passionate proficiency of the thin, much weaker Ray just three nights ago.) oh god, there is no faith or permanance or solace in love unless – unless – the mind adores, the body adores – and yet the fear is always there in my mind: tomorrow it will all be different – tomorrow I will hate the way he chuckles at a joke, or combs his hair with a dirty pocket comb. tomorrow he will see that my nose is fat and my skin is sallow, and we will both be two ugly, vain, selfish, hedonistic dissatisfied people, and the wine, and colored lights, and heated intelligent conversations will all be a fairy-tale inspired pipe dream, and the bitten apple of love will translate itself into discarded feces. tomorrow we'll start running again after the leering clockwork chameleon that looks like the prince or princess in the fairy-tales, but turns into a warted toad or a pincered cockroach when touched by mortal hands. where, where, to find that quality I long for that will grow goodly and green for fifty years – is it mind? then Ray has mind, with a weaker body; thin, with no height, and you think of flat shoes, all your life long feeling big and swollen, lying like mother earth on your back and being raped by a humming entranced insect and begetting thousands of little white eggs in a gravel pit. and you think of Florida and sun, constraints of his society, loud clothes, all shrinking, paling, before the mind, and he perhaps fickley loving delicate butterfly-like women of the insect kind. but there was the expert moving of his hands and head and tongue and the surprised knowledge that honest love could ignore defects and discrepancies of matter in the presence of lightening-crackling mind. once I thought I could live with him too. god, how I ricochet between certainties and doubts. the doubts of past convictions only cast aspersions on present assurances and maliciously suggest that those, too, shall pass into the realm of the null and void: – and then tonight the sight of the poetic one, the wanting . . . what? to conquer? to talk? this first . . . after the "don't kill me when you make love to me" . . . echoing in my ears. all these boys I love pieces of, and 3 years ago that would have been fine. but now, there is not one I know well enough, surely enough, to say, if asked: "O.K., here is a certificate guaranteeing that a Smith Phi-Bete-to-be, (maybe) potential minor poetess & story writer, one-time dilet-tante artist, reasonably healthy and attractive, alive, thinking, tall, sensuous, powerful, colorful white woman, age 21, is handing you 50 years during which she will love your faults, honor your bestialities, obey your whimsies, ignore your mistresses, nurse your progeny, paper the walls of your house with flowers, and adore you as her dying mortal god, conceive babies and new recipes in labor and travail, and remain faithful to you until you both rot and the inevitable synesthesia of death sets in." I have to be terribly sure it (marriage) is neither a glamorous gamble nor an ephemeral escape. I know none of these three boys well enough to give prognosis for a lifetime, even a vague general one. I would have to <u>live</u> with a personality over a period of frequent contact . . . the only boy I know really well is the one I know well enough that I can never marry nor love. oh a love, a growing sharing would be so good, so uncomplex. and in these rapid most complex days of speed, mood, and psychology, it is relatively impossible to "know" anyone, as it is impossible to "know" oneself. suddenly everyone else is very married and happy, and one is very alone, and bitter about eating a boiled tasteless egg by oneself every morning and painting on a red mouth to smile oh-so-sweetly at the world with.

one relies so on single symbols which supposedly presage large assump-tions. he goes to ballets, ergo he must be sensitive & artistic. he quotes poetry, ergo he must be a kindred spirit. he reads joyce, ergo he must be a genius.

let's face it, I am in danger of wanting my personal absolute to be a demigod of a man, and as there aren't many around, I often unconsciously manufacture my own. and then, I retreat and revel in poetry and literature where the reward value is tangible and accepted. I really do not think deeply. really deeply. I want a romantic nonexistant hero.

If only I knew what I wanted I could try to see about getting it. I want to live hard and good with a hard, good man. clean, brilliant and strong is how and with whom I want to live. and tonight, oh god, (I think) that I am mortal, unthinking, unworthy – and that the three men on the fringe are too far off in time and space and too like unloves and faithless, and though love be a day, I am afraid it will be only that; and though love be a day, I am afraid also that it will be more.

what to do? think & create & love people & give of self like mad. go outward in love and creation and maybe you will fall into knowing what you want simultaneously as what you want walks by your picket gate singing a never-again song with a nonchalant catch-me-quick hat aslant back on his head and a book of "how life is a flea circus" under his einstein arm. ——⫯——

187

May 13 – today I bought a raincoat – no, that was yesterday – yesterday I bought a raincoat with a frivolous pink lining that does good to my eyes because I have never ever had anything pink-colored, and it was much too expensive – I bought it with a month's news office pay, and soon I will not have any money to do anything more with because I am buying clothes because I love them and they are exactly right, if I pay enough. And I feel dry and a bit sick whenever I say "I'll take it" and the smiling woman goes away with my money because she doesn't know I really don't have money at all at all. For three villanelles I have a blue-and-white pin-striped cotton cord suit dress, a black silk date dress and a grey raincoat with a frivolous pink lining.

188 May 14 – tonight after ushering at "Ring Around the Moon" I started back alone to the house. It had just stopped raining; and I got halfway up the steps, and thought of how I would not be alone when I came in, and I turned and walked away down the sodden walk, down an alley, with stands of water in the hollows of the faulted paving, and the air warm and sweet with dogwood and flowering smells, and the lights quaint and soft, and the wet streets reflecting them. It was good to walk faceless and talk to myself again, to ask where I was going, and who I was, and to realize that I had no idea, that all I could tell you was my name, and not my heritage; my daily schedule for the next week, and not the reason for it; my plans for the summer, and not the purpose I had whittled out for my life.

I am lucky: I am at Smith because I wanted it and worked for it. I am going to be a Guest Editor on Mlle in June because I wanted it and worked for it. I am being published in Harper's because I wanted it and worked for it. Luckily I could translate wish to reality by the work.

But now, although I am a pragmatic machiavellian at heart, I find the 3 men in my life distant because I acted first and post mortemed afterward. I did not think clearly: "I want this; I must do thus to obtain this. I will hence do thus. Ergo, I shall get what I want." Stupid girl. You will never win anyone through pity. You must create the right kind of dream, the sober, adult kind of magic: illusion born from disillusion.

Is anyone anywhere happy? No, not unless they are living in a dream or in an artifice that they or someone else has made. For a time I was lulled in the arms of a blind optimism with breasts full of champagne and nipples made of caviar. I thought she was true, and that the true was the beautiful. But the true is the ugly mixed up everywhere, like a peck of dirt scattered through your life. The true is that there is no security, no artifice to stop the unsavory changes, the rat race, the death unwish – the winged chariot, the horns and motors, the Devil in the clock. Love is a desperate artifice to take the place of those two original parents who turned out not to be omnisciently right gods, but a rather pedestrian pair of muddled suburbanites who, no mater how bumblingly they tried, never could quite understand how or why you grew up to your 21st birthday. Love is not this if you make it something creatively other. But most of you are not very good at making things. "Beauty is in the eye of the beholder." What a pat speech. Why do my beheld beauties vanish and deform themselves as soon as I look twice.

I want to love somebody because I want to be loved. In a rabbit-fear I may hurl myself under the wheels of the car because the lights terrify me, and under the dark blind death of the wheels I will be safe. I am very tired, very banal, very confused. I do not know who I am tonight. I wanted to walk until I dropped and not complete the inevitable circle of coming home. I have lived in boxes above, below, and down the hall from girls who think hard, feel similarly, and long companionably, and I have not bothered to cultivate them because I did not want to, could not, sacrifice the time. People know who I am, and the harder I try to know who they are, the more I forget their names – I want to be alone, and yet there are times when the liquid eye and the cognizant grin of a small monkey would send me into a crying fit of brotherly love. I work and think alone. I live with people, and act. I love and cherish both. If I knew now what I wanted I would know when I saw it, who he was.

I want to write because I have the urge to excell in one medium of translation and expression of life. I can't be satisfied with the colossal job of merely living. Oh, no, I must order life in sonnets and sestinas and provide a verbal reflector for my 60-watt lighted head. Love is an illusion, but I would willingly fall for it if I could believe in it. Now everything seems either far and sad and cold, like a piece of shale at the bottom of a canyon – or warm and near and unthinking, like the pink dogwood. God, let me think clearly and brightly; let me live, love, and say it well in good sentences, let me someday see who I am and why I accept 4 years of food, shelter, and exams and papers without questioning more than I do. I am tired, banal, and now I am getting not only monosyllabic but also tautological. Tomorrow is another day toward death, (which can never happen to me because I am I which spells invulnerable.) Over orange juice & coffee even the embryonic suicide brightens visibly. —

[Appendix 4 contains Sylvia Plath's 19 June 1953 journal fragment about Julius and Ethel Rosenberg; Appendix 5 contains Sylvia Plath's June–July 1953 'Letter to an Over-grown, Over-protected, Scared, Spoiled Baby' – ed.]

July 6, 1953 – The time has come, my pretty maiden, to stop running away from yourself, trying to keep on a merrygoround whirlwind of activity that goes so fast you haven't time to think too much or too long. Today you made a fatal decision – <u>not</u> to go to Harvard Summer school. And you vacillated like a nervous seesaw – gulped, chose blindly – and immediately wanted to reverse a decision which is speeding into finality now already on the wings of mails, minds, and secretarial files. You are an inconsistent and very frightened hypocrite: you wanted <u>time</u> to think, to find out about yourself, your ability to write, and now that you have it: practically 3 months of godawful time, you are paralyzed, shocked, thrown into a nausea, a stasis. You are plunged so deep in your own very private little whirlpool of negativism that you can't do more than force yourself into a rote where the simplest actions become forbidding and enormous. Your mind is incapable of thinking. If you went to Harvard, all your time would be planned, diagrammed for you – practically the way it will be at Smith next year: and just now that kind of security seems desirable – it is just another way of absolving you of taking responsibilities for your own actions & planning, really, although now the issue is so confused it is hard to think <u>which</u> choice would take the most guts: and which kind of guts. Marcia is working & taking a course – you are doing neither: the woman at the vocational office said you should know shorthand: you can now learn it – you won't have it this good again, baby. You could even take psych at BU[n] if you had the guts to commute. You could be taking O'Connor's[n] novel, etc. – but why blind yourself by taking course after course: when if you are anybody, which you are no doubt not, you should <u>not</u> be bored, but should be able to think, accept, <u>affirm</u> – and not retreat into a masochistic mental hell where jealousy and fear make you want to stop eating – don't <u>ignore</u> all the people you could know, shutting yourself up in a numb defensive vacuum: but <u>please</u> yank yourself up &

don't spend years gaping in horror at the one time in your life you'll have a chance to <u>prove</u> your own discipline. Tomorrow you'll tell Gordon that he can call for you at home – various changes have taken place since you last saw him: catch perspective kid – learn shorthand; study French: THINK CONSTRUCTIVELY – and get some respect for yourself. You always said you could write a <u>Journal</u> story if you tried hard. NOW is the time to analyze, to recreate <u>in your own mind</u> – not merely to shovel the hole full of other people & their words. Now is the time to conjure up words and ideas on your own. You are frozen mentally – scared to get going, eager to crawl back to the womb. First think: here is your room – here is your life, your mind: don't panic. Begin writing, even if it is only rough & ununified. First, pick your market: <u>Journal</u> or <u>Discovery</u>? <u>Seventeen</u> or <u>Mlle</u>? Then pick a topic. Then think. If you can't think <u>outside</u> yourself, you can't write. And don't mope about saving $250 which is the price of getting to know if you are clever enough to write & improvise anyhow. Get a <u>plot</u>. Make it funny. Be big & glad for other people & make them happy. If you do nothing, make 2 people happy. Tomorrow, write Hans" & Smith Quarterly article" – each night, map out the next day's plans. If Dick could write & create alone, so can you. Pray to yourself for the guts to make the summer <u>work</u>. One <u>sale</u>: that would help. Work for that.

a.m. Right now you are sick in your head. You have called Marcia, cancelled room & she is relieved. It would have been a struggle, living there – and yet you would go calling up the director – asking to reverse a decision. Four girls would think you were unbalanced, selfish, crazy. Four girls with jobs & talk & friends. You fool – you are afraid of being alone with you own mind. You just better learn to know yourself, to make sure decisions before it is too late. 3 <u>months</u>, you think, scared to death. You want to call that man – You earned enough money to go. Why don't you go? Stop thinking selfishly of razors & self-wounds & going out and ending it all. Your room is not your prison. You are. And Smith cannot cure you; no one has the power to cure you but yourself. Be an introvert for 3 months – stop thinking of noise, names, dances – you could have bought it. The price of all this is high. Neurotic women. Fie. Get a job. Learn shorthand at night. NOTHING EVER REMAINS THE SAME –.

JULY 14 – All right, you have gone the limit – you tried today, after 2 hours only of sleep for the last two nights, to shut yourself off from responsibility altogether: you looked around and saw everybody either married or busy and happy and thinking and being creative, and you felt scared, sick, lethargic, worst of all, not wanting to cope. You saw visions of yourself in a straight jacket, and a drain on the family, murdering your mother in actuality, killing the edifice of love and respect – built up over the years in the hearts of other people – You began to do something that is against all you believe in. Impasse: male relations; (jealousy & frantic fear.) female relations: ditto. Loss of perspective humor. Colossal desire to escape, retreat, not talk to <u>anybody</u>. Thesis panic – lack of other people to be with – recrimination for past wrong choices – Fear, big & ugly & sniveling. Fear of not succeeding intellectually and academically: the worst blow to security. Fear of failing to live up to the fast & furious prize-winning pace of these last years – and any kind of creative life. Perverse desire to retreat into <u>not caring</u>. I am incapable of loving or feeling now: self-induced.

Out of it, kid. You are making monumental obstacles of what should be taken for granted – living on a past reputation –

New York: pain, parties, work. And Gary and ptomaine – and José the cruel Peruvian and Carol vomiting outside the door all over the floor – and interviews for TV shows, & competition, and beautiful models and Miss Abels:[n] (capable, and heaven knows what else.) And now this: shock. Utter nihilistic shock.

Read a story: Think. You can. You must, moreover, not continually run away while asleep – forget details – ignore problems – shut walls up between you & the world & all the gay bright girls – : please, think – snap out of this. <u>Believe</u> in some beneficent force beyond your own limited self. God, god, god: where are you? I want you, need you: the belief in you and love and mankind. You must not seek escape like this. You must think.

JOURNAL
22 November 1955 – 18 April 1956

═══

Sylvia Plath attempted to commit suicide by taking an overdose of sleeping pills on 24 August 1953. Following therapy at McLean Hospital in Belmont, Massachusetts, she returned to Smith College in February 1954 and graduated on 6 June 1955. Plath did not keep a journal during her senior year at college.

From October 1955 until June 1957, Plath attended Newnham College at Cambridge University where she read English on a Fulbright fellowship. She initially lived at Whitstead, a small house for foreign students on the grounds of Newnham College, and spent her first winter and spring breaks on the Continent. Many of the entries in the following journal are excerpts from letters to Richard Sassoon.

Excerpt from letter ▓▓▓▓▓▓
November 22, 1955

Words revolve in flame and keep the coliseum heart afire, reflecting
orange sunken suns in the secret petals of ruined arches. yes, the
glowing asbestos thorns and whistling flame flowers reflect the
cells of the scarlet heart and the coliseum burns on, without a
nero, on the brink of blackness. so words have power to open
sesame and reveal liberal piles of golden metallic suns in the
dark pit that wait to be melted and smelted in the fire of spring
which springs to fuse lumps and clods into veins of radiance.

so sylvia burns yellow dahlias on her dark altar of the sun as the
sun wanes to impotence and the world falls in winter. birds contract to frozen feathered buds on barren boughs and plants surrender
to the omnipotent white frosts which hold all colors cruelly locked
in hexagonal hearts of ice.

cf. poem

at midnight, when the moon makes blue lizard scales of roof
shingles and simple folk are bedded deep in eiderdown, she opens
the gable window with fingers frozen crisp and thin as carrots,
and scatters crumbs of white bread which skip and dwindle down
the roof to lie in angled gutters to feed the babes in the wood.
so the hungry cosmic mother sees the world shrunk to embryo again
and her children gathered sleeping back into the dark, huddling
in bulbs and pods, pale and distant as the folded beanseed to her
full milky love which freezes across the sky in a crucifix of stars.

so it costs ceres all that pain to go to gloomy dis and bargain for
proserpine again. we wander and wait in november air gray as rat
fur stiffened with frozen tears. endure, endure, and the syllables
harden like stoic white sheets struck with rigor mortis on the
clothesline of winter.

artificial fires burn here: leaping red in the heart of wineglasses,
smouldering gold in goblets of sherry, cracking crimson in the
fairytale cheeks of a rugged jewish hercules hewn fresh from the
himalayas and darjeeling to be sculpted with blazing finesse by
a feminine pygmalion whom he gluts with mangoes and dmitri
karamazov fingers blasting beethoven out of acres of piano and
striking scarlatti to skeletal crystal.

fires pale askew to pink houses under the aqua backdrop sky of
"bartholomew fair" where a certain whore slinks in a slip of
jaundice-yellow and wheedles apples and hobbyhorses from lecherous
cutpurses. water scalds and hisses in the tiny guts of the kettle
and ceres feeds the souls and stomachs of the many too many
who love satanic earthenware teasets, dishes heaped with barbed
and quartered orange pineapple and cool green globes of grapes,
and maccaroon cakes that soften and cling to the hungry mouth.

when the face of god is gone and the sun pales behind wan veils
of chill mist, she vomits at the gray neuter neutralities of limbo
and seeks the red flames and smoking snakes that devour eternally
the limbs of the damned. feeding on the furies of cassandra, she
prophesys and hears the "falling glass and topoling masonry" of
troy while hector bats her torn and tangled hair and murmurs:
"There, there, mad sister."

Words revolve in flame and keep the coliseum heart afire, reflecting orange sunken suns in the secret petals of ruined arches. yes, the glowing asbestos thorns and whistling flame flowers reflect the cells of the scarlet heart and the coliseum burns on, without a nero, on the brink of blackness. so words have power to open sesame and reveal liberal piles of golden metallic suns in the dark pit that wait to be melted and smelted in the fire of spring which springs to fuse lumps and clods into veins of radiance.

so sylvia burns yellow dahlias on her dark altar of the sun as the sun wanes to impotence and the world falls in winter. birds contract to frozen feathered buds on barren boughs and plants surrender to the omnipotent white frosts which hold all colors cruelly locked in hexagonal hearts of ice.

at midnight, when the moon makes blue lizard scales of roof shingles" and simple folk are bedded deep in eiderdown, she opens the gable window with fingers frozen crisp and thin as carrots, and scatters crumbs of white bread which skip and dwindle down the roof to lie in angled gutters to feed the babes in the wood. so the hungry cosmic mother sees the world shrunk to embryo again and her children gathered sleeping back into the dark, huddling in bulbs and pods, pale and distant as the folded beanseed to her full milky love which freezes across the sky in a crucifix of stars.

so it costs ceres all that pain to go to gloomy dis and bargain for proserpine again. we wander and wait in november air gray as rat fur stiffened with frozen tears. endure, endure, and the syllables harden like stoic white sheets struck with rigor mortis on the clothesline of winter.

artificial fires burn here: leaping red in the heart of wineglasses, smouldering gold in goblets of sherry, cracking crimson in the fairytale cheeks of a rugged jewish hercules hewn fresh from the himalayas and darjeeling to be sculpted with blazing finesse by a feminine pygmalion whom he gluts with mangoes and dmitri karamazov fingers blasting beethoven out of acres of piano and striking scarlatti to skeletal crystal.

fires pale askew to pink houses under the aqua backdrop sky of "bartholomew fair" where a certain whore slinks in a slip of jaundice-yellow and wheedles apples and hobbyhorses from lecherous cutpurses. water scalds and hisses in the tin guts of the kettle and ceres feeds the souls and stomachs of the many too many who love satanic earthenware teasets, dishes heaped with barbed and quartered orange pineapple and cool green globes of grapes, and maccaroon cakes that soften and cling to the hungry mouth.

when the face of god is gone and the sun pales behind wan veils of chill mist, she vomits at the gray neuter neutralities of limbo and seeks the red flames and smoking snakes that devour eternally the limbs of the damned. feeding on the furies of cassandra, she prophesys and hears the "falling glass and toppling masonry" of troy while hector pats her torn and tangled hair and murmurs: "There, there, mad sister."

God is on vacation with the pure transcendent sun and the searing heat that turns the flawed white body of our love to glass: look! how the riddle of the world is resolved in this menagerie of mated glass, how clean and sparkling the light blesses these pure serene ones! suddenly from the bed of mire they ascend to astonish the angels of heaven who keep the light of their love enshrined in ice.

see, see! how the mind and mated flesh can make man the envy of god, who masturbates in the infinite void his ego has made about him. but do not ask for these tomorrow. he is a jealous god and he has had them liquidated.

I have talked to various little dark men who keep giving me, at my request, booklets colored yellow and titled: sunshine holidays . . . .

do you realize that the name sassoon" is the most beautiful name in the world. it has lots of seas of grass en masse and persian moon alone in rococo lagoon of woodwind tune where passes the ebony monsoon . . . .

I am proud again, and I will have the varying wealths of the world in my hands before I come to see you again . . . I will have them, and they are being offered to me even now, on turkish tables and by dark alladins. I simply say, turning on my other flank, I do not want these jingling toys. I only want the moon that sounds in a name and the son of man that bears that name.

In the beginning was the word and the word was sassoon and it was a terrible word for it created eden and the golden age back to which fallen eva looks mingling her crystal tears with the yellow dahlias that sprout from the lips of her jaundiced adam.

be christ! she cries, and rise before my eyes while the blue marys bless us with singing. and when, she asks (for even eva is practical) will this ressurection occur?

Excerpt: December 11"

What concerns me among multitudes and multitudes of other sad questions which one had better try to lure aside with parfaits and sunshine, is that there is a certain great sorrow in me now, with as many facets as a fly's eye, and I must give birth to this monstrosity before I am light again. Otherwise I shall ressemble a dancing elephant ... I am tormented by the questions of the devils which weave my fibers with grave-frost and human-dung, and have not the ability or genius to write a big letter to the world about this. when one makes of one's own heavens and hells a few hunks of neatly typewritten paper and editors are very polite and reject it, one is, in whimsy, inclined to identify editors with god's ministers. this is fatal.

Would it be too childish of me to say: I want? But I do want: theater, light, color, paintings, wine and wonder. Yet not all these can do more than try to lure the soul from its den where it sulks in busy heaps of filth and obstinate clods of bloody pulp. I must find a core of fruitful seeds in me. I must stop identifying with the seasons, because this English winter will be the death of me.

I am watching a pale blue sky be torn across by wind fresh from the russian steppes. Why is it that I find it so difficult to accept the present moment, whole as an apple, without cutting and hacking at it to find a purpose, or setting it up on a shelf with other apples to measure its worth or trying to pickle it in brine to preserve it, and crying to find it turns all brown and is no longer simply the lovely apple I was given in the morning?

Perhaps when we find ourselves wanting everything it is because we are dangerously near to wanting nothing. There are two opposing poles of wanting nothing: When one is so full and rich and has so many inner worlds that the outer world is not necessary for joy, because joy emanates from the inner core of one's being. When one is dead and rotten inside and there is nothing in the world: not all the woman, food, sun, or mind-magic of others that can reach the wormy core of one's gutted soul planet.

I feel now as if I were building a very delicate intricate bridge quietly in the night, across the dark from one grave to another while the giant is sleeping. Help me build this o so exquisite bridge.

I want to live each day for itself like a string of colored beads, and not kill the present by cutting it up in cruel little snippets to fit some desperate architectural draft for a taj mahal in the future.

[Appendix 6 contains Sylvia Plath's 31 December 1955 – 1 January 1956 journal fragment about her vacation in France with Richard Sassoon – ed.]

January 11"

The crossing was terrible. It was fantastically rough and everywhere people lay in insular agony, retching into the bright orange basins which sloshed with curded vomit as the angry green sea smashed against the bow.

Below it was impossible, with stagnant, sweet fetid air and the stench of regurgitated slop, and people lying about groaning. I stayed above, while about 20 little girls, clad exactly alike in camel's hair coats, argyle socks, plaid kilts and scotch berets with double feathers that made them look like a crew of human turkeys, ran about giggling and vomiting as the fancy took them.

dagenham pipers

from letter january 15"

it is saturday night, turning as I write into sunday morning. the dark world balances and tips and already I can feel the dawn coming up under me.

outside it is raining and the black streets are inky with wet and crying with wind. I have just come back from a film: die letzte brücke.

It was a german-jugoslav film about the war, and the partisans fighting the germans. and the people were real people with dirty shining faces and I loved them. they were simple. they were men and both sides were wrong and both sides were right. they were human beings and they were not grace kelley, but they were beautiful from inside like joan of arc, with that kind of radiance that faith makes, and the kind that love makes.

the kind of radiance too that suddenly comes over you when I look at you dressing or shaving or reading and you are suddenly more than the daily self we must live with and love, that fleeting celestial self which shines out with the whimsical timing of angels.

that confident surge of exuberance in which I wrote you has dwindled as waves do, to the knowledge that makes me cry, just this once: such a minute fraction of this life do we live: so much is sleep, tooth-brushing, waiting for mail, for metamorphosis, for those sudden moments of incandescence: unexpected, but once one knows them, one can live life in the light of their past and the hope of their future.

in my head I know it is too simple to wish for war, for open battle but one cannot help but wish for those situations that make us heroic, living to the hilt of our total resources. our cosmic fights, which I think the end of the world is come, are so many broken shells around our growth.

sunday noon: very stingily blue whipped to white by wind from russian steppes. the mornings are god's time, and after breakfast for those five hours somehow everything is all right and most things are even possible. the afternoons however slip away faster and faster and night cheats by coming shortly after four. the dark time, the night time is worst now. sleep is like the grave, wormeaten with dreams.

January 28"

it would be easy to say I would fight for you, or steal or lie; I have a great deal of that desire to use myself to the hilt, and where, for men, fighting is a cause, for women, fighting is for men. in a crisis, it is easy to say: I will arise and be with thee. but what I would do too is the hardest thing for me, with my absurd streak of idealism and perfectionism: I do believe I would sit around with you and feed you and wait with you through all the necessary realms of tables and kingdoms of chairs and cabbage for those fantastic few moments when we are angels, and we are growing angels (which the angels in heaven never can be) and when we together make the world love itself and incandesce. I would sit around and read and write and brush my teeth, knowing in you there were the seeds of an angel, my kind of angel, with fire and swords and blazing power. why is it I find out so slowly what women are made for? it comes nudging and urging up in me like tulips bulbs in april.

February 19: Sunday night:

To whom it may concern: Every now and then there comes a time when the neutral and impersonal forces of the world turn and come together in a thunder-crack of judgment. There is no reason for the sudden terror, the feeling of condemnation, except that circumstances all mirror the inner doubt, the inner fear. Yesterday, walking quite peacefully over the Mill Lane bridge, after leaving my bike to be repaired (feeling lost, pedestrian, impotent), smiling that smile which puts a benevolent lacquer on the shuddering fear of strangers' gazes, I was suddenly turned upon by little boys making snowballs on the dam. They began to throw them at me, openly, honestly, trying to hit. They missed every time, and with that wary judgment that comes with experience, I watched the dirty snowballs coming at me, behind and in front, and, sick with wonder, kept walking slowly, determinedly, ready to parry a good hit before it struck. But none struck, and with a tolerant smile that was a superior lie, I walked on.

Today my thesaurus, which I would rather live with on a desert isle than a bible, as I have so often boasted cleverly, lay open after I'd written the rough draft of a bad, sick poem, at 545: Deception; 546: Untruth, 547: Dupe, 548: Deceiver. The clever reviewer and writer who is an ally of the generous creative opposing forces, cries with deadly precision: "Fraud, fraud." Which has been cried solidly for six months during that dark year of hell.

Yesterday night: coming in to the party at Emmanuel (ah, yes) they were hypnotizing someone named Morris in the dark, crowded room, lit with conscious bohemianism by candles in old wine bottles. The fat, yet strong, ugly boy was saying with commanding mastery and power: "When you try to go through the door there will be glass in the way. You cannot go through the door, there will be glass. When I say "gramophone" you will fall asleep again." Then he brought Morris out of the trance, and Morris tried to go through the door, but stopped. He could not go through the door, there was glass in the way. The fat boy said "Gramophone", and two laughing, nervous boys caught Morris as he fell. Then they made Morris become stiff as a steel bar; he seemed to know just how stiff that was, and went rigid on the floor.

And I talked and talked with Win:" pink-faced, blue-eyed, blond, confident, on the beginnings of love with a girl he met skiing who is engaged and going home to see about breaking it off and coming back and maybe living and traveling with him. And I learned that I was not wrong about L., and that we both love N. and I talked of R. Such games. I talked of R. as if he were dead. With a deadly nobility. And tall good-looking John" put his warm hand on my shoulder and I asked him intently about hypnotism, while Chris'" eager, shiny, red-cheeked baby-face and curly hair floated on the edge, and out of misplaced kindness I refused to go into the raw room oozing dance music with John, and went to talk chastely with Win and drink and tell Rafe who was the host with a shining face and a bowl perpetually full of fruit and liquor of a different color each time he came; "You are a wonderful host."

Then, Chris left, and in the back of talk, knelt to hug the little black-clad miniature Sally Bowles with minute black slacks and jersey and cropped blonde Joan-of-Arc hair and a long wicked cigarette holder (matching exactly her very small man Roger who was all in black like a pale ballet dancer and very little, with a review he had just written on Yeats in print in a magazine called Kayham, after Omar). Chris then sat a red-dressed girl on his lap, and then they went to dance. Meanwhile, Win and I talk very wisely and the appalling easiness of this strikes me down: I could throw everything away and make a play for John, who is now making a play for the nearest and easiest. But everybody has exactly the same smiling frightened face, with the look that says: "I'm important. If you only get to know me, you will see how important I am. Look into my eyes. Kiss me, and you will see how important I am."

I too want to be important. By being different. And these girls are all the same. Far off, I go to my coat with Win; he brings me my scarf as I wait on the stair, and Chris is being red-cheeked and dramatic and breathless and penitent. He wants to be scolded, and punished. That is too easy. That is what we all want.

I am rather high, and distant, and it is convenient to be led home across the snow-fields. It is very cold, and all the way back I am thinking: Richard, you live in this moment. You live now. You are in my guts and I am acting because you are alive. And meanwhile you are probably sleeping exhausted and happy in the arms of some brilliant whore, or maybe even the Swiss girl who wants to marry you. I cry out to you. I want to write you, of my love, that absurd faith which keeps me chaste, so chaste, that all I have ever touched or said to others becomes only the rehearsal for you, and preserved only for this. These others now pass the time, and even so little a way over the boundary, to kisses, and touches, I cry mercy and back away, frozen. I am in black, dressed more and more often in black now. I lost one of my red gloves at a cocktail party. I only have black ones left, and they are cold and comfortless.

"Richard," I say, and tell Nat," and tell Win, and Tell Chris, as I have told Mallory," and Iko," and Brian," and Martin," and David:" There Is This Boy In France. And today I told John, who is an excellent listener and who is willing to sit and hear me say how I have once been happy, and once been the highest in me, and grown to the woman I am now, all because of this boy named Richard. And John says: "I could love you violently, if I let myself." But he has not let himself. Why? Because I haven't touched him, I haven't looked into his eyes with the image he wants to see there. And I could. But I am too tired, too noble, in a perverse way. It sickens me. I wouldn't want him, even as he became a victim. So I tell him casually that I won't let it happen, playfully, because it is a stillborn child. I have given birth to so many of these.

And then, bitterly, I say: do I love Richard? Or do I use him as an excuse for a noble, lonely, unloving posture, under the perverse label of faith? Using him so, would I want him on the scene, thin, nervous, little, moody, sickly? Or would I rather cherish the strong mind and soul and blazing potency alone, refines from the marring details of the real world? Coward.

And coming into the diningroom unexpectedly at breakfast, the three bright ones turn with a queer look and go on talking the way they do when Mrs. Milne comes in, in apparent continuity, veiling the subject of their words: "so strange, just staring into the fire." And they have condemned you for being mad. Just like that. Because the fear is already there, and has been for so long. The fear that all the edges and shapes and colors of the real world that have been built up again so painfully with such a real love can dwindle in a moment of doubt, and "suddenly go out" the way the moon would in the Blake poem.

A morbid fear: that protests too much. To the doctor. I am going to the psychiatrist this week, just to meet him, to know he's there. And, ironically, I feel I need him. I need a father. I need a mother. I need some older, wiser being to cry to. I talk to God, but the sky is empty, and Orion walks by and doesn't speak. I feel like Lazarus: that story has such a fascination. Being dead, I rose up again, and even resort to the mere sensation value of being suicidal, of getting so close, of coming out of the grave with the scars and the marring mark on my cheek which (is it my imagination) grows more prominent: paling like a death-spot in the red, wind-blown skin, browning darkly in photographs, against my grave winter-pallor. And I identify too closely with my reading, with my writing. I am Nina in "Strange Interlude"; I do want to have husband, lover, father and son, all at once. And I depend too desperately on getting my poems, my little glib poems, so neat, so small, accepted by the New Yorker. To revenge myself on the blonde one, as if the mere paper dykes of print can keep out the creative flood which annihilates all envy, all mere niggling fearful jealousy. Be generous.

Yes. That is what Stephen Spender[n] misses in Cambridge criticism. And what I miss in the miserly back-biting which jokes and picks at grotesqueries: what of ourselves: Jane,[n] gesturing clumsily with knives, knocking over toasters and table silver, breaking Gordon's necklace with awkward clutching mirth, taking supper from Richard, sleep and a room and a key from me, and never caring, utterly casual. How symbolic can we get? Resentment eats, killing the food it eats. Can she resent? She is on the side of the big, conquering boys, the creative ones. We have the impetuous puppies. Could we find those others? We have our Chris, our Nat. But do we?

Generous. Yes, today, I forgave Chris. For deserting me, and hurting me a little, even as the two faceless girls he has known hurt me, only because, a woman, I fight all women for my men. My men. I am a woman, and there is no loyalty, even between mother and daughter. Both fight for the father, for the son, for the bed of mind and body. I also forgave John, for having a rotten tooth, and a lousy pallor, because he was human, and I felt "I need human kind." Even John, as he sat there, distanced by those wise words of ours, even he could be a father. And I cry so to be held by a man; some man, who is a father.

So, now I shall talk every night. To myself. To the moon. I shall walk, as I did tonight, jealous of my loneliness, in the blue-silver of the cold moon, shining brilliantly on the drifts of fresh-fallen snow, with the myriad sparkles. I talk to myself and look at the dark trees, blessedly neutral. So much easier than facing people, than having to look happy, invulnerable, clever. With masks down, I walk, talking to the moon, to the neutral impersonal force that does not hear, but merely accepts my being. And does not smite me down. I went to the bronze boy" whom I love, partly because no one really cares for him, and brushed a clot of snow from his delicate smiling face. He stood there in the moonlight, dark, with snow etching his limbs in white, in the semi-circle of the privet hedge, bearing his undulant dolphin, smiling still, balancing on one dimpled foot.

And he becomes the child in "When We Dead Awaken." And Richard will give me no child. And it is his child I could want. To bear, to have growing. The only one whom I could stand to have a child with. Yet. I have a fear, too, of bearing a deformed child, a cretin, growing dark and ugly in my belly, like that old corruption I always feared would break out from behind the bubbles of my eyes. I imagine Richard here, being with me, and my growing big with his child. I ask for less and less. I would face him, and say simply: I am sad that you are not strong, and do not swim and sail and ski, but you have a strong soul, and I will believe in you and make you invincible on this earth. Yes, I have that power. Most women do, to one degree or another. Yet the vampire is there, too. The old, primal hate. That desire to go around castrating the arrogant ones who become such children at the moment of passion.

How the circling steps in the spiral tower bring us back to where we were! I long for mother, even for Gordon, though his weaknesses, symbolized by his impotence, his misspelling, even though they sicken me. And he will be financially comfortable. And he is handsome and strong. He skis, swims, yet all the attributes of god could not console me for his weak mind and his physical weakness. God, I would almost have him just to prove he were weak, although my doubt would not let him have the chance to be strong. Unless I were very careful. I would like him to be strong, too. Only there is so little hope, it is so late.

The only perfect love I have is for my brother. Because I cannot love him physically, I shall always love him. And be jealous of his wife, too, a little. Strange, that having lived in such passion, such striking and tears, such fierce joy, I could turn so cold, so disgusted, at all the superfluous playings with others, those flash attractions that seem my doom, now, because each one brings me so much closer to Richard. And still I hope there will be some man in Europe whom I will meet and love and who will free me from this strong idol. Whom I accept even in the heart of his weakness, whom I can make strong, because he gives me a soul and mind to work with.

And now it grows late, late. And I have the old beginning-of-the-week panic, because I cannot read and think enough to meet my little academic obligations, and I have not written at all since the Vence story″ (which will be rejected with the <u>New Yorker</u> rejection of my poems, and even as I bravely say so, I hope I am lying, because my love for Richard is in the story, and my wit, a little bit, and I want to have it frozen in print, and not rejected: see, how dangerous, I again identify with rejections too much!). But how can I go on being quiet, without a soul to talk to wholly here, who is not somehow drastically involved, or near enough to at least be glad that I am unhappy. I want to cry to Richard, to all my friends at home, to come and rescue me. From my insecurity which I must fight through myself. Finishing the next year here, enjoying the pressure of reading, thinking, while at my back is always the mocking tick: A Life is Passing. My Life.

So it is. And I waste my youth and days of radiance on barren ground. How I cried that night I wanted to go to bed, and there was no one, only my dreams of Christmas, and the last year with Richard, whom I have so loved. And I drank the last of the bad sherry, and cracked a few nuts, which were all sour and withered to nothing inside, and the material, inert world mocked me. Tomorrow what? Always patching masks, making excuses for having read a bare half of what I purposed. Yet a life is passing?

I long to permeate the matter of this world: to become anchored to life by laundry and lilacs, daily bread and fried eggs, and a man, the dark-eyed stranger, who eats my food and my body and my love and goes around the world all day and comes back to find solace with me at night. Who will give me a child, that will bring me again to be a member of that race which throws snowballs at me, sensing perhaps the rot at which they strike?

Well: Elly″ is coming this summer (and mother and Mrs. Prouty) and Sue″ next fall. I love both girls, and for once, with them can be wholly woman, and we can talk and talk. I am lucky. That is not long to wait. Yet now, how much do I give? Nothing. I am selfish, scared, crying too much to save myself for my phantom writing. But at any rate it is better than last term, when I was going mad night after night being a screaming whore in a yellow dress." A mad poet. How clever of Dick Gilling;" but he is very intuitive. I had not the heart, not the flexible heart, not the guts. /But I refused to go on, knowing I could not be big, refusing to be small. I retreated, to work. And it <u>has</u> been better: 15 plays a week instead of two. Number? Not only that, but a real feeling of mastery, of occasional insight. And that is what we wait for.

Will Richard ever need me again? Part of my bargain is that I will be silent until he does. Why is it that the man must so often take the lead? Women can do so much, but apart like this, I can do nothing, shut off from writing him as I am by a kind of honor and pride (I refuse to babble any more about how I love him) and I must wait until he needs me. If ever, in the next five years. And look, with love and faith, not turning sour and cold and bitter, to help others. That is salvation. To give of love inside. To keep love of life, no matter what, and give to others. Generously.

February 20: Monday

Dear Doctor: I am feeling very sick. I have a heart in my stomach which throbs and mocks. Suddenly the simple rituals of the day balk like a stubborn horse. It gets impossible to look people in the eye: corruption may break out again? Who knows. Small talk becomes desperate.

Hostility grows, too. That dangerous, deadly venom which comes from a sick heart. Sick mind, too. The image of identity we must daily fight to impress on the neutral, or hostile, world, collapses inward; we feel crushed. Standing in line in the hall, waiting for a lousy dinner of hard-boiled egg in cheese-cream sauce, mashed potatoes and sallow parsnips, we overheard one girl say to another: "Betsy is depressed today." It seems almost an incredible relief to know that there is someone outside oneself who is not happy all the time. We must be at low ebb when we are this far into the black: that everyone else, merely because they are "other", is invulnerable. That is a damn lie.

But I am foundering in relativity again. Unsure. And it is damn uncomfortable: with men (Richard gone, no one here to love), with writing (too nervous about rejections, too desperate and scared about bad poems; but do have ideas for stories; just try soon), with girls (house bristles with suspicion and frigidity; how much is paranoia transference? the damnable thing is that they can sense insecurity and meaness like animals smell blood), with academic life (have deserted french and feel temporarily very wicked and shirking, must atone; also, feel stupid in discussion; what the hell is tragedy? I am.)

So there. With bike at repair shop, gulped down coffee-with-milk, bacon and cabbage mixed with potato, and toast, read two letters from mother which cheered me quite a bit: she is so courageous, managing grammy and the house, and building up a new life, hoping for Europe. I want to make happy days for her here. She also was encouraging about teaching. Once I started doing it I wouldn't feel so sick. That frozen inertia is my worst enemy; I get positively sick with doubt. I must break through limit after limit: learn to ski (with gordon & sue next year?) and perhaps teach at an army base this summer. It would do me a hell of a lot of good. If I went to Africa or Istanbul, I could do articles about the place on the side. Enough romance. Get to work.

Thank god the Christian Science Monitor bought the Cambridge article and drawing." They should write a letter, too, about my request to write more. New Yorker rejection of poems may smack me in the stomach any morning. God, it is pretty poor when a life depends on such ridiculous sitting ducks as those poems, ready for editors' grape shot.

Tonight must think about O'Neill's plays; sometimes, in panic, mind goes blank, world whooshes away in void, and I feel I have to run, or walk on into the night for miles till I drop exhausted. Trying to escape? Or be alone enough to unriddle the secret of the sphinx. Men forget. Said Laughing Lazarus. And I forget the moments of radiance. I must get them down in print. Make them up in print. Be honest.

Anyway, after breakfast, leaped into clothes and started off at a dog-tot to Redpath" class at Grove Lodge" through snow. Gray day, moment of joy as snow tangled with blowing hair and felt red-cheeked and healthy. Wished I'd started earlier so I could linger. Noticed rooks squatting black in snow-white fen, gray skies, black trees, mallard-green water. Impressed.

Great crowd of cars and trucks at corner by Royal Hotel. Hurried to Grove

Lodge, noticed gray pleasantness of stone; liked building. Went in, took off coat, and sat down among boys, none of whom spoke. Felt sick of staring industrially down at the desk like a female yogi. Blond boy rushes in to announce Redpath has flu. And we stayed up till two last night virtuously reading Macbeth. Which was fine. Went awestruck over old speeches: "tale of sound and fury," especially. So ironic: I pick up poetic identities of characters who commit suicide, adultery, or get murdered, and I believe completely in them for a while. What they say is True.

Well, then, a walk to town, staring as ever at the towers of King's chapel, feeling happy at Market Hill, but all stores closed, except Sayle's where I bought an identical pair of red gloves to make up for the one I lost. Can't be completely in mourning. Is it possible to love the neutral, objective world and be scared of people? Dangerous for long, but possible. I love people I don't know. I smiled at a woman coming back over the fen path, and she said, with ironic understanding, "Wonderful weather." I loved her. I didn't read madness or superficiality in the image reflected in her eyes. For once.

It is the strangers that are easiest to love at this hard time. Because they do not demand and watch, always watch. I am sick of Mallory, Iko, John, even Chris. There is nothing there for me. I am dead to them, even though I once flowered. That is the latent terror, a symptom: it is suddenly either all or nothing: either you break the surface shell into the whistling void or you don't. I want to get back to my more normal intermediate path where the substance of the world is permeated by my being: eating food, reading, writing, talking, shopping: so all is good in itself, and not just a hectic activity to cover up the fear that must face itself and duel itself to death, saying: A Life is Passing!

The horror is the sudden folding up and away of the phenomenal world, leaving nothing. Just rags. Human rooks which say: Fraud. Thank God I get tired and can sleep; if that is so, all is possible. And I like to eat. And I like to walk and love the countryside here. Only these eternal questions keep knocking at the gate of my daily reality, which I cling to like a mad lover, questions which bring the dark perilous world where all is the same, there are no distinctions, no discriminations, no space and no time: the whistling breath of eternity, not of god, but of the denying devil. So we will turn to a few thoughts on O'Neill, steel ourselves to meet accusations about French, a

New Yorker rejection, and the hostility or, even worse, utter indifference, of the people we break bread with.

Wrote one Good Poem: "Winter Landscape with Rooks": it moves, and is athletic: a psychic landscape. Began another big one, more abstract, written from the bathtub: take care it doesn't get too general. Good-night, sweet princess. You are still on your own; be stoic; don't panic; get through this hell to the generous sweet overflowing <u>giving</u> love of spring.

P.S." Winning or losing an argument, receiving an acceptance or rejection, is no proof of the validity or value of personal identity. One may be wrong, mistaken, a poor craftsman, or just ignorant – but this is no indication of the true worth of one's total human identity: past, present & future!

February 21: Tuesday

Crash! I am psychic, only not quite drastically enough. My baby "The Matisse Chapel" which I have been spending the imaginary money from and discussing with modest egoism, was rejected by the New Yorker this morning with not so much as a pencil scratch on the black-and-white doom of the printed rejection. I hid it under a pile of papers like a stillborn illegitimate baby. I shuddered at the bathos in it. Especially after I read Pete DeVries recent scintillant "Afternoon of a Faun." There are ways and ways to have a love affair. Above all, one must not be serious about it.

Still, the accommodating mind imagines that the poems, sent a week before, must be undergoing detailed scrutiny. I shall no doubt get them back tomorrow. Maybe even with a note.

February 25: Saturday

So we are scrubbed, hair washed fresh, feeling gutted and shaky; a crisis is passed. We reassemble forces, marshal a stiff squadron of optimism, and trek. On and on. Earlier in the week I started thinking about how stupid I was to have to make all those final declarations to all those boys last term. This is ridiculous; it should not be. Not that I can't choose the people I want to spend my time with, but there must have been some reason for getting into a situation where there was nothing to do but be final and obvious.

Probably it was because I was too intense with one boy after another. That same horror came with them which comes when the paraphernalia of existence whooshes away and there is just light and dark, night and day, without all the little physical quirks and warts and knobby knuckles that make the fabric of existence: either they were all or nothing. No man is all, so, ipso facto, they were nothing. That should not be.

They were also very conspicuously not Richard; I eventually came to telling them this as if they had a fatal disease and I was oh, so sorry. Fool: be didactic, now: take boys named Iko and Hamish" for what they are which may be coffee or rum and Troilus and Cressida or a sandwich on the mill race. These small particular things are good in themselves. I do not have to do them with the Only Soul in the world in the Only Body that is mine, my true one. There is a certain need of practical Machiavellian living: a casualness that must be cultivated. I was too serious for Peter, but that was mainly because he did not participate in the seriousness deeply enough to find out the gaiety beyond. Richard knows that joy, that tragic joy. And he is gone, and I should probably be glad. It would somehow be more embarassing to have him want to marry me now. I would, I think, probably say no. Why? Because both of us are moving toward security and somehow, accepting him, he might be drowned, squashed, by the simple bourgeois life I come from with its ideals for big men, conventional men: he is someone I could never live home with. Maybe someday he will want a home, but he is so damn far from it now. Our life would be so private: he would perhaps miss the blood background and social strata I don't come from; I would miss the healthy physical bigness. How important is all this? I don't know: it changes, like looking in different ends of a telescope.

Anyway, I am tired, and it is Saturday afternoon and I have all the academic reading and papers to do which I should have done two days ago, but for my misery. A lousy sinus cold that blunted up all my senses, bunged up nose, couldn't smell taste see through rheumy eyes, or even hear, which was worst, almost. And atop of this, through the hellish sleepless night of feverish sniffling and tossing, the macabre cramps of my period (curse, yes) and the wet, messy spurt of blood.

Dawn came, black and white graying into a frozen hell. I couldn't relax, nap, or anything. This was Friday, the worst, the very worst. Couldn't even read, full of drugs which battled and banged in my veins. Everywhere I heard bells, telephones not for me, doorbells with roses for all the other girls in the world. Utter despair. Ugly, red nose, no force. When I was psychically saddest, crash, the sky falls in and my body betrays.

Now, despite the twitch of a drying cold, I am cleansed, and once again, stoic, humorous. Made a few criticisms of action and had a chance to prove points this week. Ran through lists of men I knew here, and was appalled: granted, the ones I'd told to take off were not worth seeing (well, it's true), but how few I knew were! And how few I knew. So, again, I decided, again, it is time to accept the party, the tea. And Derek" asked me to a wine-party Wednesday. I froze, like usual, but said probably and went. It was, after the first scare (I always feel I turn into a gargoyle when too long alone, and that people will point) it was good. There was a fire, five guitar players, nice guys, pretty girls, one Norwegian blonde named Gretta, who sang "On top of old Smoky" in Norwegian, and a divine hot wine and gin punch with lemon and nutmeg which was good to savor and relieved the tremors I'd been having prior to the breaking of the cold. Then, too, a boy named Hamish (who is probably another Ira") asked me out next week, and, quite by chance, said he'd take me to the St. Botolph's" party (tonight).

This was enough. I had acted, and this Good Thing happened. I am a victim of prestige, too. I mean, prestige-consciousness. And the superficiality of what I have written, the glib, smug littleness, is evident. But it is not me. Not wholly. And I twinge when I see such magnificent stuff. Not because I believe I'm jealous, but because of the blonde one being In. Fear is the worst enemy. And does she fear? Assuming humanity, yes. But, like Hunter," the bone structure and coloring can take it. And hide it. If there is any.

And I have learned something from E. Lucas Meyers" although he does not know me and will never know I've learned it. His poetry is great, big, moving through technique and discipline to master it and bend it supple to his will. There is a brilliant joy, there, too, almost of an athlete, running, using all the divine flexions of his muscles in the act. Luke writes alone, much. He is serious about it; he does not talk much about it. This is the way. A way, and I believe in not being Roget's trollop, parading words and tossing off bravado for an audience.

Now, friend C. writes too, and a certain social and public view has been learned from him. But, as I remarked that frozen winter night to himself, his ego is like an unbroken puppy: scampering about spurting effusively over everything, especially if Everything is admiring. He flies socially, from girl to girl and party to party and tea to tea; God knows when he has time to write, but it is too accessible. Although, justly, some of his poems are quite fine; he misses the athletic force of Luke, though, except in one or two poems, and can't sustain discipline in his less good ones, falling apart into facilities of speech which show up like a sagging hemline on a really good dress. Luke is all tight and packed and supple and blazing. He will be great, greater than anyone of my generation whom I've read yet.

So I am, however, not worth the really good boys; or is it me? If poems were really good, there might be some chance; but, until I make something tight and riding over the limits of sweet sestinas and sonnets, away from the reflection of myself in Richard's eyes and the inevitable narrow bed, too small for a smashing act of love, until then, they can ingnore me and make up pretty jokes. The only cure for jealousy that I can see is the continual, firm positive forging of an identity and set of personal values which I believe in; in other words, if I believe it is right to go to France, it is absurd to feel pangs because Someone Else has gone to Italy. There is no compare.

The fear that my sensibility is dull, inferior, is probably justified; but I am not stupid, if I am ignorant in many ways. I will tighten up my program here, knowing as I do that it is important for me to do a small number of things well, rather than a wide number sketchily. That much of the perfectionist is still with me. In this daily game of choice and sacrifice, one needs a sure eye for the superfluous. It changes every day, too. Some days the moon is superfluous, some days, most emphatically not.

Last night, blunted as I was by agony, revolted at food and the distant bumbling noise of talk and laughter, I ran out of the dining room and walked alone back to the house. What word blue could get that dazzling drench of blue moonlight on the flat, luminous field of white snow, with the black trees against the sky, each with its particular configuration of branches? I felt shut in, imprisoned, aware that it was fine and shudderingly beautiful, but too gone with pain and aching to respond and become part of it.

The dialogue between my Writing and my Life is always in danger of becoming a slithering shifting of responsibility, of evasive rationalizing: in other words: I justified the mess I made of life by saying I'd give it order, form, beauty, writing about it; I justified my writing by saying it would be published, give me life (and prestige to life). Now, you have to begin somewhere, and it might as well be with life; a belief in me, with my limitations, and a strong punchy determination to fight to overcome one by one: like languages, to learn French, ignore Italian (asloppy knowledge of 3 languages is dilettantism) and revive German again, to build each solid. To build all solid.

Went to psychiatrist this morning and liked him: attractive, calm and considered, with that pleasant feeling of age and experience in a reservoir; felt: Father, why not? Wanted to burst out in tears and say father, father, comfort me. I told him about my break-up and found myself complaining mainly about not knowing mature people here: that's it, too! There is not one person I know here whom I admire who is older than I! In a place like Cambridge, that is scandalous. It means that there are many fine people I have not met; probably many young dons and men are mature. I don't know (and, I always ask, would they want to know me?). But at Newnham, there isn't one don I admire <u>personally</u>. The men are probably better, but there is no chance of getting them for supervisors, and they are too brilliant to indulge in that friendly commerce which Mr. Fisher," Mr. Kazin" and Mr. Gibian" were so dear about.

Well, I shall look up Beuscher's friend, and plan to see the Clarabuts at Easter. I can give them youth, enthusiasm and love to make up for the ignorances. Sometimes I feel so very stupid; yet, if I were, would I not be happy with some of the men I've met? Or is it because I'm stupid that I'm not; hardly. I long so for someone to blast over Richard; I deserve that, don't I, some sort of blazing love that I can live with. My God, I'd love to cook and make a house, and surge force into a man's dreams, and write, if he could talk and walk and work and passionately want to do his career. I can't bear to think of this potential for loving and giving going brown and sere in me. Yet the choice is so important, it frighten me a little. A lot.

Today I bought rum and marketed for cloves, lemons, and nuts and got the recipe for buttered rum, which I should have had to take me through the beginning of my cold; but I will make it soon. Hamish is so bored, he drinks. How horrible. And I drink sherry and wine by myself because I like it and I get the sensuous feeling of indulgence I do when I eat salted nuts or cheese: luxury, bliss, erotic-tinged. I suppose if I gave myself the chance I could be an alcoholic.

What I fear most, I think, is the death of the imagination. When the sky outside is merely pink, and the rooftops merely black: that photographic mind which paradoxically tells the truth, but the worthless truth, about the world. It is that synthesizing spirit, that "shaping" force, which prolifically sprouts and makes up its own worlds with more inventiveness than God which I desire. If I sit still and don't do anything, the world goes on beating like a slack drum, without meaning. We must be moving, working, making dreams to run toward; the poeverty of life without dreams is too horrible to imagine: it is that kind of madness which is worst: the kind with fancies and hallucinations would be a bosch-ish relief. I listen always for footsteps coming up the stairs and hate them if they are not for me. Why, why, can I not be an ascetic for a while, instead of always teetering on the edge of wanting complete solitude for work and reading, and, so much, so much, the gestures of hands and words of other human beings. Well, after this Racine paper, this Ronsard-purgatory, this Sophocles, I shall write: letters and prose and poetry, toward the end of the week; I must be stoic till then.

February 26: Sunday

A small note after a large orgy. It is morning, gray, most sober, with cold white puritanical eyes; looking at me. Last night I got drunk, very very beautifully drunk, and now I am shot, after six hours of warm sleep like a baby, with Racine to read, and not even the energy to type; I am getting the dts. Or something.

Hamish came in cab, and there was a tedious time standing slanted against the bar in Miller's with some ugly gat-toothed squat grinning guy named Meeson trying to be devastatingly clever and making intense devastating remarks about nothing. Hamish pale, pink and light blue eyes. I drank steadily the goblets with the red-gold Whiskey Macs, one after the other, and by the time we left an hour later, I felt that strong, silted-up force that makes one move through air like swimming, with brave ease.

Falcon's Yard," and the syncopated strut of a piano upstairs, and oh it was very Bohemian, with boys in turtle-neck sweaters and girls being blue-eye-lidded or elegant in black. Derrek was there, with guitar, and Bert" was looking shining and proud as if he had just delivered five babies, said something obvious about having drunk alot, and began talking about how Luke was satanic after we had run through the poetry in St. Botolph's and yelled about it: satanic Luke, very very drunk, with a stupid satanic smile on his pale face, dark sideburns and rumpled hair, black-and-white checked baggy pants and a loose swinging jacket, was doing that slow crazy english jive with a green-clad girl, quite black-haired and eyed and a good part pixie, and when they stopped dancing, Luke was chasing her around. Dan Huys" being very pale, frightfully pale and freckled, and me at last saying my immortal line of introduction which has been with me ever since his clever precocious slanted review: "Is this the better or worse half?" and he looking incredibly young to even think hard yet. Than Minton," so small and dark one would have to sit down to talk to him, and Weissbort," small again and very curly. Ross," immaculate and dark. They were all dark.

By this time I had spilled one drink, partly into my mouth, partly over my hands and the floor, and the jazz was beginning to get under my skin, and I started dancing with Luke and knew I was very bad, having crossed the river and banged into the trees, yelling about the poems, and he only smiling with that far-off look of a cretin satan. He wrote those things, and he was slobbing around. Well, I was slobbing around, "blub, maundering" and I didn't even have the excuse of having written those things; I suppose if you can write sestinas which bam crash through lines and rules after having raped them to the purpose, then you can be satanic and smile like a cretin beelzebub.

Then the worst happened, that big, dark, hunky boy, the only one there huge enough for me, who had been hunching around over women, and whose name I had asked the minute I had come into the room, but no one told me, came over and was looking hard in my eyes and it was Ted Hughes." I started yelling again about his poems and quoting: "most dear unscratch-able diamond" and he yelled back, colossal, in a voice that should have come from a Pole, "You like?" and asking me if I wanted brandy, and me yelling yes and backing into the next room past the smug shining blub face of dear Bert, looking as if he had delivered at least nine or ten babies, and bang the door was shut and he was sloshing brandy into a glass and I was sloshing it at the place where my mouth was when I last knew about it.

We shouted as if in a high wind, about the review, and he saying Dan knew I was beautiful, he wouldn't have written it about a cripple, and my yelling protest in which the words "sleep with the editor" occurred with startling frequency. And then it came to the fact that I was all there, wasn't I, and I stamped and screamed yes, and he had obligations in the next room, and he was working in London, earning ten pounds a week so he could later earn twelve pounds a week, and I was stamping and he was stamping on the floor, and then he kissed me bang smash on the mouth and ripped my hairband off, my lovely red hairband scarf which has weathered the sun and much love, and whose like I shall never again find, and my favorite silver earrings: hah, I shall keep, he barked. And when he kissed my neck I bit him long and hard on the cheek, and when we came out of the room, blood was running down his face. His poem "I did it, I." Such violence, and I can see how women lie down for artists. The one man in the room who was as big as his poems, huge, with hulk and dynamic chunks of words; his poems are strong and blasting like a high wind in steel girders. And I screamed in myself, thinking: oh, to give myself crashing, fighting, to you. The one man since I've lived who could blast Richard.

And now I sit here, demure and tired in brown, slightly sick at heart. I shall go on. I shall write a detailed description of shock treatment, tight, blasting short descriptions with not one smudge of coy sentimentality, and when I get enough I shall send them to David Ross. There will be no hurry, because I am too desperately vengeful now. But I will pile them up. I thought about the shock treatment description last night: the deadly sleep of her madness, and the breakfast not coming, the little details, the flashback to the shock treatment that went wrong: electrocution brought in, and the inevitable going down the subterranean hall, waking to a new world, with no name, being born again, and not of woman.

I shall never see him again, and the thorny limitations of the day crowd in like the spikes on the gates at Queens last night: I could never sleep with him anyway, with all his friends here and his close relation to them, laughing, talking, I should be the world's whore, as well as Roget's strumpet. I shall never see him, he will never look for me. He said my name, Sylvia, and banged a black grinning look into my eyes, and I would like to try just this once, my force against his. But he will never come, and the blonde one, pure and smug and favored, looks, is it with projected pity and disgust? at this drunken amorphic slut.

But Hamish was very kind and would have fought for me. It gave him a kind of glory to take me away from them, those fiends, and I am worth fighting for, I had been nice, to him, he said.

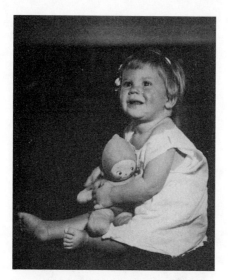

1 Sylvia Plath, October 13, 1933

2 Studio photograph of SP, aged 2, 1934

3 Otto Plath, studio portrait, 1924

4 Aurelia Schober Plath, 1972

5 SP and Marcia Brown skiing in Francestown, New Hampshire, February 1951

6 Haven House party for first-year students, May 1951. SP is third from left, front row

Baby sitter at Marblehead Mass. 1951

7 SP with Frederic Mayo and Joanne Mayo
(seated on Plath's lap) on beach, summer 1951

8 SP in her bathrobe at Haven House, 1952

9 Smith College Press Board, *Hamper*, 1952. SP is second from left, back row.

10 SP and Joan Cantor at Nauset Beach, Cape Cod, Massachusetts, August 1952

11 Studio photograph of SP, fall 1952

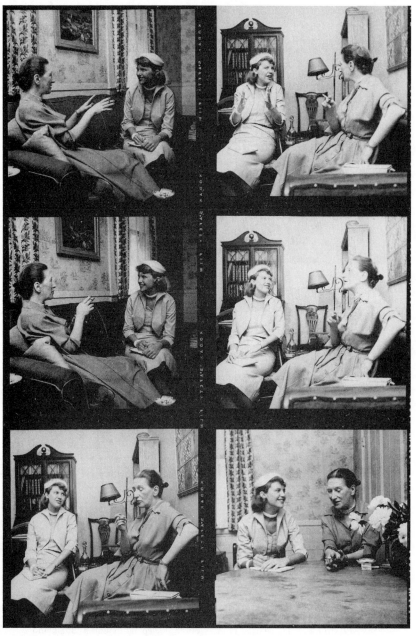

12 Contact sheet of SP interviewing Elizabeth Bowen for *Mademoiselle*, May 26, 1953

13 SP in a hallway, Smith College, 1952/1953

14 Smith College Honor Board, *Hamper*, 1953.
Seated (l. to r.): SP, Dr. Marion Frances Booth, Helen Whitcomb Randall, and
Alison L. Cook. Standing (l. to r.): Maria Canellakis and Holly Stair

15 SP at the Quadigras dance, Smith College, May 1954

16 SP in front of the President's House, Smith College, 1954

17 Marianne Moore talking to SP, April 15, 1955

18 Studio portrait of SP by Eric Stahlberg, 1955

19 SP as maid of honor at Ruth Freeman's wedding, June 11, 1955

We walked out as the blonde one was coming in, and Oswald said in his dry sarcasm something about "Tell us about bone structures" and that was the last party at Saint John's where I lost the red glove, as tonight I lost the red bandeau which I loved with all the redness in my heart. Somehow these sluttish nights make me have a violent nunlike passion to write and sequester myself. I shall sequester. I don't want to see anybody because they are not Ted Hughes and I never have been made a fool of by a man. They are phonies, Hamish said: He is the biggest seducer in Cambridge. Shall I write, and be different? Always, I grab it, the writing, hold it to me, defend, defend, against the flux, the sameness of faces. He said my name, Sylvia, in a blasting wind which shot off in the desert behind my eyes, behind his eyes, and his poems are clever and terrible and lovely.

Well, Hamish and I took an incredibly long time walking about the misty streets in the moonlight and all was blurred behind a theatrical scrim of fog, and vague boys in black gowns staggered and sang. We hid behind a car, and he said, the proctors are out after me, and I kept blithering on about having faith and being lucky, always, if you believe in something, because you can walk on water. Finally, after many strange streets which I did not know, being far far away in a land of whisky and merrydown, saying Ted to the lampposts and chiding myself with Hamish, Hamish, keeping saying it aloud, to him, because he took me away safely. We came to the gates of Queens, and I wanted like a baby to lie down and rest, just peace, peace, I kept whispering. Five boys, five late babies came up, and surrounded me, gently saying, what are you doing here, are you all right, my you smell nice, that perfume, and may we kiss you, and I just stood there huddled to the iron fence, smiling like a lost lamb and saying dear, dear, babies, and then Hamish was among them, and they climbed over and crossed the wooden bridge that Newton once put together without bolts.

Hamish helped me up on the wall, and in my tight skirt, I tried to step over the spikes; they pierced my skirt, my hands and I felt nothing, thinking from the great distance that I might at last lie on a bed of spikes and not feel it, like the yoga, like celia copplestone, crucified, near an anthill, at last, peace, and the nails went through my hands, and my legs were bare to the thigh, and I was over. The stigmata, I said, frozen, looking at those raw frigid hands that should have been bleeding. But they were not bleeding. I had gotten over in an act of sublime drunkenness and faith. And then we went to Hamish's room and lay on the floor by the fire and I was just so damn grateful for his weight on me and his mouth which was nice, and begged that he scold me, and he just said I wasn't a whore or a slut like I said but only a very silly girl and he kind of liked me and when would I learn my lesson. When? When? So it was suddenly two-thirty, and I couldn't imagine being illegal, but I was, and we managed by the light of two matches to get downstairs, and he walked out, a dark lone figure against the pale white blur of snow in the dead quiet crescent court.

He beckoned, I came walking along the outer path, through the crust of snow, breaking, hearing the dry crunch and then crossing the snow field to him, waiting for the sudden flash of light, the: hey, there, you stop! and the crack of pistols. It was dead quiet, and the cold snow was in my shoes and I felt nothing. We went through the gap in the box hedge, and Hamish tested the ice on the river; he said the porter chopped it, but it was whole, and bore us, and we crossed, free, walking home. And I heard the clocks striking three in the deathly quiet of dreaming people, and climbed the stairs somehow and went somehow after hot milk to bed.

And now it is today, and I slept only six hours and am weary and waiting till next day and next to recover. I must write Racine paper, today, dinner with Mallory (can I live) and then Ronsard desperately tomorrow.

Perhaps at dinner they will be laughing at me. Well, they are hardly white, even though they are men. But I shall be sober, oh for so long. Why won't I see him again? But I won't. I dream of banging and crashing in a high wind in London. But I want to know him sober; I want to write to him, with that kind of discipline and blaze. So I shall shut up and get some sleep tonight and tomorrow, and do so.

February 27: Monday

Briefly, most briefly. Slept late this morning, woke in dark at 11:30 feeling worthless and slack, yet stubborn. Determined to jettison all obligations for two days and recuperate. This fatigue sucks leeching at my veins. It takes more effort to write excuses than to drag around, but I confronted Miss B. after lunch, and dressed in slacks and favorite paisley velvet jersey to make me feel better, and wrote a full-page poem about the dark forces of lust: "Pursuit". It is not bad. It is dedicated to Ted Hughes.

Felt sloppy and lazy; awkward not to go out, for food, because of seeing people: there is such a difference from being able to trudge across the mucky snowfields to eat and being able to translate French and write a paper. It is as if I were hypnotized. The concentrated spurts of work I've done make me feel I've been here for eons. Yet I've let French go completely, and must do penance. I have such a damned puritanical conscience that it flays me like briars when I feel I've done wrong or haven't demanded enough of myself: I feel I've cheated myself on languages: I haven't really <u>worked</u> at learning it, and I must be tutored in German next year, instead of Italian. I must do a little reading of French (one hour) every day after this week. And two hours of writing (only, when I do poems, it eats up the whole day in a slow lust which I can't resist).

New Year's Rules: get only one supervision next term; enough time to write and read languages. Think up ideas for articles. My God, Cambridge is full of scientists, printing presses, theater groups, and all I need is guts to write about them. That's why reporting on assignments is good, because it gives an excuse to overcome the initial shyness. Perhaps I'll try out for Varsity" next term. Also I must give a party or two: sherry, tea or even dinner for 4. We'll see. Anything to <u>give out</u>.

Mother wrote today with a good letter of maxims; skeptical as always at first, I read what struck home: "If you compare yourself with others, you may become vain or bitter - - - for always there will be greater and lesser persons than yourself . . . . Beyond a wholesome discipline, be gentle with yourself. You are a child of the universe no less than the trees and the stars; you have a right to be here." Those words spoke to my heart with peace, as if in comment, kindly, on my life, my days. That first, touched on that ricocheting judgment I've made: despairing of the inferior, disintegrated men I know (who I can't consider for marriage) and blowing up the blonde one and the figure-heads all out of proportion. Envy and pride, and where's the golden mean, the man who can be mine, I his. When I start getting jealous of the five editors of <u>Mlle</u> for being married (with a pang - - - this might be me, that sweet word: success) or Philip Booth" for writing poems for the NY and having a wife and all that, it is time to build up some inner prowess; I am letting too much go vacant; I must build up a little series of sitting ducks, possible ambitions, to knock down, or I'll find <u>myself</u> sitting at the beginning of Easter vacation, addled as an egg, twiddling my thumbs. We get well first, then we work. Meanwhile, read Hopkins for solace.

March 1:" Thursday

It is somehow march and very late, and outside a warm large wind is blowing so that the trees and clouds are torn and the stars are scudding. I have
been gliding on that wind since noon, and coming back tonight, with the gas
fire wailing like the voice of a phoenix, and having read Verlaine and his
lines cursing me, and having just come newly from Cocteau's films "La Belle
et La Bête" and "Orphée" can you see how I must stop writing letters to a
dead man and put one on paper which you may tear or read or feel sorry for.

So it is. Stephen Spender was at sherry this afternoon, blue-eyed and
white-haired and long since become a statue who says "India, it depresses
me terribly" and tells of the beggars who will always be beggars throughout eternity. Young men are leaving ships full of flowers and poems, and
souls - - - delicate as snowdrops - - - duck belled white heads in my
teacups.

I can hear the wounded, miraculous furry voice of the dear bête whispering
so slow through the palace of floating curtains. And the Angel Heurtebise
and Death melt through mirrors like water. Only in your eyes did the winds
come from other planets, and it cuts me so, when you speak to me through
every word of French, through every single word I look up bleeding in the
dictionary.

I thought that your letter was all one could ask; you gave me your image,
and I made it into stories and poems; I talked about it for awhile to everyone
and told them it was a bronze statue, a bronze boy with a dolphin, who
balanced through the winter in our gardens with snow on his face, which I
brushed off every night I visited him.

I made your image wear different masks, and I played with it nightly and in
my dreams. I took your mask and put it on other faces which looked as if
they might know you when I had been drinking. I performed acts of faith to
show off: I climbed a tall spiked gate over a moat at the dead hour of three in
the morning under the moon, and the men marveled, for the spikes went
through my hands and I did not bleed.

Very simply, you were not wise to give me your image. You should know
your woman, and be kind. You expect too much of me; you know I am not

strong enough to live merely in that abstract Platonic realm out of time and flesh on the other side of all those mirrors.

I need you to do this one more thing for me. Break your image and wrench it from me. I need you to tell me in very definite concrete words that you are unavailable, that you do not want me to come to you in Paris in a few weeks or ask you to come to Italy with me or save me from death. I think I can live in this world as long as I must, and slowly learn how not to cry at night, if only you will do this one last thing for me. Please, just write me one very simple declarative sentence, the kind a woman can understand; kill your image and the hope and love I give it which keeps me frozen in the land of the bronze dead, for it gets harder and harder to free myself from that abstract tyrant named Richard who is so much more, being abstract, than he really is in this world . . . . For I must get back my soul from you; I am killing my flesh without it.

Tuesday afternoon: March 6, 1956

Break through the barriers; I am in great pain, and another shell of the so circumscribed understanding is shattered. All the neat tight desperate schedules are gone, and I got a letter from my Richard this afternoon which shot all to hell but my sudden looking in myself and finding what I feared and fought so hard not to find: I love that damn boy with all I've ever had in me and that's a hell of a lot. Worse, I can't stop; being human, even, it would take me a good two or three years to get to know anybody enough to like him enough to love him enough to marry him. So, I am in a nunnery, for all practical purposes. Worse, not in a nunnery, but surrounded by men who constantly remind me that they are not Richard; I hurt Mallory, and maybe a few others, in a fury of revulsion (and, looking at Mallory, however sorry I am for that ruthlessness of mine, I know it could be no other way now, so revolted am I).

I love him to hell and back and heaven and back, and have and do and will. Somehow, this letter killed finally all those niggling doubts: you're as tall as he; you weigh more than he; you're physically as strong & healthier; you're more athletic; your home and background and friends are too placid and conventional to accept or understand him and will color your view in time: all this: Basta!

So, out of this hurt and sickness, this mad wish to just spend everything I have to go to Paris and calmly, quietly confront him, feeling my will and my love can melt doors: out of this, I re-type the letter I wrote in answer to his which he may never read, and will probably never answer, because he seems to want a break clean and scrupulous as the edge of a guillotine:

"Only listen to me this last once." For it will be the last, and there is a terrible strength to which I am giving birth, and it is your child as it is mine, and so your listening must christen it.

The sun is flooding into my room as I write and I have spent the afternoon buying oranges and cheese and honey and being very happy after having for two weeks been very ill, because I can see every now and then how one must live in this world even if one's true full soul is not with one; I give of my intensity and passion in minute homeopathic spoonfuls to the world; to the cockney woman in the subway lavatory when I said: look I'm human and she looked in my eyes and believed me and I kissed her; and the crooked man who sells malt bread; and a little dark-haired boy running a dog which urinated on the bridge post over a pool of white swans: to all these, I can give my fantastic urges of love, in little parcels which will not hurt them or make them sick, for being too strong.

I can do this, and must do this. I hoped in a night of terror that I was not bound to you with that irrevocable love, for ever. I fought and fought to free myself as from the weight of a name that could be a baby or could be a malignant tumor; I knew not. I only feared. But although I have gone crying (god, have I) and battering my head against spikes, desperately thinking that if I were dying, and called, you might come, I have found that which I most feared, out of my weakness. I have found that it is beyond your power ever ever to free me or give me back my soul; you could have a dozen mistresses and a dozen languages and a dozen countries, and I could kick and kick; I would still not be free.

Being a woman," it is like being crucified to give up my dearest lares and penates, my "household gods": which are all the small, warm gestures of knowing and loving you: writing you (I have felt smothered, writing a kind of diary to you, and not mailing it: it is getting ominously huge, and each time is a witness of a wrestling with my worst angel) and telling you my poems (which are all for you) and little publishings, and, most terrible of all, seeing you, even for the smallest time, when you are so near, and god knows when we shall be pardoned for being so scrupulous.

This part of the woman in me, the concrete, present, immediate part, which needs the warmth of her man in bed and her man eating with her and her man thinking and communing with her soul: this part still cries to you: why, why will you not only see me and be with me while there is still this small time before those terrible years and infinite years; this woman, whom I have not recognized for 23 years, whom I have scorned and denied, comes to taunt me now, when I am weakest in my terrible discovery.

For, I am committed to you," out of my own choice (although I could not know when I let myself first grow toward you that it would hurt, hurt, hurt me so eternally) and I perhaps know now, in a way I never should have known, if you made life easy and told me I could live with you (on any terms in this world, only so it would be with you) - - - I know now how deeply, fearfully and totally I love you, beyond all compromise, beyond all the mental reservations I've had about you, even to this day.

I am not simply telling you this because I want to be noble; I very much didn't want to be noble. That most intimate immediate woman (which makes me, ironically, so much yours) tormented me into delusion: that I could ever free myself from you. Really, how ridiculous it was: how should a mistress free me. When even you, and even what gods there are, can not free me, tempting me with all kinds of men on all sides?

I thought even," at the most desperate time, when I was so sick and could not sleep, but only lie and curse the flesh, whom I was going to marry two years ago in a spluge of contrived social-conscience: we looked so well together! So he is coming to study in Germany, and I thought perhaps if I could keep him skiing and swimming I might live with him, if only he never wrote, or let me argue with him (because I always win) or looked at a bed. This cowardice terrified me; for it was that. I could not admit then, as I do now, the essential tragic fact: I love you with all my heart and soul and body; in your weakness as in your strength; and for me to love a man even in his weakness is something I have never all my life been able to do before. And if you can take that weakness in me which wrote my last cringing, begging-dog letter and admit that it belongs to the same woman who wrote the first letter in her strength and faith, and love the whole woman, you will know how I love you.

I was thinking of the few times in my life" I have felt I was all alive, tensed, using everything in me: mind and body, instead of giving away little crumbs, lest the audience be glutted with too much plum-cake.

Once, I was on the top of the ski slope, having to go down to a small figure below, and not knowing how to steer; I plunged; I flew, screaming with joy that my body braced and mastered this speed; and then a man stepped carelessly in my path and I broke my leg. Then there was the time with Wertz" when the horse galloped into the street-crossing and the stirrups came off leaving me hanging around his neck, jarred breathless, thinking in an ecstasy: is this the way the end will be? And then there are the many many times I have given myself to that fury and that death which is loving you, and I am, to my own knifing hurt, more faithful than is kind to my peace and my wholeness. I live in two worlds and as long as we are apart, I always shall.

Now that this sudden articulate awareness of my most terrible eternal predicament has come to me, I must know that you understand this and why I had to write you then and now: if you do not ever want to write to me again, send me a blank, unsigned postcard, something, anything, to let me know that you did not tear my words and burn them before knowing that I am both worse and better than you thought. I am human enough to want to be talking to the only other human who matters in this world.

I suppose I was most appalled that you should bind me to you (so that neither of us have the power to break this, through all hate, venom, disgust and all the mistresses in the world) and that you could leave me thus cut open, my heart utterly gone, without anesthetic or stitching; my vital blood was spilling on the barren table, and nothing could grow. Well, it still is spilling. And I wonder why you fear seeing me even in the time we have: for I have faith in you, and cannot believe (as I once wanted to) that it's merely for convenience, so I won't overlap with other women. Why must you be so much like Brand: so utterly intransigeant?

I could see it, if you thought your being with me would bind me to you more, or give me less freedom to find someone else, but knowing now, as I do and you must, that I am so far bled white that no mere abstinence of knives can cure me, why do you forbid our making the small, limited world we have. Why so tabu? I ask you to ask yourself this. And if you have the courage or understanding in you, to tell me.

When I was weak, there was a reason; now I see none. I see not why I should not live in Paris with you and go to your classes and read French with you. I am not any more perilous, outside myself. Why do you make our case (which is hell enough, and we have enough to test us in these coming cruel years) so utterly and absolutely rigid? I can take the even harder horror of letting myself melt into feeling again, and knowing it must freeze again, if only I can believe it is making a minute part of time and space better than it would have been by stubbornly staying always apart when we have so little time to be near.

I ask you to turn these things in your heart and mind, for I see a sudden deep question now: why do you flee me, if you know I would rather make life rich under shadow of the sword? You said before that I wanted something of you you couldn't give. Well, so I do. But now I understand what must be (which I didn't then) and understand also that my faith and love for you cannot be blunted or blinded by drinking or hurling myself into other men's beds. I found this, and know this, and what do I have?

Understanding. Love. Two worlds. I am simple enough to love the spring and think it foolish and terrible that you can deny it to us when it is the wonder of it that is uniquely ours. With that strange knowing that comes over me, like a clairvoyance, I know that I am sure of myself and my enormous and alarmingly timeless love for you; which will always be. But in a way, it is harder for me, for my body is bound to faith and love, and I feel I cannot really ever live with another man; which means I must become (since I could not be a nun) a consecrated single woman. Now if I were inclined to a career as a lawyer or journalist that would be all right.

But I am not. I am inclined to babies and bed and brilliant friends and a magnificent stimulating home where geniuses drink gin in the kitchen after a delectable dinner and read their own novels and tell about why the stock market is the way it will be and discuss scientific mysticism (which, by the way, is intriguing: in all forms: several tremendous men in botany, chemistry, math and physics, etc. here are all mystics in various ways) - - - well, anyhow, this is what I was meant to make for a man, and to give him this colossal reservoir of faith and love for him to swim in daily, and to give him children; lots of them, in great pain and pride. And I hated you most, in my unreason, for making me woman, to want this, and making me your woman alone, and then making me face the very real and terribly immediate possibility that I would have to live my life chastely as a schoolteacher who sublimated by influencing other women's children. More than anything else in the world I want to bear you a son and I go about full with the darkness of my flame, like Phedre, forbidden by what auster pudeur, what fierté?

In a way, I suppose, I felt you were like Signor Rappacini who bred his only daughter to exist solely on perilous poisonous food and atmosphere exhaled by a poisonous exotic plant: she became fatally unable to live in the normal world, and a death-menace to those who wanted to approach her from this world.

Well, that is what I became, for a while. I really cruelly wounded several people here, desperately, because I wanted to get back to that normal world and live and love in it. Well, I couldn't, and I hated them for showing me that.

Now this is all, and you must know it. But you must also let me know by some means that you know it. If you are not too scrupulous and why, now, are you? You might write me a letter and tell me honestly why, if you do not fear my childish pleadings, which are far far away and dead after today, why you refuse to let me make a few days of spring with you in Paris? I am coming, and I feel it is somehow now honestly superfluous and much too abstract and stringent of you to pretend there is left any important reason why you do not wish to see me.

I know if I were coming in a chaos, a turmoil of accusations, or even making it harder to leave you again (which it may well be, but it is possible to manage this) - - - I know then that you would have a right to forbid. But all I want is to see you, be with you, walk, talk, in a way which I imagine people past the age of love could do (although I am not pretending I would not passionately want to be with you) but we have come into the time and understanding where we could be most kind and good to each other. Even if those eternal years are upon us, why do you now refuse to see me?

I believe I can ask you this, and not have you feel that there is some disease of over-scrupulosity that makes letters reveal weakness or carry contagion. As a woman who know herself now, I ask you. And if you have courage, and look into yourself, you will answer. For I shall come, and respect your wish;

but I shall also now ask why you so wish. Do not, o do not make an artificial stasis which is unbreakable; break and bend and grow again, as I have done only today."

So I have, too, and cannot stop the crying, those flooding cathartic tears, that angle for life and hope even as my love is across that damn channel, telling me not to come. Why, why?

I am physically exhausted, and this comes, breaking my neat schedule of reading so I cannot go to bed. Unless I cut all my classes tomorrow. And Redpath, which my mind is not ready for. And yet I feel that sleep somehow now comes before all else: there is much to bear, and I must be strong and rested to be brave enough.

I read his letter and walked the wet pine-dark path tonight, with the warm rain dripping and shiny on the black leaves in the humid blurred starlight, crying and crying with this terrible pain; it hurts, father, it hurts, oh father I have never known; a father, even, they took from me.

It all sounds so simple and ridiculous: I found out today that I am deeply and for-god-knows-how-long in love with a boy who will not let me come to him out of a ferocious cold scrupulosity and not only will not let me come, when it is possible, but is going this spring away to where it will be for infinite years impossible. And he will not let me come.

And I think of that magnificent poem by James Joyce "I hear an army charging upon the land" ... and the final irrevocable lines which after that dynamic thunder of horses and whirling laughter and long green hair coming out of the sea, there is the simple series of words with all the anguish in the world:
"My heart, have you no wisdom thus to despair?
My love, my love, my love, why have you left me alone?"

If I were a man, I could write a novel about this; being a woman, why must I only cry and freeze, cry and freeze?

Let me be strong, strong with sleep and strong with intelligence and strong with bone and fiber; let me learn, through this desperation, to spread myself out: to know where and to whom to give: to Nat, to Gary, to Chris even, to Iko, to dear Gordon in his way: to give the small moments and the casual talk that very special infusion of devotion and love which make our epiphanies. Not to be bitter. Save me from that, that final wry sour lemon acid in the veins of single clever lonely women.

Let me not be desperate and throw away my honor for want of solace; let me not hide in drinking and lacerating myself on strange men; let me not be weak and tell others how bleeding I am internally; how day by day it drips, and gathers, and congeals. I am still young. Even twenty-three and a half is not to late to live anew. I don't think I'm a Celia Copplestone after all: I honestly hope that in five years I can make a new life if he is not coming; I certainly cannot just go on blindly thinking of ways in which to fill enough years so that he will come; I want somehow to live with him always: to wake and have him greet me, and bear children to him: such heavenly pride to carry his child. My god. I can't bear bathos. Let there be none; get it out, and decide what to do, and do it.

Oh someone, I run through names, thinking someone: hear me, take me to your heart, be warm and let me cry and cry and cry. And help me be strong: oh Sue, oh Mr. Fisher, oh Ruth Beuscher," oh, mother. My god. I shall probably write Elly. That will help objectify this. She knows as much as Sue; it was her bed once.

I luxuriate in this; I have been so tight and rigid since two months. Two months alone. I luxuriate in suddenly letting go and crying my insides out. I am tired and have been very discouraged by having sinus for so long, and that helps: all the despair, coming at me when I am most weak. I will read Hopkins: and, when our lives crack, and the loveliest mirror cracks, is it not right to rest, to step aside and heal; why must I rush on, dragging myself to classes: I don't really need that "escape" work offers: I need rest: I have enough, thank god, that I want to do, to read, to think about. I must have a sherry party next term, or tea, and ask Chris and Gary and Nat and Keith" (who seems so sweet) and a girl or two. The right people and right number are terribly important: so everyone will talk and communicate, and not be chaotic, or too narrow.

It is 8:30 and I am terribly tired and want only to go to bed and wake without this clutter of things to do: re-read Ghosts, think about it, read all

Electras, read and translate Ronsard, leap into Webster & Tourneur and write paper. Then next week. Next week it all slows, rides easy under apple boughs. Is there ever enough time in the world?

Some day I shall be grateful for having had two years, two years paid for (we hope) by the government to read and read what I love and study French and German and travel the far countries. Some day when I am stumbling up to cook eggs and feed milk to the baby and prepare dinner for my husband's friends, I shall pick up Bergson, or Kafka, or Joyce, and languish for the minds that are outleaping and outskipping mine.

But how so? Are these women, this Miss Burton," this old Miss Welsford" (who is coming to the end of her vigor), better for their years reading and writing articles on "The Political Tragedies of Jonson and Chapman" or books on "The Fool" and fearing the bright brilliant young ones like Dr. Krook?" I would like a life of conflict, of balancing children, sonnets, love and dirty dishes; and banging banging an affirmation of life out on pianos and ski slopes and in bed in bed in bed.

Someday. Today I lived through supervision: it is something even to live through hours of obligation now, without screaming: gently, gently, stoic one. Today, by the way, Miss Burton checked us when we impulsively said suicide was an escape (on defensive?) and she said it was a brave thing – if one could only live corruptly and miserably in this world, – to leave it. NB. So we thought. Once.

Also today, Mrs. Krook discussing redemptive power of love, which philosopher F.H. Bradley left out of his Ethical Studies (much to his weakening) and which we will hear about in DH Lawrence. Next week. And I got back my paper on "Passion as Destiny in Racine" with the comment that passion is only <u>one</u> aspect and not the fatal holocaust I made it: also mixed my metaphors re flames and cancers and appetites: well, not in that poem: which I wrote about Ted; only, like Lou Healy's poem "Circus in Three Rings" was triggered by Lou," but written for Richard.

After Dr. Krook, had good lunch at Eagle with Gary." Was only woman in dark pub atmosphere of good solid food, beer, sane talk, all-male; and was I better for it! Gary is blond, blue-eyed, most Germanic in a gentle way: a fine, analytic, slow, deliberate way of thinking: has met all the best minds everywhere, it seems: Here, studies under Daiches, Krook, maybe Lewis: has all the finest minds: E.M. Forster: well, anyway, I felt better than at any of our previous run-ins because I communicated, while intensely, at least with more calm and felt I wasn't just talking hectically at him, the way I have before, feeling he scorned my mind as female and illogical and slightly absurd.

Gary and I went on about scientific mysticism, probability in foreknowledge in cards, hypnotism, levitation, Blake (whom he admires immensely): I've read Wallace Stevens, and he's just beginning: I find myself whittling sharper edges on my talk, thinking more before speaking: trying to prove points, not just flooding in gestures: learn more of this, it's good. Gary can help, too, because, while essentially tinged with a romantic streak (almost laughable, in a nice way, he seems so pedestrian, the curse of a particular analytic temperament somehow) he is scrupulously accurate and logical; I'm having coffee with him this Thursday, tea with him & Keith next week. I must read. Read Bergson.

I was struck, even in a tedious session in a dark cubicle in Newnham with Miss Barrett" lisping sweetly to those immature girls performing an autopsy on "Les Fleurs du Mal," that I could translate Baudelaire by sight, almost immediately, except for the obvious vocabulary words I didn't know: I felt the sensuous flow of the words and meanings, and plunged in them alone, longing to read him and live with him. Maybe someday French will actually be natural to me.

Shopped this afternoon after lunch, in fickle rain and sun for mackintosh I felt I must have: suitable for spring and travel, doesn't get dirty: found ideal one, smart cut, brazen gold buttons, and bought oranges, apples, cheese, nuts and honey. Always feel happy shopping; gives me a sense of "things" somehow: taste color and touch, and a certain power and plentitude.

All this to stop crying. Also had marvelous cathartic blowup with Jane on Sunday. After she had underlined five of my new books in pencil with notes; evidently she felt that since I'd already underlined them in black, nothing further could harm them; well, I was furious, feeling my children had been raped, or beaten, by an alien. And this led to all the other things: To France (where I realize that I threw myself at Richard, making her feel superfluous: I was so desperate then! I wanted so to establish my identity across the Atlantic, and if he'd denied me then, and our love then, it would have been very bad.) At least I had the fruition of our best love yet over here.)

To St. Botolph's Review: and the evidence that there is no league of all the two I admire: Luke and Ted, and she against poems; she felt reciprocal "immorality" about sending poems to Chequer with my Chris, etc. Also felt clumsy in my presence even as I felt obtuse in hers.

Turns out we're too much alike, too much the same, ironically, to be friends closely here: One American girl who writes and is humorous and reasonably attractive & magnetic is enough in any group of Englishmen here. When we are together, it is a mutual grabbing for queenship; both of us must be unique, and we can only truly be so when apart: we overlap in too many places (especially being over here the only American girls doing our program and writing) to want to be together. So that at last is that. And the hydra is slain. Thank god. We will go on, openly, being agreeable, but not seeking each other out or writing the wrong footnotes on each other's actions. The air is cleared.

And now that the hour is nine and I've been writing the better part of the day, in a coma, not being able to breathe for crying, I shall depart, read Ghosts, bed, then tomorrow morning cut all but Redpath and read classics; then Ronsard in spare afternoon & evening hours.

Why does that green guck still spawn itself endlessly out of my head, dripping and clinging in my throat, my lungs, blocking in glutinous hunks behind my eyes: I feel sometimes I am blowing out the putrescent remains of my own decayed brains.

But in the midst of this terrible sorrow, this sickness, this weariness, this fear, I spin still: there is still the blessing of the natural world and those simply loved ones and all to read and see.

Called another Fulbright from an ad. May drive to Paris with him (is he short, deformed, ugly, ancient, married? He has a Phd from Columbia and sounded young and pragmatic). I feel I somehow must just walk to Richard's early one morning and stand there, strong and contained, and say: hello. Then I can just walk in Paris, and maybe find some people to look up, some plays to see, and then take the train to meet Gordon in Germany. Gordon will be dear and strong and heal me by his kindness, even if he knows nothing of all this aching. I refuse to be weak and tell anyone else.

We shall see. It would be a kind of final gesture to face him (Oh, yes, I still think I have power: he may be sleeping with his mistress, leaving orders for me not to be admitted, or not there, or if there, worse, refuse to see me, I am not desperate now. And that is why I feel I can honestly go. I do love him and do not see why I can't be with him to enjoy life, knowing we must leave it. We shall see.)

Come my coach. Goodnight, goodnight.

Thursday night; March 8

A small, very small word before bed. I have drunk two glasses of sherry by myself tonight and am feeling clean and scrubbed from a bath with hair freshly washed and shaken dry and silky by the fire. Today was strange. Suddenly I have been seeing a great deal of Gary Haupt.

Now there is nothing miraculous in this, except that he seems to want to see me; perhaps it is one of those cases where he was put off by my emotional, irresponsible gushing at first and is finding that I can talk lucidly and with certain perception. At any rate, he is a most calming influence and as mentioned before, I like the logical solidity of his mind; he has a fine mind.

Well, this morning I arose, descended the stairs to find a check from the travel agency about a pound less than the sum Skyways said I was supposed to get, and so planned innumerable conversations in my head to get my shillings by confronting the agency with cool, devastating words. Tomorrow, maybe. Breakfast: gagged on fishcake, couldn't manage stinking bony kipper, and so subsisted on strong acrid coffee diluted with much milk, and toast and butter and marmelade. Dressed just in time to bike off to Gary's after translating a little more Ronsard.

I love Pembroke: ran across the cobbled court and up the circular stone staircase with the gothic-arched keyhole windows that make me fell I should be wearing Elizabethan silks, and Gary was ready with homeground coffee and news to tell me, mainly re Keith and Mrs. Krook (who might have me, Gary sounded optimistic). We talked on and on about Yale and Smith and various personalities (the professors he knows are phenomenal) and also Sassoon: it gave me such a peculiar surge of illicit pleasure to casually say: oh, yes, I knew him; tell me about him. And so Gary went on and gave me a very distant opinion of why they rejected Sassoon from the Manuscript club:" he wasn't a group man; dissatisfied with Yale; giving up all to write; influence of family name, etc. I chuckled inside, and thought: o, my god. How absurd. And I love him so!

Well, we talked through Willey" (last lecture, which gave me a pang: I quite love that man) and ran to catch Krook who picked flaws in Arnold a bit, but said he began work on the consideration of Christ (humanist view) as unique man who preached gospel of redemptive power of love; went on to D.H. Lawrence & incredible fable: "Man Who Died." She read sections, felt chilled, as in last paragraph of "The Dead", as if angel had hauled me by the hair in a shiver of gooseflesh: about the temple of Isis bereaved, Isis in search. Lawrence died in Vence, where I had my mystic vision with Sassoon; I was the woman who died, and I came in touch through Sassoon that spring, that flaming of life, that resolute fury of existence. All seemed shudderingly relevant; I read in a good deal; I have lived much of this. It matters. Finished Lawrence before supper.

Well, then, after Krook, Gary asked me to Miller's to dinner, which threw me, as I'd thought I might have invaded his male environment unwantedly at the Eagle yesterday. We had cold, thick tomato juice, chicken and mushrooms in red wine casserole, roast potatoes, carrots, red wine, and finished with an exotically cooling dish of pineapple-and-icecream with coffee, talking much of English and American temperaments, painting (we'd both wanted to go to art school at one time) and going on and on. How strange; he has evidently had a very unhappy love experience with an art-student fulbright girl for whom he stayed in London all Christmas vacation. Behind his apparently dry, analytical, Germanic imperturbable face, there is this Romantic self: he almost had tears in his eyes when he said, looking away: "She didn't appreciate intelligence." Well, he certainly has that. I feel so secure with him primarily because I am absolutely devoid of any physical attraction toward him. There is no battle of the sexes, really. His mind is fine, and I find myself developing by becoming articulate with him. But he is that kind which is my total opposite: what fires are there, and there must be some rather deep smouldering ones, are by no means evident in his being: his gestures, looks, syntax. He is the exact opposite of Richard. With him, I am utterly intellectual and platonic; as much so as I've ever been; and there is, paradoxically, a safety and relief about this. Tea on Sunday, with him at Keith's, and Vienna choirboys at King's chapel Wednesday; have borrowed two books: on 17th century metaphysicals & elizabethan lyrics.

Rushed home, to Barrett, more Ronsard, slow, painstaking, but I do like; and am learning. Foul supper of dry rice, kennel-ration curry, sallow parsnips, grayed mashed potato, and cloying melted icecream with burnt caramel suace. Mrs. Lameyer writes that grammy was taken back to hospital; can't eat. Is she dying of cancer, even as I write? That dark vile mystery; I love that woman, I can't believe she could go out of the world and me not there; I can't believe home could be without her. It sickens me; afar off, I think of her, and cry. Those presences, those people loved and gone into the dark; I rail and rage against the taking of my father, whom I have never known; even his mind, his heart; his face, as a boy of 17 I love terribly. I would have loved him; and he is gone. I feel somehow much too old, with all the older ones dead before I have known them, and only the young ones, the babies, under me. I am so close to the dark. My villanelle was to my father; and the best one. I lust for the knowing of him; I looked at Redpath at that wonderful coffee session at the Anchor, and practically ripped him up to beg him to be my father; to live with the rich, chastened, wise mind of an older man. I must beware, beware, of marrying for that. Perhaps a young man with a brilliant father. I could wed both.

It grows late, and I tired, and there being cramming for Webster & Tourneur this weekend. I shall really rip about next term, being on my own, with Miss Burton Monday: fight for Krook, & plenty of free time, to write, read on my own, around criticism, metaphysicals, et. al. Am dropping, weary, but dogged; more happy for some reason. Am respecting self more.

March 9: Friday

A small something must be said about today, because as far as we're concerned, it's the first day of spring, and we can, really, breathe again and sleep through the night.

Woke up this morning after nine hours of sleep, missed Northam lecture and lingered over stale congealed egg, coffee and toast and marmelade. Felt like singing while cleaning up room: wrote a letter about how I'm forging a soul amidst great birth pangs and about how I felt concerning Sassoon to mother, included copies of two best poems: "Pursuit" and "Channel Crossing".

Also wrote her re new inspiration: application for Eugene Saxton fellowship for young writers. My whole emphasis has swung again, to a realization that if I enter this academic, critical world, I'll spend all my time reading and reading, and that I need a healthy overturning of the apple-cart, almost a refusal to read beyond a point, and to read more of what influences my writing, rather than paralyses it: contemporary work. I want to stress the living-writing life now; the academic-critical-teaching life can wait. If I write this term (having whittled my program to a bare minimum: moralists and French, perhaps German) and live in Spain a month with Elly, then return to write for a month, and take off again, I should amass enough, what with my various prizes, might make me able to write a novel (love and suicide being large part: also college environment, position of intelligent woman in world: think in chapters, stories, fight through to triumph) and poetry to keep me in discipline. I'd rather write a novel, and I could live in southern France (Vence? Grasse?) or Italy or Spain for a year and forge my soul and just read French and German and soak up art, all on my own. I've got to try that. Think of ways. All prizes: from Seventeen, to Mademoiselle, to recent poetry coups, will be invaluable; also, newspaper experience.

It's a dream. We will work toward it. It would also help getting a job in the states if I'd a novel published. Begin it this summer. Outline: intelligent woman, fight, triumph: toleration of conflict, etc. Make complex and rich and vivid. Use letters to Sassoon, etc. I'm getting excited. Make it tense & tough, and for god's sake, not sentimental.

Well, today: biked to laundromat singing and letting wind blow through hair: same chilled-champagne air as in Nice and Vence in January: clear brilliant cold light. Travel agency most nice about refund and information re trains from Paris to Munich. Bank, Heffer's: bought lots of books by Huxley: the most recent about "HEaven and Hell": of antipodes in mind: reached under hypnosis or mescalin. Post office; dropped laundry & baggage back home and went through fens where everyone was sitting out having sandwiches and ale in the sun on the mill race. Got the last 4 sandwiches at the sun-flooded Anchor and sat reading Huxley with espresso coffee. Back here now: <u>New Yorker</u> rejected poems, with a "sorry, please try again" at least. All these days of hope, it's been coming back to me regular mail. But today, fortunately, I could write ten novels and vanquish the gods; outside, tennis balls ping, birds twirp and chirr, and I must read Marlowe and Tourneur to do my last paper for Burton. Cheers for spring; for life; for a growing soul.

Saturday morning: March 10

I cannot keep still; I am on the edge; the dream comes to taunt me in the morning sun. Last night's whiskey with Hamish, glass after glass tossed down, at least five or six, is still strutting latent havoc in my veins, ready to betray me; the caffeine from the coffee this morning tenses fiber too, and I am appalled: <u>Granta</u> with bad poem by girl with same initials, ironically enough; bitterness about clique: they publish friends, always friends; must write some short sketches for them and Varsity after this next week: potent, witty, punchY: something they can't reject without being immoral.

What I want to say is: HE is here; in Cambridge. Smiling blub-faced Bert, all scrubbed and polished, met me in the street on the way to the College library: "Lucas and Ted threw stones at your window lastnight." A huge joy galloped through me; they remembered my name; it was the wrong window and I was out drinking with Hamish, but they exist in this world; I talked on a minute, Ted it seems is assigned to write a synopsis of James Joyce's "Ulysses" (!!!) and so on. I murmured something about: tell them to drop by, or something, and cycled off.

Now, tense, rebellious, with spring sprouting outside my window and playing merry hell with my blood, I have to cram for paper on Webster & Tourneur: why oh why didn't I do it yesterday. I should have known; and today will be shot to hell because he is Here and he may not bother to come again, having dates with Puddefoots or something, and I wait here, quivering like polished barbwire. If only I weren't so tired and full of feathers from that whiskey, I'd be able to cope. If he did or didn't. Probably the blonde one is lunching with him even now. Thank god Bert is hers. But He. Oh he.

Spent last session with Dr. Davy" this morning articulating: I fear oppressive and crushing forces, if I do not plot and manage and manipulate my path, joining: academic, creative & writing, and emotional & living & loving: writing makes me a small god: I re-create the flux and smash of the world through the small ordered word-patterns I make. I have powerful physical, intellectual and emotional forces which must have outlets, creative, or they turn to destruction and waste (e.g. drinking with Hamish, and making indescriminate love).

Please let him come; let me have him for this British spring. Please please.

Ran into Marain Frisch, very beautiful and fine, in French dept. of Heffer's; planned supper Tuesday night just before she left. May see her in Switzerland; coincidence, but how lovely: with Gordon, maybe?

Please let him come, and give me the resilience & guts to make him respect me, be interested, and not to throw myself at him with loudness or hysterical yelling; calmly, gently, easy baby easy. He is probably strutting the backs among crocuses now with seven Scandinavian mistresses. And I sit, spider-like, waiting, here, home; Penelope weaving webs of Webster, turning spindles of Tourneur. Oh, he is here; my black marauder; oh hungry hungry. I am so hungry for a big smashing creative burgeoning burdened love: I am here; I wait; and he plays on the banks of the river Cam like a casual faun.

March 10: Postscript

Oh the fury, the fury. Why did I even know he was here. The panther wakes and stalks again, and every sound in the house is his tread on the stair; I wrote mad girl's love song once in a mad mood like this when Mike didn't come and didn't come, and every time I am dressed in black, white and red: violent, fierce colors. All the steps coming up and running past I made into his step and cursed the usurpers that took his place. About Lou Healy I felt this smouldering desperate force that made, by persistent willing, certain situations take place.

Now I lay, burning, fevered with this disease, and the sun glared at me all at once, a lowering orange eye, blank and mocking; it set on time, I clocked it. And again the dark eats at me: the fear of being crushed in a huge dark machine, sucked dry by the grinding indifferent millstones of circumstance. He is at a party now, I know; with some girl. My face burns, and I am turning to ash, like the apples of sodom and gomorrah.

I lay and heard the steps on the stair and the knock at the door and I leapt up to welcome the fruit of my will. It was John, coming to ask me to the movies;

I wanted to see that movie, but wouldn't let myself; it will be harder to stay here and watch the clock go from eight to ten, and read the Duchess of Malfi. How I hate him; how I hate Bert for feeding my fury which I had quelled by wrenching out that poem last week.

I writhed and angered and talked to John, bidding him goodbye and sending him off; imagine, he tried to persuade me to through Copenhagen instead of Paris!

I remember the dreams I've had the last two nights: the first: trying out for a play and being in a huge gymnasium where the clowns and actors were practising. Everywhere there was the heavy circumstance of menace: I ran, huge weights were dropping on my head; I crossed the slippery floor, and afar off, laughing hobos bowled large black balls at me to knock me down; it was a terrifying time of jeopardy: similar to those moments caught between traffic, lumbering trucks and busses and bicycles coming from all angles, when I can only stand fast and shut my eyes, or blunder into a tangle of traffic and hope for luck. Black balls, black weights, wheeled vehicles, and the slippery floor: all trying to crush me, moving in heavy blundering attempts, just missing.

Then I was in my black coat and beret: Isis bereaved, Isis in search, walking a dark barren street. Into a café, searching, searching, and in a chair, hiding his face behind a newspaper, sat the dark one, suave, grinning. I stood, appalled, and he uncurled, and came with me, dark and sweet. Another dark man with the face of a slavic cretin, or a yellowed spaniard, of some indeterminate race, accosted me and said in a thick, furry voice "It is night," He thought I was a whore; I broke away, running after my Richard, who walked ahead, his back toward me.

Men's voices downstairs. I am sick, sick. With this desperate fury. God knows what will happen to me in Paris. Love turns, lust turns, into the death urge. My love is gone, gone, and I would be raped. "It is night."

March 11: Sunday morning:

Another day of hell. He is on the prowl, all the fiends are come to torment me: and I alone am escaped to tell thee. All of the eyes, the multitudes of eyes that report his being here. This morning, a male tread, a knock at the door; it is He? It was: mere Chris, after all this 10 days of absence. Only, a Chris gifted with instruments of torture: having just seen Luke and Ted down the street this very morning; they will not come. Not in the gray sober light of morning. They will not come.

But last night they came, at two in the morning, Phillipa said. Throwing mud on her window, saying my name, the two mixed: mud and my name; my name is mud. She came to look for me, but I was sleeping. Dreaming of being home in Winthrop" on a lovely new spring day, walking in pajamas down the streets of melting tar to the sea, the salt freshness, and squatting in the sea in a tangle of green weeds were clam-diggers with osier baskets, rising, one after the other, to look at me in my pajamas, and I hid in spring shame in the trellised arbors of Day's home.

Mail came through the sewer, and I got only bills. Mail and rice came through the sewer, that bubbling green mucky sewer we played in by the sea, transmuting what corruption, what slime-gilded periwinkles, into what radiant magic. They laughed and said they trusted the mail and rice coming through the sewer.

And all this while, those three boys in the dark were treating me like what whore, coming like the soldiers to Blanche DuBois and rolling in the gardens, drunk, and mixing her name with mud. Two reports today, to insert more needles in my skin. I must cram for my paper. Oh, god give me the guts to live through this week. Let me someday confront him, only confront him, to make him human, and not that black panther which struts on the forest fringes of hearsay. Such hell. They refuse to face me in daylight. I am not worth that. I must be, when if they ever come. They will not come. I don't want to eat, to go to tea today. I want to rave out in the streets and confront that big panther, to make the daylight whittle him to lifesize.

[Appendix 7 contains Sylvia Plath's 26 March 1956 – 5 April 1956 journal describing her spring vacation in Paris; Appendix 8 contains Sylvia Plath's 1 April 1956 list describing ways to win friends and influence people; Appendix 9 contains Sylvia Plath's 16 April 1956 journal fragment about Ted Hughes – ed.]

April 18"

now the forces are gathering still against me, and my dearest grandmother who took care of me all my life while mother worked is dying very very slowly and bravely of cancer, and she has not even been able to have intravenous feeding for six weeks but is living on her body, which will be all sublimed away, and then only she may die. my mother is working, teaching, cooking, driving, shoveling snow from blizzards, growing thin in the terror of her slow sorrow. I had hoped to make her strong and healthy, and now she may be too weak herself after this slow death, like my father's slow long death, to come to me. and I am here, futile, cut off from the ritual of family love and neighborhood and from giving strength and love to my dear brave grandmother's dying whom I loved above thought. and my mother will go, and there is the terror of having no parents, no older seasoned beings, to advise and love me in this world.

something very terrifying too has happened to me, which started two months ago and which needed not to have happened, just as it needed not to have happened that you wrote that you did not want to see me in paris and would not go to italy with me. when I came back to london, there seemed only this one way of happening, and I am living now in a kind of present hell and god knows what ceremonies of life or love can patch the havoc wrought. I took care, such care, and even that was not enough, for my being deserted utterly. you said that when you returned to paris, you said that you told me "brutally" your vacation would be spent. well, mine is spent too, brutally, and I am spent, giving with both hands, daily, and the blight and terror has been made in the choice and the superfluous unnecessary and howling void of your long absence. your handwriting has gone so wild and racked not all the devils could burn a meaning out of it.

[Appendix 10 contains Sylvia Plath's 26 June 1956 – 6 March 1961 journal, including drawings, descriptions, and poems written during her honeymoon in Spain and France with Ted Hughes – ed.]

Benidorm: July 15: Widow Mangada's house: pale, peach-brown stucco
on the main Avenida running along shore, facing the beach of reddish
yellow sand with all the gaily painted ~~wooden~~ cabanas making a maze
of bright blue wooden ~~legs~~ *sun* and small square patches of shadow. The
continuous poise and splash of incoming waves mark a ragged white
line of surf beyond which the morning sea blazes in the early sun,
already high and hot at ten-thirty; the ocean is cerulean toward
the horizon, vivid azure nearer shore, blue and sheened as peacock
feathers. Out in the middle of the bay juts a rock island, slanting
up from the horizon line to form a sloped triangle of orange rock
which takes the full glare of sun on its crags in the morning and
falls to purple shadow toward late afternoon.

Sun falls in flickering lines and patches on the second story
terrace through waving fans of palm leaves and the slats of
the bamboo awning. Below is the widow's garden, with dry dusty
soil from which sprout bright red geraniums, white daisies, *and*
roses; ~~and~~ spined cacti in reddish earthenware pots line the
flag-stone paths. Two blue-painted chairs and a blue table are
set under the fig-tree in the backyard in the shade; behind the
house rises the rugged purplish range of mountainous hills, dry
sandy earth covered with scrub clumps of grass.

Early in the morning, when the sun is still cool, and the breeze
is wet and salt-fresh from the sea, the native women, dressed
in black, with black stockings, go to the open market in the
center of town with their wicker baskets to bargain and buy
fresh fruit and vegetables at the ~~stalls~~: yellow plums, green
peppers, large ripe tomatoes, wreathes of garlic, bunches of
yellow and green bananas, potatoes, green beans, squashes and
melons. Gaudy striped beach towels, aprons and rope sneakers
are hung up for sale against the white adobe pueblos. Within
the dark caverns of the stores are great jugs of wine, oil and
vinegar in woven straw casings. All night the lights of the
sardine boats bob and duck out in the bay, and early in the
morning the fish market is piled high with fresh fish: silvered
sardines cost only 8 pesetas the kilo, and are heaped on the
table, ~~mixed~~ *strewn* with ~~occasional~~ *a few odd* crabs, star-fish and shells. *squid*

Doors consist of a swaying curtain of long beaded strips which
rattle apart with the entry of each customer and let in the
breeze, but not the sun. In the bread-shop, there is always the
smell of fresh loaves as, in the dark windowless inner room,
men stripped to the waist tend the glowing ovens. The milk-boy
delivers milk early in the morning, pouring his litre measure
from the large can he carries on his bicycle into each housewife's
pan which she leaves on her doorstep. Mingling with motor-scooters
bicycles and the large, shiny, grand tourist cars are the
native donkey carts, loaded with vegetables, or jugs of wine.
Workers wear sombreros, take siesta from two to four in the
afternoon in the shade of a wall, or tree, or their own carts.

The Widow's house has only cold water and no refrigerator; the
dark cool cupboard is full of ants. A shining array of aluminum
pots, pans and cooking utensils hang on the wall; one washes
dishes and vegetables in large marble basins, scrubbing them with
little snarled bunches of straw. All cooking-- fresh sardines fried
in oil, potato and onion tortillas, cafe con leche---is done on the
blue flame of an antique petrol burner.

Benidorm:" July 15: Widow Mangada's house: pale, peach-brown stucco on the main Avenida running along shore, facing the beach of reddish yellow sand with all the gaily painted cabanas making a maze of bright blue wooden stilts and small square patches of shadow. The continuous poise and splash of incoming waves mark a ragged white line of surf beyond which the morning sea blazes in the early sun, already high and hot at ten-thirty; the ocean is cerulean toward the horizon, vivid azure nearer shore, blue and sheened as peacock feathers. Out in the middle of the bay juts a rock island, slanting up from the horizon line to form a sloped triangle of orange rock which takes the full glare of sun on its crags in the morning and falls to purple shadow toward late afternoon.

Sun falls in flickering lines and patches on the second story terrace through waving fans of palm leaves and the slats of the bamboo awning. Below is the widow's garden, with dry dusty soil from which sprout bright red geraniums, white daisies, and roses; spined cacti in reddish earthenware pots line the flag-stone paths. Two blue-painted chairs and a blue table are set under the fig-tree in the backyard in the shade; behind the house rises the rugged purplish range of mountainous hills, dry sandy earth covered with scrub clumps of grass.

Early in the morning, when the sun is still cool, and the breeze is wet and salt-fresh from the sea, the native women, dressed in black, with black stockings, go to the open market in the center of town with their wicker baskets to bargain and buy fresh fruit and vegetables at the stalls: yellow plums, green peppers, large ripe tomatoes, wreathes of garlic, bunches of yellow and green bananas, potatoes, green beans, squashes and melons. Gaudy striped beach towels, aprons and rope sneakers are hung up for sale against the white adobe pueblos. Within the dark caverns of the stores are great jugs of wine, oil and vinegar in woven straw casings. All night the lights of the sardine boats bob and duck out in the bay, and early in the morning the fish market is piled high with fresh fish: silvered sardines cost only 8 pesetas the kilo, and are heaped on the table, strewn with a few odd crabs, star-fish and shells."

Doors consist of a swaying curtain of long beaded strips which rattle apart with the entry of each customer and let in the breeze, but not the sun. In the bread-shop, there is always the smell of fresh loaves as, in the dark windowless inner room, men stripped to the waist tend the glowing ovens. The milk-boy delivers milk early in the morning, pouring his litre measure from the large can he carries on his bicycle into each housewife's pan which she leaves on her doorstep. Mingling with motor-scooters bicycles and the large, shiny, grand tourist cars are the native donkey carts, loaded with vegetables, straw, or jugs of wine. Workers wear sombreros, take siesta from two to four in the afternoon in the shade of a wall, or tree, or their own carts.

The Widow's house has only cold water and no refrigerator; the dark cool cupboard is full of ants. A shining array of aluminum pots, pans and cooking utensils hang on the wall; one washes dishes and vegetables in large marble basins, scrubbing them with little snarled bunches of straw. All cooking - - fresh sardines fried in oil, potato and onion tortillas, cafe con leche - - - is done on the blue flame of an antique petrol burner.

We met Widow Mangada one Wednesday morning on the hot crowded bus jolting over the desert-dusty roads from Alicante" to Benidorm. She heard us exclaiming about the blue bay and turned from her seat in front of us to ask whether we spoke French. A little, we said, whereupon she broke explosively into description of her wonderful house by the sea, with garden and balcony-terrace and kitchen rights. She was a small, dark woman of middle age, stylishly dressed in white knitted lace over a black slip, white heeled sandals, terrifically comme il faut; her coal-black hair was done in many waves and curls, her saucer-black eyes were emphasized by blue eye-shadow and two startling black eyebrows pencilled straight slanting upwards from the bridge of her nose to her temples.

She bustled about getting native boys to put her baggage on their hand-drawn carts and hustled us to the main road, trotting slightly ahead and babbling in her peculiar French about her house, and how she was lonely and wanted to let out apartments, and she knew right away that we were "gentil". When we said we were writers and wanted a quiet place by the sea to work, she jumped to agree that she knew how it was, exactly: "I too am a writer; of love-stories and poems."

Her house, facing the cool blue blaze of the bay, was more than we had dreamed; we fell in love immediately with the smallest room, its french window-doors opening onto an balcony-terrace, perfect for writing: vines wove green leaves in the railing; a palm and a pine tree grew alongside shading one side, and a slatted bamboo awning could be drawn out to form a little roof as shelter from the direct noon sun. We knocked her down from the first price to 100 pesetas a night, figuring we could save immensely by doing our own marketing and cooking. From her rapid babble of French, mangled by a strong spanish accent, we gathered that she would trade Spanish lessons for English lessons, that she had been a teacher, and lived in France for three years.

As soon as we moved in, it became clear that Madame was not used to running a "maison" for boarders. There were three other empty rooms on the second floor which she evidently hoped to let out, for she spoke continually of how we must manage for "les autres", when they arrived. She had amassed a great quantity of white china plates, cups and saucers in the formal diningroom, and an equally large amount of aluminum pots and pans hung on hooks lining the kitchen walls, but there was absolutely no silver tableware. Senora seemed shocked that we did not carry knives, forks and spoons about with us, but brought out, finally, three elaborate place-settings of her best silver which she laid out, saying that this was only for the three of us, and she would soon go to Alicante to buy some simple kitchen silver for us and put her best silver away. Also, the problem of a small bathroom, fine for the two of us, but hardly fitted for eight, and the trouble of arranging cooking and dinner schedules on one petrol burner, seemed not to have occured to her either.

We held our breath and wished fervently that she would have no customers when she put up the sign: Apartments for rent, on our balcony-terrace. We had, at least, made sure that she would not use our balcony, which adjoined another larger room, as a selling point, by explaining that it was the only place we could write in peace, since our room was too small for a table, and the beach and garden were fine for vacationers, but not for writers' work-rooms. Occasionally, from our balcony, (where we soon took to eating meals: steaming mugs of cafe con leche in the morning, a cold picnic of bread, cheese, tomatoes and onions, fruit and milk at noon, and a cooked dinner of meat or fish with vegetables, and wine, at twilight under the moon and stars - - -) we could hear Senora conducting people around the house, speaking in her rapid staccatto French. But during the first week, although she had conducted several potential roomers about, no one had come. We had fun hazarding on the objections they might make: no hot water, one small bathroom, only an antique petrol burner - - - with such modern hotels in town, probably her price was too high: what wealthy people would be willing to market and cook? Who but poor students & writers like us? Perhaps the roomers might decide to eat out in the expensive restaurants; that was a possibility. We had found out, too, that although she had made wild, extravagant gestures when showing us about the house - - - pointing to an empty ice-less icebox, motioning out an imaginary electrical machine for making the freezing shower-water warm - - - that none of these comforts were forthcoming. We found the water from the taps was unpalatable and strange to taste; when the Senora miraculously produced a glass pitcher full of delicious sparkling water for our first dinner, we asked incredulous if it came from the taps. She burbled on evasively about the health-giving qualities of the water, and it was a full day before I caught her drawing up a pail of it from a cistern sunk deep in the kitchen, covered by a blue board. The tap water, it turned out, was "non potable".

The Senora was a fanatic about the house being "propre" for her prospective lodgers: we were to wash all dishes after meals, put them away, keep the bathroom tidy. She gave us two dishtowels to be hung behind the door, and hung up several decoy clean towels on the wall for "les autres." We were also to have a small petrol burner of our own for which we should buy petrol and matches, another dent in our desperate food budget of 40 pesetas a day for the two of us. In spite of her concern for the "propre" condition of the house, Senora washed her greasy dishes in standing cold water, often dirtier that the dishes themselves, scrubbing them with frayed tangles of straw.

Our first morning was a nightmare. I woke early, still exhausted from our continuous traveling, uneasy at the strange bed, to find no water in the taps. I tiptoed down the stone stairs to turn on the peculiar machine with odd blue-painted spigots and wires jutting out which the Senora had said "made water", turning the switch the day before, upon which there was a convincing rumble as some complicated machinery started up. I turned the switch; there was a blue flash, and acrid smoke began pouring from the box. Quickly I shut off the switch and went to knock on the Senoras door. No answer. I went upstairs and woke Ted, who was burnt scarlet from the day before in the sun.

Sleepily, Ted came down in his bathing trunks to turn the switch. There was another blue flash; no sound. He tried the light switch. No electricity. We pounded on the Senoras door. No answer. "She's either gone out or dead," I said, wishing for water to make some coffee; the milk had not yet come. "No, she'd have turned on the water if she'd gone out. She's probably lying in there refusing to get up." At last, grumpily, we went back upstairs to bed. About nine o'clock, we heard the front door open. "Probably she's sneaked around from the back to come in as if she'd been out all morning." I padded barefoot downstairs where the Senora, crisp in her white knitted dress, freshly made up black eyebrows, greeted me cheerily: "You slept well, Madame?" I was still smouldering: "There is no water," I said without preamble. "No water to wash or make coffee." She laughed a queer deep laugh which she used whenever anything went wrong, as if either I, or the water supply, were very childish and silly, but she would make it all right. She tried the light switch. "No light," she exclaimed triumphantly, as if all were solved. "It is so in all the village." "This is usual in the morning?" I asked coldly. "Pas de tout, de tout, de tout," she rattled off from under raised eyebrows, apparently just noticing my cool irony. "You must not take it so hard, Madame." She bustled into the kitchen, lifted the blue-painted lid by the sink, dropped a bucket on a string and drew up a sloshing pailful of clear water. "Plenty of water," she gurgled, "all the time." So that was where she kept her store of health-giving water; I nodded grimly and began and began to make coffee, while she ran next-door to investigate the state of affairs. I was pretty sure, that with my native inability to manage machines, I had "fused" something and blasted the whole water & electric supply in the town. Evidently it was just local, for the Senora fiddled with the machine, crowed that water was coming everywhere, and said never never to touch the machine but to call her immediately when we were worried about the water. She would fix everything.

We also had trouble with the petrol stove." For our first dinner I planned one of Ted's favorite suppers: a platter of stringbeans and fried fresh sardines which we had bought early at the fish market for 8 pesetas the kilo and kept cool in a home-made water-container of several pans covered with a wet-cloth and a plate. I put the beans on to cook, but after 20 minutes they were still as hard as they had been at first and I noticed the water wasn't even boiling; Ted doubted if there was any heat and said maybe the petrol was used up; he turned the heat higher and the flame burned a thin, smoking green. "Senora", we called. She came rushing in clucking from the living-room, whipped off bean-pot, cooking-ring and burner to reveal the damning sight of over an inch of frayed, burnt wick. We'd turned it up too high and the wick itself had been burning for lack of petrol. After filling the tank with petrol, messing about with the wick, raising the fresh part left, Senora started the burner again, tested the beans. She was not at all satisfied; running out of the room, she came back and tossed in a handful of powder which fizzed and foamed. I asked her what it was, but she just chuckled and said she had been cooking a lot longer than I and knew some "petites choses." Magic powder, I thought. Poison. "Bicarbonate of soda," Ted reassured.

Senora, we began to realize, had been accustomed to a far grander scale of living than her present circumstances. Each evening she set out to town to see about a "bonne" for cleaning house; the little girl who had been scrubbing floors the day we arrived had not showed up since. "It is the hotels," the Senora told us. "All the maids go to the hotels, they pay so much. If you have a maid, you must be very nice and careful of her feelings nowadays; she breaks your best china bowl, and you must smile and say: do not trouble yourself over it, mademoiselle." The second morning I came down to make coffee, I found the Senora in a soiled towel bathrobe, her eyebrows not yet drawn on, cleaning the stone floors with a wet mop. "I AM Not used to this," she explained. "I am used to three maids: a cook, a cleaner . . . three maids. I do not work when the front door is open, for the public to see. But when it is shut," she shrugged her shoulders, gestured comprehensively with her hands, "I do everything, everything."

In the milk-shop one day, we were trying to explain where we wanted our two litres a day delivered. The houses on the Avenida were not numbered, and it was impossible to make the delivery boy understand our elementary Spanish; finally a French-speaking neighbor was called in. "Oh," she smiled, "you live with Widow Mangada. Everybody here knows her. She dresses very stylish, with much make-up." The woman grinned as if Widow Mangada were a town character. "Does she do the cooking for you," she asked curiously. A kind of instinctive loyalty toward the Senora and her straightened circumstances sprang up in me. "Oh of course not," I exclaimed. "We do all our own cooking." The woman nodded and smiled like a cream-fed cat.

Mr. and Mrs. Ted Hughes' Writing Table: **77**
    In the center of the stone-tiled dining room,
directly under the low-hanging chandelier with its large
frosted glass bowl of light and four smaller replica
bowls, stood the heavy writing table of glossy dark polished
wood. The table top, about five feet square, was divided
lengthwise down the center by a crack which never stayed
closed, into which a drop-leaf might be inserted. At the
head of the table, Ted sat in a squarely built grandfather
chair with wicker back and seat; his realm was a welter
of sheets of typing paper and ragged cardboard-covered
notebooks; the sheets of scrap paper, scrawled across
with his assertive blue-inked script, rounded, upright,
flaired, were backs of reports on books, plays and movies
written while at Pinewood studios; typed and re-written
versions of poems, bordered with drawings of mice, ferrets
and polar bears, spread out across his half of the table.
A bottle of blue ink, perpetually open, rested on a stack
of paper. Crumpled balls of used paper lay here and there,
to be thrown into the large wooden crate placed for that
purpose in the doorway. All papers and notebooks on this
half of the table were tossed at angles, kitty-corner
and impromptu. An open cookbook lay at Ted's right elbow,
where I'd left it after finishing reading out recipes of
stewed rabbit. The other half of the table, coming into
my premises, was piled with tediously neat stacks of books
and papers, all laid prim and four-squared to the table
corners: A large blue-paper-covered notebook, much thinned,
from which typing paper was cut, topped by a ragged brown
covered Thesaurus, formed the inner row of books, close
to Ted's red covered Shakespeare, on which lay the bright
yellow wrapping paper with a black-inked rhyme which served
as birthday wrapping for a chocolate bar. Along the
edge of the table, from left to right, were a plaid round
metal box of scotch tape, a shining metal pair of sleek
scissors, an open Cassell's French dictionary on which
also opened, an underlined copy of Le Rough et Le Noire
in a yellow-bound ragged-edged paper-back edition, a bottle
of jet black ink, scrupulously screwed shut, a small
sketch book of rag paper atop Ted's anthology of Spanish
poems, and a white plastic sunglass case sewn over with
a decorative strewing of tiny white and figured shells, a few
green and pink sequins, a plastic green starfish and rounded
gleaming oval shell. The table top jutted over a border
carved with starry flower motifs and the whole stood on four
sturdy carved legs, alternating squared pieces carved with
the diagonally-petaled flower motif and cylindrical rings,
two of each; On two sides, the legs were joined by a fence
of wooden pillars, four in all, and a carved medallion in
the center depicting a frowning bearded face with handlebar
moustache.

Benidorm: July 22:" Sunday morning

It is only a little after eight thirty in the morning, and already we are becoming accustomed to our growing strict routine in the new house. Ted and I woke about seven, swatted at the hovering flies, listened to the bells of the donkey carts and the cry "Ya hoi" of the agreeable little bread woman with her basket of sugared rolls. Then I got up and took the milk we'd boiled yesterday, put it on to heat for my coffee con leche and Ted's brandy-milk, which we had with bananas and sugar. After cleaning up the kitchen and bedroom, I join Ted in our great spacious dining room which we consecrate solely to writing. The clean white plaster walls and immense dark oaken table and the cool stone tile floor and wide airy windows make it an ideal place to work without disturbance. My typing table by the little window looks out over our front porch, through the hanging leaves of the shady grape arbor to the hill of white pueblos slanting away from us.

The joy of exchanging the noisy, green neon-lit tourist boulevard by the sea, with the expensive hotels and depressing sight of idle, bored crowds, expensively dressed, sitting and dawdling over drinks as they watch other idle bored crowds pass along the promenade - - - the joy of exchanging all this for our native quarter, increases daily. Our hill road climbing up from the sea is lined with white worker's pueblos. Old tanned wrinkled women sit out in chairs at the cool of the day far into the twilight, their backs to the street, weaving thick rope nets or fine sardine-mesh. They are clad completely in black: stockings, dress, shoes, and even, for town shopping, a black mantilla.

Every morning and evening we hear the bells which herald the herd of elegant stepping black goats; yesterday I saw children clustering around the barn where one of the goats was being milked. Saturday market is the fullest of the week. Ted and I went about 8:30, the earliest we've been yet, and found all fresh and crowded and thriving, which abashed us for the lazy days we'd arrived at noon to find dried, withered vegetables. Every stand was loaded with produce, and as we passed, the saleswomen hawked their wares, crying out apples and peppers. For daring, we bought part of a large yellow summer squash (which I'd never cooked) called a calabash, I think, and two shiny purple vegetables which I imagined might be called zucchini, but not being sure, shall try to cook today according to zucchini recipe. Also loaded down with potatoes, tomatoes, eggs. The market, spread out on the beaten dirt square, included petrol stoves, all sorts and sizes of frying pans and table-ware, towels, aprons, lace shoes, coat-hangers. There was a wire cage full of nibbling brown and gray rabbits and another of clucking black and white chickens. We filled our straw market basket, feeling very proud; also bought some new fish, pescadillo, which I fried in egg and flour batter with great success.

Our new house is magnificent. We keep marveling that we bought it for the summer at the same price Widow Mangada was charging for her noisy small room, bad dirty bathroom, ant infested kitchen (all to be shared with "les autres", the piggy Spaniards) and terrace overlooking the sea (the honking staring gawking crowds on the boulevard, rather) which turned out to be the worst, not the best, feature. Ted was driven to retreat to the beds in the dark inner room, while after 10 in the morning, I was more conscious of being stared at on the balcony than of the typewriter in front of me. Now, there is utter peace. No fussy actress rushes into my new kitchen to snatch potatoes out of my hand and show me how to peel them her way, or peers under the lids of my frying pans on the petrol stove. We are left utterly tranquil. The first two days we were still recovering from our month of exterior business-rush living and the emotional turmoil of the week at the widow's; workmen hammered continually in the kitchen and bathroom, putting in the water motor for the shower, toilet and faucets. Finally, yesterday, they finished, plastered up the holes, and we have clean sparkling water, cold, but wonderful, much better than the widow's ancient faulty plumbing and wiring.

The whole house is almost an embaras de richesse: we've closed off two bedrooms, and don't use the sitting room at all. Our grand bedroom is large, cool, with a sturdy enormous dark wood bed and triple wardrobe with floorlength mirror of the same dark polished wood; against the bare white plastered walls, the effect is pleasant, spacious. The whole floor is paved with stone tiles, giving the effect of living at the cool bottom of a well. The large kitchen and pantry is my delight. Never did a new bride queen it over her deep-freeze, washing machine, pressure cooker, et. al. as I do over my one-ring petrol stove, single frying pan, cold water sink, tangles of straw for cleaning, and iceless storage pantry, where I keep my vegetables, bottles of oil, wine and vinegar, and all my cooking preparations. Yesterday I read through the vegetable section of my blessed Rombauer, mouth watering, to cull all the sauteed dishes: we have chiefly potatoes, eggs, tomatoes and onions, from which, during the summer, I hope to pull enough variety to keep Ted from roaring protest. How I love to cook; the delectable recipes in the book, with all the right touches of seasoning, and always the one ingredient which I don't have, make me long for the time when I can cook with modern range, icebox, and a variety of food. At least, if I manage on this narrow leash, I should be in heaven with the most modest of American kitchens.

Everything is going beautifully in this new place. I have a strong feeling that it is the source, and will be in the 10 full weeks to come, of creative living and writing. Yesterday Ted read me three new fables he'd just written for his fine animal book about how all the animals became:" the Tortoise one was the funniest and dearest yet; the hyena, more serious about a bitter perverted character, and the fox and dog alive with plot and marvelous Sly-Look and Four-Square. I have great hopes for this as a children's classic. Even as I write, Ted is working at the main table on the elephant and the cricket stories. Living with him is like being told a perpetual story: his mind is the biggest, most imaginative, I have ever met. I could live in its growing countries forever. I also feel a new direct pouring of energy into my own work, and shall break the jinx on my story writing this week, trying the bull-fight story and perhaps one on Widow Mangada (funny?) along with chapters in my new novel that might do for articles for Harper's; also an article, with sketches, on Benidorm for the Monitor. Must learn Spanish and translate French, too.

Never in my life have I had conditions so perfect: a magnificent handsome brilliant husband (gone are those frayed days of partial ego-satisfaction of conquering new slight men who fell easier and easier), a quiet large house with no interruptions, phone, or visitors; the sea at the bottom of the street, the hills at the top. Perfect mental and physical well-being. Each day we feel stronger, wider-awake.

The other night we climbed our road, Tomas Ortunio," for the first time. As we went up, the rows of white pueblos gave way to green orchards; we broke open the green fruit on one of the trees and found that we were in the midst of almond groves. The kernel was pale, bitter, undeveloped as yet. The soil turned dusty and reddish, spiked with dry yellow grass; an unfertile, unfriendly place, all stones and stunted twisted scrub pines. As we climbed, the sea spread out beneath us, a wide rim of blue, and the island looked closer, with sea behind it. We crossed the tracks of the little railway station, where hens scrabbled and scratched, and sat under a large pine where the wind soughed, watching the sea darken as the sun sank lower behind the purple hills at our back. Clouds scudded across the pale thin brightening white moon, which laid a paving of platinum-light on the ocean. The little green neons on the waterfront came on, and the weariness struck us as the bells of the town were striking nine. So we descended.

Yesterday, while we were marketing in the evening for wine and oil, a rain shower fell, and the lighting effects were startlingly beautiful: looking into the sun, which was shining, we saw through a silver sheet of rain a blinding shining street between dark pueblos; in the other direction, against dark clouds, the white pueblos shone, arched over by the most perfect complete rainbow I've ever seen, one end rooted in the mountains, the other in the sea. We bought a loaf of bread at our new shop, and, somehow elated by the rainbow, made our way through the fresh goat droppings to our white house with its bright border of pungent red geraniums.

Benidorm: July 23 (continued)[11]

Alone, deepening. Feeling the perceptions deepen with the tang of geranium and the full moon and the mellowing of hurt; the deep ingrowing of hurt, too far from the bitching fussing surface tempests. The hurt going in, clean as a razor, and the dark blood welling. Just the sick knowing that the wrongness was growing in the full moon. Listening, he scratches his chin, the small rasp of a beard. He is not asleep. He must come out, or there is no going in.

Up the hilly street come the last donkey carts from the village, families going home up the mountain, slow, the donkey bells jangling. A couple of laughing girls. A skinny little boy with a lean dog on a leash. A French-speaking family. A mother with a fussing white-lace frilled baby. Dark and quiet, completely still then under the full moon. A cricket somewhere. Then there is his warmth, so loved, and strange, and the drawing in to the room where wrongness is growing. Wrongness grows in the skin and makes it hard to touch. Up, angry, in the darkness, for a sweater. No sleep, smothering. Sitting in nightgown and sweater in the diningroom staring into the full moon, talking to the full moon, with wrongness growing and filling the house like a man-eating plant. The need to go out. It is very quiet. Perhaps he is asleep. Or dead. How to know how long there is before death. The fish may be poisoned, and the poison working. And two sit apart in wrongness.

What is wrong? he asks, as the sweater is yanked out, wool slacks, and raincoat. I'm going out. Do you want to come. The aloneness would be too much; desperate and foolish on the lonely roads. Asking for a doom. He dresses in dungarees and shirt and black jacket. We go out leaving the light on in the house into the glare of the full moon. I strike out hillward toward the weird soft purple mountains, where the almond trees are black and twisted against the flooded whitened landscape, all clear in the blanched light of wrongness, not day, but some beige, off-color daguerrotype. Fast, faster, up past the railway station. Turning, the sea is far and silver in the light. We sit far apart, on stones and bristling dry grass. The light is cold, cruel, and still. All could happen; the willful drowning, the murder, the killing words. The stones are rough and clear, and outlined mercilessly in the moonlight. Clouds cross over, the fields darken, and a neighboring dog yaps at two strangers. Two silent strangers. Going back, there is the growing sickness, the separate sleep, and the sour waking. And all the time the wrongness growing, creeping, choking the house, twining the tables and chairs and poisoning the knives and forks, clouding the drinking water with that lethal taint. Sun falls off-key on eyes asquint, and the world has grown crooked and sour as a lemon overnight.

In the station," Marcia had revived over a steaming mug of coffee con leche, and she found the Spanish train a complete and refreshing change in atmosphere.

Their compartment filled quickly with two Spanish soldiers, sweating in their heavy green uniforms and patent-leather hats, like pillboxes with a brim flap turned up in back; several workmen, and a dapper, ebullient chap with a small, clipped mustache who sat next to Marcia and attempted to flirt continually during the trip. Early on, one of the workmen brought out a worn leather flask filled with lukewarm wine, and passed it around to the company. Each man tilted his head back and neatly, with one hand, squirted a jet of wine into his mouth. One of the soldiers offered the flask to Tom, and Marcia was oddly proud that he managed to gulp down his jet without spilling a drop. Not wishing to refuse hospitality, Marcia, too, had taken up the flask, chorused on by the Spaniards. Tipping her head back, she managed to hit her mouth but neglected to stop squirting when she shut it, sending a spout into her eye. Everyone burst out laughing sympathetically, and Marcia felt accepted. After that, she took a drink each time the flask went round, and when she finally managed not to spill a drop there was hearty applause. The dandy next to her did tricks, making the wine run down his mustache into his mouth, swaying the jet from side to side. At each train stop, a different man got out to re-fill the flask. Marcia passed around the cheese and bread she'd bought before leaving Paris, and one of the workmen opened his rucksack and divided up tomatoes. By expressive gestures and occasional words from Marcia's pocket dictionary, they managed to hold a lively conversation with the Spaniards. One of the soldiers offered to buy any nylon stockings Marcia had with her; another commented on the passing scenery.

Feathery-gray French towns gave way to clusters of blinding white pueblos; small green fields fanned out into hot yellow plains of rye. Overhead, the noon sky blazed blue-white, and against the flat stretches of grain moved the dark figures of tanned workers in sombreros and their donkeys. Marcia exclaimed over storks nesting in church steeples, donkeys circling wells to draw water, and shepherds with crooks guarding flocks of delicately stepping goats. Occasionally they passed a herd of black bulls, roaming free and grazing at will on the open plains. Later, the land grew rocky, with queerly shaped pine trees rising on slender trunks, tapped for resin, to explode in dense, compact puffs of greenery. Tom reached for Marcia's hand across the aisle and grinned at her, his blue eyes crinkling at the corners. They'd been wanting to come to Spain, both of them, long before they'd met. And now, at last, on their honeymoon, they'd managed to scrape up enough money for a few days in Madrid and a week at the growing resort fishing-village of Benidorm, down the coast from Valencia.

By about four o'clock, the heat in the compartment was unbearable. Marcia, who usually turned to the Cape Cod sun like a plant, found herself telling Tom: "It's not the heat I can't stand, it's the dirt and the smells." The bottle of cold milk which she had brought, impractically, in her carrying-bag had soured immediately and, at a jerky stop, spilled out in a slosh of white curds on the floor; banana peels and cherry pits littered the compartment, and the stench of sweat and cheap tobacco from the workmen's hand-rolled cigarettes hung heavy in the stagnant air. For the rest of the trip, Marcia stood beside Tom in the hallway on the shaded side of the car, looking across at the white mesas lying like low-hanging clouds in the distance. Leaning out of the train window, she let the wind dry the perspiration and grime on her face, wondering if she might be condemned by some sophisticated heavenly order to wander through eternity in this present limbo - - - always dirty, hot, fatigued, longing only for a distant paradise of cold showers and clean sheets. By twilight, she was sheathed in a protective coat of numbness. Then, as she stared dull-eyed at the rocks, bare, deserted, purpling with shadow, the train swung all at once around a bend and, miraculously, a turreted palace sprang up before her. Even the Spaniards were crowding to the windows, jabbering excitedly among themselves.

"Must be the Escorial," Tom said. The palace seemed part of the natural landscape, hewn from the mauve rocks. A whole village spread out beneath it. Within an hour they were pulling into the station at Madrid.

[Appendix 10 contains Sylvia Plath's 4 August 1956 description of waves (entry 23) and Sylvia Plath's 13 August 1956 description of the bay at Benidorm, Spain (entry 26) – ed.]

Benidorm: August 14:" Tuesday

Woke in cool of morning with that usual dazed feeling, as if crawling out from a spider's web, fought upright, and revived over coffee and bananas with milk and sugar. Ted shopped for fish, bread and wine while I dressed: black linen skirt, white jersey, red belt and polka-dotted scarf to be bright and wifely for Alicante. We walked down the street, threading through fresh horse manure and the delicate peppering of goat droppings; sky blue and clear; mountains purply and cloudy-secret through favorite vista of knife-bladed green palm fronds. Old El Greco madman, thin, cadaverous, in faded red and white striped shirt, sitting as usual by water faucet. Donkey cart loading barrel of fresh water and four jugs full. Warm fresh bread smells from panaderia.

Walked past watermelon shop and wine shop to outskirts of town to begin hitching to Alicante. Bay mild blue, streaked with glassy patches of calm; boats drawn up along shore; sun beginning to heat up. Stood in dust in spotted shade at roadside; no cars for a while; bicycles and motorbikes only; bikes with box of red-crested cocks loaded on back; large hunk of swordfish steak; bundle of green-leaved branches. Crowded cars, then. Finally, two Spaniards, dark, not talking or trying to communicate to us, stopped; man next to driver got out and opened door as if he were chauffering us. Cool, pleasant ride to Villajoyosa through dusty reddish hills; overtaking donkey carts. Got out at their last stop: square of Villajoyosa, dusty, slummy; past tenements, held together by morning glory vines and geranium roots in gaudy pots; houses painted bright blue and red with white borders around windows

Villajoyosa more industrial; passed lots of garages; business just starting; plasterers casually tossing trowels of cement on wall, turning to stare at couple strolling down road; Ted in fine new khaki cotton shirt and dark pants, face pinked with sun; me tripping in wicked black heeled toeless shoes. Heat blazing now, no shade. Walked far out of town to almond groves thick with ripe nuts: green furry pods split on trees, showing brown pocked shell of nut; group of almond-pickers, their bamboo poles leaning up in trees, sitting in shade over wine-break: dungarees and sombreros; black-clad women; stared curiously too. Beyond them, we shook down a few almonds and Ted cracked them open between two stones. We sat on dusty wall and munched, rising to thumb cars; either too full or snobby; guardia civil in black patent-leather helmet & heavy green uniform biked past; we hid nuts. At last, as heat grew, a bleached blonde French couple with curly black poodle stopped to pick us up, going through Alicante.

We sat in back patting poodle, observing glimpses of blue sea through dusty red hills; reckless French driver, queer, soft, in delicately striped-textured white long-sleeved shirt, colored sunglasses and close-cropped metallic blond curly hair, looking very bleached. Wife, pretty, rounded chic French type, much bleached blonde hair, grown out dark at roots, pulled untidily back with several tortoise shell combs; narrow gold wedding band; browned with sun; arched plucked eyebrows and lively brown eyes; very merry and chichi. Man asked in accented English if we were English, and advised us that we'd have to hitch inland after Alicante, there were no coast roads.

We squealed around danger curves, passing lunbering trucks and two-wheeled donkey carts into the outskirts of Alicante: ancient fortress on hill overlooking city; clothes drying on bushes; then, beach, short, packed with people so thick under gaudy striped umbrellas that you couldn't see water; cheap garages; noisy avenue of palms; shrunk to biteable size after night-mare of first arrival, traumatic night walk along quais, and sleepless blaring room. Got out of French car, they wishing us bon voyage, and turned right on main avenue by white-coated policeman and little yellow streetcars. Vox," two flights up, cool office; pleasant dark curly haired French-speaking man at information desk; Ted began making out new application; auspicious day; young blond, slender-chinned English teacher arrived in khaki cloth suit and khaki and white pin-striped sport shirt; told us, with Spanish accent, that his mother was Spanish, father English. German boy arrived, also teacher; tall, handsome, blond sun-bleached streaks in brown curly hair; dark eyes. Came from near Hamburg; studied a year in America at U. of Illinois; taught English at Vox, also one class of German; showed me about teaching rooms, dark tables and chairs in U-shape about small blackboards; discreet blue-sea and green-tree travel posters. Most chivalrous chap; everybody very nice, encouraging about job in Madrid. Left feeling weight gone; optimistic. Concrete efforts, plans at becoming self-supporting on the way.

Began hitching just past beach; almost immediately, as we stood in shade of palms, long green German bus-car, vaguely familiar, stopped; going to Benidorm, full of fat stocky Germans. We got in third row of seats, saw blond red-cheeked little girl lying on second seat; stocky driver father turned, apologized for smell of child's urine pot, which he held up, covered, said she'd been sick. Rooted up fragments of German to talk to plump, concerned, pleasant mother who watched over child; second woman - - - grandmother? - - - fat, grizzled, neck thick as elephant's leg, sat silent in front.

Little girl, feverish, tossed in sheets, held finger; sweet child; mother explained she'd vomited, had diarrhea, convulsions - - - expressive rolling of eyes and tremors to illustrate this; they'd rushed to doctor in Alicante who said children got this sickness from the wind. Or the sun. Fine drive along shore road for first time; observed white and reddish stone houses on lonely sea front; San Juan beach; new era of projects beginning; me wanting to teach; both of us feeling world ready to sprout at fingertips, eager to work; got out at edge of Benidorm with an Aufwiedersehen.

Changed out of sweaty things to bathingsuit; tomato, pepper, onion and eggs fried for lunch; deep, exhausting nap; rose, feeling blackjacked, to recover slowly over coffee. Went across the street to get some more milk for supper; past lovely vista, white fence with plants, into house; old house, weathered peasant said milk would be ready soon. Glimpse of blue sea through fig trees, with wide green scalloped leaves, thick with green fruit; we decided to wait, Ted finding ant-track;" half an hour spent playing god.

Trail of black ants carrying straw grains or fly wings to hole; we lifted rock portal of house, threw confusion into clan; much bunching at break of new earth, retreats and fumblings. Saw two ants apparently stitched with cramp; almost transparent, beige, earth-colored spider running wildly around them, trussing them up with invisible web; ants struggling, slower; spider quick, running clockwise, counterclock wise; we tossed him another ant, bigger, which he looped in. Gave ants big dead fly, which they took with pincers, an ant to a leg, and stood, pulling? Saw still group of black ants; looked closer; all trussed to rock, twitching feebly and slowly, while black ant-spider guarded from rock, like robber baron. Big black silly beetle blundered over ants, like a rusty gentleman in pin-striped suit clambering up sand cliff.

Ancient black-clad woman, with one tooth, sunken gums baring it to the root, came to see what we were peering at; "muchos," she said, seeing the ants. Just then, a tinkling, and the flock of black and gray aristocratic goats rounded the wall of the corral with the little leprechaun of a blue-eyed milkman, in patched faded dungarees, rope sandals, and sombrero; he looked happy and pleasant; let us come into corral; new world; his world. Goats at home in bare, neat yard, drank out of water pails; black and white spotted kid. Two goats butted; one rising on hillock as if strung up from neck, poised, hung, butting down on other; playing.

Milkman's dog, still pup, tied up under fig tree; friendly, tight brown fur, floppy ears, loving and nuzzling. Goats butting again; milkman whirled, dropping stone in dead center, breaking up struggle; clucked and shooshed goats into shack: "their little house." We followed him in; dark, musky, dry, pleasant; ground cushioned with confetti-like strips of seaweed, "muy fresca"; wire netting overhead to protect from animals; milkman took goat's dug and squirted thin powerful stream with hiss, ringing into bottom of my aluminum pail. His big, pleasant, ugly black-clad wife, very broad-beamed, came out. Said she also milked goats; described frisky games of little kid with hand motions. Moon brightening through clouds as we left, clear-cut pine tree jagged against sky. Man happy, own world, out of earth; brother kept three cows on hill beyond railroad station. Left feeling good day; light yellow-green eyes of goats.

Benidorm: August 17:" Friday

Sat by bayside all morning after shopping for rabbit and myriad garnishes for gala stew. Sun hot on bare back; bay sheltered by high white cliff topped by white stucco and plaster pueblos, cubist study with colored clothes drying on lines on many leveled porches; cave-dwellings made of salt-crystal; sound of tubs of water being poured down cliff; dirty dish water sloshing in dark wet patches on sandy cliff; women lugging large pails of garbage: egg shells, melon rinds; fish heads, to empty in ocean along mole of rugged stones stretching sheltering arm into bay; water blazing blue in the sun, dark prussian streaks; smell of dead fish; confetti strips of seaweed drying in hummocky banks; burning sand under footsoles, beach pebbled black with creosote along water line.

In calm sheltered bay, small green and white motor boats and rowboats dipped; several large fishing boats moored; sardine boats drawn up in row on shore: full of coiled rope; three to four large global lights strung in loose wire mesh hung from metal rods above stern of boats; drew three boats in black line design; blotted out memory of maliciously blurred drawing yesterday; small square sails, gaff rigged boats; large rotting hulls, splayed open like fish skeletons in varying stages of decomposition; bubbles of creosote melted in sun; smell of tar, dead fish.

Clock bells striking hour and half hour from moorish castle. Keyhole blue-mosaic windows of house on cliff; sand strewn with feathery gray flakes of seaweedstrips, prickly grass clumps; mountains faint, misted, cloud white hung over tops; structured by sun to dimension. Cries of children swimming, fishing.

Fishermen's boys: skinny legged, lean, brown; bold and shy; loveable puppies: scrambled up behind me sitting perched on scalding deck of boat, nudged, chattered, pushed each other over boat edge; I turned and grinned at the littlest, with big brown eyes and peeling nose, pink and brown patches of skin, tow head, husky voice; he catapulted back into a bank of dry seaweed on the afterdeck and the other little boys laughed; big, bright awake eyes, dancing, merry; curious, and shy too; patched faded overalls; lean and brown and agile; pokes and fisticuffs. Mice and squirrel and cocker spaniel faces.

Fisherman coming in, coiling lines; wealthy German taking color photographs of his catch, laid out flapping and glistening in flat box: fish of all shapes and sizes: Fish: sheened and wet in sun, colored and speckled and striated like rare glistening shells: small tight-fleshed fish with black streaks on shimmering pale blue sides; spined ugly mouthed brown speckled fish; wicked black Moray eel with triangular head, black nasty eyes and gorgeous yellow brocaded back; red and pink shots of light from fins. Swimmer wading out of sea gripping squirming small octopus which twined and writhed long hanging legs; absurd bullet head; cracked octopus down on shore, legs piling and coiling, gift to fisherman.

Strolled past rows of cabanas: fat tan bulging women, lipstick, earrings, rubbing oil into mounds of flesh packed into tight black bathingsuits; bandy legged, paunchy staring hairy men; very pale fat woman in dark glasses and florid two piece yellow flowered bathing suit rubbing lotion into double layered fat of midriff; old woman in vile pale lavender suit washing toes warped with bunions in wash of waves on shore; fat swarthy little boy with greasy black hair and religious medal around neck bobbing on rise and fall of waves in red inner tube. Ginger-headed albino man with dead white skin, edged with painful pink, sitting swathed to the waist in striped beach towel, large sunglasses.

Tuna and beans in cream sauce for birthday lunch; new green honeydew melon: not as good as yesterday (probably, by freak of fortune, the best most delectable melon in the world), wild cold honey-flavored melon-flesh; creamy texture, refreshing, sweet the way sunlight would taste, coming through the clear glassy green bulk of waves.

Tonight: long deep nap, dropping of end of pier into hypnotized sleep, plummeting deep into dark with rock around ankles; groggy dazed doped waking, spinning warm sick giddiness; cleared head with washing and cold drink of water; sweaty, reserve of energy growing. Gulped scalding coffee, like surgeon before difficult new operation to be performed for first time. Got out ingredients from larder: Ted lit carbon fire, glowing to red coals in black oven, after much smoking and glowering clouds; scraped carrots naked, cut onion, squushy tomato; cooked down strips of salt pork, floured pink tight rabbit flesh; seared rabbit to savoury brown, chunked in big kettle; made rich dense gravy from drippings, adding flour, salt, boiling water, two packets of condensed soup - - - vegetable and beef and chicken, glass and a half of wine at Ted's insistence; added sauce to kettle with can of peas, onions, tomato & carrots. Boiled and bubbled, savoury, steaming and delectable. Presents: ponky-pooh chocolate for breakfast; pink-flowery-wifely-wrapped suave Madrid tie: gold & black for lunch; Hemingway leather wine flask, full, for dinner.

Mr. and Mrs. Ted Hughes' Writing Table:

In the center of the stone-tiled dining room, directly under the low-hanging chandelier with its large frosted glass bowl of light and four smaller replica bowls, stood the heavy writing table of glossy dark polished wood. The table top, about five feet square, was divided lengthwise down the center by a crack which never stayed closed, into which a drop-leaf might be inserted. At the head of the table, Ted sat in a squarely built grandfather chair with wicker back and seat; his realm was a welter of sheets of typing paper and ragged cardboard-covered notebooks; the sheets of scrap paper, scrawled across with his assertive blue-inked script, rounded, upright, flaired, were backs of reports on books, plays and movies written while at Pinewood studios;" typed and re-written versions of poems, bordered with drawings of mice, ferrets and polar bears, spread out across his half of the table. A bottle of blue ink, perpetually open, rested on a stack of paper. Crumpled balls of used paper lay here and there, to be thrown into the large wooden crate placed for that purpose in the doorway. All papers and notebooks on this half of the table were tossed at angles, kitty-corner and impromptu. An open cookbook lay at Ted's right elbow, where I'd left it after finishing reading out recipes of stewed rabbit. The other half of the table, coming into my premises, was piled with tediously neat stacks of books and papers, all laid prim and four-squared to the table corners: A large blue-paper-covered notebook, much thinned, from which typing paper was cut, topped by a ragged brown covered Thesaurus, formed the inner row of books, close to Ted's red covered Shakespeare, on which lay the bright yellow wrapping paper with a black-inked rhyme which served as birthday wrapping for a chocolate bar. Along the edge of the table, from left to right, were a plaid round metal box of scotch tape, a shining metal pair of sleek scissors, an open Cassell's French dictionary on which also opened, an underlined copy of Le Rouge et Le Noire in a yellow-bound ragged-edged paper-back edition, a bottle of jet black ink, scrupulously screwed shut, a small sketch book of rag paper atop Ted's anthology of Spanish poems, and a white plastic sunglasses case sewn over with a decorative strewing of tiny white and figured shells, a few green and pink sequins, a plastic green starfish and rounded, gleaming oval shell. The table top jutted over a border carved with starry flower motifs and the whole stood on four sturdy carved legs, alternating squared pieces carved with the diagonally-petaled flower motif and cylindrical rings, two of each; On two sides, the legs were joined by a fence of wooden pillars, four in all, and a carved medallion in the center depicting a frowning bearded face with handlebar moustache.

[Appendix 10 contains Sylvia Plath's 18 August 1956 description of Benidorm, Spain (entries 27–28) – ed.]

Paris: August 26:"

Ile de la Cite: down steps, out to green empty park; eight a.m.: early gray morning after rain, dark stains on pavement drying light gray; sit on quai by bank and drink from leather wine-skin; fisherman drops line, lets float go down with slow river Seine, draws in flipping silver gudgeon, puts in white cloth sack. Across river, barges moored on opposite bank; woman in flat shoes, yellow sweater and blue dress drops aluminum bucket over edge of boat into water, jerks cord, sloshes it about, draws it up spilling water; swabs deck with mop, throws dirty water over side; hangs up washing. Bookstalls are opening; green sycamores in spotted leopard yellow light.

Exhausted; lifted skirt under bridge, behind truck, secure in noise of falling water and urinated on sidewalk; ate greasy good last of tuna sandwich. Fatigue growing; back to hotel, up Rue de Buci to buy fruit. Stood before stand of peaches, moustached dark man rapidly filling bags. Little impatient gray-haired woman behind: Advancez, messieur-dame. We demanded a kilo of red peaches. Ladedum, toute le monde demande les rouges, chanted the oily man, rappidly filling our bag with green peaches. I looked in the bag while his back was turned to take the money; I found a solid rock-hard green peach; I put it back and took a red one. The man turned just as the hostile little woman made a rattling noise of furious warning to him, like a snake about to strike. One is not allowed to choose, the man raged, grabbing the bag back and rudely dumping the hard green peaches on the counter. We fumed, sick at the outrage, meanness and utter illogic; bought a kilo of delicious yellow pears touched with red, and another kilo of peaches at the nearest corner stand.

At the hotel, at twelve ten, our room was not ready; the mellow, full-lipped feline faced concierge made little moues of regret: they are americans and I cannot wake them; I have called. We sprawled in stiff wooden chairs, uphol-stered in red-flowered material. Near tears. Only a bed. The stiff cramped limbs of the train ache and return. Concierge brings two little glasses: "I saw you had a bottle of milk," she placates. We drink a bottle down. Slimy dark curly Jewish Americans saunter down, expensive tweed jackets; "let's sneak out and not pay." The culprits. To bed, deep dream sleep. Rain on roof outside window, gray light, deep covers and warm blankets. Rain and nip of autumn in air; nostalgia, itch to work better and bigger. That crisp edge of autumn. Must work and produce in print before return. Several stories And articles.

[Appendix 10 contains Sylvia Plath's 26 August 1956 description of the Hôtel des Deux Continents, Paris (entry 30) and notes from her September 1956 visit to York-shire (entries 31–32) where she probably wrote the following draft of an article about her experiences in Benidorm, Spain – ed.]

Sketchbook of a Spanish Summer"

After a bitter British winter, we sought the heart of sunlight in the small Spanish fishing village of Benidorm on the Mediterranean sea for a summer of studying and sketching. Here, in spite of the tourist hotels along the waterfront, the natives live as simply and peacefully as they have for centuries, fishing, farming, and tending their chickens, rabbits, and goats.

We woke early each morning to hear the high thin jangle of goat bells as the goatherd across the street led his flock of elegantly-stepping black goats to pasture. "Ya hoi!" came the shout of the little bread-woman as she strolled by with a great basket of fragrant fresh rolls over her arm. Daily, after breakfast, we walked downtown to shop at the peasant market. (Kitchens in Spain are a far cry from those in America: only the wealthy possess iceboxes, which are proudly displayed in the livingroom; dishes are washed in cold water with tangles of straw; and a one-ring petrol stove must cope with everything from <u>café con leche</u> to rich rabbit stew.)

The open air peasant market begins at sunup. Natives set out their wares on little wooden tables or straw mats at a hilly crossroads between white pueblos that sparkle like salt crystal in the sun. Black-clad peasant women bargain with the vendors for watermelons, purple figs wrapped in their own scalloped leaves, yellow plums, green peppers, wreathes of garlic, and speckled cactus fruit. Two straw baskets hung on a balance serve as scales and rough stones are used as weights. Live rabbits crouch in wire cages, with silken brown fur and noses quivering, to be sold for stew. One woman holds a squawking, flapping black chicken upside down by the legs while she calmly goes about the rest of her shopping. Strung up on wires against the pueblo walls are gaudy striped beach towels, rope sandals, and delicate white cobwebs of handmade lace. Higher on the hill, a man is selling petrol stoves, earthenware jugs and coathangers.

The fish market is a fresh adventure every day, varying according to the previous night's catch. Every evening, at dusk, the lights of the sardine boats dip and shine out at sea like floating stars. In the morning, counters are piled with silvery sardines, strewn with a few odd crabs and shells. Strange fish of all shapes and sizes lie side by side, speckled or striated, with a rainbow sheen on their fins. There are small fish with black streaks on shimmering pale blue scales, fish glinting pink and red, and a Moray eel with wicked black eyes and a splendid yellow brocade patterning its dark back. We never quite had the courage to select our dinner from the pile of baby octopuses, their long legs tangled and twined like a heap of slippery worms.

All our food and drink came from the farms around us. When we needed extra milk for supper one evening, we crossed the street to wait for the goatherd. Soon a musical tinkling sounded in the distance, and the flock of aristocratic black goats rounded the wall of the corral, followed by the goatherd, who resembled a smiling Spanish leprechaun in patched, faded dungarees, rope sandals, and a sombrero. He invited us into the corral to watch the milking. The goatherd's pup, with tight brown fur and floppy ears, yipped greeting from the shade of the fig tree where it was tied. The goatherd clucked and shooed his goats into what he called "their little casa." Following him into the dark, musky, pleasant interior, we found the ground softly carpeted with with confetti-like strips of freshly dried seaweed. Then the goatherd began to milk one of the black goats, squirting out a thin powerful stream of milk which hissed and rang in the bottom of our aluminum pail.

Modern innovations in Benidorm have not disturbed the rhythm of native customs. Although motor-scooters and a few large, grand tourist cars now crowd the narrow streets, the main traffic is donkey carts, loaded with vegetables, straw, or jugs of oil, wine and water. Delivery men continue to bicycle along on their routes, one with a crate of red-crested cocks, another with a large slab of swordfish in his basket. While drinking water is drawn from wells in the more modern houses, on our hill, the natives still congregate to fill their great earthenware jugs from the town pump.

By noon, the glare of the Spanish sun is so bright that it is difficult to raise one's eyes. All glitters white: sky, streets, and houses seem to glow with an inner radiance. From three to five, after a late lunch, all shops are closed and work halts for siesta time. Later, in the cool of the day, the old tanned, wrinkled women sit outside their doorways in wooden chairs, backs to the street, weaving nets of thick rope or fine mesh. In spite of the heat, they are always clad completely in black: shoes, stockings, dresses, and, for town shopping, often a black mantilla.

Only once in our whole summer of clear blue sunny days did a rain cloud pass. During the sudden, brief shower the lighting effects were startlingly beautiful. Looking toward the sun, which was still visible, we saw through a silver sheet of rain a dazzling drenched street between dark pueblos; in the opposite direction, against a backdrop of dark clouds, white pueblos shone under the arch of a perfect rainbow, one end rooted in the mountains, the other in the sea.

Every vistas in Benidorm was brilliant with color. From the front porch of our house, latticed by an arbor of purpling grapes and green leaves, we could glimpse an azure corner of the Mediterranean, glossy as peacock feathers. Behind the village the encircling hills, rose in a scrim of mist against the still blue sky. Our garden itself was like a painter's palette: white daisies and pungent red geraniums sprouted under the jagged green fronds of a palm tree, while vivid indigo morning glories hung like a tapestry along the wall.

Late one afternoon we walked up into the hills for a twilight view of the sea. The rows of white pueblos gave way to almond groves, each tree thick with ripe nuts; the green furry pods split open, showing the pocked brown shell inside. We shook down a few nuts, cracked them between two stones, and munched the kernels as we went along. Farther on, the dusty reddish soil was spiked with dry yellow grass and scattered with stones; twisted scrub pines grew on the bare summits of the hills. As we climbed, the bay of Benidorm spread out beneath us, a wide crescent of blue.

Crossing the tracks of the little railway station where hens scrabbled and scratched, we sat under a large pine, listening to the wind sough in the branches and watching the sea darken as the sun sank lower behind the purple hills at our back. Clouds scudded luminous across the brightening white moon which laid a paving of platinum light on the ocean. The little green neons on the waterfront blinked on and the bells of the clock tower were striking as we descended.

Now, back in the midst of a chilly British autumn, with drifting gray mists and bleak winds, the memory of this Spanish summer turns in our mind with a blaze of color and light like an inward sun, to warm us through the long winter.

[Appendix 10 contains Sylvia Plath's October 1956 descriptions of Cambridge, England (entries 33–34), as well as ideas for novels and poems (entries 35–36) – ed.]

See last pages: Fish & chip shop

Cambridge: January 3: Walk to Granchester:

Clear mild day with water-color blue skies. Past last row of
identical stone houses, road becomes muddy track with standing
puddles of water. Walking into sun, low horizontal light shining
on grass, River Granta, meadows of stiff dried beige sedge
rustling in little breeze. Through creaking wooden stile. Squint
into sun; brilliant green grass meadows stretching flat away on
both sides of the river, color iridescent, floating almost in a
green radiance above the grass itself. Sky reflecting pale watery
blues in flooded fields, crooked runnels and ponds. Rural quiet
scene. No people. Ahead, path gleaming silver in the light,
green meadows blazing, framed between dark willows; cows coming,
like dark silhouettes against the sun-bright grasslands, grazing,
placid bulks, tails twined and clotted with mud. Red hawthorn
berries vivid on the bare tall bushes bordering the mud-quagged
path. Eerie moss-green, unearthly neon green trunk of slender
elderberry tree. Tiny English robin, olive-green back, big
liquid dark eye, orange bib. Old man straight as a poker biking
with white toy terrier on leash beside him, trotting through
the mud puddles. Very still air. Sound of hounds barking in
the distance. Gazing back toward Cambridge---minute spires of
King's Chapel white in the sun over the bare treetops, pinnacles
of frosting. Clear air, gentle landscape. Christmas dollhouse,
drude, gaudy, displayed in window of children's playroom.

January 10: Brilliant clear blue invigorating day. To heart of
town. Sun pale warm orange on buildings of Newnham Village. Fens
clear green, rooks nests bared in trees, wet dew standing
transparent on every branch, across white-painted wooden bridges.
Wind rattling dry rushes. Ducks dipping on river in front of
Garden House Hotel, shiny green heads of mallards and speckled
brown dames. Wetness on tarred sidewalk reflecting blue glaze
from pale sky. Water whipped white by mill race. Noise of
continuous rushing. Pale blue-painted Anchor. Orangy plaster of
Mill pub. Through lane under old red brick buildings of Queens'.
Past butchers of Silver Street: cow hulks, strings of sausages,
halves of pigs hung in small window. Up King's Parade, bright
green bare stretch of lawn in front of chapel, bright white
sun on greek facade of senate house. Sun full on daffodils, budding
pink and lavendar hyacinths in Market Hill. Petty Cury: crowded,
one-way street. The big clock over Samuel's jewelers. Butcher's,
bookshop, shoe stores, fish market. Trucks, bikes, people walking
in street, sidewalks to narrow. Alleyways. Alexandra House. Man
carring plucked chicken by neck, red comb dangling like ruffled
scallops of blood. Clear day. Brisk. Pure air. Gilded hands on
clock over King's gate, lacy pinnacled spires. Biking back into
the great white glare of sun. Children running through poplar
glade in fens.

Gowst Chance

Cambridge: January 3: Walk to Granchester:"
Clear mild day with water-color blue skies. Past last row of identical stone houses, road becomes muddy track with standing puddles of water. Walking into sun, low horizontal light shining on grass, River Granta, meadows of stiff dried beige sedge rustling in little breeze. Through creaking wooden stile. Squint into sun; brilliant green grass meadows stretching flat away on both sides of the river, color iridescent, floating almost in a green radiance above the grass itself. Sky reflecting pale watery blues in flooded fields, crooked runnels and ponds. Rural quiet scene. No people. Ahead, path gleaming silver in the light, green meadows blazing, framed between dark willows; cows coming, like dark silhouettes against the sun-bright grasslands, grazing, placid bulks, tails twined and clotted with mud. Red hawthorn berries vivid on the bare tall bushes bordering the mud-quagged path. Eerie moss-green, unearthly neon green trunk of slender elderberry tree. Tiny English robin, olive-green back, big liquid dark eye, orange bib. Old man straight as a poker biking with white toy terrier on leash beside him, trotting through the mud puddles. Very still air. Sound of hounds barking in the distance. Gazing back toward Cambridge - - - minute spires of King's Chapel white in the sun over the bare treetops, pinnacles of frosting. Clear air, gentle landscape. Christmas dollhouse, crude, gaudy, displayed in window of children's playroom.

January 10: Brilliant clear blue invigorating day. To heart of town. Sun pale warm orange on buildings of Newnham Village. Fens clear green, rooks nests bared in trees, wet dew standing transparent on every branch, across white-painted wooden bridges. Wind rattling dry rushes. Ducks dipping on river in front of Garden House Hotel, shiny green heads of mallards and speckled brown dames. Wetness on tarred sidewalk reflecting blue glaze from pale sky. Water whipped white by mill race. Noise of continuous rushing. Pale blue-painted Anchor. Orangy plaster of Mill pub. Through lane under old red brick buildings of Queens'. Past butchers of Silver Street: cow hulks, strings of sausages, halves of pigs hung in small window. Up King's parade, bright green bare stretch of lawn in front of chapel, bright white sun on greek facade of senate house. Sun full on daffodils, budding pink and lavendar hyacinths in Market Hill. Petty Cury: crowded, one-way street. The big clock over Samuel's jewelers. Butcher's, bookshop, shoe stores, fish market. Trucks, bikes, people walking in street, sidewalks to narrow. Alleyways. Alexandra House. Man carring plucked chicken by neck, red comb dangling like ruffled scallops of blood. Clear day. Brisk. Pure air. Gilded hands on clock over King's gate, lacy pinnacled spires. Biking back into the great white glare of sun. Children running through poplar glade in fens.

Cambridge Diary

Monday afternoon: February 25:
Hello, hello. It is about time I sat down and described some things: Cambridge, people, ideas. The years whirl by, & I am nowhere nearer articulating them than two years ago. I used to sit on my doorstep in Wellesley, & mourn my local stasis: If, I muttered to myself, I could Travel & meet Interesting People, oh, what I wouldn't write! How I would astound them all.

Now, I have lived in Cambridge, London & Yorkshire; Paris, Nice & Munich; Venice & Rome; Madrid, Alicante, Benidorm. Whiz. Where am I? A novel. To begin. Poems are moment's monuments: I am splitting the seams of my fancy terza rima. I need Plot: people growing: banging into each other & into circumstances: stewpot citizens: growing & hurting & loving & making the best of various bad jobs.

So this American girl comes to Cambridge to find herself. To be herself. She stays a year, goes through great depression in winter. Much nature & town description, loving detail. Cambridge emerges. So does Paris & Rome. All is subtly symbolic. She runs through several men - - - a femme fatale in her way: types: stolid Yale man critic Kraut-head Gary Haupt; little thin sickly exotic wealthy Richard; combine Gary & Gordon; Richard & Lou Healy. Safe versus not safe. And of course: the big, blasting dangerous love. Also, double theme: combine Nancy Hunter & Jane: grave problem of identity. Peripheral boys: characters for amusement. Chris Levenson: lispy puppy.

Every day from now till exams: at least 2 to 3 solid pages describing a remembered incident with characters & conversation & descriptions. Forget about plot. Make it a vivid diary of reminiscence. Short chapters. By the time I go home there should be thus 300 pages. Revise over summer. Then either Harper's or Atlantic contest.

See each scene deep, love it like a complex faceted jewel. Get the light, shadow & vivid color. Set scene the night before. Sleep on it, write it in the morning.

But first: some quick notes on the present island. I am restless. Eager. Yet unproductive. Outside: a blue clear cold day that makes me want to be wandering through wooden stiles by the hawthorn hedges and squirrel tree to Granchester. But I biked to town today to shop: bank, P.O. where I mailed off two batches of Ted's poems, freshly typed, to the SRL" & Poetry. Loaded my black patent leather bag with sherry, cream cheese (for grammy's apricot tarts), thyme, basil, bay leaves (for Wendy's" exotic stews - - - a facsimile of which now simmers on the stove), golden wafers (such an elegant name for Ritz crackers), apples and green pears.

I was getting worried about becoming too happily stodgily practical: instead of studying Locke, for instance, or writing - - - I go make an apple pie, or study the Joy of Cooking, reading it like a rare novel. Whoa, I said to myself. You will escape into domesticity & stifle yourself by falling headfirst into a bowl of cookie batter. And just now I pick up the blessed diary of Virginia Woolf which I bought with a battery of her novels saturday with Ted. And she works off her depression over rejections from Harper's (no less! - - - and I hardly can believe that the Big Ones get rejected, too!) by cleaning out the kitchen. And cooks haddock & sausage. Bless her. I feel my life linked to her, somehow. I love her - - - from reading Mrs. Dalloway for Mr. Crockett - - - and I can still hear Elizabeth Drew's voice sending a shiver down my back in the huge Smith class-room, reading from To The Lighthouse. But her suicide, I felt I was reduplicating in that black summer of 1953. Only I couldn't drown. I suppose I'll always be over-vulnerable, slightly paranoid. But I'm also so damn healthy & resilient. And apple-pie happy. Only I've got to write. I feel sick, this week, of having written nothing lately. The Novel got to be such a big idea, I got panicked.

But: I know & feel & have lived so much: and am so wise, yes, in living for my age: having blasted through conventional morality, and come to my own morality. Which is the commitment to body & mind: to faith in battering out a good life. No God but the sun, anyway. I want to be one of the Makaris: with Ted. Books & Babies & Beef stews.

The parrafin heater dear Dr. Krook loaned us gurgles down its lucent blue petrol and the glowing red wire dome warms the room. Afternoon sun reflects from the windows of the duplicate brick houses across the street. Birds whistle & chirr. Above the orange brick chimneys & chimney pots, white clouds drift and fray in a rare blue sky. God, it is Cambridge. Let me get it down in these next three months - - - the end of my 22 months in England. And I told myself, coming over, I must find myself: my man and my career: before coming home. Otherwise - - - I'll just never come home.

And now: both! As I never dreamed: a sudden recognition scene. Act of faith. And I am married to a poet. We came together in that church of the chimney sweeps with nothing but love & hope & our own selves: Ted in his old black corduroy jacket & me in mother's gift of a pink knit dress. Pink rose & black tie. An empty church in watery yellow-gray light of rainy London. Outside, the crowd of thick-ankled tweed-coated mothers & pale, jabbering children waiting for the bus to take them on a church outing to the Zoo.

And here I am: Mrs. Hughes. And wife of a published poet. O I knew it would happen - - - but never thought so miraculously soon. Saturday, February 23rd, just almost an exact year from our first cataclysmic meeting at the St. Botolph's party, we woke late, grumpy & full of backwash tides of sleep, depressed over Ted's 3 rejections of poems from the Nation (after 3 acceptances in a row, a stupid letter from ML Rosenthal," rejecting them for the wrong reasons), Partisan Review (oh, so interesting, but we are simply cram-full with poems) & Virginia Quarterly. Ted is an excellent poet: full of blood & discipline, like Yeats. Only why won't these editors see it??? I muttered to myself. They accept bad flat poems, with no music, no color - - - only bad prose statements about bad subjects: unpleasant, nasty, uncommitted.

And then, while we were going about the domestic trivialities - - - Ted tying his tie in the livingroom, me heating milk for coffee, the Telegram came.

Ted's book of poems - - - The Hawk In The Rain - - - has won the Harper's first publication contest under the 3 judges: W.H.Auden, Stephen Spender & Marianne Moore! Even as I write this, I am incredulous. The little scared people reject. The big unscared practising poets accept. I knew there would be something like this to welcome us to New York! We will publish a book-shelf of books between us before we perish! And a batch of brilliant healthy children! I can hardly wait to see the letter of award (which has not yet come) & learn details of publication. To smell the print off the pages!

I am so glad Ted is first. All my pat theories against marrying a writer dissolve with Ted: his rejections more than double my sorrow & his acceptances rejoice me more than mine - - - it is as if he is the perfect male counterpart to my own self: each of us giving the other an extension of the life we believe in living: never becoming slaves to routine, secure jobs, money: but writing constantly, walking the world with every pore open, & living with love & faith. It sounds so paragon. But I honestly believe we are: apart, we rotted in luxury, adored & spoiled by lovers. Cruelly walking over them. Together, we are the most faithful, creative, healthy simple couple imaginable!

All Saturday was a daze of joy & conjecture. We burnt a whole pot of milk to a black bubbling acrid crisp on the stove in the process of calling up our mothers - - - Ted's in Yorkshire, mine in America. Then we had salad & ham & clear pungent cider at the Eagle pub, sitting on the rough wooden seats by the blue & purple fire, listening idly to nearby conversations, staring up at the tawny orangey ceiling, smoked over with air squadron numbers. It was pouring rain, but under our umbrella we strode radiating. Browsed in Bowes & Bowes where they treat me like Queen Elizabeth, I'm such a good customer with my blessed £56 book-allowance, loaded arms with V. Woolf, tea at the Copper Kettle with the steamy windows, round tables facing rough glass windows bordered by green potted plants, looking out at the sugar crystal pinnacles of King's, & the gilt hands on the King's clock over the gateway.

We dressed up for a gala supper at the King's parade restaurant: much better than Miller's - - - all plushy, quiet, efficient. Escargots? oh yes, madam. And pheasant. & venison. We being at the end of resources, settled for the routine dinner - - - chicken soup, good & creamy, delicious stuffed tomatoes, turkey with the usual unredeemed chip potatoes & overcooked dried peas, or canned. Chablis & iced lemon mousse transfigured it all. We idled, nibbled, dreamed aloud.

The ceiling was black, patterned with bursts of white stars, very fine. A lattice of white painted wood protected the little dining room from the traffic of waiters. Kitchen doors whooshed, stiff little men with waxed moustaches brought wine, lighted candles burned, the brazier hissed like a caged snake. Ted looked clean-cut, dark, handsome & utterly lovable in the flickering light. We commented on the other guests - - - a wall-eyed blond, horsy maleish woman, Breuguel-nosed woman with potato features. We figured out the pools & lost again. But we wouldn't trade our book publishing news for pools any day. Reeled home in rain & orange mist of Fen Causeway lights. Mystic white swans, bending necks underwater of iron bridge, sucking, floating, white diamonds. Eerie with white reptilian necks. Creatures of another world. I wanted to provoke one from that white-swan calm & indifference.

All right. Enough of this talking about and about. Present. Observe & present.

Scene for tomorrow: precise description of departure from Paris in spring with gordon: farewell to giovanni:" doubts, horrid stifled depression; grim train ride; elegant meal; flavorless life; snow in Munich; frightening surgical hotel. Describe Paris room, breakfast. Get weak, flabbiness in Gordon's nature; scorn & disgust of girl; forecast of failure of trip ahead. "You'll never marry, if you're like this." Taunts & undermines weak manhood, lack of purpose. Pivot-point of decision.

Sweet dreams.

February 26: Tuesday
It is about 7:30. Have been awake since black 3:30, Ted sneezing & fighting off cold; frigid gray dawn. Mind incredibly quick. Placing poems. Visions of books: poems, novels. Are we destined to be as successful as I picture? Or is it a wish-dream? Got up as brash, nerve-raking alarm ground off at 6 to make bad egg-nog. Grim argument over silly question, Ted maintaining it would be good to read a bad book deeply for 2 years in prison - - - one would learn by one's true experience it was wrong. Me saying it was better to have nothing to look at than a bad book: that only those with critical apparatus beforehand would be able to discern badness, & what good would it do them. He criticizing my Earthenware Head poem. Bad time for criticism. Me with no new poem to right on yet. O for vacation. Enough hacking. Begin.

Monday: March 4
I am stymied, stuck, at a stasis. Some paralysis of the head has got me frozen. Perhaps the vision of 3 papers to do in one week, and all English literature to read and re-read in less than 3 months has stunned me idiotic. As if I can

escape by going numb and daring to begin nothing. Everything seems held up, what is it?

Mail doesn't come. I haven't had an acceptance since October 1st. And I have piles of poems and stories out. Not to mention my book of poems. Even Ted's letter about winning the contest, with its award details, hasn't come, so even vicarious pleasure is shorn from me. Bills come. I write nothing. The novel, or rather, the 3-page a day stint, is atrocious. I can't get at it. I am writing with a blunt pencil tied on a mile-long stick, at something far off over the horizon line. Will I break through someday? At least if I get 300 pages written by the end of May, I'll have the creaking, gushing skeleton plot of the whole thing. Then I can write slowly, re-writing each chapter, carefully with a subtle structured style. If I can ever find a subtle structured style.

It's hopeless to "get life" if you don't keep notebooks. I am angry now because, except for snow, I forget what the trip from France to Munich was like. I keep being true-confessional. All interior "she felts" and appallingly awkward. Again, I feel the gulf between my desire & ambition and my naked abilities. But I will doggedly write my 3 pages a day, even if my supervisors scorn me. Only it would help my morale no end to feel it was a good novel. But it's not a novel now. Just straight blither. But the girl will have to get through a year of life in 3 months of mine. And then, two months this summer to re-write, carefully, knowing what I'm trying to do. I might as well be glad of the plot. I really don't know much but that. And plot's hard for me, so good.

But I feel now, again, that I can never write a good story or a good poem. Much less bad ones. All is static. My exams oppress. I get into a rut, unable to yank my mind out of it. I love it here so. How to get it.

Biked today, this morning, up Queen's road: on left, hedged green playing field, red humped brick roofs of Newnham, bare trees with black clots of rookeries, pink blossoms like little sticky puffs of snow on black boughs. Purple and yellow crocuses in bloom by the long low red brick almshouse with its arched doorways, a face in stone carved at each corner of the lintel. The dangerous curve, blind, by the garage, a right turn, and over the while-railinged bridge, bumpy wood boards, past the Jolly Miller. Cocker-spaniel racing. Ducks whickering past my ear. Canoes and punts drawn up on the mud bank under the Granta's grey stone. Poplars shooting up on the right.

Green swatches of grass, up onto the tarred path along the little river. Blue and green faint hazes blowing in the sun, all bluish, greenish. Some students in black gowns drinking beer on the stone bridge by the pale blue Anchor over the rush of the mill race, tossing the crusts of ham sandwiches to the milling, splashing ducks. Clear, crisp. Vestige of mists. Up shaded silver street, past white butcher. Gilt hands on church clock. Ahead: King's parade. Senate house white, blurred by mist on ground. Potted plants, faces behind steamed windows of Copper Kettle, like fish in an aquarium.

I feel really uncreative. After talking with Mary Ellen Chase," I self-paralyze myself & wonder what I've got in my head. How to teach anyone anything? That would do me the most good, I think. The day by day teaching. Looked at in one gulp, it terrifies. As does the Novel. The Exams. But hour by hour, day by day, life becomes possible. But I am dry, dry and sterile. How is it it does not show? I feel Mary Ellen Chase, even, with dozens of 2nd rate novels, best-sellers. I have not one. I must produce. But it is too usual to write about the lack of ideas for writing. Ted showed such brilliant insight when he said I needed at least a year in place to settle - - - but to change every year or so to stimulate to new writing. That is so true.

If I can digest changes, in my novel. Not swell tumid with inarticulateness. As I am now. Or to gibbering - - my old blue devil - - - black-white, black-white. I get quite appalled when I realize my whole being, in its recusing and refusing after my 3-years struggle to build it flexible and strong again, my whole being has grown and interwound so completely with Ted's that if anything were to happen to him, I do not see how I could live. I would either go mad, or kill myself. I cannot conceive of life without him. After twenty-five years of searching in the best places, there is just no one like him. Who fits. Who fits so perfectly and is so perfectly the male being complement to me. Oh, speak. I am so stupid. Really stupid.

Yet what do other people talk of? Other people - - - like the Scots, yesterday, in their dream white-house with the rainbow prism livingroom - - - they seem tedious, dull. What purpose have they? We have our life, our love, our writing. And project after project.

I could write a terrific novel. The tone is the problem. I'd like it to be serious, tragic, yet gay & rich & creative. I need a master, several masters. Lawrence, except in Women in Love, is too bare, too journalistic in his style. Henry

James too elaborate, too calm & well-mannered. Joyce Cary I like. I have that fresh, brazen, colloquial voice. Or J.D. Salinger. But that needs an "I" speaker, which is so limiting. Or Jack Burden. I have time. I must tell myself I have time.

Only the weight of Irwin Shaw and Peter De Vries and all the witty clever, serious, prolific ones oppresses me. I feel, were it not for Ted, I'd sell my soul. It is so ironic to think of nobly writing and writing on this novel, and sacrificing friends & leisure & turning out a bad bad novel. But I feel I could write a best-seller. I'm sure of it in a kind of reverse way: I am sick with what I am writing - - - but am sure it can grow, be re-written to an art-work. In it's small way. About the voyage of a girl through destruction, hatred and despair to seek and to find the meaning of the redemptive power of love. But the horror is that cheapness and slick-love would be the result of the thing badly written. Well-written, sex could be noble & gut-shaking. Badly, it is true-confession. And no amount of introspection can cure it.

I suppose I will get these papers done, & for a while get rid of this albatross of pressure & write well in vacation. I've done it before - - the papers, & not died. But I must get back into the world of my creative mind: otherwise, in the world of pies & shin beef, I die. The great vampire cook extracts the nourishment & I grow fat on the corruption of matter, mere mindless matter. I must be lean & write & make worlds beside this to live in.

Monday: March 11, 1957:
Quarter past six. New routine beginning again. Better keep it up this time: namely, to hack ourself a day to ourselves from six to eight, then five to eight. Writing to ourselves. Woke to the long fire-engine alarm that shreds my skin off to the quick nerve. A silvern burble and twit and blither of myriad birds outside secret in the blue misted light. The pure virgin joy of waking early and all others but us asleep.

Now, from the livingroom, on my left out through the windows, the sleeping identical brick houses, knitted together in one long row, are swimming, weltering, in a thinning blue air, like some fabulous sunken undersea twilight.

I have thought: a pox on my "She thought-she felt" banal novel. Read "The Horse's Mouth": that's it. For now at least. Break into a limited, folksy, vivid style that limits the girl, defines her: humor, vivid, but serious: "at bottom really grave." Wife of Bath. Better read "Herself Surprised". Make your own style, don't copy. But a richer Laundromat Affair style. And watch it be a best seller. Much easier to work at: style will define material. Most difficult part: style. Vivid direct descriptions. First person: perhaps I can get away with third.

I am wicked, sick: a week behind. But will do 5 pages a day until plodding I catch up. Use words as poet uses words. <u>That</u> is it! Gulley Jimson is an artist with words, too - - - or, rather Joyce Cary is. But I must be a word-artist. The heroine. Like Stephen Dedalus walking by the sea: ooo-ee-ooo-siss. Hising their petticoats.

Now: a quick description: to be in the Cambridge-spring part of the book. Fish and chip shop on a rainy night:

Turned onto the Fen Causeway" in black warm blowing mist. Orange lights reflecting in puddles, lurid orange suns, spinning orange cocoons out of the thick mist. Orange rain drops. An unnatural color. She gritted her teeth, patting her hair. Soggy, rain-wet. On the left, the sunken Sheep's green, weltering in full brooks and standing ponds, shoved its poplars whoosh into the ragging mists. Those poplars. On clear nights, full of stars, leaning, pointing, big stars caught in the branches. Or angels. On those nights, stuck shining with angels. Remember Tinka Bell. Looked like a firefly glow till you got up close. Little lady then, shining dainty, with dragonfly wings.

Squinting, the black, slippery tree branches looked to circle the orange streetlamps. Spinning a net of branches, spiderwebbing orange.

"Why do the branches go round the lights?"

"The lights," he said, his pale orange profile cutting itself ahead into the black, "reflect on the branches going round, not the others."

She plunged her hand into his pocket. Orange light made patent-leather strips on his shiny leather coat. They crossed the bare highway by the Royal Hotel, the brick ugly and leprous orange. Across a little iron-railinged bridge by the Botannical Gardens.

"I hate orange lights. They make the town sick."

"Some council. Some one or two fat men sitting. Orange lights proposed. Easier to see in snowstorms, one or two snowstorms. And fogs. For the drivers. And we, have to walk about in the foul orange mess. Like orange lepers."

No one was out in the rain. The streets shone, and blue-white lights shone on the narrow criss-cross streets off the main highway with its globed orange pedestrain crossing lights ticking and blinking of their own accord by the black and white painted strip, bordered with metal studs.

Russell Street. Ahead, far up on the right. Light spilt out in a warm puddle. Two men climbed into the light, into the bright white doorway of the fish and chip shop.

"Do you have money?"

"No. I wish you'd take care of us."

"Take care!"

He stopped dead, the rain falling softly, wetly. He shoved his hand into his trouser pocket, his jacket pocket. He brought out a handful of coppers.

"Count it up."

"Six-pence, and thruppence. And three, four pennies. How much is one fish? And I was so wanting fish."

He hoisted up his coat, feeling into another pocket. And brought up another sixpence.

"All. Absolutely. Damn!" The gun barrel shone from inside his sweater. He hauled at it, fixing it steady.

"Careful." She drew his black wool scarf to hide it. "Do come in with me. It'll look suspicious if you stay outside."

"A hell of a lot more suspicious if I walk in with a gun sticking out of my coat. Why can't you get the stuff yourself?"

"I hate going in alone."

They stopped in front of the little door to the shop. Through the steamed glass, the white, square interior glittered, dazzling. They blinked, and he thrust open the glassed door.

Two boys in leather jackets lounged against the counter, staring openly. She pulled her black gown up on her shoulders. It was always slipping back, catching her arms behind like a straightjacket.

The pale thin man behind the counter lifted up a wire basket of hissing French fries. The pleasant woman beside him smiled, questioning. He was staring off to the side, seeing salmon jumping. Something. She nudged him. "Hey."

"One fish. Six pennyworth of chips."

"Plaice or cod?" the woman asked.

The girl smiled at her.

"Cod," the boy said.

"I just thought you might like plaice," the woman told the girl. She took a paper bag, half filled it with crisped brown chips, and a fried slab of cod. "Give it back to me after you've put the vinegar on."

The girl picked up the cracked metal tin of salt and snowed it into the bag. Then, taking the cut-glass bottle of vinegar, she showered the fish, lifted the edge of it, and doused the potatoes. She handed the bag back to the woman, who wrapped it up in a sheaf of newspaper.

The boy counted out the change. They had twopence left.

"'Night." They pushed out into the wet dark. Slowly, she unwound the newspaper, finding the mouth of the paper bag.

"Here." He reached in and broke off a steaming hunk of fish, tilting his head back, and dropping it into his mouth. She burnt her fingers, pulling off part of the fried skin, with the fish sticking succulent to her fingers. She licked them, as they strolled slowly down Russell Street.

"I'd rather eat fish and chips on a rainy night than anything," she said, offering him the bag again. "Take some chips too. They're all at the bottom." She cradled the bag against her, feeling the warmth. A warm center against the rain.

The chips were soaked with vinegar.

"Is that the monastary?"

They came to a long brick building on the left, with light spilling out from behind drawn blinds. "Yes," he said.

Radio music blared from behind the curtains. She stopped dead.

"The monks are meditating," he walked on ahead, his hands shoved into his pockets, to the street corner. But she froze the scene in her eye.

The glass lantern, the streetlight at the end of the street, against a brick wall, lit up the white background of the sign: "St. Elegius Street". Black letters. So neat. Always, I must remember this: the clear light in the square of iron ribs and glass. How fresh that sign shows.

A burst of laughter from the radio. And then deep, resonant chimes. "Hark to the chimes. Come bow your head . . . " Over the radio. That camp grace they always sang.

"Is it Big Ben?" she called, softly, to his turned back.

"Yes."

She waited. The hour began to strike.

Bong. Bong. Bong. Would it finish. The rain fell lightly.

Bong. Bong. Someone, an old woman, pulled the curtain of the monastary and stared out.

Bong. The girl stood, ready to run.

Bong. The sound held her, hauling up a sight of the Thames walk below

Haymarket. The black chains, the black walls, the lights hanging in transparent green tree leaves.

Bong. Bong.

"Nine o'clock," the boy said.

She came up to him, and pushed her hand back into his, in his pocket, digging her nails in between his fingers. They walked on, peering in cracks of window curtains into lighted rooms.

"Would you live in that house?"

"It's a garage." She stared up at the second floor window of the little brick building. The curtains weren't drawn, and she glimpsed red hangings stark against white-painted walls. A boy, an Indian, with dark hair and a red sweater, moved into the window space and beyond. One wall was painted plum color.

"The young architect owns it."

"I'd like it. Snug. Water-tight."

They came out onto the main road, into the orange mists.

"Let's walk back through the horse park," she said. "The orange grits my teeth. I feel positively sick at it."

"That way's a mud trough."

"We've got boots on."

They turned left, cutting across the highway, through the stile. Horses were grazing, dark shapes against the orange light, backs bend, manes flowing. Moving slowly over the wet grasses, ankle keep in low webs of orange fen fog.

[Appendix 11 contains Sylvia Plath's June 1957 – June 1960 journal, including her June 1957 descriptions of London (entry 4) and descriptions of fellow passengers on the *Queen Elizabeth II*, crossing the Atlantic Ocean to New York (entries 5–7) – ed.]

JOURNAL
15 July 1957 – 21 August 1957

———

Plath completed her B.A. degree at Cambridge University in June 1957. Plath and Hughes crossed the Atlantic Ocean on the Queen Elizabeth II, *arriving in New York on 25 June 1957. After a reception in Wellesley, Massachusetts, they spent the rest of the summer on Cape Cod, Massachusetts, within cycling distance of Nauset Light and Coast Guard beaches.*

July 15, 1957: The virginal page, white. The first: broken into
and sent packing. All the dreams, the promises: wait till I can
write again, and then the painful, botched rape of the first page.
Nothing said. A warmup. A directive. It is almost noon, and through
the short spined green pines the sky is a luminous overhung gray.
Some bastard's radio jazzes out of the trees: like the green eyed
stinging flies: God has to remind us this isn't heaven by a long shot.
So he increases the radios and lethal flies.

Slowly, with great hurt, like giving birth to some endless and
primeval baby, I lie and let the sensations spring up, look at
themselves and record themselves in words: the blind moves in and
out on the window with a slight breeze, pale yellow-brown, tawn,
and the curtains move, cotton with yellow sunburst Flowers and
black twigs on a white ground. We have not yet got good coffee, but
the fatigue is slowly sinking in us, after two days of heavy sleep,
sogged with bad dreams: diabolically real: Haven house, the feet of
Smith girls past the room, which becomes a prison, always giving out
on a public corridor, no private exits. The leer: the slow subtly
faithless smile, and the horror of the worst, the dream of the worst,
come at last into its own. Waking is heaven, with its certainties.
Why these dreams? These last exorcisings of the horrors and fears
beginning when my father died and the bottom fell out. I am just now
restored. I have been restored for over a year, and still the dreams
are'nt quite sure of it. They aren't for I'm not. And I suppose never
will be. Except that we will be living a safe life, no gin parties,
no drunk ego-panderings. If I write stories, poems, and the novel.
All I need to do is work, break open the deep mines of experience and
imagination, let the words come and speak it all, sounding themselves
and tasting themselves.

Each of these magic seven weeks: writing: not the novel yet, until
I'm warmed up. Now the stories. Fiction for the Atlantic Monthly
to be ready for Dan Aaron's introduction to Sam Lawrence: two stories
at least: The Eye-Beam One : like Kafka, simply told, symbolic, yet
very realistic. How one is always and irrevocably alone. The askew
distortions of the private eye. Set in Cambridge. And another:
perhaps a version of the waitress story: only I haven't got it here.
Make it up. Naturalistic. Jewel prose. Make out little paragraphs of
what happens to whom. Then think it clear. Write it.

Harper's article on Student life at Cambridge: Assignment: Cantab.
Witty, incidental: vignettes. Men and women situation. Cold, food.
Eccentricities. Social circles. Decentralized. All for profs, not
students.

Slick stories: money-makers: very gay, lively with lots of family.
Use Aldriches, baby-sitting experiences. Summer living in with family
on beach: Cantors. Very fast pitch. Rewrite Laundromat Affair. Also,
diabolic sister story. How she comes in, jealous of younger brother's
marriage, not like the old days. Funny rather giddy characters. Try
also one very serious one: emotional: lady on ship-board? New York
secretary: setting, Queen Elizabeth. Yes.

Novel: FALCON YARD: central image: love, a falcon, striking once and
for all: blood sacrifice: falcon yard, central chapter of book: the
irrefutable meeting and experience. Emblem: lord & lady riding smiling
with falcon on wrist. Get impersonal into Judith, create other characters
who act in their own right & not just as projections of her...

July 15, 1957: The virginal page, white. The first: broken into and sent packing. All the dreams, the promises: wait till I can write again, and then the painful, botched rape of the first page. Nothing said. A warmup. A directive. It is almost noon, and through the short spined green pines the sky is a luminous overhung gray. Some bastard's radio jazzes out of the trees: like the green eyed stinging flies: God has to remind us this isn't heaven by a long shot. So he increases the radios and lethal flies.

Slowly, with great hurt, like giving birth to some endless and primeval baby, I lie and let the sensations spring up, look at themselves and record themselves in words: the blind moves in and out on the window with a slight breeze, pale yellow-brown, tawn, and the curtains move, cotton with yellow sunburst flowers and black twigs on a white ground. We have not yet got good coffee, but the fatigue is slowly sinking in us, after two days of heavy sleep, sogged with bad dreams: diabolically real: Haven house, the feet of Smith girls past the room, which becomes a prison, always giving out on a public corridor, no private exits. The leer: the slow subtly faithless smile, and the horror of the worst, the dream of the worst, come at last into its own. Waking is heaven, with its certainties. Why these dreams? These last exorcisings of the horrors and fears beginning when my father died and the bottom fell out. I am just now restored. I have been restored for over a year, and still the dreams are'nt quite sure of it. They aren't for I'm not. And I suppose never will be. Except that we will be living a safe life, no gin parties, no drunk ego-panderings. If I write stories, poems, and the novel. All I need to do is work, break open the deep mines of experience and imagination, let the words come and speak it all, sounding themselves and tasting themselves.

Each of these magic seven weeks: writing: not the novel yet, until I'm warmed up. Now the stories. Fiction for the Atlantic Monthly to be ready for Dan Aaron's[n] introduction to Sam Lawrence:[n] two stories at least: The Eye*Beam One: like Kafka, simply told, symbolic, yet very realistic. How one is always and irrevocably alone. The askew distortions of the private eye. Set in Cambridge. And another: perhaps a version of the waitress story: only I haven't got it here. Make it up. Naturalistic. Jewel prose. Make out little paragraphs of what happens to whom. Then think it clear. Write it.

283

Harper's article on Student life at Cambridge: Assignment: Cantab. Witty, incidental: vignettes. Men and women situation. Cold, food. Eccentricities. Social circles. Decentralized. All for profs, not students.

Slick stories: money-makers: very gay, lively with lots of family. Use Aldriches, baby-sitting experiences. Summer living in with family on beach: Cantors. Very fast pitch. Rewrite Laundromat Affair. Also, diabolic sister story. How she comes in, jealous of younger brother's marriage, not like the old days. Funny rather giddy characters. Try also one very serious one: emotional: lady on ship-board? New York secretary: setting, Queen Elizabeth. Yes.

Novel: <u>FALCON YARD</u>: central image: <u>love, a falcon</u>, striking once and for all: blood sacrifice: falcon yard, central chapter of book: the irrefutable meeting and experience. <u>Emblem</u>: lord & lady riding smiling with falcon on wrist. Get impersonal into Judith, create other characters who act in their own right & not just as projections of her ...

Cape Cod

Wednesday: July 17:

No skipping after today: a page diary to warmup. All joy for me: love, fame, life work, and, I assume, children, depends on the central need of my nature: to be articulate, to hammer out the great surges of experience jammed, dammed, crammed in me over the last five years, and before that, although before that it wasn't so desperate for there was a slower flow of experience, digestible enough to be written out in short stories and poems, when I had a certain slickness that is enviable now, although that slickness would now never enclose and present the experience welling up in me full and rich as fruit on a blue and white pottery platter. Anyway, if I am not writing, as I haven't been this last half year, my imagination stops, blocks up, chokes me, until all reading mocks me (others wrote it, I didn't), cooking and eating disgusts me (mere physical activity without any mind in it) and the only thing that sustains me, yet is not enjoyed fully, is the endless deep love I live in. And the unique and almost bottomless understanding of Ted. Without that, I would rush about, seeking solace, never finding it, and not keeping the steady quiet deadly determined center I have even now at the end of one of my greatest droughts: It Will Come. If I Work.

Poems are bad to begin with: elaborate ones especially: they freeze me too soon on too little. Better, little exercise poems in description that don't demand philosophic bear-traps of logical development. Like small poems about the skate, the cow by moonlight, a la the Sow. Very physical in the sense that the worlds are bodied forth in my words, not stated in abstractions, or denotative wit on three clear levels. Small descriptions where the words have an aura of mystic power: of Naming the name of a quality: spindly, prickling, sleek, splayed, wan, luminous, bellied. Say them aloud always. Make them irrefutable.

Then: the magazine story: written seriously, but easily, because it is easier to manipulate strictly limited characters, almost cariacatures, some of them, than the diary I of the novel, who must also become, in her way limited, but only so that she can grow to the vision I have now of life, which tomorrow will be a fuller vision, and tomorrow.

Yesterday was the first day of work: a bad day. Spent time on a very desperately elaborate psychological idea and wrote maybe one good image (the boy with the whole ocean bottled in his head) to a raft of brittle, stilted artificial stuff. Not touching on my deep self. This bad beginning depressed me inordinately. It made me not hungry nor want to cook, because of the bestialness of eating and cooking with out keen thought and creation. The beach: too late, after a hot walk along a gravelly, sunny, sidewalk on Route 6, the deathly pink, yellow and pistachio colored cars shooting by like killer instruments from the mehcanical tempo of another planet. Broken glass, then the scrub pine shadowing Bracket road, the whisk of bird and squirrel in underbrush, green berried shrubs, and the rough tar. A great blue span of Atlantic under the cliff at Nauset Light, and a swim in the warmish green seeweeded water, rising and falling with the tall waves at tide turn. Lay in sun far up beach, but the sun was cold, and the wind colder. The boom, boom of great guns throbbing in the throat, then the ride back, bad-tempered. Making mayonnaise, and it coming out well. Fine. Then, grubbing over supper, with the badly begun poem like an albatross round the neck of the day, nothing else. And the tables and chairs insulting the way they are when a human being tries to live their merely phenomenal life and miserably doesn't succeed. They go smug, I-told-you-so.

Now it is near ten, and the morning yet untried, unbroken. The feeling one must get up earlier and earlier to get ahead of the day, which by one o'clock is determined. Last night: finished "The Waves", which disturbed, almost angered by the endless sun, waves, birds, and the strange uneveness of description - - - a heavy, ungainly ugly sentence next to a fluent, pure running one. But then the hair-raising fineness of the last 50 pages: Bernard's summary, an essay on life, on the problem: the deadness of a being to whom nothing can happen, who no longer creates, creates, against the casting down. That moment of illumination, fusion, creation: We made this: against the whole falling apart, away, and the coming again to make and make in the face of the flux: making of the moment something of permanence. That is the life-work. I underlined & underlined: reread that. I shall go better than she. No children until I have done it. My health is making stories, poems, novels, of experience: that is why, or, rather, that is why it is good, that I have suffered & been to hell, although not to all the hells. I cannot life for life itself: but for the words which stay the flux. My life, I feel, will not be lived until there are books and stories which relive it perpetually in time. I forget too easily how it was, and shrink to the horror of the here and now, with no past and no future. Writing breaks open the vaults of the dead and the skies behind which the prophesying angels hide. The mind makes and makes, spinning its web.

Write down the passing thought, the passing observation. How Mrs. Spaulding," with her heavy-lidded blue eyes, her long braid of gray hair, wants her life written: so much happened. The San Francisco earthquake and fire, with her mother giving away the baked beans and bread to refugees, and she crying and wanting to keep the beans; hearing a sound like railway trains jamming into each other on a siding, seeing her doll-cradle rock, grabbing the doll, her mother grabbing her into the bed. Her husband dropping dead. Her having an operation, coming out of the hospital to dry her hair at her friend's house, and have it set. Her second husband walks in the door, sees her long hair hanging: what a beautiful sight. The little child getting sick and missing him. His wife dying on the same day her husband did. All this: raw, material. To be useful. Also, images of life: like Woolf found. But she: too ephemeral, needing the earth. I will be stronger: I will write until I begin to speak my deep self, and then have children, and speak still deeper. The life of the creative mind first, then the creative body. For the latter is nothing to me without the first, and the first thrives on the rich earth roots of the latter. Every day, writing. No matter how bad. Something will come. I have been spoiled to think it will come too soon: without work & sweat. Well, now for 40 days I work & sweat. Write, read, sun & swim. Oh, to live like this. We will work. And he sets the sea of my life steady, flooding it with the deep rich color of his mind and his love and constant amaze at his perfect being: as if I had conjured, at last, a god from the slack tides, coming up with his spear shining, and the cockleshells and rare fish trailing in his wake, and he trailing the world: for my earth goddess, he the sun, the sea, the black complement power: yang to yin. The sky is clear blue, and the needles of the pine shine white and steely. The ground is orange-red with fallen pine needles, and the robins and chipmunks steal their color from this red earth.

[Appendix 11 contains Sylvia Plath's June 1957 – June 1960 journal, including descriptions of pine cones (entry 12), descriptions of the Spauldings with a drawing of a corn vase (entry 26), and notes for a story 'The Great Big Nothing' about a New York secretary crossing the Atlantic Ocean by ship (entry 27) – ed.]

July 18, 1957:

A brief before-bed fling to say how lousy today was. After the night drive with Spauldings last evening, the gnats biting itches into the bone, the late greasy dishes, the Woolf sting in Jacob's Room put off because of it, a strange sleep. No more dreams of queen and king for a day with valets bringing in racks of white suits, jackets, etc. for Ted & ballgowns and tiaras for me. A semi-plangent dream of children, sullen, cloudy, oppressed, squatting and being eel-catchers. Then a pleasant view of Ted's rosy mother" holding a lovely droll baby, with two older children at her right side, me taking the cheeks of the baby & squeezing them into a comical dear O-face: her children or mine?

Very tired, contrasted with the crisp blue new morning. Bowls of coffee made with milk and a morning of futile shilly-shallying over the mother's helper story, with the characters obstinate, not moving or speaking, and me with no definite idea of who they are: shall Sassy be a shy bookworm, dominated by mother, who comes out of her shell & gets a man? Or a tomboy terror, very athletic, who falls in love for the first time against her mother's directions, with a nice simple guy. God knows. About three stories are pulling me: mother dominates daughter, only nineteen years older, or twenty: girl 17, mother 37: mother flirts with girl's dates. Girl fights for freedom & integrity. Sat Eve Post" story: suddenly possible as I think about it. Get tension of scenes with mother during Ira and Gordon crisis. Rebellion. Car keys. Psychiatrist. Details: Dr. Beuscher: baby. Girl comes back to self, can be good daughter. Sees vision of mothers hardships. Yes yes. This is a good one. A subject. Dramatic. Serious. Enough of the hyphenated society names. Mental hospital background. Danger. Dynamite under high tension. Mothers character. At first menacing, later pathetic, moving. Seen from outside first, then inside. Girl comes back: grown bigger: ready to be bigger. Like mother, yet furious about it. Wants to be different. Bleaches hair. Policemen. Annoying her. Story in newspapers. After suicide attempt. Earthy Dr. Beuscher. Nowhere to go. Back to school. Then what? Something. Laborious charts. MOTHER-DAUGHTER. Troubles. Graphic. A real story. "Trouble-making Mother".

Okay. An idea. Just when you thought nothing had come. Or could. In six weeks you better be on a pile of written mss. Do it. Like Kazin said, this summary about what it is just isn't the story. It's playing about. But for me to break open an idea in summary is at this early stage a life-saving event. Not to scratch on the glassy surface of my head begging an idea to hatch, complete as a day-old chicken, on the blank page. Even the mother's helper story should do something. Fresh, brazen stubborn girl Sassy? Get to kernel of character: what motivates her to do what? Conflict: Stages. Mother wants Sassy to be social success instead of what she is and to like right boy: chooses Chuck. Enter Lynn & Gary. Mother wants Lynn to help Sassy be social by setting example. Mother & Lynn vs. Sassy. Freshness, scene set for change. Sassy falls for Gary who falls for Lynn who is pinned & static. Lynn perceives this: helps sassy get Gary (on shipwreck) and Mother lose chuck. Shifts field. Own boyfriend comes back. Mother is shown the light. How clear, how lovely. Now just write the damn thing.

Another: THE DAY OF THE TWENTY-FOUR CAKES: Either Kafka litmag serious or SATEVEPOST aim high: woman at end of rope with husband, children: lost sense of order in universe, all meaningless, loss of hopes: quarrel with husband: loose ends, bills, problems, dead end. Wavering between running away or committing suicide: stayed by need to create an order: slowly, methodically begins to bake cakes, one each hour, calls store for eggs, etc. from midnight to midnight. Husband comes home: new understanding. She can go on making order in her limited way: beautiful cakes: can't bear to leave them. Try both styles: do it to your heart's content.

July 20, 1957: Saturday

A new era has begun: it is not yet seven thirty. I have my four hour morning ahead, whole as a pie. And I am slowly, amazedly, beginning to delight again in the workings of my own mind: which has been shut off like an untidy corpse under the floorboards during the last half year of exam cramming, slovenly Eltisley living, tight budgeting, arranging of moving: us, great trunks, hundreds of books and little thin delicate expensive pottery cups. A space of paralysis. And now, aching, but surer and surer, I feel the wells of experience and thought spurting up, welling quietly, with little clear sounds of juiciness. How the phrases come to me: I have begun the story about the Trouble-Making Mother, and instead of scratching at a bare plastic surface which resists my nails, I am sitting in the heart of it, pouring it out, untidily, all right, but it comes, and the ordering and shaping of it will come. And then the tale of the twenty-four cakes will come.

Ted is wonderful: how to get it down? All of a piece, smelling lovely as a baby, a hay field, strawberries under leaves, and smooth white, browning to tan, with his great lion head of hair erupting. We are clean now, daily bathing the muck of Eltisley, which will always signify spiders in clots of dust, black coal sludge sticking brick floors, smeared windows, pale yellow-orange walls, untidy Sassoons" - - - bathing that muck off from our bones in the great salt tides of the Atlantic, the hot sun.

We dream: and my dreams get better. Newnham last night, clear, not low-skied, fetid, as in my old exam dreams. Neutral, verging on pleasant: books on robins, queer birds, and exam folio on natural design: pressed flowers: sheafs of pressed pink and yellow trumpet flowers, wild and small. Podgy examiners, Miss Cohen," Miss Morris." And waking, with my skin not yet quite on, to Ted bringing cold orange juice to quench sleep-thirst, and the bowls of coffee, green china-glass bowls.

In his dream we walked a meadow: a baby tiger, and a tiger beyond a hedge. A tiger-man, with a great Chinesey yellow face knocking at the door with a gun. Ted defending, bluffing with an empty rifle: I could kill a tiger with snipe shot at this distance. Magnificence. For the Novel.

Virginia Woolf helps. Her novels make mine possible: I find myself describing: episodes: you don't have to follow your Judith Greenwood to breakfast, lunch, dinner, or tell about her train rides, unless the flash forwards her, reveals her. Make her enigmatic: who is that blond girl: she is a bitch: she is the white goddess." Make her a statement of the generation. Which is you.

Episodes: exterior: the white wedding cakes halls of Newnham: concrete as no one has been concrete: the American innocence on the saturated spot of history. Worn walks, scooped stone steps: scooped by whom: famous names? Innocence beyond innocence, having passed intact through the disintegrating forces of lust, vanity, hate, ambition: plenitude, having passed through penury. No garden before the fall: but a garden hand-made after it. Gary Haupt: distressingly pedantic, bearish: would be a critic, trying to read "When I was young and easy under the apple boughs." Satirize him: shuffle, sinus, water blue eyes and faint whitish-yellow cast to skin: simple life: potato and steak. Heavy books by Yale professors inscribed: to Gary, in appreciation of his work in English ... his affair with an older, ugly girl-artist who was past mistress of a loose, libertine poet and couldn't get over it. All for the novel. Beginning Monday: try for 7 or 8 pages a day.

The Girl In the Mirror
Menagerie with a Red Fox

July 25: Thursday:
How we cling to these days of July: August is a September month" (there, I've got so used to writing "mother" in the last days that it nips out to usurp all words beginning with "m"). Today: clear, flung, blue, pine-chills, orange needles underfoot. Writing weather, after three days of murking clouds, rain: silver tinselly rain, all theatrical and limpid big drops on Monday, then the deluge, cold, straight, and quite magnificent. We sat out on the dripping porch in chairs, rain pooling the green-plastic seat covers, smearing the screens with translucent panes of water, seeping into the dry fissured ground. Sunday was heaven: a mark in life, a clear line on a clean page: we were rested, writing free, tan, quite enchanted with our work, the sky, and our finding a sandbar, all smooth and shallow to bathe on between Nauset Light and Coast Guard beach: we played: floating, my hands and feet bobbing like corks, my hair wet from my forehead, trailing to bait the fishes. A surge of glory and power. Then back to work. Writing and scrawling corrections, retyping, my story on the Trouble-Making Mother: close to my experience, getting a neat slice out of a big pothering deepdish pie; all takes place in one day: change of mind the crux. Begins at pitch of tension, series of flashbacks triggered by telephone calls: characters all vivid, present: Curt's house, Jason, mother, doctor Karen: all working and weaving in and out. I must say, I'm surprised at the story: it's more gripping, I think, than anything I've ever done. No more burble about Platinum Summers manipulated from

behind my eye with a ten-foot pole. Real, dramatic crises. A growth in the main character. Things and emblems of importance. I got depressed with the ending on Tuesday: four pages of anti-climactic question and answer between Doctor and Sara, dry and chopped logical as an adding machine: now, you've decided this, how do you feel about that. Bad as a rich involved poem with a bare flat two-line moral tacked on the end: this is the truth kiddies, without any fancy stuff. Well, Tuesday night & yesterday morning I thought & found the answer: keep the audience guessing: fast, quick end, gathered up into the dramatic sheath of the story. I think I made it. Sent it off to the SatEvePost: start at the top. Try McCalls, Ladies home J., Good Housekeeping, Womans Day, before getting blue. If they wrote little praises about my style in other stories, but wished for a more serious subject, why, this is my best styled story and has enough seriousness, identity problems, fury, love etc. to be a winner. If I got only one story accepted, I'd have a bulwark to lean my foot against between me and the last published one: my infancy, in 1952, five years ago. I would be helped by that: it would cast an aura of immediate potential over my present strugglings and catapult me out of the adolescent market into my own among all the money-earning brain-loaded adults. But, if not, I must work, and not whine. In five years after five years of steady work, I might have grounds to complain. Not now, after my first good story for five years, with hardly a word written in between.

The artist's life nourishes itself on the particular, the concrete: that came to me last night as I despaired about writing poems on the concept of the seven deadly sins and told myself to get rid of the killing idea: this must be a great work of philosophy. Start with the mat-green fungus in the pine woods yesterday: words about it, describing it, and a poem will come. Daily, simply, and then it wont lour in the distance, an untouchable object. Write about the cow, Mrs. Spauldings heavy eyelids, the smell of vanilla flavouring in a brown bottle. That's where the magic mountains begin.

July 29: Monday"

Gail	Jenny	Judith
Hilda	Jennifer	Phyllis
Isabel	Joyce	Rachel
		Ruth
		Sybil
		Sibyl
		Vivian

Back again at ten-thirty, angry because it's ten thirty and the laundry to be done this afternoon and me hung between the equal and conscience-twanging pulls of at least five demanding stories: the Twenty-Four cake story (McCalls or SatEvePost naturalism and introspection), the Eye-Beam story (Atlantic Monthly: weird, very Kafka symbolic: girl gets speck in eye for a week: world is put away far off, and she realizes the irrevocable nature of her own loneliness: relation to suitor), the novel Falcon Yard (to begin o horror at the beginning and write through how? whose style? to the end, incorporating the turgid mass already written and avoiding the sentimentality of the love affair: take a lesson from Hemingway), the mother's helper story to finish and type up with the Laundromat one for the Journal, and the Harper's article which makes me shudder and revolt every time I think of Harper's with a very very guilty conscience. The panacea: getting deep into one story and involved, as in the Trouble-Making Mother one, so the others are ipso facto, shut out for a week.

Five more weeks. The day after the day after tomorrow it is August. And no lesson plans, no grammar studied. Now to get out of the chill paralysis. Realize that only one day and one book must be taught at a time. And I'll have the time. Get into novel deep enough so it will go on at the same time."

After Friday of cooking, whipping yellow oil into yellow egg yolks to make mayonnaise, white sugar into white egg whites to make meringue, yellow butter into yellow custard, and whipped cream folded in to make yellow and white custard, and on and on, I am back to a certain stoic stance: to begin again and write and read in the afternoons and evenings and to hell with the beach for a while. Any idiot can waste the summer getting tan only to lose it.

The cake-story: Ellen Stockbridge, at twenty-nine has three children: Blair, age 2, Penny, age 4, and Peter, age 7. Jock, her strong-willed, taciturn but loving husband is a salesman of office furniture, rising fast, with a need to make business trips. Problem: Ellen has sacrificed her own personality (talent: looks) to making good family and home for Jock. By contrast with her younger sister, Franny, she sees how dowdy she is: Franny is single, a secretary for a law firm, who can afford a pink and white convertible, and is hardening into a kind of bright, brazen, spinsterishness. Franny's men: Ellen married Jock after the war and started having kids, always behind on the budget. Resentment: Jock rumored or seen lunching with his secretary: on Franny's type: nothing to care for but herself. Ellen, after a quarrel with Jock who is leaving on a salestrip over the weekend (she's not sure if it's with secretary) decides to leave him: to go to the city and work, and take care of herself and perhaps come back all sleek and lovely again. Not children's fault*yet, somehow it is: they don't think of her as a person, just a mother: convenient. She calls Franny to mind kids for a day, says she's going into town shopping. Compelled to leave something for children: their favorite cakes: starts baking. By compulsion, feels the need to keep on, orders four dozen eggs, confectioners sugar, measures out vanilla, baking powder: sense of order, neatness, creativeness. Born homemaker, sense of dignity, richness: knowledge that she's what Jock really needs and wants. Trusts him to see it, too. He walks in that night, having cut short his trip. Saturday: starts in morning at eight. Ends around midnight. Jock comes home, walks into kitchen: she is vital, flushed from baking, at peace with herself. Knows she will stick with him, and that he has truly come back to her. The last train to the city: she is dressed: just putting frosting on cupcakes. August saturday.

It is, o god, August 9th: a Friday, uncomfortably near the uprooting of roots, a clear blue-white morning about 9:30, and me coldly and gingerly writing about 14 lines on my long lumbering dialogue verse poem with two people arguing over a ouija board. It is quite conversational sounding in spite of the elaborate 7-line pentameter stanzas rhyming ababcbc and is more ambitious than anything I've ever done, although I feel to be doing it like a patchwork quilt, without anything more than the general idea it should come out a rectangular shape, but not seeing how the logical varicolored pieces should fit. At least it gets me out of that incredible sense of constriction which I have on trying to find subjects for small bad poems, and feeling always that they should be perfect, which gives me that slick shiny artificial look. So I will try to wean myself into doing daily poetic exercises with a hell-who-cares-if-they're-published feeling. That's my trouble. I see it very clear now: bridging the gap between a bright published adolescent which died at 20 and a potentially talented & mature adult who begins writing about 25. It is tempting to cling to the old lyric sentimental stuff: the prose shows how far I am behind: I haven't published a story for 5 years. The prose is not so easy to come into maturity as the poetry which, by its smallness & my practise with form, can look complete. The main problem is breaking open rich, real subjects to myself & forgetting there is any audience but me & Ted.

I have never in my life, except that deadly summer of 1953, & fall, gone through such a black lethal two weeks. I couldn't write a word about it, although I did in my head. The horror, day by day more sure, of being pregnant. Remembering my growing casualness about contraception, as if it couldn't happen to me then: clang, clang, one door after another banged shut with the overhanging terror which, I know now, would end me, probably Ted, and our writing & our possible impregnable togetherness. The glittering and coming realities: my job at Smith, which I need more than anything to give me a sense of reality, or serving, specifically, from day to day, and meeting minds & working & practising with them; our apartment in Northampton which we'd have to leave because of the baby; our future, Ted with no job, me with no job, the avalanche of bills putting us into debt, and, worst of all, hating and hating the intruder when, four years from now, say, we could be the best parents possible. Also, the idea of 20 years of misery and a child being unloved, as it inadvertently, through our fault, killed our spiritual and psychic selves by freezing them into a stasis out of the necessity of sacrificing everything to earning money. This we lived in, sickly, from day to day, counting the days over the longest times I'd gone: 35 days, 40 days, and then the crying sessions in the doctor's office, the blood test Sunday, in avalanches of rain & thunder, riding the streaming roads, up to our knees on our bikes in the dips filling inch by inch with rainwater, drenched to the skin, bent to break under the lightning. I pictured final judgment on a bridge: a thundercrack & last pyre of electricity. But nothing happened. Nothing, till Monday when, after a busy, deceptive morning of shopping, I sat at the typewriter and the hot drench itself began, the red stain dreamed for and longed for during the white sterile ominous minutes of the six weeks. And the swearing to whatever gods or fates there be, that I would never complain or bewail anything as long as the baby didn't come: the ultimate worst, aside from physical mutilations and sicknesses and deaths, or the loss of love.

And, punctually, I got the next worseness to cope with a day later: Yesterday, the rejection of my poetry book,[n] after an almost malicious false alarm from mother, and after half a year of hoping and yes, even counting on the damn thing. It was like receiving back the body of a cancerous lover whom you hoped dead, safely, at the morgue, in a wreath of flowers to commemorate the past.

It Came Back. And with the misery of knowing half of the poems, published ones, weren't any longer, or in two years would definitely not be, passable in myself because of their bland ladylike archness or slightness. And I become linked to the damn book again, weeding it out like an overgrown garden: once the weeds were scenic, but not any more. And if A.C.Rich[n] wasn't so dull, and Donald Hall[n] so dull, and they putting in a hundred pages of dull published poems, I wouldn't feel so lousy. It would have backed me up at Smith in my work, given me that toehold on my adult work instead of making me go on from a five year gap, and only 16 poems published in the last year.

Worst: it gets me feeling so sorry for myself, that I get concerned about Ted: Ted's success, which I must cope with this fall with my job, loving it, and him to have it, but feeling so wishfully that I could make both of us feel better by having it with him. I'd rather have it this way, if either of us was successful: that's why I could marry him, knowing he was a better poet than I and that I would never have to restrain my little gift, but could push it and work it to the utmost, and still feel him ahead. I must work for a state in myself which is stoic: the old state of working & waiting. I have had the most unfortunate hap: the bright glittery youth from 17 to 20 and then the break-up and the dead lull while I fight to make the experiences of my early maturity available to my typewriter.

Yesterday: I faced another fact square on: I have not only been grossly spoiled: I haven't worked at all. Not one tenth hard enough. This I know now: it was outlined by our visit to the two young writers Mrs. Cantor sent over: they are both through with the first draft of novels, 350 pages of typing: now that's, simply mechanically, a hell of a lot of typing not to mention writing & rewriting. They have had six months, to our six weeks. So what. I haven't used six weeks. I haven't written a poem for six months until this long exercise in freer speech and extended subject, and haven't written a story since October except for one, the Trouble-Making mother, which is a slick story, but one I consider good, which was rejected without a word from the SatEvePost, and a flashy light one about a mother's helper which I consider artificial, and not worth rewriting and which will, in a week, no doubt come back from the Ladies' Home Journal along with the little laundromat affair. So what have I written: bad conscience about Mademoiselle and Harper's and the Atlantic plagues me: they'd print anything I wrote that was good enough. So all I have to do is work. Mavis Gallant[n] wrote every night for ten years after work to get regular in the New Yorker, although she gave up everything. But, to salve my conscience, I must feel the pain of work a little more & have five stories pile up here, five or ten poems there, before I start even hoping to publish, and then, not counting on it: write every story, not to publish, but to be a better writer, and ipso facto, closer to publishing. Also: don't panic. I'd rather not live in this gift luxury of the Cape, with the beach & the sun always calling, and me feeling guilty to stay in out of the sun as I would have to in the inland town, but more guilty to go out in the sun when I haven't worked at writing like a dog. That is what I need to end this horror: the horror of being talented and having no recent work I'm proud of, or even have to show. Next summer, better to sweat in Hamp" & save money & work on novel so I'll be worth a year's grant to work on, say, a verse play. Now I've started this dialogue, I am interested in verse plays. TV: try that. But be honest. No more mother's helper stories with phony plots. It wasn't all phony, but slicked over, without the quirks, to move fast. And Ted will be proud of me, which is what I want. He doesn't care about the flashy success, but about me & my writing. Which will see me through.

Wednesday: August 21, 1957

A low, sultry day. The sky a luminous white glower of light. I am caught in the six days before this is over. Stops and starts. In love with Henry James: Beast in the Jungle robs me of fear of job because of love of story, always trying to present it in mind, as to a class. The first week will be the worst, but from Sept. 1st on, I'll outline my first four weeks & prepare them in detail & become familiar with the library again. So there. Once I get into the blissful concreteness of this job, my life will catapult into a new phase: that I know. Experience, various students, specific problems. The blessed edges and rounds of the real, the factual.

Every day to jot down notes: a husband uses the birthday card from his mother-in-law as a penwiper. Whole relationship jumps into focus. Kindly unadmired unloved mother-in-law. Problem of aging parents.

Yesterday: the weird spectacle of fiddler crabs in the mud-pools off Rock Harbor creek: a mud flat at low tide, surrounded by a margin of dried brittle marsh grass, stretching away into the yellow-green salt marsh. Mud, damp toward center, alive with the rustle and carapaced scuttle of green-black fiddler crabs, like an evil cross between spiders and lobsters and crickets, bearing one gigantic pale green claw and walking sideways. At our approaching footsteps, they crabs near the bank scuttled up it, into holes in the black mucky earth, and into the grass roots, and the crabs in the soggy black center of the dried pool dug themselves into the mud, under little mud lids until only claws jutted from the little cliff of the bank, and elbows and eyes looked out of the myriad holes among the roots of the dry grasses and the drying clustered musselshells, like some crustaceous bulbs among the tussocks. An image: weird, of another world, with its own queer habits, of mud, lumped, under-peopled with quiet crabs.

A light vivid Harper's article on Cambridge. A couple of short colorful articles on Eastham to go with drawings of Mrs. Spaulding and beachplums, boats beached in Rock Harbor, and two corn vases.

A story: told with infinite detail, but must <u>move</u>: The corn vases. To balance long sentences, have short fluid sentences. Mrs. McFague, a stolid, good-hearted Cape Codder, indefatigable talker, memory runs back to Frisco quake, thrown together with young couple in her cottages without car, takes them shopping, to doctor's. Sense of her simplicity, yet she hides riches: antiques: two corn vases in trailer, amid poverty. Lazy, unimaginative, sickly husband: get in story of second marriage through present talk: husband with abscessed ear: visitors descend on them: Mrs. McFague's lack of will-power, contrast with Tookie, who would consider such an invasion outrageous. Mrs. McFague comes back to find children playing with corn vases, utter weakminded wills of parents. Main theme: parental weakness. Mrs. McFague sends them off. Tookie, no children, English husband.

[Appendix 11 (entry 41) contains Sylvia Plath's notes for a short story 'Mama McFague & the Corn Vase Girl' – ed.]

Friday night, February 21: Simply the fact that I write in here, able to hold a pen, proves, I suppose, the ability to go on living. For some reason fatigue accumulated this week like a leaden sludge into which I sink. Horns outside in the ghoul-green tinny light, shrieks, laughs and absortive chants "If you can't hear us, we'll yell a little louder." And the louder yell. The restless uneasy rush of car-tires, cushioned gears engaging. How one looks to morning, early morning, six, five, while the great populous city lies dumb, sunk in predawn slumber. Those fresh blue bird-burbling Cambridge dawns - no birds here, but exhaust & tired men grinding to work. Whoops, now. And people cramming in and out of the brick church at all hours. Today the last lap, thanks to George Washington. Woke after 9 hours sleep still exhausted & rebellious, not wanting to drag my drugged body to a lecture platform: a problem of identity: ted says: "In twenty-five minutes you'll be talking to a class." I dawdled over coffee in the thick brown pottery mug, waiting for the coffee-revelation, which didn't come, bang, into clothes, torn webbed stockings, out into the dull-mat-finished gray morning raw as an oyster & jamming into gear to the parking lot, the gold hand on the clock tower on college hall standing at 9. Ran up ice path gritted with sand, bang, bell rang, into class in a daze, with faces looking up, expecting me to say something, + me not there, blank, bored, hearing my voice lead out blithes on ironic structure of the Oedipus which I realize I don't understand myself: it is folly to try to outwit the gods. Or: we are all predestined - or still: we have free will & must be responsible.

NOTEBOOK –

August 28, 1957 – "The fullness thereof" –

Aug 30: Item: weak-willed girl who is always "put-upon" by high-power salesmanship of others until, in this high-pressure age, she is a product "not-herself" – her clothes, hairdo, job, men, etc. are really her mother's, sister's, brother's & townspeople's concept of what should be "just right" for nice little Sara, Millie, Bridget, or whatever. Few abortive attempts at rebellion or rejection of other's deciding for her are repulsed, overcome or come out ironically – e.g. perfume-counter girl gives her wrong sultry perfume (girl thought she wanted "sultry")[n] instead of wrong "sweet-feminine" perfume) – pushed into going around with sister's old boyfriend, into engagement – suddenly stops – some strange man shocks her out of it – somehow asserts self – striking interior same – but has been fostered in sweet, bloussy little-girl exterior – changes & integrates.

Sept. 6 – First morning up early. Clear day, light yellowing, cold, among elm leaves. Last night: walk in odd primeval greening park – dark twisted rocks, crunch of acorns underfoot, every sprig of fallen bough shaping itself to squirrels. Now: coffee-vision, in spite of Ted using coffee percolator wrong, making poisonous brew, milk boiling over, mislaying percolator directions, waiting for desk (desk comes, all squat, ugly; doesn't fit doorway; men take door down, still doesn't fit; joy! it was so ugly; will bring up little desk from home with vineleaves on it). Story: woman with poet husband who writes about love, passion – she, after glow of vanity & joy, finds out he isn't writing about her (as her friends think) but about Dream Woman Muse.

Sept 12 – Last night: the horror of unknown physical pain, accelerating – the swollen back gum, blistered, loose, bleeding; the ripped stomach muscle from hoisting furniture: like a knife, turning, pivoting on a knife, that throbbed; then the left-over beef stew, with the white blobs of salt pork, fat, greasy & the hot faint rushes of fever at the sight of bacon fat, melted in the pan, and the pork sausages, exuding & oozing their own fat – the clenched fear: hernia, hemorrhage looming, and the horror of ether, the razor slitting the stomach, and life throbbing away, red flood by red flood – I lay, crouched, kneeling on the khaki quilt on the livingroom floor where there was air, remembering Spain & the poisonous red Spanish sausage; the channel crossing & the tuna sandwich & wine & acrid vomit in the nose, searing the throat & me crawling under the chairs; the Atlantic crossing & me kneeling on the floor of the little cabin under the electric light & the vomit shooting out across the room from the rich dinner, the lobster & pecans & martinis – now, in the bathroom, kneeling on the floor, thinking of fat, of the salt pork & fatty marrow larding the thick soup, & retching, dryly: "Salt pork," I said, & then it came, the first dilute retch of stew, dissolved in water, then the clench, then the ejection. Ted held my head, my stomach, over the white bowl of the toilet. Then I washed my face, the fatty fumes cleared, I could sleep, exhausted, cool, till the sun of morning, pale & slanted through the venetian blinds, & the sound of leaves, falling –

Poem: Crucifixes – Lawrence's essay : "an atmosphere of pain" – prismatic variety of Christs' – but: mainly: No transfiguration – blood & pain & misery or staunch bitter rebellion of body – but no peace, no transfiguration – atmosphere of fear of physical pain – wincing from the knife – the loss of identity which is slavery to physical pain. Brutal, passionate flesh – Matisse crucifix – pain smoothed away, identity smoothed away in pain – pure fusion – no remainder – flesh sublimed to gold – "meaning of own souls anguish" – "human attempts at deciphering the riddle of pain" – 'blood": "florid & ornate" – ugly, unredeemed, ironic – waiting in corridors – cross of flesh x spirit – minor daily crosses –

Story: two – ① Moor setting – walk to Haworth, to Wuthering Heights – physical, rich, heavy-booted detail – blisters, grouse – picnic – honey soaking through brown paper bag – fear, aloneness – goal – cairn of black stones, small, contracted – their dream of each other, she & he – Elly & red-headed artist – strength of Elly? Strength – each alone – bracken, marsh – tea in deep cleft of valley – dark, cats – story of lost woman – match-flare of courage in the dark – moor sheep – bus-wait opposite spiritualists – ghosts & reality on moor – difference in stone house for four – aloneness & difference of experience – tell from four points of view – each with different vision of day, changing – house: absolute reality, but clustered with ghosts – eternal paradox of identity – lens focussing disparate rays: medium – of unknown clustering forces – influence of ghosts, stars – Elly: theatrical: self, star: Cathy: actress – red-head stolid artist: portrait painter: realist – face of things, not spirit – Poet: Ted – metaphor for decay, aloneness – spiritist: Sibyl – cluster

of ghost – <u>possessed by</u> house, not house possessed by her (as with others) –
Will Greenough
Curt Fleischmann
Evi Glidden
Sibyl Moss"

②– Woman's mag – American wife of British writer – insecure – theatrical
brilliant friend from NYC touring, comes up – threat – brings boyfriend –
walk to heights – responsibility – brings out good in Elly? Strength – ? <u>House
of Wind</u> – Elly – symbol of outer world – can she meet it? Jealousy – to face
responsibility or not? Said she wouldn't go home untill she found career or
man – elaborate plot – not married – engaged: visiting fiancées parents –
humble – Elly: spectacular – really loves her – overcomes selfishness: faith in
fiancé: no attraction for social life – friendship with Elly – from tentative
jealousy & enmity – she is ahead, not behind, & will stay ahead – <u>committed</u>
– Evi Larkin," Jill Holly Ford, Julian Gascoigne, Chandler Whipple

"Four Corners of a Windy House" –
Trip to & from Wuthering Heights told by four characters – each seeing
different facet of absolute reality – which is nearest truth? Evi (egoistic
actress), Leroy / Curt (realist prosaic artist), William (creative poet – half-
dust, half-deity), Sibyl (dreamy pale medium of spirit forces) – The house
stood. The black stones cast no shadow. Vary tones of voice, style, observations of others – Leroy – he-man
Curt → Evi (her beauty, vivid life – Sibyl too pale, ethereal)
Evi → Will (he can create beautiful words, roles, for her)
Will → Evi / Sibyl (his muse, versus his woman – flesh & spirit,)
Sibyl → all & none – visionary, flesh transparent – assumes responsibility,
pain & suffering –

Crime & Punishment –
Poem: ghosts: can only appear to sick, not healthy men of earth, men of this
world – fragments of other-world.

[Appendix 12 contains Sylvia Plath's 1 October 1957 'Letter to a demon'; Appendix
13 contains Sylvia Plath's 5 November 1957 journal fragment – ed.]

January 4, 1958: New Year four days gone, along with resolutions of a page
a day, describing mood, fatigue, orange peel or color of bathtub water after
a week's scrub. Penalty, and escape, both: four pages to catch up. Air lifts,

clears. The black yellow-streaked smother of October, November, December gone & clear New Year's air come – so cold it turns bare shins, ears and cheeks to a bone of ice-ache. Yet sun, lying now on the fresh white paint of the store-room door, reflecting in the umber-ugly paint coating the floorboards, and shafting a slant on the mauve-rusty rosy lavendar rug from the west gable window. <u>Changes</u>: what breaks windows to thin air, blue views, in a smother-box? A red twilly shirt for Christmas: Chinese red with black-line scrolls and oriental green ferns to wear every day against light blue walls. Ted's job chance at teaching just as long & just as much as we need. $1000 or $2000 clear savings for Europe. Vicarious joy at Ted's writing which opens promise for me too: <u>New Yorker's</u> 3rd poem acceptance & a short story for <u>Jack & Jill</u>. 1958: The year I stop teaching & start writing. Ted's faith: don't expect: just write, listen to self, scribble. Fear about that: dumb silence. Yet: so what? It will take months to get my inner world peopled, and the people moving. How else to do it but plunge out of this safe scheduled time-clock wage-check world into my own voids. Distant planets spin. I dream too much of fame, posturings, a novel published, not people gesturing, speaking, growing & cracking into print. But with no job, no money worries, why the black lid should lift. Look at life with humor: easy to say: things open up: know people: horizons extend: Max Goldberg" yesterday, little, round, ugly yet a light in him: the dark grist mill boards & tales of the steelworkers course in humanities: "It's a fish-story, so why not end it. Fish is caught." "Naw, prof, there's a fight going on?" "Where?" Pounds chest: "In here! In here!"

Notes for <u>Jack & Jill</u> story: "Changeabout in Mrs. Cherry's Kitchen" – Suddenly, Ted & I looked at things from our unborn children's point of view. Take gadgets: a modern pot & kettle story. Shiny modern gadgets are overspecialized – long to do others tasks. Toaster, iron, waffle-maker, refrigerator, egg beater, electric fry-pan, blender. One midnight fairies or equivalent grant wish to change-about. Iron wants to make waffles, dips point for dents; refrigerator tired of foods, decides to freeze clothes, toaster tired of toast, wants to bake fancy cake. Egg beater dizzy with whirring around decides to iron ruffly white blouse. Roasting spit wants to bake cookies. Dish-washer wants to cook. Disturbance caused by jealousy, return gladly after whirlwind experiment to doing best of own job. Coffee-maker Pixies or elves who churn milk & sour cream go to work one midnight – or one day of year when each machine can do what it wishes – have a vacation. This year they choose to change their jobs. Complex, perhaps, but possible?

Night visions: the fire and coughing – zebra stripes of light laid on walls and angled ceilings from venetian blinds: <u>Falcon Yard</u>: rise above pure central line diary – lyric cry no: but rich, humorous satire. Reconstruction. Gary Haupt among the many. Tables to bump into. Cameo – dear perspectives. Get back to perfect rhythms & words binging & bonging in themselves: green, thin, whine – then phrases, then sentences. Place doesn't matter – it's the inner life: Ted & me. Me on my own with him. Above decorum & circumspection. Poetry book finished, stories (<u>Journal & Atlantic</u>), & first draft <u>at least</u> of novel. Then attempt at novel grant – Saxton ideally, not royalty advance sort, for year in Italy. Now the unpleasant hairy work – Mr. Hill" refusing job, Pelner to be rid of, Dostoevsky to do & course books to outline.

The moment I stop, stop the itch of dreams and dream-lulling, squirrelish money-counting, paralysis sets in: paralysis of alternatives: to make up a scene? To describe a childhood incident by memory? I have no memory. Yes, there was a circle of lilac bushes outside Freeman's yellow house." Begin there: 10 years of childhood before the slick adolescent years, & then my diaries to work on: to reconstruct. Two popular trees, green & orange striped awnings. I never learned to look at details. Recreate life lived: that is renewed life. The incident goes down, a grit in the eye of god, and is wept forth a hundred years and a day hence, a globed iridescent pearl world – turn the glass globe and the snow falls slowly through ronds of quartz air. Metaphors crowd. Pellets of fact drop into the mind's glass of clear liquor and unfold petal by petal, red, blue, green, or pink and white – paper flowers creating an illusion of a world. Every world crowns its own kings, laurels it own gods. A Hans Anderson book cover opens its worlds: the snowqueen, bluewhite as ice, flies in a sleigh through her snow-thick air: our hearts are ice. Always: sludge, offal, shit against palaces of diamond. That man could dream god and heaven: how mud labors. We burn in our own fire. To voice that. And the horror: the strange bird who knows Longfellow, perches on a wire with a backdrop of English green-bushed landscapes. The white-bearded grandfather drowning in the sea-surge, the warm, slow, sticky rollers; the terror of paper crackling & expanding before the burnt-out black grate: whence these images, these dreams? Worlds – shut-off by car-bustle, calendar-dictation. A world hung in a Christmas ornament, washed gilt, a world silvered & distended in the belly of my pewter teapot: open Alice's door, work & sweat to pry open gates & speak out words & worlds.

Each day an exercise, or a stream-of-consciousness ramble? Hates crackle and brandish against me: unsettling the image of brilliance. My face I know not. One day ugly as a frog the mirror blurts it back: thick-pored skin, coarse as a sieve, exuding soft spots of pus, points of dirt, hard kernels of impurity – a coarse grating. No milk-drawn silk. Hair blued with oil-slick, nose crusted with hair and green or brown crusts. Eye-whites yellowed, corners crusted, ears a whorl of soft wax. We exude. Spotted bodies. Yet days in a dim or distant light we burn clear of our shackles and stand, burning and speaking like gods. The surface texture of life can de dead, was dead for me. My voice halted, my skin felt the pounds & pounds pressure of other I's on every inch, wrinkled, puckered, sank in on itself. Now to grow out. To suck up & master the surface & heart of worlds & wrestle with making my own. To speak <u>morally</u> for it is a moral. A moral of growth. Fern butting its head on concrete of here & now & ramming its way through. To get the faces bodies acts and names & make them live. To live as hard as we can, extending, & writing better. This summer: no job, or only very part time job. German study & French reading. Reading own books: Berkeley, Freud, Sociology. Most of all: <u>myths & folktales & poetry</u> & <u>anthropology</u>. History even. Knowing Boston. Boston diary: taste, touch, street names. Six o'clock rings, belling from the church where all the funerals come. Rooms. Every room a world. To be god: to be every life before we die: a dream to drive men mad. But to be one person, one woman – to live, suffer, bear children & learn others lives & make them into print worlds spinning like planets in the minds of other men.

<u>Incident</u>: The day I hung Johanna from the trapeze: her blue wool jumper & hoarse voice: mother looking out of the brown stucco house. Child sadism. Digging to china. Name: Days, O'Kelly's, Lanes, Ella Mason, Florence Brown. The old woods & the garnetts in their sewer-hole. The Eldracka's and Rinki the fat dachshund. Our stretch of beach. The sewer-hole. The green rock. Johnson Avenue. Jimmy Beale & his drowned sister. Vacant lot – field of raspberries & daisies. Catalpa tree. Collecting tin cans & keys for war effort. Joan MacDonald's & baking mud pies. Each memory dragged up drags up another. Exercise: not just naming but recreating. Lights of Boston airport & planes. Superman. Lights on runway. Red berries on fir trees. Wandering jew & iris roots. Not enough, not enough. Teachers & school. Camp. What I know. Mary Coffee. Mary Ventura. Mrs. Meehan's Mad Boy: art teacher and her 30 year old son. Then the big expansion – Cape Cod camp summers – Vineyard. The moors and Cambridge. Paris &

Benidorm – to master these places and the people. Abortion. Suicide. Affairs. Cruelty. All those I know. How everything shrinks on return – you can't go home again. Winthrop shrunk, dulled, wrinkled its dense hide: all those rainbow extensions of dreams lost luster, shells out of water, color blanching out. Is it that our minds colored the streets and children then & do so no longer? We must fight to return to that early mind – intellectually we play with fables that once has us sweating under sheets – the emotional, feeling drench of wonder goes – in our minds we must recreate it, even while we measure baking powder for a hurry-up cake & calculate next months expenses. A god in breathes himself in everything. Practice: <u>Be</u> a chair, a toothbrush, a jar of coffee from the inside out: <u>know</u> by feeling in.

<u>Tuesday night: January 7</u>: All day, or two days, you lay under the maple-table and heard tears, phones ring, tea pouring from a pewter pot. Why not lie there until you rot or get thrown out with the rubbish, book? A wreck on a shoal, time and tears vicissituding round about you, surging and sliding cool and blue-distant. Lie there, catching dust, pale rose and lavendar scruff from the rug, blank-paged and my voice quiet, choked in. Or to pass on air, blown with the other cries and complaints, to some limbo in the far nebulae. Anyhow: by dint of squandering some ink here, after counting your pages, you should see me through to the spring, to my so-called liberty – from what I seem to know, but for what I can only dream. Writing stories & poems is hardly so far-fetched. But talking about it hypothetically is grim: a thing. Today, outside now, snow descends. This is where I came in. Dry taps on window. A greenish light from the lamps & flakes blowing oblique in the cone of light. An auspicious beginning for work tomorrow. After sun all week. And my lectures as usual, to prepare tomorrow morning – felt and feel mad, petulant, like a sick wasp – cough still & can't sleep till late at night, feel grogged & drugged till noon. Yet will I work & get through. One day at a time. After a brief bold encounter with Chas. Hill yesterday, blue and squinch-toothed, & his icy self, a call from Mr. Fisher & my stupid discussion this morning in the high white atticky study, all book-crammed, & his 7 volume novel in black thesis books with white lettering that I know must be so ghastly. The gossip. One gets sick trying to conjecture it. The eleven o'clock coffee break & the gossip. All the inferences: The Institution will regard you as irresponsible. Two-year conventions. Rot. I am in a cotton-wool wrap. All is lost on me – all double entendres. "I have divided loyalties," I say. "I am your friend," he says. "No one but me will tell you this. – Oh, by the way, may I tell all this to Mr. Hill". "I resigned twice", he

said. "Once because of gossip that I was sleeping with students. President Nielson called up & found there were 10 in my class: 'Hell, Fisher, that's too much even for you.'" Now he is living deserted by his 3rd Smith wife for his selfishness. His vanity is as palpable as his neat white moustache. "It's all in your mind," he says, "about anxiety. I have it from various sources." If they deal in inference, hint, threat, double entendre, gossip. I'm sick of it. They mean vaguely well, somehow. But have no idea what is for my own good, only theirs. "What do you need to write?" Gibian asks over tea. Do I need to write anything? Or do I need time & blood? I need a full head, full of people. First know myself, deep, all I have gathered to me of otherness in time & place. Once Whitstead was real, my green-rugged room with the yellow walls & window opening onto Orion and the green garden and flowering trees, then the smoky Paris blue room like the inside of a delphinium with the thin nervous boy & figs and oranges & beggars in the streets banging their heads at 2 am., then the Nice balcony over the garage, the dust & grease and carrot peels of Rugby street on my wedding night, Eltisley avenue, with the gloomy hall, the weight of coats, the coal dust. Now this pink-rose-walled room. This too shall pass, laying eggs of better days. I have in me these seeds of life.

Wednesday night: January 8: Codeine, opium, drawn from opiates, took me from my cough and aches and lifted me, with no pain, into the core of a cocoon all warm and yet abstracted from my body, a point of consciousness sleeping in lulled chaos, unshaped, undefined, unlimited. Dreamed, though, thanks to blue Mr. Hill: in Winthrop, in the Freeman's old diningroom, but it was all redecorated "like a bedroom" I said ungraciously, in blue: ruffled blue plastic curtains, blue quilted walls, and bluey lights (a recall of my Paris blue-room of yesterday?) I missed my three o'clock class, and saw the big clock whir, trying to get free, but it was too late to postpone the class by a call. Then it was twenty past three, twenty of four, and I debated, and it was four, and the faculty meeting to face, late, the smoke, all of them together. – Woke, afar off, uncaring, to the bright light, thick-piled snow, shedding a whiteness, a light upward. Slowly, carelessly, codeine-careless, drank thick sweet cold orange juice Ted brought out of the white bowl with the blue rim, gagged on a stale month-old egg (we must get our own chickens, cocka-doodle and a warm fresh egg for dody's cup), drank languidly the cooling coffee in the wide brown cup. Then Ted left for Amherst & his interview-lunch, me riffling through old poems, drifting, dreamlike, wondering if I was crazy or just more casual about my work. Underlined notes in Crime &

Punishment, angry again to be behind, weak, after a vacation renewing others blood & leisure. Lonely lunch of bottled potato salad on dry lettuce, canned cup of chicken & rice soup, chicken bits some sort of spiced cat-flesh. How I hated canned soups – so uniform, always feel cheated. I'll make my own more & more, & my own dark bread. Lousy mail: insult mail: letter returned of mine to Warren for more postage, request for Dostoevsky book from library: gives nothing: takes postage, takes book. Wrapped great black mohair scarf around neck like piled fur, donned red gloves & crunched out in snow. Chill. Crisp. Crunch of cars chains, grinding, buzzing on packed snow trodden to a glaze of ice. Coffee alone in coffee shop. Pleasant blur. Dark. A few girls, one plump blonde & pink-faced; one queer one in a red & white striped knit cap sheathing her hair, and gold circle earrings, dungarees & high boots: obviously a lady-pirate. Music souping from jukebox, melancholy, embracing. Felt alone. Defiant. Very old and distant from those days I crowded in with Sue Weller, Hunter, my friends & schemes & sorrows. How I can go, meeting & exorcising my own ghosts here! I've made some new ones now. Mr. Petersson" on the door step – genial, amazingly intuitive: about Ted's trying to find a job, "demoralizing", he said, "waiting about & not working. Hard on you." Ah, yes, I breathed. The tone to take now. Class fresh & rosy. After 3 coffees. Judith Noland from Tulsa, Oklahoma: on Bessie McAlpine: buxom smiling Bessie, beside me in Art 13, social, responsible, her horrible wrist with the brown patch-scar & the black shaved hair always sprouting. Bessie married "the catch of the town", they had a swimming pool, children loved her, but they had a Volkswagon & she fell out of the door & she got killed. How I felt here then, her life, abundant, crushed, quenched, extinguished. I felt it like the spurt of my own blood, & my life, like a proud, desperate foot, on her neck. A double view. Muse. Set dream-seeds. It's enough to live life, to botch it, without dreaming it double, botches worse. Dream of flying. Of alphabet lands. Clean worlds, dream worlds –

Sunday night: January 12: Fumings of humiliation, burned and reburned, heartburn, as if I could relive a scene again & over, respeak it, forge it to my own model, and hurl it out, grit into pearl. Grit into art. Blundering, booted, to the little coffee shop table, past muffled chairs, braced under draped coats. The intimate group of three, James" leaving, black-haired, squinting, not speaking, air sizzling with unspoken remarks, "Do you really hate it here so much?" The pale British Joan," green-rimmed spectacles, green-painted fingernails, furred, with great dangling gold Aztec earrings, shaped like cubist angels, meaning remarks & meaning looks – Sally's" great flat pale hands, like air-bourne white-bellied flounder backs freckled, gesturing, stub-nails enameled with gilt paint. Superior. Condescending. Rude pink white-mustached Fisher: "Shame on you", grinning foolishly, pointing to red lipstick caked in a crescent on a coffee-cup – "The mark of the beast." All the back-references to common experience – "Is this yours" – persian-lamb fezzed Monas" holding up a pale tan pigskin pouch stamped in a red & green and gold pattern. "No, I wish it were. Is it Susie's? Is it Judy's?" Parties. Dinners. Lady with fishy eyes. "It's all in your mind," Fisher says. "I have it from various sources". In polite society a lady doesn't punch or spit. So I turn to my work. Dismissed without a word from the exam committee, hearing Sally superciliously advising me not to tell my students questions, I am justifiably outraged. Spite. Meanness, what else. How I am exorcising them from my system. Like bile. See Aaron & get it out. See Marlies" about exam & get it out. The girls stand by. Even the big nasty, blank-faced in her raccoon coat turned good, two & one-half hours of good talk Friday. Satur-day exhausted, nerves frayed. Sleepless. Threw you, book, down, punched with fist. Kicked, punched. Violence seethed. Joy to murder someone, pure scapegoat. But pacified during necessity to work. Work redeems. Work saves. Baked a lemon meringue pie, cooled lemon custard & crust on cold bathroom windowsill, stirring in black night & stars. Set table, candles, glasses sparking crystal barred crystal on yellow woven cloth. Making order, the rugs smoothed clean, maple-wood tables & dark tables cleared. Shaping a meal, people, I grew back to joy. I serve. Elly, dark haired, hair down in an unbraided sheaf, thick white sweater, Indian brown face, mobile, but too volatile, no quiet, an act, a throwing around. How deep & to what peace come those waters? Her strength, her resiliance, is of rubber, she rebounds, reshapes. He, too good. Of granite, face rock-set. Hair tight, black, knife-cut to skull. Eyes dark, still, but beautiful when he laughs, warming. Leonard." Adoring Austin Warren followed him to Michigan. Good meal. White wine, clam & sour cream. Red wine, roast beef, corn & mashed potatoes with onions whipped in. Salad. Pie & coffee. I make, made. This is shaping & it redeems. Bitter cold out, cold an ache in the lungs, a palpable weight on the face, fingers, shins. How black. Chilled through before sped to Sage." Citizen Kane. The boor-boy with hat slouched, banaging Elly, kissing her mouth, Leonard stiffening & looking stony – off, me making a face at him. A dark house. Moving, black barbwire, textured x's against a gray sky, wider mesh, carved barriers, devices, and K monogrammed in steel. Xanadu. A man slowly striding out, before a great mirror, & men striding, smaller & smaller, down an avenue of mirrors, greying, the shadow of a man cast back, moving in the glass of mirrors. A glass globe containing a world of snow, turned, falling snow, thick, in a crystal world. Asleep on a frigid midnight, last codeine taken, I deserved it, the sure deep doped sleep. <u>Sunday</u>: woke from deepness, fresh, stronger – ready to battle. A clear bright day. Up, emerging from daze, elbow-deep into last night's dishes, thick sweet orange juice. Wonder: bright, primary grade kindergarten orange: foods all colors, vivid, except bright blue. Red (apples, tomatoes, beef), orange (carrots, sweet potatoes), yellow (butter, squash), green (lettuce, spinach, beans), purple (plums, eggplant). Only blueberries. Why? Ted's gruel, coffee. Then our walk. Booted, alone, in the iced drinkable air, cry glories, eye awakens. Children coasting on highschool hill, on round beaten metal shields. Blue bright shadows on snow. Snow-packed crunchy smooth. No people. Houses tawdry, metal numbers on porch posts rusted, run rust into cream-painted wood. Left over green wreaths & red plastic bows, silvered pinecones. A house with kelly-green painted chimneys. We strode, talking of grants, of Italy, freeing ourselves step by step. A ginger-orange cat on a doorstep, yellow door, red-spoked wheel. A pale blue stucco house. A yellow one, high up a hill, and the purple cones, rounded, of the Holyoke range standing on the horizon. Coils of rusty christmas light wires & round wicker baskets of discarded red, green, yellow & blue bulbs. Blazing blue sky, icicles sculpted, spearing from eaves. New, no one we know, we the wanderers. Cut pine boughs & woodchips, sharp-scented. Back to baking, cup-cakes & cookies for McKee" & Spofford" tea. Typed old stories & verse dialogue to send off. Dug out some rough novel episodes. Some joy. Mainly despair. So single-viewed & sentimental: diary-like & vain. Will try now writing over each chapter as a story, with definite motion & climax, building up minor characters so they become actors, not just observed, like wallpaper, by the girl's eye. Sibyl as name pretentious. Try Dody: dody Ventura." Dody being a foolish anagram for Dido," of whom she may be a cariacature. Good to get mind going on this. Will try, now I'm freed from deathly obligation to kill myself over classes by the general stench of huff & spite of The Institution & its members. No incident – such as biting, is more than melodrama or bathos unless prose lifts it, wreathes it, makes eyes pearls. Work on a chapter at a time: "Friday Night in Falcon Yard." Twenty pages each. Point of view. Not just personal. External world in. Leonard, not Ian. Story symbolic – closer to nightmare of personal vision: solipsist: thus will stand on itself, not just on relation to plot. Purple roses on my white flannel nightgown, pink roses on quatre-foil pink ground of wallpaper. Glory nothing, pools and violins on a mountaintop nothing unless the mind seethes, picks up color, conversation, like lint & gets it down. How to describe a face, even? One girl in the class differentiated from another? Dark, light? Judy Hofmann, in jodpuhrs, heavy-boned, pale-blue-ringed eyes, white or plaid wool shirts, wiry brown hair. Her writing careful, big. Not enough. How does she live? Does she knit? Read true confessions. Oh, it is this indwelling with others, this meticulous gripping of detail to anchor the vague, unseen flaws & faults in internal geography, that must be done daily. Exercise, practise. Set tasks.

January 14: Tuesday: A small draft of deadly night air seeping through the white-painted metal slats of the venetian blinds sets me coughing, wheezing, with an ominous click and whistle deep in my lungs. Resolutions to get ahead in Dostoevsky fail. Tomorrow morning in four hours I must outline 2 hours of lecture. Now I am uncaring, more & more, about Smith social life. I will lead my own: Sunday teas, dinners later for U. of M. teachers – and my work. Even, I'll try, if the prose isn't too bad. Poems are out: too depressing. If they're bad, they're bad. Prose is never quite hopeless. The poetry ms. came thumping back unprized from the $1000 contest. Who won? I'd like to know. The second defeat. Must watch where it goes the third time. But I got rid of my gloom, & sulking sorrows by spending the day typing sheafs of Ted's new poems. I live in him until I live on my own. Starting June 1st. Will I have any ideas then? I've been living in a vaccuum for half a year, not writing for a year. Rust gags me. How I long again to be prolific. To whirl worlds in my head. Will I promise for 150 more days how I'll write, or take courage & start now? Something deep, plunging, is held back. Voice frozen. Today: gray, dun, wan – no light, all light ingathered, mat surface. Laundry & whirring white machines; grocery store & piles of cellophaned liver & celery, potatoes & cauliflower, exciting the desire, increasing the need. Left car to have fender undented. Name list of queer good names (cf. last page). Walk with Ted home – soot lying in a gray grit-cloak on snow, dog urine-stains bright yellow, holes pissed at heat into banks of snow. And in late afternoon, sleet beginning, dry, like white sand on the windows & the wind curling its wail around the sleet-sugared eaves. Bobs of snow.

January 20, Monday: Wicked, my hand halted, each night at writing, I fell away into sleep, book unwritten in. Woke today, at noon, coming drugged to the surface, after a lost weekend. All the deep rooted yawns. Plunged to the depths of my fatigue, and now: bushels of words. I skim the surface of my brain, writing. Prose now. Working over the kernel chapter of my novel, to crouch it & clench it together in a story. Friday night in Flacon Yard. A girl wedded to the statue of a dream, cinderella in her ring of flames, mail-clad in her unassaultable ego, meets a man who with a kiss breaks her statue, makes man-sleepings weaker than kisses, and changes forever the rhythm of her ways. Get in minor characters, round them out. Mrs. Guinea. Miss Minchell. Hamish. Monklike Derrick. American versus British. Can I do it. Over a year maybe I can. Style is the thing. "I love you" needs my own language. Then, too, "Mrs. McFague & The Corn Vase Girl" – meaty, mad character & its Sacred Object. Guarded through an invasion by the barbarian hordes in Tookie's Cabin. A mild woman driven to the end of her tether. How to end it? Crisis: Tookie confronts child lifting corn-vase. Pauses. Vase drops. Child screams. "She hit me." Who is to blame? Mrs. McFague lives in the web of her past, the corn-vase girl the idol round which she moves. Her dream house. Never built. Her sluggard husband, unhelpful. Oh, quicken prose. Tookie's eye, but naive, young – married. Half-bored, half-sympathetic with Mrs. McFague. Ted writing today, livingroom rug, clean-swept, mauve, littered under papers of poems, stories. His Yorkshire tales: a new forte; Jack & Jill bought his fairy-tale "Billy Hook & the Three Souvenirs." More & more we will write. God get me in my own heaven, he in his.

Free now, of a sudden, from classes, papers. Half the year over & spring to come, I turn, selfish, to my own writing. Reading a glut of SatEvePost stories till my eyes ached these past days I realized the gap in my writing & theirs. My world is flat thin pasteboard, theirs full of babies, odd old dowagers, queer jobs & job-lingo instead of set-pieces ending in "I love you." To live, to gossip, to work worlds in words. I can do it. If I sweat enough. Today, after creamy hot milk-coffee, fat lucent bacon on cracked wheat toast, we drove in the icy blue air to Williamsburg, to Goshen, snow piled high & white into the woods coming down to the roadside. We took a side road after Goshen, snow-packed, glistening bumpy, but sanded. "Fresh eggs." a sign said. Blue hills like a humped still sea in the distance and not a soul, not a footprint in the snow outside the tidy houses. A brown house, fresh chocolate paint, and yellow doors. But not a dog-bark, not a smoke twist. Past black & white cows stamping, steaming, down by a snow-banked brook, stamped brown, pissed yellow, stained at the lip of the dark waters. Past dirty white frame houses and banks of black-speckled snow. Those lives indoors. God, to lift up the lid of heads. Sky plowed in blue furrows, clouding white. An orchard on a high-domed white hill, trees brown-black whorls of branches. Never close enough – Never the eye close enough to the crack between brown-painted floor & white wall-base molding where pale balls of furry gray dust hide. My arm aches now. To bed to read on in <u>Look Homeward Angel</u> & tomorrow to finish rough draft of falcon yard story, type Ted's two. Supper with Arvin[n] & Spofford. Wash hair. Shop? Wednesday, study again.

January 21: Tuesday: Under a mauve-based lamp, vase shaped with curlycue handles, and a sallow rayed oil-paper shade, the ruck of salves and creams, blue bottled noxema, spicy, hygenic; red-capped thick cream deodorant; a great buff-colored round box of talcum powder with a dusty fawn corduroy top; a plastic covered cartridge of touch-of-genius red lipstick; a cheap gilt gift-mirror, face down to show a back embroidered with green and pale blue and pink flowers on sheened stems, plastic covered to keep unsoiled the feminine pastels. Of such is the kingdom of concreteness. What can I see else in this room from my pillow-perch, back to the window, black-spaced night and Route 9 carlights shut out by the rattly metal slats of the venetian blinds, undusted, gritted with soot & minute bits of grime and hair from the inside of passerbys' nostrils. A fake white-wood bureau three drawers high, with a gilt-bright handle on every drawer, juts out of the alcove, holding the odd items of our essential toilette. A white painted door open, paneled, with gray shadows geometric, tidy. A kitchen chair, seat and back padded & covered in tomato-red plastic, draped variously with black velvet slacks, two lace-topped slips of white nylon with broken shoulder-strap, ragged edged pink wool pants, a dark green and blue and black striped jersey, the corner of a brown & white checked wool jacket, all mounded over the red chair back. Chromium bent bars form four gleaming bright chair legs. A pale blond wood cabinet with one drawer & one shelf on which reposes the unnatural pale neon green clock radio, with black numbers, white hands for minutes & a red second hand circling the dial. An umber-painted floor. Quatrefoil rose wallpaper. O rose room.

The doorbell's rasp today, hot water steaming toward tea and the bright blue-white light, almost incandescent, of twilit snow. A cardboard wrapped packet of a record for Ted, compliments of Oscar Williams,[n] whom we have never met. His dead poetess-wife's face looms pale, high-cheekboned, with lowered eyes, out of the shiny record-cover with the eulogies on the back. For what reason? To haunt us with her live words, her live voice, her live face, she who lies some-where rotten, unstitching stitch by stitch? He sends her paintings, her words, to us. So, blown ghost, she comes to our tea, more substantial then many inarticulate mortals. That is strange: the deadness of a stranger who is somehow never dead – the knife of death unfelt, the immortals hover in our heads. Dinner out then at the pale green-painted faculty club. Stuffy. Vacant. Botany professors forking raw tongue with dowdy seat-spread wives. Newton Arvin, bright, balding, a strange, quirked lovely man, pink, in his brown suit, & classical Ned Spofford with his thin responsive face, black Indian-short crew-cut and black sparking eyes, pale, pointed face, giving out light, and his hawk-hooked nose. Spooned up watery red soup, talked of Cambridge England, ghost-haunted, how far from right deep speech. Then the uncuttable tough florid-pink tongue, the watery orange turnip, mashed potato, slippery dressinged lettuce, lucent & fresh as a drink of water. Apple pie & cheese & coffee. Just now, as I remember I had coffee, I waken, wide-eyed. Sleet coming down with a dry rustle, turning to beads of water on our hair. Must invite hordes of nice people to dinner, many dinners. Pair them right & ask them.

Jealous one I am, green-eyed, spite-seething. Read the six women poets in the "new poets of england and america." Dull, turgid. Except for May Swenson & Adrienne Rich, not one better or more-published than me. I have the quiet righteous malice of one with better poems than other women's reputations have been made by. Wait till June. June? I shall fall rust-tongued long before then. Somehow, to write poems, I need all my time forever ahead of me – no meals to get, no books to prepare. I plot, calculate: twenty poems now my nucleus. Thirty more in a bigger, freer, tougher voice: work on rhythms mostly, for freedom, yet sung, delectability of speaking as in succulent chicken. No coyness, archaic cutie tricks. Break on them in a year with a book of forty or fifty – a poem every ten days. Prose sustains me. I can mess it, mush it, rewrite it, pick it up any times – rhythms are slacker, more variable, it doesn't die so soon. So I will try reworking summer stuff: The Falcon Yard chapter. Yet it is a novel chapter somehow: slack, uncritical, too many characters in it. Must make some conflict. I am at least making more minor characters come alive: Mrs. Guinea, Miss Minchell, Hamish. Must avoid the exotico-romantico-glory-glory slop. Get in gem-bright details. What is my voice? Woolfish, alas, but tough. Please, tough, without any moral other than that growth is good. Faith too is good. I am too a puritan at heart. I see the back of the black head of a stranger dark against the light of the livingroom, band of white collar, black sweater, black trousers & shoes. He sighs, reads out of my vision, a floorboard creaks under his foot. This one I have chosen & am forever wedded to him.

Perhaps the remedy for suppressed talent is to become queer: queer and isolate, yet somehow able to maintain one's queerness while feeding food & words to all the world's others. How long is it since bull-sessions about ideas? Where are the violent argumentative friends? Of seventeen, of yesteryear? Now Marcia is set in her dogmatic complacency, loyal to weak Mike," jealous as a female fawn-colored bulldog, netted in by supermarkets, libraries and job-routine. Entertaining? Probably. Childless, but evidently unwillingly. She shells some resentment under her brisk breezy talk. I am too simple to call it envy: "Do all your students think you're just wonderful and traveled & a writer?" Acid-baths. Given time & a Mikeless Marcia I'll attack her next year & get at her good innards. Innocence my mask. It always was, in her eyes, I the great dreamy unsophisticated & helpless thus unchallenging lout-girl. She, so pragmatic, now markets & cooks with no more savoir faire than I, I wife my husband, work my classes & "write." She remembers two things of me: I always chose books for the color & texture of their covers and I wore curlers and an old aqua bathrobe. To my roommate, with love. I wish she hadn't married Mike. Then she wouldn't have to shrink so small. I wonder if, shut in a room, I could write for a year. I panic: no experience! Yet what couldn't I dredge up from my mind? Hospitals & mad women. Shock treatment & insulin trances. Tonsils & teeth out. Petting, parking, a mismanaged loss of virginity and the accident ward, various abortive loves in New York, Paris, Nice. I make up forgotten details. Faces and violence. Bites and wry words. Try these.

Catch up I will tonight, each blank page a curse to my crimes, a spur to my remedies. I gabble on, exhort, create little. Too tired, for example, to take down notes on six new people and a new house breached Saturday night. I walk, blindered, eyes lowered. Life loses me. A bad night – Ted not getting name, address, hour or reason for invitation right. We went dinnerless, late, to cold apple cider in icy metal cups colored neon pink, green, brass – enough to sicken, in little crocheted cup bottom-drawers. Bowls of buttered popcorn, needing salt, by the red-toothed grin of a wood fire behind a clever black grille curtain that pulled open & shut on a drawstring. Queer good greenish seeds, like wheat-seeds – what called? Whisker-nuts? Then cold spicy squash or pumpkin pie with cold whipped cream served on little nervous legged tables. A dark-green walled room with panels of red-gold wood.

Driftwood decorating a thick-woven indian table mat; a piano with yellowed music. A sandy big-eyed dog. Broken people, yawn-brewing. Kind, soft, weak dark Bob Tucker," weak-handsome, voice driven to a whisper: a writer? All acclaimed his critical prose. He spoke of Iowa & writer's workshops. Pale, flabby hands? (Cf. Arvin's tonight, warm & hard as rivets). His pretty white-skinned wife, big, placid, with auburn hair & red-brown rich eyes, kind, maternal, with little gilt pink-rhinestoney earrings – the wrong touch: why do I see it, snob that I am? Smith-snob, I spot frills & cheap decor. But the house, good, rugged, masculine, with its rumored brooks, hills & more brooks with reeds & brazen invading deer-hunters. Sid Kaplan," mean, spiteful, bitten & pompous about Leonard Baskin." Gods create, let what moles will carp, carp. Queer & off-kilter in a nasty-tasting metallic blue suit. His wife dark ugly, toothy, but warm, funny & nice. Then the other "young couple", names lost in the rush of introductions behind standing & shifting figures. He, dark, black, warmly Jewish, not broken like Tucker, but alive with bushy black eyebrows & black wet eyes, dry-hot. She, a big-boned simpering teacher, great pale thickish legs & arms, an attractive teal-blue dress, fitting breasts, waist, flaring full. A broth of reddish-brown hair standing in a fluffy bang off her forehead & round about her head. A big generous painted mouth & sculpted pencilled brows. She, obviously used to queening, knowing, a striking female teacher among ugly men, gazed away from me, almost obsessively. At last looked direct and blurted, "Do you know Nicholas de Stael." Unfortunately for her, I knew him very well, having gone, that terrible April in Paris, to a posthumous exhibit of his work at the crumbling, scandalously falling-down new museum of modern art on the Seine & viewed his painting, sitting, drawing line facsimiles & color notes of boats against a dark green sky, pale flavous and slender bumpy pears arranged, three, on a dark purple and green ground, blue squared Paris rooftops, black & white balancing brushstrokes, I adoring, alone, lonely, absorbing all that paint, reading how he jumped off a cliff at the Cap d'Antibes. What drove him? All those hot reds & blues and yellows spurting from his fingertips? What vision of madness in a mad world? There, benched, I met Karl & god-knows her name, yes, Joan, dark-haired, slightly buck-toothed, nervous – he wrote then & asked if he had a chance – a divorce? How I laughed when I saw the two of them. Mother Hubbard. All this the name of de Stael jolted up. Yes, how well I knew him. Oh, it all depends what period.

January 22: Wednesday: Absolutely blind fuming sick. Anger, envy and humiliation. A green seethe of malice through the veins. To faculty meeting, rushing through a gray mizzle, past the Alumnae House, no place to park, around behind the college, bumping, rumping through sleety frozen ruts. Alone, going alone, among strangers. Month by month, colder shoulders. No eyes met mine. I picked up a cup of coffee in the crowded room among faces more strange than in September. Alone. Loneliness burned. Feeling like a naughty presumptuous student. Marlies in a white jumper & red-dark patterned blouse. Sweet, deft: simply can't come. Wendell[n] & I are doing a text-book. Havent you heard? Eyes, dark, lifted to Wendell's round simper. A roomful of smoke and orange-seated black-painted chairs. Sat beside a vaguely familiar woman in the very front, no one between me and the president. Foisted forward. Stared intently at gilt leaved trees, orange-gilt columns, a bronze frieze of stags, stags and an archer, bow-bent. Intolerable, unintelligible bickering about plusses & minuses, graduate grades. On the backcloth a greek with white-silver feet fluted to a maid, coyly kicking one white leg out of her Greek robe. Pink & orange & gilded maidens. And a story, a lousy sentimental novel chapter 30 pages long & utterly worthless at my back: on this I lavish my hours, this be my defense, my sign of genius against those people who know somehow miraculously how to be together, au courant, at one. Haven't you heard? Mr Hill has twins. So life spins on outside my nets. I spotted Alison,[n] ran for her after – meeting – she turned, dark, a stranger. "Alison", Wendell took her over, "are you driving down?" She knew. He knew. I am deaf, dumb. Strode into slush, blind. Into snow & gray mizzle. All the faces of my student shining days turned the other way. Shall I give, unwitting, dinners? To invite them to entertain us? Ted sits opposite: make his problems mine. Shut up in public those bloody private wounds. Salvation in work. What if my work is lousy? I want to rush into print any odd tripe. Words, words, to stop the deluge through the thumbhole in the dike. This be my secret place. All my life have I not been outside? Ranged against well-meaning foes? Desperate, intense: why do I find groups impossible? Do I even want them? Is it because I cannot match them, tongue-shy, brain-small, that I delude my dreams into grand novels and poems to astound? I must bridge the gap between adolescent glitter & mature glow. O steady. Steady on. I have my one man. To help him I will.

Sunday night: January 26: A blank day of cooking & gusts of drowsiness. Mother gone on a broth of renewed communication: suddenly it comes over me – how much life is shuttered & buckled in the tongues of those we patronize & take forgranted. "How did Marion's madness come on her?"

We asked. The dining room stood dark, windowless, guarding its shadows, and the two uneven red candles, one tall, one short, stuck into the green-bottles, wax-crusted, made a tawdry yellow light, as candles do, warring against the faintest gray daylight. Marion became a religious fanatic and one morning, shortly before Pearl Harbor, began to prophesy: she was Christ, she was Ghandi, she would not let her husband touch her. Mother listened to her, lying on her back, shut-eyed, with no food, no drink, talk, talk, talking for ten hours without a stop. A mental hospital for two years, the visits from Bill: "Stop chasing after butterflies and come home to take up your real responsibilities." Relapses, set-backs. He and his "perfect marriage" – never once did she contradict him or counter his wishes. She, her own heroine, living sainthoods, martyrdoms, novel sagas. Married to the wrong man, twenty-one years older than she. He, wiry, scrawny, "Pop", with that skin disease puffing his hands dry, red, flaking the skin off. Cigar wet dark: brown in his down-dumped mouth. Piles of old <u>Saturday Evening Posts</u> in his dark, gloomed study with the dust-spreckled desk, the cot. And all those meticulous oil paintings, gilt-framed in dining-room, living-room, & den, of antique schooners, myriad-sailed on the high crest of jewel-blue & precisely foaming seas. How he, dead, lives on, and is unshaped, reshaped, made again. To see those old venerable originals before we die – Edith Sitwell, TS Eliot, Robert Frost: all the slick forties & fifties give us is gin-drinking politic poetry-pandering businessmen. We woke & evoked memories. Mother: loved in absence, somehow strange & hated in presence. The sterile forced pathetic smell of a woman without a man, pitied, yet despised for the very lack which constitutes her tragedy. So she left, happier. One so starved for other people's lives may well sip up our overflow. Once I am doing "my own work" will I be less selfish? – Will I be what? Maker of myself. Unshut my clam-shell reticences? All my diaries are spattered with undone imperatives, directives: This summer: read French, relearn & read German. Life. People: eyes & ears not shut, as they are now, I apart, aware of apartness & a strange oddity that makes my coffee-shop talk laughable – we are inviting people to dinner: four a week, 16 a month: I shall not go sick or nervous or over-effusive – I shall merely cook a damn good dinner & serve it & hope people talk well, eat well & get on well. Ted & I are strangers to them, they, strangers to us, but friends & interknit to themselves. So what. I must get out of my baby's nightmare, whip up menus with casual ease, seat people dividing up couples, male, female, male. And also think. This term – I am reading & correcting exams for Arvin's course (will it be $100? $300?) & so will reread all Hawthorne, Melville & James: good for me, to bring my mind together with his. Ted's courses begin Wednesday at the U. of M. It will be good honing & discipline for his mind – to articulate, to come up against forms of poetry & prose in words before college people. We will work hard this term, courage, Oh courage, but only 4 months seems not so long, to pile up, we hope, at least $3000 saved from our salaries & $1000 from writing. My miserable tense knotted sleepless nights now, no sleep till dawning & then a formless drugged morning, must go. Last night I recall a vague, tedious weird nightmare of the London Plague, or of the Plague & fire combined. Classes missed & bungled. Must do Joyce & plays this week, after correcting. Read quarterlies. Such a Sunday-night garbage this is. Early tomorrow, my exam. Then the deluge: correct all afternoon. Tonight: black wet rain: world of glisten & slop – rushed out after Ted talked with Gibian over the phone to read a good review of his book in the Virginia Quarterly. How my voice must change to be heard: brash, concrete. Away with blue moony soup-fogs. Tomorrow night, observe each wall corner, color & character at the Tuckers. My feet are cold. Back quirk better.

NB: A postscript. Wrote, all day Friday, through versions & versions to finished version of "Change-About in Mrs. Cherry's Kitchen" – mailed in hope & fatalistic despair, to Jack & Jill. For some reason, for no reason, it will be rejected: just to make this year of unacceptance complete. Sewanee rejection, according to mother, already in the mail. I have gritted so long, I can grit about 4 months longer. Anyhow, I had a delightful Friday with Mrs. Cherry & made a little world, which really pleased me. That, in itself should be A Great Good Thing. Now, idea notes for future essays at children's tales:

THE SNOW CIRCUS: A Christmas contest for the best snow animal on a street: giraffes, camels, elephants, and so on – personalities of children realistic & important, – some keen rivalry, suspense. Animals come alive at night and make a circus? Something to get in excitement & plot-structure. Xmas Eve.

THE FRINGE-DWELLER: À la James (whose story "Altar of the Dead") I've just finished reading though I should be doing Joyce. Girl, aging girl, is haunted by own nothingness & devours views from windows (stories, movies, overheard talk & sights in the street, pictures in newspapers, etc.) with continuous feeling she is "just about", miraculously, to come into her OWN – her own life. A kind of benign & pathetic vampire, she sucks her vicarious being from a catholic multitude of sources. A pane of glass, a door, an unheard name of a stranger on a bus, keeps her, is <u>all</u> that keeps her from putting on this miraculous, marvelous name, identity & life. Awakes to voices, nail-taps outside her coffin. She her own tomb. To <u>realize</u> in particulars, concretest detail.

<u>Monday night: February 3</u>: A round white moon smaller than a penny blue-beaming through the bathroom window slats. So far behind I am, must do day's stint if not all ten, to keep the evil half-year from piling & avalanching up. To say what? I am eye, or my eyes, having cracked and twisted their muscles over seventy blue booklets of hastily-scribbled drivel of botched significance I now go rapidly pace-pace-apace through the book I dreamily campus-wandered with myself, some five years ago, the <u>Portrait of The Artist</u>, word-encanting, descanting. Now, Macchiavel, I rip through, to organize: how to present, vividly, the act of creation which takes place? I snort out onto white waiting fingers a greeny clot of snot, transparent eggwhite-set with a red veinburst of blood, wipe it behind the bedpost head. No Stephen I. Spent ten minutes at least tonight scrubbing my fingers to bare bones over that damn black-faced pot I burned the stew's carrots & potatoes to – it shines now, with a few scum-black etches, after my dumping that ghastly green poison-smelling abrasive cleaner in, scrubbing in a slosh of suds, dumping bogwater out & beginning again. Today: jammed. First day of term: of second term. Term I end: half-year done & year spinning through snow & mountains of bare trees into dogwood & apple orchards flowering which we must sleep in. Up, weary, groaning protest, out of my second night of dreaming I walk in late to Arvin's class, Miss Van der Poel's″ & get huffed looks, annoyed averted heads, irritated eyes. Dreamed also I met & somehow loved the unmet & hence unloved Leonard Baskin in some strange house, his wife pale as death, her hands blackening with that terrible nameless disease. Ted says he will be, red, fat. No. Saw floating in a dream his 'Large Dead Man', fat, obscene, puffing. Stone-grey. I gushed, purple, spontaneous passages, prose-praise. Hell, Baskin, said, you read all that in a book. I got up out of that fading, faded world of guilt & illicit and unconsummated love and missed appointments to a world of ice-bright sun, ice-air & drawing on my mesh, run-spidered stockings, said to myself – this is the real world where clocks can't skip an hour as you look at them horrorstruck, the great date unkept. Cold new orange juice. Toast & bacon. Scalding coffee. Registrar's office & rush of girl's – wrote stupid D-card for Aston. Skipped to Arvin's lecture: he, friendly, pink – misplacing Melville's name with James', Hawthorne's with Melville's, getting through ½ of the

first lecture I had taken down four years ago. But pleasant to listen to, secure, I, insecure at the back-corner of the class. Curious eyes on me. Cold gimlets. So what: above that, married gold ring, heels silk stockings, hair up: how I confront myself & disbelieve. I am again behind, cramming: only till next weekend, then the next. O spring vacation. Sometimes, secure, I wonder we don't stay here, Ted teaching (ho) at Amherst, or Holyoke (he has had inquiries from both) & me here. A joint income of $8 thousand. But even as I wake from the nice comfort, I see my own death & his & ours smiling at us with candied smile: The Smiler. How a distant self must, vain & queenly, dream of being a great dramatic Dunn″ or Drew-type teacher, loved, wise, white-headed & wrinkled, a many-wrinkled wisdom. After Arvin, art & the sudden surprise – Böcklin's "Island of the Dead" –

Tuesday morning: February 4: To continue where my pen fell from my hand & I fell asleep: "The Island of The Dead", read about in Strindberg's "Ghost Sonata" – an island, chunks of marble, angular pale stone, set in the pale wash of a sea, and tall, black-dark cypresses rising like steeples of death from the center of the island – a shrouded figure, standing, swaddled from head to foot in white, being rowed just to shore, outined, a white ghost-form, against the vibrant darkness of the cypresses. Strange visions. A lonely island – some One buried there, or the island of all, invisible, essence of air in the dank caverns of cypress boughs. O gothic. I listen to Arvin, & shall go presently, out in the soft-falling dry slow snow to listen to him this morning, pretending to Ted I've taken a taxi. Will my Jack & Jill story be rejected this week? Now, in time, I know not, but hope. Soon, even in the compass of these pages, shall I know, & hope not? Time has brought this book and my tender spoiled untried unworked vein of life in a leap from the blind sick hell of September & October to the weary but cavalier unpreparation of early February. Six weeks more of snow & sleet. O keep healthy. I breathe among dry coughs & clotted noses. I must, on the morning coffee-surge of exultation & omnipotence, begin my novel this summer & sweat it out like a school-year – rough draft done by Christmas. And poems. No reason why I shouldn't surpass at least the facile Isabella Gardner″& even the lesbian & fanciful & jeweled Elizabeth Bishop in America. If I sweat the summer out.

I love this book, black point of pen skidding over smooth paper. Shall catch up & keep up. Each day brings jam-packed muches to muse on, to describe. Ted has written a long-lined long-versed strong poem on "Dick Straight-up." The similar slow majestic unstrident cadences of "Everyman's

Odyssey" – next year, I feel we shall come into our own. One acceptance now would wing me through this year. Will my students find me out? I think not. I've been through the worst, the hells of explaining snippets of ambiguous, ambivalent William James on 3 days & nights of no-sleep and the visiting sweet professors trying conspicuously to be inconspicuous in the last row. Shall I write a SatEvePost story about plagiarism? Trala. They write enough about doctor's, why not about teachers? Not noble & heroic enough? We operate on young girls' souls, not their esophagi. Tonight I shall somehow manage dinner for 5 & coffee for an extra two with ease. My trusty angel-topped lemon meringue pie – if I serve a dinner once a week I lose my nervousness. So if they come by duty they come by duty. I know not. Like the Sultans:" saw their black flasheyed Jamie in a vision: I want one like that. After this book-year, after next-Europe-year, a baby-year? Four years of marriage childless is enough for us? Yes, I think I shall have guts by then. The Merwins want no children – to be free. Free to be narrow, selfish & confined in age. I will write like mad for 2 years – & be writing when Gerald 2nd or Warren 2nd is born, what to call the girl? O dreamer. I waved, knocked, knocked on the cold windowglass & waved to Ted moving out into view below, black coated, black haired, fawn-haunched & shouldered in the crisp-stamped falling snow. Fevered, how I love that one.

Tuesday night: February 4th:" So it is over, the stretched smiles & wearying wonder: why don't they go home? Tired, too, tired we, Ted quietening after coffee and me hearing the silence growing under the talk – have I thought one intelligent thought, felt one flash of intuited wisdom? Yes o yes, but I am weary, too weary to speak, write or think. A grim grind I see ahead: how to give to it the best & the best extract sharp as juice of lemon. I make a damn good lemon meringue pie. Praise for day: ran down to Mrs. McKee's twilit bric-a-brac bitseyed apartment to bake meringue – smoke among the prism-ed gilt-flowered candelabra and innumerable pots of green plants & hanging vines – clam dip eternally & Mr. Arvin pink & bright making crackers of it, Florence beautiful and pale in her black corduroy maternity dress, bulging, woman, her stockings up to the knee, lace-gartered, her shape being black, almost absent, undefined, only her tragic face, tremulous & that funny cracked onconsistent nasal voice. Roast beef, onion potatoes, corn & mush-rooms, green salad, white wine & red & the pie. Mrs. Aaron came in green stockings, red heeled shoes, a red & green plaid skirt & green (or red?) top, knitting a neutral tan thing. Mrs. McKee had finished a thumbless pale blue baby-mitten. Yes, the Jack & Jill rejection came. How I intuit ahead. No

323

reason, but all my pink-potted dreams gone kaputt. But with it a strange letter from Art News asking for a poem on art & speaking of an "honorarium" of $50-$75 – a consolation prize? I shall submerge in Gauguin – the red-caped medicine man, the naked girl lying with the strange fox, Jacob wrestling with his angel on a red arena ringed by the starched white winged caps of Breton peasant women. O will this week end, to my one day, my Sunday, of rest? Will I somehow prepare my classes on Joyce, yet undone? I drive to the breaking point, but have tested & tried myself & only say: the end will come. A year to write in – to read Everything. Will it come & we do it? Answer me, book. Today: Matisse, exploding in pink cloths & vibrant rich pink shadows, pale peach pewter & smoky yellow lemons, violent orange tangerines & green limes, black-shadowed & the interiors: oriental flowery – pale lavenders & yellow walls with a window giving out onto Riviera blue – a bright blue double-pear-shape of a violin case – streaks of light from the sun outside, pale fingers – the boy at the scrolled piano with the green metronome shape of the outdoor world – color: a palm tree exploding outside a window in yellow & green & black jets, framed by rich black red-patterned draperies. A blue world of round blue trees, hatpins & a lamp. Enough. I shall sit & stare at Gauguin in the library, limit my field & try to rest, then write it. Don't count gold hens before egg shell congeals. Walked to class today – snow stopped: hard, clear, icy shackles of air – face burned agreeably all through Arvin. <u>Look up</u>: in Boston: angels or muses floating light as handkerchiefs in a Monday wind under 5 arches – in a green rural scene by Puvis de Chavannes in the public library. Shopped: piled glut of meat (is it real), vegetables (are they rubber?) into our frost-coated icebox. Cooked & cleaned. Tea quietens. I deserve a year, two years, to live my own self into being: which, in less than 4 months, I'll take.

<u>Wednesday, February 5</u>: Weary, wicked, unprepared on Joyce for tomorrow, steeped in hot tub, scrubbing of skin scum & greenly soaking, hot, the kinks & cranks out of my system. Am I living half alive? I am so tired, after last night, & the mound of dishes, after the pressure-cooker of patchwork last-minute preparation – always the vision of how much better I could be doing – & I <u>could</u> be: knocking them agog, that I feel in a dream, a fog, out of which familiar faces loom, smiling, helloing, eyeing each other with a secret knowledge. An aspirin dulled an eye-ache, headache of fatigue. Be good next week – tomorrow slap together 2 chapters, two hours of Joyce discussion – Crackling he peels off his sweater. White skin, black hair. This morning I dreamed of the new face, the only one, somehow, who is lovely dark-liquid

eyed, faintly sallow-skinned, golden with green shadows – holding hands & driving through students effused with an ineffable sweetness & euphoria, & then to wake to no lonely bed but the touch of my own man, & the faces on our dreaming lovers change & tremble into the image of morning like the face reflected on an unquiet pool gathering & gathering together its fragments into a scarcely trembling visage into the final inevitable knit stillness. After the sweat and fury of the bed, weary we, drugged, dregged – gulping half a cup of coffee, one bite of beachplum-jam-spread toast, sticky body of sweats and exudings & odors into worn thick wools, sheathed. And sick, shocked, through ice-blue air, over crusty shrunk snowdrifts, to Arvin's lecture, shutting the door, & shutting the door on late students, spoiled faces, sweet faces, ugly faces – far I am now. So what, I say. A morning of guilt, baby fiends, black veils – and I, I sluggard, take it in, now, my afternoon hour to be done tomorrow. Secret sin: I envy, covet, lust – wander lost, red-heeled, red-gloved, black-flowing-coated, catching my image in shop windows, car windows, a stranger, sharper-visaged stranger than I knew. I have a feeling this year will seem a dream when done. I have some great nostalgia for my lost Smith-teacher self, perhaps because this job is now secure, bitable-size, & the new looming threat of a new life in a new (for me) city at the one trade which won't be cheated or "got-by" with patch-up jobs, waits, blank-paged: o speak. What then? What now? How much easier, how much smiling deadlier, to scrape & scrub a living off the lush trees of Joyce, of James. Morning, too, of Matisse odalisques, patterned fabrics, vibrant, blue-flowered – tambourines, bare skin, breast-round, nipplies – rosettes of red lace & the skirls & convoluted swirls of big palmy oaky leaves. The Vence chapel: a day of days. I in Nice-bought gray slacks & a thick too-tight white sweater crying on the curb under the blue sky with doves coo-rooing in dovecotes, chickens strutting white & the orange bright as planets in the glossy dark green pagodas of trees, and the thin sick replica of the dark mobile jew who soft-steps through dream, face-changer, from greasy-haired imbecile in summer German class, to rich sick inbred scion of a fox-hunting family to the warm volatile present face that pale, greenish-gold in the dim stair-well, foreign, unaware of its twist to rubber postures of love, unaware even of the movie seen together in the real time world. A hot hour of exam rehash. Deposited check in a raw wind.

Saturday: February 8: A cold one a.m. hour, with a big wind moving the windows in their frames, & the reflected room in the dark pane, the clear pane darkened against blackness, wagged in and out with the shake-shake of the wind. A groggy underdone undone state between two provinces of sleep. We went to see the "Pickwick Papers" with Paul Roche" last night. Shin-deep in dry-crystalled snow, we strode out bent-headed, into an air thick with snow, the greenish-tinted light of streetlamps illuminating cones of greenish-white slanting flakes. Paul, raspy-voiced, hoarse-coughing, his blond marceled hair & scarf, his glassy wide blue eyes. Weak – all his adonis-boy looks lost, seedy, coarse-pored, with skin too-bright-orange & seamed as if grease-paint were cracking. The move, a jog of anecdotes & cariacature faces – good but slight, & the mass lace & lily bridal at the end – an evening-after at Paul's, the sky still snowing & deeper drifts dry, cold white, covering the old dirty clumps & road-lining ridges of snow – Clar-issa" blonde & sullen, her hair down, sheened metallic gilt in the dim light – a dark blue sweater, harlequin striped bermuda shorts – red, green & yellow, & long navy-blue stockings, she in a pout, not speaking, serving coffee to all 3 but not me because I can't drink coffee after 4 and her red mouth glisten-ing in a silken pout. She is going according to Paul to have a baby in Septem-ber. Not expected? Hindering their plans to live in Greece, to travel. Paul: maybe I'll be going on over myself to find a house. A crack, a separation. Clarissa left, while Paul adventures alone, in his charming gallant fashion, living off Colonel Bodley & John Sweeney" in Boston, free, free. Wangling meetings & Guggenheim recommendations from William Carlos Williams, ee cummings, Marianne Moore: I gossiped. The red-valentine-colored couch with white wood bordered back curving I coveted, for the first time feeling with the Roches, inner & closer to consolidation of forces than they. Paul spoke of Bob Petersson's asking him if he wouldn't like to be in the classics department, Pat Hecht's" "Knowing more about Greek plays", or pretend-ing to, than he. Lovely babies they have, but Paul is a cracked & opportunist dandy, no poet, his poems all full of lily's & and nymphs and white souls of Yeats blooming in hyacinths. Anyhow, the new sense of power & maturity growing in me from coping with this job, & cooking & keeping house, puts me far from the nervous insecure miserable idiot I was last September. Four months has done this. I work. Ted works. We master our jobs & are, we feel, good teachers, natural teachers – this: the danger. The sense of elaborate exclusion, the unseeing gaze of Joan Bramwell & calculated insolence & patronizing stance of Sally Sears I shall be free from: I don't like it, yet I don't like them enough to court lost favor – when did the change come? With my bursting into tears in front of Marlies? Humiliations stomached like rotten fruit. I grow through them & beyond. My work must engross me these next four months – plays & poems, reading for Arvin, working on a poem for Art

News – black-clad, I walk alone, & so what: cariacature green-nailed Joan and pale freckle-spreckled Sally in stories. A new life of my own I shall make, from words, colors & feelings. Merwin's high Boston apartment opens its wide-viewed windows like the deck of a ship.

<u>Sunday: February 9</u>: Night, nearing nine. Outside: laughter of boys, the brooom-brooom of a car revving up. Today spent itself in a stupor, twilit, fortified by coffee & scalding tea: a series of cleansings – the icebox, the bedroom, the desk, the bathroom, slowly, slowly, ordering – trying to keep the "filth of life at a distance" – washing hair, self, stockings & blouses, patching the ravages of a week, reading to catch up with my first week of Hawthorne stories – writing, for the first time, a long letter to Olwyn," feeling colors, rhythms, words joining & moving in patterns that please my ear, my eye. Why am I free to write her? My identity is shaping, forming itself – I feel stories sprout, reading the collection of <u>New Yorker</u> stories – yes, I shall, in the fulness of time, be among them – the poetesses, the authoresses, – I must meantime this June beginning, learn about planets & horoscopes to be in the proper starred house: I'll wish I had learned if I don't: tarot pack, too. Maybe I should stay alone, unparalysed, & work myself into mystic & clairvoyant trances, to get to know Beacon Hill, Boston, & get its fabric into words. I can. Will. Now to do what I must, then to do what I want: this book too becomes a litany of dreams, of directives & imperatives. I need not to be more with others, but to be more & more deeply, richly alone. Recreating worlds. In four months I shall be in another house, another life: only not to waste what we are given – scholarship is too easy: why, I wonder, with a bit more reading, couldn't I take over Arvin's lectures? But to make my own voice, my own vision, that's another matter: do it I must. No outdoors today: hands scrubbed dry & nails polishless over tub, sink, toilet, crockery. A grease smell of garlic bread, good & tanged, drenched French-vinagered & onioned salad, stewed & sauced chicken, fish & peas. And the fatty wax-smoked smell of candle-wicks snipped out and smoking. Must shop, go to classes, finish 3 chapter Joyce outline tomorrow. Put books on reserve. Now for a picture, enough of this blithering about calendar engagements: I am here: black velvet slacks stuck with lint, worn & threadbare slippers, dun-fuzzed with dark brown leopard spots on a pale tan ground, gilt bordered, then the polished blond-brown woodwork of the Whelans" maple coffee table, the dull inner glow of white & silver highlights on the pewter sugar bowl with its domed lid & cupola peak, then the dented-red-skinned apples, mealy & synthetic tasting. Ted in the great red

chair by the white bookcase of novels, his hair rumpled front, dark brown, but tighter than ever, & his face blue-greening along the jaw: those faces he makes: owls, monsters: <u>The Man Who Made Faces</u>: a symbolic story? Who are we, really? In his dark green sweater, white & green banded at the cuffs, bent over the pink tablet, black trousers, grey socks of pale thick wool, shoes black, cracked, shining in the light. He poises, pen in right hand, propping his chin, elbow on the tablet and the chartreuse-shaded light behind him. All about, in a three-quarter circle, papers, airmail letters, books, torn pink scraps of tissue, typed poems. I, chilled, feel his warmth & hairy belly & sweet skin smells haul me over to be held & hugged: HUG his shirts instruct, at the inner neckband, coming back from the Laundry starched & bound. Another story for <u>The New Yorker</u>: the evocation of my seventeenth summer, the spurt of blood of my period & the twins painting the house, the farm work and Ilo's kiss. A synthesis: the coming of age. A matter of moment: get MEChase to tell me where to send NY stories, to whom. I shall in a year do it.

I catch up: each night, now, I must capture one taste, one touch, one vision from the ruck of the day's garbage. How all this life would vanish, evaporate, if I didn't clutch at it, cling to it, while I still remember some twinge or glory. Books & lessons surround me: hours of work. Who am I? A freshman in college cramming history & feeling no identity, no rest? I shall ruminate like a cow: only that life end not before I am born: the windows jerk & sound in their frames. I shiver, chilled, the grave-chill against the simple heat of my flesh: how did I get to be this big, complete self, with the long-boned span of arm & leg, the scarred imperfect skin? I remember thick mal-shaped adolescence & the colors of my remembering return with a vivid outline: high school, junior high, elementary school, camps & the fern-huts with Betsy: hanging Joanna: I must recall, recall, out of the stuff is writing made, out of the recollected stuff of life. Get one central symbol, on central vision of change, & work it into a distilled essential whole. I have lived so much that what is needed now is not living anew outwardly, but living inward, recalling & calling up the coming out party at the Buckleys," the chauffeur driving us through the blazing October Connecticut hills in the gray rain; Jimmy Beale's & Paula Brown's snowsuit: images fused of the superman. Images of shame and exultation. "Get hold of a thing & shove your head into it" Ted says just now. I weary & will take hot milk to bed and read more Hawthorne. My lips are drying, chapped, & I bite them raw. I dreamed I had long stinging scratches down the fingers of my right hand, but looking down saw my hands white & whole & no red blood-scabbed lines at all.

Tuesday, February 10: Moments before I leave, nostrils clinching with cold, on the walk to Arvin, Van der Poel. Yesterday, in spite of sleep over the weekend, weary, depressed: am I getting a persecution-complex from Sears' & Bramwell's obvious snubs, Monas's knowing mock-deferent looks? so that when Tony Hecht" rattled off: "O-you-energetic-girl-coming-to-campus-when-you-don't-have-classes" with a pale monkey-sneer I took it as calculated mockery? The second time he said it: once or twice too many. I yanked together shredded words meaning nothing: "You should talk", & next time will ask if he'll give me a time table & accuse him of poverty-struck small chat, & using the same old line: I talked to myself, back-talked to him, driving downtown to bank, where the lady savingsclerk was sassy over the English check, but I refused to raise my voice, bitchy-thing; to the First National where the bill looked colossal, padded; to the laundry where my laundry wasn't dried. An afternoon of dim gray light, ice-chill – we walked briefly to the greenhouse at the end of Woodlawn watching a thin gray squirrel lope across the road, our cheeks knobbing to ice, & drank tea, the purging boiling innard-bath of tea, while Ted outlined his Molière & I struggled through outlining this week's first chapter of Joyce – two more to go, & Sophocles. Then the Wheelwright" lecture on depth experience & symbols – a listing of six fancy terms – plurisignation, indirection, archetypes, emergence by juxtaposition – all translatable to freshman English level – a few jokes, no burning radiance. We went home after: Northern lights red-lit the sky, a fountain of blood-red, gauzing & drifting over Cassiopeia's chair, and the sky to the right a wierd frosty greeny-white, odd-minted radiance. Tonight, another dinner.

Monday Night: February 17: A moment, caught, in the stillness of waiting for guests – Wendell to come, & Ted gone to pick up Paul & Clarissa. My own tigress perfume & the dull-avocado green of my skirt and bright turquoise & gold-lined & white & black paisley patterned jersey warm & snug on me & the white wine drunk during smoothing on thick white marshmellowy frosting singing thin in my veins – oh the absolute free willingness unleashed which wine brings. The apartment clean-carpeted and empty, bowls of sour cream & onion, pots of tomato & meat sauce, garlic butter, hot water, waiting, waiting. Soon the rude bell-buzz will sound & after, after, to hell with Sophocles, I shall pick you up & go on with you, to catch up. Last week, almost caught up I was, but night by night I, weary, dropped my pen & fell to sleep, aching, onto the pillow, like a great kink of knotty muscles & sinews, to be undone in sleep night long. A nightmare to record, spun, it seems out of various linked daily threads. Ted called Mrs. Van der Poel last night to ask her to dinner; in her art class I had seen suffering Christs & corrupt judges & lawyers by Rouault (who died this last Wednesday night) & under these pictures a title or blurb written in French explaining the theme; then a black & white valentine from Elly with a photo-montage of lovers, of three men behind barbwire at a Concentration Camp clipped from the Times from a review which I read about tortures & black trains bearing victims to the furnace – all this I traced into my terrible primitive-drawing dream, a series, like flipped pictures in a book, of black-line drawings (almost like cartoon stick figures) on a white ground of all varieties of tortures – hangings, flayings, eye-gouging, and, in a bright crude blood red, lines & spots indicating the flow of blood – all the stick figures having red-hands to the wrist & being depicted in crude animation with "La torture" written in bastard dream-French under the drawings. Woke, dragging out of the horror of the sequence, to gray morning light in our rose walled room, sucked back, and they flashed on the screen again, & then woke & lay, horizontal, safe, out of the dream-movie hearing the early morning traffic on route 9 outside the window.

– Yesterday, Sunday. A dim gloomed day after Saturday's usual drugged sleep-drunken afternoon sleep & dulled evening pottering. A blizzard, whooing and wailing, jiggling the windows in their sockets & blowing snow horizontal, each window giving out onto a white world; crumbling into a whirl, whorl of white crumbs & twirling on itself. The church bells sounding noon & six in all this & we, gratefully, cancelling U. of Mass tea, & supper at Holyoke with this friend of Ted's called Antoine." How Ted got his friends I don't know – they are so small & wistful & half-drowned compared to him – Danny Weissbort & Than Minton & Dan Huws & David Ross all writing meek miserable adoring letters from London, all self-conscious, grubbing, sorrowing with no knit forces & disciplines – their demons formless and pale like grubs under turned stones and their genii asleep on the dark side of the cold moon.

Tuesday morning: February 18: A morning, early, of bright snow-light, very white & sheer, coming in at the windows – shafted and cleansing. The shakiness of late last night & the residue of sickness at too much wine cleared off by a drink of prickly fizzing water and a mug of hot quenching & calming coffee. Soon I walk out into the nostril-freezing weather to Arvin & Van der Poel, and before I go, I shall relish & cherish our apartment, cleaned, still, from yesterday, fragrant, and how glad I am I did all the meat sauce-greasy red-and-yellow fat-smeared plates last night in my after-banquet fervor & left them not until this morning. Paul's queer bottle of German wine, empty now, looking rather like a speckled brown thermos, heavy & stonelike, with its dull black-speckled brown sheen & yellow label depicting swans, golden grapes, top hats and castles in a kind of heraldic emblem – May-Wine flavored with woodruff (a flower, like woodbine?) tasting of liquid honey & crushed nectarous flowers, chill thin and sweet – stands sentinel. Today, I must cram & do my two days of Sophocles & prepare Webster so I can assign them next week's. I have a day off, bless it, with Washington's Birthday & must read the DHLawrence thesis then & outline up to spring vacation. How clear & cleansed & happy I feel. Why? Last night's dinner cleared such air – Wendell an unexpected ally & miraculous gossip, so richly he held forth, & Paul & blond witchy dear Clarissa, her red mouth opening & curling like a petalled flower or a fleshly sea anemone, & Paul, gilded as always, but not quite so seedy, his blue eyes marred with red, his blond curls rough & Rossetti-like, cherubic, curling, his pale jacket & pale buff sweater setting off his gilt and gaudy head. Have I said I saw him running down the stairs of Seelye out into last week's falling snow with a bright absinthe-green suit on that made his eyes the clear unearthly & slightly unpleasant acid green of a churned winter ocean full of icecakes. We talked, & I must never again start drinking wine before my guests come – I slowed, but sickened late. Till midnight they stayed & Wendell favored us with department secrets – how Robert & Charles & Newton & Elizabeth & Dan have the Power, how Newton & Fisher (who married 3 of his students & once too had gold gilding curls) are anti-feminist which outrages Miss Hornbeak" (of course, no real women these) and how Eleanor Lincoln refused to be department chairman until she was made professor, & about old rivalries & also how good my freshman english classes were, in glowing terms which was of course very pleasant, especially when I view how fantastically far I've come from the living sleepless nightmares recorded on typed paper last October & November – I have mastered, now, the art of casualness & self-confidence & march a mistress of my soul through the white-furzed snows of Paradise Hill and the snow-hung Botanic gardens. I can, I brag boast & maintain, manage my girls, even the obstreperous Alice – I shall somehow manage to do Sophocles & the thesis & this week no matter what go to that art museum & break down my other fear, how childish & stare stare at Rousseau & Gauguin & write somehow a poem to send along with my earthenware head poem.

"The Earthenware Head"

<u>Tuesday noon</u>: The church bells have begun and done their noon hour chiming and I, back from the clear sheer blue air, unaccountably exhilarated, poise on the brink of grim work, leafing through my calendar, counting 4 weeks to spring vacation, seven & a half weeks until my books begin. I had a vision in the dark art lecture room today of <u>the</u> title of my book of poems, commemorated above. It came to me suddenly with great clarity that "The Earthenware Head" was the right title, the only title. It is derived, organically, from the title & subject of my poem "The Lady & The Earthenware Head", and takes on for me the compelling mystic aura of a sacred object, a terrible and holy token of identity sucking into itself magnet wise the farflung words which link & fuse to make up my own queer & grotesque world – out of earth, clay, matter, the head shapes its poems & prophecies, as the earth-flesh wears in time, the head swells ponderous with gathered wisdoms. Also, I discover, with my crazy eye for anagrams that the initials spell T–E–H– which is simply "to Edward Hughes", or Ted, which is of course my dedication. I dream, with this keen spirit-whetting air, of a creative spring. So I shall live & create, worthy of Ruth Beuscher & Doris Krook and myself and Ted & my art. Which is word-making, world-making. This book title gives me such staying power (perhaps these very pages will see the overturn of my dream, or even its acceptance in the frame of the real world). At any rate, I see the earthenware head, rough, crude, powerful & radiant, of dusky orange-red terracotta color, flushed with vigor and its hair heavy, electric. Rough terracotta color, stamped with jagged black and white designs, signifying earth, & the words which shape it. Somehow this new title spells for me the release from the old crystal-brittle & sugar-faceted voice of "Circus in Three Rings" and "Two Lovers & a Beachcomber", those two elaborate metaphysical conceits for triple-ringed life – birth love & deaths and for love and philosophy, sense & spirit. Now pray god I live through this windy season and come into my own in June: three and a half months, how the year dwindles. To get through this week and thesis. I feel great works which may speak from me. Am I a dreamer only? I feel beginning cadences & rhythms of speech to set world-fabrics in motion. Let me keep my eye off publication & simply write stories that have to be written. We reject the Merwins' flat: the rejection grows, green

reddens & plop, it drops full plump into our laps – the noisy street, the filthy bathroom, dark bedroom & no doubt Dido's hairpins & hairscruffs in all the floorboard cracks, also two months extra rent & no furniture. No thanks. We will perhaps stay here in June & stick up for top floor, light & a view, quiet & preferably furnished. Notes. Of Van Voris:* pale with a mouth like snail spread for sliding – a man who always keeps the expression on his face for a moment too long. My poems thin to a bare spare twenty, even those with quaint archaic turns of speech. How far I feel from them, from poems. O to get in voice again, this book a wailing wall. What thoughts few as they are, revolve in my head? The Double: The Earthenware Head (jutting forth from the African masks & doll-masks on Mrs. Van der Poel's screen, with their blank eyes rounded with phosphor circles, and their insect heads & diminutive pincer mouths) – how all photograph-portraits do catch our souls – part of a past world, a window onto the air and furniture of our own sunken worlds, & so to the mirror-twin, Muse.

Thursday morning: February 20: This morning, gray, dulled, triple-pained, the pain of the blood-spirt, the aching ague of a tired body, & the aesthetic & moral pain of a badly botched unprepared tragedy beginning – because of what? Because of papers all weekend, dinner & cooking Monday? I know not. But must despair not. Worst here, worse can't come. Must take it easy: decide whether to linger on Oedipus & be thorough & leave Antigone till next week. Perhaps best: think I will. Must somehow then argue out the subtleties of Oedipus before 3 p.m. & will then read papers more in earlier classes. Department meeting yesterday grim & somehow headless without Machine-man Hill. Nobody knew what motions were there or how to word them – Arvin, Fisher, Dunn missing & giving it the air of an old lady's meeting with a crew of young instructors. I alone & perhaps willfully so – walking off – and I would very much like to know how to be casual & friendly – but how do I know the rituals of these people – the drinks & visits & coffees? I never talk to them about classes, which would be fun, or anything else. Miss Drew said, as everybody said, why not stay here to teach & ask for a diminished program if Ted likes teaching? In the smoked night atmosphere, with its weary nightmare glaze, her kind thin gray face with brown brilliant eyes (and she over seventy!) seemed to give no answer & my replies to be inane – I want all my time, time for a year, the first year since I was four years old, to work and read on my own. And away from Smith. Away from my past, away from this glass-fronted, girl-studded and collegiate town. Anonymity. Boston. Here the only people to see are the twenty people on the faculty whom I just don't want to see another year. Will I write a word? Yes. By the time I write in here again this ghastly day will be over, I having walked out my dreamy drugged state & given three classes, botched & unsure. The next three weeks, however, I shall prepare violently & fully a week ahead if it's the last thing I do. O resolves. The three red apples, yellow speckled, thumb-dinted brown, mock me. I myself am the vessel of tragic experience. I muse not enough on the mysteries of Oedipus – I, weary, resolving the best & bringing, out of my sloth, envy and weakness, my own ruins. What do the gods ask? I must dress, rise, & send my body out. A year of writing: I shall create people, slimy & funny & noble, & give it a year of my life: the poems also: The Earthenware Head & Falcon Yard. The mystery of time past: I hear Redpath, small, neat & legal-logical in his black gown pronouncing in French "Antigone" & feel like weeping – for him, for his white-haired black-eyed delicate ancient mother, for the thin green spring weather in a wash over the riverside willows. Let me not be sentimental, let the distance in time give me humor and irony and a shrewd, if loving, eye – let the people: Jane Baltzell (whom I have just written to, come & take my place) and Barry Fudger" & Chris Levenson & Ildiko Hayes" & Judy Linton" & Dan Massey" & Ben Nash" – let all their names – Gary Haupt – Mallory Wober – John Lythgoe – Keith Middlemass – Luke Meyers – take on the aura, magnetic & radiant, of sacred objects & move solid in the time & space of Cambridge. Even Sally Sears (Sarah Burns) & Joan Bramwell must be in, intervolved in the mysteries of time past & identity. Paul Klee – in art – the twittering line – "The ghosts departure" – a gesture of farewell from the blue spaces from a bundle of sheets & a new moon & green planet. A third to Rousseau & Gauguin – a twittering, leafy world. "Goat" And the end of the Marionette," a little yellow soul in star-gilded infinity floating

Friday night, February 21: Simply the fact that I write in here able to hold a pen, proves, I suppose, the ability to go on living. For some reason fatigue accumulated this week like a leaden sludge into which I sink. Horns outside in the ghoul-green tinny light, shrieks, laughs and abortive chants "Iˇf yòu càn't hèar ŭs, wĕ'll yèll ă lìttlĕ louder." And the louder yell. The restless uneasy rush of car-tires, cushioned gears engaging. How one looks to morning, early morning, six, five, while the great populous city lies dumb, sunk in predawn slumber. Those fresh blue bird-burbling Cambridge dawns – no birds here, but exhaust & tired men grinding to work. Whoops, now. And people cramming in and out of the brick church at all hours. Today – the last lap, thanks to George Washington. Woke after 9 hours sleep still exhausted

& rebellious, not wanting to drag my drugged body to a lecture platform: a problem of identity: Ted says: "In twenty-five minutes you'll be talking to a class." I dawdled over coffee in the thick brown pottery mug, waiting for the coffee-revelation, which didn't come, bang, into clothes, torn webbed stockings, out into the dull-mat-finished gray morning, raw as an oyster & jamming into gear to the parking lot, the gold hand on the clock tower on college hall standing at 9. Ran up ice path gritted with sand, bang, bell rang, into class in a daze, with faces looking up, expecting me to say something, & me not there, blank, bored, hearing my voice lead out blither on ironic structure of the Oedipus which I realize I don't understand myself: It is folly to try to outwit the gods. Or: we are all predestined – or still: we have free will & must be responsible. How glad I was, when bell rang. Free to shop. Just as I drove into the snow-piled parking lot behind the first National & got out to stride to the back door, hands bare & tucked futiley into my coat sleeves, coat blowing open & wind on my bare throat, the heavy metal apparatus of the swinging door hinge came loose & hit a woman on the head: she stood, singled out in a muddy maroon colored coat, ugly, violated: "It struck my head", & as I pushed into the store, past starers, a nasty mean mealy mouthed man, chest stuck out under a blue monogrammed jacket & a face blotched & pale as bad sausage, came pushing out to repair, to right, to make amends. After shopping, drove uptown, searching for coffee, drugstore closed at top of street, went into the next where I saw tall red-leather stools & icecream taps: "No coffee" smiled the unctuous-lipped attendant & I strode out, down to the glitter of Newberrys where in the warm interior air, scented variously of cheap gardenia perfumes, salted cashew nuts and plastic leathers, I sat with a stingy three-quarter cup of good enough "Newberry's famous coffee" and a little glass finger jug of milk, sipped it scalding, & drove back to campus & my 11 o'clock in the tiny white room which I like most of all simply because of its intimacy, clean whiteness & pleasant lighting. I am sure I teach better in that room, just as I am sure I teach better in certain dresses whose colors & textures war not against my body & my thought. Home, fallen, falling, to a lunch of cold chicken, potato cakes, lima beans in cheese sauce, green salad & white wine, drugged, half-drunk, I fell in bed to the sound of knocking, tapping & hammering downstairs, nightmare dreams in halls echoing with the sound of the hammer, & waking each hour to fall back again into sweaty velvet, bad sour and acid tastes, headache sharp & vinous – to drag up groggily & foul fur-tongued at 4:30 & make tea, cleansing myself with scalding amber-tinted water. A walk then, in the dusk, warmer, warm enough to walk around the park of black-green trees dark against the phosphor of the snow & blue watered sky. Sudden: a new moon like a cup coming from clouds & gathering into itself the blaze, whitened & purified, of sunk sun which still flushed the west with light. The brilliant crescent forming a chalice between the tall black pine branches: we will yet see a moon in Rome like this one. The car balking again, not shifting to second or third, the tire flat – and we seeing Fred the mean-eyed wiry thug garageman tinkering with it to destroy it, deceitful, malice-filled, like the vampire cook in the 'ghost sonata', with his bottle of soy-sauce filling the car, greasing it, oiling it. How we are at the mercy of the one's with 'know-how'. A day in a life – such gray grit, and I feel apart from myself, split, a shadow, and yet when I think of what I have taught & what I will teach, the titles have still a radiant glow & the excitement & not the dead weary plod of today. I have gotten back the life-vision, whatever that is, which enables people to live out their lives & not go mad. I am married to a man whom I miraculously love as much as life & I have an excellent job & profession (this one year), so the cocoon of childhood and adolescence is broken – I have two university degrees & now will turn to my own profession & devote a year to steady apprenticeship, and to the symbolic counterpart, our children. Sometimes I shiver in a preview of the pain & the terror of childbirth, but it will come & I live through it.

<u>Saturday night: February 22</u>: Occasionally the unquiet of the cars oppresses, as on yesterday, today. The window shakes, the night is black, & there is a new moon. All day I have been putting off reading that D.H.Lawrence thesis by reading "The Marble Faun" & I shall read the thesis through before bedtime tonight, check it tomorrow & have the report written by tomorrow noon & take it to the library & read in some Jacobean books & get my class notes done by Monday night: all this book is is resolves, which proceed to breakage & despair. "The Marble Faun", tedious, a Roman guidebook, & yet with a sylvan and gothic charm – moonlit coliseum, skull-mortared crypts, statues & paintings, masques & carnivals, & Donatello with his leaf-shaped furry ears – I love having read it because of my Roman time & walked again through St. Peter's & felt the mass of stone and gold and weighted jewels rise up in one massive fist to strike me. George Washington's birthday & the only feeling I have: a surly resentment that there is no mail. I ran up and down the outside stair at least three times and then the two o'clock streets had such a blank finished all-gone look that I called the Post Office and received the confirmation of my suspicions. A scattered dull day – the answer to: what is life? Do we always grind through the present, doomed

to throw a gold haze of fond retrospect over the past – (those images of myself, for example, that floating april day in Paris on the Place du tertre, wine & veal in sunlight with Tony," when I was without doubt most miserable before the horrors of Venice & Rome and the bloom of my best Cambridge spring & the vision of love) or ahead to the unshaped future, spinning its dreams of novels & books of poems & Rome with Ted out of a lumpish mist. All day I have run about, a hundred times, to kiss him in his niche or in his bath, to sniff his smell of bread & grapes and kiss his delectable places.

Sunday night: February 23: This must be the 26th February 23rd I have lived through: over a quarter of a century of Februaries, and would I could cut a slice of recollection back through them all & trace the spiraling stair of my ascent adultward – or is it a descent? I feel I have lived enough to last my life in musings, tracings of crossings & re-crossings with people, mad and sane, stupid and brilliant, beautiful and grotesque, infant and antique, cold and hot, pragmatic and dream-ridden, dead and alive. My house of days and masks is rich enough so that I might and must spend years fishing, hauling up the pearl-eyed, horny, scaled and sea-bearded monsters sunk long, long in the sargasso of my imagination. I feel myself grip on my past as if it were my life: I shall make it my future business: every casual wooden monkey-carving, every pane of orange-and-purple nubbled glass on my grandmother's stair-landing window, every white hexagonal bathroom tile found by Warren & me on our way digging to China, becomes radiant, magnetic, sucking meaning to it and shining with strange significance: unriddle the riddle: why is every doll's shoelace a revelation? Every wishing-box dream an annunciation? Because these are the sunk relics of my lost selves that I must weave, word-wise, into future fabrics. Today, from coffee till tea time at six, I read in "Lady Chatterley's Lover", drawn back again with the joy of a woman living with her own game-keeper, and "Women in Love" & "Sons & Lovers". Love, love: why do I feel I would have known & loved Lawrence – how many women must feel this & be wrong! I opened The Rainbow which I have never read & was sucked into the concluding Ursula & Skrebensky episode & sank back, breath knocked out of me, as I read of their London hotel, their Paris trip, their riverside loving while Ursula studied at college. This is the stuff of my life – my life, different, but no less brilliant & splendid, and the flow of my story will take me beyond this in my way – arrogant? I felt mystically that if I read Woolf, read Lawrence – (these two, why? – their vision, so different, is so like mine) – I can be itched and kindled to a great work: burgeoning, fat with the texture & substance of life: this my call, my work: this gives my being a name, a meaning: "to make of the moment something permanent": I, in my sphere, taking my place beside Ruth Beuscher & Doris Krook in theirs – neither psychologist-priestess nor philosopher-teacher but a blending of both rich vocations in my own word-ed world. A book dedicated to each of them. Fool. Dreamer. When my first novel is written & accepted (a year hence? longer?) I shall permit myself the luxury of writing above: "I am no lier." I worked on two pages of carefully worded criticism of the Lawrence thesis: feel I am right, but wonder as always: will they see? will they scornfully smile me into the wrong? No: I stated clearly my case and I feel there is a good case made. Cups of scalding tea: how it rests me. We walked out about seven into the pleasant mild-cold still night to the library: the campus snow-blue, lit from myriad windows, deserted. Cleared, cleansed, stung fresh-cheeked, chill, we walked the creaking-cricking plank paths through the botanical gardens: while Ted delivered thesis & book I walked four times round the triangle flanked by Lawrence House, the Students' Building & the street running from Paradise Pond to college hall, meeting no one, secretly gleeful & in control, summon-ing all my past green, gilded, grey, sad, sodden and loveless, ecstatic, & in-love selves to be with me & rejoice. We came home ravenous, to devour seared steak, quenching chef salad, wine, luxurious lucent green figs in thick chilled cream.

Monday night: February 24: Weary, work not done, week scarcely begun: such mortal falls, the edge of heat keeps up so short a time. Yet today gathered into itself (approximating as it does the second anniversary (25th to be exact) of our meeting at the Botolph's party and the anniversary of the acceptance of Ted's book via telegram as winner of the NYC poetry center contest) some symbolic good joint-fortune. Mademoiselle, under the per-sona of Cyrilly Abels, wrote to accept one poem from each of us for a total of $60. Ted's "Pennines in April" & my "November Graveyard" – spring & winter on the moors, birth & death, or, rather, reversing the order, death & resurrection. My first acceptance for about a year: I feel the swing into the freedom of June begin – shall doggedly send out remaining 5 or 6 poems until I find some home for the best: but this came, linking our literary for-tunes in the best way: I must work to get a book of poems together by next February at least. Ted drove me through a warm wet grey despondent morn-ing to Arvin's lecture – I am sure I know "The Scarlet Letter by heart. Then: good introduction to Picasso – blue period (Old Guitarist, Laundress, Old Man at table) and the magnificent rose-vermilion period – saltimbanques, pale, delicate, poised & lovely. Don't like the mad distortions of his 40's with my deep self much – world of sprung cuckoo-clocks – all machinery & blare & schizophrenic people parceled out in patches & lines like dead goods: macabre visual puns. Grubbed a bit at critical texts of Webster & Tourneur – ironically: just where I was after meeting Ted two years ago! Then a hot bath, shampoo – urge to clean house – will vacuum tomorrow: substitute spiritual purges – all afternoon noting critical books. Weary. Made meat loaf, juicy, & prepared two stewed chickens for tomorrow. Ted & I walked briefly in slush. Class notes tomorrow: must – & dinner –

Thursday morning: February 27: Moments snatched, & wildly snatched, between duty & duty. Outside, across the blunted pyramid of the red tile roof next to our windows great flakes of snow drift, out into which I trudge, momently, to my 9 o'clock class, another play still to read & outline, The Duchess of Malfi barely done by 1 am, and me sleepless, dreaming all the brief five hour morning, porcupine quills in the pillow, of counting beast and bird images and listing them on a never-filled sheet. My despair with The Duchess is that she is so rich, so dazzling, with diamonds and pearls, that I can't linger enough over her. Must slight The Revenger's Tragedy – give it 20 minutes tomorrow so next week will be cleared for Ibsen. A rather dull dinner this week – never have three men & one woman who must cook – Antoine a thin miserable scruffy & pathetic slip of a Frenchman – going to Morocco – next year from Holyoke. Ned Spofford shy, bright, but not rich in levels – a thin and bright brittle young man – I feel the girls must go to his head – he speaks surprisingly of his 'charm', or 'charm' that appeals to them. No more dinners. Maybe Max & Sylvan," but to hell with Marlies & them all. Except for her, we've paid the givers back & she doesn't deserve a day of mine. A day a week I've squandered. No more. Arvin's exam comes up with, in effect, a week of correcting for me to do. I am unfairly angry because I thought the job would pay $300 where it pays $100, and my art poem, if I wrote it, would almost meet, with hours of pleasure squandered, the sum. Faculty meeting long, smoky, controversial – Bill Scott," myopic, pale, fallen-chinned physics professor very like the Mad Hatter with his bitten slice of bread & butter. Sometimes I wonder, are they all dodos? Surprises: Stanley 'fired' – one year appointment ending next year: he, volatile, enthusiastic, 'immature', they secretly jealous of him spending over a year on a 'non-academic' project – a novel. What, alas & hoho, must they think of me? A complete traitor. I go to buttress myself from snow in boots & woollens. Pray for my safe return.

<u>Thursday night (Feb. 27 con)</u> Weary, weary to tears, a pen hardly held – the walk through warmish air and wet vertical snow, slipping, treacherously just not breaking my ankle, four times, five times, on the gliddery streets. My morning classes good on <u>Antigone</u>, in spite of the 9 o'clock latecomers – symmetrical, just finishing on bell-stroke, and a pleasant coffee-hour, for the first time benevolent & cordial. The companionship, enjoyed, of Fisher (always harping, like senex amans, on his first wife – "The one who wrote the cookbooks", Pelham and Belchertown being the "seats of incest in Hampshire county", February being an expensive month "because of St. Valentine's Day", women being more obscene than men –) Joan, silly and rather giddy, & Sally nice if she would be nice – Dan & Elizabeth & Philip Wheelwright, telling his indelible stories & anecdotes – and then my blessed responsive 11 o'clock. But then rain, grit, waiting on for Ted in the steamy reading room of periodicals, weary, wearier, a lambchop lunch & Dan Aaron, infinitely nice & infinitely well-meaning – tempting: me teaching here part-time, even proposing Ted teaching here, even proposing a grant – advance on my book. My book. And, breathless, late, crack-voiced, with my dazzle-shot Duchess and a class of dumb dolts, unread & stupid – I must get other people to ask questions, answer, & not try to begin to reply to their idiocies – a weary horror of a day – and tomorrow simply bearable because after it comes Saturday & by god's sake I <u>will</u> prepare Ibsen. Tonight, hearing Paul, in the crowded Browsing Room, urbane, curly headed, Dante Gabriel Rosetti or Pre-Raphaelite – all lily-crisp & appreciate, about "Virginia" – she I feel cold facing, but merging with, I too, merging. With the rhythms of days & words. Talk. Pipe dreams. A grave wish. And so, eyesore & tetchy, to bed & tomorrow less grim.

<u>Friday Night: February 28:</u> Vinously blurred, letting lamb fat and blood congeal to pale grease on the scattered plates, wine sediment curd in the bottom of glasses. Today, for some reason blest, day done with, & the reward, shining, of no extra preparation for tomorrow, and turning, wistful, toward writing – rereading the thin, thinning nucleus of my poetry book – "The Earthenware Head" & feeling, proud, how steady are the few poems I am keeping on – a sure twenty, sixteen of them already published (except for the damn, damned dilatory London Magazine). Rereading my long excerpt "Friday Night in Falcon Yard", too lumbering, leisurely, too artificial, too much in it: yet: this I will revise, condense, for spring vacation time, as I write that art poem, to a short story to send out, starting with <u>Sewanee</u>: I've put too many extraneous characters in, like Zaida and Evelyn and Mrs. Guinea – to be

a tight story: I feel the novel could take them: yet they must act, be functional, not just dispensable paragraph cariacatures as they are now: I must get Gary moving, and Rachel – not just static figures floating on Dody's Sargasso brain. Today: "the last day of February" said Miss Lincoln, & a green shoot sprang up in me as I wrote: March 1st, predating my letter-with-poems to the <u>Partisan</u> review – will send poems out tirelessly – should get at <u>least</u> 4 more accepted to make an even 20 – "Lady & Earthenware Head", "Lesson in Vengeance", "All The Dead Dears", & "Resolve" – <u>hopefully</u>. Classes better: 9'oclock on time, but rather slow. 11'oclock pure joy. 3'oclock, half-absent – no doubt because of my whirling words about a quiz yesterday – well, Ill drop a short shocker on them first thing next week. Hoho how quaint is malice. Rain. Wet rain. Grit & slush rubbing in my boots. No parking spaces in town. To bank. Then tea & a lukewarm bath, and the luxurious unfolding into my own evening & time.

<u>Saturday morning: March 1</u>:" A groaning start: sky grey, air grey as the day – dirty dishwater in the kitchen, all the curded cups and grease-filmed glasses. Blankets untucked and the insecurity of pulling at them for cover, for heat, and they plucking loose, sliding away. Woke, sheet wound in a thick noose around my neck. Sipped, aching, skin-tendered, my coffee while Ted's upper lip gouted thick red drops and runs of blood: he cut it. Nausea turned me from honey & toast: empty-stomached I go forth to class: when I come back the week will of force be ended. I yearn to my writing: must work to get my central novel chapter published as a story. It is surface skimmed now: It must gather mosses, mother-of-pearl sheen, in the sargasso of my imagination, emerging richly crusted, symbols gathering potency. I shall be late to class: can I bear up the sky? This morning after Ted left I blest his diminishing black figure – turned to chanting verses & got magnificent sense of power: learned the brief "call for the robin redbreast & the wren," "Thou art a box of wormseed," and began "Hark, now everything is still" – how to describe it – ? The surge of joy and mastery as If I had discovered a particularly effective, efficacious prayer: some demons & geniis fuse, answering, when I chant. I will learn Eliot, Yeats, Dunbar – chanted the "Lament of the Makaris" on the toilet. I will learn Ransome, Shakespeare, Blake and Thomas and Hopkins – all those who said to words "stand stable here" and made of the moment, of the hustle and jostle of grey, anonymous and sliding words a vocabulary to staunch wounds, to bind up broken limbs and "set the skull back about the head" – my own husband-in-poetry's words: I am married to a poet: miracle of my green age. Where breathes in the same body, a poet and a proper man, but in Ted?

<u>Sunday night: March 2:</u> Again, late: it will be twelve before I sleep. A strange, stopped day: Ted & I having morning coffee – black & bitter-edged, with the Bramwells in their uncomfortable second-floor flat, chairs turned wrong-side-to, records scattered, white marble fireplace angular & function-less. James is leaving for their home in France tomorrow. Ted met him in the library yesterday, a few seconds before I came into the periodical room from my last class of the week: I looked into the room through the glass door before I opened it, saw no black-coated Ted, pushed the door open, saw James' back in brown & white tweed coat, then Ted, dark, disheveled & with that queer electric invisible radiance he gives off as he did that first day I saw him over two years ago: to think, irony of ironies, that two years ago I was feverishly studying Webster & Tourneur for my supervisions (which very plays I am this week examining my students on) and furiously, desper-ately, talking myself into a crazy belief that I would somehow manage to see Ted & imprint my mark ineffacably on him before he left for Australia and murder his pale freckled mistress named Shirley. Let all rivals forever be called Shirley. How, now, sitting here in the calm cleared livingroom where we have our ordered teas, I feel I have wrested chaos and despair – and all the wasteful accident of life – into a rich and meaningful pattern – the light through this door, into the dark dim pink-walled dining alcove, shines to our bedroom & bright from his writing of poems in the swept spacious bedroom the chink of light through the crack in between the doorframe & door betrays him to me: & suddenly all, or most, of that long 35 page chapter which should be – the events at least – the core of my novel, seem cheap & easily come-by – all that sensational jabber about winds & doors & walls banging away and back. But that was the <u>psychic</u> equivalent of the whole experience: how does Woolf do it? How does Lawrence do it? I come down to learn of those two: Lawrence, because of the rich physical passion – fields of force – and the real <u>presence</u> of leaves and earth and beasts and weathers, sap-rich, and Woolf because of that almost sexless, neurotic <u>luminousness</u> – the catching of objects: chairs, tables & the figures on a street corner, and the infusion of radiance: a shimmer of the plasm that <u>is</u> life. I cannot & must not copy either. God knows what tone I shall strike. Close to a prose-poem of balanced, cadenced words and meanings, of street-corners and lights and people but not merely romantic, not merely cariacature, not merely a diary: <u>not</u>, ostensibly, autobiography: in one year I must so douse this experience in my mind, imbue it with distance, create cool shrewd views of it, so that it becomes reshapen. All this – digression: James, the subject: yesterday, a broken man, his craggy sallow face, with its look of genial corrugated black

lines – hair, brows, wrinkles & dark grain of shaven beard, his bright, mirthful black eyes – all seemed broken, askew. Ted said his hand was weak and cold as snails. "When are you leaving America?" I felt impelled to ask first, meaning, of course, when in summer. "Monday", he said. He can't work here, can't write here. He talked loudly, in an audible whisper & I wanted to quiet him, & get out of there, with the dilly girls listening over their periodicals. A chink opened into his hell: what it must be to decide him to leave, & how absurdly vindicated I felt, remembering Joan's mean-toned "Why are you going? – Don't you like it here?" How can James leave her? This always puzzles me. I need Ted to smell & kiss & sleep with & read by as I need bread & wine. I like James: one of the few men here whose life doesn't seem available, processed in uniform, cellophane-wrapped blocks, like synthetic orange cheese: James has the authentic, cave-aged, mold-ripened smell of the real thing. And yet, not a man, not completely. Joan seems young & thin for him. At coffee this morning he seemed restored, jovial. We talked of bulls & bullfights, after the two movies – on Goya & bullfighting – last night. I borrowed James' autobiography & finished it tonight: 250 pages, "The Unfinished Man" – about his experiences as a conscientious objector during the war: desultory beginning, here, there, Stockholm, Finland & all told about, characters portrayed, not actually moving & talking on their own, but talked about, half-emerged, like a frieze of flushed marble. And women: he seems to run from them – his wife queerly in the background, diminishing to America, to divorce; his child evaporating. A "told-about" love affair with a queer Finnish girl, death-oriented, who commits suicide (was he to blame, partly? did it really happen?) and a rather illuminating statement that he ("like most men") believes that loving a woman eternally isn't incompatible with leaving her: loving, leaving – a lovely consonance. I don't see it: and my man doesn't. The quiet of midnight settles over Route 9. Already it is tomorrow & the days I cross off with such vicious glee, – just as I toss, with premature eagerness, empty bottles of wine & honey into the waste basket to be neat & clear of clogging half-full jars – are those of my youngness & my promise. I believe, whether in madness or in half-truth, that if I live for a year with the two years of my life & learning at Cambridge I can write & rewrite a good novel. Ten times this 35 page chapter & rewriting & rewriting. Goal set: June 1959: a novel & a book of poems. I can not draw on James' drama: war, nations, parachute drops, hospitals in trenches – my woman's ammunition is chiefly psychic & aesthetic: love & lookings.

Monday Night: March 3: Late again, just after eleven, but I rested an hour this afternoon, drugged with fatigue from little sleep last night and a groggy, practically breakfastless morning. All day it has rained & misted, rained and misted: warm, grey, the snow dirty, porous, diminishing: until by teatime a thick wet white suspension of mist muffled trees and people, a ghost-white world. Drove in rain to laundry, enjoyed Arvin on "The Marble Faun" and the slides of colored Picasso & Juan Gris, a delight to eyes, music of line motifs, color planes, vibrations: abstract language: interpenetration, synthetic, analytic cubism. Then the laundry wasn't ready &, peeved, I drove home. A chapter – story from Luke's novel arrived, badly typed, no margins, scrawled corrections, & badly proofread. But the droll humor, the atmosphere of London & country which seeps indefinably in through the indirect statement: all this is delicate & fine. The incidents & intrigues are something I could never dream up – unless, I add, I worked at it: money stolen, & three charming characters posing as geneologists for a rich American lady with much money & little silver mirrors all over her shoes. Nothing so dull & obvious & central as love or sex or hate: but deft, oblique. As always, coming unexpectedly upon the good work of a friend or acquaintance, I itch to emulate, to sequester. Got a queer and most overpowering urge today to write, or typewrite, my whole novel on the pink, stiff, lovely-textured Smith memorandum pads of 100 sheets each: a fetish: somehow, seeing a hunk of that pink paper, different from all the endless reams of white bond, my task seems finite, special, rose-cast. Bought a rose bulb for the bedroom light today & have already robbed enough notebooks from the supply closet for one & 1/2 drafts of a 350 page novel. Will I do it. Broke the jinx of my first lesson & got a quiz made up & "Ghosts" outlined. Must rip through other two plays tomorrow & then to the blinding deluge of Arvins exams –

Wednesday: March 5: Just afternoon, the church clock having struck twelve, and my week's lesson pages on Ibsen done – for the first time, a week ahead: must do this from now on: it takes such a curse of haste & hit-or-miss of the teaching half of the week. Sun: bright if weak – for the first time in days of rain and mist: snows swindled to still diminishing white patches and crusts and bare green stretches of grass, sodden, muddy, emerging. Slept, half-conscious, through Arvin's class and Art, weary, almost sick with fatigue & feeling now restored, renewed to begin the next two weeks: and then the blessing of spring vacation: to write my art poem & a whole week to outline the poetry course – and all through that eight week period the joy of knowing the end of May is at hand: I found the two pained & torturous typewritten sheets I wrote in October and November when trying to keep myself from flying into black bits – how new, now, is my confidence: I can endure – endure through weaknesses, bad days, imperfections and fatigue: and do my work without running away or crying: mercy I can no more. If, knocking on wood (where does that come from?) I can survive in health till spring vacation, all shall be well. Even now, faced with 54 of Arvin's exams for which I must do a good bit of reading before I can cope, and then the second DHLawrence thesis to read on top of that – plus mid-semester grades. March 17th should be a liberation of sorts: winter-shackles thrown off. Money pours in: salary check mysteriously gone up, – (Arvin's work? for exams?) Our bank account from salarys mounts to $700, our poetry earning since September shall soon touch $850 & auspiciously reach their set-aim by June: we are going to try for poetry contests, jingle contests – trifling sums, but my gripping acquisitive sense thrives: I knew America would do this for us. Ted, yesterday had two poems "Of Cats" & "Relic" accepted enthusiastically by Harper's – not one rejection yet in the last three batches – pray that The Yale Review and the London Magazine will not be recalcitrant: strange what vicarious pleasure I get from Ted's acceptances: pure sheer joy: almost as if he were holding the field open, keeping a foot in the door to the golden world, & thus keeping a place for me. Aim: to have my art poems: one to three (Gauguin, Klee & Rousseau) – completed by the end of March. I shall spend time in the art library: at last. I feel my mind, my imagination, nudging, sprouting, prying & peering. The old anonymous millionairess" seen this morning coming from the ugly boxed orangey stucco house next door, hobbling on one crutch down her path to the gleaming black limousine breathing o-so-gently at the curb, burdened, bent, she, under the weight and bulk of a glossy mink coat, bending to get into the back of the car, as the rotund, rosy white-haired chauffeur held the door open for her. A bent mink-laden lady. And the mind runs, curious, into the crack in the door behind her: where does she come from, who is she? what loves and sorrows are strung on her rosary of hours? Ask the gardener, ask the cook, ask the maid: all the rough, useful retainers who keep a clockwork ritual of grace in a graceless house, barren-roomed and desolate.

– Ted read his poems at the University last night – a queerly unsatisfying affair: a small glittery room in the-hive-roomed student union, with the rumble & distraction of a meeting going on next-door, and three other 'poets' – except for Dave Clarke," who rises to a gloss & delicacy of ear and philosophical play, embarassingly bad – Ted shone: the room dead-still for his reading – he came third: and I felt the genuine gooseflesh, the tears filling my lids, the hair standing like quills: I married a real poet, and my life is redeemed: to love, serve & create. But there, everybody walks & lives in rooms with such low ceilings he who is a foot taller is no god, but an embarassing and uneasy visitation.

<u>Saturday night: March 8</u>: One of those nights when I wonder if I am alive, or have been ever. The noise of the cars on the pike is like a bad fever: Ted sickish, flagging in discontent: "I want to get clear of this life: trapped." I think. Will we be less trapped in Boston? I dislike apartments, suburbs. I want to walk directly out my front door into earth and into air free from exhaust. And I: what am I but a glorified automaton hearing myself, through a vast space of weariness, speak from the shell speaking-trumpet that is my mouth the dead words about life, suffering, and deep knowledge and ritual sacrifice. What is it that teaching kills? The juice, the sap – the substance of revelation: by making even the insoluble questions & multiple possible answers take on the granite assured stance of dogma. It does not kill this quick of life in students who come, each year, fresh, quick, to be awakened & pass on – but it kills the quick in me by forcing to formula the great visions, the great collocations and cadences of words and meanings. The good teacher, the proper teacher, must be everliving in faith and ever-renewed in creative energy to keep the sap packed in herself, himself, as well as the work. I do not have the energy, or will to use the energy I have, and it would take all, to keep this flame alive. I am living & teaching on rereadings, on notes of other people, sour as heartburn, between two unachieved shapes: between the original teacher & the original writer: neither. And America wears me, wearies me. I am sick of the Cape, sick of Wellesley: all America seems one line of cars, moving, with people jammed in them, from one-gas-station to one diner and on. I must periodically refresh myself in this crass, crude, energetic, demanding & competetive new-country bath, but I am, In my deep soul, happiest on the moors – my deepest soul-scape, in the hills by the Spanish Mediterranean, in the old, history-crusted & still gracious, spacious cities: Paris, Rome. I slept, as always on Saturday afternoons, the sick vinous thick-furred sleep of exhaustion. Woke, dazed, to pare potatoes into cool white ovoids, carrots into long conical spears, onions slippery glossed & bulbous popped & cracked from their rattle-paper skins. Writing a good poem will affect me like a celestial love-affair: Will it happen? Will one come. In a little over a week I should begin: free: on my first vacation. Finished marking the 55 Hawthorne exams in half the time, simply by sorting them out according to answers to each of the four

questions: hope there are no grave repercussions, furors – how arbitrary the whole system of marking is! Tomorrow the Lawrence thesis: then the Strindberg plays to do, then my own papers to correct. I can see chinks of light: of a new life. Will there be pain? The birth-giving pain is not yet known. Last night, weary, up the odd Gothic blind stair-well to Arvins for drinks: Fisher & the Gibians: dull, desultory talk about aborigines & me going out on the incoming of politics. Arvin: bald-head pink, eyes & mouth dry slits as on some carved rubicund mask: a Baskin wood-cut: huge, mammothed in the hall: a bulbous streaked head, stained, scarred, owl-eyed – "tormented man", and a great, feathered, clawed fierce-eyed owl sitting in an intolerable eternal niche of air above the head. Ted does not like Arvin: I sense an acrid repulsion between the two men – he senses a lizard, snakiness & I, half-caught in this vision, see Arvin: dry, fingering his key-ring compulsively in class, bright hard eyes red-rimmed, turned cruel, lecherous, hypnotic & holding me caught like the gnome Loerke held. Fisher, arms flapping, ridiculous, jumping up as if to urinate or be sick, only to leave, leaving his pipe, his drink half-finished. "He's done that all year," said the Gibians.

Monday night: March 10: Exhausted: is there ever a day otherwise. Alfred Kazin to dinner tonight: he: broken, somehow, embittered & unhappy: greying, his resonance diminished. Lovable still: and he and Ann," his wife too a writer, another couple to speak to in this world. How babies complicate life: he paying also for a son. Ted is queerly sick still: how hopeless, helpless I feel with Ted pale, raggle-haired, miserable-visaged and there no clear malady, no clear remedy. He coughs, sweats, feels sick to his stomach. Pale and sweet and distant he looks. I think: a week from today I shall be resting, rested, and in my "vacation", able for a week to write on a poem for days, without feeling assignments too near: only 8 weeks of poetry to prepare, seventy papers to correct, and all Melville to read, which should be joy, of sorts. A Rousseau poem: a green-leaved world. With the naked lady on her red velvet couch in the jungle's middle: how close to this I come. Today, all I feel like doing is sleep. I fall on the bed, drugged, with this queer sickish greeny-vinous fatigue. Drugged, gugged, stogged and sludged with weariness. My life is a discipline, a prison: I live for my own work, without which I am nothing. My writing. Nothing matters but Ted, Ted's writing & my writing. Wise, he is, and I, too, growing wiser. We will remold, melt & remold our plans to give us better writing space. My nails are splitting and chipping. A bad sign. I suppose I really haven't had a vacation all year: Thanksgiving a black-wept nightmare & Christmas the low blow of pneumonia and since then a struggle to keep health. Almost asleep in Newton's class: must be up early, to laundry & to steal more pink pads of paper tomorrow. Kazin: at home with us, talking of reviews: his life: a second wife, blonde & he being proud of her, touchingly. What is a life where in one dreams of Fisher, furtive, in pink & gaudy purple & green houses, and Dunn & racks & racks of dresses.

Tuesday afternoon, March 11: Something got me in its grip these last three afternoons. Today, too, I slumped into bed, unable to hold my head up after lunch, and so into a sick stupor of a sleep. A mild March day with an edge of cold hid in wind-stir, in the angle of shadow, a dazed squirrel hopping ungainly, half out of it hide, shoulders moulting and furry haunches. A thin green-yellow wash of light underlying bare ground, bare trees, warmly luminous and promising. O how my own life shines, beckons, as if I were caught, revolving, on a wheel, locked in the steel-toothed jaws of my schedule. Well, since January I have been holding a dialogue with myself & girding myself to stand fast without running. Now I am at a saturation point: fed-up. The thought of outlining three hours of Strindberg plays this week appals me. While Strindberg should be most fun of all. I turn to these pages as toward a cool fluid drink of water – as being closest to my life – words must sound, sing, mean: I hear a tin cup chink on a fountain brim as I say "drink." I must grow ingrown, queer, simply from indwelling and playing true to my own gnomes and demons. I count & recount calendar weeks as if an idiot telling beads toward the second coming. Will they dream up some holiday chore for me or no? All I hear is the distant unquiet roararoar of a plane and the screak and whoosh of traffic outside our window which seems to have increased with the last few days – and the holler and hullabaloo of highschool letting out. Today, overslept caught in some gross and oppressive nightmare involving maps and pale sandy deserts and people in cars – a sense of guilt, bad-faith, embarrassment and sallow sulphurous misery brooding over all. Listened to the same Arvin lecture on <u>Mardi</u> I heard four years ago & a lecture on the pure abstractionist Mondrian: as warm as Platonic linoleum-squares.

Thursday morning, March 13: This morning in my one hour before trudging to class, instead of cramming notes on the play I must give this afternoon, one of my favorites, "The Ghost Sonata", I sit, warm, drowsy & at the other side of the shakes, writing here, trying to build up a calm center. Yesterday was a horror – Ted said something about the moon and Saturn to explain the curse which strung me tight as a wire and twanged unmercifully. Too tired for the saving humor, downed, doused in my vital quick. Piddling at averages, income tax forms, anything to keep from the pain of thinking about my play preparations, and after that, my 64 papers to correct, my thesis, my mid-semester grades. Until late on Monday I must bear up: and today, keep a deep, quiet core & not get fratchy or angry. Yesterday I sheepishly cut Arvin (and why not?) and Art (my own loss) and sat scribbling long introductory pages – summarizing Ibsen. Introducing, Naturalism, Strindberg, grinding into "Miss Julie" – which remains to be finished today & the "Ghost Sonata" notes written between morning classes, the "Dreamplay" notes written over tea. Conserve, conserve. Alice Zinc, fresh, brazen, stupid – questions – sneering, spoiled, "What is the message?" and weary, my dikes down, she, and the myriad smug-grinned girls & shop-keepers and professors people my waking dreams. A bad class, asking for extensions as if English were an extra-curricular course waiveable if they have other exams. Today: sit deep. Trust to a renewal of fervor & force over spring vacation, with May 22 as the finis date. Quarrel with Ted over sewing on buttons on jackets (which I must do), wearing his gray suit, and such trivia, he getting up from sickness, me going down into it. Gulping a chicken wing & a mess of spinach & bacon, all, all, turning to poison. "Dreamplay" – ambitious production – the Daughter dancing descent through a scrim of clouds, her voice stiff & stagey, and the scenery creaking & thumping in its changes. The smoke-faced lawyer rich-voiced, lending depth – the Deans of the Faculties humorous, but the irony of the play being that it is all true in my own life. We had just finished quarreling about buttons & haircuts (like their salads and such as a basis for divorce), and especially the repetition of schooling the officer goes through – teaching & learning forever that twice-two is - - - what? And I, sitting too in the same seats I occupied three, four, five, six, seven years ago teaching what I learned one, two, three, four years ago, with less vigor than I studied and learned – living among ghosts and familiar faces I pretend not to recognize: Mrs. William Shakespeare, my housemother, in front of us; Alison Cook the skeletal ghostly Warden to the rear; my own class dean & now the dean of my own students – waiting dinner at her place for us tomorrow; along with Miss Lincoln who persisted in giving me a B in Milton. And at faculty meeting in the afternoon the sense of all their talk about the Alpha Society & Award having been gone over in my reign as 'bright student' – and the graduate fellowships as well. All rolling over on itself, tasting of sourdough, tasting of heartburn. Now I must leap into my clothes and stride to class, early, to steal three pink books: yes, for my novel: have just read the sensationalist trash which is "Nightwood" – all perverts, all ranting, melodramatic: "The Sex God forgot" – self-pity. Like the stage whine of the "dream-Play" – Pity us: Oh, Oh, Oh: Mankind is pitiable – Ted is trying for a Saxton grant & has an excellent draft for a project – if <u>only</u> this would happen – to justify America for him: his <u>Jack &</u> <u>Jill</u> story came back, but with a nice letter from the editor. O for a Saxton: on it we would somehow live & <u>both</u> furiously write.

<u>Friday afternoon: March 14</u>: Outside the grinding & sloshing of cars in soggy winter-weather – trees, houses, cars, are white-sided, snow-sided. As if to mock my final days before spring vacation snow kept falling thick and wet, whitening the air, climbing shin-deep. Trudge, body. Deep sleep last night and queer nightmares – fragmented rememberings at breakfast: of Newton Arvin: withered, mysterious, villainous. Shrunken heads to piece together clues to deceptions: heads lolly-pop size, withered, painted ruddy over the shrunk corruption of approaching death. Dark elevations of floors & stairs in unlit libraries. Pursuit, guilt. Cars on the familiar home turnpike: vegetables thrown in anger & vengeance. Rhubarb stalks & blunt warted brown potatoes: vengeance on a competing country vegetable stand sapping their custom away. A vivified awakening after 10 hours of sleep & the queer dark & white empty campus at nine, not a soul, not a car – a nightmare sequence preparing, the class building unlit. Cleared up: student mass-meeting. A dull day: cramming down notes on the Dreamplay. My after-noon class turgid, over half not having read the play & me quiet but feeling my head pounding on a blank, spoiled, ignorant wall. And a battle coming home: the car skidding, slipping, up the treacherous college lane hill over the pond where once before we skidded, turning, poised perilous. Jaded, satur-ated, stale: I mark time, mark the slogging obstacle course of these last days: tomorrow: classes, then the dubious bliss of correcting papers, writing a thesis report. Then a week solid, after Monday, of writing on a new poem: a poem for a contest: 350 lines: an exercise to set me free: 10 small poems in one large one titled, from Wallace Stevens: "Mules That Angels Ride" – with, I hope, the naturalness & implicit form (without glassy brittleness) of my "Black Rook" poem: Inspiration & Vision expressed through Matter: Human Bodies, Art (painting), tables & chairs.

<u>Saturday Morning: March 15</u>: If I survive to return to write again here after noon today, my own classes will, for a blessed two-and-a-half weeks, be

suspended. I am strongly tempted to get more & more casual & curt about them & more and more involved in my writing. The day after tomorrow I begin. Last night all my stomach turned sour and rancid: Ted & I slogged through lakes of mud concealed by a wet foot of snow to get to Miss Schnieders" for dinner: a warm fire-lit livingroom, a curving vermilion velvet sofa, mat grey walls, and the rooms, painted like the inside of pastel beads, stretching away in little colored cells of light: peach, pale green. A huge supper: lamb, buttery potatoes, carrots & cheese covered broccoli, apple cake & cream. I sat at a little table in a stiff low-backed white chair between Tony Hecht & Reinhart Lettau," Reinhart by far the kindest & most honest of the two, his ears sticking out directly from his head, his teeth crooked, his eyes behind thick glasses, but fine-souled & pleasantly sturdy, blond & Germanic in all his outer ugliness. Tony: urbane, hair professionally curled & just barely tinct with grey, as if an outline – he has had three grants to write in Europe & is pocketing his Hudson while continuing to work & teach which galled Ted & me – his taking a year of writing, as it were, from another poet. We talked of Ionesco, the war, Tony on one side, Reinhart on the other. Home to read in the rich & vivid first novel by Peter Fiebleman "A Place Without Twilight". I must learn from him: a beautifully produced book: clear simple cover: white; black print & stark medallion design: girl, stylized, back-to, regarding face in mirror the mat good blue of the page edges. A rich honest book: the smell of magnolia, the taste of sugar cane, the look of a stunned raccoon.

<u>Saturday evening</u>: And so I have survived. It is well after eleven, the radiators dead cold and the air unproductive and chill. Fell into bed & slept as usual this afternoon with Ted: a drunken sleep-sodden drowning. I am surrounded by papers to correct & must grind on two more days, but, at home, at least, with no class preparation. Then to clean house like a tornado: If I conjecture rightly, I will feel a blow on the head, see a track of comet sparks, & wake up confronting my three o'clock class, stammering unprepared nothings about Gerard Manley Hopkins. A gray day: walking to class, snow spitting, half asleep in my lectures, letting the flow of impulse carry the boat, adrift, drifting. Reading <u>When We Dead Awaken</u> in between, in the cold, angular gloom of my library office. A peculiar hunger and thirst upon me: steak and salad and red wine tonight. I am yet in a dream, unproductive, weary. Got a notice from the Guggenheim people & the Houghton Mifflin awards – hopeless to concern myself about until I have written my two books by the end of next year. Ted getting a phone call this afternoon from blessèd paternal

white-haired Jack Sweeney asking Ted to read at Harvard on the Morris (Maurice?) Grey readership on Friday April 11th for the princely sum of $100 and expenses! One hour of his own poems: to us this looks like professional glory. Greasy dishes pile up in the kitchen, the garbage can overflows with coffee grounds, rancid fat, rotting fruit rinds & vegetable scrapings: a world of stinks, blemishes, idle dreams, fatigue and sickness: to death. I feel like a dead person offered the fruits and riches & joys of the world only if she will get up and walk. Will my legs be sturdy? My trial period approaches. To bed, now & resolutely to work tomorrow. Save, conserve: wisdom knowledge, smells & insights for the page: to wrestle through slick shellacked façades to the real shapes and smells and meanings behind the masks.

Tuesday morning: March 18: Almost, not quite, let down to rest. I am about to dress, to trudge to Arvin and the white whale after a delinquency of two days. But so: I am getting paid little enough money for ruining my eyes – they blear, blur and twitch from sandy grains. How lovely it will be to spend my mornings, after coffee, working on poems, an art poem (I must get books on Rousseau, Gauguin, Klee) and a long poem about the spirit, luminous, making itself manifest in art, in houses and trees and faces: "Mules That Angels Ride". Two days of crammed correcting of papers – arbitrary, how arbitrary are marks: sixty papers: never again shall I ask for more than a two page paper. And averaging nine marks for all: Ted did that. And typing out a thesis report. Very black. Last night – aching, dazed, too numb to feel or cry, I took a hot bath: therapy: the kinks wore out, and I rose purged, for a day, of the sticky collection of sweat and exudings, powdered, in a fresh-laundered torn white-cotton nightgown with tiny purple roses sprigged over it. From now on nothing will be so bad. I'll wash my hair today & start cleaning house. When will I feel my liberty? Perhaps not till tomorrow, after my last class to attend, perhaps not till sleep on Thursday. In the past two days, Sunday & Monday, Ted & I have had, respectively, dinner and tea (and lecture) with two American "poets". Queerness of queernesses. Peter Viereck" & George Abbe." Sunday afternoon we drove across the wide flat ice-gray Connecticut River & into the snowcovered Holyoke range with its bristles of bare winter trees and up into the ugly black-smeared brick atrocities of Victorian Holyoke. Antoine lives in a faculty house facing out over white snow-fields into the purpling and bristled hills. We shouldered into his tiny room with its cot and, surprisingly, real fireplace with a log burning red. Walls covered with odd and tawdry papers: the sheet of an old piece of music, a print in color of an ancient French unicorn tapestry, theater bills. Two women teachers: a young, soft dark-haired girl in a coverup dress of electric blue: Evelyn" someone, who teaches modern philosophy & lisps somewhat, slightly bucktoothed. And Miss Mill," a fat dowdy fixed lady, with gray hair that looked as if it needed dusting, an ugly, or, rather, nondescript, suit and layers of spreckled fat skin. She proceeded, over sherry and a nut or two from a glass jar which Antoine passed around, to relate the story of Dylan Thomas' visit to Holyoke in raucous, shrill tones which allowed of no interruptions: a woman who never listens, a horrible woman, shaped in hard round bullet shapes, squat, unsympathetic as a dry toad. Dirty decaying teeth, hands with that worn glisten of flesh unmarried old ladies have: a glitter of rhinestones somewhere, a pin, or chain. We talked of nothing: the Dylan Thomas story lasted till dinnertime, & Evelyn, bearing a platter of white cut bread covered with a grey-pink paté specked with something black, led us down the ugly brown stairs to an uncomfortable private diningroom, a too-varnished, too-polished mahogany table & skittery stiff-backed chairs. I drank, quickly, & never modestly demurred when Antoine came round with the red wine. An ugly fattish yellow dolt-faced girl with purplish acne waited on us. I sat on Antoine's left, facing the irrepressible Miss Mill who evidently had taken an immediate dislike to me & whom I proceeded to ignore. "Peter's here," Evelyn softly & joyously exclaimed. And my first impression was: he's a madman. He gave the impression of being too brightly colored blue & yellow, and ravaged by years of sandblasting. Goggle, electric-blue frog eyes, a pocked, vivid tan coarse-pored skin, short blondish hair, and a pale sleazy whitish-cream jacket that didn't hang right & gave him a cockeyed, humpbacked look. Heavy black leather ski-type boots, or perhaps, hiking boots, and, again pants that hung as on bandy-legs. He began to talk immediately in a rather high, grating voice: frank, fanatic & open. I spent the mealtime talking with him, raising my voice, too: everybody giggled, gulped wine (except Miss Mill) and raised their voices. I began to go pleasantly erotic, feeling my body compact and sinewy, feeling like seducing a hundred men. But immediately, I turn to Ted: all I have to do is think of that first night I saw him, and that's it. Viereck raved: politics, Ezra Pound: we agreed a man was all of a piece, couldn't really compartmentalize himself, airtight. Viereck (winner of at least two Guggenheims) raved against the giving of Guggenheims to old safe famous people & advocated their bestowal on poets who spent the money on women & drink & were politically radical. We all flowed upstairs again (Viereck having, in the course of the meal – (thick slabs of roast beef, watery string beans, roast potato & some ghastly icecream, vanilla rounds with a green shamrock of mint-flavored icecream in the middle) – put on greenish-hued sunglasses). Viereck promptly pulled down the blinds of the window, all except one long thin strip of window, & cut out the snow-blinding view: the left strip showed stark and delicately-colored, like a Japanese watercolor – lavendar mountains, white plains of snow, & a stipple of bushes, grasses & trees perfect as lines of a calligraph. We drank black, bitter espresso coffee which Antoine made in a queer chromium-tubed pot, and then brandy. Antoine passed a glass jar of pink, green, yellow & lavendar easter-egg candies. We left then. Viereck shaking hands goodbye & miraculously leaving my hand full of a bunch of his pamphlets on poetry & politics his "Americana."

Thursday morning: March 20: My first morning: blank pages: a blank page. Tired still, but warm & comfortable. Resolved not to go out: outside the slithering soggy sound of cars speeding through wet. Snow falling when I woke: black varnishing the slick roads, but hanging to tree and roof top in icy shackles. I give myself a week – through next Wednesday: and give up the idea of the long contest. Have narrowed down poem subjects to Klee (five paintings and etchings) and Rousseau (two paintings) & will try, arbitrarily, one a day. Each subject appeals, deeply, to me. Must drop them in my mind and let them grow rich, encrusted. And choose: choose one today. I sit in a stupor – torn, torn: a pure whole week, and me so far from my deep self, from the demon within, that I sit giddy on a painted surface. Yesterday: sat in the art libe soaking & seeping in pictures. I think I will try to buy the Paul Klee Book. Or at least, get it over the weekend. Reminders now, of the seawrack of the past week: the most sickening, the most embarrassing of experiences: Monday – tea with George Abbe at the Roches & a horror of a lecture in the Browsing Room. Paul, with his professional dewy blue-eyed look and his commercially gilded and curled blond hair on his erect, dainty-boned aristocrat head looking as if it had been struck on a greek coin that since had blurred & thinned from too much public barter and fingering. "One of the finest minor poets in America", Paul breathed over the phone. Abbe sickened Ted & me the minute he walked into Paul's livingroom, with his slick nervous smile, his jittery huckster-hand jingling money in his pants' pocket. Clarissa, apparently recently recovered from a sulk of tears, slouched about in a baggy white sweatshirt and a blue & white full skirt, and baby-buttoned black ballet shoes, like Miss Muffet in a private tantrum. And the lecture: I writhed, bristled. In that dark-wooded and antique room, with its dim light and worn, deep comfortable chairs and darkened oriental rugs, with the hollow-coffined grandfather clock ticking its sepulchral ticks and the oil-portrait of Mary Ellen Chase leaning forward, as if out of the gilt restraining frame, her white hair an aureole, a luminous nimbus, George Abbe garbled his bible of crudities to the literary Mademoiselle Defarges of Smith knitting his slick and commercial words into cable-stitched sweaters and multi-colored argyles. Intolerable: catchpenny phrases "This is the point, do you get it, I'll just tie this up." George Abbe, it develops, has a handy little storage-closet (personal, private) called the 'Subconscious', or, more glibly, the 'Subliminal' where he tosses all his old dreams, his ideas and visions. Buzz, snip, handy little demons get to work, and presto! a few hours, days or months later he writes out a poem – zip-zip. What's it mean? I dunno. – You tell me. He reads some of his own trash: a jeweled dog & a boy licking a sticky lollypop. What's it mean? A poem's gotta move – He gets boys in academy to write him interpretations of his own poems: "fabulous!" he tosses a sheaf of paper on the table, waves a poem about the animal, March, with its "pussy-willow eyes" in "the latest issue of the <u>Atlantic</u>". Brags: "I've just sold this to Poetry London-New York." The more interpretations a poem has the better a poem it is. Why, anyone can write: He even wrote a poem in twenty minutes on stage for a show called "Creation While You Watch" – one guy improvised mood music, another painted while George Abbe fished up a mood poem in his unconscious & wrote it on the blackboard – that's pressure-cooker poetry par excellence. Ted & I got sicker & sicker. George Abbe got more & more hectic: read one or two crapulous dull & affected passages from his new novel 'The Winter House': about his boyhood, sob. Everything he wrote, or read here, was about his boyhood. His poor father: a country pastor, with only a thousand dollars a year for a salary. His own insecurity: he jumps about, yaps, jingles his money, voice rising strident: "I was insecure, still am. Can't stand being away from <u>people</u>. Get scared." On writing poetry on blackboards in public: "Wonderful! You know, the way you can worship better in church, with a hundred people around, then you can in nature." A poseur: every poem is an ulcer: or, every ulcer should have been a poem: he quotes his friend John Ciardi in "The Canadian Businessman". As if poetry were some kind of therapeutic public purge or excretion. Ted & I left, disgusted, to go home to our private & exacting demons who demand every conscious and deep-rooted discipline, and work, and rewriting & knowledge.

– A sequel: lunch at the Roche's yesterday: started from coffee with Clarissa and various unsatisfactory gossip, she having a third baby in Mexico while Paul goes to Greece, gallivanting & translating, & to England. While I kept pouring my coffee from the saucer back into the cup, after the children, knocked the table, I came to the conclusion that both Pandora and the fat dolt-headed Poter are idiots: Pandora is cute, like Clarissa, but dull as a blond doll: "Brown doggie bite," she vouch safed. Poter ran about, fat-headed, goggle-blue-eyed & drooling: all extroverted – no inner, self contained play – futile, purposeless flinging about. Ted came. And Paul, in his creamy-absinthe-tweed suit which brings to a crescendo of color the outlandish mint-tinge of his eyes. Then Pat Hecht & serious, pained, wordless baby Jason. Pat pale, studiedly casual in torn sneakers & pleasant as razor-blades. Too much salt in a fruit salad. We ate, grumpily, & left.

<u>Friday afternoon: March 28</u>: A whole week, and I haven't written here, nor picked up the book. For good reason. For the first time a lapse of writing here spells writing. I was taken by a frenzy a week ago Thursday, my first real day of vacation, and the frenzy has continued ever since: writing and writing: I wrote eight poems in the last eight days, long poems, lyrical poems, and thunderous poems: poems breaking open my real experience of life in the last five years: life which has been shut up, untouchable, in a rococo crystal cage, not to be touched. I feel these are the best poems I have ever done. Occasionally I lifted my head, ached, felt exhausted. Saturday I groaned, took pellets of bufferin, stitched in the worst cramps and faintness for months, which no pills dulled, and wrote nothing: that night we went to a dull dinner at the Roche's with Dorothy Wrinch" who acted like a gray-haired idiot, goggling, going through her little-grey-haired-misunderstood-genius-scientist-act. She obviously does not care for Ted: he is too honest and simple and strong and un-Oxford & untwittery for her. She obviously was miffed I said I'd call her for coffee and never did: but I won't, either. I don't care a damn for her & won't waste poem-time on people I can't stand. One night, late, we walked out and saw the lurid orange glow of a fire down below the highschool. I dragged Ted to it, hoping for houses, in a holocaust, parents jumping out of the window with babies, but nothing such: a neighborhood burning a communal acreage of scrubby grass field, flames orange on darkness, friendly shouts across the flaming waste land, silhouettes of men and children firing a border with tufts of lit grasses, beating out a blaze with brooms as it jeopardized a fence. We walked round, and stood where a householder stood grimly & doggedly wetting his chrysanthemum stalks and letting the waters run into a little dyke or ditch, separating his patch of

lawn from the crackling red-lit weed stalks. The fire was oddly satisfying. I longed for an incident, an accident. What unleashed desire there must be in one for general carnage. I walk around the streets, braced and ready and almost wishing to test my eye and fiber on tragedy – a child crushed by a car, a house on fire, someone thrown into a tree by a horse. Nothing happens: I walk the razor's edge of jeopardy. Today: bright sun and a benevolence in the air: the scritch and roar of men sweeping up the winter's leavings of sand from the street into waiting trucks. The park with a pale greenish light, full of innumerable squirrels, silvery, sun-dazed, picking up twigs & chasing each other. We walked around and around under the silvery treeboles and great dark pines. Crows wheeled, shiny-black and cawing. I found a bright bluejay feather, banded across, blue and black. We crunched acorns, pine cones underfoot, and projected years of writing: years and years of writing and traveling. I sent off a group of eight poems, seven of them new, under the title "Mules That Angels Ride" (the vision arrives astride the symbol, the illumination comes through a mask of mud, clear and shining) to a Wallace Stevens Contest: will this spring bear fruit? As so many springs have done? I mailed 5 poems today to Howard Moss at the New Yorker – three of them what I would call "sure things." One, a sestina, I wrote yesterday – my first & only good sestina – and the subject fit it: on Rousseau's last painting, "The Dream" – which I titled: "Yadwigha, On A Red Couch, Among Lilies: A Sestina for the Douanier."

Saturday morning: March 29: A horrible hangover and nightmare morning: ironically clear, sunny brisk fresh day, green buds on the lilac standing bright in the six o'clock sun. Last night we foolishly drank martinis – my first for at least two years – like water. Then pizza and beer. Ugh. I took alka seltzer last night, that sparkling clear cool drink, and fell into a lousy sleep. Dreamed, for about the second time, a horrid dream of teaching, which means I am oppressed by work & must do my work: I dreamed I was home in Wellesley with mother, hypnotized, as usual, before the clock, which said past nine, drove in a coffee-gulped rush to Seelye. Parked just beside college hall & ran across the lawn: could see the dark disgusted face of Ann Bradley looking out of the second floor classroom window: she was wearing a navyblue sweatshirt, and her face greasy, as if coated with a thin layer of transparent snot. Ran upstairs, breathless, to find a huge class of fifty, most of them strangers, as for the beginning of a new term, and stacks of classcards on my desk. Tried to cover lateness & unpreparedness by reading the attendance cards. Class restive, defiant socialites. The cards were not arranged alphabetically & had unpronounceable names and as I started reading them, turned into an immense bundle of scarves & belts, with names embroidered & sewn on them every which way. A smug indignant girl like Liz Robertson tossing her soft brown hair: That's not the way to say my name! Sylvie Koval & Sue Badian appearing, like angels in the hostile mob. Me picking up a green & white Saturday Review with black print which suddenly appeared on the desk & trying to read the titles of sections which were written in a queer patois French: Ezra Pound's translation of T.S. Eliot. I saw Miss Drew: pale, mournful, cadaverous, in the classroom at the rear, observing, skeptical. I realized the Saturday Review was dated March 7th & would be unavailable. Miss Drew got up to leave, drawing a scarf around her tall, thin head and said: "I just don't see how you're going to do this." The bell rang, confusion, snickers, and I woke up, mouth swollen huge & black, tongue furred. Ran to the bathroom for another alka seltzer & stuck out my tongue: looked perfectly normal. But feel sick, self-disgusted as I would be if I wantonly poisoned myself, or shortened my life. No more drinks for me: martinis are lethal. Ugh. Just beer, cold and thirst-quenching, would have been so lovely. Ugh. I drank coffee, sniffed eagerly of the cool fresh morning as Ted left for his last day of work before vacation (his). Looked through & through my calendar: eight weeks: seven actual teaching weeks. Each week will diminish my pile of preparation: Hopkins, Yeats, Eliot, Thomas, Auden, Crowe Ransom, e e cummings. I should have fun if I face preparations & do them very tight, very well. Must do a list of definitions for the first day. Illustrate on board. How much better the day looks as I wake: it moves by steady laws which are as much for me as against me. Eight weeks. This work, teaching, has done me much good: I can tell from the way my poems spouted this last week: a broad wide voice thunders and sings of joy, sorrow and the deep visions of queer and terrible and exotic worlds. Marty & Mike came for dinner Thursday night: they both much better – radiant – none of the nasty & petty jealousy of Christmas at tea. Marty strangely radiant: her eyes black & lustrous: they cannot have a baby, she told me in the kitchen, would I recommend her when they adopt one? Tears jetted out of my eyes: Marty, of all, who should have her own baby: they tried & tried & she says they would be the scientific miracle of the century if they had a child.

[Six sentences omitted by ed.]

A judgment, unspoken but perpetually present. The only worse, worst: to have an idiot or crippled child of one's own. Will I have them? Will mine be all-right? Ted's family is full of madness – suicide, idiots & mine has a diabetic father, grandmother died of cancer, mother with ulcers & tumors, aunt unable to conceive after three miscarriages, uncle with heart trouble. Oh glory glory. I live still, and so does Warren. Well, they came & went, & I felt sick, struck, after hearing that: as if I saw in Marty's life, from the winter days that freshman midsemester eight long years go when Mike was in England & I took her picture beside the "Mike" she'd written in the snow to the summer day he came home to Marblehead and she waited for him at Blodgett's in a pink piqué dress and all glowing-brown tan: to know, in retrospect, a doom was on them, chastens & subdues. I sit, this morning, yellow-green of color, and sickish, in Ted's big dark green & red plaid woolen bathrobe and the house is chill, but clean, except for a pan of dirty glasses we drank out of all during the night to ease our dehydration. We want to buy art books. de Chirico. Paul Klee. I have written two poems on paintings by de Chirico which sieze my imagination – "The Disquieting Muses" and "On the Decline of Oracles" (after his early painting, "The Enigma of the Oracle") and two on paintings by Rousseau – a green & moony-mood-piece, "Snakecharmer", & my last poem of the eight, as I've said, a sestina on Yadwigha of "The Dream". I shall copy here some quotations from a translated prose-poem by de Chirico, or from his diaries, which have unique power to move me, one of which, the first, is the epigraph to my poem "On the Decline of Oracles":

---

(1) "Inside a ruined temple the broken statue of a god spoke a mysterious language."

(2) "Ferrara" the old ghetto where one could find candy & cookies in exceedingly strange & metaphysical shapes."

(3) "Day is breaking. This is the hour of the enigma. This is also the hour of prehistory. The fancied song, the revelatory song of the last, morning dream of the prophet asleep at the foot of the sacred column, near the cold, white simulacrum of god."

(4) "What shall I love unless it be the Enigma?"

And everywhere in Chirico city, the trapped train puffing its cloud in a labyrinth of heavy arches, vaults, arcades. The statue, recumbent, of Ariadne, deserted, asleep, in the center of empty, mysteriously-shadowed squares. And the long shadows cast by unseen figures – human or of stone it is impossible to tell. Ted is right, infallibly, when he criticizes my poems & suggests, here, there, the right world – "marvelingly" instead of "admiringly", and so on. Arrogant, I think I have written lines which qualify me to be The Poetess of America (as Ted will be The Poet of England and her dominions). Who rivals? Well, in history – Sappho, Elizabeth Barrett Browning, Christina Rossetti, Amy Lowell, Emily Dickinson, Edna St. Vincent Millay – all dead. Now: Edith Sitwell & Marianne Moore, the ageing giantesses & poetic godmothers. Phyllis McGinley is out – light verse: she's sold herself. Rather: May Swenson, Isabella Gardner, & most close, Adrienne Cecile Rich – who will soon be eclipsed by these eight poems: I am eager, chafing, sure of my gift, wanting only to train & teach it – I'll count the magazines & money I break open by these best eight poems from now on. We'll see.

Tuesday night: April 1st: An absolutely grim and grey and sorrowful barren day. Woke home in Wellesley in my straight single bed to steaming of radiators. A rainy mizzle introducing April. Chill. A dull wait at the dentist reading articles in Mlle & gritting how well I could write them if only given time. A painful and routine session with Dr. Gulbrandsen – pale, stare-eyed, like a gentle blond pig, digging my gums to blood that I swallowed, not to be bothersome, cleaning and not bothering to look for cavities. I must have a low pain threshhold. All day my gums have ached, my left shoulder has ached from the first polio shot, my eyes have ached from bad lights and driving glare. After a bowl of hot corn chowder with mother we started back to Hamp with a full thermos of hot coffee. Grey low clouds blurred the hilltops & the landscape loomed all shades and lovely changes of purple, lavender – bare, still, and trees here yellow-twigged, here twigged bright red. We sipped scalding coffee, felt grey and diffuse as the wet weather. Counted twelve Volkswagon's on the two & three-quarter hour trip. Home to no mail but a mimeographed circular notifying me how there will be lessons for women in investing money in stocks. Ha. Everything in-between – no acceptances or rejections. No writing freedom. No energy or inclination to do my Hopkins lessons which I must have ready for the day after tomorrow at 9 am. Ugh. Tearful. Sore. Grumpy with Ted who sometimes strikes my finicky nerves as coarse – scratching, nose-picking, with unwashed, unkempt hair & a dogmatic grumpiness – all unnecessary & unpleasant, about which I am nagging if I say anything. And I am much worse – petulant, procrastinating, chafing with ill will at the inevitable grind beginning again.

Sunday night: April 6: A mean miserable cold: I turned out the light at eight-thirty after two aspirins expecting they would knock me out. No such luck.

Head swimming and dull with a day-full of absolutely fake & useless buff-erin & codethricin or some such idiotic name I sneeze and sneeze, wet and soggy, piling up sodden frayed Kleenex tissues, throat aching, eyes twitching & an allergic sneezy twitch inside my head, lips swollen, nose sore. And this weekend I had planned to rest up & get ahead on my work. Now, by the time I am breathing & on my feet it will be time to teach again. All yesterday afternoon & today I have been too ratty miserable to do anything but hunch in bed & sneeze & twitch and read the latest women's magazines – McCall's & the Ladies Home Journal: irony upon irony: McCall's, the "magazine of togetherness" is running a series of articles on illegitimate babies & abor-tions, an article on "Why Men Desert Their Wives"; three stories & articles considered, seriously here, humorously there, suicide from boredom, des-pair, or embarassment. The serial story, "Summer Place", by Sloan-the-Man-in-the-Grey-Flannel-Suit Wilson is about a miserable middle-aged woman named, significantly enough, Sylvia, who commits adultery with the man she should have married twenty years ago but didn't because she was foolish & didn't realized when he raped her at the age of sixteen that they were meant for each other – adultery, love affairs, childless women, incom-municative & sullen couples – "Can this marriage be saved?" The psycholo-gist asks of two selfish, stupid, incompatible people who were idiots to marry in the first place. It came over me with a slow wonder that all these articles & stories are based on the idea that passionate & spiritual love is the only thing on earth worth having & that it is next to impossible to find and even harder to keep, once caught. I turned to Ted, who is as close & warm & dear as can be, closer, warmer, dearer than I ever was to myself – who sees me sick, ugly, sallow, sneezy & hugs me, holds me, cooks me a veal chop & brings bowls of iced pineapple, steaming coffee at breakfast, tea at teatime. I feel, miraculously, I have the impossible, the wonderful – I am perfectly at one with Ted, body & soul, as the ridiculous song says – our vocation is writing, our love is each other – and the world is ours to explore. How did I ever live in those barren, desperate days of dating, experimenting, hearing mother warn me I was too critical, that I set my sights too high & would be an old maid. Well, perhaps I would have been if Ted hadn't been born. I am, at bottom, simple, credulous, feminine & loving to be mastered, cared for – but I will kill with my mind, my ice-eye, anyone who is weak, false, sickly in soul – and so I have done. Our needs – of solitude, quiet, long walks, good meat, all our days to write in – few friends, but fine ones who measure nothing by externals – all these agree & blend. May my demons & seraphs guard me on the right way and we live long toward white hair & creative wisdom & die in a flash of light in each other's arms. He uses me – uses all of me so I am lit and glowing with love like a fire, and this is all I looked for all my life – to be able to give of my love, my spontaneous joy, unreservedly, with no holding back for fear of his, misuse, betrayal. And so, in the lousy shut-in world of this cold, last night & put on my new white nylon night-gown with red roses, very small, embroidered on the collar, & filled Ted's slippers with a chocolate rabbit & ten tiny chocolate eggs, each wrapped" in a different color of tinfoil – green spots on silver, gold mottling, streaked peacock blue. I believe he has eaten them all. I think I shall sit up all night & force myself to read or write untill this drugged, dregged twitching goes. Pray God Ted doesn't catch this for his reading in Cambridge on Friday. Today, as so many days this year, & so many days in my life, has been a horrid painful limbo. Woke after a sleep & queer nightmare – of seeing a new comet or satellite – round, but conical, with the point behind it 🌑 like a faceted diamond. I was up somewhere on a dark high place watching it pass over head like a diamond moon, moving rapidly out of sight & then, suddenly, there were a series of short sharp jerks & I saw the planet halted in a series of still-shot framed exposures, which for some reason was a sight not granted to the human eye, & at once I was lifted, up, my stomach & face toward earth, as if hung perpendicular in mid-air of a room with a pole through my middle & someone twirling me about on it. I looked down at Ted's kahki legs stretched out on a chair, & the bodies of other faceless people crowding the room & my whole equilibrium went off, giddy, as I spun & they spun below & I heard surgical, distant, stellar voices discussing me & my experimental predicament & planning what to do next. I spun, screaming, sick & woke up to a knife-cutting sore throat, a headache which is now at its height, & a swollen, streaming nose. Tried to write a poem about a fool on April Fool's day, but was too weak & drugged to lift a pen, so it didn't work. Feel very blue. Hate wasting a weekend like this. To hell. This makes me want a Spanish climate. To breathe. Pored over Beardsley. Felt utterly fin de siècle & fin de moi-même.

An hour later, feverish, doped, I sit up still. Easter night. Stirred only this morning to watch the Catholic red-brick church across the street disgorge its crowds into the thin softly greening April rain – umbrellas flowered, pink, yellow, blue, green, and women came in white gloves with flowers pinned to their coat shoulders. Now, still, the traffic runs. Must I utterly squander in conscious misery a whole day & night every two weeks of my life? Lord knows where this wet drippy mucous spins itself from. Nothing to do but wake & endure & blink away the twichery water. I count my calendar, miraculously having lived through a week on Hopkins teaching – knowing full well 3 poems a day is no "work" for them, as most of them don't work at all. Cathy Fey, the sullen white-fleshed slob in a straw man's hat coming late, coughing loudly & insolently, swigging medecine or brandy from a brown bottle. Anne Bradley "in a mood", snotty, vague. Well I love Hopkins' poetry, will read, expound & not waste myself on the worst of them but simply mark them down. The best – my whole 11 o'clock – then, Sally Lawrence, Sue Badian, Jane Campbell, Sylvie Koval, Topsy Resnick – for these live & joyous & working girls I give thanks. Will I ever stop these wet sneezes? The one thing I have done more than I ever thought I would do is write those eight good poems over spring vacation & my book swells to 30 poems & 48 typewritten double-spaced pages. I aim for 30 more poems by next December 31st, the year's end: a book then & hopefully, all the poems accepted for publication. What ratty stuff gets printed in these quarterlies! If I get rejected from The New Yorker this week, will promptly send batch to the Atlantic, then Harper's.

Monday: April 7: Still in bed, weak & headachey & miserable – utterly useless & stupid with this cold which has ruined inexcusably two-and-a-half perfectly good, cherishable days of my precious week. I am at the point now of not caring: to hell with it: I am lousy miserable with a fever of almost a hundred & a head ringed with the devil's own iron garter. Good love-making today, morning & afternoon, all hot and hard and lovely. Ted washed the mountain of collected dishes & Elly came – stylish, sexy, quieter yet still an actress in extremely high black heels with pin-point spikes, a tight black dress, cocktail type, which showed bare shoulder & black bra straps, and a deep smoky bluey-purple cashmere sweater worn like a cape. She stayed over three hours, played to Ted, whom I am sure she comes to see anyway, and I sat up, drinking glass after glass of iced white wine & feeling exhausted. I made a mess of tuna mayonnaise, mashed potatoes & corn & onions, very good & fortifying after no food all day, and lolled in the big green chair. Ellie rose & took off all the various skits & entertainments she has seen recently & I felt oddly casual: her job with John Crosby on the Herald Tribune sounds "thrilling" and dangerous – I should think he'd want to have an affair with her, but except for idle curiosity to hear about how these queer people live – lesbians & homosexuals – I couldn't care less. I am sick of everything – of feeling forever tired, sick, nose grated raw, throat swollen & smarting, eyes watery & twitchy, body lethargic & wan white &

the job of preparation crammed & crowded again although I would, virtuously, have done it by now if well. Sent off more entries to Dole & Heinz contest. How nice to win five Ford cars, a two-week trip to Paris, all debts paid & a $10,000 nest egg. Will we? How I wish.

Tuesday: April 8: Still in bed, still feeling lousy & sneezing like the Great Twitch the minute I get up in Ted's woolen bathrobe, my long practical & unlovely peach flannel nightgown & black wool knee socks. This cold has no right to still be wet & snuffly after three days. Instead of raining, as it did yesterday, it is cold & clear & sunny. Woke out of a queer hectic unremembered dream at crack, literally, of dawn – almost night, still, but that queer clear new blue undersea light heralding the change – birds, rudimentary, chirp-churping in dark pines & the waned streetlights an ungodly luminous pale green color. Washed in the half-light, the east sky a lightening cold ice bluegreen. Have been wandering around all morning since Ted left at seven thirty after making me a cup of coffee in that lovely glossy white china Stangl pottery cup with the pink tulip on one side & the light blue springing forget-me-not on the other. Slipped into my dirty red down-at-the-heel ballet shoes (which I must throw out) & tried to sit in the relatively clean & unfeverish livingroom after wandering about collecting dirty plates & glasses & stacking them intricately in the yellow plastic dish pan. No good. Began to sneeze, wetly stream, the left side of my head hardening to unbreathable concrete. Back to bed, with the elegant black mohair shawl Ted gave me draped around my shoulders. Made myself a pot of too-strong tea & drank three cups while I read Frank Sousa's story about two drunk women which is a steal from Salinger's "Uncle Wiggily in Connecticut" and then read "Uncle Wiggily in Connecticut" and four or five other Salinger stories. I have no energy. Feel strong as a wet nylon stocking. And not half as clean. Ted's key is at last turning in the lock.

Thursday: April 10: It is a race between me & the taxi: I am feeling exactly as bad, wet and snuffly as I felt Sunday, only a good bit more worn down & tired. Five more teaching hours to last out today & tomorrow morning & then the 3 free-cuts & home posthaste at noon tomorrow to stop at the blessed doctors & get some cure for this pernicious, persistent infection. The April weather looks lovely. But outside yesterday a pernicious chill raw wind hacked at my head & I relapsed to blockheaded runny agony last night. My nosedrops are almost gone – I must somehow conserve them till tomorrow morning. My afternoon class yesterday must have sensed I was feeling lousy, for they were gentle & responsive. If this 9 am class doesn't respond, I shall simply give them the information with the minimum strain. Ted is wonderful: stands by, hugs, makes coffee & clears up dishes. God be thanked for a husband who can stand a sniveling weak-sick wife & care for her in sickness & health, for better & for much much worse. He is my life now, my male muse, my pole-star centering me steady & right. O god, if I stayed in the whole week (& not just a measly four days) I would posthaste recover but I must hear Ted read at Harvard tomorrow (& look forward to meeting the long looked-at poetess Adrienne Cecile Rich) that I will not be on sick-leave now for it would make my leaving tomorrow impossible & improbable & involve me unpleasantly with the department again. Yesterday – how casual, how cool I am become – I received my first acceptance from The Ladies' Home Journal of a poem: This doesn't really count at all for my book, but is pleasantly lucrative: They pay me $10 a line (I thought I would get only beginner's rate $3 a line & so was left breathless today with a $140 check – feel as if I'd sold an unsightly yet solidly lucrative pink-flowered pig.

Saturday night: April 12: A week from the start of my cold & its exhausting & painful continuing I am now in bed at home, tired, almost too tired to write or form letters, & too tired to do justice to yesterday – our trip up from Northampton in a white whirlwind of sopping horizontal snow banging straight into our windshield – The reading of Ted's at Harvard with the small loyal audience & the drinks at Jack Sweeney's with Mairé and Adrienne Cecile Rich & her husband Al Conrad[n] & the wine-floating supper of shrimp & chicken cacciatore at Felicia's just off Hanover Street. I am fighting the last shreds of cold with newly & too-late acquired cocaine drops

Sunday afternoon: April 13th: Back in Northampton – still slightly out of focus, eager, in spite of vestigial fatigue, to hear from poems sent out, from innumerable contests entered with great gullibility – the dole pineapple & heinz ketchup contests close this week, but the French's mustard, fruit-blended oatmeal & slenderella & Libby-tomato juice contests don't close till the end of May. We stand to win five cars, two weeks in Paris, a year's free food, and innumerable iceboxes & refrigerators and all our debts paid. Glory glory. I suppose nobody intelligent or poor ever wins. I suppose people named Ponter Hughes never win. We woke to sunlight & April thaw this morning & told each other our literary dreams – each of us had a dream within a dream. I dreamt – and much more forgotten – we were visiting the author of the other "Feast of Lupercal" (Ted's projected title for his second book – Mairé told us her cousin had just published a novel by that name) – who turned out to be a young black-haired greekish-italian in a white toga with a face combining the babyish softness about cheeks & mouth of Phil McCurdy, the vigor of the young Orson Welles & the glamorous obvious sex-appeal of Peter S. Fiebleman. He was holding a feast in his court – a twelve-storied greek-façaded palace full of bright modern art paintings (a recall of Sweeney's rooms?) I forget the rest: it was colored, radiant, full of promise. I am attaining, with my return of health & the stubborn break-through of spring, the first real deep-rooted peace & joy I have known since early childhood, when I dreamt complete technicolor stories and fairy tales. TODAY: is an anniversary. Two years ago, on Black Friday the 13th, I took a plane from Rome through the mist-shrouded sky of Europe, to London – renounced Gordon, Sassoon – my old life – & took up Ted and my resurrec-tion came about with that green and incredible Cambridge spring. How I must write it up in my novel – and in various stories for McCall's & the New Yorker – I can do it: these eight spring-vacation poems have given me con-fidence that my mind & my talent has been growing underneath my griefs and agonies and drudgeries – as if my demons and angels guarded and increased whatever gifts I ignored, forgot and despaired of during the black year, which has turned out to be the most maturing & courage-making year yet – I could have dreamed up no test more difficult. The week ahead bulks huge – cramming Melville today & tomorrow before the deluge of Arvin's Tuesday exam & 55 books to correct. Then my own load of 65 poetry papers. But with each week the year diminishes & my writing time nears. How my projects will wax & multiply! I have a feeling that after two years of sweat, study, bleared-eyes & dogged work we will somehow become creative children of Fortune.

We have finished tea, and the late afternoon Sunday sun lights the blue-lined page opposite and causes the red armchair to incandesce like ruby. I can write for the woman's slicks: More & more this comes over me – as easily as I wrote for Seventeen, while keeping my art intact: I shall call myself Sylvan Hughes – pleasantly woodsy, colorful – yet sexless & close to my own name: a perfectly euphonious magazine name. The drive back: warm, sunny & a new start: hills an incredible vivid purple & snow-capped in the blue dis-tance; flooded groves with trees up to mid-trunk in mirroring wet blue; a dead rabbit, a dead black & white skunk with its four little feet crisped up; twenty-seven doughty bug-nosed Volkswagons – we are doing a spontaneous statistical survey of them. Now, hearing Ted type in the bedroom, untidy because of unwashed hair & the pink scruff & scraps on the rug, I postpone Melville, yearn to write a poem with the resurge of spring & my health this one day which two years ago brought me my dream, my love, my artist & my artist's life. Friday now – in reminiscence. I blurred & pushed through cold rain and my two morning classes, forgetting to pass out any mimeographed sheets for the poetry lecture tomorrow. My nine o'clock class was cold, unsatisfactory, refractory. My eleven o'clock was a delight, responsive, humorous – bringing visitors all listening & eager. Two of my best students asked Ted & me to dinner this week & next week, so we should save more money – I hope to hit a new low budget of $200 this month: ten days in New York in June will probably cost a good bit even if we have no extra rent & just food & entertainment. Now at last about Friday: we fought through a horizontal whirlwind of sleet which covered my whole-part of the window as the windshield wiper wasn't working & made me furiously twittery since I saw only the vast looming shapes of approaching trucks through the semi-opaque lid of sleet and each shape seemed, coming, looming, a menace, a possible death. We pushed on, eating good steak sandwiches, drinking from the thermos of scalding coffee, and counting Volkswagons like snow-going beetles. After two and three-quarters hours of begging Ted to go ten-miles-an-hour-less than fifty, we came to the narrowing & familiar wood-road, Weston Road. We drove beyond Elmwood to the Fells drugstore where I stepped out into slush-damned brown puddles of icewater ankle deep. Ran in & bought a dry shampoo to cure my greasy hair. Home to Elmwood and unloading of sacks, drank off last of brandy. To Brownlee's, then, where we bared left arms for our second polio shots, secured a prescription for cocaine, then on through laggard traffic, to Cambridge & Jack Sweeney, waiting, gracious, whitehaired, loveable, in the quiet sanctum of the poetry room. We slogged in ice mud & rivulets. Fell into a taxi & rode to Radcliffe's Longfellow hall. Sepulchral. Deserted. I imagined no one would come. Followed a white-dressed attendant down echoing marble-speckled & polished halls to a lavatory where a thick horse-bodied Radcliffe girl was combing her hair. There was no gilded liquid soap in glass bulbs above the sink – only rough honest dirt-expunging borax. And the bracing odor of disinfectant. Back to the hall to shake hands with Harry Levin's dark, vigorous small Russian wife: "Harry is onder ze wedder. I bring a good ear." We went in, after greeting Mrs. Cantor, Marty & Mike, & Carol Pierson," and the room blurred before my eyes. Very big room, very sparsely peopled – listeners scattered. I followed Mrs. Levin & saw

Mairé's luminous pallor, gold hair done in a low chignon, and a quaint small hat of black and russet feathers like a bird-down cloche. Ted began, (after a fine & precise introduction by Jack, mentioning the steel-factory night-watchman work & the job as a rose-gardener) to read. I felt cold, felt the audience thin & cold. The poems, which I knew by heart, sent the inevitable chill of awe & wonder over me: the foolish tears jumped to my eyes. Mrs. Levin squirmed, reached for her pocketbook & scribbled something in pencil on a rattling envelope, asked me to repeat the title of "The Thought-fox." Afar off, somewhere, a clock struck five. Ted spoke of out-Tennysoning Tennyson – the audience laughed, a pleasant muted burble. Laughed & warmed. I began to relax: new poems gave good surprise – "To Paint a Waterlily": clear, lyric – rich & yet craggy. He ended on "Acrobats" – a perfect metaphor, really, for himself as a poetic acrobat-genius & the desirous & in many cases envious audience. A burst of warm genuine applause. Jack went up & asked Ted to read another. He did "The Casualty". I knew, with the same clairvoyance I had two years ago envisioning this foothold, how in ten years Ted would have a packed Harvard stadium audience to applaud and adore. The audience broke up & suddenly seemed all friends – Peter Davison," Mrs. Bragg (now Harry Levin's secretary), Gordon Lameyer (no doubt jealous as hell, but noble, in his way, to come – pulling out a leaflet about his big-money project – The Framingham Music Circus which will make him rich & for which he has raised hundreds of thousands of dollars in backing). Phil McCurdy, chastened, boyish-faced, married to Marla with a baby girl & teaching Biology in Brookline High, illustrating science text books for Scribner's, offering us a joint trip to Maine on a friend's yacht this summer which I hope might come true. Mother – thin & somehow frail – & bluet-eyed Mrs. Prouty: "Isn't Ted wonderful." Philip Booth: a new meeting for the first time – he, handsome & strangely nice-guy innocent looking: we exchanged compliments, spoke of his aunt & the aging Smith psychiatrist Dr. Booth – he hemmed at my asking if he'd teach at Wellesley next year & admitted, with some joy, to just having heard he'd been granted a Guggenheim. But he & his wife & kids will be around next year. Hope to meet again. Adrienne Cecile Rich: little, round & stumpy, all vibrant short black hair, great sparking black eyes and a tulip-red umbrella: honest, frank forthright & even opinionated. The crowd thinned, & the Sweeney's, Ted & I & Adrienne slogged through rain to a taxi, switched (Jack, Ted & I) to our sodden Plymouth, & soon were tiptoeing gingerly down the red-brick cobbles of Walnut Street's hilly decline to Jack's polished hall, all slippery black & white linoleum. His apartment reached in the thin gilt barred elevator. Adrienne & Mairé there – also the doe-eyed tan Al Conrad, an economist at Harvard, whom I felt cold & awkward with at first. I in my old & trusted lavendar tweed dress, pale, with bright turquoise & white weave & blue & silver beads. Two bourbons & water on ice. Found out that the two huge paintings leaping out of the left wall were original Picasso's (c. 1924) The brown, cream & black composition on the right, with its sinister black mask – a Juan Gris. And, in the library, the springing blue-green oil of a rider on a horse ("The Singing Rider") by old Jack Yeats, just dead – WB's brother – "rather like Soutine – like Kokoshka" (whom I would know not, were it not for Mrs. Van der Poel). I felt distant from everyone. Feverish in lavender tweed. We left then, in Al's great station-wagon for "Supper at Felicia's". A blur of lights, neons. We parked on Hanover Street – a Paris bistro-street of shops & diners. Walked, heads down, down a narrow street, past the wonderful room of a bake shop, a greased paper, like butter frosting lidding one window, a bare interior, a heavy wooden trestle table covered with yellow-browned round cakes, large, middling, small, and two men in white aprons laying white frosting on a three-tiered square cake. Then a narrow doorway with "Felicia's" printed over it, a crowd of ladies – who would emphatically consider themselves 'girls' – probably a crew of telephone-operators – one with a corsage: set old-maidy or borderline-tarty faces: "Betty Clarke?" "Betty Andrews"? They gathered galoshes & umbrellas at the top of the stair-head & left. We sat, I with Jack on my left, Al on my right. Began with a bottle of fine dry Italian white wine shaped like a blue-glass urn. Antipasto – shrimps hot in red sauce & Felicia herself like an honest actress, hawk nose, bright peach-pink sweater & lipstick & powder to match, reeled off the menus "fettucini, linguina." I talked to Al about trudo, tuberculosis, deep, deeper, enjoying him. A long time, through chicken cacciatore with queer pieces of bone & white chunk meat. Then switched to Jack, who asked me to make a recording in June, on Friday the 13th.

April 14: Monday night: Still feeling too sogged & groggy, although convalescent, to wash hair and self. And very weary. I got up to sunshine and through a cold succulent honeyed pink grapefruit, a duty half of toast with bacon & pellets of overcooked chicken liver & milky no-coffee coffee. Came early to the dark yellowed halls of Seelye & relieved the history supply shelf of yet another pink book. Arvin's classroom at 8:45 stood empty a moment. I sat in my front-corner seat by the window and contemplated the bright chrome yellow expanse of Alexander's empire: to be a baker in one of the minor outposts: the mind quails at such expanding spaces in such bottomless times. I wondered uneasily, as after a long illness when one adjusts one's delicate hearing and sickroom vision to the crude noise and glare of the health-gifted world, if I were in the right room, if this were the day of the test by some fluke, & I misplaced. No: Arvin took out his jangling keyring, and I picked up in my 1954 notes his 1958 thread. Weary: on Melville's short tales. I am rereading "Moby Dick" in preparation for the exam deluge tomorrow – am whelmed and wondrous at the swimming Biblical & craggy Shakespearean cadences, the rich & lustrous & fragrant recreation of spermaceti, ambergris – miracle, marvel, the ton-thunderous leviathan. One of my few wishes: to be (safe, coward I am) aboard a whale ship through the process of turning a monster to light & heat. Shopped, meditative, strolling with my wicker cart & plucking off the labeled & logically shelved provender: no wheat-garnering & deer-slaying alas, all cellophaned & mute, identity-less. A groggy afternoon: a feverish nap claimed me. Then the rather good Eng 11 lecture by Maynard Mack. Made a huge fish soup. Park-walked at sunset. A pheasant cried at our feet, started, flew long-tailed. Found two blue jay feathers

Tuesday night: April 15: Washed at last, hair clean & slightly damp rolled up on 3 handkerchiefs – blood alive & roseate warm from bath, jagged nails filed smooth & freshly painted with transparent laquer. Powdered. In new knee-length white nylon gown with the red rosebudded shawl collar which would fit me equally well, perhaps better, if I were pregnant. An undermining day. Walked to Arvin's to collect exams. To art: Orozco: the murals at Dartmouth the history of the Indians. A Christ-the-tiger hacking down his own cross & the statues of classicism, Buddhism. The great white god Quetzlcoatl banishing the false crew of gods of death, magic, fire, storms. Sorted exams for Arvin. Steaming & savory fish soup for lunch, smacking good all onion-essence, chunks of soaked fish & potato steaming, hot, bacon bits, buttery crackers foundering in it. A warm day – buds cracking miraculously – fat green buds on bush (lilac?) by verandah. Scrawled down some notes on Yeats in the gloomy corner of my office. Got just about nowhere: felt rebellious: wanted to sit, read deep at leisure. Am appalled at the turgid essays on Yeats: about & about & about – all take one farther & farther from the poems. I long for peace, solitude: to read his poems through aloud. Read only the great poets: let their voices live in my ear & not the dregs & academic twiddle & pish of the young modern grey-flannel suit poets. Felt sterile. No energy to work. A frightening lassitude. Have not outlined this week's poems – must tomorrow a.m. And then Arvin's exams. And then my own student papers. And a dinner or some such every night. I tell myself that this will be my worst week this year. After all, every thing lets up and diminishes after this. Torturous wait for mail: no mail but the infernal flannel-stuffing of circulars. Ted out at Paul's – I too weary – for reading of Paul's "Oedipus." I yawn. Wait up.

Thursday morning: April 17: time, almost time, to rise, dress & go to meet my morning classes. Still, when I wake up, (and the sun shines bright in our room shortly after six) I feel as if I were rising from a grave, gathering my moldy, worm-riddled limbs into a final effort. Yesterday was poor – felt shot – worked on a couple of Yeats poems for class preparation & read & read in him: the scalp crawled, the hair stood up. He is genuine: an anti-type of Eliot, and I do enjoy Eliot, Yeats is lyrical and sharp, clear, rock-cut. I think the reason why my favorite poems of my own are "The Disquieting Muses" & "On the Decline of Oracles" is because they have that good lyrical ten-sion: crammed speech and music at once: brain & beautiful body at once. More & more I realize how I must stop teaching & devote myself to writing: my deep self must seclude, sequester, to produce lyrics & poems of high pitch intensity – differing from the neat prosy gray-suited poems of Donald Hall, et. al. I am unrecognized. The New Yorker has not replied to the ms. I sent off two & a half weeks ago. The Art News has not answered the two poems I sent them: I run for mail & get mocked by a handful of dull space-consuming circulars addressed to "Professor Hughes" and advertising tedi-ous books on the art of writing an intelligible sentence. I have the joyous feeling of leashed power – also the feeling that within a year or two I should be 'recognized' – as I am not at all now, though I sit on poems richer than any Adrienne Cecile Rich. I amuse myself, am all itch & eager fury for the end of my term. My 3 o'clock yesterday, except for the bland useless Liz, very kind, agreeable, cooperative – much fun indeed, surprisingly. I always feel better after my week's first class: a jinx of chilliness broken & me in heat – also – the week begun, must grind to an end & after this: only 4 ½ weeks of joyous poets & poems. Park walk yesterday noon: first tulip cracked its green bud sheath & opened red silk and purple-black stamens to sun –

Tuesday morning: April 22: Must shortly leap into clothes & out into the pearl-grey, dull-grey morning to Arvin out of politeness and to Baskin on Rodin out of interest. I will also catch up in here on my crammed Friday. Yesterday was wiped out by the cramps & drug-stitched stupor of my first day of the curse, as it is so aptly called. Do animals in heat bleed, feel pain? Or is it that sedentary blue-stockinged ladies have come so far from the beast-state that they must pay by hurt, as the little mermaid had to pay when she traded her fish-tail for a girl's white legs? Sunday also blotted out – by housecleaning. I'd forborne to ask Mrs. McKee for the vacuum for quite some time & the result was increasing unpleasant tremors of repulsion at the scruffy, palpably <u>dirty</u> rugs, floors & dust-thick surfaces. So Sunday: the purge – scrubbed the bathroom, the kitchen – defrosted icebox, scrubbed floor. Moved bed to alcove in bedroom unearthing great balls & tangles of dust & hair, but now have the look of a new room – great space – will be cooler in summer. Sorted books, magazines, papers & finally the vacuum to purify all. Now feel clear of soul. How the old maxim must have taken profound root: cleanliness is next to godliness. An absurd quarrel with Ted Sunday night as we were dressing to go to Wiggin's – he accusing me of throwing away his awful old cufflinks "as I had done away with his coat", and, for that matter, his book on Witches, since I never could stand the torture parts. None of this being true. He wouldn't say it was foolish, I, as stubborn, wouldn't forget. So I ran out, sickened. Couldn't drive anywhere. Came back. Ted had gone out. Sat in the park – all vast, dark, ominously full of silent Teds, or no Ted – nightcrawler hunters came with flashlights. I called, wandered. Then saw his figure striding down Woodlawn under street lamps and raced after, paralleling his course hidden by the row of pines edging the woods. He paused, stared, and if he weren't my husband I would have run from him as a killer. I stood behind the last fat fir tree & wagged the branches on each side till he came over. We raced to dress, to Wiggins. To a supper that was spoiled by our extreme budget consciousness – that a snack we could have managed for very little amounted to nine dollars – thank goodness, we felt, we had $3.50 credit from the Welcome Wagon. We did love the great iced raw oysters on their scraggly-lace, blue-eyed peacockish shells & the little bottle of strange sauteurne. But the mushrooms tasted like rubber. And the relishes were good, and the lobster, but the salad tasteless, the tomatoes hothouse synthetic. Ah, how frugal we are become. Lucky we're both puritans & great misers: Lord knows, we need to be.

– Evening: A day of misery: <u>The New Yorker</u> rejection of all the poems (O, Howard Moss, or "They" liked <u>The Disquieting Muses</u> & The Rousseau Sestina) – a burning sense of injustice, sobs, sorrow: desire to fight back, & no time or energy to do so till June. No work done: none – all my papers to correct & three hours of preparation to do. Finished What Maisie Knew: ironically, Henry James' biography comforts me & I long to make known to him his posthumous reputation – he wrote, in pain, gave all his life (which is more than I could think of doing – I have Ted, will have children – but few friends) & the critics insulted & mocked him, readers didn't read him. I am made, crudely, for success. Does failure whet my blade? I read, baked a chocolate cake with white frosting, wrote letters to Marty, my student whose knee is being operated on today, Peter Davison (& sent him the rejected poems – wishing I could try Harper's first) & now, after a grey sticky unsatisfactory & profitless day, go oily-haired, bloody-gutted & unprepared-for class to bed.

Saturday morning: April 26: Almost time to walk out into the end of April – Monther's birthday – to my 9 o'clock which I feel very loth to confront, weary as I am & have been this week. "Among School Children" today. This week I drudged. Having drudged on Arvin's scrawled exams last week, cleaned this Augean stable of a house Sunday, crumped out with the curse Monday, shuddered & gloomed over the New Yorker rejection all sticky grey lethal Tuesday and cut Arvin & Art rudely Wednesday to cram preparation & begin my own jam-packed correcting of 64 papers which I slaved at, blearing my eyes, until yesterday noon. Was sick-tired last night: additional fury & humiliation, anguish & anger: Stanley Sultan (who always looks to me as if, with his black-liquid eyes & hair & golden skin – he had just climbed out of a barrel of warm whale oil) told me the girl whose Lawrence thesis I had voted, with misgivings for my generosity – a low cum, received a summa, the highest grade possible. He had voted MAGNA. Putting aside my more picayune scruples, I could see a MAGNA, even wish I had given it a MAGNA & the other a SUMMA (which will probably fail) – but a SUMMA! never – the conclusion was lousy: hasty, a messy plum-pudding with pits. O how they must amuse themselves: it is as if, after ruining my clear eyes for a week over Arvin's exams, he simply re-marked them all – a waste. Next year I would know better, but, of course, won't be here. Such small situations must be sucked up & lost in the sun's burning & mammoth belly. Goodbye to it. How is this for the title of a poetry book, such as my firsts THE EVERLASTING MONDAY? Surprisingly, it appeals: the christian story of the man bearing faggots in the moon: the epigraph: "Thou shalt have an everlasting Monday & stand in the moon" – the Yeatsian idea of work, becoming, fused with static being: a work & a life of eternal Mondays, eternal launderings & fresh starts

<u>Tuesday morning: April 29</u>: Called back, just as I was going out to a wet grey plodding office hour – and the hour most pleasantly cancelled. I have been dilatory, and it shows: I am ten days behind here. So will cram in something before I set out again to Arvin, with Mrs. Van der Poel's cane. How strange I delayed in going till 5 of eight, the moment Donna called. Felt, as usual, exhausted this morning & fell back into those horrid dreams of getting up to make a school deadline, waking up & being still in the dream & it being still later. Dreamed Chris Levenson called up to ask me to do some sort of poetry reading (of other people's poems, characteristically) & I delayed, dawdled into clothes & arrived late (a memory from the close of "The Bostonians"? – the angry, eager audience stamping out its impatience for the tardy & never-to-be-speaker Verena?) and saw a peculiar 'rhythmic' dance going on past the hour for classes to begin with several of my weakest students – Al Arnott, Emmy Pettway, etc. – doing an awkward unlearned dance with a rope (preparatory to tarring & feathering me?) in green, pale green nymph-suits. I must have anemia, or mononucleosis, or some dread insidious disease: I stayed in bed all yesterday with Ted bringing me meals (Arvin had called to say there would be no class) & read till I finished <u>The Bostonians</u>, and here I am, deeply exhausted as ever. Sunday also was a blue day: weary, depressed: is it partly because I am so close to freedom (which is actually a different tyranny: insecurity) and as yet unable to bridge the gap, as I did that one week of spring vacation, with productive writing? Perhaps: teaching, even 28 weeks, was secure as a machine running on atomic energy. Writing, once I get into it, I hope, will be deeper, surer, richer & more life-giving than anything I have ever done before.

Amazing how warm a gauze of nylon stocking is: just decided not to go bare-legged and suddenly stopped sneezing. If only Ted doesn't object too much to the noise, I will enjoy the summer here in spite of the constant traffic. When I am blue – as yesterday, I think about death, about having to die having lived awake to so little of the world – of the dreams of glory – lives of great authors, moviestars, psychiatrists. People who don't have to grub for money. Then I think of my gross fears at having a baby which I suppose center around that crucial episode at the Boston Lying-In so many years ago when that anonymous groaning woman, shaved & painted all colors, got cut, blood ran, water broke, & the baby came with bloody veins & urinated in the doctor's face. Every woman does it: so I cower & want, want & cower. I also think of how far I fall short from the ideal of Doris Krook – what a slipshod part time scholar I am – no nun, no devotee. And how, on the other hand, very far I fall short from writing – how many thousand publish in the New Yorker, the Sat Eve Post, who work, study, get material, and I, I dream & boast I could do it but don't & maybe can't. What else? O the desire to write a novel & a book of poems before a baby. The desire also for money which I am miserly about, not buying clothes, nor frills, although I could go wild doing so – startling dresses & frivolously colored shoes to match. Amazing how money would simplify problems like ours. We wouldn't go wild at all, but write & travel & study all our lives – which I hope we do anyway. And have a house apart, by the side of no road, with country about & a study & walls of book-cases. –

Wednesday: April 30: Clock rounding fast, faster, toward midnight and I am more than usually sick of being tired. In twenty minutes it will be Mayday which, as I so wittily explained to my class, means Distress, or 'M'aidez' in the airforce, and hence exam day. Thank heaven: I couldn't stand a full week of lecturing. Today: cold, after thickening rain last night. Cold & sunny. It seems I've been running about all day – more & more tired in the morning. A dash to Arvin in time to hear roughly the same things about The Bostonians I heard four years ago. Cheated my conscience & skipped art & the earnest Spanish Gordon[n] from the Spanish department who explained so well yesterday how Goya the rationalist who drew witches & monsters did exist. Drove straight down town in the chill, brilliant light – to the bank, to buy 3 jerseys @ $1.98 to renew my 'teaching wardrobe' for the ensuing month – a bright medium blue with a shock almost purple, a white, and a scoop neck with thin horizontal red, white & blue stripes. Home & spent the next hours typing up a florid, unbalanced & embarassingly serious obvious version of a central incident in my novel: this summer I will study under Henry James & George Eliot for social surface, decorum: this I think I need, not the absurd "I love you kid let's go to bed" which equates every Jack and Jill with every other, but a complex, rich, colored & subtle syntactical structure to contain, to chalice the thought & feeling of each second. Horrid dull mail today, but yesterday's of pleasure & interest: Ted's four poems in a place of honor (after Robert Penn Warren & before WS Merwin, et al) in the Spring Sewanee – also a review of his book, among 20 others, in the same issue – the critic criticizes the maelstroms & cataclysms, but echoes Eliot & says "very considerable promise". Oscar Williams will end his new revised edition of Modern Poetry with Ted's poems (three) & PEN accepted my "Sow" for their annual with Ted's "Thrushes."

<u>Thursday: MAYDAY</u>: A scrambled page to profit from coffee-consciousness and moments before starting out for class: I shall try, later, to record that memorable Friday recording poems in Springfield with Lee Anderson," plus the Glascock Reading & party at Holyoke, with the cast of characters present. All holds fire: my poems at <u>Art News</u> & <u>The Atlantic</u> (editor's gone gallivanting to Europe), Ted's two good stories at <u>The Atlantic</u>. Woke as usual, feeling sick and half-dead, eyes stuck together, a taste of winding sheets on my tongue after a horrible dream involving, among other things, Warren being blown to death by a rocket. Ted, my saviour, emerging out of the néant with a tall mug of hot coffee which sip, by sip, rallied me to the day as he sat at the foot of the bed dressed for teaching, about to drive off – I blink every time I see him afresh. This is the man the unsatisfied ladies scan the stories in the <u>Ladies' Home Journal</u> for, the man women read romantic women's novels for: oh he is unbelievable & the more so because he is my husband & I somehow love cooking for him (make a lemon layer cake last night) and being secretary, and all. And, riffling through all the other men in the world who bore me with their partialness, the only one. How to make it sound special? Other than sentimental, in my novel: a gross problem. Am giving exams today, so must go early to write on board – but to record, here, a conscious change of tone, of heart: suddenly realized I am no longer a teacher – oh, I have a month & a day to go, but just as I jitterily <u>became</u> a teacher a month before my first class, so my prophetic Pans & Kevas are free already, and their impatient tugs toward writing at every itch applied by reading Marianne Moore, Wallace Stevens, etc., disturb my equilibrium – Suddenly I no longer <u>care</u> – let the <u>Wasteland</u> run how it may – I am already in another world – or between two worlds, one dead, the other dying to be born. We are treated as ghosts by permanent members of the faculty – as shadows already departed with no flesh & blood interest in their future. I ignore classes till the last minute, want to hastily bundle them off, and wonder how I can stand the next three weeks. After today, <u>exactly</u> three weeks. I chafe, itch, die to get to my writing. Yet must and must, dead though I am to it, now leave and perform the gestures which will mislead them into giving me my salary for the next perilous month of waiting.

– A little later: exactly three weeks from today – and this book will see it, I finish classes. I feel strange after today, so tired I long only for sleep – and must still stay in stockings to leave momently for student supper at Park House. Ted received a terse, or rather, wordless, communication from <u>The Nation</u> in the noon mail: a proof, on the Nation's usual smutchy blotting paper, of his poem "Historian": it is a difficult, different, abstract poem, but I have come to like it immensely. Today was streaks & patches – sallies out thrice during exams to shop & read, between exams to glimpse at magazines – all miscellaneous patches & pieces. And the day, from a cold morning overcast with a jigsaw puzzle of high tight clouds, blew away with clouds, presented a clear sun, blue sky and cool wind. I am ridiculously apathetic about my work – distant, bemused, feeling, as I said, a ghost of the world I am working in, casting no shadow. And living thus a living death, which I shall expatiate upon at length as we deal with TS Eliot this week and next. How I shall live until May 22nd I wonder. The Arvin exams till June 1st present no problem: it is the platform preaching that wearies.

<u>Saturday: May 3</u>: That weariness, that Saturday death came upon us again and now after an afternoon of drugged and agony-stitched sleep, we sit over the remains of cold steak and hot cheese crackers and white wine – tired still, but slept in pain enough to sleep in peace. Read a bit of William Dunbar, a bit of "The White Godess" and unearthed a whole series of subtle symbolic names for our children whose souls haunt me – that my hurt & my two legs could be the doorway for walking, talking human beings – it seems too strange and fearful. We thought: Gwyn, Alison, Vivien, Marian, Farrar, Gawain. All white goddesses and knights. A cold drear day. Half my nine o'clock absent & a rather productive hour with the weaker ones. Rain, then, cold, a green cast to puddles – treeleaf reflections & the campus full of fathers – odd ugly men, fat wealthy men, grey aristocratic men: negro chauffeurs and cadillacs and black hired limousines. No fresh man fathers though – we shopped for bread, butter & lettuce & came home in a chill shower. After a supper, or lunch, of mashed potatoes & sausage we fell in bed, made love and slept, a sick, pained near-death sleep. I feel occasionally my skull will crack, fatigue is continuous – I only go from less exhausted to more exhausted & back again. Tomorrow I must correct all my exams which I should do in one day – they're short & all on the same subject. Then a close outline of <u>The Wasteland</u> which should take all week. I pick up my ms. of poetry & leaf through it, unable to invent, to create – all my projected nostalgia for my students can't shake the conviction that teaching is a smiling public-service vampire that drinks blood & brain without a thank you.

<u>Monday – May 5th</u>: Close to eleven, I am untransformed Cinderella home alone after scrub-jobs waiting for Ted. Felt tired today: nothing new, but not even desirous of going out tonight with priss-mouthed pale queer Antoine

from Holyoke, Ted's friend, so Ted didn't push, but went, neither of us eating any supper, and I forgoing the Amherst play. I finished the rather easy job of marking the exams on "The Equilibrists", scrubbed a stack of dishes, dusted dining & living & bed rooms, washed hair, bathed in lukewarm water, lacquered my nails. Wish I could at same time have gone to see the Anouilh play – I am superstitious about separations from Ted, even for an hour. I think I must live in his heat and presence, for his smells and words – as if all my senses fed involuntarily on him and deprived for more than a few hours, I languish, wither, die to the world. We had the car fixed today – muffler & exhaust pipe renewed after several days of jet-puttputt noises & eardrum pressure as if we were climbing dangerous altitudes. The muffler has been broken almost all year, so I am convinced carbon monoxide was seeping into the car – it always smelt just a tinge strange & sickish – and slowly, day by day, keeping us doped, drugged, exhausted – I write about nothing but weariness (the door downstairs creaks, a step, a key on the lock & Ted mounting) and nothing of the colored days & nights – such as the Friday with Lee Anderson and the Glascock reading. Last Friday Ted & I bundled into George Gibian's beachwagon with Kay," Marlies Danziger (whom I greeted coolly, remembering my gauche sobstory to her last fall, and her refusal of tea, supper) and briefly Elizabeth Drew (who left when she considered the show might have music & modern dance) to Holyoke to see Denis Johnston's" production of "Finnegan's Wake". It was a cold night – an incredible twilight along the river & mountain road. The Holyoke range lit purple in the paling light – all mauves, reddish-lavenders, and a strange greening spume tipped and stippled the trees. Water, river water and flooded flats reflected orange-gilt or flat pale blue. A moon loomed, as if set off like a balloon a moment before. We hung around the ugly Holyoke hall for half an hour, joking & gossiping. The seats were highly uncomfortable – not graded up toward the back, so it was impossible to see the floor of the stage, and grossly creaky. "Finnegan's Wake": strange: impossible to hear half the words for the creaking of the irritable chairs, and the words heard and unseen hard to decipher the puns of – liked best, of course, the parts I'd read – the riverrun opening, the 'tell me of Anna Livia', the stone & elm scene at the river with the washerwomen, the Mookse & the Cripes, the Ondt & the Gracehoper. Some scenes did make me shiver, the words carried all the creaks, too-loud records & cricked neck before them – but the rest of it was trying to catch the mumblety-peg jabber of a cosmic doubleacrostic in the heart of a thunderstorm. Whisky at Marlies' and gossip – the sense that they eventually choose poems for their classes to read because of the battery of 'examples' of irony, metaphor, zeugma, etc. Have begun "The Wings of the Dove" and begun with the pale blue-eyed witch – named Kate Croy who is passive as yet, though shrewd-sighted, between the self-interested exploitist tactics of her sister, father and Aunt Lowder, but she will soon, I trust, begin to take on the exploiter's role. O money. For want of it or for excess of it what crimes and sufferings are enacted in the Jamesian sphere. I must get my moral code in my novel: I have one – but lack the structure of a well-defined society to give tension to rebellion: convention must work for me in this.

Tuesday morning: May 6: Time, I think, there will be for a page before leaving for Arvin: I shall end this week firm in duty by going to Arvin & Art all three days. Woke as usual, eyes stuck shut and dear Ted to bring coffee and a roast-beef sandwich. I dressed, conscious of color and the loveliness of being thin and feeling slink, swank and luxurious in good fits and rich materials. For the first time put on my red silk stockings with red shoes – they feel amazing, or, rather, the color feels amazing – almost incandescent fire silk-sheathing my legs: I can't stop looking – the stocking goes almost flesh-color, but gathers rose and glows at the edges of the leg as it cuts its shape on air, concentrating the crimson on the rounding-away, shifting as I shift. Quite satisfactory. I shall wear my white pleated wool skirt and deep lovely median blue jersey with the square neck to hear Robert Lowell[n] this afternoon: read some of his poems last night & had oddly a similar reaction (excitement, joy, admiration, curiosity to meet & praise) as when I first read Ted's poems in St. Botolph's: taste the phrases: tough, knotty, blazing with color & fury, most eminently sayable: "where braced pig-iron dragons grip / The blizzard to their rigor mortis." Oh god, after coffee, even I feel my voice will come out strong and colored as that! Want today to write about our Sunday night with Leonard & Esther[n] Baskin whom, suddenly and well, we met. Sunday a grumpy day, stogged in the middle of exams with grey wet weather and chill. Took Ted over to Sylvan's after supper to read the poems turned in for the spring contests and money prizes. Paul Roche was there, his face that bright artificial orangey tan, his eyes marbley-blue and his hair like rather pampered & crimped wheat – I feel curious as to his machinations, his avowedly 'voluminous' correspondence & ability to meet people. Marie[n] there also, lovely today, soft and soft-haired, not the sorrowing and eldering-faced Marie she often is.

Saturday midnight: May 10: The day is passing over into Sunday. We fell sighing and aching into bed about three o'clock this afternoon in the pink-grey room, venetian blinds drawn, and I dreamed strangely, but not at all unpleasantly. Paul Roche figured in my dreams which centered around the Smith College Library – he with mint-green eyes in his mint green tweed suit – in an English Department Meeting room resembling the coffee shop, with booths, sat a shoddy, fat refugee-sort of old man fumbling over a paper-bag lunch – he was rather like Max Goldberg asking Lowell to teach his class – but not with any of Max's crude exploitation-shark aura – a pathetic 'Bartleby-the-Scrivener' look. Smith refused to pay him a year's salary – he wasted, starved. We took up a collection & presented him with a great lavender-tinted glass jar of Ovaltine marked $2.19 on the cover: nourishing at least. Later, Ted & I were sitting out on the lush green lawn in deck chairs between the library and Hatfield with some other faculty people who kept observing that the heavy scent of sweet grass (I think the lawn was somehow ours) smelt of the heat of love, the heart of the love-bed. I could see Max, minus his despicable qualities, in the old man when I woke later, at 8:30, but whence his lovable & pitiable self? The jar may well be a transfer from the gigantic jar in the center of the library entrance filling with dollar bills for African students scholarships" which my conscience has been nagging me to contribute to. And the smells – an amusing transference of my obsession with Ted's delicious fragrances which are to me lovelier than any field of new-cut grasses? We woke in darkness, the sky a memory of orange light, and had tea – toasted tuna-salad sandwiches and some excellent canned peaches. I shall soon go to bed & hope to wake rested tomorrow to clean house and prepare my final three lessons. It seems impossible I should ever say these words, but say them I do now, and deserve to. Twelve days from now (it is just turned Sunday morning) I shall be teaching my last classes, and must make them good ones. I need to lie out much in the sun, roast and rest and write. This week's mail has been atrocious – flannel & unwanted invitations. My classes today were thin – half the girls there only. I had to do most of the work & got through 'The Fire Sermon' sooner than I thought I would. Saw Sylvan displaying a tarot pack – like mine – to George Gibian and Joan Bramwell at the crossroads between library and Seelye. I am become a fiend for money. Greedily I add up & readd our bank balance from writing, our checking balance from salaries – between the two we have about $ three thousand and hope to have $4 thousand saved by Sept. 1st when we must somehow start to bring in new money. If only by a freak we could win one of these oatmeal-naming contests or get Ted that Saxton! Ironically, if we had a year to write, we could earn the next year, and so on, until we were at least able to bargain for better jobs. I need to curb my lust for buying dresses ("for New York") only by recalling our budget & keeping it whittled thin. We expect so much! and <u>need</u> so much – teaching 3 or 4 days a week with over 3 months of paid vacation seems a gift, now I think of it. But we need <u>all</u> our time for writing now. A road to freedom – or, more freedom than we have: how many incidental grubbing writers publish a story monthly, a poem weekly – & we must dedicate ourselves & work & work. Today we sat in the park – clear, chilly Mayday – high blue sky and apple-blossoms out. Watched black frogs in pond – two sleek ones – who surfaced, eyes high on heads, to stare at us. Children behind a tree sang – song insults and hootings.

<u>Sunday: May 11</u>: Mother's day, mother calling late last night to thank us for pink camellia & pink roses. Queer mother – stiff about helping us come to Boston. Her conscious mind always split off, at war with her unconscious: her dreams of terrible insecurity, of losing the house – her guarded praise at our getting poems published, as if this were one more nail in the coffin of our resolve to drown as poets and refuse all 'secure' teaching work. Today I rose & made breakfast – coffee, and toast & bacon, and chilled peaches & pineapple. Then making love, hearing the cars come and go in regular battalions, to and from the hourly masses. Another title for my book: <u>Full Fathom Five</u>. It seems to me dozens of books must have this title, but I can't offhand remember any. It relates more richly to my life and imagery than anything else I've dreamed up: has the background of <u>The Tempest</u>, the association of the sea, which is a central metaphor for my childhood, my poems and the artist's subconscious, to the father image – relating to my own father, the buried male muse & god-creator risen to be my mate in Ted, to the sea-father neptune – and the pearls and coral highly-wrought to art: pearls sea-changed from the ubiquitous grit of sorrow and dull routine. I am going on with <u>The Wings of the Dove</u> and ravenously devouring a thousand page anthology of magnificent folk & fairy tales of all nations, my mind again re-peopling itself with magics and monsters – I cram them in. O, only left to myself, what a poet I will flay myself into. I shall begin by setting myself magic objects to write on: sea-bearded bodies – and begin thus, digging into the reaches of my deep submerged head, "and It's old and old it's sad and old it's sad and weary I go back to you, my cold father, my cold mad father, my cold mad feary father ... " so Joyce says, so the river flows to the paternal source of godhead.

<u>Tuesday morning: May 13</u>:" Thirteen days behind schedule in here. I have been listening to my mind's streaming thoughts all morning and have an

hour – two hours, to myself before Ted comes home from work. The queerness, the richness which rises to my mind in these mornings – my first free
from Arvin & Art – seems so quick, so complex, as to defy setting down. I
have had more & more to write, accumulating, gathering, and yet am held,
tight, tense, galled, in tether. This week on my calendar looms full and
scrawled with meeting, dinners, classes, and the deluge of my last and long
papers to come and engulf the weekend – then next week – two days & my
classes done with, only James to fill up on and then Arvin's last exams. I
can't shape into writing now: my superficial mind must keep itself up: nine
months dwindle to nine weeks, which obligingly dwindle to the present nine
days. Partly this, keeps me from writing (tried a bad dull poem Sunday about
our landlady which was deadly, dogged & depressed me terribly: as soon as
I produce a bad one – within these strictures of time: knowing I can't try
again, knowing I can't throw it away, prodigal, & start afresh the next hour
– I hear my chittering ogres and efrits or whatever mocking me in just the
same insinuating, patronizing tone of George Gibian or Mrs. Van der Poel:
'why not write summers? what makes you think you can, or want, or will
write anyway? You have shown little, you may show less',) my two allies
are: Ted, and time to myself to perfect the crude personal roughness, generali-
ty & superficiality of that 35 page description of falcon yard I sent to New
World Writing. Henry James teaches me hourly – he is too fine for me – but
then, I am so crude and loud that his lesson can only serve to make me less
crude, not more fine – teaches me how life is circuitous, rich, sentences and
acts laden with all the riches of meaning and implication. Well, I am half
through The Wings of the Dove: Millie seems to me so damnably good: a
kind of wealthy Patsy O'Neil: even Patsy will be grist for my mill. But Millie
is so noble: she sees and sees and will not flinch or be mean, be small: like
Maggie Verver she will not indulge "the vulgar heat of her wrong." With
which, under which, I should explode. By being 'simple', aren't they, by that
very quality, being highly wrought? O if my Dody might be complex: the
trouble with amorality is that it sets up no tensions except the rather simple
one of the inavailability of what is wanted: once this is provided, the tensions are swamped in a rather gross all-embracing flood. I must erect a real
china shop, only not fake, for my splendid bulls. I read of Millie with her
ominous as-yet-undefined illness. And I can scarcely lift a pen. I don't write
here partly for that reason: the thought of penmanship exhausts me. I feel to
have undulant fever, but my temperature is perfectly normal: I am too tired
to read, too tired to write, too tired to prepare my last three lessons, which I
should at least strain myself for. I wander in my bathrobe & wool socks

about the cold, beautifully bare and clean apartment: how cleanliness rests my soul. I have an arduous apprenticeship to begin this summer. Writing a volume of poems, writing a novel – is so <u>small</u> in one sense: in comparison to the quality & quantity of others. And nothing, maliciously, evilly, confirms my ambition. I have an ominously red, sore & swollen eyelid, a queer red spot on my lip – and this ennervating fatigue like a secret and destructive fever – can I do my dreams justice? <u>The Atlantic</u>, <u>Harper's</u>, <u>Art News</u> – all are silent on the head of my poems. And John Lehmann[n] won't publish, it seems, those he accepted over a year ago. I brace myself for the large, fat envelopes, the polite, encouraging, yet inevitable rejection. The air is empty, vacant, and its restrained surprises will no doubt prove most unpleasant. Well, I have a year. Lord knows how good I would feel if Ted's Saxton came through – I hate the idea of his working – it would quite take half the joy from my own dedication. Outside, after, ten days of rain, a cold clean wind and flashes of green leaves, of sunlight. There is a doggedness in me that resents even these last two weeks & longs for liberation, won't run about dithering up preparation. I spent all yesterday rushing about, shopping, scouring, making a runny but delicious custard-meringue-raspberry pie. Paul & Clarissa came, Clarissa five months pregnant, thickening under a black loose shirt, her hair bright gilt, Paul, double, probably quite wicked (we learned he has an older brother & sister: a fact difficult to adjust to our strong impression of his singularity – heard how he lay naked in the rose-garden at Clarissa's mansion in Saginaw, crocheted, while intently observing TV, a light blue wool cape for Pandora with PR embroidered on it in white angora and a bunny tail at the back). Why are the Roche's so intriguing, though Paul is an obvious, a palpable sham, and Clarissa is simple, even deluded? Their show is diverting – they are 'sports' – odd quantities on a slate of evens. Less intelligent, less rich in mind & such than many others here, they loom absorbing as any eccentric. We go to see them to learn more – to 'place' them, for they have places, queer, but nonetheless, places. Paul – who wouldn't like to know what goes on in his head – what machinations lead him to set about doing Greek translations, for example? to impress Clarissa's parents, to stall (until they come across handsomely by leaving a fortune) under the aura of a specialist scholar's life work? One can't help wanting to know. He is 'successful' in getting money, getting an audience, although Smith at large has seen through the gaudy clothwork, and I, that one night at Sylvan's, saw the orange, blond, blue-eyed mask slip and naked hate, or perversion, glare out with the stilled malice of a cougar about to spring. To kill. Paul is thirty-one. He has published nothing since the book of fables & the novel six years ago – what does he do? The translations are a front: he uses a lexicon. Stanley claims to have seen the lexicon & Louis MacNiece's translation on his desk, open, and his own page a kind of elaborate synthesis. So he is a fraud. One suspects, one knows, this – and yet one wonders: how, so beautifully, does he keep it up? Keep it up in face of outright insults which he, it appears, frankly recognizes, admits – as he & Clarissa admitted to us not long ago that people drop them, have resoundingly dropped them: "Oh they come over, but they never ask us back." What swallowings of pride must this mean – must the open admission, still more, mean – to such socially conscious people? Ted & I are aware of a great dearth of invitations, of Tony Hecht even, one might say, owing us a dinner – but the reaction, partly sour, is also a relieved one – I'm sick of dinners – their cost, what one pays – is only socially fixed, repaid, by one's having to spend more & more of oneself, and this I am through with. It comes home, strongly, how exterior relations impoverish if one is not heart-deep in one's own work. Bless Ted for being like me in this and demanding, with a sauce of good other people, our sequestering, our dedication. How the problems, and I knock wood as I write, of a handsome and gifted-poet husband, then, fray to mist, because of Ted's being himself, and me, one hopes, my own self. The church bell on the Church of the Blessed Sacrament opposite is just bonging out its queer version of twelve noon. I am now dressed in my red Christmas shirt with its subtle pattern of paisley black, green and grey foliage, and my very subtle smoky green skirt, deep grey-green, like a military color. I feel better for dressing: that poem by Yeats comes to mind – the one about our restlessness: always longing for the next, the different season: our longing being the longing for the tomb. And so tonight I will long to get in bed and to sleep: Ted's witchy Aunt Alice[n] illustrates this admirably when she stays in bed for no reason except that there's no reason to get up if one only has to go back to bed again. I made a great dinner last night: the lamb was tough, though. Mrs. Van der Poel came: black, tiny, elegant, her grey hair curled into spit, or kiss curls, her heels high, her fur opulent, a highly trained & soulless silver poodle with a taste for modern art: her relations seem to suggest linkage to primary colors, the garish Leger city scapes where women are turbine-engines. I never felt such an inimical presence as Mrs. Van der Poel's. She makes me feel large, soft, and agreeably doltish. She is sterile, absolutely barren. Her coming, I feel, was forced. She said, when she first refused that she'd 'love to come another time', which I took up as a dogged duty – to give her the <u>chance</u> for another time, and after three or four shiftings, which I should have interpreted as refusal, she came, sat, chittered.

About art, artists, notably Baskin – nothing. Either one wasn't worth her wisdom, or she wasn't in the mood, or she doesn't <u>have</u> the best kind of wisdom: she can put everything into bright, neat words, and this is killing. One suspects her dry bright tidy little voice could find a lucid epithet for the worst chaos. One wonders about her vanished husband. Priscilla: the name does, for her. One supposes she keeps the Van der Poel for its high tone. Ted and I both came away with the strong impression that she dislikes Leonard Baskin. Why? She possesses an admirable, huge Baskin "Hanging Man", she invited him to give three lectures on sculpture for her classes; she is, however, a Professor, a chairman of the department, and he a creative artist with an avowed scorn of offices-in-the-art-building, department meetings, and such. At any event, she exuded dislike. I can't, nor can Ted, spot the sentence, the clause, but it was evident.

– Just now, restless, unproductive, I was wandering about the bare clean apartment eating a piece of buttered toast and strawberry jam when, stopping wolfish by the bathroom venetian blind, as I always do, to eye the vista for the mailman, I heard a burst of prophetic whistling and the man himself exploded, as it were, into view with his light blue shirt and beaten leather shoulder-pouch. I ran to get ready to go downstairs and felt him pause, so hurried to the livingroom gable window. And there, as suddenly sprung up, was Ted in his dark green corduroy jacket waylaying the man and demanding mail. From the window I could see it was nothing, nor was it – a handful of flannel: circulars – soap-coupons, Sears sales, a letter from mother of stale news she'd already relayed over the phone, a card from Oscar Williams inviting us to a cocktail party in New York on the impossible last day of my classes. No news. I feel a nervous havoc in my veins – and am close to starving myself – Ted's influence here is marked. When he won't eat I all too easily find it a bother to prepare food for myself and so fail in nourishment and sleep. A dull and useless day, dream-dictated. Went to the library for an office-hour with Sylvie Koval – found myself uttering pompous nothings. Browsed in magazines while hours fled, stomped home bare-legged in the grey cold, rain threatening. Miss Hornbeak a horn beak, cold as dry-ice.

<u>May 14</u>: Wednesday: Grim night. My eyelid's hot stinging itch has spread, in actuality, or by sympathetic imagining nerves, to all my body – scalp, leg, stomach: as if an itch, infectious, lit and burned, lit and burned. I feel like scratching my skin off. And a dull torpor shutting me in my own prison of

highstrung depression. Is it because I feel a ghost – ? My influence waning with my classes who have no exam, but one paper and then no need to work or listen. At the faculty meeting I marveled so much time had passed and I was in my same aloneness, only further in, as if a transparent lid enveloped me & shut up all others whose faces have no personal meaning for me – they are going on next year, I am gone already in spirit, if lingering in a locust-itchy-crawly body. I feel about to break out in leprousy: nervous: hearing stairs creak: dying of cowardice – ready for all the lights mysteriously to go out and the horror of a monster to take me: nightmares haunt me: Joan of Arc's face as she feels the fire and the world blurs out in a smoke, a pall of horror. I wait for Ted's return from Paul's reading of Oedipus. I itch. I feel between two worlds, as Arnold writes – "one dead, the other powerless to be born": all seems thus futile – my teaching has lost its savor: I feel the students are gone & have none of the satisfaction as a teacher of planning a better more vital course next year: that is done. Then, on the other hand, I have nothing but a handful of poems – so unsatisfactory, so limiting, when I study Eliot, Yeats, even Auden and Ransom – and the few written in spring vacation to link me umbilically to a new-not-yet-born world of writing – only the five-year distant adolescent successes in writing: a gap. Will I fill it, go beyond? I am hamstrung: papers to come, senior exams & Arvin's. My eyes are killing me – what is wrong with them. No mail – only letter from Patsy which holds out New York – a vision of time – a bridge from a dead world to a newborn one.

May 19: Monday: Only it isn't Monday at all, but now Thursday the 22nd of May and I through with my last classes & a hot bath and disabused of many ideals, visions and faiths. Irony: the mature stance which covers up the maudlin ladies' magazine blurt of tears. Disgust. Yes, that's more like it: revulsion at much in myself and more in Ted, whose vanity is not dead, but thrives. Irony: in almost two years he has turned me from a crazy perfection-ist and promiscuous human-being-lover, to a misanthrope, and – at Tony's, at Paul's, a nasty, catty and malicious misanthrope. How he praised this in me: I at last "saw" the real world. So I put the two of us in our separate, oh infinitely superior world: we are so nice, naturally, too nice-'smilers'. So we are now, in society, nasty & cruel & calculated – oh, not first off, but only when attacked. No more brave innocent blinkings – all tooth and nail. And just as I rose to a peak of nastiness for perhaps the first time in my life – I have never been catty professionally & publicly, I got the final insight: not only am I just as nasty as everybody else, but so is Ted. A liar and a vain smiler. How it works: how irony is the spice of life. My novel will hardly end with love & marriage: it will be a story, like James', of the workers & the worked, the exploiters & the exploited: of vanity and cruelty: with a ronde, a circle of lies & abuse in a beautiful world gone bad. The irony I record here, for the novel, but also for the <u>Ladies' Home Journal</u>. I am no Maggie Verver. I feel the vulgar heat of my wrong enough to gag, to spit the venom I've swallowed: but I'll take my cue from Maggie, bless the girl. How the irony builds up – every time I made one of my foolish bland statements I felt a chill, a dark rubber-visaged frog-faced fate, ready to loom up at the fulness of the moment, to confront me with some horror as yet unseen, unforseen. And all this time it has been going on, on the far edges of my intuition. I confided my faith in Ted, and why is the wife the last to see her husband's ulcer? Because she has the most faith, the carefully & lovingly nurtured blind faith that turns unquestioning to follow the course of the sun, hearing no outside cries of thirst from the desert, no curses in the wasteland. I saw James leave Joan Bramwell, or, rather, saw Joan pack him off because of a mad affair, diabolical, with the Lamia S——, and Joan's thin wavery voice confessing her suffering, her gladness in spite of all of what she has learned, her humiliations, her sanity – hated – in the face of madness, S——'s keeping James out till midnight after the movies, Joan calling & asking him home, & James coming: S—— calling later & saying that she had bashed her hands through the window & that they were bleeding badly – her ugly raised wrist-scars. O, I said in a bright clear voice: "I am the only woman on the faculty who has a husband" – Joan's is a weak vain elderly rat & doesn't count, is gone; Marlies doesn't live with hers except on weekends. Well, mine is a liar, a vain smiler, a twister. I look at Lowell's first book: Jean Stafford[n] then. Well, at least she writes for <u>The New Yorker</u> – a good career, a good living – or maybe she's in a madhouse even as I speak, she's been an alcoholic. Who knows who Ted's next book will be dedicated to? His navel. His penis. I first saw him vain, a smiler. And here after all these years is the old nick. Well, start with the background to the facts – the misanthropy felt for all except Ted & myself, the faith in Ted & myself & distrust of all others. Add last night – Ted reading the part of Creon for Paul's translation of <u>Oedipus</u> & practically telling me not to come. (May 22) I said all right, but rebelled. I am superstitious about not hearing Ted read. I raced through my second set of papers (and still have another to go) and leapt up, as if drawn on a leash, and started running, down the stairs, out into the warm, heavy lilac-scented may dark. The new moon stared at me over the trees – its shadow of whole-ness clearly drawn. I ran, skimming, although deep in long tension &

exhaustion, as if I would fly, my heart a hurting fisted lump in my chest. I ran on, not stopping, down the bumpy, steep hill by Paradise Pond, saw a rabbit, fuzzed, brown, in the bushes behind the Botany Building. I ran on up to the lighted colonial front of Sage hall, white columns glowing in the electric lights, not a person in sight, empty echoing pavements. The hall was glaring: two people, a fat girl & ugly man, were in the side booth running a tape of music for the recording. I tiptoed in, slipped into a seat in back, and tried to still the funny knocking of my heart & my rasping breath. Ted stood on the left of the stage, far off, next to Bill Van Voris, in the center, as Oedipus. Chris Denney[n] in elegant black and Paul, rumpled & gilt-curled head erect on his lily stalk neck, beside her. Paul's voice came ghostly over the tape – (like his novel, the satyr entering the body of the novitiate & loving him up) which he answered. Ted looked slovenly: his suit jacket wrinkled as if being pulled from behind, his pants hanging, unbelted, in great folds, his hair black & greasy in the light. The minute I came in he knew it, and I knew he knew it, and his voice let the reading down. He was ashamed of something. He gave the last line with the expression of a limp dishtowel & I felt this faint flare of disgust, of misgiving. There he stood, next to the corrupt, white snail-faced Van Voris whose voice luxuriated over the words: loins, incest, bed, foul. I felt as if I had stepped barefoot into a pit of sliming, crawling worms. I felt like hawking & spitting. Ted knew whom he stood beside, and whose words he read. He shrank, slouched away from it. But he could have gotten out of it before. Long before. Paul would love to have Philip Wheelwright read Creon. Ted didn't come to meet me afterwards. I stood in front, went out behind & asked the janitor where the readers were. He had to tell me. In a small lighted room Bill Van Voris slumped in a loose boneless position, legs stuck straight out, on a flowery-upholstered couch. Ted sat with a mean wrong face over the piano, banging out a strident one-finger tune, hunched, a tune I'd never heard before. Nor had I seen that odd, lousy smile since Falcon Yard. Oh yes, the preying ones, how I shall manage it. He didn't speak. He wouldn't come away. I sat down. We went then. Clarissa had been cold & nasty: Pat Hecht had possibly revenged herself by telling Clarissa all the nasty things we'd said of Paul, leaving in politic fashion, Tony's insults out. Anyway, it was a stale, rancid evening, just as the evening with the Hechts had been. Which more of in the course of this. So it was an accident. So Ted was ashamed of appearing on the platform in the company of lice. So today is my last day. Or was. Armed with various poems by Ransom, cummings & Sitwell, I went to class, received applause in the exact volume of my enjoyment of the class – a spatter at 9, a thunderous burst at

11, and something in between both extremes at 3. I had made a kind of ceremonial stab at asking Ted to drive down with me till I got through this afternoon, so I could see him & rejoice the very minute I got through my first class. So we went. I was teaching, among other things, 'parting without sequel': how perfect – I moralized about the joy of revenge, the dangerous luxury of hate and malice, and how, even when malice & venom are 'richly deserved', the indulgence of these emotions can, alas, be ruinous. Ah Ransom. All boomerangs. Before class I had twenty minutes. Ted arranged to bring books into the library & meet me in the car: to be waiting there till my classes ended. I went alone into the coffee shop which was almost deserted. A few girls. And the back of the head of Bill Van Voris. He did not see me come in, nor ask for coffee, although I was almost within his view. But the girl he was sitting with in the booth opposite him could see me. She had very fine black eyes, black hair, and a pale white skin, and was being very serious. I took my coffee up and did not attract Bill's attention, but sat down in the booth directly in back of him, facing the back of his head and his student. Ha, I thought, listening, or, rather, hearing. I sipped my coffee and thought of Jackie" whose skin is dough color with fine tight wrinkles, whose hair is mousecolor whose eyes are of indeterminate color behind tortoise-shell rimmed glasses. Who is not perhaps as cultivatedly 'intellectual' as Bill's students. I noted Bill's back well: the tasteful thin-grain corduroy jacket fitting his broad masculine shoulders, a light-cinnamon color, tweedy or tobacco color, his pale bull neck, the little springing crisp whorls of his dark very-close cropped hair. He was talking in his way: silly, pretentious, oh yes fatuous. She stammered prettily, as I left my ears unshuttered: Something about "The hero . . . the comic as distinct from the classic Hero." "Comic?" Bill's voice cracked up, a whisper, or wheeze nuzzled somewhere in it. "You mean . . . " she faltered, dark eyes asking for help. "Satiric", Bill proposed, all sure wisdom. I felt a stir, a desire to tap his shoulder, lean over & tell him to come off it, comic heroes were fine, satire didn't hold a monopoly. But I shut up. Bill quickly swerved to Restoration drama. Sniffing, inhaling the daisies in his own field. "Morality. Of course, all that material for jokes, that wonderful opportunity for bawdy jokes. Men and men leaving their wives." The girl responded, geared for the supreme, the most intense understanding: "O, I know, I know". They were still talking when I left the coffeeshop for my class. At which I almost talked myself hoarse. I could see Al Fisher, sitting in the same seat, & me opposite, that official sexual rapport. Al Fisher and his dynasties of students: students made mistresses. Students made wives. And now, his silly, fatuous vain smile. When Bill gets tenure –

probably not much but play about till then – he will begin Smith mistresses. Or maybe Jacky will die: she has death, and great pain written on her stretched mouth: grim gripped lips and eyes that measure, reserved, cold, the chances she takes and has to take and will take. These images piled up. I felt tempted to drop in at the library before class and share with Ted my amusing insight, my ringside seat at Van Voris and the Seductive Smith girl: or William S. is bad agayne. But I went to class. When I came out, I ran to the parking lot, half-expecting to meet Ted on the way to the car, but more sure of finding him inside. I peered through a perspective of car windows but saw no dark head. Our car was empty and the emptiness struck me as odd, particularly on this day which we have counted toward for twenty-eight weeks. I did see Bill, after what was probably over an hour and a half, bidding a warm smiling goodbye to his student between the green lilac bushes framing the path from the coffee shop to the parking lot. He began coming toward me & I quickly turned my back on him and got into the car which I drove up to the library, figuring Ted would be in the reading room, oblivious of time, immersed in The New Yorker article by Edmund Wilson. He was not there. I kept meeting left-over students of mine from my three-oclock class. I had an odd impulse to drive home, but I was not destined to anything shocking in the apartment yet, although I have been prepared to be. As I came striding out of the cold shadow of the library, my bare arms chilled, I had one of those intuitive visions. I knew what I would see, what I would of necessity meet, and I have known for a very long time, although not sure of the place or date of the first confrontation. Ted was coming up the road from Paradise Pond where girls take their boys to neck on weekends. He was walking with a broad, intense smile, eyes into the uplifted doe-eyes of a strange girl with brownish hair, a large lipsticked grin, and bare thick legs in khaki Bermuda shorts. I saw this in several sharp flashes, like blows. I could not tell the color of the girls eyes, but Ted could, and his smile, though open and engaging as the girl's was, took on an ugliness in context. His stance next to Van Voris clicked into place, his smile became too white-hot, became fatuous, admiration-seeking. He was gesturing, just finishing an observation, an explanation. The girl's eyes souped up giddy applause. She saw me coming. Her eye started to guilt and she began to run, literally, without a goodbye, Ted making no effort to introduce her, as I'm sure Bill would have. She hasn't learned to be deceitful yet in her first look, but she'll learn fast. He thought her name was Sheila; once he thought my name was Shirley: o all the twists of the tongue – the smiles. Strange, but jealousy in me turned to disgust. The late comings home, my vision, while brushing my hair, of a black-horned grinning wolf all came clear, fused, and I gagged at what I saw. I am no smiler anymore. But Ted is. His aesthetic distance from his girls so betrayed by his leaning stance, leaning into the eyes of adoration – not old adoration, but new, fresh, unadulterated. Or, perhaps adulterated. Van Voris looks white. Lily-handed. Why is it I so despise this brand of male vanity? Even Richard had it, small, sickly & impotent as he was at nineteen. Only he was rich, had family and so security: a lineage of men able to buy better wives than they deserved. As Joan said: Ego and Narcissus. Vanitas, vanitatum. I know what Ruth would tell me, and I feel I can now tell her. No, I won't jump out of a window or drive Warren's car into a tree, or fill the garage at home with carbon monoxide & save expense, or slit my wrists & lie in the bath. I am disabused of all faith, and see too clearly. I can teach, and will write and write well. I can get in a year of that, perhaps, before other choices follow. Then there are the various-and few-people I love a little. And my own dogged and inexplicable sense of dignity, integrity that must be kept. I have run too long on trust funds. I am bankrupt in that line.

– Later, much later. Some time the next morning. The fake excuses. Vague confusions about name & class. All fake. All false. And the guilty look of stunned awareness of the wrong presence. So I can't sleep. Partly out of shock myself at the cheapness of vanity, the heavy ham act: oh yes, Stanley, very clever: matinee idol: hanging over, great inert heavy male flesh: "Let's make up." O such good fuckings. Why so weary, so slack all winter? Ageing or spending. Fake. Sham ham. No explanations, only obfuscations. That is what I cannot stand, why I cannot sleep. He snorts & snores even now in smug sleep. And the complete refusal to explain. What Kazin said that spring evening was true: that's why Ted jumped at him. Only Kazin was wrong in one particular: it wasn't Smith girls. No – the eager leaning open grin and my vision of Van Voris with this – of Fisher, later, yes. Dishonesty – a rift. All stupidity & frankness on my side: what a fool one is to sincerely love. Not to cheat. To two time. It is awful to want to go away and to want to go nowhere. I made the most amusing, ironic & fatal step in trusting Ted was unlike other vain and obfuscating and self-indulgent men. I have served a purpose, spent money, mother's money, which hurts most, to buy him clothes, to buy him a half year, eight months of writing, typed hundreds of times his poems. Well, so much have I done for modern British & American poetry. What I cannot forgive is dishonesty – and no matter what, or how hard, I would rather know the truth of which I today had such a clear & devastating vision from his mouth than hear foul evasions, blurrings and rattiness. I have a life to finish up here. But what about life without trust – the sense that love is a lie and all joyous sacrifice is ugly duty. I am so tired. My last day, and I cannot sleep for shaking at horror. He is shamed, shameful and shames me & my trust, which is no plea in a world of liars and cheats and broken or vanity-ridden men. Love has been an inexhaustible spring for my nourishment and now I gag. Wrong, wrong: the vulgar heat of it: the picture of fatuous attention, doe-eyed rollings of smiles, startled recognition, flight – all cannot be denied. Only clearly explained. I do not want to ask for what should be given before the heavy hammy American cheap slang "let's make up." The heavy too jocular-jocularity. This is the vain, selfish face & voice I first saw and the Yorkshire Beacon boy, the sweet & daily companion is gone. Why should he be proud of my recent nastiness to Hecht & Van Voris if it isn't a judgment on his own inner corruption. For I smell it. The house stinks of it. And my vision fills in the blurred latenesses with oh yes Frank Sousa. I know. I know worse for knowing all myself & he not telling me or understanding what it is to know. His picking his nose, peeling off his nails & leaving them about, his greasy unkempt hair – what does this matter? Why did I make his concerns my own & wish to see him his best & finest, I won't bother now; the dirt is too deep for Halo shampoo & lux soap, the raggedness too far-frayed for the neat nip of trimming shears. He does not care. He is sulking as he began to after I came to the reading. His accepting that & keeping up to it showed how far down he has gone. He wants to go down, to leave me to hunt for him on my last moment of teaching to celebrate the end of a year of teaching by learning what my intuition clears for me like a pool of clearing water after the mud settles. O I see the frogs on the mud-bed. And the corruption in warts on their slick and unctuous black hides. So what now.

June 11: Wednesday: A green cool rainy night: peace & concord almost a month behind in this book, but much to tell – I have avoided writing here because of the rough & nightmarish entry I must take up from – but I take up & knit up the raveled ends. I had a sprained thumb, Ted bloody clawmarks, for a week, and I remember hurling a glass with all my force across a dark room; instead of shattering the glass rebounded and remained intact: I got hit and saw stars – for the first time – blinding red & white stars exploding in the black void of snarls & bitings. Air cleared. We are intact. And nothing – no wishes for money, children, security, even total possession – nothing is worth jeopardizing what I have which is so much the angels might well envy it. I corrected, sullenly, my eyes red with a stinging itchy rash, honors papers – simply putting in time in the garden of the faculty club – they could all be 'summas' or 'cums' for all I cared – under Miss Hornbeaks' acid eye. And then Arvin's exams which I finished, along with all my obligations at Smith, about 10 days ago, on Sunday June 1st. We have half of June, then July and August clear to write, but the looming blackness of no Saxton for Ted. The irony is that his own editor at Harper's is adviser to the trustees and his project although most warmly approved, is ineligible because of the very qualification we thought would win for him – his Harper-published book. So I shall try for a Saxton for 10-months & Ted for a Guggenheim this next year – he trying to rank TS Eliot, WH Auden, Marianne Moore, etc., behind him. I don't want to live in the country this year, but in Boston, near people, lights, sights, shops, a river, Cambridge, theater, editors, publishers – where we won't need a car & will be well away from Smith. So we will gamble – on a possible Saxton for me & at least on Boston jobs if we aren't earning, by writing, but that last only a death's door resort. We must keep round-trip ship-fare for Europe intact, and our mystic $1,400 of poetry earnings. I am just getting used to peace: no people, no assignments, no students. Peace, at least after our visit home to apartment hunt this weekend, & me to make a recording at Harvard & to celebrate our 2nd wedding anniversary – how can I say this calmly? This was a central problem in my other book, and here it begins well into marriage. An incident today to start a train of remembering our wearying and also rejuvenating week in New York which cleared out Smith cobwebs: we went at twilight to walk in the green Park – (I have just written a good syllabic poem on the 'Child's Park Stones' as juxtaposed to the ephemeral orange & fuchsia azaleas and feel the park is my favorite place in America.) The evening was dim, light grey with wet humid mist, swimming green. I took a pair of silver-plated scissors in my raincoat pocket with the intent to cut another rose – yellow, if possible – from the rose garden (by the stone lion's head fountain) just come into bloom – a rose to begin to unbud as the red, almost black-red rose now giving out prodigal scent in our livingroom. We walked round on the road to the stucco house & were about to descend to the rose garden when we heard a loud crackling sound as of the breaking of twigs. We thought it must be a man we'd seen in another part of the park coming through the thick rhododendron groves from the frog-pond. The yellow roses were blowzy, blasted, no bud in view. I leaned to snip a pink bud, one petal uncurling, and three hulking girls came out of the rhododendron grove, oddly sheepish, hunched in light manilla-colored raincoats. We stood regnant in our rose-garden and stared them down. They shambled, in whispered converse, to the formal garden of white peonies & red geraniums, stood at a loss under a white arbor. "I'll bet they're wanting to steal some flowers", Ted said. Then the girls evidently agreed to walk off. I saw an orange rosebud, odd, which I've never before seen, and bent to clip it, a bud of orange velvet, after the girls were out of sight. The grey sky lowered, thunder rumbled in the pines, and a warm soft rain began to fall greyly as if gently squeezed from a grey sponge. We started home through the rhododendron groves where the girls had come out. I saw, as we had half-envisioned, but yet saw with a shock, a newspaper loaded with scarlet rhododendron blossoms neatly tucked behind a bush. I began to get angry. We walked farther, and saw another newspaper crammed full of bright pink rhododendrons. I had a wild impulse, which I should have followed to satisfy my blood lust, to take up all the rhododendron flowers and set them afloat in the frog-pond like rootless lilies to spite the guilty-pickers & preserve the flowers as long as they would be preserved in water for the public eye. I picked up bunches of the scarlet ones, but Ted, also angry, wouldn't have it. But as we passed the pond and had come out onto open grass, we both turned back, of one accord to put the blossoms in the pond. As I must have sensed, the girls were back – we heard muffled laughter & the cracking of branches broken carelessly. We came up slowly with evil eyes. I felt blood-lust – sassy girls, three of them – "O, here's a big one", a girl ostentatiously said. "Why are you picking them?" Ted asked. "For a dance. We need them for a dance." They half-thought we would approve. "Don't you think you'd better stop?" Ted asked, "this is a public park." Then the little one got brassy & fairly sneered "This isn't your park." "Nor yours," I retorted, wanting strangely to claw off her raincoat, smack her face, read the emblem of her school on her jersey & send her to jail. "You might as well pull up the bush by its roots." She glared at me & I gave her a mad wild still stony glare that snuffed hers out. Showily she directed another girl to get the other rhododendrons. We followed them to the pond, where they stood, consulted, then doubled back on their tracks. We followed to the edge of the rhododendron grove in the rain, lightning flashed, almost clear red, and we saw them hurrying down to a waiting car & loading the rhododendrons into the openback trunk. We let them go. If we made them uncomfortable it is almost enough. But we were angry. And I wondered at my split morality. Here I had an orange and a pink rosebud in my pocket and a full red rose squandering its savors at home, & I felt like killing a girl stealing armfuls of rhododendrons for a dance: I guess I feel my one rose a week is aesthetic joy for me & Ted & sorrow or loss for no one – yellow roses are gone blowzy – why not conserve one bud through full bloom to blowzy death & replace it with another: to possess & love an immortal many-colored rose during rose-season while leaving a gardenful – but these girls were ripping up whole bushes – that crudeness & wholesale selfishness disgusted & angered me. I have a violence in me that is hot as death-blood. I can kill myself or – I know it now – even kill another. I could kill a woman, or wound a man. I think I could. I gritted to control my hands, but had a flash of bloody stars in my head as I stared that sassy girl down, and a blood-longing to fly at her & tear her to bloody beating bits.

<u>Friday, June 20</u>: My motto here might well be "My spirits, as in a dream, are all bound up." I have been, and am, battling depression. It is as if my life were magically run by two electric currents: joyous positive and despairing negative – which ever is running at the moment dominates my life, floods it. I am now flooded with despair, almost hysteria, as if I were smothering. As if a great muscular owl were sitting on my chest, its talons clenching & constricting my heart. I knew this fresh life would be harder, much harder, than teaching – but I have weapons, & self-knowledge is the best of them. I was blackly hysterical last fall, beginning my job: the outside demands exacted my blood, and I feared. Now, a totally different situation, yet the same in emotional content – I have fourteen months "completely free" for the first time in my life, reasonable financial security, and the magic and hourly company of a husband so magnificent, sweet-smelling, big, creative in a giant way, that I imagine I made him up – only he offers so much extra surprise that I know he is real and deep as an iceberg in its element. So I have all this, and my limbs are paralyzed: inside demands exact my blood, and I fear – because I have to <u>make up</u> my demands: the hardest responsibility in the world: there is no outer recalcitrant material to blame for snags and failures, only the bristling inner recalcitrance: sloth, fear, vanity, meekness. I know, even as I wrote last fall, that if I face & command this experience & <u>produce</u> a book of poems, stories, a novel, learn German & read Shakespeare & Aztec anthropology and the origin of the species – as I faced & commanded the different demands of teaching, I shall never be afraid again of myself. And if I am not afraid of my self – of my own craven fears & wincings – I shall have little left in the world to be afraid of – of accident, disease, war, yes – but not of my standing up to it. This is, of course, a manner of whistling in the dark. I have even longed for that most fearsome first woman's ordeal: having a baby – to elude my demanding demons & have a constant excuse for lack of production in writing. I must first conquer my writing & experience, & then will deserve to conquer childbirth.

Paralysis. Once the outer tensions are gone: I sit on a cold grey June day in welcome of the green gloom of leaves, I fall back & back into myself, dredging deep, longing to revisit my first hometown: Winthrop, not Wellesley. Jamaica Plain, even: the names are become talismans. The church clock, or is it angelus? strikes twelve in its queer measured sequences of bells. I have let almost a month slip by – going to New York, to Wellesley & apartment hunting. Frittering. Being with people. I say it is people I need, yet what good have they done me? Perhaps, as I try a story, I shall discover. I lean on the window, forhead to the glass, waiting for the blue-uniformed mailman to walk out from the house, having left letters of acceptance. I dreamt about Stanley Sultan last night, laughing & slapping his thighs in recounting a movie he saw where the eternal Sid Caesar, on the forty-ninth floor of his apartment building, answered the exorbitant demands of his ritzy sweetheart & found a bee-tree (memory of the Bronx Zoo?) in the city, but the bees flew & police men had to chase them with ariel nets. I also dreamed the Atlantic rejected my two poems. If life is prosaic – there seem, of late, to be greasy dishes & pots forever piled in the sink – at least dreams should be colored, wondrous. I go suspended in the void, the vacuum, the exhaust of the year's teaching machine which speeds off clicking and purring. I must, again for the first time and for the longest time, tightly & creatively structure my days – fill myself with reading & writing projects – keep a clean & well-run house, get rid of my slovenly sickness. We found, this week, an 'ideal' apartment – ideal aesthetically if not in high price & kitchen crammed against one wall of the livingroom. But the view, oh the view, yes the view. Two tiny rooms for $115 a month, and yet light, quiet & a sixth floor Beacon Hill View to the river, with two Bay windows, one each for Ted & me to write in. I await only Marianne Moore's letter before I can send off my application for a Saxton grant, which would just cover an economical ten months of our contracted year & relieve my puritan conscience completely about the rent. The rented Beacon Hill flat gives our summer free peace. I write here, because I am paralyzed everywhere else. Compulsive. As if in reaction to the dance, the tarentella of the teaching year, my mind shuts against knowledge, study: I fritter, gliddery – pick up this & that, wipe a dish, stir up some mayonnaise, jump at the imagined note of the mailman's whistle above the roar of traffic. I am disappointed with my poems: they pall. I have only a few over 25 and want a solid forty. I have distant subjects. I haven't opened my experience up. I keep discarding & discarding. My mind is barren of ideas & I must scavenge themes as a magpie must: scraps and oddments. I feel paltry, wanting in richness. Fearful, inadequate desperate. As if my mind clicked into a "fix", which stood frozen, blindered. And I must slowly, slowly set my lands in order: make my dream of self with poems, breast-sucking babies, a wife-of-bath calm, humor and resilience, come clear with time. I face no school-scheduled year, but the hardest year where all choosing is mine, all making and all delays, defautings, shyings off and all tardy sloths.

★June 25th: Wednesday★ A starred day, probably the first in this whole book. I was going to write here yesterday, but was in a teary, blue wits' end mood. Today I sat to type back letters & more of Ted's & my poems to send out. Seated at the typewriter, I saw the lovely light blue shirt of the mailman going into the front walk of the millionairess next door, so I ran downstairs. One letter stuck up out of the mailbox, and I saw The New Yorker on the left corner in dark print. My eyes dazed over. I raced alternatives through my head: I had sent a stamped envelope with my last poems, so they must have lost it & returned the rejects in one of their own envelopes. Or it must be a letter for Ted about copyrights. I ripped the letter from the box. It felt shockingly, hopefully thin. I tore it open right there on the steps, over mammoth marshmellow Mrs. Whalen sitting in the green yard with her two pale artificially cute little boys in their swimsuits jumping in and out of the rubber circular portable swimmingpool and bouncing a gaudy striped ball. The black thick print of Howard Moss's letter banged into my brain. I saw "MUSSEL-HUNTER AT ROCK HARBOR seems to me a marvelous poem & I'm happy to say we're taking it for the New Yorker ... " – at this realization of ten years of hopeful wishful waits (& subsequent rejections) I ran yipping upstairs to Ted & jumping about like a Mexican bean. It was only moments later, calming a little, that I finished the sentence " . . . as well as NOCTURNE, which we also think extremely fine". Two POEMS – not only that, two of my longest – 91 and 45 lines respectively: they'll have to use front-spots for both & are buying them in spite of having a full load of summer poems & not for filler. This shot of joy conquers an old dragon & should see me through the next months of writing on the crest of a creative wave.

Thursday: June 26: The first day of swelter: grey, wet, warm rain making a slither of the streets. A dog barks far off. The milk bottles sweat drops, the butter slumps. The house begins to look untidy again. I think I shall bathe tonight & clean it tomorrow. Drove with Ted this afternoon to the roadside fruit & vegetable market and made the effort I've avoided – loaded up on beets, asparagus, strawberries, new potatoes, chicory – all to be cooked, prepared. In the A & P I rushed to the magazine rack & there was Ted's story 'Billy Hook and the Three Souvenirs' in the July issue of Jack & Jill. The story was sumptuously presented: two fine lively color pictures & two half-tone drawings: gay & magic. Looked up spiders and crabs and owls in the sticky deserted gloom of the college library: pleasant to feel ownership of it in sodden summer. Wrote a brief poem this morning – "Owl over Main Street" in syllabic verse. Could be better. The beginning is a bit lyrical for the subject and the last verse might be expanded. I should leave poems to lie, to be rescrawled, & not be so eager to stick them in my book. I'd like a good fifteen to twenty poems more. That owl we heard on our midnight walk around town – the great feathered underside of the bird's body, its wide wing spread over the telephone wires – a ghoulish skrwack. Also: the black spider in Spain knotting ants around its rock. Visions of violence. The animal world seems to me more & more intriguing. Odd dreams: drank from a plastic cylindrical bottle with a red tip & realized in horror it was starch-poison I put in it – waited for my stomach to wrench & wither, ran to icebox, remembering about antidotes, & swallowed a raw egg whole: Ted says it's a symbolic dream of conception. Also, last night – a musical comedy & a hundred Danny Kayes. Pulled a piece of skin off my lip & my lips began welling blood, lip-shape – my whole mouth a skinless welling of brilliant red blood.

Tuesday: July 1st: The sticky weather, sulphurous, sultry, has begun with a flow of blood: began yesterday. I shut my head to the dopey blur of sense, to the cramp, & climbed Mount Holyoke with Ted. Hot, drenched green. I found words & phrases from my "Above the Oxbow" poem right & making the scene righter: "leaf-shuttered escarpments". We sweat, and looked for animals, but saw only squirrel heads & tails to account for occasional brush crashes. Then, on the bend in the tar road after the birches, by the path to 'Taylor's Notch', we saw the grey furred grubbing shape that puzzled us so in the road on our drive a few days ago: a humped, short-legged, stump-tailed rattish-faced creature. When we were almost upon it, snuffling rapt, as it was, at something in the road, it lumbered slowly & awkwardly into the fern & stopped. Ted walked round to the other side of the animal & started trying to catch it by throwing his raincoat over it. He jumped forward, the coat spread like a cloak & fell onto the creature, but it scrabbled across the road & into the fern backed by a ledge where it turned to face us, shaking piteously & making a chattering clack-sound with its long yellow rodentine lower teeth, fat & squat, like a mother full of babies. I longed to pat it, to feed it a leaf, to make it somehow apprehend our love, but it feared & stood its ground valiant, a fierce, scared rodent. We decided it was a wood chuck, a groundhog, & left it in the fern in pity. A haze blurred Hadley fields to a muzzy green, the river flowed – dull molten pewter. The whole interior of Prospect House was walled with reliquaria – a hundred years ago, after the Civil War, Abraham Lincoln, Jenny Lind, went up in the snow-smashed funicular railway. A newspaper of 1916 recapitulated history. We staggered down to fly-blown barns & hen stench on the flat river-level farms below.

Thursday: July 4:" Grey, for once, a sunless blessing after two days of still, suffocating air and sweat dripping at every move, prickling when sitting still and sticking my back to the chair-backs. I have been writing poems steadily & feel the blessed dawn of a desire to write prose beginning: bought a literary Mlle to whet my emulous urge – don't feel angry now: have my own time. I am rejecting more & more poems from my book which is now titled after what I consider one of my best & curiously moving poems about my father-sea-god muse: Full Fathom Five. "The Earthenware Head" is out: once, in England, "my best poem": too fancy, glassy, patchy & rigid – it embarrasses me now – with its ten elaborate epithets for head in 5 verses. I suppose now my star piece is "Mussel Hunter at Rock Harbor": the author's proofs came from The New Yorker yesterday, three long columns of them in the blessed New Yorker print which I've envisioned for so long. My next ambition is to get a story in The New Yorker – five, ten more years work. A horrid two-day noise of an electric saw cutting a tree down & up at the priests' angered & disturbed these days, the truck is gone & I hope for peace – the traffic is regular & soft enough to be minimal. I began German – two hours a day, on July 1st. Have started translating Grimm's fairytales, making a vocab list, but must work now on the grammar lessons – have forgotten all verb & noun-case forms, but am surprised enough I can get the sense of a story after two years of not touching it. My life is in my hands. I'm plowing through penguin books on Aztecs, the personality of animals, Man & the Vertebrates. So much to read, but this year I will make out schedules, lists – that is a help. Ted has given me several poetry subjects & assignments which are highly exciting: I've already written a good short poem on the groundhog & on landowners & am eager for others.

Friday: July 4: Independence day: how many people know from what they are free, by what they are imprisoned. Cool air, Canadian air, changed the atmosphere in the night & I woke to cool weather, cool enough for hot tea & sweatshirt. I woke to feed our baby bird. Yesterday, with this queer suffocating hysteria on me – partly, I think, from not writing prose – stories, my novel – I walked out with Ted in the dense humid air. He stopped by a tree on the street. There on bare ground, on its back, scrawny wings at a desperate stretch, a baby bird, fallen from its nest, convulsed in what looked like a death-shudder. I was sick with its hurt, nauseous. Ted carried it home cradled in his hand, and it looked out with a bright dark eye. We put it in a small box of cardboard, stuffed with a dishtowel & bits of soft paper to simulate a nest. The bird shook & shook. It seemed to be off balance, fell on its back. Every moment I expected the breath in its scrawny chest to stop. But no. We tried to feed it with bread soaked in milk on a toothpick, but it sneezed, didn't swallow. Then we went downtown & bought fresh ground steak, very like worm shapes, I thought. As we came up the stairs the bird squawked piteously & opened its yellow froggish beak wide as itself, so its head wasn't visible behind the fork-tongued opening. Without thinking, I shoved a sizeable piece of meat down the bird's throat. The beak closed on my fingertip, the tongue seemed to suck my finger, & the mouth, empty, opened again. Now I feed the bird fearlessly with meat & bread & it eats often & well, sleeping inbetween two-hourly feedings & looking a bit more like a proper bird. However small, it is an extension of life, of sensibility & identity. When I am ready for a baby it will be wonderful. But not until then. Wickedly didn't do German for the last two days, in a spell of perversity & paralysis.

Last night Ted & I did PAN for the first time in America. We were rested, warm, happy in our work & the overturned brandy glass responded admirably, oddly, often with charming humor. Even if our own hot subconscious pushes it (It says, when asked, that it is "like us"), we had more fun than a movie. There are so many questions to ask it. I wonder how much is our own intuition working, and how much queer accident, and how much 'my father's spirit.' PAN informed us my book of poems will be published by Knopf, not World (They are 'liars' at World – a strange note: do I feel this?) Also: fifty poems for my book. We will have two sons before we have a girl & should name the boys Owen, or Gawen, the girl Rosalie. Pan recited a poem of his own called 'Moist', stated his favorite poem of Ted's is "Pike" ("I like fish", and of mine is "Mussel-Hunter" ("Kolossus likes it.") Kolossus is Pan's "family god." He advises me to 'lose myself in reading' when depressed (it's the 'hot weather') and claims my novel will be about love, & I should start writing it in November. Among other penetrating observations, Pan said I should write on the poem-subject 'Lorelei' because they are my 'Own Kin'. So today, for fun, I did so, remembering the plaintive German song mother used to play & sing to us beginning "Ich weiss nicht was soll es bedeuten ... " The subject appealed to me doubly (or triply): the German legend of the Rhine sirens, the Sea-Childhood symbol, and the death-wish involved in the song's beauty. The poem devoured my day, but I feel it is a book poem & am pleased with it. <u>Must</u> agonizingly begin prose – an irony, this paralysis, while day by day I do poems – and also other reading – or I will be unable to speak human speech, lost as I am in my inner wordless Sargasso.

<u>Monday: July 7</u>: I am evidently going through a stage in beginning writing similar to my two months of hysteria in beginning teaching last fall. A sickness, frenzy of resentment at everything, but myself at the bottom. I lie wakeful at night, wake exhausted with that sense of razor-shaved nerves. I must be my own doctor. I must cure this very destructive paralysis & ruinous brooding & daydreaming. If I want to write, this is hardly the way to behave – in horror of it, frozen by it. The ghost of the unborn novel is a Medusa-head. Witty or simply observant character notes come to me. But I have no idea how to begin. I shall, perhaps, just begin. I am somewhere in me sure I should write a good 'book poem' a day – but that is nonense – I go wild when I spend a day writing a bad twelve lines – as I did yesterday. My danger, partly, I think, is becoming too dependent on Ted. He is didactic, fanatic – this last I see most when we are with other people who can judge him in a more balanced way than I – such as Leonard Baskin, for example. It is as if I were sucked into a tempting but disastrous whirlpool. Between us there are no barriers – it is rather as if neither of us – or especially myself – had any skin, or one skin between us & kept bumping into and abrading each other. I enjoy it when Ted is off for a bit. I can build up my own inner life, my own thoughts, without his continuous 'What are you thinking? What are you going to do now?' which makes me promptly & recalcitrantly stop thinking and doing. We are amazingly compatible. But I must be myself – make myself & not let myself be made by him. He gives orders – mutually exclusive: read ballads an hour, read Shakespeare an hour, read history an hour, think an hour & then 'you read nothing in hour-bits, read things straight through'. His fanatacism & complete lack of balance & moderation is illustrated by his stiff neck got from his 'exercises' – which evidently are strenuous enough to disable him.

Another grey day. The small black bird sneezing, jumping frantically out of his box & falling over his feet onto his head – can't walk, can't fly. What to do? I sit with him under this book, dozing on my stomach between my thighs. Yesterday – a sick suffocating day – we went on a green drive through 'backwoods' New England to Chesterfield Gorge, where our odd Child's Park rocks are supposed to come from. A green gloom – a sog-needled pine wood falling sheer away in rocks to a rocky bottom – a 'roll-rock highroad' – amber water clear, sluicing over oval & round stones – odd potholes & wavy formations worn in the rocks – how old? how old? We saw ants, at the river edge, & walked in our sneakers over the stones. The water, brown, peaty-green. A black frog – as I imagine obsidian-carvings – crouched on a stone. A stream welled deep in lush thick grass clumps. On the path we found a dead mole – the first I have ever seen – a tiny creature with bare flat feet, looking like a tiny man's, and pallid white pushy-looking hands – a delicate snout & its sausage-shaped body all covered with exquisite grey-blue velvety fur. We also found a dead red squirrel, perfect, its eye glazed in death, and stiff. I felt somehow nonexistent – had a sudden joy in talking to a grease-stained husky garage mechanic boy. He seemed real. Unless the self has enormous centering power, it flies off in all directions through space without the bracing & regulating tensions of necessary work, other people & their lives. But I won't get my writing schedule from outside – it must come from within. I'll leave off poems for a bit – finish the books I'm now in the middle of (at least five!) do German (that I can do) & write a kitchen article (for Atlantic's Accent on Living?), a Harper's Cambridge Student Life article – a story 'The Return' & suddenly attack my novel from the middle. O for a plot.

Wednesday: July 9: Freshly bathed, it being early for once & not too hot. We are recovering after a week of the bird. Last night we killed him. It was terrible. He wheezed, lay on one side like a stove-in ship in his shit streaks, tail feathers drabbled, rallying to open his mouth, convulsing. What was it? I held him in my hand, cradling his warm heart-beat & feeling sick to the pit of my stomach: Ted no better – I let him take the bird for a day & he was as sick as I. We hadn't slept for a week, listening for his scrabble in the box, waking at blue dawn & hearing him flutter his pin-feather wings against the cardboard sides. We couldn't see what was wrong with his leg – only that it had folded, useless, under his stomach. We walked out through the park – not wanting to go back to the house & the sick bird. We went to the tree where we'd found him & looked up to see if there was a nest – we'd been too upset to look when we picked him up a week ago. From a dark hole about ten feet up in the trunk a small brownish birdface looked, then vanished. A white shit shot out in a neat arc onto the sidewalk. So that was where our little bird had his habit of backing to the edge of his papers. I resented the hale whole birds in the tree. We went home: the bird peeped feebly, rallied to peck at our fingers. Ted fixed our rubber bath hose to the gas jet on the stove & taped the other end into a cardboard box. I could not look & cried & cried. Suffering is tyrannous. I felt desperate to get the sickly little bird off our necks, miserable at his persistent pluck & sweet temper. I looked in. Ted had taken the bird out too soon & it lay in his hand on its back, opening & shutting its beak terribly & waving its upturned feet. Five minutes later he brought it to me, composed, perfect & beautiful in death. We walked in the dark blueing night of the park, lifted one of the druid stones, dug a hole in its crater, buried him & rolled the stone back. We left ferns & a green firefly on the grave, felt the stone roll of our hearts.

Prose writing has become a phobia to me: my mind shuts & I clench. I can't, or won't, come clear with a plot. Must put poetry aside & begin a story tomorrow, today was useless, a wash of exhaustion after the bird. Always excuses. I wrote what I consider a 'book poem' about my runaway ride in Cambridge on the horse Sam: a 'hard' subject for me, horses alien to me, yet the dare-devil change in Sam & my hanging on god knows how is a kind of revelation: it worked well. Hard as my little gored picador poem was hard. But now I can't write as I used to – generally, philosophically, with "thoughts that found a mare of mermaid hair / tangling in the tide's green fall". – I have to write my "Lorelei" – to <u>present</u> the mermaids, invoke them. Make them real. I write my good poems too fast – they are on objects, not <u>themes</u>, thus concrete, limited. Good enough, but I must extend. I must start outlining a story plot: obviously it takes time – I half expect to fly to the typewriter & begin. Central conflict – my life is full of it. Start there. Marriage: Courtship. Jealousy. Settings I know: try Wellesley – suburbia. Cambridge apartment: Lou Healy, <u>Sat Eve Post</u> style. Jealousy: sister of newlywed husband. Poor poet. Couple divided over baby: why fear? Not like other men. Suburban neighborhood. I have fragments. Vignettes. Mrs. Spaulding is a story herself. I must note backgrounds jobs against which my people can move. Plagiarism in college. Young teacher. Decision to make. Start with that: 15 to 20 pages a week. Why not? Ambivalent position. Romance involved. Campus setting. I know this. Make a page of story plots & subjects tomorrow. That's what – a paragraph on each – style & sort.

Also several on "The Return". Use Baskin. Ho ho. Everyone here. Aaron's cocktail party. S————, James & Joan triangle. From whose point of view? Think, Think. Study sympathy point of view – emotional center –

<u>Saturday: July 12</u>: I feel a change in my life: of rhythm & expectancy, and now, at 11 in the morning, tired, very, yet steady after our great talk last night. A change has come: will it tell, a month from now, a year from now? It is, I think, not a false start. But a revision of an old, crippling delusion into a sturdy-shoed, slow-plodding common sense program. Yesterday was the nadir. All day I had been sitting at an abstract poem about mirrors & identity which I hated, felt chilled, desperate, about, my month's momentum (over 10 poems in that time) run down, a rejection from <u>The Kenyon</u> sealing hopelessness. I began, realizing poetry was an excuse & escape from writing prose. I looked at my sentence notes for stories, much like the notes jotted here on the opposite page: I picked the most 'promising' subject – the secretary returning on the ship from Europe, her dreams tested & shattered. She was not gorgeous, wealthy, but small, almost stodgy, with few good features & a poor temperament. The slicks leaned over me: demanding romance, romance – should she be gorgeous? Should Mrs. Aldrich, so normal & plodding & good with her seven children, have an affair with young, sweet Mr. Cruikshank" across the street? I ran through my experience for ready-made 'big' themes: there were none: E——'s abortion? Marty's lack of a child? Sue Weller's weepy courtship with Whitney? All paled, palled – a glassy coverlid getting in the way of my touching them. Too undramatic. Or was my outlook too undramatic? Where was life? It dissipated, vanished into thin air, & my life stood weighed & found wanting because it had no ready-made novel plot, because I couldn't simply sit down at the typewriter & by sheer genius & will power begin a novel dense & fascinating today & finish next month. Where, how, with what & for what to begin? No incident in my life seemed ready to stand up for even a 20 page story. I sat paralyzed, feeling no person in the world to speak to, but off totally from humanity in a self-induced vacuum. I felt sicker & sicker. I couldn't happily be anything but a writer & I couldn't be a writer: I couldn't even set down one sentence: I was paralyzed with fear, with deadly hysteria. I sat in the hot kitchen, unable to blame lack of time, the sultry July weather, anything but myself. The white hardboiled egg, the green head of lettuce, the two suave pink veal chops dared me to do anything with them, to make a meal out of them, to alter their single, leaden identity into a digestible meal. I had been living in an idle dream of <u>being a writer</u>. And here stupid housewives & people with

polio were getting their stories into the Satevepost. I went into Ted, utterly shattered, & asked him to tackle the veal chops. And burst into tears. Useless, goodfornothing. We talked it out, analyzed it. I felt the lead tons of the world lift. I have been spoiled, so spoiled by my early success with Seventeen, with Harper's & Mademoiselle, I figured if I ever worked over a story & it didn't sell, or wrote a piece for practise & couldn't market it, something was wrong. I was gifted, talented – oh, all the editors said so – so why couldn't I expect big returns for every minute of writing. A cracking good story a week? I demanded a 20-page plot about a top-of-the-head subject that didn't engage me. Now, every day, I am writing 5 pages, about 1,500 words on a small vignette, a scene charged with emotion, conflict & that is that: to make these small bits of life, which I discarded as trivial, not serious 'plot material'. I cannot correct faults in rhythm, in realization – in thin air. I spend 3 hours & shall from now on, in writing, not letting a bad or slight subject engulf the day. I began with a woman menaced by a dog this morning. I bite off what I can chew. The first try is awkward, gets little mood, but it begins. Nora Marple is the sort of woman dogs growl at. Here life begins. Out of 30 exercises, perhaps a character: out of 100, perhaps the seed of a story. I shall doggedly work, wait & expect the minimum.

Thursday: June 17:[n] After two days of no-schedule, disrupted by our seeing Baskins, Rodman[n] & the intolerable stuffy lazy Clark's with their mean, mealy-mouthed Quakerism, I sit down on a clear cold sunny day with nothing to beef at except the slick sick feeling which won't leave. It comes & goes. I feel I could crack open mines of life – in my daily writing sketches, in my reading & planning, if only I could get rid of my absolutist panic. I have, continually, the sense that this time is invaluable, & the opposite sense that I am paralyzed to use it: or will use it wastefully & blindly. I have all the world's reading on my back, instead of a possible book a day. I must discipline myself to concentrate on certain authors, certain fields, lest I welter, knowing nothing and everything. Across the street there is the chink, chunk of hammers on nails, the tap of hammers on wood. Men are on the scaffolding. I am neither a no-nothing nor a bohemian, but I find myself wishing, wishing, to have a corner of my own: something I can know about, write about well. All I have ever read thins and vanishes: I do not amass, remember. I shall this year work for steady small growth, nothing spectacular, & the ridding of this panic. The windows shake in their sockets from some unheard detonation. Ted says they are breaking the sound barrier. Somewhere I have a vision, not of thwarting, of meanness, but of fulness, of a maturer, riper placidity, a humor to bear nightmare, an ordering, reshaping faculty which steadies & fears not. A housewife – with children & writing & reading in the midst of business, but fully, with good friends who are makers in some way. The more I do, the more I can do. I should choose first the few things I wish to learn: German, poets & poetry, novels & novelists, art & artists. French also. Are they making or breaking across the street there? All fears are figments: I make them up.

(July 17) Marianne Moore sent a queerly ambiguous spiteful letter in answer to my poems & request that she be a reference for my Saxton. So spiteful it is hard to believe it: comments of absolutely no clear meaning or help, resonant only with great unpleasantness: "don't be so grisly", "I only brush away the flies" (this for my graveyard poem), "you are too unrelenting" (in "Mussel-Hunter"). And certain pointed remarks about "typing being a bugbear", so she sends back the poems we sent. I cannot believe she got so tart & acidy simply because I sent her carbon copies ("clear", she remarks). This, I realize, must be my great & stupid error – sending carbons to the American Lady of Letters. Perhaps I thus queered my chance of a Saxton. I hope not. O such clear days & earliness should be the repository for work & work. There is no heartening in the mail. The Baskins Sunday – we walked over, was desultory, Esther in a sullen, or sick mood. Ted & I sat on the grass under the trees by the back porch, Esther on the chaise with the blond, blue-eyed naked cherub Tobias whom we watched, admired & centered our afternoon around. Janet Aaron came. Tan very brown, lean as a rake, with her raspy, sarcastic drawl – she looks like a woman who has found it ridiculous to commit herself to a single emotional stance in anything, but must always ride high heavy irony. Tobias spent the afternoon opening her wicker pocket book & spreading its contents on the grass – pennies, film wrapped in silver paper, a gaudy slick postcard of a man fishing, green stamps (Tobias got these stuck to his stomach & rear), two lipsticks, a compact, pencils (he appropriated these). When the scraps of paper & ruck were all spread in the grass, Tobias sprinkled dirt joyously in the bowl of watermelon. Leonard & Esther seem to me so strong – how have they agreed to be so strong – Esther is dying, I guess. I think much of her. She needs to urinate every half-hour & didn't go in, but told Ted to go look at Tobias in the rubber-tub of water while she shakily stood & let down her pants & sat at the side of the chaise, letting the urine dribble into the grass, her back pale, with red blotches, perhaps from sitting so. Leonard & Ted threw green small apples fallen from the tree at the bust of the laurelled, rotund poet Laureate. Leonard mimicked

Tony: "I haven't gone into the physiology of this." Ted hit the Laureate square on the chin. Janet left: she knows Isabella Gardner (niece, great-niece? of the Boston museum Isabella), some poet named John Hay. The afternoon waned. Leonard took Janet & Ted & me to his studio in the long brick carriage house. The doorway was overgrown with leaves, the room inside light, with a green overcast from the leaves bordering the windows. Dead men, bronzes, lay in an irregular row on the floor. Two stone-carvings stood on pedestals – one – the 'Ricardo de Napoli'? a smiling, bald wise merchanty man on a nubbled pillar, with an exquisitely carved penis the only other protuberance on the oblong column beside his head. "Deàth, Sated" – an apish, thick, hunched, barrel-set monster with sketched stare & grimace sketched white on the grey stone. Then, on its back on two sawhorses, dominating the room, a great angel, wingless. The floor was slippery with shavings. Leonard got Ted to lift the angel & Janet & I cleared the shavings from under its thick-blocked yet uncarven feet. Upright, the angel shouldered us into the corners & dominated the room. A sketch, profile, hung on the wall, showed the angel's outline superimposed on the numbered layers of laminated walnut wood. The angel was half again as high as we were, stood, head bald, eyes orientally hooded, face smoothed, smile wise beyond sorrowing, arms folded & belly rounded, weight lofted up on firm, slender arch of legs as if he stood on inches of air. His shoulders were pegged to receive the wings, the rich dark-honey walnut wood glows golden in my memory. In the corner, the square-edged wing-shapes, like the rockers of a child's wooden rocking-horse, uncarved & still crude. What to do but take it in, in praise, amaze. I like the stone-carvings best. Esther seemed weary. Janet left. I helped Esther to the door, she leaning on my arm, shaking, using her black cane with the gilt eagle-head. The screen door opened out, pushing us off the steps, but she balanced, the door scraping her as Lester opened it. "It's terribly hard." "I know, I know," Leonard almost impatiently, hushed her, took her in. We shilly-shallied about supper, left then, for the promise of meeting again tomorrow over Rodman. Monday I wrote for the third day a beginning of a piece that pleased me, instead of leaving me dead-cold & despairing, caring nothing. A flowery beginning to the runaway horse. I must finish it this morning: have done no writing but caught up here, & am already wasting my German hours. Monday I baked a cake, vanilla, with lemon icing. It was raining & seems to have rained all month. I sat at Baskins with Esther, watching her undress & wash Tobias. Rodman came in with Baskin: a surprise: no fat oily Jewish intellectual but a thin, wiry, tan fellow with dark, queerly vulnerable brown eyes, very lean, almost hollow-chested. His girl strangely simian, self-possessed, pretty and sevenish, green-eyed, with thick brown curly hair. She drew pictures – odd ladies under stars in whirly skirts. Their pug dog, Pudgy, they left outside tied to a wicker garden chair in the failing wet twilight. For the first time we were with Baskins when they were with somebody that knew them less than we. We ate cheese & ham sandwiches, fruit compote & my cake. Baskin ragged Rodman: "You're so vulnerable," repented, & showed him photographs, and us, of his drawings, wood cuts & sculptures. Rodman had an article on James Kearns, Aubrey Schwartz & Baskin in Arts in America. I liked Schwartz's "Crying Vendor," Baskin's "Darkened Man". How much of horror, of despair, of death, springs from Esther's shaking, dying, muscles going, bit by bit. We took Rodman to his hotel & came back. A magical evening, Esther talked to me: Tobias a curse & a blessing. She got much worse in her seventh month, couldn't walk – she misses carrying him very much, In the kitchen, Leonard carved at a woodblock, talked to Ted. Likes Ted's poem "Pike" & will do a broad sheet of it he says. We looked, after midnight, toward two, through one magnificent volume of Flora Londonensis, or something like – magnificent flowers, queer & delightful writing about their use, habitats. We left with "Tobias & the Angel", "Man with Forsythia", "Avarice" – the priest under the wolf-head, and several fine cuts of Blake & Samuel Palmer. I almost don't want to go back, for fear all meetings must fall short of this one. Rodman for breakfast Tuesday – his little girl leaving her scrambled eggs & soggy toast, Pudgy eating some vile dogfood ("the best") in the kitchen & Rodman in a too-bright, too-crisp cotton checked shirt, socks & leather sandals, drinking much coffee & we dragging bit by bit, information out of him. Although he has authored anthologies of poetry, the authorative book on Haiti (& has one appearing on Mexico this fall), he seems to know everything about nothing. Divorced from his wife (a wild society, motor-cycling Polack), he seems petrified, with no emotional center, no deep flux of rapport. Serious, tenacious, scared: "Going to Martha's Vineyard – I play tennis, four, five hours a day." His child, too wise, too much his puppet

Saturday: July 19: Paralysis still with me. It is as if my mind stopped & let the phenomena of nature-shiny green rosebugs and orange toadstools & screaking woodpeckers – roll over me like a juggernaut – as if I had to plunge to the bottom of non-existence, of absolute fear, before I can rise again. My worst habit is my fear & my destructive rationalizing. Suddenly my life which always had clearly defined immediate & long-range objectives – a Smith scholarship, a Smith degree, a won poetry or story contest, a

Fulbright, a Europe trip, a lover, a husband – has, or appears to have none. I dimly would like to write (or is it to have written?) a novel, short stories, a book of poems. And fearfully, dimly, would like to have a child: a bloodily breached twenty-year plan of purpose. Lines occur to me & stop dead: "The tiger lily's spotted throat." And then it is an echo of Eliot's "The tiger in the tiger pit," to the syllable & the consonance. I observe: "The mulberry berries redden under leaves." And stop. I think the worst thing is to exteriorize these jitterings & so will try to shut up & not blither to Ted. His sympathy is a constant temptation. I am made to be busy, gay, doing crazy jobs & writing this & that – stories & poems & nursing babies. How to catapult myself into this? When I stop, moving, other lives & single-track aims shoulder me into shadow. I am fixed, fixated on neatness – I can't take things as they come, or make them come as I choose. Will this pass like a sickness? I wish I could get some womanly impartial advice on this. Defensively, I say I know nothing: lids shut over my mind. And this is the old way of lying: I can't be responsible, I know nothing. Grub-white mulberries redden under leaves. Teaching was good for me: it structured my mind & forced me to be articulate. If I don't settle my trouble from within, no outside shower of fortune will make the grass grow. I feel under opiates, hashish – heavy with paralysis – all objects slipping from numb fingers, as in a bad dream. Even when I sit at my typewriter, I feel as if what I wrote were written by an imbecile ten miles off. I am on the bird now, and have been for two days; I have written eighteen pages of confused repetitious observation: Miriam felt this, Owen said that, the bird did this. I have not gotten to the dramatic part where they kill & bury the bird whose sickness has come to dominate their lives. I am sure of the solidity of the subject, but not sure of the emotional line & crisis of my story: yet it will be a story. Tomorrow morning I will finish it & begin it over again, drawing structure out of it. I must be ghastly to live with. Incompetence sickens me to scorn, disgusts me, & I am a bungler, who has taken a bad turn in fortune – rejected by an adult world, part of nothing – of neither an external career of Ted's – his internal career when written out, perhaps – nor a career of my own, nor, vicariously, the life of friends, nor part of motherhood – I long for an external view of myself & my room to confirm its reality. Vague aims – to write – fall stillborn. I sense a talent, sense a limited fixity of view stifling me now. I would be supremely happy, I tell myself, if I could only get 'in the swing' of writing stories. I have two ideas: bless them – enough for a summer: a serious bird-story where the bird becomes a tormenting spirit & by its small sick pulse darkens & twists two lives – and the story I'll get all the factual background for when I visit

Spaulding's on the Cape: I want to learn <u>how</u> she built & designed those cottages. Work & work on human interest of how she'll get a house herself. Saving her pennies, antiques – Lester's illnesses. Humbly, I can begin these things. Start in two realities that move me, probe their depths, angles, dwell on them. I want to know all kinds of people, to have the talent ready, practised, ordered, to use them, to ask them the right questions. I forget. I must not for get, not panic, but walk about bold & curious & observant as a newspaper reporter, developing my way of articulation & ordering, losing nothing, not sitting under a snail-shell.

<u>Sunday: July 27</u>: A grey day, cool, gentle. The strangling noose of worry, of hysteria, paralysis, is miraculously gone. Doggedly, I have waited it out, and doggedly, been rewarded. The prose does not prosper. I am rewriting an old story, a two-year old story, for "The Return", amazed at the lush, gaudy, giddy romantic rhetoric. I have written four or five quite good poems this past ten days, after a sterile hysterical ten days of non-production. The poems are, I think, deeper, more sobre, sombre (yet well colored) than any I've yet done. I've written two about Benidorm, which was closed to me as a poem subject till now. I think I am opening up new subjects & have, instead of a desperate high-keyed rhetoric, a plainer, realer poetry. I've about 29 poems for my book – a perpetual maximum it seems, but have discarded already half of those written in my hectic April vacation week, & several written since, my earliest being 'Faunus', 'Strumpet Song', which I wrote just after I met Ted. I have a peculiar and very ennervating fever, and have had, these last days. I have been ridiculously exhausted every morning, as if waking out of a coma, a queer deathlike state, when Ted brings me juice – and that, late enough, about ten o'clock, after ten hours of sleep. What is it? I am in the prime of life, my best years ahead to work in, to write poems & have children, and I am exhausted, a dull, electric burning dessicating my skull, my bloodstream. Will I write here in perfect health from our little Boston apartment in a month & more? I hope so. I feel I am beginning solidly & calmly to face the work ahead, expecting a minimum of produce with a maximum of work study & devotion. Read some of Hardy's poems with Ted at tea – a moving, highly kindred mind, Hardy's, especially 'An Ancient to Ancient's,' & Last Words to a Dumb Friend."

<u>August 1: Friday</u>: A new month. Hot, lush, tropical-rainy weather until today, today bright and clearly autumnal. The drive back to Hamp strangely repetitive – as if a regression, we almost asphyxiated by the faulty car.

Moving is upon us – also, the need to plunge deeply into life: it is not coming, it is perpetually here: here and gone. Dreaded the beach today with the Van Voris family & found it oddly charming. The substance of their family – I find stimulating, restful & rich in its own way: life in a natural sequence. Swam in the lukewarm limpid lake with the children, mainly playing. In dense, green-dark pinegroves sat pleasantly dazed in woodsmoke eating hamburgs & watermelon as if in a dream, conversation flowing to Paris, to Dublin, to California. I am not especially drawn to the children, but enjoyed them & wish I could get my life clear-edged so I could have some. I have a queer growing hunger for a baby. I feel an immaturity there, where a teen-age mother is farther advanced in womanhood than I. If this year I work & slave & get perhaps a practical skill together with writing, perhaps I will break open several worlds. The Van Voris's obviously plan a long stay: they have painted their house blissful shades – monterey red, white, hot orange & have fine-textured fabrics, burlapy linens with stylized prints & so on. They are good, Jacky, especially, whom I like. She is a solid girl, must work & work. I feel I can get so much from them by simply asking & listening & being <u>kind</u>. Story material. But write the story. Start with the here & now. The trip to the doctor, the x-ray & blood-test, seemed ironically to exorcise my fever. So I sat all evening in a wet suit, covered by Bill's eminently fine Dublin sweater. I wonder what one needs to sacrifice to have money for a home & children – is it a sacrifice? We need, both of us, to be alas, wealthy, simply to ever have a family. I must work on those women's story's & even stenotyping.

<u>August 2: Saturday</u>: I have a strong feeling of sickness, of which I am heartily sick. A life of doing nothing is death. Our life is ridiculously ingrown, sedentary. Ted has fanatic ideas – he wants to get thin & eats jam, sugar, sweet things in great amounts, simply walks, won't hear of any plausible or implausible exercise – <u>Later: Sunday morning</u>: it is as if I needed crises of some sort to exercise my fiber. I find all cool, clear & possible this morning. The great fault of America – this part of it – is its air of pressure: expectancy of conformity. It is hard for me to realize that Dot & Frank probably don't like Ted simply because he "won't get a job, a steady career." I have actually married exactly the sort of man I most admire. I will shut up about the future for a year & face work & encourage Ted's work in which I have the greatest of faith. I find myself horrified at voicing the American dream of a home & children – my visions of a home, of course, being an artist's estate, in a perfect privacy of wilderness acres, on the coast of Maine. I will no doubt be an impractical vagabond wife & mother, a manner of exile. I must work for

an inner serenity & stability which will bear me through the roughest of weathers externally: A calm, sustaining, optimistic philosophy which does not depend on a lifelong street address within easy driving distance of an American supermarket. And what fun to see England with Ted, to live in Italy, the South of France. If I can work this year like mad & get <u>one</u> woman's story published, a book of poems finished, I will be pleased: also, review & read German & French. Ironically, I have my own dream, which is mine, & not the American dream. I want to write funny & tender women's storys. I must be also, funny & tender & not a desperate woman, like mother. Security is inside me & in Ted's warmth. The smell & feel of him is worth a private fortune a year & how lucky I am – there are no rules for this kind of wifeliness – I must make them up as I go along & will do so.

<u>August 3: Sunday</u>: Felt a sudden ridiculous desire this morning to investigate the Catholic Church – so much in it I would not be able to accept: I would need a Jesuit to argue me – I am yet young, strong – must seek adventure & not depend on a companion. As for children – I'll be happier to have worked a year on writing, had a holiday – before I begin with them: once I have a baby, I won't be able to go on writing unless I have a firm foundation for it. The apartment, small as it is, will encourage little house work & cooking. Peace, I must tell myself, so it becomes an instinctive sense, peace is interior, radiating outward. I must keep note books of people, places – to recall them. Now: a plane drones, cars whoosh by, a few birds are chirping, a car door bangs, Ted has just thrown down a paper, sighed, & his pen is scratching rapidly. I must learn to lead my own life with him, but not lean on him for every move. <u>Note</u>: A woman of twenty-five feels the shock of her age simply by saying: if I live as long as I have already lived I shall be fifty. <u>Note</u>: The sort of woman who, when it begins to rain and while it rains, can think only of open windows – car windows, second floor windows, everywhere – open windows, and the rain pouring in at a vicious slant, ruining woodwork, wallpaper, books & furniture irreparably.

Yesterday we sat in the rose garden at sundown, a lovely incandescent time, reminiscent of Yorkshire, of those late afternoons in granchester meadows watching the water-voles. Rose leaves red, deep-red tipped, the flowers in the formal garden white, yellow, lit up by the horizontal rays. A rainbow in the fountain. A man approaches a young woman in Trafalgar Square: "Pardon me. But you're standing on the wrong side of the fountain". "Why, sir, what do you mean?" He takes her around & shows her the rainbow waiting as therapy? A venomous blow-up with the landlady, Mrs. Whalen. Insane accusations on her part, tremulous retorts & disgust on mine: a shaming encounter: behind our back, while we were at the Cape, she took the living-room rug to be cleaned (which I had told her we had a right to as floor covering, it being a 'furnished apartment') & substituted a filthy summer straw mat whose spots & stains loomed to meet the eye. She also took all the curtains. Deceit, insult, fury: last night we discovered this – or, rather, this morning – as we drove back at night through mist & cold black woods – I had a panic fear in the dark middle of the wood: we saw two deer: Ted one, I, that & another: white head & ears pricked up, eyes glowing green, trans-fixed by the car-lights. After the long rainy trip to & from NYC in one day Monday to pick up Warren, this was the last exhaustion – woke hollow at noon after a bare seven hours sleep – coffee only, & then we got stupidly involved reading magazines in the library at Smith which always sickens me: vitriol between critics, writers, politicians: an arsonist burned to black crisp depicted in Life in the space before death, his skin hanging & curling away like peeled black paint; cremation fires burning in the dead eyes of Anne Franck: horror on horror, injustice on cruelty – all accessible, various – how can the soul keep from flying to fragments – disintegrating, in one wild dispersal? We read, dibbled, for hours – on no food, fools we – shopped – peaches, corn. Then, as I half-sensed it, Mrs. Whalen had to come up – bad conscience about rug & curtains? Fury, rather, about our leaving the house windows open – she plumped her fat white bulk on the stairs, breathed, ranted – we let her go on – 'apartment in a mess, terrible shape' – we took her up: "what, exactly, was the mess?" She hemmed, hawed – greasy wall by kitchen sink, dirty venetian blind in bathroom – moved, obviously, by the desire to circuit accusations of spying: 'she'd just seen this on running through' – we'd left the apartment in apple pie order. 'Have you looked under the bed?' I said. I felt exhausted, starved, too stupid & sick to be clever & neat – she had no right to criticize the place – which is equivalent to criticizing my housework – no damage to the house: I would have picked up, but after the rug episode feel like smearing filth over it: I am not cool either. She yattered about Mrs. Yates" calling up: 'the bathroom screen fell down on Mrs. McKee's roof' – she fumed: Ted quietly said it had no doubt fallen down in the storm while we were away. Then we were 'uncooperative' – & so on. 'Get down off your high horse' she told me: "I'm just a kitchen maid, I never had an education ... " This spilled out, & Mrs. McKee's hand was apparent here – our companionable chats against Mrs. Whalen's compulsive laundry & lack of aesthetics had turned to Mrs. McKee's purpose. She, I learned, helped Whalen drag the 'heavy' rug upstairs – as if it was a favor to us! Then 'Jim won't speak to you, he's so mad. He's Irish.' As if greasy walls were his business – they will be now. The humor of this gradually seeps in on me – it shoots off, objectifies – the venomous three – Whalen, McKee & Yates: I shall write about this & cariacature them all three: spite, hate being the theme in its various unsightly forms – including my own spite, which is indignant, vicious – 'I don't see any dirty fingerprints on the wall,' Mrs. McKee observed when she was up here for tea a month ago – story from her point of view – spite & machinations of lazy, unhappy woman. 'Frog' collection – green plants. All fury, grist for the mill. I shall rest & , resting more & more, see it whole.

I am in the middle of a book on demoniacal possession – cases extremely diverting – but also inspiring – metaphors for states of human experience as well as the experience itself – as Aphrodite is the personification of lust & rending passion, so these visions of demons are the objective figures of angers, remorse, panic: Possession: Demoniacal & Other: Oesterreich."
(94) 'Four years ago C. was one day going home from her work when she met in the street the apparition of a woman which spoke to her. Suddenly something like a cold wind blew down her neck as she was speaking, & she at once became as if dumb. Later her voice returned, but very hoarse & shrill." . . . "She then loses the sense of her individuality". (106) Possession by fox: "Neither excommunication nor censing nor any other endeavor succeeded, the fox saying ironically that he was too clever to be taken in by such manœuvres. Nevertheless he consented to come out freely from the starved body of the sick person if a plentiful feast was offered to him. 'How was it to be arranged?' On a certain day at four o'clock there were to be placed in a temple sacred to foxes & situated twelve kilometres away two vessels of rice prepared in a particular way, of cheese, cooked with beans, together with a great quantity of roast mice & raw vegetables, all favourite dishes of magic foxes: then he would leave the body of the girl exactly at the prescribed time'. Of Achilles (Janet hypnotizes 'devil') (116) "Although the patient appeared possessed, his malady was not possession but the emotion of remorse. This was true of many possessed persons, the devil being for them merely the incarnation of their regrets, remorse, terrors & vices."

To brood over this, to use & change it, not let it flow through like a seive."
Our Boston flat we saw in rain yesterday – lovely afternoon with the Jacobs

girl talking of her work with problem children & adolescents in NYC – the place a dream, elegant view – better than we remembered it – four nights away: it waits, we will work.

August 28: Thursday: A chill clear morning. Yesterday's anger has clearer, finer edges now: I could have said more than I did better than I did, but in four days we will be off & all here will lose its emotional tension & become a flat memory only, to be ordered, embellished by the chameleon mind. Dreamed last night I was beginning my novel – "What is there to look to?" Dody Ventura said – a beginning conversation – then, a sentence, a paragraph, inserted first of all of description to 'place', to 'set' the scene: a girl's search for her dead father – for an outside authority which must be developed, instead, from the inside. Midnight: still tired, but curiously elated, as if absolved from suffocation – projects bubble: Boston & our flat seems as fine, finer than Widow Mangada's Mediterranean hideout or our Paris Left Bank room. Suddenly I like people, can be nice, natural. We lolled over supper: cold chicken, summer squash, cabbage – sat in the twilit rose garden – a cricket chirred from the ivy on the stone wall, stone flagstones between which grass grew long, roses of pink and yellow, color gone in the grey blueing twilight to a faintly luminous pallor, the fountain plinking, five arcs on the summer house temple, the stone lionhead set in the wall, a ferocious grimace set in stone. I think I am growing more casual – am I? Or is this a lull in a merry go round of panic blackouts, to take all for what it is & delight in the small pleasures – a good dog poem by Ted: a green afternoon with Esther Baskin & Tobias under the trees, apples fallen, rotting on the ground, reading her essay of the bat, Ted's proof of the pike poem – Tobias blond, pink, cherubic, smiling, crowing, crawling, taking the papers from my purse & scattering them about – an atmosphere of books, poems, wood engravings, statues. Tea & cookies at the Clarkes – they opening up, mimicking Mary's father – Mr. Godfrey, the old drunken lawyer in the stander-by of those days of fury I remember. Now we are quieter, placider, ageing. A day of hopes & frustrations – wherein we have, in effect, made & lost £300. A letter from the Guiness Brewery this morning saying Ted had won the first prize for the best poem in England by a living author this past year – an honor & a sum equalling his book's revenue. The phoneman came & installed the phone – to be "connected up at the central office later." We three left on the clear, sultry morning on the crest of promise, elation – rode a round on the swan boats trailed by squabbling, ravenous brown-speckled ducks, pontificating about novels, writing, ways of living. Walked Washington Street, turned away from dark, cavernous bars with "No Ladies Allowed." Crowds in Filene's. We sat over beers & swordfish & fried scallops in a Commercial Street tavern: gradually the sickening understanding grew on me that "The Thought-Fox" was not technically eligible for the money because it had first been published in The New Yorker in America, not Britain. We wandered, disconsolate across the broad, truck-crowded, railroad tracked Atlantic Street to the wharves – T-Wharf, with its sagging houses, rickety wooden balconies, windowboxes of petunias & geraniums. At the third floor "Blue Ship Tea Room" overlooking the harbor, we treated ourselves to delicious desserts & tea & read the menu advertising venison, whale & bear steak. The tables were covered with bright stylized Pequod-Moby Dick prints. Saw crates of crabs – lithe, shiny, spreckled, unloaded into barrels "to cook" the little syphylitic man loading them told me. One crab fell outside the crate, sidled to the edge of the wharf & dropped down, pale stomach up, into the black, garbage & oil slicked water to sink out of sight. We saw a cat, tiger, meowing by barrels of haddock heads in front of the ship-loading markets. Walked up Hanover Street: a surprising Italiana – children everywhere, on curbs, jumping through those new round hoops that serve to twirl in, jump through, roll & no doubt much more: Paul Revere mall – a flash reminisce of a Roman square – endless pastry shops – elaborate wedding cakes, inedible cream-filled cakes. We stopped at a clam bar, a sort of Italian fish & chip shop & had 5 quahogs apiece, sitting on red stools at the high narrow counter, watching the dark sallow-skinned boy whipping the quahogs open with a knife, loosen them & set them on a white, blue-patterned plate around half a lemon – salty, gritty, but good. Crossing under the great highway artery, past "Mama Anna's" where we went with the Sweeney's – we discovered the open markets – the first "foreign" market I've seen in America – cheaper than Paris, more highpowered than Benidorm – stacks of peaches, oranges, tomatoes, squash – each stall undercutting the other – peppers, onions – one-third, one-half cheaper than the posh Beacon Hill shops. Cellars-full of meat, chickens, beefs – overcoming, weight upon weight of goods – I must price, weigh, haggle. We bought pork, bananas, tomatoes. War is talked of again – Chinese communists, fareast-news breaks in grimly. Moonshot rivalry. Death sentence of negro stealing $1.95. How? Hatred, madness, bigotry. One cannot retreat. Miss America beauty pageant fashion chaos – three contestants wear same gown. Phone not on when we came home. A wearying comedy of errors. Dozed in heat. Rose exhausted to drink tea, make an apple pie. Luke & Ted talk in livingroom – I too tired – Boston: nooks, crannies. Stimuli, to discover, to expand – but also to contract, work – I have done nothing, little. This eight hundred dollars gleams, vanishes – irony upon the Saxton irony. I must rest this week end & start writing. Mellifluous Schumann. Eyes droop – what will come of this new year –?

Thursday: September 11: A pleasant day – clear, blue, early on, and magnificently fresh. Clouding over later, with a wicked wind. Yesterday was lost in a fog of pain, cramps, curses & dopey-sickness from too much useless bufferin. Time slips shockingly by with our 'schedule' unbegun as yet – and nothing but a whole year, undivided, ahead: the discipline demanded is enormous. I have been tired, feverish, cramped. We have spent a lot of money already – on shoes (I bought mine too tight as usual & got frightful heel blisters from my 'walking shoes' on our first walk at midnight through Scollay Square – we saw gypsies, madams, a paddy-wagon, a lit tattoo-shop, a fat man, facing the window straddled on a chair, head propped on folded arms, braced, wincing, as the tattooer (– a beautiful devoted man with oddly pale, kindled blue-eyes whom I pointed out yesterday, when he wasn't at work, as a murderer-type) took up a fresh electric needle. We joined a crowd at the window – a guy beside us said: "Never paid a thing for a tattoo but this one on my arm. Five dollars. A tiger head." The models of the tattoers art were pinned on the wall in the form of drawings – girls, American flags, innumerable serpents. It is late now – our kitchen curtains are up – cutting off kitchen distractions from my workroom: crisp, starched. I love the dark green of the walls, the bare floors, the dark woods & comfortable couch. Impressions are so rich, so new, hard to assemble – the assault of experience – innumerable characters seen, overheard, edges of multitudinous lives – sights: the grotesque & ornate brownstone Trinity Church next & under the enormous clean grey granite of John Hancock. Beethoven's piano sonata twenty-six, twenty-seven sound from the bedroom. How little one knows, learns – I cling to compulsive orders, am easily nonplussed, confused, suspicious. Already I look at job adds. I must write – every morning, an^n exercise, meticulous recapturing, embroidering on an event, an experience the day before: our goldfish dying – our freeing the last one in the Public Garden pond last night, watching the ridiculous, funny snowwhite Aylesbury duck billing among two proud, hostile white swans – no other common brown ducks to be seen – mucking about in the grass with its bill snorting even, like a hog at apples. After ten days of a comedy, frustrating, of errors with the phone company: this I must write up, I got furious – felt the whole order of reality and responsibility crumbling: wrote a succinct, eloquent letter to the 'manager'. I felt, glumly, nothing would happen, but the letter freed my anger, straitlaced in the jargon of decorum – quoting names of operators, times of calls, never saying "lies", but far worse, "misinformation". Today, about two, strange oceanic roars and diminuendos sounded over the previously dead line – a dial tone, dim ringings – although no numbers I dialed took effect. At last, after a ten-day silence in which the instrument had diminished to a ridiculous toy, a ring. "All-righty", a repairman said, utterly heartening. (all my senses are shaken up, tittillated, here) – I must force myself into new experiences – a good part-time job – not deadening, if any. I have not yet assimilated enough to retire, to write, alone. A paradox: life stimulates one, refreshes a sense of people, places, events – yet must be shut off during the actual writing time. Sonata no. 28. Liz Taylor is getting Eddie Fisher away from Debbie Reynolds who appears cherubic, round-faced, wronged, in pincurls and houserobe – Mike Todd barely cold. How odd these events affect one so. Why? Analogies? I would like to squander money on hair styling, clothes. Yet know power is in work and thought. The rest is pleasant frill. I love too much, too wholly, too simply for any cleverness. Use imagination. Write and work to please. No criticism or nagging. Shut eyes to dirty hair, ragged nails. He is a genius. I his wife.

Sunday morning: September 14: two weeks here have inexplicably withered away. Yesterday we both bogged in a black depression – the late nights, listening sporadically to Beethoven piano sonatas – ruining our mornings, the afternoon sun too bright and accusing for tired eyes, meals running all off-schedule – and me with my old panic fear sitting firm on my back – who am I? What shall I do? The difficult time between twenty-five years of school routine and the fear of dilatory, dilotante days – the city calls – experience and people call, and must be shut out by a rule from within. Tomorrow, Monday, the schedule must begin – regular meals, shoppings, launderings – writing prose and poems in the morning, studying German and French in the afternoon, reading aloud an hour, reading in the evenings. Drawing and walking excursions. I must be happy first in my own work and struggle to that end, so my life does not hang on Ted's. The novel would be best to begin this next month. My <u>New Yorker</u> poems were a minor triumph. Who else in the world could I live with & love? Nobody. I picked a hard way which has to be all self-mapped out & must <u>not</u> nag (ergo: mention haircuts, washes, nail-filings, future money-making plans, children – anything Ted doesn't like: this is nagging); he, of course, can nag me about light meals, straight-necks, writing exercises, from his superior seat. The famed & fatal jealousy of professionals – luckily he is ahead of me so far I never need fear the old superiority heel-grinding – in weak-neck impulse. Perhaps fame will make him insufferable. I will work for its not doing so. Must work & get out of paralysis – write & show him nothing: novel, stories & poems. A misty, furred, grey-sunny Sunday. Must lose paralysis & catapult into small efforts – life for its own sake. A nightmare sequence – jazz breaking through Beethoven, soap opera downstairs shattering profound vocational medita-tion. Do we, vampire-like, feed on each other? A wall, sound-proof, must mount between us. Strangers in our study, lovers in bed. Rocks in the bed. Why? He sleeps like a sweet-smelling baby, passion gone into the heat of his skin. If I write eleven more good poems I will have a book. Try a poem a day: send book to Keightley – ten more during the year – a fifty poem book – while the crass Snodgrasses publish & gain fame. Ted fought for publication before his book which was an open sesame – gathering prizes & fame. And so do I now fight – but have broken three doors open since June: <u>New Yorker</u>, <u>Sewanee</u> & <u>Nation</u>: one a month. I feel, suddenly today, the absence of fear – the sense of slow, plodding self-dedication. This book led me through a year of struggle & mastery. Perhaps the book I am about to begin will do something akin. Smile, write in secret, showing no one. Amass a great deal. Novel. Poems. Stories. Then send about. Let no book-wishing show – work. I must move myself first, before I move others – a woman famous among women.

<u>Monday: September 15</u>: Brag of bravado, & the fear is on. A panic, absolute & obliterating: here all diaries end – the vines on the brick wall opposite end in a branch like a bent green snake. Names, words, are power. I am afraid. Of what? Life without having lived, chiefly. What matters? Wind wuthering in a screen. If I could funnel this into a novel, this fear, this horror – a frog sits on my belly. Stop & ask why you wash, why you dress, you go wild – it is as if love, pleasure, opportunity surrounded me, and I were blind. I talk

hysterically – or feel I will explode: I am in a fix: how to get out of it? Some little daily external ritual – I am too ingrown – as if I no longer knew how to talk to anyone but Ted – sat with my face to a wall, a mirror. My odd publications here & there argue writing is no vain dream, but a provable talent – I am in a vicious circle – too much alone, with no fresh exterior experiences except the walking around, about, staring at people who seem, simply because they are other, to be enviable – the responsibility of my future weighs, terrifies. Why should it? Why can't I be pragmatic, common? At the end of a teaching day, no matter the reversals, I had earned ten dollars – motive enough, in many minds. I need a vocation & to feel productive & I feel useless. Ignorant. To develop writing when I feel my soul is bitty, scatty, tawdry? Why aren't I conceited enough to enjoy what I can do & not feel fear? Lawrence bodies the world in his words. Hope, careers – writing is too much for me: I don't want a job until I am happy with writing – yet feel desperate to get a job – to fill myself up with some external reality – where people accept phone bills, meal-getting, babies, marriage, as part of the purpose to the universe. A purposeless woman with dreams of grandeur. My one want: to do work I enjoy – must keep clear of any confiding in mother: she is a source of great depression – a beacon of terrible warning

Thursday: September 18: Much happier today – why? Life begins, minutely, to take care of itself – an odd impulse brings a flood of joy, life – queer nice slightly sinister people: at the tattooist's. Also, even though I got up 'late', nineish, on the wet grey day, & felt the usual morning sickness 'what shall I do today that is worthwhile?', I got right to work after coffee & wrote 5 pages analyzing P.D. – one or two well-turned sentences. Then I sat & read on my "Bird In The House" story which was so lumbering & bad I felt I could improve it – worked meticulously on 5 pages & felt better by lunch. A fine mail, even though I got a snotty letter from Weeks rejecting my snake-charmer ("although bewitched by the sinuosity, etc., etc.), for Ted had a lovely check of $150 for "Dick Straightup", which makes, with the "Thought-Fox Prize", about $1,000 earned this September. Walked out to deposit check & I got more & more drawn to the tattooist shop – it was chill, about to rain, but Ted acquiesced. We found the place with the display window on Scallay Square & stood outside, I pointing to the panther head, the peacocks, the serpents on the wall. The tattooist, with a pale, odd little fellow inside, were looking at us. Then the tattooist came to the door in black cowboy boots, a soiled cotton shirt & tight black chino pants. "You can't see good enough from out there. Come on in." We went, gog-eyed, into the little shop, brightly lit, tawdry: I shall spend all next morning writing it up. I got the man talking – about butterfly tattoos, rose tattoos, rabbit hunt tattoos – wax tattoos – he showed us pictures of Miss Stella – tattooed all over – brocade – orientals. I watched him tattoo a cut in his hand, a black, red, green & brown eagle & "Japan" on a sailor's arm, "Ruth" on a school-boy's arm – I almost fainted, had smelling salts. The pale, rather excellent little professorial man – who was trying out new springs in the machine, hung round about – rose tattoos, eagle tattoos spin in my head – we'll go back. Life begins to justify itself – bit by bit – slowly I'll build it.

Saturday: September 27: I shall end these pages, I hope, in a more placid, optimistic mind than heretofore. After yesterday's climax of frustration – dazing, humid heat, late rising, botched haircutting, overloading of groceries & staggering up the steep Hancock Street to the jeers of passing policemen, the insolence of an ugly little landlady when I asked, breathless & pained if she had a phone ("Ve don do dat here, let strangers into da livingroom" – whereupon she trotted up the steps & into the house as if I had a contagious disease, swept a well-aimed dust wad behind her, in my direction & slammed the door), the ride offered in the nick of time – Ted's depression, the laundry to collect, which got smutty on the line up stairs, the usual depressing call from mother, depressing because of her hardships at work, her unspoken nervousness about our fortunes, my lack of a job – and the sense of nothing written, nothing read, nothing done – after all this, today dawned cool, grey with consoling rain, limiting alternatives. We stayed in – writing, consolidating our splayed selves. I diagnosed, & Ted diagnosed my disease of doldrums – & I feel better, as if I can now start to cope: like a soldier, demobbed, I am cut loose of over twenty steady years of schooling & let free into civilian life – as yet, newly, I hardly know what to do with myself. I start, like a race horse at the bugle, or whatever, hearing about schools opening – I get weird impulses to rush to Harvard, to Yale, begging them to take me on for a Phd, a master's, anything – only to take my life out of my own clumsy hands. I am going to work, doggedly, all year, at my own pace, being a civilian, thinking, writing, more & more intensely, with more & more purpose, & not merely dreaming, ego-safe, about the magnificent writer I could be. I have worked hard today on my bird story – words come right, rhythms come right, here, there & it is a beginning of a new life.

October 14; Tuesday: A moment snatched, two & a half weeks later, chicken & squash ready in the oven for Ted's return from the library, back achey, eyes bleary from new job. I went out to three agencies a week ago Monday, got the first job I was interviewed for Tuesday – more hours than I wanted, & low pay, but with compensations of fascinating work & no home work – typing records in the psychiatric clinic at Mass. General, answering phones, meeting & dispatching a staff of over twenty-five doctors & a continual flow of patients – it is exhausting, now I'm new to it, but gives my day, & Ted's, an objective structure. Got a rejection of poems I thought a "sure thing" at the New Yorker & haven't had time or energy to brood – or write! But I figure the job is good for me – all my desires to be analyzed myself, except for occasional brief returns of the panic-bird – are evaporating: paradoxically, my objective daily view of troubled patients through the records objectifies my own view of myself. I shall try to enter into this schedule a wedge of writing – to expand it. I feel my whole sense & understanding of people being deepened & enriched by this: as if I had my wish & opened up the souls of the people in Boston & read them deep. A woman today – fat, fearing death – dreaming of three things – her dead father, her dead friend (dead in childbirth, rheumatic fever), her own funeral – she, in the coffin, & also standing & weeping among the onlookers. Her son falling downstairs & fracturing his skull, drinking poison (D.D.T.) – her mother in the house when it exploded, burning to death – Fear: the main god: fear of elevators, snakes, loneliness – a poem on the faces of fear. Relevant note from Defoe's Journal of the Plague Year: " ... it was the opinion of others that it (the plague) might be distinguished by the party's breathing up on a piece of glass, where, the breath's condensing, there might living creatures be seen by a microscope, of strange, monstrous & frightful shapes, such as dragons, snakes, serpents & devils, horrible to behold." – The chaemeras of the sick mind also.

[Appendix 14 contains Sylvia Plath's 'Hospital Notes' – ed.]

Names:	Helene Burm	Children's Names
Glen Fallows	Ida Budrow	Boys: Farrar
Mr. Moggio	Wilner Broadnax	Gawain
★Dody Ventura	Betty Mimno	Merlin
Spofford	Harlan Allard	Girls: Alison
Sara Burns (S.S.)	Bridget / Les Nawn	Gwyn
Gerard Fee	Jasper Miniter	Liadan
Nancy Veale	Albert Quern	Vivien
Joe McCoola	Florence Pursley	Marian

Mrs. Marple
M.B. Derr
Maurya Hughes
Chrystl
Madame Mesmin
Otto Emil
Glasby-Boole
Nettleton
Mrs. Whorley
Mrs. Groobey"
Melvina Keeler
Drusilla Fox
Alvina Walsh
Evelyn Smalley
Phillipa Forder
Gail Greenough
Heather Hyde
Lois Marshall
Myrtle McFague
Maurya Moher
Miriam Phelps
Priscilla Steele
Sadie Lane ★
Candy Garth
Myrtle Pettijohn

William Quigg
Roger Slawsby
Orrin Teed
Leona Weagle
Katherine Welby
Arvis Whitley
Sidney Whitkin
Morris Pliskin
Vernon Plumley
Thaxter Polk
Grace Ludden
George Lufkin
Hairn Kennett
Henry Kiggen
Rebecca Gormley
Cyril Greenidge
David Grell
Phyllis Griffin
Hazel Grigsby
Hyman Doodlesack
Primilla Greenleaf
Earl Dooks
Sadie Dooling
Herbert Fothergill
Isabella Foye

Barbara Higby, Higden
Elva Hogquist
Minna Holland

JOURNAL

12 December 1958 – 15 November 1959

——

In 1959, Plath worked part-time for the chairman of the department of Sanskrit and Indian studies at Harvard University, audited Robert Lowell's poetry writing course at Boston University, and continued therapy with Dr Ruth Beuscher. Plath and Hughes conceived Frieda Rebecca Hughes in June. During the summer, they drove across Canada and the United States to visit Plath's aunt Frieda Plath Heinrichs and her husband Walter J. Heinrichs in California. From 9 September to 19 November, Plath and Hughes were guests at Yaddo, an artist's colony in Saratoga Springs, New York. They moved back to England in December.

If I am going to pay money for her time & brain as if I were going
to a supervision in life & emotions & what to do with both, I am
going to work like hell, question, probe sludge & crap & allow
myself to get the most out of it.

Ever since Wednesday I have been feeling like a "new person".
Like a shot of brandy went home, a sniff of cocaine, hit me where
I live and I am alive & so-there. Better than shock treatment:
"I give you permission to hate your mother."

"I hate her, doctor." So I feel terrific. In a smarmy matriarchy
of togetherness it is hard to get a sanction to hate one's mother
expecially a sanction one believes in. I believe in RB's because
she is a clever woman who knows her business & I admire her. She
is for me "a permissive mother figure." I can tell her anything,
and she won't turn a hair or scold or withhold her listening which
is a pleasant substitute for love.

But although it makes me feel good as hell to express my hostility
for my mother, frees me from the Panic Bird on my heart and my
typewriter (why?), I can't go through life calling RB up from
Paris, London, the wilds of Maine long-distance: "Doctor, can I
still go on hating my mother?" "Of course you can: hate her hate
her hate her." "Thank you, doctor. I sure do hate her."

What do I do? I don't imagine time will make me love her. I can
pity her: she's had a lousy life; she doesn't know she's a walking
vampire, but that is only pity. Not love.

On top she is all smarmy nice: she gave herself to her children,
and now by God they can give themselves back to her: why should
they make her worry worry worry? She's had a hard life: married
a man, with the pre-thirty jitters on her, who was older than her
own mother, with a wife out West. Married in Reno. He got sick
the minute the priest told them they could kiss. Sick and sicker.
She figured he was such a brute she couldnt, didn't love him.
Stood in the shower forcing herself to enjoy the hot water on her
body because she hated his guts. He wouldn't go to a doctor,
wouldn't believe in God and heiled Hitler in the privacy of his home.
She suffered. Married to a man she didn't love. The Children were
her salvation. She put them First. Herself bound to the track
naked and the train called Life coming with a frown and a choo-choo
around the bend. "I am bloody bloody bloody. Look what they do to
me. I have ulcers, see how I bleed. My husband whom I hate is
in the hospital with gangrene and diabetes and a beard and they
cut his leg off and he disgusts me and he may live a cripple and
wouldn't I hate that. Let him die."(He died.)"The blood clot hit
his brain and wasn't it lucky he died because what a bother he'd
be around the house, a living idiot and me having to support him
in addition to the two children."

She came home crying like an angel one night and woke me up and
told me Daddy was gone, he was what they called dead, and we'd
never see him again, but the three of us would stick together
and have a jolly life anyhow, to spite his face. He didn't leave
hardly enough money to bury him because he lost on the stocks,
just like her own father did, and wasn't it awful. Men men men.

NOTES ON INTERVIEWS WITH RB: Friday, December 12th:

If I am going to pay money for her time & brain as if I were going to a supervision in life & emotions & what to do with both, I am going to work like hell, question, probe sludge & crap & allow myself to get the most out of it.

Ever since Wednesday I have been feeling like a "new person". Like a shot of brandy went home, a sniff of cocaine, hit me where I live and I am alive & so-there. Better than shock treatment: "I give you permission to hate your mother."

"I hate her, doctor." So I feel terrific. In a smarmy matriarchy of togetherness it is hard to get a sanction to hate one's mother especially a sanction one believes in. I believe in RB's because she is a clever woman who knows her business & I admire her. She is for me "a permissive mother figure." I can tell her anything, and she won't turn a hair or scold or withold her listening which is a pleasant substitute for love.

But although it makes me feel good as hell to express my hostility for my mother, frees me from the Panic Bird on my heart and my typewriter (why?), I can't go through life calling RB up from Paris, London, the wilds of Maine long-distance: "Doctor, can I still go on hating my mother?" "Of course you can: hate her hate her hate her." "Thank you, doctor. I sure do hate her."

What do I do? I don't imagine time will make me love her. I can pity her: she's had a lousy life; she doesn't know she's a walking vampire. But that is only pity. Not love.

On top she is all smarmy nice: she gave herself to her children, and now by God they can give themselves back to her: why should they make her worry worry worry? She's had a hard life: married a man, with the pre-thirty jitters on her, who was older than her own mother, with a wife out West. Married in Reno. He got sick the minute the priest told them they could kiss. Sick and sicker. She figured he was such a brute she couldn't, didn't love him. Stood in the shower forcing herself to enjoy the hot water on her body because she hated his guts. He wouldn't go to a doctor, wouldn't believe in God and heiled Hitler in the privacy of his home. She suffered. Married to a man she didn't love. The Children were her salvation. She put them First. Herself bound to the track naked and the train called Life coming with a frown and a choo-choo around the bend. "I am bloody bloody bloody. Look what they do to me. I have ulcers, see how I bleed. My husband whom I hate is in the hospital with gangrene and diabetes and a beard and they cut his leg off and he disgusts me and he may live a cripple and wouldn't I hate that. Let him die." (He died.) "The blood clot hit his brain and wasn't it lucky he died because what a bother he'd be around the house, a living idiot and me having to support him in addition to the two children."

She came home crying like an angel one night and woke me up and told me Daddy was gone, he was what they called dead, and we'd never see him again, but the three of us would stick together and have a jolly life anyhow, to spite his face. He didn't leave hardly enough money to bury him because he lost on the stocks, just like her own father did, and wasn't it awful. Men men men.

Life was hell. She had to work. Work and be a mother too, a man and a woman in one sweet ulcerous ball. She pinched. Scraped. Wore the same old coat. But the children had new school clothes and shoes that fit. Piano lessons, viola lessons, French horn lessons. They went to Scouts. They went to summer camp and learned to sail. One of them went to private school on scholarship and got good marks. In all honesty and with her whole unhappy heart she worked to give those two innocent little children the world of joy she'd never had. She'd had a lousy world. But they went to college, the best in the Nation, on scholarship and work and part of her money, and didn't have to study nasty business subjects. One day they would marry for love love love and have plenty of money and everything would be honey sweet. They wouldn't even have to support her in her old age.

The little white house on the corner with a family full of women. So many women, the house stank of them. The grandfather lived and worked at the country club, but the grandmother stayed home and cooked like a grandmother should. The father dead and rotten in the grave he barely paid for, and the mother working for bread like no poor woman should have to and being a good mother on top of it. The brother away at private school and the sister going to public school because there there were men (but nobody liked her until she was sweet sixteen) and she wanted to: she always did what she wanted to. A stink of women: lysol, cologne, rose water and glycerine, cocoa butter on the nipples so they won't crack, lipstick red on all three mouths.

Me, I never knew the love of a father, the love of a steady blood-related man after the age of eight. My mother killed the only man who'd love me steady through life: came in one morning with tears of nobility in her eyes and told me he was gone for good. I hate her for that.

I hate her because he wasn't loved by her. He was an ogre. But I miss him. He was old, but she married an old man to be my father. It was her fault. Damn her eyes.

I hated men because they didn't stay around and love me like a father: I could prick holes in them & show they were no father-material. I made them propose and then showed them they hadn't a chance. I hated men because they didn't have to suffer like a woman did. They could die or go to Spain. They could have fun while a woman had birth pangs. They could gamble while a woman skimped on the butter on the bread. Men, nasty lousy men. They took all they could get and then had temper tantrums or died or went to Spain like Mrs. So-and-so's husband with his lusty lips.

Get a nice little, safe little, sweet little loving little imitation man who'll give you babies and bread and a secure roof and a green lawn and money money money every month. Compromise. A smart girl can't have everything she wants. Take second best. Take anything nice you think you can manage and sweetly master. Don't let him get mad or die or go to Paris with his sexy secretary. Be sure he's nice nice nice.

So mother never had a husband she loved. She had a sick, mean-because-he-was-sick, poor louse, bearded-near-death "Man I knew once". She killed him (The Father) by marrying him too old, by marrying him sick to death and dying, by burying him every day since in her heart, mind and words.

So what does she know about love? Nothing. You should have it. You should get it. It's nice. But what is it?

Well, somebody makes you feel Secure. House, money, babies: all the old anchors. A Steady Job. Insurance against acts of god, madmen, burglars, murderers, cancer. Her mother died of cancer. Her daughter tried to kill herself and had to disgrace her by going to a mental hospital: bad, naughty ungrateful girl. She didn't have enough insurance. Something Went Wrong. How could the fates punish her so if she was so very noble and good?

It was her daughter's fault partly. She had a dream: her daughter was all gaudy-dressed about to go out and be a chorus girl, a prostitute too, prob-ably. (She had a lover, didn't she? She necked and petted and flew to New York to visit Estonian artists and Persian Jew wealthy boys and her pants were wet with the sticky white filth of desire. Put her in a cell, that's all you could do. She's not _my_ daughter. Not my nice girl. Where did that girl go?) The Husband, brought alive in dream to relive the curse of his old angers, slammed out of the house in rage that the daughter was going to be a chorus girl. The poor Mother runs along the sand beach, her feet sinking in the sand of life, her moneybag open and the money and coins falling into the sand, turning to sand. The father had driven, in a fury, to spite her, off the road bridge and was floating dead, face down and bloated, in the slosh of ocean water by the pillars of the country club. Everybody was looking down from the pier at them. Everybody knew everything.

She gave her daughter books by noble women called "The Case For Chas-tity". She told her any man who was worth his salt cared for a woman to be a virgin if she were to be his wife, no matter how many crops of wild oats he'd sown on his own.

What did her Daughter do? She slept with people, hugged them and kissed them. Turned down the nicest boys whom she would have married like a shot & got older and still didn't marry anybody. She was too sharp and smart-tongued for any nice man to stand. Oh, she was a cross to bear.

Now this is what I feel my mother felt. I feel her apprehension, her anger, her jealousy, her hatred. I feel no love, only the Idea of Love, and that she thinks she loves me like she should. She'd do anything for me, wouldn't she?

I have done practically everything she said I couldn't do and be happy at the same time and here I am, almost happy.

Except when I feel guilty, feel I shouldn't be happy, because I'm not doing what all the mother figures in my life would have me do. I hate them then. I get very sad about not doing what everybody and all my white-haired old mothers want in their old age.

So how do I express my hate for my mother? In my deepest emotions I think of her as an enemy: somebody who "killed" my father, my first male ally in the world. She is a murderess of maleness. I lay in my bed when I thought my mind was going blank forever and thought what a luxury it would be to kill her, to strangle her skinny veined throat which could never be big enough to protect me from the world. But I was too nice for murder. I tried to murder myself: to keep from being an embarrassment to the ones I loved and from living myself in a mindless hell. How thoughtful: Do unto yourself as you would do to others. I'd kill her, so I killed myself.

I felt cheated: I wasn't loved but all the signs said I was loved: the world said I was loved: the powers-that-were said I was loved. My mother had sacrificed her life for me. A sacrifice I didn't want. My brother and I made her sign a promise she'd never marry. When we were seven and nine. Too bad she didn't break it. She'd be off my neck.

I could pass her in the street and not say a word, she depresses me so. But she is my mother.

What to do with her, with the hostility, undying, which I feel for her? I want, as ever, to grab my life from out under her hot itchy hands. My life, my writing, my husband, my unconceived baby. She's a killer. Watch out. She's deadly as a cobra under that shiny greengold hood.

She is worried about me and the man I married. How awful we are, to make her worry. We had good jobs and were earning between us about six thousand a year. My god. And we deliberately and with full possession of our senses threw these jobs (and no doubt our careers as teachers) over to live without lifting a finger. Writing. What would we do: next year, twenty years from now: when the babies came. We got re-offered the jobs (lucky the colleges weren't perfectly furious with us and banging the doors shut) and turned them down again! We were crazy one way or another. What would the aunts and uncles say. What would the neighbors say? She would take that job teaching English at Smith: if only she had had a chance like that. She said this. She wants to be me: she wants me to be her: she wants to crawl into my stomach and be my baby and ride along. But I must go her way.

I'll have my own babies, thank you.

I'll have my own husband, thank you. You won't kill him the way you killed my father. He has a soul, he has sex strong as it comes. He isn't going to die so soon. So keep out. Your breath stinks worse than Undertaker's Basement when it comes to trying to rear a soul in its perfect freedom. You won't make my husband mad by raving about houses and babies. You won't make him ashamed by offering me $300 for a course in stenotyping for my birthday (by implication, so I can work and earn money because he probably never will). My husband supports me in soul, body and by feeding me bread and poems. I happen to love him. I can't hug him enough. I love his work and he fascinates me every minute because he is new and changing minute by minute and making new things every day. He wants me to change and make things too. What I make and how I change is up to me. He says Okay he is glad.

The Man: RB says: "Would you have the guts to admit you'd made a wrong choice?" In a husband. I would. But nothing in me gets scared or worried at this question. I feel good with my husband: I like his warmth and his bigness and his being-there and his making and his jokes and stories and what he reads and how he likes fishing and walks and pigs and foxes and little animals and is honest and not vain or fame-crazy and how he shows his gladness for what I cook him and joy for when I make something, a poem or a cake, and how he is troubled when I am unhappy and wants to do anything so I can fight out my soul-battles and grow up with courage and a philosophical ease. I love his good smell and his body that fits with mine as if they were made in the same body-shop to do just that. What is only pieces, doled out here and there to this boy and that boy, that made me like pieces of them, is all jammed together in my husband. So I don't want to look around any more: I don't need to look around for anything.

What doesn't he have? A steady job that brings in seven thousand a year. A private income. All the stuff that lots of money buys. He has his brains, his heat, his love for his work and his talent for it and no fortune and no steady income. How ghastly.

He can and will make money when he wants it and needs it. He won't put it first, that's all. Too much else comes first for him. Why should he put money first? I don't see why.

So he has all I could ask for. I could have had money and men with steady jobs. But they were dull, or sick, or vain, or spoiled. They made me gag in the long run. What I wanted was inside a person that made you perfectly happy with them if you were naked on the Sahara: they were strong and loving in soul and body. Simple and tough.

So I knew what I wanted when I saw it. I needed, after thirteen long years of having no man who could take all my love and give me a steady flow of love in return, a man who would make a perfect circuit of love and all else with me. I found one. I didn't have to compromise and accept a sweet balding insurance salesman or an impotent teacher or a dumb conceited doctor like mother said I would. I did what I felt the one thing and married the man I felt the only man I could love, and want to see do what he wanted in this world, and want to cook for and bear children for and write with. I did just what mother told me not to do: I didn't compromise. And I was, to all appearances, happy with him, mother thought.

This must baffle mother. How can I be happy when I did something so dangerous as follow my own heart and mind regardless of her experienced advice and Mary-Ellen Chase's disapproval and the pragmatic American world's cold eye: but what does he do for a living? He lives, people. That's what he does.

Very few people do this any more. It's too risky. First of all, it's a hell of a responsibility to be yourself. It's much easier to be somebody else or nobody at all. Or to give your soul to god like St. Therese and say: the one thing I fear is doing my own will. Do it for me, God.

There are problems and questions which rise to the surface out of this.

Mother: What to do with your hate for your mother and all mother figures? What to do when you feel guilty for not doing what they say, because, after all, they have gone out of their way to help you? Where do you look for a mother-person who is wise and who can tell you what you ought to know about facts of life like babies and how to produce them?

The only person I know and trust for this is RB. She won't tell me what to do: she'll help me find out and learn what is in myself and what I (not she) can best do with it.

435

I hate my mother: yet I pity her. How shall I act toward her without feeling a hypocrite? Or cruel?

* * *

Writing: My chain of fear-logic goes like this: I want to write stories and poems and a novel and be Ted's wife and a mother to our babies. I want Ted to write as he wants and live where he wants and be my husband and a father to our babies.

We can't now and maybe never will earn a living by our writing which is the one profession we want. What will we do for money without sacrificing our energy and time to it and hurting our work? Then, worst:

What if our work isn't good enough? We get rejections. Isn't this the world's telling us we shouldn't bother to be writers? How can we <u>know</u> if we work now hard and develop ourselves we will be more than mediocre? Isn't this the world's revenge on us for sticking our neck out? We can never know until we've worked, written. We have no guarantee we'll get a Writer's Degree. Weren't the mothers and businessmen right after all? Shouldn't we have avoided these disquieting questions and taken steady jobs and secured a good future for the kiddies?

Not unless we want to be bitter all our lives. Not unless we want to feel wistfully: What a writer I <u>might</u> have been, if only. If only I'd had to guts to try and work and shoulder the insecurity all that trial and work implied.

Writing is a religious act: it is an ordering, a reforming, a relearning and reloving of people and the world as they are and as they might be. A shaping which does not pass away like a day of typing or a day of teaching. The writing lasts: it goes about on its own in the world. People read it: react to it as to a person, a philosophy, a religion, a flower: they like it, or do not. It helps them, or it does not. It feels to intensify living: you give more, probe, ask, look, learn, and shape this: you get more: monsters, answers, color and form, knowledge. You do it for itself first. If it brings in money, how nice. You do not do it first for money. Money isn't why you sit down at the typewriter. Not that you don't want it. It is only too lovely when a profession pays for your bread and butter. With writing, it is maybe, maybe-not. How to live with such insecurity? With what is worst, the occasional lack or loss of faith in the writing itself? How to live with these things?

436

The worst thing, worse than all of them, would be to live with not writing. So how to live with the lesser devils and keep them lesser?

Miscellania: "Does Ted want you to get better?" Yes. He does. He wants me to see RB and is excited about my upswing in emotion and joy. He wants me to fight my devils with the best weapons I can muster and to win.

RB says:
There is a difference between dissatisfaction with yourself and anger, depression. You can be dissatisfied and do something about it: if you don't know German, you can learn it. If you haven't worked at writing, you can work at it. If you are angry at someone else, and repress it, you get depressed. Who am I angry at? Myself. No, not yourself. Who is it? It is my mother and all the mothers I have known who have wanted me to be what I have not felt like really being from my heart and at the society which seems to want us to be what we do not want to be from our hearts: I am angry at these people and images.

I do not seem to be able to live up to them. Because I don't want to.

What do they seem to want? Concern with a steady job that earns money, cars, good schools, TV, iceboxes and dishwashers and security First. With us these things are nice enough, but they come second. Yet we are scared. We do need money to eat and have a place to live and children, and writing may never and doesn't now give us enough. Society sticks its so-there tongue out at us.

Why don't we teach like most writers? It seems teaching takes all our time and energy. We didn't do a thing teaching last year. Satisfaction with passive explication of the great works. Kills and drys one out. Makes everything seem explainable.

Main Questions:
What to do with hate for mother.
What to do for money & where to live: practical.
What to do with fear of writing: why fear? Fear of not being a success? Fear of world casually saying we're wrong in rejections.
Ideas of maleness: conservation of creative power (sex & writing).
Why do I freeze in fear my mind & writing: say, look, no head, what can you expect of a girl with no head?

Why don't I write a novel?"

Images of society: the Writer and Poet is excusable only if he is Successful. Makes Money.

Why do I feel I should have a PhD, that I am aimless, brainless without one, when I know what is inside is the only credential necessary for my identity? NB: I do not hit often: once or twice.

How to express anger creatively?

Fear of losing male totem: what roots?

RB: You have always been afraid of premature choices cutting off other choices. Mother's choices cut her life down to a dry chittering stalk of fear.

NOTEBOOK NOTES

Saturday morning
December 13, 1958

So learn about life. Cut yourself a big slice with the silver server, a big slice of pie. Learn how the leaves grow on the trees. Open your eyes. The thin new moon is on its back over the green Cities' Service cloverleaf and the lit brick hills of Watertown, God's luminous fingernail, a shut angel's eyelid. Learn how the moon goes down in the night frost before Christmas. Open your nostrils. Smell snow. Let life happen.

Never felt guilty for bedding with one, losing virginity and going to the Emergency Ward in a spurt spurt of blood, playing with this one and that. Why? Why? I didn't have an idea, I had feelings. I had feelings and found out what I wanted and found the one only I wanted and knew it not with my head but with the heat of rightness, salt-sharp and sure as mice in cheese.

Graphic story: the deflowering. What it is like. Welcome of pain, experience. Phonecall. Pay bill.

Seen on walk down Atlantic Avenue: A black hearse rounding the corner by the coffee house in a cinder-block garage under a corrugated tin roof. Velvet curtains like at the opera, and patentleather black as Lothario's dancing shoe. Among the ten ton trucks by the railroad station, this suave funeral parlor sedan, greased and groomed. Why, whereto? We walked, and the trucks rattled by grazing our flanks. Across the street the hearse had stopped, drawn up back to the open door of the railway express shed. Men in black coats and derby's were sliding a redwood coffin off the rollers into the shed. Heavy, heavy. We stopped, stared, fingers freezing in our gloves, our breath spelling Indian puffs on the grey still deathly air. One black-coated man wore the permanent expression of grief stony on his face, an out-of-work actor perpetually reliving the role where he bursts in and tells that the brave army is cut to bits, that little Eyolf is gone after the rat wife and nothing but his crutch is left on the water to cross his wet bed. Grey hair, a long vein-mottled face, hollow eyesockets and fixed Greek-tragedy eyes and a mouth-mask of absolute misery: but static, frozen. He helps a red-faced, round-cheeked cherry nosed man, whose face would break into smiles if his black coat and round topped black hat didn't keep him solemn as the job requires in the eyes of the watching public. We watched. The reddened richwood coffin slid into a packing crate of pale wood on a suitcase and trunk trolley. The packing crate had copper fluted handles on either side. A square wood lid fitted over the gap the coffin entered and tightened snugly with copper wing nuts like shiny butterflies. The round-faced man climbed on top of the packing crate and laboriously penciled some directives on the top: Christmas mail to somebody out West. Fragile: Perishable Goods: Handle With Care: Headside Up: Keep In a Cool, Dry Place. Whose body? Somebody bumped off? Some husband, father, lover, whore? The last Dickensians. The last caricaturers of grief whose faces never alter from the one grimace. They sell their fixed selves like a commodity of great value to the legions of the bereaved, whisper, console, condole: "At a time like this, nothing but the best."

A dark-faced, dark-haired girl at the door with a basket full of Christmas greens and artificial red flowers. Her face brightens: "You bought from me last year." No, baby, I wasn't here last year. "Feel." She holds out a pot, a small earthenware pot full of greens and the big red flowers. "Do you make them yourself?" I ask. A moment's hesitation: "Yes." I got Ted. The man decides in this house. No, he said. "Will you help me?" No. We pondered. Misers. Scrooge. Why not give? If we gave, if we gave to the open buckets, the janging bells, we would have nothing for ourselves. We feel too hard-put in a world of money to give to flowerpots of greens: the world is making us worry about work for a living. Yet, if we had money, would give, give. A Puritan sense: they exhibit Christmas sympathies, as do the shops. Besides, her coat looked warmer than mine. Did she notice the ragged holes in Ted's sweater elbows, his shirt sticking out.

Acorn Street: the shadowed alley cobbled with river stones the sun never shines on. Here the red-jacketed black poodles and silky angora-sweatered pugs lead their masters and mistresses and hump to crap. A Hill of millionaires being led around by fancy dogs looking for a place to crap. A man in black coat and hat follows his pompon eared poodle up the cobbled street halfway. The poodle squats. Good boy. After the poodle is through, the man bends and does something with a newspaper to the fresh turd. Is he sweeping snow over it, like a cat scratches sand over its excrement, neatly, neatly. Or is he gathering up the crap in the newspaper and carrying it home, or to the nearest ashcan? Mysteries never to be penetrated.

A gay incursion: looking out the window for the mailman: can see, over the second cup of coffee his brass buttons and round blue hat and blue-clad paunch. Can see his bulging brown leather mail satchel, scratched and blotched by the variable Boston weathers. Ran down in the elevator. A thin airmail letter after a fall of rejection for Saxton fellowship, Harper's rejection, Encounter rejection, Atlantic rejection, and book rejection from the World Publishing House. An acceptance of three poems with a charming warm admiring letter from John Lehmann. Lorelei, The Disquieting Muses, The Snakecharmer: all my romantic lyricals. I knew his taste. How nice, how fine. That crack of courage. That foothold. And the sense to know I must change, be careless, deep in my writing.

Blue shadows of trees looped on the sunwhite snow of the park in Lousyberg Square: the toga-Greek statue clutching his stone sheet in the frost. Clear air. Bless Boston, my birthtown. Give me the guts to begin again here my second quarter century of life and live to the hilt.

I may have a baby someday: I feel quite smiley about it. Where has the old scare gone? I still feel a deep awe of the pain. Will I live to tell of it?

Work. Work. Hysterical teary-bright call from mother. Warren's pattern of collapsed romances. My heart aches, dull, frozen: she is ruining him: his dull, secure life: he was good, did what the good woman said, and why should I the naughty one be happy? I am. She begged us to "come and live in her house for awhile if we wanted a change." She wants to make the most of us, afterall she feels, fears, we may go away at any minute.

NOTEBOOKS

Tuesday morning
December 16

Nine thirtyish: have rewritten and rewritten <u>Johnny Panic And The Bible Of Dreams</u> and am going to start sending it out now. I think I can bear up under rejections: hope only that I get letters of commentary. I want it to go about. It's so queer and quite slangy that I think it may have a chance somewhere. Will send it out 10 times before I get sorry: by then, I should have two or three more stories.

It snowed this weekend. We woke up, Monday, to see against the far grey mountain range of buildings across the park innumerable white flakes, John Hancock's blurred totally off the skyline and the snow on the rooftops mounding up, blowing against our windows, and the grind and repetitious slither of car-wheels revolving stuck in our canyon alley. Today, grey skies, but all very light up here with the white snow sharply etched on all the angles of rooftops, gutters, gables, chimneys, and the orange-and-rusty-black chimneypots smoking in small plumes all over lower Beacon Hill. The river basin thick almost luminous white.

Have been happier this week than for six months. It is as if RB saying "I give you permission to hate your mother" also said "I give you permission to be happy." Why the connection? Is it dangerous to be happy? One feels that is mother's secret life-philosophy: the minute you dare to be happy fate smacks you a low blow: about Warren's romance (he got a letter yesterday & read it to mother over the phone, a letter "making everything all right") "That's just the way my life was, the minute you think things are bad enough, something awful happens to make it worse." I am enjoying myself with a great lessening of worry: the dregs of dissatisfaction with myself: not writing enough, not working hard, not reading hard, studying German - - - are things I can do if I want & will do. It is the hate, the paralyzing fear, that gets in my way and stops me. Once that is worked clear of, I will flow. My life may at last get into my writing. As it did in the Johnny Panic story.

Got an old New World Writing, Frank O'Connor's stories, and three Ionesco plays yesterday on our walk out. O'Connor's stories an inspiration of technique; "sure things". I feel it is as important to read what is being written now, good things (Herb Gold is good) to get out of my old-fashioned classroom idiom: She felt, she said. Prim, prim. Read "Amedee" and laughed aloud. The growing corpse: the mushrooms: met with by all the petty-bourgeois platitudes usually used up on trivia. The accepting the horrific and ridiculous as if it were the daily newspaper delivery. Is it to say that platitudes take the edge off our real horrors so that we are all blinded to them, our corpses and poisonous mushrooms?

Truman Capote this weekend: a baby-boy, must be in his middle thirties. Big head, as of a prematurely delivered baby, an embryo, big white forehead, little drawstring mouth, shock of blond hair, minty skippy fairy body in black jacket, velvet or corduroy, couldn't tell from where we sat. Ted & men hated the homosexual part of him with more than usual fury. Something else: jealousy at his success? If he weren't successful there would be nothing to anger at. I was very amused, very moved, only Holiday Golightly left me more chilly than when I read her.

Harvard couple at Gerta's[n] party & Fassett's[n] afterward: a great cowish Norwegian wife, daughter of a seacaptain, who in certain lights and angles looked beautiful, notably in profile, with a strong nose, fair complexion, glinty blond hair, and mink coat; I think it was mink, a sparky slithery fur. I kept thinking she must be beautiful, but then her heavy chin, almost round full face got in the way, her stuckout stomach (another baby) and thick legs; then she became cowish. She talked of her husband to Ted; I talked to the husband. He doesn't like animals, not "doesn't like", but just "doesn't care"; Agatha's remarkable tiger kitten did some amazing skippings and dancings and attacked Bimbo, who knocked the kitten down with a paw and seemed about to eat him till the kitten writhed & mewled pitiably and rolled off; Scylla, the mother, on the way to the kitten to solace it, stalked past the reclining Bimbo and, as an afterthought, gave him a malicious, vengeful cuff. Startling; not the revenge, so much as the thought-out retention of anger, the wait between the act and the cuff. This egg-head, Richard Gill,[n] tutor in Economics at Leverett House, looked blankly at the kitten as if a chair were simply moving from one place to another in a house full of walking chairs and so what. I feel a whole level of sensibility is missing in people like this. He hates traveling, went to Harvard for a BA, got his PHD from Harvard, lives and teaches at Harvard now, not just in town, but in a dormitory; dotes on his children, hates to travel. His wife says he can't find his way anywhere, not even to the Beacon Hill Kitchen when they lived on the Hill, so she had to pick him up at home and lead him there, never meet him there. He talks solely of himself. He has had stories in the Atlantic, and the New Yorker wrote and asked for some, and he publishes there. Knows and dotes on Frank O'Connor, took his course in writing, then assisted him for two years. "A story must have a character that bends, like a crowbar. Some outside incident must send him off in another, very different direction from which he is going in at the beginning of the story."

Advice. I must take it. Just what I need: character changes. That is "plot". Theme.

People: Mrs. McKee, Mrs. Doom: expect the worst: relation to Greek tragic chorus. Expects worst of human nature: sad feeling of having lived up to the worst she expects, by throwing away the pie server, laughing at her. She is drawn by misfortune, draws it to her. Does she also draw the worst in people out? Is it, in the end, her fault for being as she is, not fate's fault? The collection of frogs, knicknacks, magazines. Daughter's suicide attempt. Son's failing out of schools. Red sport's cars. Episode of rug, landlady; hunting for pie server; minute description of the pond. The Pie-Server Incident

The Champion Spinach-Picker: Ilo Pill, artist; introduction to sex. Background of farm. Honesty. Mary Coffee. Sense of shame. Stupid faith. Tempting of danger. Revelation: limits. "Lord knows how mother got my brother and me the farm-jobs, but she managed it." DPs. Estonians. Negroes.

I-stories about Winthrop. Recreate town. Father, atheist; the Catholic Conways, and Lalleys. Jimmy Beale, Jimmy Booth, Sonney, Sheldon: the Jews. Penitentiary.

Paul Roche: his green suit and green eyes; the great sponger; get him in, wife, children: revelation about him.

NOTEBOOK

Wednesday am
December 17

A LHJ story, The Button Quarrel? Ask RB about psychological need to fight, express hostility between husband & wife. A story of an "advanced" couple, no children, woman with career, above sewing on buttons, cooking.

Husband thinks he agrees. Fight over sewing on buttons. Not really fight about that. Fight about his deep-rooted conventional ideas of womanhood, like all the rest of the men, wants them pregnant and in the kitchen. Wants to shame her in public; told from point of view of wise elderly matron? advice? ah, what is it.

Angry at RB for changing appointment to tomorrow. Shall I tell her? Makes me feel: she does it because I am not paying money. She does it and is symbolically witholding herself, breaking a "promise", like mother not loving me, breaking her "promise" of being a loving mother each time I speak to her or talk to her. That she shifts me about because she knows I'll agree nicely & take it, and that it implies I can be conveniently manipulated. A sense of my insecurity with her accentuated by floating, changeable hours and places. The question: is she trying to do this, or aware of how I might feel about it, or simply practically arranging appointments?

A tirade with Ted over Jane Truslow," "You know her," "How can I be expected to know which one?" and buttons, his telling Marcia and Mike that I: hide shirts, rip up torn socks, never sew on buttons. His motive: I thought that would make you do it! So he thought by shaming me, he could manipulate me. My reaction: a greater stubbornness than ever, just as his reaction is when I try to manipulate him into doing something, ergo, changing seats at Truman Capote. It would have been better looking-at Capote to change seats, it would be better wearing-shirts-and-coats for Ted for me to sew on his buttons: what makes, or made, both acts impossible was the sense that the other was putting more in his decision than the act itself: it was a victory one over the other, not an issue of theater seats and buttons. I face this. I feel to know it. But he doesn't. Just as he tells me, when he wants to manipulate me one way (eg, to stop "nagging", which means talking about anything he doesn't like) that I am like my mother, which is sure to get an emotional reaction, even if it's not true. I hate my mother, therefore his surest triumph and easy-way to get me to do what he wants is to tell me I'm just-like-my-mother whenever I do or don't do something he wants. Realizing this is half the battle against it. Will he admit it to himself? I'm just as bad. Dirty hands, dirty hands.

Marcia and Mike: Unpleasant: the hidden corpse of Amedee grows with meaning.

[Six sentences omitted by ed.]

444

Both of us must feel partly that the other isn't filling a conventional role: he isn't "earning bread and butter" in any reliable way, I'm not "sewing on buttons and darning socks" by the hearthside. He hasn't even got us a hearth; I haven't even sewed a button.

Friday morning: December 26, 1958:

About to see Beuscher. A cold after-Christmas morning. A good Christmas. Because, Ted says, I was merry. I played, teased, welcomed mother. I may hate her, but that's not all. I pity and love her too. After all, as the story goes, she's my mother. "She can't encroach unless you're encroachable on." So my hate and fear derive from my own insecurity. Which is? And how to combat it?

Fear of making early choices which close off alternatives. Not afraid of marrying Ted, because he is flexible, won't shut me in. Problem: we both want to write, have a year. Then what? Not odd jobs. A steady money-earning profession: psychology?

How to develop my independence? Not tell him everything. Hard, seeing him all the time, not leading outer life.

Fear: access after seeing people at Harvard: feeling I've put myself out of the running. Why can't I throw myself into writing? Because I am afraid of failure before I begin.

Old need of giving mother accomplishments, getting reward of love.

I do fight with Ted: two acrid fights. The real reasons: we both worry about money: we have enough till next September 1st. Then what? How to keep concerns about money and profession from destroying the year we have?

Neither of us wants a job connected with English: not magazine, publishing, newspaper or teaching: not now, teaching.

Problem of Ted and America. He doesn't see how to use it yet. I feel his depression. Don't want to force or manipulate him into anything he doesn't want. Yet he worries too, only is not articulate about it.

Don't know where we want to live. What profession we will work into. How much to count on writing. Poetry unlucrative. Maybe children's books.

Ted: steady, kind, loving, warm, intelligent, creative. But we are both too ingrown: prefer books too often to people. Anti-security compulsion.

Problem: knowing what we want: conflicting wants. Country versus city, America versus England and Europe, expensive tastes versus no money, lots of children versus no help.

If I can build up myself and my work I will be a contribution to our pair, not a dependent and weak half.

Hate of mother, jealousy of brother: only when I am dubious of the way of life to substitute into the place of the life they seem to favor. They will accept it, but we must be sure of our way. We are not; I am not. Discouragement about work. Haven't really worked at writing. Fear of aimless intellectual frittering. Need for a profession dealing with people on a level not superficial.

Jealousy over men: why jealous of Ted. Mother can't take him. Other women can. I must not be selfless: develop a sense of self. A solidness that can't be attacked.

NOTEBOOK

December 27, 1958
Saturday

Yesterday had a session with Beuscher quite long, and very deep. I dug up things which hurt and made me cry. Why do I cry with her and only with her? I am experiencing a grief reaction for something I have only recently begun to admit isn't there: a mother's love. Nothing I do (marrying, saying "I have a husband so I really didn't want yours"; writing: "here is a book for you, it is yours, like my toidy products and you can praise and love me now") can change her way of being with me which I experience as a total absence of love. What, then, do I expect in the way of love? Do I feel what I expect when I see RB? Is that why I cry? Because even her professional kindness strikes me as more to what I want than what I feel in mother? I have lost a father and his love early; feel angry at her because of this and feel she feels I killed him (her dream about me being a chorus girl and his driving off and drowning himself). I dreamed often of losing her, and these childhood nightmares stand out; I dreamed the other night of running after Ted through a huge hospital, knowing he was with another woman, going into mad wards and looking for him everywhere: what makes you think it was Ted? It had his face but it was my father, my mother.

I identify him with my father at certain times, and these times take on great importance: eg that one fight at the end of the school year when I found him not-there on the special day and with another woman. I had a furious access of rage. He knew how I love him and felt, and yet wasn't there. Isn't this an image of what I feel my father did to me? I think it may be. The reason I haven't discussed it with Ted is that the situation hasn't come up again and it is not a characteristic of his: if it were, I would feel wronged in my trust on him. It was an incident only that drew forth echoes, not the complete withdrawal of my father who deserted me forever. Ask: why didn't I talk about it afterwards? Is this a plausible interpretation. If it had come up since, it would be recollected by the stir-up of similar incidents and fears. Ted, insofar as he is a male presence is a substitute for my father: but in no other way. Images of his faithlessness with women echo my fear of my father's relation with my mother and Lady Death.

How fascinating all this is. Why can't I master it and manipulate it and lose my superficiality which is a careful protective gloss against it?

Read Freud's "Mourning and Melancholia" this morning after Ted left for the library. An almost exact description of my feelings and reasons for suicide: a transferred murderous impulse from my mother onto myself: the "vampire" metaphor Freud uses, "draining the ego": that is exactly the feeling I have getting in the way of my writing: mother's clutch. I mask my self-abasement (a transferred hate of her) and weave it with my own real dissatisfactions in myself until it becomes very difficult to distinguish what is really bogus criticism from what is really a changeable liability. How can I get rid of this depression: by refusing to believe she has any power over me, like the old witches for whom one sets out plates of milk and honey. This is not easily done. How is it done? Talking and becoming aware of what is what and studying it is a help.

RB; You are trying to do two mutually incompatible things this year. 1) spite your mother. 2) write. To spite your mother, you don't write because you feel you have to give the stories to her, or that she will appropriate them. (As I was afraid of having her around to appropriate my baby, because I didn't want it to be hers). So I can't write. And I hate her because my not writing plays into her hands and argues that she is right, I was foolish not to teach, or do something secure, when what I have renounced security for is nonexistent. My rejection-fear is bound up with the fear that this will mean my rejection by her, for not succeeding: perhaps that is why they are so terrible. The saving thing is, Ted doesn't care about the rejections except insofar as they bother me. So my work is to have fun in my work and to FEEL THAT MY WORKS ARE MINE. She may use them, put them about her room when published, but I did them and she has nothing to do with them.

It is not that I myself do not want to succeed. I do. But I do not need success with the desperation I have felt for it: that is an infusion of fear that successlessness means no approval from mother: and approval, with mother, has been equated for me with love, however true that is.

WHY DON'T I FEEL SHE LOVES ME? WHAT DO I EXPECT BY "LOVE" FROM HER? WHAT IS IT I DON'T GET THAT MAKES ME CRY? I think I have always felt she uses me as an extension of herself; that when I commit suicide, or try to, it is a "shame" to her, an accusation: which it was, of course. An accusation that her love was defective. Feeling too, of competing with Warren: the looming image of Harvard is equated with him. How, by the way, does mother understand my committing suicide? As a result of my not writing, no doubt. I felt I couldn't write because she would appropriate it. Is that all? I felt if I didn't write nobody would accept me as a human being. Writing, then, was a substitute for myself: if you don't love me, love my writing & love me for my writing. It is also much more: a way of ordering and reordering the chaos of experience.

When I am cured of my witch-belief, I will be able to tell her of writing without a flinch and still feel it mine. She is a sad old woman. Not a witch.

A fear also that she might appropriate Ted as hers and kill him, or kill him through me? In spirit or maleness is as bad as physically. For me he is infinitely preservable.

Is our desire to investigate psychology a desire to get Beuscher's power and handle it ourselves? It is an exciting and helpful power. "You are never the same afterwards: it is a Pandora's box: nothing is simple anymore."

MY WRITING IS MY WRITING IS MY WRITING. Whatever elements there were in it of getting her approval I must no longer use it for that. I must not expect her love for it. She will use it as she has always used it, but this must not upset me. I must change, not she. Why is telling her of a success so unsatisfying: because one success is never enough: when you love, you have an indefinite lease of it. When you approve, you only approve single acts. Thus approval has a short dateline. The question is: so much for that, good, but now, what is the next thing?

WHAT DO I FEEL GUILTY ABOUT? Having a man, being happy: she has lost both man and happiness and had to make do with Warren and me substituted for the man, and our happiness substituted for her own.

My happiness in certain ways is not useable for her: it goes against her pronouncements and implies she is wrong, or was wrong. She envies me for what I have done. It reflects back on her past and suggests she is to blame for what happened to herself, for not making a better choice on this and that. Re my announcement of the Smith offer repeated: I only wish somebody would offer me a job like that.

One reason I could keep up such a satisfactory letter-relationship with her while in England was we could both verbalize our desired image of ourselves in relation to each other: interest and sincere love, and never feel the emotional currents at war with these verbally expressed feelings. I feel her disapproval. But I feel it countries away too. When she dies, what will I feel? I wish her death so I could be sure of what I am: so I could know that what feelings I have, even though some resemble hers, are really my own. Now I find it hard to distinguish between the semblance and the reality.

WHY HAVE I PERSISTED IN THE DELUSION THAT I COULD WIN HER LOVE (APPROVAL) TILL SUCH A LATE DATE? NOTHING I DO WILL CHANGE HER. DO I GRIEVE NOW BECAUSE I REALIZE THE IMPOSSIBILITY OF THIS?

What little maxim can I repeat to myself to get my writing going under the proper auspices?

I resent her too because she has given me only useless information about life in the world, and all the useful woman-wisdom I must seek elsewhere and make up for myself. Her information is based on a fear for security and all advice pushes toward the end and goal of security and final answers.

The ash bits from the black wired box seiving the red-brick chimney soot are winking and somersaulting down, bright white like snowflakes in the shadow of the building, caught by the sun. This I enjoy.

One reason all people at Harvard are a reproach to me and make me jealous: because I identify them with Warren? How to stop this.

PROBLEM: The same act may be good or not good depending on its emotional content. Such as coitus. Such as giving presents. Such as choosing a job.

WHAT IS THE MATURE THING TO DO WITH HATE FOR MOTHER? Does the need to express it recede with a mature awareness I can't expect love from her, therefore will not hate her for not giving it? Does all hate pass off into benevolent pity?

Ted & I are introverts and need a kind of external stimulus such as a job to get us into deep contact with people: even in superficial contact such as smalltalk which is pleasurable. Like my saga with the wise Louise. Writing as a profession turns us inward: we don't do reportage, criticism, freelance research. Poetry is the most ingrown and intense of the creative arts. Not much money in it, and that windfalls. Teaching is another distortion: it selects an abstract subject: a subject "about reality, spiritual and physical", organizes it into courses, simplifies the deluge of literature by time-divisions and subject-divisions and style-divisions. Makes organized a small bit of it all and repeats that for twenty years. Psychology, I imagine, supplies more reality-situations: the people you deal with are bothered with a variety of things, people and ideas, not just the symbolism of James Joyce. They have different jobs; different things are good for them. They do not take the Exam of Life together in the same room: each is different. There is no common grade scale. They have common problems but none is exactly the same. This requires an extension of other-awareness. Whatever Ted does, I would like to submit myself to it. It would require a long discipleship. However, I don't want to enter it until I have convinced myself I am writing and writing for my own pleasure and to express insights to others also, and learning techniques.

Ted and I talked about jobs yesterday: He is as pathological as I am in his own way: compulsive against society so he envisions "getting a job" as a kind of prison-term. Yet says now his job at Cambridge was a rich experience which he then took as death. I would be pleased if he found something that he liked. What is so terrible about earning a regular wage? He admits it feels good. He is afraid of the Image: so many have regular jobs and are dead why wouldn't it kill him? If he has his writing established in this year, I don't think it would kill him. But he doesn't want the sort of job, no more do I, that I/he could walk into without much preparation; a job to do with writing.

We agreed on a Friday afternoon blow-up: all problems and not only that, but praise: counting week's good things. Projecting constructive things for the next week. This week. We had a very good f'ing. Enormously good, perhaps the best yet. We read over an hour of King Lear over tea. I read four Ionesco plays: The Bald Soprano, Jack, The Lesson, The Chairs: terrifying and funny: playing on our old own conventions and banalities and making them carried to the last extreme to show, by the discrepancy between real and real-to-the-last-thrust, how funny we are and how far gone. "We eat well because we live in a suburb of London and our name is Smith." A family crisis: a boy won't submit and say he adores hashed brown potatoes: the smallness of the object contrasted with the totality of emotion involved on all sides: a ridicule, a terror. Now all I need to do is start writing without thinking it's for mother to get affection from her! How can I do this: where is my purity of motive? Ted won't need to get out of the house when I'm sure I'm not using his writing to get approval too and sure I'm myself and not him.

Reason I want RB to talk first? Desire not to have responsibility of analysis rest on me? I want to ask questions & will: it is my work and my advantage to work on it. Immense peace today after talk with her, deep grief expression: when will that last end?

NOTEBOOK

December 28
Sunday

Before nine. Oatmeal eaten, and two cups of coffee. Had my coffee vision in bed. Began clearly to remember Dick Norton. A possible theme: virgin girl brought up in idealism expects virginity from boy her family raves about as pure. He is going to be a doctor, a pillar of society; he is already swinging toward conventionalism. Takes her through lectures on sickle cell anemia, moon-faced babies in jars, cadavers, baby born. She doesn't flinch. What she flinches at is his affair with a waitress. She hates him for it. Jealous. Sees no reason for being a virgin herself. What's the point in being a virgin? Argument with him: humor. She won't marry him. What are her motives? He is a hypocrite. "Well, should I go around telling folks?" Kiss the earth and beg pardon. No, that wouldn't be enough. The modern woman: demands as much experience as the modern man.

How to recognize a story? There is so much experience but the real outcome tyrannizes over it. Louise, or this girl, has a terrific capacity for tolerating experience. What she can't tolerate is his having an experience she can't have. What does this motivate her to do? Sleep with another man. How can you know a man is potent unless you sleep with him before you're married. She has learned about contraception. How does this experience change her? Emergency Ward, she loses her virginity. Symbolic act to match experience of fiancee. Roommate wise about men. Divorce is a reason for testing people out before you're married to them. Influence of roommate. Payment of hospital, by deflowerer. How does this end?

Went to library yesterday afternoon with Ted. Looked up requirements for a PhD in psychology. It would take about six years. A prodigious prospect. Two years for prerequisites, languages for MA. Four years for the rest, it might be three. The work of applying, figuring out programs, etc., and not to mention money, a formidable thing. Awesome to confront a program of study which is so monumental: all human experience. Still, it was good to face what it would mean. I wonder if the statistics would overwhelm me.

Turn, with a kind of relief, to the business of learning a craft. I am reading Frank O'Connor's stories not just with the first innocence, letting it come at me, but with a kind of growing awareness of what he is doing technically. I will imitate until I can feel I'm using what he can teach. His stories are so clearly "constructed": not a whit unused: a narrative flow. That is what I most need and most miss. I write a sort of imagey static prose: like the tattoo story: I understand for the first time why he didn't accept me for his course with my Minton story: I should have sent the Perfect-Setup or the sorority story. They had plot, people changing, learning something. My trouble with Johanna Bean is that I have about three themes, none clear.

The main theme: hanging is the symbolic rejection of fictitious goodness. Feeling of badness in world unconquerable by good: war, death, disease: horror radio programs. Badness in self. Johanna a scapegoat: model of goodness. How do you defend yourself in case of attack? By fighting back. Johanna doesn't fight back; is helpless, foolish. Change of ethic in child. Sees something more problematic than mother makes it. Leroy: Maureen, participate. Where does guilt lie? In Johanna? Games: psychodrama. Close relation of girl and father.

NOTEBOOK

December 31
Wednesday

The last day of 1958: clear and heavenly blue: the day, bland, offers beauty: all weathers are lovely, if only the inner weather reflects and endows loveliness. A question: do I love laziness more than I love the feeling of accomplishing work (writing, learning German, French; studying)? It seems that way. I take the path of least resistance and curl up with a book. Everyone else seems to be doing valuable work: social work, cancer research, teaching, degree getting, mothering. What can I do?

Have been working on the Leroy-biting story, without much idea where it will end: yet as I write, day by day, two pages or so, and brood, new ideas come up. The hanging of Johanna Bean promises not to come in here at all. A story must have a SINGLE THEME: although a theme can be underlined by related material. My present theme seems to be the awareness of a complicated guilt system whereby Germans in a Jewish and Catholic community are made to feel, in a scapegoat fashion, the pain, psychically, the Jews are made to feel in Germany by Germans without religion. The child can't understand the larger framework. How does her father come into this? How is she guilty for her father's deportation to a detention camp? As this is how I think the story must end? Johanna will come in on her own with the trapeze, Uncle Frank, and the fiction of perfect goodness. Also, the story about "The Little Mining Town In Colorado". My writing is quite uncolored. Is the interest in it only mine?

I am still dallying a good two hours too much before working: sewing on The Button, making a bed, watering a plant. Still sick on waking and will be till the story is more interesting than my own self-musings.

Ted read my signature on the letter to his parents as "woe" instead of love. He was right, it looked surprising: the left hand knows not what the right writes. It would make me quite happy if he would find some steady something he liked to do. DN's mother was not so wrong about a man supplying direction and a woman the warm emotional power of faith and love. I feel we are as yet directionless (not inside, so much as in a peopled community way - - - we belong nowhere because we have not given of ourselves to any place wholeheartedly, not committed ourselves).

Ted labored all yesterday afternoon and evening making a wolf-mask out of Agatha's old, falling-apart sealskin. It is remarkably fuzzy and wolfish. About the party tonight: the sense of not wanting to go: the Unknown, everybody buying fabulous costumes and toys to go with them. I haven't even got a red hood or a basket, which is all I need, but can't see spending even a couple of $$/

Am reading St. Therese's autobiography: a terror of the contradiction of "relic and pomp admiration" and the pure soul. Where, where is Jesus. Maybe only the nuns and monks come near, but even they have this horrid self-satisfied greed for misfortune which in it's own way is perverse as greed for happines in this world: such as T's "precious blessing" of her father's cerebral paralysis and madness: a welcome cross to bear!

The only way to stop envying others is to have a self of joy. All creation is jammed in the selfish soul.

I think I am pregnant: I wonder when and if I will feel it.

[Appendix 10 contains Sylvia Plath's December 1958 list of words and names (entry 42a), notes about Top Withens (entry 42b), notes about Saint Thérèse de Lisieux and

454

Saint Teresa of Avila (entries 44–46), notes for Plath's poems 'The Bull of Bendylaw', 'Point Shirley', and 'Goatsucker' (entry 47); Appendix 11 contains a fragment from 'Point Shirley' (entry 41) – ed.]

NOTEBOOK

January 3, 1959
Saturday

As usual after an hour with RB, digging, felt I'd been watching or participating in a Greek play: a cleansing and an exhaustion. I wish I could keep the revelations, such as they are, fresh in mind. Relieved she suggested $5 for an hour. Enough, considerable for me. Yet not outrageous, so it is punishment. Felt brief panic at the thought she would not take me on or try to refer me to someone else.

All my life I have been "stood up" emotionally by the people I loved most: daddy dying and leaving me, mother somehow not there. So I endow the smallest incidents of lateness, for example, in other people I love, with an emotional content of coldness, indication that I am not important to them. Realizing this, I wasn't angry or bothered she was late. The terror of my last day of teaching last May, when this happened, especially with the face of that girl. If it happened more often, I would find it a character fault, but it doesn't seem to have happened.

Twister: I don't care if T gives me presents as proof of _my_ affection. What comes to mind? Hugging. I have never found anybody who could stand to accept the daily demonstrative love I feel in me, and give back as good as I gave. She said well: so you wouldn't be left on a limb with your love hanging out. Afraid of having love all unaccepted, left over. Shame at this.

At McLean I had an inner life going on all the time but wouldn't admit it. If I had know this, I would have praised the Lord. I needed permission to admit I lived. Why?

Why, after the "amazingly short" three or so shock treatments did I rocket uphill? Why did I feel I needed to be punished, to punish myself. Why do I feel now I should be guilty, unhappy: and feel guilty if I am not? Why do I feel immediately happy after talking to RB? Able to enjoy every little thing: shopped for meat, a victory for me, and got what I wanted: veal, chicken, hamburg. My need to punish myself might, horribly, go to the length of deliberately and to spite my face disappointing T in this way or that. That would be my worst punishment. That and not writing. Knowing this is the first guard against it.

What do I expect or want from mother? Hugging, mother's milk? But that is impossible to all of us now. Why should I want it still. What can I do with this want. How can I transfer it to something I can have?

A great, stark, bloody play acting itself out over and over again behind the sunny facade of our daily rituals, birth, marriage, death, behind parents and schools and beds and tables of food: the dark, cruel, murderous shades, the demon-animals, the Hungers.

Attitude to things: like a mother, I dont want anyone to say anything against T, not that he is lazy or shiftless: I know he works, and hard, but it doesn't show to the observer, for whom writing is sitting home, drinking coffee and piddling about. A play.

ASK ABOUT MOTHER-LOVE: Why these feelings. Why guilt: as if sex, even legally indulged in, should be "paid for" by pain. I would probably interpret pain as a judgment: birth-pain, even a deformed child. Magical fear mother will become a child, my child: an old hag child.

NOTEBOOK

January 7, 1959
Wednesday

The abstract kills, the concrete saves (try inverting this thesis tomorrow). How an Idea of what Should Be or What One Should Be Doing can drive an eating, excreting two-legged beast to misery-). How dusting, washing daily dishes, talking to people who are not mad and dust and wash and feel life is as it should be helps.

Boston is filthy: a drift of weekly soot on the windows, the windows smeared with greasy cooking exhalations, dust under the bed and all over, appearing miraculously every day, thrown and shaken out the window, and seeping in again.

Don't wake up in the morning because I want to go back to the womb. From now on: see if this is possible: set alarm for 7:30 and get up then, tired or not. Rip through breakfast and housecleaning (bed and dishes, mopping or whatever) by 8:30. Ted got coffee and oatmeal today: he doesn't like to do it, but does it. I am a fool to let him. Alarm-setting gets over the bother of waking at ragged odd hours around nine.

Be writing before 9 (nine), that takes the curse off it. It is now almost 11. I have washed two sweaters, the bathroom floor, mopped, done a day's dishes, made the bed, folded the laundry and stared in horror at my face: it is a face old before its time.

Nose podgy as a leaking sausage: big pores full of pus and dirt, red blotches, the peculiar brown mole on my under-chin which I would like to have excised. Memory of that girl's face in the Med School movie, with a little black beauty wart: this wart is malignant: she will be dead in a week. Hair untrained, merely brown and childishly put up: don't know what else to do with it. No bone structure. Body needs a wash, skin the worst: it is this climate: chapping cold, dessicating hot: I need to be tan, all-over brown, and then my skin clears and I am all right. I need to have written a novel, a book of poems, a LHJ or NY story, and I will be poreless and radiant. My wart will be non-malignant.

Reading "The Horse's Mouth": hard to get into. I see why it didn't sell much here: too rich a surface, all knots and spurtings of philosophy, but only as emanation from the bumpy colored surface of life, not imposed on it. Plot not spare and obvious, but a spate of anecdotes. Podgy old Sara eternal as Eve, Alison, wife of bath. This old battered hide: needs a brain and a creative verve to make it liveable in, a heater in the ratty house.

Read Aino tales: primitive: all at penis-fetish, anus-fetish, mouth-fetish stage. Marvelous untouched humor, primal: bang, bang you're dead. Stories of alter-ego: same thing done by two people, only one is rich by it, other poor and dead: difference, attitude of mind only. NB.

The first thing is the early rising. Also, telling Ted nothing. DOING. Finished, almost, story of Shadow: no Johanna Bean in it at all. Despair: have ideas: lack of know-how. Also, lack of ideas. How many girls go to sleep on marrying after college: see them twenty-five years later with their dew-eyes turned ice, same look, no growing except in outside accretions, like the shell of a barnacle. Beware.

NOTEBOOK

january 8
Thursday

A poor day again. The old sickness on me and a morning dissipated in phone calls and calculatings with the money down $1,000. A deep wish to leap to Columbia and get a Phd. And make money by working. I don't know if I'm the sort to stay home all day and write. I think my head will get soft if I have no outer walls to measure it against. Or that I will stop speaking the human language.

Very bad dreams lately. One just after my period last week of losing my month-old baby: a transparent meaning. The baby, formed just like a baby, only small as a hand, died in my stomach and fell forward: I looked down at my bare belly and saw the round bump of its head in my right side, bulging out like a burst appendix. It was delivered with little pain, dead. Then I saw two babies, a big nine month one, and a little one month one with a blind white-piggish face nuzzling against it: a transfer image, no doubt, from Rosalind's[n] cat and kittens a few days before: the little baby was a funny shape, like a kitten with white skin instead of fur. But my baby was dead. I think a baby would make me forget myself in a good way. Yet I must find myself.

Every now and then I get the feeling I could do a good work. Yet what have I done. What I have done, nonetheless, is quite good, some of it, and with work I should do better. One indication: one story accepted. Lord knows what is happening to me: I am dying of inertia.

Is it a defense, not working: then I can't be criticized for what I do. Why am I passive? Why don't I go out and work? I am inherently lazy. Teaching looks a blessed relief after this burden. Any way, we don't get out and meet people. Ted stays in and brings in little but books. I am going sloppy. I will wash hair and shower tonight. How to bring my life together in a strong way? Not to wander and squander. So little I know of the world.

Nothing to measure myself against: no community to be part of. Ted refuses

458

any church. Still, why can't I go alone. Find out and go alone. Other people are a salvation. It is up to me.

Last night's horror: Stephen Fassett in it, stiff and sad. Walking by gravestones, dragging them away with a rope: a corridor, with dead corpses being wheeled down it, half decayed, their faces all mottled and falling away, yet clothed in coats, hats, and so on. We got pushed into the stream, and horror, the dead were moving. A dead corpse, all grinning and filth being propelled along standing by another man almost as bad, then a lump of flesh, stunted, round, with black cloves, or nails stuck in all over it, and only one long apish swinging arm, reaching out for alms. I woke screaming: the horror of the deformed and dead, alive as we are, and I among them, in the filth and swarming corruption of the flesh. I feel, am mad as any writer must in one way be: why not make it real? I am too close to the bourgeois society of suburbia: too close to people I know: I must sever myself from them, or be part of their world: this half-and-half compromise is intolerable. If only Ted wanted to do something. Saw a career he'd enjoy. But I wonder: he says "get a job" as if it were a prison sentence. I feel the weight on me. The old misery of money seeping away. A cold corpse between me and any work at all. I need a flow of life on the outside, a child, a job, a community I know from preacher to baker. Not this drift of fairytales.

NOTEBOOK

January 10
Saturday

Almost eleven. The infuriating irregular noise of the electricians snaking their wire up the column beside my sink, rolling the wire downstairs. There can be only two more apartments on our side to fix, but the noise is deafening. How disruptions annoy. They shouldn't but they do: anything an excuse can hinge onto. At least we don't live on the bottom floor: they must hear all eight floors being fixed.

I have proceeded very little distance in my resolution. I am at least making the oatmeal and coffee, but this morning, after a late night yesterday with Marty & Mike & Roger & Joan Stein" we slept till 9:30.

Cried yesterday morning: as if it were an hour for keening: why is crying so pleasurable? I feel clean, absolutely purged after it. As if I had a grief to get

459

over with, some deep sorrow. I cried about other mothers coming to take care of their daughters for a while, with babies. Talked of how I could let her have her limited pleasure if I were "grown-up" enough not to feel jeopardized by her manipulating me. I sidestepped this problem ingeniously: talked of MEChase, Lesbians, (what does a woman see in another woman that she doesn't see in a man: tenderness). I am also afraid of MEC: you must hate her, fear her: you think all old women are magical witches.

The crux is my desire to be manipulated. Whence does it come, how can I triumph over it? Why is my flow of inner life so blocked? How can I free it? How can I find myself & be sure of my identity?

Next time: start by asking if my stubborn shut-mouth at the beginning is an attempt to force RB to talk first, take the running of the hour out of my hands: she won't talk first, makes me. And I eventually do.

How can I stop fearing other people? How can I know who I am? How to let my native sense of meaning flow and connect with people and the world? Why this sense of horror, coming over me? Fear? If Ted had a positive program, joy in his work - - - a work that would serve as a connection with people, a place, it would help: while uncommitted, I am faced with dozens of possibilities, places, ways: fear of death by premature choice, cutting off of alternatives. How to say: I choose this, & not fear the consequences.

Rejection of my Johnny Panic story without a note from the Yale Review: all my little dreams of publishing it there vanished: so writing is still used as a proof of my identity. Bitterness at achievement of others.

Glimmer last night of pleasure, which slipped away: Agatha's top floor room, the grey snow-light of evening coming, the tea, the enclosed feeling of peace, old carpets, old sofa, old smoothed chairs: don't share sorrow with Ted of rejection: he worries about me, I make up problems. Talk of poetry, cats, Ted reading Smart's poem on cats. Martini at Marty's seeing her print blouse and slacks she is sewing, a real honest wish to make something like that myself. Yet a rebellion at the time on it. Interest in making clothes for children. Why can't I read Yeats, Hopkins, if I love them. Why do I punish myself by not looking at them? I think I will get a Phd in English & teach poetry.

Talked also with RB of victorian women who fear men: men treat women as brainless chattels: have seen so many romances end in this sort of thing, waste of a woman, they don't believe marriage can work without woman becoming maid, servant, nurse, and losing brain. Ulcers: desire for dependency & feeling it is wrong to be dependent: you reject food (mother's milk), dependency, and yet get dependency by being sick: it's the ulcer to blame, not you.

Where is joy. Joy in frogs, not in Idea of people looking at my frog poem. Why must I punish myself, or save myself, by pretending I am stupid and can't feel? (The damn electrician sounds to be sawing the house in). Would pregnancy bring a kind of peace? I would, she says, probably have a depression after my first baby if I didn't get rid of it now. Expecting mother to see how it really feels to be a mother. She not able to oblige.

Promiscuity: my ingenious, evasive self-deceiving explanation: I had to give out affection in small doses so it would be accepted, not all to one person, who couldn't take it. Very queer. The fact that belies this is that I found no pleasure in anything except my relation with R, and that was a monogamous affair for me while it lasted. So I was trying to be like a man: able to take or leave sex, with this one and that. I got even. But really wasn't meant for it. What about exhibitionism? The whore, a male-type woman? For all-comers?

She praises me, and I feel hungry for it: I castigate myself so completely. What a mess I am.

To see what to expect from mother, etc., accept it and know how to deal with it. This presupposes an independence and sense of identity in myself, which I have not got. This is the main issue.

I come away with more questions than when I go in. Will send her a check at the end of the month.

The rejection a blow. Sanctions my utter lack of faith which puts me in a despair. Shows the writing for itself is not first. Yet what joys, loves I have known. And how they are part of the world.

I have hated men because I felt them physically necessary: hated them because they would degrade me, by their attitude: women shouldn't think, shouldn't be unfaithful (but their husbands may be), must stay home, cook wash. Many men need a woman to be like this. Only the weak ones don't, so many strong women marry a weak one, to have children, and their own way at once. If I could once see how to write a story, a novel, to get something of my feeling over, I would not despair. If writing is not an outlet, what is.

The noise, the noise: is this the last cable? A fury of anger and frustration and self-pity.

Felt a joy yesterday, soon clouded.

NOTEBOOK

January 10, 1959
Saturday

Postscript: Am reading the book of Job: great peace derived therefrom. Shall read the Bible: symbolic meaning, even though the belief in a moral God-structured universe not there. Live As If it were? A great device.

Will not tell Ted of rejection: will not make gloom concrete: that is an indulgence. He gets bothered because I am bothered and then I feel bad for his being bothered and so on. Will just quietly send it out again Monday. The mailman wrinkled it by jamming it in the box. Must speak to him.

January 20, 1959
WEDnesday

Peculiar peace this morning: all is grey and dripping wet. We have a new cat whose needs and miaows are becoming a part of consciousness. I tried shutting it in the bedroom, but it cried and cried. It loves human warmth, cries to get in bed with us. A little stary tiger now curled drowsy blue-eyed on the couch. Playful, adventurous, named Sappho.

A muddled week. Warren for a good dinner Saturday, roast beef, creamed spinach in broth, and a superb lemon meringue pie. A movie at the Brattle with the magnificent moueish Giulietta Massina, the Nights of Cabiria. Not the single power and terror of La Strada, but excellence, humor, her beauty and sudden raffish down-lippings. Sunday, a walk rapidly to T-wharf, the stench, the docked ships. Back to C——'s cave-like cool long apartment which I love, the expensive furniture and openness: talk, with a visiting Bennington senior working her stint in boston, the olive, long face, blue-black Jewish hair in a back braid, like Esther Brooks' hair, a kind of thick woven blue and white serape, black and grey striped tapered slacks and bare ankles, little pointy black leather Italian shoes. A weak kindly escort, Ed Cohn, too gentle, too sweet and soft. Qualms about the PhD. C——'s fearsome veering: the affair with the married architect next door ("his wife tried to kill me, to strangle me") and the simultaneous "I don't want to sound fickle but" she'd marry an associate professor of Columbia in Sociology at the drop of a proposal. She would do it, too. How curious one is about these friends committed to other lives, and what they will choose and do.

Monday, to Rosalind Wilson's to get the cat: a warm basketful by the fireplace, all drowsing, prowling on furry rugs. We took the littlest livest tiger.

A moment with Elizabeth Harkwicke" and Robert Lowell: she charming and highstrung, mimicking their subnormal Irish housegirl whom they have at last let go, he kissing her tenderly before leaving, calling her he would be late, and all the winsome fondnesses of a devoted husband. He with his stories about Dylan Thomas, the two bald men in Iowa, Thomas putting his hands on each head: I can tell the two of you apart because one wears glasses, and one's a good fellow and the others a dry turd. Lowell's half-whisper and sliding glance. Peter Brooks," his tall wrinkled soft kind charming face, falling here and there, nerves: his iceblue eyed pouty blonde ballerina wife, Gerta K. saying to her "Next to me I hear you're the biggest bitch in Cambridge." Lowell: "You should tell her: you're boasting."

Finished a poem this weekend, Point Shirley, Revisited, on my grandmother. Oddly powerful and moving to me in spite of the rigid formal structure. Evocative. Not so one dimensional. Spent a really pleasant afternoon, rainy, in the library looking up Goatsuckers for a poem for Esther's night creatures book. Much more than on frogs, and much more congenial a subject. I have eight lines of a sonnet on the bird, very alliterative and colored. The problem this morning is the sestet.

I feel oddly happy. To enjoy the present as if I had never lived and would tomorrow be dead, instead of "Jam tomorrow, jam yesterday, never jam today". The secret of peace: a devout worship of the moment. Ironically: with most people this is what comes naturally.

Very tired after late night with Lowell. Argument with Agatha, very silly: her argument with Steve, snatching a record out of his hand. I see both points, Agatha's emotionally and Steve's considered and by far more sanely balanced one. And love them both.

With Ted: only utter faith and belief, and my own work. I make up problems, all unnecessary. I do not reverence the present time. Tomorrow: Ask RB why I need to have a problem. Why she was late? What am I hiding about "other people" to protect myself? Why am I so jealous of others. I am me, and the rain is lovely on these chimneys.

My projects falter. I will go from now on to the library and read for four hours every afternoon: no phone, no visitors. That will give me a peace. Will study German. This is a main wish and concern.

We decided to live in England. I really want this. Ted will be his best there. I shall demand an icebox and a good dentist, but love it. Hopefully a big sonorous place in the country in easy distance of London, where I may work. I would so much like to. I will read novels by Lessing and Murdoch, also Bianca VanOrden. Sometimes life seems so meanderingly pleasant. And then I castigate myself for laziness. For not working for a PhD like J. or on a third book like ACR or having four children and a profession, or this, or that. All ridiculous. In worry I do nothing.

Joy: show joy & enjoy: then others will be joyful. Bitterness the one sin. That and the ever-prevalant sloth.

NOTEBOOK

January 27
Tuesday

The world in itself, with its gentle siftings of white snow, the first real snow yet, on the rooftops, pleating and patching, blurring with the plumes of chimney smoke and vanishing into a close grey distance with John Hancock and the Charles River Basin - - - all this is more than these mean, crooked eyes deserve.

A month of the New year evaporated. Read Wilbur" and Rich this morning. Wilbur a bland turning of pleasaunces, a fresh speaking and picturing with incalculable grace and all sweet, pure, clear, fabulous, the maestro with the imperceptible marcel. Robert Lowell after this is like good strong shocking brandy after a too lucidly sweet dinner wine, desert wine.

I speak with RB of being little, as if I were a homunculus. I made an appointment to cut and permanent my hair yesterday and canceled it. Unable to impose my will and wish on a professional hairdresser. Mother with her usual miffed, tragic look, dropped by a book. I didn't ask her up. I'm not working, only studying to change my ways of writing poems. A disgust for my work. My poems begin on one track, in one dimension and never surprise or shock or even much please. The world is all left out. World's criticism had a point: too much dreams, shadowy underworlds.

To ask RB what I can do to sift out grown self from contracted baby feelings, jolting jealousies. Learn German, Italian. Joy. How much and how many in this life want merely "a good deal." A selfinterested shuffling of the cards in the right, plush-enough combination. I am worried about being lazy if happy, worried about being self-deluding if working on anything. So little myself all other identities threaten me. Dreamer forever. Robert Lowell and his wife and the Fassetts are coming to dinner this week. I am wondering what to serve them all in one dish. Lemon meringue pie. Will read Hardwickes stories at the library. I want their success without their spirit or work.

How externals seem to fill worlds of people like Shirley N." Her baby, its walks and talks, her making of rugs and her skating and swimming. What cares she for any spirit or religion: it isn't an issue: social life is what she does. I am panicked at the separation from Mother Academia, although I remember I thought I'd never get through studying for exams. The challenge of marrying a man whose way of life is what I admire and want and am too lazy to live up to. I do no German, no French. Is this because it is easier for me to complain I don't do it than to do it?

Frittered an afternoon at Agatha's: twilight, after listening to the dull-reading Wilbur, the gimicky Cummings, all sentimentality gliding up and down the scale, none of his early solid poems, All In Green My Love Went Riding, and the satires. Tea and sweet cake and the twilit gossip, with the cats licking sugar crumbs from their lips: her frantic debate with a smug

German psychoanalyst who excused the Nazis, Hitler (he was thwarted in school, all bad things begin with good intentions). Her running, tearing her hair, moaning. Her wearing a thick coat always in the house, like a caul, a womb-sack. She is mad, hysterical. Her opinions are emotional statements, woe to the one who misses the current. Must make a reading list. Have read two Brecht plays: always a surprise, a shock and pleasure: the dramatizing of "issues" embodied in the real world. Good, good. Will begin to make a rug today. To step on.

NOTEBOOK

January 28
Wednesday

A clear blue day, a close-clipped furze of white snow crisping all the cock-eyed angles of roof and chimney below, and the river white. Sun behind the building to the left, striking a gold-dollar glow from a domed tower I don't know the name of. If I can only write a page, half a page, here every day and keep myself counting blessings and working slowly to come into a better life.

Oddly happy yesterday, in spite of a bad morning, when I think I did nothing but work on a silly poem about a bull-ocean which evades all direct statement of anything under the pretense of symbolic allegory. Read ACRich today, finished her book of poems in half an hour: they stimulate me: they are easy, yet professional, full of infelicities and numb gesturings at something, but instinct with "philosophy", what I need. Sudden desire to do a series of Cambridge and Benidorm poems. Am I crude to say "the New Yorker sort." That means something.

Amazingly happy afternoon with Shirley yesterday. Took subway out. Smoky day, smoke white against snowfilled sky, smoke greyblack against pale twilight sky coming back. Brought my bundle of woolens and began to make the braided rug: immense pleasure cutting the good thick stuffs, wrestling with the material and getting a braid begun. Talked easily about babies, fertility, amazingly frank and pleasant. Have always wanted to "make something" by hand, where other women sew and knit and embroider, and this I feel is my thing. John sat in highchair, Shirley fed and bathed and bedded him, very easily. He was loving to me, hugging me and rubbing his forehead against mine. Felt part of young womanhood. How odd, men don't interest me at all now, only women and womentalk. It is as if Ted were my representative in the world of men. Must read some Sociology, Spock on babies. All questions answered.

Can I do the poems? By a kind of contagion?

Came home & happily made a quick hamburg supper. Lowells coming tomorrow and all the cleaning and planning for that I put off till tonight. Must get my hair cut next week. Symbolic: get over instinct to be dowdy lip-biting little girl. Get bathrobe and slippers and nightgown & work on femininity.

Read and translate at library in the afternoon. Last night I took a shower and braided on my rug while listening to Beethovens second symphony. Maybe I will learn something.

The cat is biting more now, but after mackerel this morning most endearingly climbed up my shoulder and nuzzled. Must try poems. DO NOT SHOW ANY TO TED. I sometimes feel a paralysis come over me: his opinion is so important to me. Didn't show him the bull one: a small victory. Also, be growing into a habit of happiness. That will work also. A check, $10 from the Nation for "Frog Autumn." Welcome. Am happy about living in England: to go to Europe at the drop of a channel-crossing ticket: I really want that. How odd: I would have been amazed five, ten years ago at the thought of this. And delighted. Must use Beuscher to the hilt.

Friday
February 13, 1959

First time I've had the heart to write in here for weeks. A lousy green depressing cold. Cried with the old stone-drop gloom with RB yesterday. She said I don't work as well so bad: I think I'm going to get well and then I feel I can't; need to be punished. Get a job, in Cambridge, somewhere, in a 10 day limit. I dream of bookstores, design research. That would be something. It is seven thirty. We have had orange juice, oatmeal, coffee for the first time in weeks of late sloppy risings and Ted's exile to the library. We are fools. The alarm on, we shower and rise. Five hours from seven to twelve is all we need for writing. She says: you won't write. This is so, not that I can't, although I say I cant.

Have been reading Faulkner. At last. Sanctuary and beginning the collected stories and excerpts. Will go on a jag. Absolutely flawless descriptive style: and much description: dogs, their smells, fuckings and terrors. Scenes. Whorehouse interiors. Colors, humor and above all a fast plot: rape with corn cobs, sexual deviation, humans shot and burned alive, he gets it in. And where are my small incidents, the blood poured from the shoes?

Sent Johnny Panic to Accent. Just to get it printed would give me a lift. Hornbook took "The Bull of Bendylaw": an auspice for my book at the Yale thing? I need to get rid of these poems some way.

Am going to Marty's this morning but never again anything in the morning except RB: my sunday confession.

The cat trying to get into my lap: it is spoiled by loving & hugging.

Shirley's story: her telling Mrs. N all about sex, Mrs. N reading sex books and telling her something helpful about women getting climaxes, which the indefatigable Mrs. N gets at fifty and after. "Did it help?" "Shirley tells me everything." The idealization of Dick, her favorite son, and Joanne," who can do no wrong: they go to New York, they sail, and no one worries about the money: Mrs. N's borrowings of cribs and scales and toidy seats for Shirley's baby. Making her feel ashamed. The terrible mother. Dick and Joanne's measured three-hour shift visits to both pairs of parents. The "hunting for the oar" at twilight.

C———'s sicknesses, calling Marty. Her affair with the married architect, moving out of the house. Stories from mad points of view. Free myself. The guilt, need for punishment is absurd. I am a victim of original sin, which is the natural human sloth, part of the human predicament. The cat stands up like a woodchuck in my lap and licks the space bar as if that would keep me loving it on my lap.

Stanley Kunitz," his bright white Cambridge apartment with the blood-red burlap curtains and the violent depthless red-accented paintings of his New Greenwich Village wife, who called him: Uh-huh, uh-huh, bye honey. His queer astigmatism, dismissing all poets but himself and the old Roethke and Penn Warren, especially women, whose success must be particularly distasteful to him. The experience of the New England Poetry Society meeting, their spending two hours on their little reading of members trash, tea, a hare-lipped Poetry Editor of the Saturday Evening post advising about submissions, before letting Kunitz read and then the unanswered telephone outside the door ringing throughout. Dinner at the horrible Hotel Commander with Isabella Gardner and the Fassets and Kunitz and fur-sleeved gross-faced Gerta.

February 19
Thursday

The North Wind doth blow. Grey and the snowflakes blowing suddenly like bits of white paper. Ann Hopkins" white-and-black spotted fixed female cat trying to get settled in smaller and smaller boxes, finally managing, and hiding its head in foetal position for a cat, I imagine. Then crawling up under her red bedspread and lying under it in the middle of the bed, and inert red lump. Queer: born with flying-squirrel flaps and too many thumbs, which bunch out from its feet.

A misery. Wrote a Granchester poem of pure description. I must get philosophy in. Until I do I shall lag behind ACR. A fury of frustration, some inhibition keeping me from writing what I really feel. I began a poem on "Suicide Off Egg Rock" but set up such a strict verse form that all power was lost: my nose so close I couldn't see what I was doing. An anesthetizing of feeling. Keeping me from work on a novel. To forget myself for the work, instead of nudging the work to be my reason for being and my self.

Dinners and parties all this week which I am glad to forgo from now on. Heard Wilbur read: oddly, I was bored to death. I enjoy his poems more when I read them myself: his voice is dull, playing a joke on the poem with the audience, his clever poems on the Mind Cave-Bat and Lamarck merely ingenious. Eighteenth century manners. Stanley Kunitz, in his best three or four poems much much finer. Stanley getting $15,000 from the Ford foundation for two years of writing what he wants where he wants. We hearing nothing from the Guggenheim. I, sitting here as if brainless wanting both a baby and a career but god knows what if it isn't writing. What inner decision, what inner murder or prison-break must I commit if I want to speak from my true deep voice in writing (which I somehow boggle at spelling)" and not feel this jam up of feeling behind a glass-dam fancy-facade of numb dumb wordage. Somewhat cheered by the Spectator printing my two small poems. I think success would be heartening now. But, most heartening, the feeling I were breaking out of my glass caul. What am I afraid of? Growing old and dying without being Somebody? It is good for me to be away from the natural stellar position at Smith. I look queerly forward to living in England: hope I can work for some weekly in London, publish in the women's magazines, maybe. England seems so small and digestible from here.

Typing frees me. Before Beuscher I obviously shall not write, so shall try writing letters. Courage, courage. It is as if I have been pushing myself so hard for so many years, I am slack once the outer demand is gone, resting only, I hope. Then to work on German and French. If I could work into prose, I might be able to whip my life into better shapes. Have tried getting up at 6:30 most mornings this week and Ted is happier, and I also. Even if I don't write. Part of it is I feel I should add a couple of powerful poems to the volume I am sending off to the Yale Contest this next week and this paralyses me. Better send the book off and free myself of it.

Try writing one page of talk every day. Enchanting child at Arthur and Geraldine (Kohlenberger?):[n] her Fuzzy Bronco, the queer stub-faced cats. Like another animal. Engel's[n] second novel: there will be a great silence about it. Yes, that would be worst.

Wednesday
February 25

The anniversary of our meeting, third. Last night a miserable dowie dowie fight over nothing, our usual gloom. I am ready to blame it all on myself. The day is an accusation. Pure and clear and ready to be the day of creation, snow white on all the roof tops and the sun on it and the sky a high clear blue bell jar.

Lousy dreams. Forget last nights. Gary Haupt was in it, refusing to speak and passing by with a stiff accusing and sallow face as if he smelt something bad. The other night it was men in costume, bright cummerbunds, knickers and white blouses, having a penalty given them, and not carried out, and suddenly forty years later they were lined up, I saw them small in the distance, and a man with his back to me and a great sword in his hand went down the line hacking off their legs at the knees, whereupon the men fell down like ninepins with their legstumps and lower legs scattered. I believe they were supposed to dig their own graves on the leg stumps. This is too much. The world is so big so big so big. I need to feel a meaning and productiveness in my life.

Got somewhere last week with RB I think. The resurrection of the awful Woodrow Wilson interview at Harvard. What I fear worst is failure, and this is stopping me from trying to write because then I don't have to blame failure on my writing: it is a last ditch defense, not quite the last - - - the last is when the words dissolve and the letters crawl away. Knowing this, how can I go to work? Transfer this knowledge to my inmost demons?

Ted's thinking idea good. I listed five subjects and got no farther than Egg Rock. Wrote a ghastly poem in strictly varying line lengths with no feeling in it although the scene was fraught with emotion. Then did it over, much better: got something of what I wanted. Pulled. To the neat easy ACRich lyricism, to the graphic description of the world. My main thing now is to start with real things: real emotions, and leave out the baby gods, the old men of the sea, the thin people, the knights, the moon-mothers, the mad maudlins, the lorelei, the hermits, and get into me, Ted, friends, mother and brother and father and family. The real world. Real situations, behind which the great gods play the drama of blood, lust and death.

Lowell's class yesterday a great disappointment: I said a few mealymouthed things, a few BU students yattered nothings I wouldn't let my Smith freshmen say without challenge. Lowell good in his mildly feminine ineffectual fashion. Felt a regression. The main thing is hearing the other student's poems & his reaction to mine. I need an outsider: feel like the recluse who comes out into the world with a life-saving gospel to find everybody has learned a new language in the meantime and can't understand a word he's saying.

When I write my first LHJ story I will have made a step forward. I don't have to be a bourgeois mother to do it either. The reason I don't write them is that it is safer from rejection not to - - - then I haven't the opportunity to be in jeopardy.

Reason I didn't like Monroe Engel on first look was his Harvard position and resemblance to the head of the WW committee. And his appointment is not renewed and his novel not reviewed. My god. The poor man.

O to break out into prose.

Saturday
February 28

7:30, a fog closing in, all the buildings melted away except the rooftops and chimneys immediately below the window. The mists of error. Stayed in bed yesterday with this peculiar fatigue I am sure comes from a weariness that I have no story plots and do not make any up. I have the time to write and am piling up brick by brick, a guilt. Yet I have written two good poems, better in their way, particularly the last, than any I have written: Point Shirley, and Suicide Off Egg Rock. Why can't I bring love back into my poems: start even with persona, if I am afraid.

Nightmare before going to RB this week: train broke down in subway in a fire of blue sparks, got on wrong track, driving in old car with Ted, drove into deep snowdrift and the car fell apart, struggled to a telephone after 11, her maid answered, and I felt she was home, either knowing this would happen and thus not coming out, or pretending she wasn't home. Bought blue shoes on the way back from seeing her. Relived with all the emotion the episode at the hospital in Carlisle. Murderous emotions in a child can't be dealt with through reason, in an adult they can.

Read Faulkner yesterday, after Tostoi's superb Death of Ivan Ilyitch, a sustained full-pitch rendering of the beast-man's fear and horror of dying. Is Ivan's knowledge, in a flash, at the last, that his life has been all wrong, a steady downgrade in just those points he thought it most a success, redemptive in any sense? He dies in peace, or at least, in a sudden recession of fear, in an access of light. But was the pain intended to bring this about? I think not. Suffering is because it is, the voice answers. The Bear a magnificent story except for the infuriating, confused (deliberately and unneedfully) fourth section, a bumbling apocalyptic rant about landownership and God and Ikkemotubbe and such rot. The rest, a clear, honest recreation of an archetypal image, the great Bear with the man's name, who is, in his way, large as Moby Dick.

Fog blowing by the window in great poufs now.

Try to get into a story. Forget self and give blood to creation.

NOTEBOOK

Monday, March 9

After a lugubrious session with RB, much freed. Good weather, good bits of news. If I don't stop crying she'll have me tied up. Got idea on the trolley for a poem because of my ravaged face: called The Ravaged Face. A line came, too. Wrote it down and then the five lines of a sestet. Wrote the first eight lines after coming back from a fine afternoon in Winthrop yesterday. I rather like it - - - it has the forthrightness of "Suicide Off Egg Rock". Also finished a New Yorkerish but romantic iambic pentameter imitation of Roethke's Yeats' poems. Rather weak, not, I think, book material, but I'll send it to the NY and see what they think.

A clear blue day in Winthrop. Went to my father's grave, a very depressing sight. Three grave yards separated by streets, all made within the last fifty years or so, ugly crude block stones, headstones together, as if the dead were sleeping head to head in a poorhouse. In the third yard, on a flat grassy area looking across a sallow barren stretch to rows of wooden tenements I found the flat stone, "Otto E. Plath: 1885–1940", right beside the path, where it would be walked over. Felt cheated. My temptation to dig him up. To prove he existed and really was dead. How far gone would he be? No trees, no peace, his headstone jammed up against the body on the other side. Left shortly. It is good to have the place in mind.

Walked over rocks along the oceanside under Water Tower Hill. Out on the sandbar I found the same colony of thick white and orangey snailshells. Got wet-footed and frigid handed collecting. Ted out at the end of the bar, in black coat, defining the distance of stones and stones humped out of the sea. Walked the seawall to Deer Island: hey, you can't go any farther, the guard said. We talked to the young chap in the hexagonal house on the shore, like a summerhouse, a glassed-in bandstand. Glimpsed the floral pattern of a comfortable armchair inside. He told us there was a piggery on the island, an chickens and cattle and, in the summer, corn, beans and garden greens. Gossiped about high realestate on the shore, his seniority on the job, the easy three to eleven shift. Came back & followed fire engines down Cornhill where there had been a great fire, which was still smouldering. The gutted brick building was blackened and hollow, smoke fanning in spasmodic whiffs from the eaves. Icicles hung from all the windowledges.

My desire for a career apart from writing. Writing impossible as my one thing, it is so dried up, so often. I would like to study comparative literature. The discipline of a PhD attracts me in my foolhardiness, or of reporting for weeklies, or of reviewing. I must use my brain in the world, not just at home on private things.

Great cramps, stirrings. It is still just period time, but I have even waves of nausea. Am I pregnant? That would queer my jobs for a while I guess. If only I could come to the novel, or at least the Journal stories. Maybe some good pregnant poems, if I know I really am.

March 20
Friday

Yesterday a nadir of sorts. Woke up to cat's early mewling around six. Cramps. Pregnant I thought. Not, such luck. After a long 40 day period of hope, the old blood cramps and spilt fertility. I had lulled myself into a fattening calm and this was a blow. Especially with Marty's troubles and adopting a child, and Shirley's second one on the way: I'd like four in a row. Then dopey, and the cramps all day. I am getting nowhere with RB. I feel I deliberately put myself into a self-pitying helpless state. Next week. What good does talking about my father do? It may be a minor cartharsis that lasts a day or two but I don't get insight talking to myself. What insight am I trying to get to free what? If my emotional twists are at the bottom of misery, how can I get to know what they are and what to do with them? She can't make me write, or if I do write, write well. She can give me more directives or insight in what I am doing and for what general ends I am doing it. I regress terribly there. I may have all the answers to my questions in myself but I need some catalyst to get them into my consciousness.

Then a brooding soup lunch and a horrid afternoon at work: made two mistakes in the income tax letters which must be typed over & spelt a word wrong I'd asked for twice on an applications blank. Very annoying. He had got me coffee too. Wicked self. Well, he was fool enough to hire me. I felt doped, grumpy. RB said cramps are all mental after arguing against natural childbirth, saying pain was real.

I cry at everything. Simply to spite myself and embarrass myself. Finished two poems, a long one, "Electra on Azalea Path" and "Metaphors for a Pregnant Woman", ironic, nine lines, nine syllables in each. They are never perfect, but I think have goodnesses. Criticism of 4 of my poems in Lowell's class: criticism of rhetoric. He sets me up with Ann Sexton," an honor, I suppose. Well, about time. She has very good things, and they get better, though there is a lot of loose stuff.

A desire to get my hair cut attractively instead of this mousy pony tail. Will no doubt go out and get a pageboy cut as of old. Is it money keeps me back? Must get fixed up before I go to Holyoke. Four weeks that gives me.

Refusal to write. I just don't. Except for these few poems, which have been coming thicker and better. I see the right state of mind like a never never land ahead of me. That casual, gay verve. Alas alas. I maunch on chagrins.

Desire for intellectual career. Have not touched German: to learn that would be a great triumph for me. The morning is fresh & blue. Incredible months ahead, of clearness. Produce, produce. To get the Yale thing would be good. No word from the Guggenheim. If not Yale this year, Lamont the next.

Do odds & ends today. Old panic back yesterday. What am I and what am I doing in world? Write another NYorker story. Or any story. Look up German concentration, I mean American detention camps. Read TS Eliot.

Finished the Tolkien trilogy. A triumph. A battle of the pans and kevas. I don't know when I have been so moved.

Sunday
March 29

Sitting here on a blue clear cold morning, Easter, I believe, and the risen Christ meaning only a parable of human renewal and nothing of immortality. My hair resembling its old self but newly cut in too-short bangs. The old brooding stasis of prose: I am full, but paralyzed to know what to do with it:

to say: a New Yorker or Journal story only stiffens me. I must do them for the fun of it.

An article-story: the Day I Died. And one of C——'s intrigues, The Alley: John Singer Sargent's mistress, Miss Salley. Egan and his mad child-wife.

A pleasanter day at my job this last, with the great grey-crewcutted DHH Ingalls" giving me two offprints of articles on Sanskrit poetry. Meeting Ted for beer afterwards & he working on his fox story anthology for the first time.

I want to begin my Bed Book. Something freezes me from my real spirit: is it fear of failure, fear of being vulnerable? I must melt it. I will get out some more children's book this week. I would rather publish this than a book of poems.

Lovely supper with Marcia and Mike on the depressing day we realized we'd done the wrong thing about the Guggenheim budget: and Ted getting into what Booth said were the final finals: a horror, we didn't demand enough and said we weren't going to Rome, thinking: they'll never give it us to go back to England. So we wrote back, changed budget and added Rome again, and now are hopeless: they'll think us ridiculous and vacillating and not give the money. Maybe, though, his letter was a letter of warning: giving us time to change? O o o. C—— waiting also for grants; Marcia and Mike glowing, about adopted baby in the offing?

Here are stories: the beautiful popular girl who can't get married. The homeloving childloving couple who cant have children. O yes, and the born-writer who can't write.

Got at some deep things with Beuscher: facing dark and terrible things: those dreams of deformity and death. If I really think I killed and castrated my father may all my dreams of deformed and tortured people be my guilty visions of him or fears of punishment for me? And how to lay them? To stop them operating through the rest of my life?

I have a vision of the poems I would write, but do not. When will they come?

Made, after Marcia, an elegant and delectable refrigerator cheesecake. All rots, however. These witless clear mornings. If I could get into prose, into children's books, it would be a salvation. If I could have simple fun doing it.

Thursday
April 23

As with April, spring manifests itself in joyous news. I am tired, having got up and out of Ted's work-room by 7, after two weeks of pre- and post-Guggenheim lethargy. We are transfigured. After a near-miss, a query and paltering over the budget and the place of travel, we got it, and rounded off to the farthest thousand, $5,000, which seems incredibly princely to us. After an invitation to Yaddo for two months in September and October, which we at first interpreted as a consolation prize. Guggenheim day: Friday April 10.

Also, yesterday, my second acceptance from the New Yorker: a pleasant two: the Watercolor of Granchester Meadows which I wrote bucolically "for" them, and Man in Black, the only "love" poem in my book, and the book-poem which I wrote only a little over a month ago at one of my fruitful visits to Winthrop. Must do justice to my father's grave. Have rejected the Electra poem from my book. Too forced and rhetorical. A leaf from Ann Sexton's book would do here. She has none of my clenches and an ease of phrase, and an honesty. I have my 40 unattackable poems. I think. And a joy about them of sorts. Although I would love more potent ones. All the Smith ones are miserable death-wishes. The ones here, however grey (Companionable Ills, Owl) have a verve and life-joy.

I am still blocked about prose. A novel still scares me. Have been reading "Passage to India" for the first time and admiring the miraculous flow and ease of it. To have the time to show the placing of a red card on a black, the change of daylight and the geography of certain hills: the blessings of the novelists wide untidy landscape art. It would be a certain therapy. But if I do some good stories, that is the way toward the mountain. I do not yet do them.

I think too much yet about What Kind they should be and Where I should

477

publish them. Poems now are an evasion too. I have my book as such and must not take the easy way of sitting a morning before a poem in evasion from my children's Bed Book which I long and yet fear to begin. Part of my passiveness. If you are dead, no one can criticize you, or, if they do, it doesn't hurt.

The "dead black" in my poem may be a transference from the visit to my father's grave.

Worked and worked with Beuscher: the skip of a week gave me courage and momentum: stayed awake the whole night before thinking over what I have come through and to. Concentrated on my suicide: a knot in which much is caught. Weary still from the absolutely deadening weekend in Northampton and Holyoke. The strain of Stanley's intolerable position. How to overcome my naivete in writing? Read others and think hard. Never step outside my own voice, such as I know it.

I think: a Wuthering Heights article for red-shoe money. Correct the word in my Monitor poem. Start a poem for the bed book. A story on the hospital. About the affair of Starbuck" & Sexton. A double story, August Lighthill and the Other Women. Also about the children, seen through Jan's eyes. Here is horror. And all the details. Get life in spurts in stories, then the novel will come. A way. By the time I get to Yaddo, three good publishable stories and the Bed Book done!

April 25
Saturday

Clear day, dragged up as usual early, but exhausted, too much so to write, so worked on polishing up essay on Withens only to be stopped in title from final typing by not knowing spelling Withens or Withins.

Two visits yesterday: to Mrs. Lamb, the terrible invalid downstairs who has lived in her small two-room apartment for 25 years and not been out of her room for two years. Her great monstrous fat body propped on a worn green plush chair with oddly high legs, so her elephantine legs, in thick beige stockings, could be propped on a footstool. The little cleaning woman ("so poor, just herself and her sister, they have nothing. I gave her some icecream my taximan brought today") going out as I came in seemed to have accomplished nothing. A sickening smell of medecines, stuffiness, old lady-sweat, as of rooms not opened for years. Dusty black telephones appeared in every corner, obviously so she wouldn't have to put herself out unduly to answer them. She wore a navyblue dress over her bulk with white buttons, innumerable white buttons, marching down the front and holding the material together with effort, little looped openings pulling at every notch. Her big-jowled face rested on her chest, queerly warted, and her greasy grey-yellowed hair hung in short strings ("I wanted to have a hairdresser come permanent it today, but she couldn't come, I hope you don't mind"). The smell gave me a headache. The room itself seemed a nightmare, an impossibility below our clean bright sweet-smelling place, and the more of a nightmare in being identical in shape with it. In spite of the cleaning woman, an oppressive sense of filth. Between Mrs. Lamb's high chair and the window were piles of dusty papers, mementos, boxes, from which she rummaged old pictures of her son, her grandchildren, her daughter in Egypt, dressed in jodphurs, taking pictures of the natives on the desert, and pictures of herself as an unbelievably attractive young girl in an hourglass dress, pouty and sultry, with, as her negro maid said "A Mae West figure". The old, dark surface of the photo, taken 50 years ago? Cast me into a pool of reveries, that such beauty should come to such a horrid mountain of immovable flesh, unable, because of her fat, to move out of her room for four years.

The room: exactly like ours, but repulsive. A black swatch of blistered paint on the icebox, and black soot and grease smears fanning away from the stove on the walls and ceilings, the window frames hanging with soot and the windows too smeared to see through. A little fake green christmas tree with soapflakes and tinsel stood on a small table beside a clock. Bare floor, no rugs. She came from the family of Shaws, her son married a Shaw (no relation) and her daughter (about 45?) had a young man, also a Shaw, Louis Agassiz Shaw (Junior), and her daughter-in-laws uncle, or father, was also, oddly enough, named Louis Agassiz Shaw. I shuddered to think of the state of the bedroom. She severed the muscles of her legs in jumping out of a car and stepping on a board walk unfastened at one end. Stories of burglars upstairs, her dog Crumpet saved from asphyxiation at the Animal Rescue League, the Count and Countess de Longay in our apartment, an old glassed-in bookcase: Castles of England. Daughter came, warm, solid, much improved atmosphere; left after two hours.

479

May 3, 1959
Sunday

A Day of Yawns after a fantastic spell of work from coffee to midnight last night. I am now hungrily putting the last minutes of cooking onto breaded veal in cream, green parsley rice and rather soggy yellow squash, and very weary. Washed hair. Retyped pages, a messy job, on the volume of poems I should be turning in to Houghton Mifflin this week. But AS is there ahead of me, with her lover GS writing New Yorker odes to her and both of them together: felt our triple martini afternoons at the Ritz breaking up. That memorable afternoon at G's monastic and miserly room on Pinckney "You shouldn't have left us": where is responsibility to lie? I left, yet felt like a brown winged moth around a rather meagre candle flame, drawn. That is over. As Snodgrass would say.

I wrote a book yesterday. Maybe I'll write a postscript on top of this in the next month and say I've sold it. Yes, after half a year of procrastinating, bad feeling and paralysis, I got to it yesterday morning, having lines in my head here and there, and Wide-Awake Will and Stay-Uppity Sue very real, and bang. I chose ten beds out of the long list of too fancy and ingenious and abstract a list of beds, and once I'd begun I was away and didn't stop till I typed out and mailed it (8 double spaced pages only!) to the Atlantic Press. The Bed Book, by Sylvia Plath.

Funny how doing it has freed me. It was a bat, a bad-conscience bat brooding in my head. If I didn't do it I would do nothing. A ready-made good idea and an editor writing to say she couldn't get the idea out of her head. So I did it. I feel if the Atlantic is stupid enough to reject it someone else will snap it up, and better so, if they will also take my poems. I have two ideas, one about a Lonesome Park and the other about a Town on a Very Steep Hill (for Christmas or Easter). Maybe I can work out one of those before I get my first rejection of the ms. Suddenly it frees me - - - and Ted too. I can go to the magazine rack this morning and get a NY Times, a NYorker, a Writers Mag and not feel drowned or sick. Me, I will make my place, a queer, rather smallish place, but room and view enough to be happy in.

The Monitor's accepting my first article "The Kitchen of the Fig Tree" for the Home Forum Page opened up a vista of $50 checks for an extension of my letter-writing habits. I have "A Walk to Withins" written and ready, and an idea for "Watching the Water Voles." They are Christian Scientist in their religious article and rather pagan on the rest of the page.

Read article on radium-dial painters, doomed in the amazingly radium-stupid 20's to die of internal radiation, in the NYorker. A STORY by Sylvia Townsend Warner. The usual flawlessly realized stuff with a pathos-or-bathos point "The Quality of Mercy". I think I could, with work and thought, write for them. But am far far from it. This week have kept all mornings free and must work on my Sweetie Pie story and figure what it's about. Sometimes, with the NYorker, I'm not so sure that matters! My joy now will be my first Children's Book accepted, and my first New Yorker story. All this throws the lugubrious balance away from my book of poems which may well improve by more maturing. If it only won the Yale, all would be fine. This year, I think, is a year of maturing. I am joyous in affirming my writing at last.

Wednesday
May 13, 1959

How many mornings pass like this one? Seed-time, I say. I read my note-books on Spain, take out a leaflet about "The Discontented Mayor" (prod-ded by an Esquire article on Spain) and browse and muse over working it up into a short-short vignette for Esquire or possibly Mlle. About to turn to that infuriating story which isn't sure of its own point "Sweetie Pie & The Gutter Men". Very good possibilities, if only I can get it out of its last-summer fix. Wrote a pretty-pretty poem yesterday "In Midas' Country", one of those ideal New Yorker pieces. Ironic to see if they buy/ Wish I'd hear from "Johnny Panic": I think that is publishable. Cooler and grey, with that city-canyon wetness after a spring rain.

Bothered about RB: I seem to want to cover everything up, like a cat its little crappings with sand, perhaps before leaving for California?

Well, I must bring up those pressure points: suicide, deflowering, T's sister, and present writing; lack of rooted social life, yet not minding it; lack of children. Today. Also concern about mind getting lazy. Learning languages.

My "Bull of Bendylaw" book of poems is much better arranged. Also, at this rate, with "Arts In Society" accepting "Sculptor", "The Goring" (which I was beginning to think unsalable) and "Aftermath", I have only 13 poems to publish before all 45 are in print, and these poems should not be too hard to sell.

Ten, the clocks strike. Yesterday was tropical: rain, fearful humidity, sweating, low ragged wet clouds, heat lightning. We tossed till midnight when a cooler air set in.

Mailed the ms. of Ted's Children's Book "Meet My Folks!" both to Harper's and Faber's. This book should sell like hotcakes. I reread my notes about Ted's children's fables written three summers ago in Spain, how they should be a classic, and now see how obviously unsalable they were in such form, and hope my judgments have matured as I think they have. Well, in my book of 45 poems there are only 10 surviving of the book I sent Auden at the Yale Series two summers ago. And I have written a lot more than 35 since then, too.

Now, to see what work I can accomplish before I leave for RB.

Monday
May 18

Set-back last week. Got Monitor article on watervoles rejected which I too lightly and confidently predicted would earn me an easy $50. I am not wise to even such a common market? It did me good. I got mad, then grim, then industrious and resigned. Finished, all of a piece, "Sweetie Pie and the Gutter Men" which has been on my back for about, almost, a year. Have ideas, ideas. I think it is a damn good story. Much more accomplished, working three characters, conversation, than "Johnny Panic" which I have not got back from Accent yet, sent sometime last fall. Am waiting to get name of story editor of NY from Stanley. It will be by far the best story I have sent them yet.

Ted & I have our two children's books sent off, not a word, of course, yet. His to Harper's and Faber's, mine to the Atlantic Press. I have rumbling ideas for "The Lonesome Park", only must figure how to get people in it.

Changed title of poetry book in an inspiration to "The Devil of The Stairs", which I hope has never been used before. "The Bull of Bendylaw", which was catching, had an obscure point, the idea of energy breaking through ceremonial forms, but this title encompasses my book & "Explains" the poems of despair, which is as deceitful as hope is. Hope this goes through.

Dreamed last night of being a matron with seven daughters, like dolls, whom I was to dress in party dresses all graded rose-colors, yet I found blue and purple dresses among the yellow and pink. Great confusion. Have they their gloves, their pocketmoney in their pocketbooks. One daughter was large, blond, freckled, Arden Tapley, only how changed from her innocent youth. Dreamt also George Starbuck had a book of poems published by Houghton Mifflin, a spectacular book, full of fat substantial poems I hadn't seen, called "Music Man". The endpapers were decorated as in a childrens book, ducks, colored Jack Horners, etc. He also send an envelope full of profound jottings on scraps of paper: To my dear friends. Zany epigrams and the like.

Worked on my braided rug the last two days after a stall of a couple of months. A lovely thing, the rich new blues and reds and red-and-black weaves I got with Shirley. Looks like a stained glass window. Shall risk having it cleaned today, I think.

Idea for novel, still titled <u>Falcon Yard</u>: story of three women, or mainly one: C——, with her illegitimate baby and mental hospital, just as Marty, her closest tagalong friend was discovering she couldn't have a baby. Story of C——'s alley, which will be named Falcon Yard. Much easier to work up because not personal. At Yaddo? Must read more contemporary novels.

Last night, down Hanover Street by all the elaborate Italian florists, with their great paper bouquets of flowers, heart-shaped and scalloped, and the innumerable pastery shops with seven-tiered wedding cakes, came upon "<u>Moon Street</u>". A poem or story deserves that name.

Wednesday
May 20th

All I need now is to hear that GS or MK" has won the Yale and get a rejection of my children's book. AS has her book accepted at HM and this afternoon will be drinking champagne. Also an essay accepted by PJHH," the copy-cat. But who's to criticize a more successful copy-cat. Not to mention a poetry reading at McLean. And GS at supper last night smug as a cream-fed cat, very pleased indeed, for AS is in a sense his answer to me. And now my essay, on Withins, will come back from PJHH, and my green-eyed fury prevent me from working. Or drive me into hibernation & more work. Tell T nothing. He generalized about the article on water-voles he hadn't read, expatiating from Pjhh's note: Oh, all your stuff, the trouble with it is it's too general. So I won't bother showing him the story on Sweetie Pie I've done, keep the viper out of the household & send it out on my own. My first accepted story would give me intense joy: but even without it, I shall plod on and on, free as I am at present and for a year of the need to work, free as yet of children. Fight last night, he not bothering to perceive how intolerable it is to me to work (ho, have I worked? very little) and feel everything stagnating on my desk, and I lying awake and tense, the air fearfully wet and hot, the sheets damp and heavy. Got up finally and read all of Philip Roth's "Goodbye Columbus" which except for the first novella I found excellent, rich, and always fascinating, entertaining. Even laughed. Got to bed at 3. Bad sleep. Woke to the same hostile silences. He did make coffee. Banged about. I showered and felt better and in this sweet nauseous thick air am waiting to get mail, rejections, to go to B (am very ashamed to tell her of immediate jealousies - - - the result of my extra-professional fondness for her, which has inhibited me) and then the Sultans will disarrange the day, and the Booths for dinner. He should be some comfort, he is nice, if almost pathetically serious and earnest.

What to do with anger, ask her. One thing to say: Yes, I want the world's praise, money & love, and am furious with anyone, especially with anyone I know or has had a similar experience, getting ahead of me. Well, what to do when this surges up over & over? Last night I knew that mother didn't matter - - - she is all for me, but I have dissipated her image and she becomes all editors and publishers and critics and the World, and I want acceptance there, and to feel my work good and well-taken. Which ironically freezes me at my work, corrupts my nunnish labor of work-for-itself-as-its-own-reward. Hit this today.

Learn from Roth. Study, study. Go inward. There it is pure. Or may be, one day.

Shower, keep clean, enjoy colors and animals. People, if possible. How I love the Baskins. The only people I feel are a miracle of humanity and integrity, with no smarm. I MUST WRITE ABOUT THE THINGS OF THE WORLD WITH NO GLAZING. I know enough about love, hate, catastrophe to do so.

Braided violently on rug, which is at cleaner's, and felt anger flow harmlessly away into the cords of bright soft colored wool. It will be not a prayer rug but an anger rug. Only hope the cleaner's today do a good job. That is a relief, to have that to do. Think I will go to the sailing place. By myself.

Monday
May 25

Again, again, the grumpy fruitless cramps. The two or three odd days of hope blasted and all to begin again. My Maudlin poem is a prophetic little piece. I get the pleasure of a prayer in saying it: Gibbets with her curse the moon's man. Of course it would wait till today, when I was going to make lunch at Marcia's (which I shall call to cancel) then my job at Harvard then the Poetry Society with the triumphant AS & GS and then dinner with Hitchen" and some woman or other which I shall have to cook up. Oh crud. The two things I would like are a book (or story in the NY) accepted and a baby. After all my surmising about Marcia and Mike I don't feel like going through anything similar myself. Must not be accusing, although I feel like it.

Max" came yesterday. Odd, how I dislike him. A horrible rich unction to his voice. A mental effort to say he may be exemplary, but his aura is all wrong. I couldn't look at him. He made me sick. Short, too-white skin, red hair, a sense of flabbiness, not any bite or grit. I don't want to see him again. Except that I would like to see where my father went to school in Wisconsin.

The gripes don't let up in spite of aspirin. Aspirin make me feel sick. It will be a bad day all round. My face looks yellow and podgy as cheese.

Reading V. Woolf's The Years. With rain, she can unite a family, here in London, there in the country, in Oxford. But too disparate. By skipping five, eleven, years, and from person to person, suddenly a little girl is in her fifties with grey hair, and so we learn time passes, all moves. But the descriptions, the observations, the feelings caught and let slip, are fine, a luminous web catching it all in, this is life, this is time.

I now am in pain, and a grinding frustrated pain. Earlier in the morning, the sun, coming over the buildings in the east caught and illuminated to a bright virid glow the ivy, the new ivy, on the red brick wall of the garden below in Acorn Street. The leaves in Louisberg Square are so thick now I can only see the greek togaed statue as a nobbed pale grey stone, with dapples of light and shadow. Dare I take another pill? If the pain would shut up; but then I'd be sicker.

Brains for supper last night. Ugh, I gag to think of it. I made them with a pungent wine sauce and they were ghastly. Even Ted couldn't eat all of them. Soft, flabby, obscene meat: food for mental invalids. Gah.

ANother fresh May morning gone to hell, for no reason but this crampiness. If childbirth pangs are real, why aren't cramps real? And why should I have them if I think they're ridiculous?

The chicken, raw, wrapped in paper in the icebox, dropped a drop of blood on my pristine white cheesecake. Dreamed of catching a very tiny white rabbit last night: a menstruating dream?

Sunday
May 31

A heavenly, clear, cool Sunday, a clean calendar for the week ahead, and a magnificent sense of space, creative power and virtue. Virtue. I wonder if it will be rewarded. I have written six stories this year, and the three best of them in the last two weeks! (Order: Johnny Panic and the Bible of Dreams, The Fifteen Dollar Eagle, The Shadow, Sweetie Pie and the Gutter Men, Above the Oxbow, and "This Earth Our Hospital"). Very good titles. I have a list of even better. Ideas flock where one plants a single seed.

I feel that this month I have conquered my Panic Bird. I am a calm, happy and serene writer. With a pleasant sense of learning and being better with every story, and at the same time the spurred tension that comes from knowing they fall short, in this way or that, from what I see ahead, ten stories, twenty stories from now.

I have done, this year, what I said I would: overcome my fear of facing a blank page day after day, acknowledging myself, in my deepest emotions, a

486

writer, come what may: rejections or curtailed budgets. My best story is "This Earth Our Hospital" (I seem jam full of Eliot titles, having changed the title on my book of poems to "The Devil Of The Stairs"). Full of humor, highly colored characters, good, rhythmic conversation. An amazing advance from "Johnny Panic", set in the same place, but told all as an essay, with only one or two other characters.

I think of a book, or a book of stories: "This Earth Our Hospital". That is what I would call it, pray nobody beats me to it. I weep with joy.

Last night I sent off my application from here for a TV writing grant. Oddly enough, it would cause such complications in our plans that I half don't want it, yet it would mean an income, combined of $10,000 the year. I have an amazingly interesting biography, am young, promising. Why won't they give me one of the five? Money, money. I like CBS, too. They are more inventive than most stations. Another test, like Mlle's June month - - - only more dangerous: would I pass, keep myself intact? Interesting.

Sent off "Above the Oxbow" which I wrote up from an "exercise" I did last July and which moved me very much, and "This Earth Our Hospital" to the Atlantic, a very good contrast. If they don't take the latter story they're crazy. It should be a Best American Short Story.

Amusingly, and significantly, these two stories at the Atlantic free me from an over-emphasis on the two at the New Yorker, which I feel now will probably be rejected. I will have two more and better stories out by the time I hear from the Atlantic, and slowly pile them up. I feel to have come, for the first time in my life, to a break through into that placid, creative Wife of Bath humored Sea I only saw in glimpses from a very narrow, reef-crammed strait. The house is clean, polished. My assignments are off, and I have a list of others to begin:

The System & I: a humorous essay about 3 or 4 run-ins with socialized medicine. The Little Mining Town In Colorado: about a young girl's plunge into the hothouse world of soap-opera while she is bedded with rheumatic fever: relation with her parents and her very strong nurse figure (this suggested by Steve Fasset's account of his nurse, who really didn't want him to get well, he was her life for 15 years and in such a sybaritic, no, no, such a symbiotic relationship pattern found it intolerable when he opposed his will to hers). Point at which soap-opera and real-worlds fuse, and then separate.

The Discontented Mayor: A vignette in Spain, American boy and girl living together, interview with mayor. No more than ten pages, full of color and character. Broken mayor. (to Harper's, Esquire).

Lord Baden-Powell and the Mad Dogs: (New Yorker, Esquire): 7–10 pages, cocktail party setting in weird room at Elizabeth's with Jim, builds up fake story, his crippling, his way of getting back at the world. Mostly conversation. Sense of fakeness, who is gullible, who is deceived. His way of limiting the healthy members of the world, getting back at them.

Emmet Hummel and the Hoi Polloi: an essay about the annoying experiences with common tradespeople, sense of persecution, contrast to the cheery Reader's Digest. Example, perhaps concluding example: eating boiled eggs at breakfast in boarding house, cracks off the top, sounds hollow: nothing in egg: puts in salt, pepper, butter. Everyone else is eating eggs. He cannot jump up and shout: Fraud, fraud, I have no egg. Simply puts the spoon to his mouth, makes motions of eating. No one notices him. Other incidents: Subway newstand lady and Magazine. He thumbs through, waiting for train. Wants to see who has written an article. She asks, May I help you in a prodding way. He says, just a minute, I want to see if something is in here. She attends to others. He holds up magazine & five dollar bill, but she deliberately avoids him. Then train comes clanging in. He puts magazine down, thinking it will take too long for her to change the bill, but magically she is there, taking the bill. The train opens its doors and people crowd up to the woman: she takes dimes, changes quarters. Excuse me, excuse me, my change please. She looks satisfied, keeps on taking money. Finally, after everybody almost has got on the train, she counts out four dollar bills and change onto the papers so he has to scramble to pick them up. Rushes away after she says "You kept me waiting so long sir, choosing your magazine, and you expect me to hurry with your change." Furious. Thinks up devastating answers all the way home on the train. But knows the futility of this: he won't be back to that same station, and if he ever is, the lady won't be the same.

Similar encounter in public market with peaches: inability to buy the ones he wants. Sense of his own sensitivity always losing out against the coarse, cheating practicality of the common people. Clerk in a bank, or some such. Neat adding up of figures, no problems. Immaculate, spartan, chaste.

Diggers of house across the street. Babies in boarding house cry. Emmet asks when they'll be through: "What's it to you, buddy." Policeman rude also. Goes through green light, turns yellow. Called over. Policeman makes out ticket in spite of his protests. I guess I better begin on Emmet Hummel. A New Yorker piece? If only I were one of their people.

Supper at Frances Minturn Howard's" on Mount Vernon Street. The sense of old, subtle elegance. Red plush sofas, tarnished, yet glinting silver tea paper on the walls. Oil miniatures of cousins, Julia Ward Howe background. A supper, light and delectable, of ham, succulent with fat and cloves and crust, asparagus, and a thread-thin noodle cooked in chicken broth and browned with cheese and bread crumbs. Vanilla ice cream, fresh strawberries and finger-size jelly rolls for dessert.

Her garden: a cool white-painted well. Spanish wrought iron flower-pot holders. A brick flowerbed built up all around. Tall, Dutch tulips, just past their prime. Ivy, a fountain with a dolphin. A frog in the shrubbery. Solomon's seal. Bleeding hearts. And the brick walls whitewashed to the height of a room, giving a light, spanish patio effect. Dutchmen's pipe, or some such vine forming a lattice of green leaves over the brick wall at the back. A great tree, what is it, those mosquito trees, Tree of Heaven, plunging up to the light between the buildings. Rum and lemon juice, and the cool elegant plopping of the water.

Talk: Tom? Is it, Howard, a radio Ham, stories of men in Louisburg Square with ham radios, presidents of companies, heads of the Sheraton Hotels. People who want islands so they will be sought out from all over the world. Calling CQ CQ, calling CQ. Memories of George Sassoon in Cambridge and his set, his radio ham's pallor. The Horseless Age: magazine of 1904 with all the old cars. Tom's father knew Wright brothers, man who invented the Stanley Steamer, men who utilized ammonia deposits in refrigerators in a creative way. We talked of Lindbergh, the chaste hero of two continents, the case of the kidnapping of his child. The electrocuted murderess of her husband in some Schneider-Grey case or other, a very clumsy affair. Teletype machines. Steve's hand-elevator when he had rheumatic fever. The man who slept in the zoo with the monkeys (no, that was another time at Agatha's, I should have put that down while I remembered it). Pink brocade draperies. Oriental cups, oriental screens. Must learn names of the proper carpets and so on.

Now for Ingalls: his mother determined to redecorate the house, making the South Side into a separate house for Ingalls & his wife. Says to Doctor: "Well I don't suppose if I have only a year or so to live it would be much use to decorate. What do you advise me to do?" Doctor Jarman reported to have said "Don't redecorate." Cruelly confirming her suspicions. Now she wants to redecorate the livingroom to make it more livable for herself. Problem of her Idees Fixe after last bout of pneumonia: her wheelchair, being wheeled around in the Circle by a handiman.

The Night Watchman with Problems: feet hurt, has to sit down, always falls asleep when he sits down. Falls in love with all the Hotel's telephone operators, sends them presents.

Mr. Munyer: Fine laces, leathers, etc. etc. Complaining letter: rent of shop raising now three times, to $7000. Not as many display windows as shoe shop, and no fans now. Atmospheric condition so serious that customers just step in and step out again it is so intolerably humid, with-out looking around. Airconditioning said to cost close to two-thousand dollars. He doesn't want to pay, for it will only go into increasing value of shop for hotel, nothing he can take away with him, and nobody will rent the shop if it's not air-conditioned. His twenty-five year build-up of customers, his yearly trip for fine leathers and laces to Vienna. Aggrieved, aggrieved. His "Levantine indirection".

Taffee: Ingalls daughter in Germany. Applications to Radcliffe for year after next. What will she do this year? Be a Gaststudent in Germany? Ingalls 15 year old boy at Nobel and Greenough: his car Puddle-Jumper.

The ski lodge: expensive lanterns. 6 hundred $ sofas, chairs, counters, carpets, draperies. Cork floors. Fireplaces. Snow-making machine. Trestle lift. Change of advertising agents. Genteel bungling of old agents: "gentle ladies to babysit": he changes all this.

Jain monks in India; seeable only in 3-month rainy season as they have a vow to move on every night otherwise. Elaborate metaphorical pleas for money and scholarships at Harvard from Poona, Agra, etc. Indian fairy-tales, bad translations of the great poets.

Jane & Peter: Sense of something wrong. She redoing whole house where Peter's mistress lived for two years. They are repainting, buying original paintings - - - a Lawrence Sisson of worm-diggers. Very funny, now that I think of it. His tragic burnt-out fire poem in the Atlantic (also odd, with Ted's poem supposedly accepted last fall when Peter's were rejected not out yet) which Jane snorts at: "When did you write it?" Does she know all about his mistress. Or, for that matter, about me? God, story-situation after situation. Only to make them, to define them.

I feel in a braiding-rug mood today. Very sleepy, as after a good love-making, after all that writing this week. My poems are so far in the background now. It is a very healthy antidote, this prose, to the poems' intense limitations.

Rain last night drawing away visibly, street by street: it is raining every-where, pouring great whited lines, then not raining on Willow Street, but raining on Chesnut Street and the park, then not raining on Chestnut Street, but raining on the park, then the rain and clouds folding up completely and packing off. A grey, silvered sunset, everything faintly luminous and glisten-ing, but the heat unrelieved. Baby ducklings bobbing comically on the Embankment. We kept counting six, six, everytime we got a number a couple going down and couple more bobbing up. Suddenly there were eight, and they all paddled away to the breakwater islands to go to bed.

A happier sense of life, not hectic, but very slow and sure, than I have ever had. That sea, calm, with sun bland on it. Containing and receiving all the reefy, narrow straits in its great reservoir of peace.

June 6
Saturday

After a spurt of unaccustomed exercise yesterday in Gloucester Harbor, rowing in the cold, without enough layers of sweaters to keep from shaking with chill, and catching not one fish, although a boat of two male rowers passed by holding up a string of mammoth white-bellied flounders and a pan of the same, I fell aching into bed last night and slept as if blackjacked.

Dreamt one dream I remember, as apposite and ironical to this morning's mail. Read J.D.SAlinger's long "Seymour: An Introduction" last night and today, put off at first by the rant at the beginning about Kafka, Kierkegaard, etc., but increasingly enchanted. Dreamed, oh how amusedly, that I picked up a New Yorker, opened to about the third story (not in the back, this was important, but with a whole front page, on the right, to itself) and read "This Earth - - - That House, That Hospital" in the deeply endearing New Yorker-heading type, rather like painstakingly inked hand-lettering. Felt a heart palpitation (my sleep becomes such a reasonable facsimile of my waking life) and thought "That's my title, or a corruption of it". And of course, it is: an alteration of "This Earth Our Hospital" and either a very good or an abominable variation of it. Read on: my own prose: only it was the "Sweetie Pie" story, the back-yard tale, with the would-be Salinger child in it. Beuscher congratulating me. Mother turning away, saying: "I don't know, I just can't seem to feel anything about it at all." Which shows, I think, that RB has become my mother. Felt radiant, a New Yorker glow lighting my face. Precisely analogous to that young British Society girl Susan who, after being deflowered in a canoe house, asks her handsome young deflowerer: Don't I look Different? Oh, I looked different. A pale, affluent nimbus emanating from my generally podgy and dough-colored face.

This morning woke to get a letter in the mail from the estimable Dudley Fitts," which I numbly translated to be a kind refusal of "The Bull of Bendy-law", saying I missed "by a whisper", was the alternate, but my lack of technical finish (!) was what deterred him, my roughness, indecision, my drift in all but four or five poems. When my main flaw is a machinelike syllabic death-blow. A real sense of Bad Luck. Will I ever be liked for anything other than the wrong reasons? My book is as finished as it will ever be. And after the Hudson acceptance, I have great hopes that all 46 poems will be accepted within a few months. So what. I have no champions. They will find a lack of this, or that, or something or other. How few of my superiors do I respect the opinions of anyhow. Lowell a case in point. How few, if any, will see what I am working at, overcoming. How ironic, that all my work to overcome my easy poeticisms merely convinces them that I am rough, anti-poetic, unpoetic. My God.

I am grim, sour. Rejection will follow rejection. I am only a little better equipped to take them than a year, two years ago. I am still at the low point of consoling myself by the assurance that Dudley Fitts is a fool, who wouldn't know a syllabic verse if he saw one. Well, now to the rounds. To Knopf, Viking, Harcourt, Brace.

Wednesday
June 10

Three poetry rejections this morning: Paris Review, New Yorker, and Christian Science Monitor. Notes, nice notes. The main thing being to send them out rapidly again. Just as I think: ah, I shall have no trouble getting these accepted, bang. Sent my book of poems, The Devil Of The Stairs, off to Knopf on Monday, June 8th. How unpopular I am. Will send a bunch to the Nation. Well, have made Sewanee, Partisan, Hudson this year. And another 2 to the New Yorker. The CSMonitor likes my last essay, the one on Withens. Must get Folks into any others I do. Folks and facts. Send my poems next to Harcourt, Brace. Philip Booth's history of lots of publisher's rejections. Then the Lamont prize. Maybe I can play the same game.

Day in Winthrop, fishing. Cold. Caught two crabs (Ted did) and a skate, foul-lipped face on a flat fish. Came home with 15 pounds of fresh cod thanks to a moustached, wooden-footed acquaintance of the sea who went out 16 miles and came back with a boat full which he halved with us. Gulls hanging, voracious, tugging at the fish-guts he tossed, wolfing a foot-long intestine in a few flying gulps. Crying, and hanging on the wind over our heads.

Notes: Woman on the bus with three children and a fourth on the way. Loud shrew voice: Princess, Princess, you can't stand up there.

A woman who secretly deprives her husband of the best, largest plate of food: eats the marrow out of his bones literally.

People who grow a whole colony of avocado tree-plants along the shelf by the shower in the bathroom.

Must do a couple more stories so I won't be sad, overly sad, when the one's I've done come back from the New Yorker, Atlantic, etc. How many thousands of people as writers more successful than I. If I don't write in spite of this, in spite of rejections, I don't deserve acceptances.

Felt broken on the rack after yesterdays wind, rowing. Good feeling. Every-thing in life takes tang from it: hot tea, hot bath, freshest ever cod-fish sauteed with hot potatoes. Reading in bed. Warm comforts. Began Lonely Crowd this morning, an antidote to V. Woolf's tiresome The Years, finished last night. She flits, she throws out her gossamer nets. Rose, at age 9, sneaks to the store in the evening alone. Then she is fat, grey-haired, 59, snatching at remarks, lights, colors. Surely, this is not Life, not even real life: there is not even the Ladies' Magazine entrance into sustained loves, jealousies, boredoms. The recreation is that of the most superficial observer at a party of dull old women who have never spilt blood. That is what one misses in Woolf. Her potatoes and sausage. What is her love, her childless life, like, that she misses it, except in Mrs. Ramsey, Clarissa Dalloway. Surely if it is valid there, she should not keep losing it to lighting effects followed over the general geographic area of England, which are fine, painstaking, but in the last ditch, school-essay things. Out of this fragmentary welter the best works rise. Of course life is fragmentary, deaf people not hearing the point, lovers laughing at each other over nonsense, but she shows no deeper current under the badinage.

What to discuss with RB? Work, desire for work of meaning. To learn German. To write, be a Renaissance woman.

Saturday
June 13

A rainy, sticky unweddingy day. Three years ago, on such a day in London, Ted and I were tracking down our clergyman in front of Charles Dickens house.

Stayed up till about 3 this morning, feeling again the top of my head would come off, it was so full, so full of knowledge. Found out yesterday, George Starbuck won the Yale. He sure this proves him the Best. Calling up, "O, didn't I tell you". I had inured myself to a better book than mine, but this seemed a rank travesty, and John Holmes" well-involved in it. Asking us out to night spots with him and Galway Kinnell," the one dense and utterly unfavorable reviewer Ted had ("not one important or finished poem in the book") to celebrate Kinnell's acceptance by Houghton Mifflin and submission to the Lamont Awards. Of course he will win.

Drank tea, ate steak and fried potatoes about 10 pm, the steak, of course, the first mealy-mouth steak we've got from DeLuca. Read COSMO-POLITAN from cover to cover. Two mental-health articles. I must write one about a college girl suicide. THE DAY I DIED.

And a story, a novel even. Must get out SNAKE PIT. There is an increasing market for mental-hospital stuff. I am a fool if I don't relive, recreate it.

Mailmen below everywhere in the rain, in their short-sleeved light blue shirts and prophetic hats. O for a word, a transfiguring word. I regressed, but am getting back where my Self and my need to publicly affirm its Success Powers is melting out of my view, and the world, with my great curiosity in it, my need to observe, clinically, pain, sorrow, jealousy, conversaion, is coming back and I, that limiting blank wall, am irrevelant.

My Heart Leaps Up When I Behold A Mailman On The Street.

For RB: It is not when I have a baby, but that I have one, and more, which is of supreme importance to me. I have always been extremely fond of the definition of Death which says it is: Inaccessibility to Experience, a Jamesian view, but so good. And for a woman to be deprived of the Great Experience her body is formed to partake of, to nourish, is a great and wasting Death. After all, a man need physically do no more than have the usual intercourse to become a father. A woman has 9 months of becoming something other than herself, of separating from this otherness, of feeding it and being a source of milk and honey to it. To be deprived of this is a death indeed. And to consummate love by bearing the child of the loved one is far profounder than any orgasm or intellectual rapport.

Also, about Ambition: universal, driving Ambition; how to harness it, not be a Phaeton to its galloping horses. To keep in that state of itch which is comfortable: goals far enough ahead to be stimulating, near enough to be attainable with discipline and hard work, and self-generating enough to offer new goals and distances when one is achieved. And to work like a ditch-digger to spade up new areas of sensibility and knowledge and awareness.

Monday
June 15

A frigid grey morning, cold wet snivelling winds. I am still dazed by our being back on schedule. Yesterday: a very Pleasant day. We got up early. Ted got raisin bread at the store & we drank hot tea with the crisp fruity toast, sogged in butter. Outside: whipping rains, black skies, cracks and bumbles of thunder. I worked all day on his "Courting of Petty Quinnett" story, which I think is marvelous: perfectly plotted, the race of the three women for the fortune and the husband, each with a character pattern that involves, inevitably, her dropping out, in one way or another, of the race. Ted's mother & sons relation very well done. The fine apparition of Mad Ann Pilling in a red ball dress on the old cart horse. He has a book of stories here: Yorkshire tales. I am very proud and excited. Where to sell it? Some audience would be delighted. I think, if it passes Harper's, Harper's Bazaar, I'll try the Ladies' Home Journal even, and Cosmopolitan, then Mlle, then, finally, the New Yorker, the Atlantic. It is an off-beat story, but I should think eminently publishable.

I rise and sit again. No mailman of course. Have finished the Frankau novel, also excellent: Cara and the Duchess magnificent eccentricas come to colored, mad life. Fine foil to the sensitive drolly grave Penelope Wells and the serious Don. Read Jean Stafford, so much more human than Elizabeth Hardwicke. Hardwicke's characters utterly unlikeable in any way. A sense of the superior position of writer and reader - - - even the baby, as Agatha shrewdly observed, although it only appears for a paragraph, is a nasty louse, unredeemed. Stafford full of color, warmth, humor, even her witches and child-thiefs are human, humorous, part of the world, not small flat cutouts with sticky eyelashes. What strikes me about that collection of four New Yorker writers is their density. I tried to approach this, and, I think, did, in my "Sweetie Pie" story, and, in another way, in my hospital story, but my "Shadow" story reads mighty thin, mighty pale.

Today: reminisences of Cantors outdoor wedding. The great tent in the garden with leaf silhouettes on the roof, freshly planted mignonette, baby's-breath. Daisy bunches on little ribboned posts, a red-carpet, green-and-white-striped canopy from the street. Guests: men with canes, ladies in white straw hats, white gloves, pastel linens. Mrs. C's electric blue roses, electric blue shoes, electric blue hat of a great cabbge rose sitting smack on top of her head with a sequinned veil frilled out around it like a corolla of fishnet, the vivid turquoise feathers repeating the motif of turquoise on the print dress. Her tall elegance: "Kahalil Gibran, by the Prophet". The Christian Science Service: by a renegade Unitarian minister: service made up by the young people. Readings from Gibran, Science and Health, something about the masculine and feminine principles. Dangerous and ambiguous reading from Gibran about needing to stay separate, Laurentian. Leave out "in sickness and in health". Musicians: organ, violin, bass fiddle, hidden in shrubbery with soprano. Aria "Overhead the Moon is Beaming" from Student Prince. "Thank Heaven for Little Girls", "Wonderful Guy", "The Girl That I Marry" at reception. Line. Yellow sunflower dresses, straw hats, green velvet ribbons and green shoes. Undoctored punch, tables miraculously up in yard: spun sugar, shoe and rose shaped ices, mushrooms, caviar, lobster puffs, asparagus rolls.

Notes: "Do you remember my dream?" A giddy woman who has mildly prophetic dreams. Lives in dreams. THE BIG DREAMER. Just looked up my old story, THE WISHING BOX: not bad. One or two places quite amusing. But the real world in it isn't real enough. It is too much a fable. Good idea, though.

MENTAL HOSPITAL STORIES: Lazarus theme. Come back from the dead. Kicking off thermometers. Violent ward. LAZARUS MY LOVE.

I think I see Our Mailman, the one with the redolent cigars. Resign, resign, myself to rejection from the New Yorker, even though I dreamed I saw my obstetrician story published under the title of my hospital story at the Atlantic.

I feel insufferable impatience. This week my Bed Book should be either accepted or rejected by the Atlantic Press, I have sent my revision to Emilie McLeod." After the grim news Starbuck got the Yale, to which I am now resigned, if disappointed in Fitts' judgment, and that Maxine K also got a letter from Henry Holt (and how many other women also?) I feel very dubious about wanting to be published by Holt: a pride, a sense that I wouldn't want it unless they put me up for the Lamont. If only Knopf accepted my book I'd say hell to the Lamont. Knopf, or Harcourt, Brace or Macmillan (maybe) or Viking. If only Rosenthal would write me about Macmillan. But my book, grim as it is, needs a prize to sell it.

NOW: the story about George, J— and Ann, and the children. An insuffer-able woman (myself of course) gets involved in the separated family. She thinks G will be fondest of her, tells mad wife (she's <u>sick</u>, I mean, really <u>sick</u>) it is of course Ann, feels very clever. Then finds out, when A's book is accepted, it is really A, gets furious. Calls up society, or gets sociologist friend to call up society for prevention of cruelty for children, never really finds out if they get through. Day in park. Children can't speak, finds herself throwing peanuts to pigeons etc. Ducks, squirrels, children blank-staring and oblivious. Smell bad, girl urinates on bench. I wouldn't be surprised to read tomorrow in the paper how that little girl was <u>killed</u> falling from that roof. Of course she never does read any such thing. Her good will perverted, conditional on pity that would generate from self if G was her lover, when cheated of that, it becomes nasty busybodiness. THE OLYMPIANS. Poor, married poets in Ritz bar.

THE SILVER PIE SERVER: Mrs. Guinea and Sadie Peregrine: war of two old shuttledoors and battlecocks. Loneliness and meanness of two. Odd friendship. Frogs: cold, slimy pets. Thoughts, emotions of Mrs. Guinea. Gloomy, lugubrious. Rug-changing incident. Vengeance on young happy couple upstairs, always arguing, crying, but apparently happy. Broken leg. They search for pie-server, but do not find it. Symbol of propriety of gloom, Mrs. Doom.

PS: Nothing in mail but circulars from the Poetry Society, and a little card, which I like, from AKnopf, the usual about receiving the ms., every care taken except in fire, flood. With a Borzoi dog. Only pray I hear from them before the damn H. Holt.

Ann Peregrine was as methodical about committing suicide as she was about cleaning house.

June 16
Tuesday

A discovery. I'd already discovered it, but didn't know what it meant. A discovery, a name: SADIE PEREGRINE. I had her being Mrs. Whatsis in the beginnings of my Silver Pieserver story. Suddenly she became the heroine of my Novel <u>Falcon Yard</u>. Oh, the irony. Oh, the character. In the first place: SP, my initials. Just thought of this. Then, Peregrine Falcon. Oh, Oh. Let nobody have thought of this. And Sadie: sadistic. La. Wanderer. She is enough, this Sadie Peregrine, to write the novel at Yaddo while I fish for bass.

Read over stories written in Spain yesterday. Very depressed. They are so DULL. Who'd want to read them. The circumstances, Widow Mangada, the Prado, the Black Bull, the Stick Man, live in my mind highly colored. But the telling is so boring. I almost wept. What if these four stories I have just finished are as boring to editors as my 3 1956 stories to the 1959 me?

OUR THIRD WEDDING ANNIVERSARY TODAY. Ted lost our good umbrella (his first wedding present to me was an umbrella, this lost one a different one, about the third, as we have lost several) yesterday in the Book Store while buying our anniversary present to each other: Will Grohmann's Paul Klee book. Superb. The Seafarer in full color.

I bob up for the mailman. Surely, symbolically, today a book acceptance will come. More likely a story rejection from the New Yorker. Why did I dream my obstetrician story would get in? One of those gruesome dreams-in-reverse of the fact, no doubt, like my dreaming of getting money before the Saxton rejections.

Arts Festival: Gagaku Japanese Dancers. Weird, odd, but I went into a trance. The high pipey, drumskin music, jars of water, blown reeds. The raised royal stage. Red cinnabar, gold. And the stepping and bowing, the delicate stylized patterns of four and two. Orange sleeves, planes of embroidered color. Headdresses of gold and silver. The animal-faced prince. The lovely dance before the cave of the sun-goddess, with a bough of green to which was attached a white circlet, shaping the air, now against the green, now hanging from it, a supplication. Then the sabers, the spears. A cold, wet night, the soil squishy underfoot, people with woolen rugs, hats, scarves, layers of sweaters. A few drops of chill rain. Low dark skies. Winds of merciless damp.

Remember: do not feel shut out of your past. Especially the summer of the Mayos. Remember every detail of that: a story is in that. And in Ilo and the farm summer. My god. God, I think I'll Start on that. Mary Coffee. The damn thing is, I have the goddam subjects, but am thumbs and loose ends trying to realize them, order them. Tell it in third person, for god's sake.

Saturday
June 20

Everything has gone barren. I am part of the world's ash, something from which nothing can grow, nothing can flower or come to fruit. In the lovely words of 20th century medicine, I can't ovulate. Or don't. Didn't this month, didn't last month. For ten years I may have been having cramps and for nothing. I have worked, bled, knocked my head on walls to break through to where I am now. With the one man in the world right for me, the one man I could love. I would bear children until my change of life if that were possible. I want a house of our children, little animals, flowers, vegetables, fruits. I want to be an Earth Mother in the deepest richest sense. I have turned from being an intellectual, a career woman: all that is ash to me. And what do I meet in myself? Ash. Ash and more ash.

I will enter in to the horrible clinical cycle of diagramming intercourse, rushing to be analyzed when I've had a period, when I've had intercourse. Getting injections of this and that, hormones, thyroid, becoming something other than myself, becoming synthetic. My body a testtube. "People who haven't conceived in six months have a problem, dearie" the doctor said. And, taking out the little stick with cotton on the end from my cervix held it up to his assistant nurse: "Black as black". If I had ovulated it would be green. Same test, ironically, used to diagnose diabetes. Green, the color of life and eggs and sugar fluid. "He found the exact day I ovulated" the nurse told me. "It's a wonderful test, less expensive, easier." Ha. Suddenly the deep foundations of my being are gnawn. I have come, with great pain and effort, to the point where my desires and emotions and thoughts center around what the normal woman's center around, and what do I find? Barrenness.

Suddenly everything is ominous, ironic, deadly. If I could not have children - - - and if I do not ovulate how can I? - - - how can they make me? - - - I would be dead. Dead to my woman's body. Intercourse would be dead, a dead-end. My pleasure no pleasure, a mockery. My writing a hollow and failing substitute for real life, real feeling, instead of a pleasant extra, a bonus flowering and fruiting. Ted should be a patriarch. I a mother. My love for him, to express our love, us, through my body, the doors of my body, utterly thwarted. To say I am abnormally pessimistic about this is to say that any woman should face not ovulating with a cavalier grin. Or "a sense of humor". Ha again.

I see no mailman. A lovely clear morning. I cried and cried. Last night, today. How can I keep Ted wedded to a barren woman? Barren barren. His last poem, the title poem of his book, being a ceremony to make a barren woman fertile: "Flung from the chain of the living, the Past killed in her, the Future plucked out." "Touch this frozen one." My god. And his children's book, on the same day as I went to the doctor, yesterday, getting the long praising letter from T.S.Eliot. "Meet My Folks!" And no child, not even the beginnings or the hopes of one to dedicate it to. And my "Bed Book": not accepted yet, but it will be, whether the cloudy McLeod rejects it or not, and I dedicating it to Marty's adopted twins. My god. This is the one thing in the world I can't face. It is worse than a horrible disease. Esther has multiple sclerosis, but she has children. J— is crazy, raped, but she has children. C— is unmarried, sick, but she has a child. And I, come to the time, the great good time of love whereof children are the crown and glory, sit here, chewing my nails. I simply don't know what to do. All joy and hope is gone.

WEDNESDAY: SEPTEMBER 16:"

Woke out of a warm dream to hear Ted rustling and moving, getting his fishing things together. Dark, more sleep, then the red sun in my eyes, horizontal beams through the dark pines. The faint, brimming nausea gone, which has troubled me the past days. Air clear enough for angels. The wet dews gleaming on the rusty pine needles underfoot, standing on the looped plant stems in pale drops. The great dining room handsome: the dark-beamed ceiling, the high carved chairs and mammoth tables; the terra-cotta plaster in a frieze above the polished woods. Honey oozing out of the comb, steaming coffee on the hot-plate. Boiled eggs and butter. Through the leaded windows the green hills melting into blue, and the frost-white marble statues at the garden fountain. I shall miss this grandeur when we move above the garage - - - the gilded old velvets of pillows, and the glow of worn rich carpets, the indoor fountain, the stained glass, the oil paintings of the Trask children, the moony sea, George Washington.

A terrible depression yesterday. Visions of my life petering out into a kind of soft-brained stupor from lack of use. Disgust with the 17 page story I just finished: a stiff artificial piece about a man killed by a bear, ostensibly because his wife willed it to happen, but none of the deep emotional undercurrents gone into or developed. As if little hygenic transparent lids shut out the seethe and deep-grounded swell of my experience. Putting up pretty

artificial statues. I can't get outside myself. Even in the tattoo story I did better: got an outside world. Poems are nowhere:
Outside the window the wet fern

I said to myself yesterday, reading Arthur Miller in Ted's studio my footsoles scorching on the stove. I feel a helplessness when I think of my writing being nothing, coming to nothing: for I have no other job - - - not teaching, not publishing. And a guilt grows in me to have all my time my own. I want to store money like a squirrel stores nuts. Yet what would money do. We have elegant dinners here: sweetbreads, sausages, bacon and mushrooms; ham and mealy orange sweet potatoes; chicken and garden beans. I walked in the vegetable garden, beans hanging on the bushes, squash, yellow and orange, fattening in the dapple of leaves, corn, grapes purpling on the vine, parsley, rhubarb. And wondered where the solid, confident purposeful days of my youth vanished. How shall I come into the right, rich full-fruited world of middle-age. Unless I work. And get rid of the accusing, never-satisfied gods who surround me like a crown of thorns. Forget myself, myself. Become a vehicle of the world, a tongue, a voice. Abandon my ego.

Try a first-person story and forget John Updike and Nadine Gordimer. Forget the results, the markets. Love only what you do, and make. Learn German. Don't let indolence, the forerunner of death, take over. Enough has happened, enough people entered your life, to make stories, many stories, even a book. So let them onto the page and let them work out their destinies.

In the morning light, all is possible; even becoming a god.

Yaddo: Library:" Second Floor

Dark paneled wainscots up to door-lintels. White plaster strip above that. Dark wood molding. White plaster ceiling, no ceiling fixtures. Three squarish persian carpets on the floor – busy with blues, reds, greens on dark blue or pale yellow ground. Dark red stair carpet. Magazine table (Sewanee, Kenyon, Art News, Musical Quarterly, Paris Review etc) covered with red, mauve, navy & buff patterned carpet over the dark oval table with ringed wood legs. Table flanked by two heavy arm chairs, open work wood sides, red plush back & seat cushion tacked to wood. Bust of Homere on dark mottled green marble pillar in corner. Ornate gilt wall lamp fixture with petals of streaked pink & white glass for the bowl of it – exotic magnolia petals. All scrolls & filigree leaves.

Square marble-topped end table with carved open work ebony wood, shelf for a gilt-lettered Websters. A piece of pink-veined petrified rock. Pane of stained glass on either side of sliding doors opening onto porch – gold & green medallion with gold torches & border – watered-semiopaque glass background. Dim oil portrait of Katrina with bare spiritual white bosom & shoulders in dim frame – oval portrait above windowless window seat. Old-gold velvet mat & pillows. Round table, more periodicals, flanked by armchairs, straightbacked & covered in yellow brocade – two more of these chairs down the room by another carved round table supporting a fat yellow & white figured contemporary lamp; its white silk shade encased in cellophane. A great gilt-framed painting of a dark-shadowed headland against a deep blue cloud-crossed sky above a heavy, long table with columnar legs, covered by a blue & white patterned rug. On it, Nation, New Republic, miniature of the winged victory. Giant pitcher with dolphin mouth, gilt figurehead angel under it, over worked with white dragons, cherubs & winged monsters on a dark blue ground – Wainscotted Stair coming down from above. On the newel, another elaborate lamp in form of a grecian vase with bas relief of naked nymphs – two nymps with goat-hooves holding respectively a goblet & a grape cluster toward lamp bowl of frilled pink candy-glass. On stair-landing: large stained glass window of woman in blue gown, float in white draperies & fillet of pearls binding auburn hair holding hands to a sky of stone-shaped clouds – green lawn, blue & white sky. Carpet glows blood red. Trickle of fountain below stairs. Glassed-in reading porch with three great-arched windows looking into thick green pinetrees – slatted wooden summer chairs. Saccharine gilded statue in greek robes & laurel bearing sign Amor & Caritas. Dark hall to bedrooms. Window of little bull's eyes, leaded. Ornate sideboard – enclosing Bayreuth beersteins – gilded bow-legs, gilded wood set with innumerable round, oval & leaf-shaped mirrors

[drawing of sideboard – ed.]

Glass atlas of stars & constellations painted with birds, men
horses in yellow & blue & green – equinoxes marked in red on wrought iron
pedestal –
Centaurus, Lupus Scorpio, Cancer, Taurus Capricornus, Sagittarius
Pegasus, Andromeda, Lynx, Leo.

Glass atlas of stars of
constellations painted
w on birds, their
horses in yellow &
blue & green –
equinoxes marked
in red on wrought
iron pedestal –
Centaurus, lupus
Scorpio, Cancer, Taurus
Capricornus Sagittarius
Pegasus, andromeda, lynx, leo.

Engravings over fireplace –
Veduta dell' esterno della gran basilica
de S. pietro in vaticano
    (Piranesi architetto fec.)
Veduta del Sepolcro di Cajo Cestio
Veduta del Castello dell' acqua Paola
    sul Monte Aureo
Veduta della vasta Fontana di Trevi
    anticamente detta l'acqua Vergine

White walls, dark wood-framed engravings
ruddy orange carpet – yellow chairs.
Fat bellied cherubs carved on desk
tall candlesticks with holder like Ladies
leg o' mutton sleeve – glossy green
stones set in fine vents.

Alcove – wall-statue of angel
over large cherubs-head-
gilded wood "priere" – hands
of angel steepled in prayer.
Engraving of masts & Italian sea ships
"Veduta del Porto di Ripa
Grande"
Old photos of children in openwork
quadruple wood screen – carved
    wood flowers & figures

Engraving – veduta del
campidoglio di franko

Silver vase – tiffany – on image
of Greek vas with classical
figures, horses, & shields chariot

Engravings over fireplace –

Veduta dell'esterno della gran basilica de S. pietro in vaticano (Piranesi Architetto fec.)
Veduta del Sepolcro di Cajo Cestio
Veduta del Castello dell'Acqua Paola sul Montre Aureo
Veduta della vasta Fontana di trevi . . anticamente detta Vacqua Vergine

[drawing of candlestick – ed.]

White walls, dark wood-framed engravings – ruddy orange carpet – yellow chairs. Fat bellied cherubs carved on desk – tall candlesticks with holder like ladies leg o'mutton sleeve – glossy green stones set in fine vents –

Alcove – wall-statue of angel over large cherubs – head – gilded wood "priere" – hands of angel steepled in prayer
Engraving of masts & italianate ships – "Veduta del Porto di Ripa Grande"
Old photos of children in openwork quadruple wood screen – carved wood flowers & leaves

[drawing of screen – ed.]

Engraving – veduta del campidoglio di fianko

Silver vase – tiffany – on image of Greek vas with classical figures, horses, shields, chariot

[drawing of vase – ed.]

Chair inlaid with panels of light wood, diamonds & flowers & leaf-sprigs in white & red on black –

[drawing of chair – ed.]

FRIDAY: SEPTEMBER 25:

Again woke to hear Ted readying for fishing. Foolishly griped at being woken: that's enough to make a man kill his wife. Why should he stay in bed

soundless till I choose to stir? Absurd. Yet I woke from a bad dream. O I'm full of them. Keep them to myself or I'll drive the world morbid. I gave birth, with one large cramp, to a normal sized baby, only it was not quite a five months baby. I asked at the counter if it was all right, if anything was wrong, and the nurse said: "Oh, it has nest of uterus in its nose, but nothing is wrong with the heart." How is that. Symbolic of smother in the womb? Image of mother dead with the Eye Bank having cut her eyes out. Not a dream, but a vision. I feel self-repressed again. The old fall disease. I haven't done German since I came. Haven't studied art books. As if I needed a teacher's sanction for it.

Spent an hour or so yesterday writing down notes about Yaddo library, for they will close the magnificent mansion this weekend after all the guests come. The famous Board. John Cheever, Robert Penn Warren. I have nothing to say to them. It would not matter if I had a sort of rich inner life, but that is a blank. Would getting a degree help me? I'd have to know a lot more, study, keep juggling my understandings, but why can't I do this on my own? Where is my will-power? The Idea of a life gets in the way of my life. As if my interest in English had crippled me: yet it supports myriads of professors, and they make a life. Always this desperate need to have a job, a work to steady my sense of purpose.

Yesterday, the great thick tiger cat that always waylays us by the garage and bit at Ted the last time we patted it, bit Mrs. Mansion so badly on the hand that she had to go to the hospital. They are going to kill the cat, I think. It is nowhere in sight. Mrs. A." going to kill hers, too, she announced suddenly at supper: "It's cramped my style. She's lived nine years, that's long enough." A queer cold thing for her to come out with suddenly.

Telling of old Miss Pardee," Katrina's maid-of-all, getting senile. Visited her sister in Connecticut and in Grand Central lost all sense of who she was or where she was going. Had to be identified by papers she carried in purse. Lived in West House & didn't travel after that. Then her older, more senile sister's companion died, and she got ready to go again to see her: dressed in black coat, hat, with bag over arm waiting for taxi two hours ahead of time. Mrs. A. thought she'd have to use force to keep her from leaving. Called sister's place, and woman told sister situation: freezing cold up at Yaddo, Miss P. not well, insisted on going. "Why," said the sister, "she's already been and gone." Mrs. A. told Miss P. this: "Your sisters says you've already been and gone." Miss P. looked and looked at her, didn't miss her eye. Then said: "Well, then, I guess I'd better take off my things." And so by such antique meanderings the sisters cancelled each other out.

Wrote one good poem so far: an imagist piece on the dead snake. Am working on a rambling memoir of Cornucopia. Will try farm story in character of simple girl next: read Eudora Welty aloud. Much more color and world to her than to Jean Stafford, somehow.

Wasps gather and swarm in skylight, then disappear. My flesh crawls. Sun pure through spaces of pines, bright on needles. Crows caw. Birds warble. List incidents for possible stories. Read for poem subjects. Next to snake poem, my book poems <u>are</u> all about ghosts and otherworldly miasmas - - - R.Frost would not take it, I am sure, but I wish they'd hurry and let me know.

SATURDAY: SEPTEMBER 26:

A clear, fresh day, with the cool nip back again. Newton says Smith classes started Wednesday. Seeing him was enough to bring back my old teaching nightmares: a lounging, bored class, about to be dismissed, me noticing a student ressembling Ellen Bartlett, to whom I had given a C, had a story in the New Yorker (like the story in Mademoiselle about Car'line) and me promising to reconsider her mark on these grounds. Probably a meld of my sense of this vibrant new Ellen Currie, Jean Stafford's New Yorker stories which I'd just been reading, and Newton's recall to the old treadmill.

All the cats are being killed: three of them. The old grumpy one for biting Mrs. Mansions hand. Mrs. Ames' because it cramps her style, and the new white-booted puss because it's a bother: we think we heard George shoot her the other day.

On the back of the screen door of the mansion this morning, as if flung and frozen there, a frost moth: all white furred, legs, body, antennae, with grey and white wings. Lovely exotic esquimau creature.

Listened to Schwartzkopf singing Schubert Lieder last night in the music room. Immensely moved, Who is Sylvia, and "Mein ruh ist hin" recognizable, words here and there: a strong sense of my own past, from which I am alienated by ignorance of language which I find difficult to break through.

Reading much Eudora Welty, Jean Stafford, must go through Katherine Anne Porter. Read "A Worn Path", "Livvie", "The Whistle" aloud. That is a way to feel on my tongue what I admire. "The Interior Castle" a lurid, terrifying recreation of intolerable pain.

Bored at waiting to hear from mail. Two children's books: the Bed Book now seems limited and thin. Max Nix seems rather ordinary. Yet I dream of a transfiguration: a letter of acceptance. No word from H. Holt about poems yet. Robert Frost probably hasn't bothered to say NO yet. I have a queer feeling about them: they can't decide for themselves. So they won't be for it.

Must get into deep stories where all experience becomes usable to me. Tell from one person's point of view: start with self and extend outwards: then my life will be fascinating, not a glassed-in cage. If only I could break through in one story. Johnny Panic too much a fantasy. If only I could get it real.

A farm story: Ilo, the Jeness brothers, Mary Coffee. A Mayo story: baby-sitter in complicated family: the Pillars. A mad story: college would-be suicide. A Double story: involvement with roommate. Once I did one good one, I would break in. The Tattooist story at Sewanee an encouragement. Has a glow now it never would have had otherwise. If only my Cornucopia story could get a climax. It is a rambly diary.

Detail: the pond fish like black willow leaves lying in green glass. A leaf twirling by itself in a still wood. Remember experiences: faithfully: detail. Get college: that glow, that luster. A thing not known again. And I shut experience off. Remember pain. Joy. First love. Disillusion with a heroine. Live in bright worlds of past, then you will make them up from a feather, a word, the color of an old woman's eye.

A silver pie server story.

SEPTEMBER 28: MONDAY:

Wakeful last night. Tossed and turned. New Yorker fever, as if I could by main force and study weld my sensibility into some kind of articulateness which would be publishable: and yet my two best stories I think this year are the Fifteen Dollar Eagle and Johnny Panic - - - both first person, slangy. Dreams of grandeur. Asking TSE's sanction for using the Devil of the Stairs as title for my book. Writing the Adelaide book. Getting my two children's books accepted. Oh my. Opened memory. Recalling, wording, summer at Mayo's. If I work this year, without cease, at opening out my own experience, I should come up with something. My whole trouble is shutting my experience off, sitting with a blank mind. I must go in search of times past. Then all time present will be endowed with special form and meaning.

Dreams: lately. A rejection of my book of poems by Holt, with three IBM type cards (like the Gulf oil bill I sent back), no five cards, enclosed with adverse comments by Borestone type readers: poems too depressing, too grim, no lyricism, they much prefer celebrations of life: O clear and lovely day, etc. etc. Even so, last night I mentally composed a letter to Dudley Fitts about sending my book to the Yales again. Sure I'd win, of course. A dream last night of my father making an iron statue of a deer, which had a flaw in the casting of the metal. The deer came alive and lay with a broken neck. Had to be shot. Blamed father for killing it, through faulty art. Relation to sick cats around here?

KA Porter cant speak or eat with people when she is writing.

I have a bad ear. Feels full of water or crackly cotton.

A horrid priest came to the back door of the mansion yesterday, raw, bright red face looked to have gone under carrot scraper. Black coat, white neckband. Asked for Jim Shannon." I didn't know where he was. He chewed gum of some sort, harrumphed, rubbed some coins together. Asked me to show him and wife (?) around mansion. I grew cold, said I was not authorized to do so. What are you, a writer? A repulsive ignorant and oddly disgusting man.

Dreams of grandeur also: NY accepting drawings. Giving sanction to my running about drawing chairs and baskets.

Inertia at beginning stories. How to organize them? Plunge, plunge into pillars story. Send for diary.

Sent, in spite of all, three stories to Atlantic today. A kind of game, for of course Peter D will reject me. I am sure he would not let Weeks publish a thing I wrote. If only they would accept Ted's Petty Quinnet. I am so impatient. Yet the one important thing is to pile up good work. If IF I could break onto a meaningful prose, that expressed my feelings, I would be free. Free to have a wonderful life. I am desperate when I am verbally repressed. Must lure myself into ways and ways of loquacity. Must WORK the stuff. Work over Pillars story now. Rework and rearrange it. My Cornucopia "story" is merely an essay on the impossibility of perfect happiness. Yet it hardly rams the point home. Pleasant enough places, but rough and undramatic. My first job to open my real experience like an old wound; then to extend it; then to invent on the drop of a feather, a whole multicolored bird. Study, study one or two NY's. Like the now-prolific Mavis G.

TUESDAY: SEPTEMBER 29

A smoggy rainy day. Somnolent bird twitters. A weight upon me of the prose solidity of the professional story tellers: something I haven't come near. A lingering breakfast in the garage room: reminiscent of a private dormitory, an institution, a mental home. The waxed linoleum, the straight strawbacked chairs, the ash trays and bookcases, and mammoth blue-glass grapes. Looked at the two pages of my Pillars story I wrote yesterday and felt disgust at the thinness of them. The glaze again. Prohibiting the density of feeling getting in. I must be so overconscious of markets and places to send things that I can write nothing honest and really satisfying. My feverish dreams are mere figments; I neither write nor work nor study.

Of course I depend on the mirror of the world. I have one poem I am sure of, the snake one. Other than that, no subjects. The world is a blank page. I don't even know the names of the pine trees, and, worse, make no real effort to learn. Or the stars. Or the flowers. Read May Swenson's[n] book yesterday. Several poems I liked: Snow by Morning and a fine imagist piece At Breakfast, on the egg. Elegant and clever sound effects, vivid images: but in the poem about artists and their shapes, textures and colors, this seems a mere virtuosity with little root. Almanac I liked too, about the world's history measured by the moon a hammer made on a thumbnail.

I write as if an eye were upon me. That is fatal. New Yorker rejected my two exercises: as if they knew that's what they were. Are still "considering" Christmas poem, although I am sure they will not take that. The adrenalin of failure. A black hornet sits on the screen, scratching and polishing its yellowed head. Again the rains fall on rooftops the color of a pool table.

If I could cut from my brain the phantom of competition, the ego-center of self-consciousness, and become a vehicle, a pure vehicle of others, the outer world. My interest in other people is too often one of comparison, not of pure intrigue with the unique otherness of identity. Here, ideally, I should forget the outer world of appearances, publishing, checks, success. And be true to an inner heart. Yet I fight against a simple-mindedness, a narcissism, a protective shell against competing, against being found wanting.

To write for itself, to do things for the joy of them. What a gift of the gods.

Create Agatha: a mad, passionate Agatha. Immediately I want her husband to keep bees, and I know nothing of bees. My father knew it all.

How much of life I have known: love, disillusion, madness, hatred, murderous passions.

How to be honest. I see beginnings, flashes, yet how to organize them knowledgably, to finish them. I will write mad stories. But honest. I know the horror of primal feelings, obsessions. A ten page diatribe against the Dark Mother. The Mummy. Mother of shadows.

An analysis of the Electra complex.

WEDNESDAY: SEPTEMBER 30:

When I woke this morning in the dark, humid bedroom, hearing the rain beating down on all sides, it seemed to me I was cured. Cured of the shuddering heartbeat which has plagued these last two days so that I could hardly think, or read, for holding my hand to my heart. A wild bird pulsed there, caught in a cage of bone, about to burst through, shaking my whole body with each throb. I began to want to hit my heart, pierce it, if only to stop that ridiculous throb which seemed to wish to leap out of my chest and be gone to make its own way in the world. I lay, warm, my hand between my breasts, cherishing the surfacing from sleep and the peaceful steady unobtrusive beat of my rested heart. I rose, expecting at every moment to be shaken, and indeed I was not. I have been at rest since waking.

It is raining. Steady straight streams of rain falling, falling, slicking the green tarpaper roofflats, the pink and blue and lavender slates of the slant roof, looping down in runnels, taking the color of the slates and tiles like a chameleon water. Falling in little white rings in the puddles on my porch. Dropping a scrim of pale lines between me and the pines, filling the distance with a watery luminous grey.

Began, just yesterday, two pages about The Mummy. If I can do this honestly. Twenty page chapters out of nightmare land. Then I will pile them up and think about weird quarterlies to take them. They are absolutely uncommercial: no story line, no steady grammar like Paul Engle chooses to be Best American. Started reading Blackberry Winter, stories by Sylvia Berkman: encouraged. They are almost without conversation, action. Just moods. Dream moons, rain moods, very introverted and even maudlin. Well, I must leave dreams of money and grandeur alone. If I can only get some horror into this mother story.

SATURDAY: OCTOBER 3:

The weather has cooled: the pine needles have fallen to make a thick orangey-light carpet underfoot on the roads. A grey squirrel I watched before dressing undo a pinecone like an artichoke, leaf by leaf. No mail. Only Teds PettyQ back from the Atlantic with a snotty note from PD. Blue mists in the apple orchard. No poems. The mummy story dubious. Is it simply feminine frills, is there any terror in it? Would be more if it were real? Set with real externals? As it is, it is the monologue of a mad woman. Dreams: the night before last, a terrible two-day rush to pack for the ship to leave for Europe: missing Ted here, there, the hour passing and me still stuffing odd sweaters and books in my typewriter case. Last night I lived among jews. Religious service, drinking milk from a gold chalice & repeating a name: the congregation drank milk also at the same time from little cups. I wished they put honey in it. Sitting with three pregnant women. My mother furious at my pregnancy, mockingly bringing out a huge wraparound skirt to illustrate my grossness. PD in this too. Shaving my legs under table: father, Jewish, at head: you will please not bring your scimitar to table. Very odd.

Did launder clothes yesterday. Must do handwash today. Go over Ted's two stories. Either draw or do German.

SUNDAY: OCTOBER 4:

Marilyn Monroe appeared to me last night in a dream as a kind of fairy godmother. An occasion of "chatting" with audience much as the occasion with Eliot will turn out, I suppose. I spoke, almost in tears, of how much she and Arthur Miller meant to us, although they could, of course, not know us at all. She gave me an expert manicure. I had not washed my hair, and asked her about hairdressers, saying no matter where I went, they always imposed a horrid cut on me. She invited me to visit her during the Christmas holidays, promising a new, flowering life.

Finished the Mummy story, really a simple account of symbolic and horrid fantasies. Then was electrified this morning, when I made an effort to come out of my lethargy and actually wash a pile of laundry and my hair, to read in Jung case-history confirmations of certain images in my story. The child who dreamt of a loving, beautiful mother as a witch or animal: the mother going mad in later life, grunting like pigs, barking like dogs, growling like bears, in a fit of lycanthropy. The word "chessboard" used in an identical situation: of a supposedly loving but ambitious mother who manipulated the child on the "chessboard of her egotism": I had used "chessboard of her desire". Then the image of the eating mother, or grandmother: all mouth, as in Red Riding Hood (and I had used the image of the wolf). All this relates in a most meaningful way my instinctive images with perfectly valid psychological analysis. However, I am the victim, rather than the analyst. My "fiction" is only a naked recreation of what I felt, as a child and later, must be true.

Now, forget salable stories. Write to recreate a mood, an incident. If this is done with color and feeling, it becomes a story. So try recollecting: the time of fever and near death in Benidorm. The color, feelings of that time. The She. Then the search for RS in Paris, the precocious little boy Bonalumi Francis. Recreate those two for a starter. The landlady, her dog. All that. The main thing, color and mood: where to begin and end. In search of times past. Out of that will spring other things: the green peach incident, the spilt gasoline, the Matisse chapel. Not to manipulate the experience but to let it unfold and recreate itself with all the tenuous, peculiar associations the logical mind would short-circuit.

TUESDAY: OCTOBER 6:

Yesterday very bad oppressed. Heavy skies, grey, but with no release. Spent the day writing a syllabic exercise in delicacy about Polly's tree. Coy, but rather fun. Read pound aloud and was rapt. A religious power given by memorizing. Will try to learn a long and a short each day. Best to read them in the morning first thing, review over lunch and chatechize at tea. I would have him as a master. The irrefutable, implacable, uncounted uncontrived line. Statement like a whiplash. God.

Of course Henry Holt rejected my book last night with the most equivocal of letters. I wept, simply because I want to get rid of the book, mummify it in print so that everything I want to write now doesn't get sucked in its maw. Ted suggested: start a new book. All right, I shall start with snake, and simply send out the old book over and over. Also a wordless, even formless rejection of Max Nix, which does bore me. An inexcusable thing.

George Starbuck's immortal love poem to Anne Sexton in the NY this week. A reminder.

A fine rain falling now. Gordon Binkerd" saying: this is cedar, this pine, this blue spruce. Woke to a warm darkness, the grey waterlight barely filtering through the dense green pines. All this month the umber needles have fallen in fine siftings to cover the paths with an orange-tawny plush.

Rain thickening. The lovely released sound, trickles, drops, tattoos. I do like my Mummy story even if it is mad. If I can break into a style, poignant, clear, evoking experience. I shy from bringing myself to it. Try today. A New Yorker story, simply because it movingly recreates a day, and event. Is it because the avenue of memory is so painful that I do not walk down it, grey, laden with sorrow, vanished beauties and dreams? The skies and rooftops of Paris, the green Seine, the frieze of the British Museum in London. Once, once, I began, all would be well. One story: shall I set a year to work? Then, if all is not reached, a year after that? One story, and I would have begun. I flit now from one subject to another: the farm? the Mayos? Spain? Paris? I must choose one. The only stories I can bear to reread are The Wishing Box, Johnny Panic, The Mummy and the Tattooist. All the others - - the Oxbow, the Cornucopia one, the Fifty Ninth Bear, and Sweetie Pie and the Hospital one - - - are duller than tears. Begin, begin.

OCTOBER 10: Saturday

Observations: in the late solid rains, the seven-day rains, three toadstools pushed up out of the sodden pineneedles in front of West House. Big as oranges, rounded battering rams, they fisted themselves through the soil, a few dark brown twigs sticking to them. They were orange-ruddy at the top, as if the color pooled there, with porous lemon, pale lemon stems and virginal white underpleats, the tops tufted also in pale lemon. Now they are spread flat and gross, orange plates with hairy yellow warts.

One bluejay comes, cocks on the railing, a rare stipple of turquoise white and black and deep blue, and eats all my bread crumbs.

Walk yesterday with Ted up the road. A dead baby snake. A live brown-and-green beveled garter snake. Winged ants. Innumerable leaping and scuttling crickets that ran for shade or shelter under the instep of our shoes. A deserted house-site, vile suede-furred leafy plants pushed up through the macadam. Milkweed pods blackened with tar. The hot steamy drench of the day. Blue mists proliferating over the bland clear silver ponds.

Dream of Mrs. Mansion: after she gave Gordon the plate with two fat encrusted pork chops. There was a great frosted layer cake. By mistake it was sent to the Old Ladies' Home in town and eaten all but four pieces. I came upon her just as she was setting it out for the servants tea and chided her: the artists were so few, they would like the remaining cake. Finally I won out. Got a piece.

New Yorker accepted the Winter's Tale poem. Felt pleased, especially after Harper's rejection.

Feel oddly barren. My sickness is when words draw in their horns and the physical world refuses to be ordered, recreated, arranged and selected. I am a victim of it then, not a master.

Am reading Elizabeth Bishop with great admiration. Her fine originality, always surprising, never rigid, flowing, juicier than Marianne Moore, who is her godmother.

The incredible dense irrefutable structure of Iris Murdoch's novels: her placing people, their minds and observations, here, here, and revealing it all. Also, her lighting effects: deft, always luminous. Her words: iridescent, radiant, bright, etc.

When will I break into a new line of poetry? Feel trite. If only I could get one

20 Ted Hughes and SP
in Yorkshire, 1956

21 Ted Hughes and SP
in Paris, August 1956

22 SP in Cambridge, England, 1956

23, 24 SP sailing into New York harbor on the
Queen Elizabeth II, June 25, 1957

25 SP reading her poems in *The New Yorker*, August 1958

26 Smith College English Department, *Hamper*, 1958. Seated (l. to r.): Fisher, Drew, Lincoln, Arvin, Dunn, Hill, Hornbeak, Williams, Petersson. Standing (l. to r.): Aaron, Randall, Danzinger, Borroff, Sears, SP, Johnson, Roche, Bramwell, Sultan, Hecht, Van Voris, Schendler

27 Ted Hughes and SP in their Boston apartment, 1958

28 SP camping at Rock Lake, Algonquin
Provincial Park, Ontario, Canada, July 1959

29 SP feeding deer, Algonquin Provincial Park, Ontario, Canada, July 1959

30 SP drawing in the harbor at Cornucopia, Wisconsin, July 1959

31 SP rowing on Yellowstone Lake, Yellowstone National Park, Wyoming, July 1959

32 SP at Jackson Lake, Grand Teton National Park, Wyoming, July 1959

33 Ted Hughes and SP in Concord, Massachusetts, December 1959

34 SP and Frieda in the living room
at Court Green, December 1961

35 SP and Frieda outside the front door of Court Green, December 1961

36 SP with Frieda and Nicholas on the lawn at Court Green, August 1962

37 SP and Nicholas in Devonshire, December 1962

38 SP, Frieda, and Nicholas among the daffodils at Court Green, April 22, 1962

good story. I dream too much, work too little. My drawing is gone to pot, yet I must remember I always do bad drawings at the first.

German and French would give me self-respect, why dont I act on this.

OCTOBER 13: Tuesday

Very depressed today. Unable to write a thing. Menacing gods. I feel outcast on a cold star, unable to feel anything but an awful helpless numbness. I look down into the warm, earthy world. Into a nest of lovers' beds, baby cribs, meal tables, all the solid commerce of life in this earth, and feel apart, enclosed in a wall of glass. Caught between the hope and promise of my work - - - the one or two stories that seem to catch something, the one or two poems that build a little colored island of words - - - and the hopeless gap between that promise, and the real world of other peoples poems and stories and novels. My shaping spirit of imagination is far from me. At least I have begun my German. Painful, as if "part were cut out of my brain". I am of course at fault. Anesthetizing myself again, and pretending nothing is there. There is the curse of this vanity. My inability to lose myself in a character, a situation. Always myself, myself. What good does it do to be published, if I am producing nothing? If only a group of people were more important to me that the Idea of a Novel, I might begin a novel. Little artificial stories that get nothing of the feeling, the drama even of life. When they should be realer, more intense than life. And I am prepared for nothing else. Am dead already. Pretend an interest in astrology, botany, which I never follow up. When I go home I must teach myself the Tarot pack, the stars, German conversation. Add French to my studying. This comes so natural to some people. Ted is my salvation. He is so rare, so special, how could anyone else stand me! Of course, otherwise I might get a PhD, teach in New York, or work at a career. It is hard, with our unplanned drifting, to do much in this way.

Another thing that horrifies me is the way I forget: I once knew Plato well, James Joyce, and so on and so on. If one doesn't apply knowledge, doesn't review, keep it up, it sinks into a Sargasso and encrusts with barnacles. A job that would plunge me in other lives would be a help. A reporter, a sociologist, anything. Maybe in England I will have some luck. They are, in a sense, less "professional" than we are here. More open to the amateur. At least I think so.

I can't reconcile myself to the smalltime. How easy it is to get ten dollars here and there from the Monitor for poems and drawings. Two poems accepted this morning: my "exercises" on Yaddo and Magnolia Shoals. Yet I hunger after nebulous vision of success. Publication of my poetry book, my children's book. As if the old god of love I hunted by winning prizes in childhood had grown more mammoth and unsatiable still. Must stop this. Grow enamoured of the orange toadstool, the blue mountain, and feel them solid, make something of them. Keep away from editors and writers: make a life outside the world of professionals from which I work.

I write nothing about the people here. Typical. Polly:" alternately young and old: blondish, with a sweet spinsterish face, a tight nimbus of curls, white gilt-threaded shawls, a slight lisp, way of holding her eyes modestly down. A tragedy in her life? She learns astrology, talks of progressions, of black times when she kept saying "I wish I were dead." Did her lover die in the war? Is she totally bound to her mother? Her sick mother, her divorced brother, and the dogs? She wears black a good deal - - - scoop-necked black dresses. Take a lesson from Ted. He works and works. Rewrites, struggles, loses himself. I must work for independence. Make him proud. Keep my sorrows and despairs to myself. Work and work for self-respect: study language, read avidly. Work, not expect miracles to follow on a hastily-written nothing.

OCTOBER 19, 1959: Monday

Most of my trouble is a recession of my old audacity, unselfconscious brazenness. A self-hypnotic state of boldness and vigor annihilates my lugubrious oozings of top-of-the-head matter. I tried Ted's "exercise": deep-breathing, concentration on stream-of-conscious objects, these last days, and wrote two poems that pleased me. One a poem to Nicholas," and one the old father-worship subject. But different. Wierder. I see a picture, a weather, in these poems. Took "Medallion" out of the early book and made up my mind to start a second book, regardless. I might have a better chance in the Yales this year. Depending on Fitts' conscience. The main thing is to get rid of the idea what I write now is for the old book. That soggy book. So I have three poems for the new, temporarily called THE COLOSSUS and other poems.

Involvement with Mavis Gallant. Her novel on a daughter-mother relation, the daughter committing suicide. A novel, brazen, arrogant, would be a solution to my days, to a year of life. If I did not short-circuit by sitting judgment as I wrote, always rejecting before I open my mouth. The main concern: a character who is not myself - - - that becomes a stereotype, mournful, narcissistic.

A beautiful blue day. Pure soul weather. Frosty, and my Harcourt form rejection. Ted says: You are so negative. Gets cross, desperate. I am my own master. I am a fool to be jealous of phantoms. Should maunder in my own way. These three new poems are heartening. Yesterday not so good - - - too linked to the prose vision of the garden in my Mummy story. Must not wait for mail for it ruins the day. Work without vision of world's judgment. I shall do it yet.

Another thing: to stop concern only with own "position" in world. Another phantom. I am. That is enough. I have a good way of looking I can develop if only I forget about an audience.

Ted is the ideal, the one possible person.

Worked on German for two days, then let up when I wrote poems. Must keep on with it. It is hard. So are most things worth doing.

Immerse self in characters, feelings of others - - - not to look at them through plate glass. Get to the bottom of deceptions, emotions.

The florid cinnamon-scented oil-colored world of St. Jean Perse.

Old wish to get reward for elimination. That is evident. Old rivalry with brother. All men are my brothers. And competition is engrained in the world. Separate baby and poem from decay and rot. They are made, living, good-in-themselves, and very keepable.

Children might humanize me. But I must rely on them for nothing. Fable of children changing existence and character as absurd as fable of marriage doing it. Here I am, the same old sour-dough. Eight years till I am thirty-five, I should work in that time: stories, NYorker or otherwise. A novel. A children's book. With joy and renaissance enthusiasm. It is possible. Up to me.

OCTOBER 22: THURSDAY:

A walk today before writing, after breakfast. The sheer color of the trees: caves of yellow, red plumes. Deep breaths of still frosty air. A purging, a baptism. I think at times it is possible to get close to the world, to love it. Warm in bed with Ted I feel animal solaces. What is life? For me it is so little ideas. Ideas are tyrants to me: the ideas of my jealous, queen-bitch superego: what I should, what I ought.

Ambitious seeds of a long poem made up of separate sections: Poem on her Birthday. To be a dwelling on madhouse, nature: meanings of tools, greenhouses, florist shops, tunnels, vivid and disjointed. An adventure. Never over. Developing. Rebirth. Despair. Old women. Block it out.

Two dead moles in the road. One about ten yards from the other. Dead, chewed of their juices, caskets of shapeless smoke-blue fur, with the white, clawlike hands, the human palms, and the little pointy corkscrew noses sticking up. They fight to the death Ted says. Then a fox chewed them.

The shed of the hydraulic ram. Black, glistening with wet: gouts of water. And the spiderwebs, loops and luminous strings, holding the whole thing up to the rafters. Magic, against principles of physics.

No mail. Who am I. Why should a poet be a novelist? Why not?

Dream, shards of which remain: my father come to life again. My mother having a little son: my confusion: this son of mine is a twin to her son. The uncle of an age with his nephew. My brother of an age with my child. O the tangles of that old bed.

Drew a surgical picture of the greenhouse stove yesterday and a few flowerpots. An amazing consolation. Must get more intimate with it, That greenhouse is a mine of subjects. Watering cans, gourds and squashes and pumpkins. Beheaded cabbages inverted from the rafters, wormy purple outer leaves. Tools: rakes, hoes, brooms, shovels. The superb identity, selfhood of things.

To be honest with what I know and have known. To be true to my own weirdnesses. Record. I used to be able to convey feelings, scenes of youth; life so complicated now. Work at it.

OCTOBER 23: Friday: Yesterday: an exercise begun, in grimness, turning into a fine, new thing: first of a series of madhouse poems. October in the toolshed. Roethke's influence, yet mine. Ted's criticisms absolutely right. Mentioned publishing poetry to M.COwley" last night: his wry, tragic grimace told me: he's seen my book, or heard of it, and rejected or will reject it. Dream of Luke's painting: florid, elegant ballade landscape in silvered blues and greens of peasant Corsican nativity with Adam and Eve leaning out of the long grass to look. A luminous pink-white light on the scalloped and easy leaves, round caverns of pale blue shadow. Fine, welcoming letter from an editor at Heinemann on seeing my London magazine poems, which begin the magazine: hope springs. England offers new comforts. I could write a novel there. So I say, so I say. Without this commercial American superego. My tempo is British. Wet, wet walk with Ted. Blue drippings, dulled green lakes, dim yellow reflections.

NOVEMBER 1: SUNDAY

A wet, fresh air, grey skies. All the colors of the last weeks dulled to smoke-purple and blunt umbers. Dreamed several nights ago of having a five-mounths (born at five months?) old blond baby boy named Dennis riding, facing me, my hips, a heavy sweet-smelling child. The double amazement: that he was so beautiful and healthy and so little trouble. Ted claims this is a rebirth of my deep soul. Auspicious. Dreamed last night a confused dream of two youths, juvenile delinquents, on a dark lawn in front of our old Winthrop house, throwing our saucepan of milk out. In a fury, I flew at one and actually started tearing him apart with my teeth and hands. The other had said he was going into the house, and I thought he would ruin it and hurt mother. (Triggered by seeing the children out for Halloween last night, the gang of adolescents?)

I wonder about the poems I am doing. They seem moving, interesting, but I wonder how deep they are. The absence of a tightly reasoned and rhythmed logic bothers me. Yet frees me.

It now starts to rain. Big drops.

Last night we drove - - - Polly, Howard," Gordon, a red-headed librarian from Skidmore and her date - - - to Scotia to see Ingmar Bergman's The Magician. Not as gripping and terrifying as the Seventh Seal, but fine, magnificently entertaining. Photography, haunting scenes and characters faces strong - - - recognized the cast of the other film. Why can't America, even England, produce something like the good Swedish and Italian and Japanese films? The corruption of the capitalist civilization? The lack of any knowledge of deep humanity?

Feel unlike writing anything today. A horror that I am really at bottom uninterested in people: the reason I don't write stories. Only a few psychological fantasias. Know very little about lives of others. Polly's ghost: the old superintendant standing at the foot of her bed in full moonlight holding a baby. She later finding a picture of him in same posture, holding a lamb.

Get out big Botany book at home. What an inertia has overcome me: a sense of fatality: the difficulty of learning out of school.

Ted's dreams about killing animals: bears, donkeys, kittens. Me or the baby? Starting to type his play. Illadvised, said yesterday wished it were realistic. Of course, I want a broadway hit in my cheap surface mind, an easy street. He has revised and really improved the children's book Meet My Folks! I feel we must find a publisher here, yet the macabre is so outside our tradition. There again, the real world must give the wonder. My Bed Book will probably fail because of no human, or child, interest - - - no plot.

Well, I do not feel like working today. The typewriter needs a new ribbon. Badly.

WEDNESDAY: NOVEMBER 4:

Paralysis again. How I waste my days. I feel a terrific blocking and chilling go through me like anesthesia. I wonder, will I ever be rid of Johnny Panic? Ten years from my successful seventeen, and a cold voice says: What have you done, what have you done? When I take an equally cold look, I see that I have studied, thought, and somehow not done anything more than teach a year: my mind lies fallow. I don't look forward to a life of reading, and rereading, with no mentor or pupil but myself. I have written one or two unpleasant psychological stories: Johnny Panic and The Mummy, which might well justify printing, a light tour de force about the tattooist, and that is all since Sunday at the Mintons' seven years ago. Where is that fine, free arrogant careless rapture. A cold mizzle of despair settles down on me when I try to think even of a story.

Miraculously I wrote seven poems in my POEM FOR A BIRTHDAY sequence, and the two little ones before it, The Manor Garden and The Colossus, I find colorful and amusing. But my manuscript of my book seems dead to me. So far off, so far gone. It has almost no chance of finding a publisher: just sent it out to the seventh, and unless Dudley Fitts relents this year and gives me the Yale award, which I just missed last year, there is nothing for it but to try to publish it in England and forget America. Or send it to Macmillan or Wesleyan paperbacks and forget prizes, which might well be a good thing. I think I should try the Yales, therefore hope I won't get it accepted as an entry to the Lamont, which I have even less chance of winning - - - that would cancel both. Comparing it to Booths book, O'Gorman's book, etc., and Starbuck's, I do feel I am not without merit.

I shall perish if I can write about noone but myself. Where is my old bawdy vigor and interest in the world around me? I am not meant for this monastary living. Find always traces of passive dependence: on Ted, on people around me. A desire even while I write poems about it, to have someone decide my life, tell me what to do, praise me for doing it. I know this is absurd. Yet what do I do about it?

If I can't build up pleasures in myself: seeing and learning about painting, old civilizations, birds, trees, flowers, French, German - - - what shall I do? My wanting to write books annihilates the original root impulse that would have me bravely and blunderingly working on them. When Johnny Panic sits on my heart, I can't be witty, or original, or creative.

To give myself respect, I should study botany, birds and trees: get little booklets and learn them, walk out in the world. Open my eyes. Write a daily diary about people, feelings, insights. Speculate about others. Plot events. Also learn astrology and tarot. Seriously. Take German lessons wherever I am, and read French. Maybe learn to ride a horse or to ski. This won't save me, but will increase my breathing space. And a job, a part-time job: editing or something of the sort, in London. I hate the thought of being a dilettante. Yet if I got a Phd & taught, I'd never write. And writing is my health; if I could once break through my cold-selfconsciousness and enjoy things for their own sake, not for what presents and acclaim I may receive. B was right: I avoid doing things, because if I do not do them, I can't be said to fail at them. A coward's custard.

Pleasant dream of return to London: renting a room with the bed in a garden of daffodils, waking to soil smells and bright yellow flowers. The Doers intrigue me. I would be one of them. If I wrote a good children's book, a book or two of poems, a story or two: a beginning.

NOVEMBER 7, 1959: Saturday

Despair. Impasse. I had a vision last night of our swimming in the Salt Lake: a solid beautiful thing. I thought: this light, this sensation is part of no story. It is a thing in itself and worthy of being worked out in words. If I could do that, get back the old joy, it would not matter what became of it. The problem is not my success, but my joy. A dead thing.

My Mummy story came back from NW Writing with a mimeographed rejection. It is a very bitter, often melodramatic story, simply an account. I have built up my old brother-rivalry praise-seeking impulses to something amounting to a great stone god-block. Ten years after my first talent-burst on the world, when everything flowed supply to my touch. I could create the Minton's seven years ago because I forgot myself in them.

Dangerous to be so close to Ted day in day out. I have no life separate from his, am likely to become a mere accessory. Important to take German lessons, go out on my own, think, work on my own. Lead separate lives. I must have a life that supports me inside. This place a kind of terrible nunnery for me. I hate our room: the sterile whites of it, the beds filling the whole place. Loved the little crowded Boston apartment, even though J. Panic visited me there.

What horrifies me most is the idea of being useless: well-educated, brilliantly promising, and fading out into an indifferent middle-age. Instead of working at writing, I freeze in dreams, unable to take disillusion of rejections. Absurd. I am inclined to go passive, and let Ted be my social self. Simply because we are never apart. Now, for example: the several things I can do apart from him: study German, write, read, walk alone in the woods or go to town. How many couples could stand to be so together? The minute we get to London I must strike out on my own. I'd be better off teaching than writing a couple of mediocre poems a year, a few mad, self-centered stories. Reading, studying, "making your own mind" all by oneself is just not my best way. I need the reality of other people, work, to fulfil myself. Must never become a mere mother and housewife. Challenge of baby when I am so unformed and unproductive as a writer. A fear for the meaning and purpose of my life. I will hate a child that substitutes itself for my own purpose: so I must make my own. Ted is weary of my talk of astrology and tarot and wanting to learn, and then not bothering to work on my own. I'm tired of it too. And tired of the terrific drifting uncertainty of our lives. Which, I suppose, from his point of view, is not at all uncertain, for his vocation of writing is so much stronger than mine.

My poems pall. A jay swallows my crumbs on the wet porch. My head is a batallion of fixes. I don't even dare open Yeats, Eliot - - - the old fresh joys, for the pain I have remembering my first bright encounters. Less able to lose myself. And myself is the more suited for quick losing.

Independent, self-possessed M.S. Ageless. Birdwatching before breakfast. What does she find for herself? Chess games. My old admiration for the strong, if Lesbian, woman. The relief of limitation as a price for balance and surety.

Take hold. Study German today. The ribbon is terrible. So am I. I have the one person I could ever love in this world. Now I must work to be a person worthy of that.

NOVEMBER 11: WEDNESDAY"

I only write here when I am at wits' end, in a cul de sac. Never when I am happy. As I am today. Partly the weather. A still morning, bright sun, clear blue sky. We went for a walk after breakfast. Frost stiffend and outlined the grassblades with white, and the whorls and rosettes of leaves and weeds. The rose garden shone in the sun, the thorny stems, with dead red leaves, bound together. The white statues are all encased in little wooden huts, like out-houses, against the ravages of winter and vandals. In the shadow of the pool wall, the grass was white and crisp, but in the sun, the frost had melted and the grass glittered bright green with wet. We saw two black and white woodpeckers with red caps (which kind, exactly?) in the tall pines, tapping crisp as thimbles on a window pane.

In the wood, by the brook, the slim grey boles of the saplings were bare, a few dry brown leaves twirled, and the cascade of water sprayed and froze: clear ice shackling the branches, blown back in icicle sprays, knobbed in bubbles on the moss. A kind of wild, twisted glass sculpture.

Felt warm in my tweeds, pleasantly fat-stomached. The baby is a pleasure to dream on. My panics are seldom. If only I can get a doctor I trust, firm, capable and kind, and a hospital where I will know what is going on, I shall be all right. It can't last much more than 24 hours. And if the baby is sound and healthy.

Finished typing Ted's play* this week. 84 pages. Very lively and somehow I see it going on in my head. I should think an experimental theater would put it on - - - the one fault, the long set speeches, mainly the Kaiser's. But they are good speeches.

Woodpile: cut limbs, heartwood pink as salmon, great fraying shards of bark. Textures of rough and smooth.

I am eager to leave here. 11 weeks is too much. Ted loves it though. If I were writing a novel it would be okay. But even then, I like the bother and stimulus of ordinary life, friends, plays, town-walking, etc. Dry grasses and blue woodsmoke sailing by my window. I'd like to work in London. A novel, a novel. I'd send it to a British publisher first. Feel my first book of poems should be published, however limited. I wrote a good poem this week on our walk Sunday to the burnt-out spa. A second book poem. How it consoles me, the idea of a second book with these new poems: The Manor Garden, The Colossus, The Burnt-out Spa, the seven Birthday poems, and perhaps Medallion, if I don't stick in in my present book. If I were accepted by a publisher for the Lamont, I would feel a need to throw all my new poems in to bolster the book. For the Yales I do not feel such a need. Well, three months till the Yales open.

Excited about practical matters of packing and traveling, seeing people. I hate our room here: white, surgical, a hospital. Have, in two months, written three stories, none very satisfactory, about ten or twelve good new poems, a bad, impossible children's book. When I am off alone I become more inhuman. Need width of interests, stimulus, demands. Distractions, yes. The fight to go to two good movies here ridiculous: there is the big station wagon they won't use. To live in city or country? I am excited about England. When I think of living in America, I just can't imagine where: hate suburbs, country too lonely, city too expensive and full of dog turds. I can imagine living in London, in a quiet square, taking children to the fine Parks. Moving to country right outside, still being near. Every day life begins anew.

NOVEMBER 12: THURSDAY

A note only. My optimism rises. No longer do I ask the impossible. I am happy with smaller things, and perhaps that is a sign, a clue. Weary today, after a 1 o'clock night, I will spend my time typing up a few stories. I shall send Monteith" three after all, I think. The one story I want to get published now is Johnny Panic. I will also try the Fifty-Ninth Bear, The Mummy and The Beggars on principle. Last night found out Lehmann accepted my story THIS EARTH OUR HOSPITAL. Have changed the title to THE DAUGH-TERS OF BLOSSOM STREET. A much better thing. This is satisfying. The story is amateurish in very many ways, but not too thin in texture. I'm putting my old things, the thin ones, out of circulation. Skipped back from the garage in the blue light of a fuzzy moon, a warmish, windy night. Fin-ished the blue mole poem yesterday to our satisfaction. Every day is a renewed prayer that the god exists, that he will visit with increased force and clarity. I want to write about people, moving situations. If only I could combine the humorous verve of my two recently accepted stories with the serious prose style of the Mintons, I should be pleased. Want to write about George Starbuck, his wife, the days with R. in Paris. If only I could break through my numb cold glibness that comes when I try to make a declarative sentence. Color it up, thicken it.

Excited this morning about Teds caning story: the most difficult and success-ful he's done yet. I was really moved reading it out with him and seeing, really seeing, how it should go, what words were taboo, what paragraph needed omission to make it leap together. Now, it is as good as could be. If only the New Yorker would take it. It seems, finally, subtle and deft enough. If he finishes the Mambrett story we will have done a lot. Only I must start stories. Keep a notebook of physical events. My visit to the tattoo shop and my job at the hospital supplied me with two good stories. So should my

Boston experience. If only I can go deep enough. A party at Agatha's, Starbuck's wife. The gardens. Oh, God, how good to get it all. Slowly, slowly catch the monkey. Small doses of acceptance help. Perhaps telling stories to children will help me do a few books there.

We are coming along. If only we could work out a place to live, and jobs we liked, to keep us steady.

Last night: the two arty instructors at Skidmore. An old turn-of-the-century house, mansard roofs, high-ceilinged, narrow and awkwardly shaped rooms. White and grey painted walls with an underfigure in the plaster. A grey, white and black Mexican rug. Low tables made of wood and bricks. A rope lion, braided tail, hemp ruff. A great red earthenware floor vase, with a cone shaped base topped in an ovoid bowl, with predatory, scalloped border, incurving claws. A red, orange and yellow modern painting of a sunset, no forms, all hot oils blending. A mobile, unmoving, overhead, like a formula for an atom: balls of white stereofoam on a squared lattice of sticks. The girls: the elder, ageless, with dark, old-maidish bun, skinny, flat chested, short, with flat black shoes and a nondescript beige dress with maroon velvet belt, which doubled her in on it. Glasses, a bright, luminous face, a speech instructor: "Oh, Mr. Binkerd, the music sets such a <u>mood</u>!" The other, younger, arty, quite pretty with delicately heeled blue shoes, a loose fashionable hairdo, blue-shadowed eyes, glasses also, a stylish grey-blue sweater and skirt, a silver mexican necklace, elaborate, in good taste. Sultry manner. Teaches weaving and jewelry making. May in the other room: freckled, in herself, a tough little nut. I imagined the situation of two lesbians: the one winning a woman with child from an apparently happy marriage. Why is it impossible to think of two women of middle-age living together without Lesbianism the solution, the motive?

NOVEMBER 14: SATURDAY

A good walk this morning. Got up in time for breakfast at 8 and the mail came early as if to reward us. Warm blowy grey weather. Odd elation. Note this. Whenever we are about to move, this stirring and excitement comes, as if the old environment would keep the sludge and inertia of the self, and the bare new self slip shining into a better life.

We went round the lakes to find the gate into the Whitney's race track. NO

HUNTING OR TRESPASSING said the odd gate in the woods: why opening into yaddo pines? We walked out by boarded-up white houses with blue-black shutters and crescent moons carved in them. The bleak stables with numbered doors, like a shut white-shingled promenade. Open skies, for a change, after the fir-shut domes at Yaddo.

We walked out on the bland, sandy track. Pale purple and bluish hills melted in the grey distance. The black twiggy thickets of the bare treetops. Leaves rattled in the wind. A black bird flew up to a bow. Burnt corn cobs, old corn shalks. A black flapping scarecrow on crossed staves made out of a man's tattered coat and a pair of faded, whitened dungarees. Waved vacant arms.

Saw dogs, two, tongues hanging, exploring a copse of saplings and bracken. The yellow-brown, dessicated color of the land. Found cartridge shells. Fox tracks, deer prints in the soft sand. The green, brilliant underbed of the lakes. Mole hills and tunnels webbing the Yaddo lawn. Felt into a hole, both ways, with my finger after breaking into the tunnel.

Wrote an exercise on mushrooms yesterday which Ted likes. And I do to. My absolute lack of judgment when I've written something: whether it's trash or genius.

Exhausted today after several late nights. Fit to write nothing. Dreams last night troubled: mother and Warren in puritannical, harsh, snoopy poses. I bit her arm (repeat of my biting the delinquent), and she was old, thin, every-watchful. Warren discovering me about to bed with someone whose name was Partisan Review. Old shames and guilts.

But a sense of joy and eagerness at living in England. Partly, too, because of the recent hospitality my poems, and my story, have found there. Much closer to my mind.

Yaddo

NOVEMBER 15: SUNDAY

Have had a series of bad, sleepless nights. The coming unsettling? As a result, tired, without force, full of a sour lassitude. Late last night made the mistake of having coffee, thinking it would keep me awake for the movie.

We didn't go, and I lay in a morbid twit till the hollow dark of the morning, full of evil dreams of dying in childbirth in a strange hospital unable to see Ted, or having a blue baby, or a deformed baby, which they wouldn't let me see.

My one salvation is to enter into other characters in stories: the only three stories I am prepared to see published are all told in first person. The thing is, to develop other first persons. My Beggars story a travesty: sentimental, stiff, without any interest at all. And the horror is that there was danger, interest. Slangy language is one way of breaking my drawingroom inhibitions. Have I learned anything since college writing days? Only in poetry. There I have.

Ted's good story on the caning. Very fine, very difficult. He advances, unencumbered by any fake image of what the world expects of him. Last night, consoling, holding me. Loving made my nerves melt and sleep. I woke drained, as after a terrible emotional crisis. Today am good for little. Submerged in reviews of reviews. How good is it to read other people? Of other people? Read their stories, their poems, not reviews. I am well away from the world of critics and professors. Must root in life itself. Yet Iris Murdoch has a brilliant professorial intellect operating in her work. Mesmerize myself into forgetting the waiting world. the IDEAS kill the little green shoots of the work itself. I have experienced love, sorrow, madness, and if I cannot make these experiences meaningful, no new experience will help me.

A bad day. A bad time. State of mind most important for work. A blithe, itchy eager state where the poem itself, the story itself is supreme.

[Appendix 10 contains Sylvia Plath's observations on the 1960 obscenity trial of *Lady Chatterley's Lover* and notes concerning Plath's 1961 appendectomy at St Pancras Hospital in London; Appendix 11 contains Plath's descriptions and drawings of Trafalgar Square in London; Appendix 15 contains Plath's 1962 descriptions of her neighbors in North Tawton, Devonshire – ed.]

Journal Fragment
17–19 October 1951

1951

7:30 p.m. Wednesday, October 17 –
 I don't know why I should be so hideously gloomy, but I have that miserable "nobody-loves-me" feeling. I've been up here in the infirmary for a day and a half, now, and really my head feels much better, not so stuffed and all. But still I feel very shaky, especially when I get up, from all the pills they've given me, maybe. Tomorrow I get up for my first written which I've stupidly put off studying for by reading old <u>New Yorker</u> magazines. Also I've got a luncheon date with somebody from <u>Mademoiselle</u>, who's meeting all the thousands of girls who want to enter the College Board Contest. I can't think of a thing to wear. All my clothes are brown, navy or velvet. No matching accessories. Hell, how I've piddled off money, penny by penny, for unmatching items. How can I expect to criticize the country's leading fashion mag when I can't even dress correctly myself? To top it off, I've just talked to mother over the phone, and made her unhappy, Dick unhappy, me unhappy. Instead of whizzing off for a gala weekend Friday, with Carol, for Dick, clinic, party at HMS," etc., I languish. Not even <u>really</u> sick up here, which I could bear. No. I <u>could</u> go home if I wanted too. But it would be a strain on my health & my academic work. As is, I'm shaky. I've two weeks back work to catch up on. It's the "best thing" as far as common sense is concerned to go to bed early Saturday night, to work all weekend. But heck, I keep thinking of me dancing with Dick in my black velvet, and meeting his fascinating friends . . . oh, well. Brace up. Build up your body and be ready to meet the next party, the next boy, the next weekend with renewed strength. As it is now, I'm too well to be really ill and pampered, too groggy to make being up worthwhile. Siniusitis plunges me in manic depression. But

at least the lower I go the sooner I'll reach bottom & start the upgrade againt.

12 Friday –

Now all this dolorousness may be normal, being as I just got out of the infirmary today and still carry a head packed full of mucous, leaving me groggy and shaken. But suddenly all my courses are way out of hand – I've missed too much, and am at least a week behind in all of them. Not only that, I don't know whether or not I'll be on Press Board, or whether I can sell stockings in my spare time, which I haven't any of. Then too, how will I ever find time to work at the mental hospital? I am torn by a desire to really get to know the girls in my house – and chat and play bridge now & then. But worst of all, I have this terrible responsibility of being an A-student (everybody labels me as such – what hollow mockery!) and I don't see how I can keep up my front. Last year, at least, I had two easy courses. This year government[n] has thrown me completely – Freshman are brightly articulate in section. Religion is demanding – I am a week behind, fouled up my first written. In art, I've missed a good 10 hours work. No matter how much time I spend over there, I'll never get above a B- my most optimistic mark. My English lit course is plainly above me unless I go to seminars & read lots of extra stuff. My creative writing course demands what I love – work and time. But how to combine weekends with Dick, intense work, sociability and, above all, health? God knows. Now I know why Ann left. How can I ever think with this load of hard mucous in my head? Where is my strength coming from?

6 Friday – Letter from Constantine! Fate, fate! Now to soaring, now to the heights! Will I become the wife of a handsome dark haired Russian oil magnate-to-be?? And what of the blonde Greek God cutting cadavers in the heart of Boston? Life, life, where is thy sting!

She is about thirty-two years old, and you wouldn't bother noticing her features unless she started talking to you about herself, which she did. You see, I'm on the second floor of the infirmary, and except for two basal metabolism cases that came in for the morning[n] I'm the only girl up here. They say they keep the second floor for colds; they're adding on a new wing down the other end of the hall, and I can hear the hammering from where I sit on the sun deck. One of the men came into my room yesterday to help the nurse catch a wasp. His name was Victor, and he was a cheerful gray little fellow in blue overalls that were too big for him. He kept telling me about how wasps wouldn't sting you if you didn't bother them, and the nurse kept laughing and saying how one wasp flew right at her and stung her face without her even getting near it.

Well anyhow, like I started out to say, this day nurse came in for the first time this morning to take my temperature and to give me my inhalation. So while she was making the bed she laughed to herself as though remembering something special and awfully funny. So I asked her what she was laughing at and she said it was about how her boyfriend was wearing leather shoes last night and slipped on the stairs of the Valley Arena with two glasses of beer. Did he spill, I asked. Only a little on her suit and she didn't mind, she said. Then she started talking about how she changed nursing schools and didn't finish her three year course but was taking an 18 month course that had everything but the operating room only she didn't tell the students about it because they might lose confidence. We were looking at a cartoon book, and she laughed and said about how one picture reminded her of seeing her first delivery. She didn't want to be there watching, so she always hid in a room washing instruments or something, but this time the head nurse made her stand right where she couldn't walk away or anything. And then she remembered how they used to watch bodies being cut up, and she said how her mother hadn't ever told her anything about how men looked, so when the doctor began to take off the sheet and cut off tissue after tissue she went and gagged in a shocked tone, and everybody turned and looked at her. Her mother ought to have told her something first, seeing as she even had brothers.

Then she told about how she had something wrong with her left eye and no one in her family would back her up to have an operation on it. Finally her aunt in New York told her to, and she went to the doctor. The second time he cut her eye he did it too much and so when she looked she had double vision and that was bad because of crossing streets. So the doctor said if she'd let him cut once more he fix it, and she did. Now when she looks at you with her brown eyes you think she's staring over your head until you see how her right eye is really fixed on you after all. Did it hurt you, I asked. She said they only gave her novacaine and nembutal so she could still be wide awake enough to turn her head at the right time.

What's your boy friend like, I asked her then. Oh, Joe, she said. Last night he got real romantic. And she bridled, her head to one side and her chin stuck back into her neck with a silly toothy grin. I noticed that her teeth were crowded one in front of the other, real close together. She had good big breasts though, and they bulged up under the starched sexless white uniform so you could see how some guy might want to get real romantic. How did you meet him, I asked, thinking that if she would talk that question would do it. It did.

She met him at a square dance. Grace and Jane got her to go on her Saturday night off and said, who knows, Betty, you might meet some nice fella. So she was standing waiting for a square to begin when this guy walks up to her and asks her to be his partner. Oh, no, she says to herself, you're too old for me. Well, she never squaredanced before, so he took her up to the loft and showed her a few steps. She smiles to herself and tells how he asked where she lived first and then when she was off. She started going out with him, and it seemed like he was divorced and had two kids. One was with the mother, and the other little girl was with him. She was eight years old, and had trouble with her feet. The only thing was, she was being brought up a Polish Nationalist which is like the Catholic belief, only the Poles allow their priests to marry.

Joe was awful considerate, but still you've got to be careful of these married men and their emotions; they're kind of wary about getting married again, so you've got to make sure just what they're planning. Joe wouldn't get married till his mother died anyway, because she's only given a year more to live. And now after his brother died just last week it was hardly decent to go planning anything like that. Still, it would be only five weeks more that Betty could stay up here, and it would be so nice if the two of them could take a cottage down the beach for a week just by themselves.

It was a funny thing, but they'd had pictures of Joe's brother's funeral taken since the sick mother couldn't get out of bed. Betty was having them developed, but she really wished they wouldn't come out because she didn't want to have to look at them. As a matter of fact, Joe's brother didn't _really_ die, but he committed suicide. Shot himself in the abdomen. So that's why they kept the funeral pretty quiet. He must have had a lot of pain after he did it; it showed in his face.

Why did he do it, I wonder, I asked. Well, he left six kids and a sick wife in the hospital. Seems he'd lost his job, and when he got another he'd figured he couldn't support them all being as they were living in a tenement anyway. Some people can take just so much and no more. Betty didn't know her, but it seemed like the wife was the sort of woman who made a lot out of every little ache and pain. She had ulcers on her legs from having so many children in a row. Well, take six kids from one to ten years old and figure it out. A kid every year or two, just about. Joe's brother looked awful old, about sixty, and him only thirty-five. So now he's dead, and Joe really shouldn't leave town for a week or two. Even if Betty <u>would</u> like to go to the shore for a week. It would be so nice, and they might even take the kid along, only they couldn't have as much fun that way. So they could get a double cottage – you've got to be so careful when you're single.

So she'd wait till July before she'd push the issue about getting married. After all, it's a man's job to do the asking.

Then the supervising nurse came in and said, "Miss. Gill," will you take switchboard duty from one to two." Miss Gill hadn't heard the stealthy antiseptic approach of the official white soft-soled shoes, so she broke off saying how she kind of liked Joe being as she'd been going with him for two years. She became very subservient and official, pouring a glass of thick syrupy cough medicine, and picking up crumpled kleenex. She said, "Yes, of course," and bustled out of the room, her breasts jiggling softly under the starched white bib of her uniform.

APPENDIX 2

Back to School Commandments

(1) I will not overwhelm him by breathless over-enthusiasm.
(2) I will not throw myself at him physically.
(3) I <u>will</u> be moderate, yet intense, and interested.

Back to School Commandments
(1) Keep a CHEERFUL FRONT continuously.
(2) <u>Science</u> – don't get upset. You have to get an A so you have to learn this. You <u>can</u>: You proved it by getting 2 good test marks.
(3) <u>Unit</u> – Don't panic. Ask for an extension if you need it. Write allegory paper this weekend. You were in infirmary a week if he needs excuses.
(4) <u>Davis</u>″ – ask for extension if you need it. You've done enough words theoretically anyway. Do paper for him in exam period.
(5) See Schnieders. Be calm, even if it is a matter of life & death.
(6) Get <u>Mlle</u> written.
(7) DO EXERCISES
(8) Get a lot of sleep: afternoon naps if necessary
(9) Remember: 5 months is not eternity. 2 months is not eternity. Even if it looks that way now.
(10) Attitude is everything: so KEEP CHEERFUL, even if you fail your science, your unit, get a hateful <u>silence</u> <u>from</u> <u>Myron</u>, no dates, no praise, no love, nothing. There is a certain clinical satisfaction in seeing just how bad things can get.

P.S. Remember – you're a hell of a lot better off than 9/10 of the world anyway!
    Love,
      Syl

Journal Fragments
24 March 1953 – 9 April 1953

slickers bloom like synthetic crocuses on campus: yellow, blue, red, and god knows what else. buds on trees are most bucolic and sylvan. rain could be parisian if it cared to.

I have glimpsed NYC for but one brief weekend in my locally anesthetized life, and spend most of my time in intellectual dishevelment in the rustic Smith pastures; hence anything you care to tell me in advance about the civilized customs of the city will be inordinately appreciated.
march 24

friday I got an idear. I am now in the midst of writing the biggest true Confession" I have ever written, all for the remote possibility of gaignigh (that word the lady said is: gaining, as in weight) filthy lucer. a contest in True Story is in the offing, with all sorts of Big Money prizes. being a most mercenary individual, because mercenary can buy trips to europe, theaters, chop houses, and other Ill Famed what-nots, I am trying out for it. all you have to do, the blurb ways, is write the story of your life or somebody else's life from the heart. and a sexy old heart it is. grammar and spelling mistakes won't count in the judging, says the rules, only it must be written in english, and not on onion skin paper or in pencil. I dunno why that last rule. mebbe people have been gluing onion rinds together and getting a large purge out of writing from the heart on that with a stubby pencil. anyhow, sylvia just finished the rough draft of a whopping true Confession of over 40 (you can count them) pages, trying to capture the style, and let me tell you, my supercilious attitude about the people who write Confessions has diminished. it takes a good tight plot and a slick ease that are not picked up over night like

a cheap whore. so tomorrow, I rewrite the monstrosity I have just illegitimately (everything gets done illegitimately amid great conflict) delivered.

sunday night,
april 5, 1953

life is amazingly simplified, now that the recalcitrant forsythia has at last
decided to come and blurt out springtime in petalled fountains of yellow. in
spite of reams of papers to be written, life has snitched a cocaine sniff of sun-
worship and salt air, and all looks promising.

april 9, 1953

APPENDIX 4

Journal Fragment

19 June 1953

June 19, 1953

All right, so the headlines blare the two of them are going to be killed" at eleven o'clock tonight. So I am sick at the stomach. I remember the journalists report, sickeningly factual, of the electrocution of a condemned man, of the unconcealed fascination on the faces of the onlookers, of the details, the shocking physical facts about the death, the scream, the smoke, the bare honest unemotional reporting that gripped the guts because of the things it didn't say.

The tall beautiful catlike girl who wore an original hat to work every day rose to one elbow from where she had been napping on the divan in the conference room, yawned and said with beautiful bored nastiness: "I'm so glad they are going to die." She gazed vaguely and very smugly around the room, closed her enormous green eyes and went back to sleep.

The phones are ringing as usual, and the people planning to leave for the country over the long weekend, and everybody is lackadaisacal and rather glad and nobody very much thinks about how big a human life is, with all the nerves and sinews and reactions and responses that it took centuries and centuries to evolve.

They were going to kill people with those atomic secrets. It is good for them to die. So that we can have the priority of killing people with those atomic secrets which are so very jealously and specially and inhumanly ours.

There is no yelling, no horror, no great rebellion. That is the appalling thing. The execution will take place tonight; it is too bad that it could not be televised ... so much more realistic and beneficial than the run-of-the mill crime program. Two real people being executed. No matter. The largest emotional reaction over the United States will be a rather large, democratic, infinitely bored and casual and complacent yawn.

APPENDIX 5

Letter

June – July 1953

June . . . July, 1953
Letter to an Over-grown, Over-protected, Scared, Spoiled Baby:

This is the immediate time for a decision: whether or not to go to Harvard Summer School. It is not the time to lose the appetite, feel empty, jealous of everyone in the world because they have fortunately been born inside themselves and not inside you.

It is a time to balance finances, weighty problems: objectives and plans for the future, to decide on relative importances. I am not a wealthy girl; I have a very small amount of money with which to meet next year's college expenses. The outgo this last month, and the amount spent on clothes ate up just about all of my winnings and prizes. Originally, my biggest satisfaction was that I would not have to get a job this summer and could sit down and write and learn shorthand, a practical skill that I could not afford to go to school to take, and that mother could teach me in my own backyard . . . that I could keep up along with typing and thus never be at wit's end for a job. When I apply for jobs after college, or after graduate school, I will want to know typing and shorthand . . . my bargaining power will be much better.

Then I decided I would go to Harvard Summer School for several reasons: I wanted to take Frank O'Connor's writing course because I thought that I might be able to sell some of the stories I wrote for it. I also decided to try elementary psychology so the way would be open to take psych courses later, if I wanted to. I could thus combine the practical and the creative. Now the O'Connor course is closed to me. Yet I still want the chance to write on my own, even if the prospect scares me to death because it means thinking and working on my own. So I would not want to take the full program of study, and thereby lose the main chance to have a "go" at writing for the most auspicious time in years . . . and probably the only such long time in at least a year. This is the summer where I build up a backlog. O.K. so I'd have to give up my scholarship to summer school, which means paying the same price for one course, which I might not give a damn about in the long run, or might agonize over every time I thought of the money (about $250) going out for it. I would have literally not more than $100 to $200 left at the end of my senior year . . . a mere pittance.

If I went to summer school, I would be meeting new people, no doubt queer people and nice people; I would have the library, and the "activities" and Cambridge. It might be a very nice luxury. Yet, I would be seeing Sally," and Jane, and hearing about their fascinating jobs, and feeling, in spite of myself, guilty as all hell: and sourly spending $250 is something that in reality I do not care to do. Either choice I make will have to be followed out with a scheduled program, a creative and very disciplined outlook, or I am not worth the paper this is written on.

If I live at home, I will be alone all summer, unless I seek out neighbors. I will be not earning money, and not really spending money. I will have to be cheerful and constructive, and schedule my day much harder than if at Harvard. I will learn about shopping and cooking, and try to make mother's vacation happy and good. That in itself would be worthwhile. I will work two hours a day at shorthand, and brush up my typing. I will write for three or four hours Each Day, and read for the same amount of time from a reading list I draw up carefully, so I won't read hit or miss.

I do not want to think that I am staying home because of fear: jealously of Marcia and Mike, of Sally and Jane in their casual productive job-home. I like to be busy, to work hard, and I would in contrast feel lazy and guilty, as I said. Which shows how weak I am in one way.

Face this realistically. I will have to give up my scholarship if I go to Harvard. Honestly, I could not tell the people at Smith I had one. How can I ask for money from them for a graduate year (If I want and need one) if I have spent $250 and earned nothing. Now, I can always say I worked for the month of June, and took free shorthand for the rest of the summer. Logically, this is a much more politic thing to do. The decision is my own.

I have to be creatively "existential". It is damn hard, because I keep wanting to crawl back into the womb. Living good takes hard work and planning and Imagination.

I Do Not Think that one psych course, in my financial setup, is worth $250. I was desperate to learn something beside English. I can read on my own, although it is hard to crack one's mind in discipline.

If I can't dream up plots in my own room and backyard, I won't be able to dream them up anywhere. I am of course, as I said, afraid to try writing on my own, because of the huge possibilities of failure. But I am going to. I will read "Seventeen's" and write a story for them. Also for the "Ladies Home". Also maybe for Accent on Living, and the New Yorker. The more I think of it, the more creative I will be at home, without all the big guilts and sapping jealousies if I pampered my original whim and went to Harvard now that my whole scheme is altered by not taking O'Connor's course.

In the middle of the summer, I will begin reading Joyce, so that I'll have a bulk read in time to begin thinking about the writing of my theses chapters, right at the beginning of the fall. I Will Not Lie Fallow or be Lazy. And at home, I will not have the little man in my head mocking: is this worth it, worth it, worth it, this course for $250, while your mother does all the work at home.

I must make choices clearly, honestly, without getting sick so I can't eat, which is in itself a defense mechanism that wants to revert to childhood tactics to get sympathy and avoid responsibility.

At home, I must not also begin dreaming up idealistic pictures of summerschool, envy of Marcia, who after all has a job to justify her rich summer (and who last summer had a hell of a time).

And by the way, everything in life is writable about if you have the outgoing guts to do it, and the imagination to improvise. The worst enemy to creativity is self-doubt. And you are so obsessed by your coming necessity to be independent, to face the great huge man-eating world, that you are paralyzed: your whole body and spirit revolts against having to commit yourself to a particular roll, to a particular life which Might Not bring out the Best you have in you. Living takes a very different set of responses and attitudes from this academic hedony ... and you have to be able to make a real creative life for Yourself, before you can expect anyone Else to provide one ready-made for you. You big baby.

Hardest thing is to know where and how to Give of Yourself ... and that's a problem to ponder this summer.

Can you earn money writing? You have, in the teen age group, but the competition in the slicks is phenomenal (cf. Mrs. Davis). The Literary Market seems at once harder and more aesthetically rewarding.

I AM NOT GOING TO HARVARD SUMMER SCHOOL.

I will learn shorthand, typing, and write and read and write and read, and talk to myself about attitudes, see the Aldriches and neighbors, and be nice and friendly and outgoing, and forget my damn egocentered self in trying to learn and understand about what makes life rich and what is most important

APPENDIX 6

Journal Fragment
31 December 1955 – 1 January 1956

New Year's Eve: 1956:"

Cold roast beef, hunks of bread and red wine in a fat glass carafe for supper in the Gare de Lyon: outside the window, trains steaming in their cradled tracks, people running, rushing with duffle bags, suitcases; an already out of date Christmas tree blinking colored lights on and off in chains: is it a code? Colored lights saying Merry Christmas in morse code? to the initiate who know. There is some rhythm hidden for those who wait and watch the flashing combinations of red, green and blue lights.

Carrying bags, square gray vanity case, olivetti, black umbrella, climbing steep steps to train, lugging cases, compartments filling with joking sailors in blue, stocky wrinkled peasants pulling ham sandwiches out of bulky leather bags. Finally, a blue compartment 3rd class, settling in, tearing off the loue tags and feeling guilty. Eight o'clock. Whistles, people pushing past compartment, bumping suitcases. A porter bringing luggage for a couple: vivacious blonde in big gray fur coat, unshaven legs, caramel=colored loafers and black skirt and jersey, slightly untidy, rather enchanting, playing up to her companion, a stolid restful man, rather stocky, with a pleasant ugly face which became beautifully alive and craggy when he smiled. At last, the shriek of whistles, the yell of porters and the moment of intuitive silence. The train began to move. Off into the night, with the blackness of a strange land knifing past. In my mind, a map of France, irregularly squarish, with a minute Eiffel Tower marking Paris toward the north, and a line of railway tracks, like a zipper, speeding open to the south, to Marseille, to Nice and the Cote d'Azur where perhaps in the realm of absolute fact the sun is shining and the sky is turquoise. Away from sodden mud and cutting winds of gray Cambridge, away from the freezing white frosts of a cold gray london, where the sun hung in the white mists like a bloody egg yolk. Away from the rain and wet feet of Paris, with colored lights wavering in the gutters running with water and the Seine flowed gray and sluggish by the quais and Notre Dame lifted two towers to a lowering, thick, curded gray sky.

On the train: staring hypnotised at the blackness outside the window, feeling the incomparable rhythmic language of the wheels, clacking out nursery rhymes, summing up the moments of the mind like the chant of a broken record: saying over and over: god is dead, god is dead. going, going, going. and the pure bliss of this, the erotic rocking of the coach. France splits open like a ripe fig in the mind; we are raping the land, we are not stopping. The pretty blonde turns out the light and it is warm and dark in the compartment with the blinds into the narrow corridor pulled down, and the night landscape outside the window slowly slowly coming alive in a chiaroscuro of shadows and stars. For we are leaving the thick clouds and smoky ceiling, we are plunging through into clear moonlight, first edging the thinning clouds like curded cream, then breaking forth pure and clear, in a spinning blueness. Single lights and clusters in villages. Then the weird whiteness of roads, as if made of broken white shells, or trails of bread crumbs left by the babes in the woods. Stars now too against the sky, turning in spirals, growing to look like Van=Gogh stars, and the strange black trees, wind=blown, tortuous, twisted, idiosyncratic pen-sketches against the sky: cypresses. And quarries, steep like a cubist painting in blocks and slanting roof=lines and rectangular whitish shacks, bleached in the light, with geometric shadows. Then blackness again, and land lying flat under the clear moon.

Drowsing for a while, stretched out on my back on the narrow compartment seat, with the good weight of Sassoon, sleeping fitfully, on my breast. And underneath always the tireless language of the train wheels, rocking us gently, within a network of steel. Slowing, calming, into lights of Lyon, and rousing from a dizzy coma to jump down the steep train steps onto the platform where vendors are selling bottled drinks and sandwiches. We buy a bottle of red wine and two large soft rolls of white bread with ham inside. We are very hungry and rip into the large soft sandwiches with our teeth, drinking down the wine in a white paper cup, finishing the peanuts we brought in a little paper bag and the cellophane parcel of dried figs, and finally the three small tangerines, which we peel, smelling the sharp fragrance as the porous skin tears open, spitting the slippery white seeds into a brown paper bag which we put under the seat with the empty wine bottle and the crisp little coats of peanuts, scattered about whispering underfoot.

Hours leap or delay on the luminous dial of Sassoon's watch. Between dozing and waking to stare out into the night, straining to see, to evoke the colors locked into the all-comprehensive blackness, France runs past. Secret, hidden, giving only the moon, rocky hills now, with clotted patches of whiteness, perhaps snow, probably not. Then, lifting my head sleepily once, suddenly the moon shining incredibly on water. Marseille. The Mediterranean. At last, unbelievable, the moon on that sea, that azure sea I dreamed about on maps in the sixth grade, surrounded by the pink, yellow, green and caramel countries the pyramids and the Sphinx, the holy land, the classic white ruins of the greeks, the bleeding bulls of spain, and the stylized pairs of boys and girls in native costume, holding hands, splendid in embroidered silks.

The Mediterranean. Sleep again, and at last the pink vin rosé light of dawn along the back of the hills in a strange country. Red earth, orange tiled villas in yellow and peach and aqua, and the blast, the blue blast of the sea on the right. The Cote d'Azur. A new country, a new year: spiked with green explosions of palms, cacti sprouting vegetable octopuses with spiky tentacles, and the red sun rising like the eye of God out of a screaming blue sea.

Breakfast in the dining car, after balancing along the aisles of countless train=cars, staring in at sleepy people in their compartments, stiff and yawning from the night spent dozing upright. A sense of keeness on the surface, sleeplessness, because of the blaze of new shapes, new color. Fresh orange juice, crisp croissons with little yellow snails of bland butter, bacon and eggs sizzling in a tin platter, and large, generous mugs of steaming café au lait, reclaiming us from shaky fatigue, infusing solidity, resilience. And always, the incredible shocks of blue coastline moving past us beyond the window: blue curved inlets, steep reddish hills, planted with palms, their bark like pineapple skin, and the pastel colored villas, with shutters boarded up: turquoise, salmon pink, with the black wrought iron arabesques of frivolous balconies, drawn with the bizarre finesse of Steinberg. Green steep hills in back of us, and the sun bleaching the pastel fronts of the villas – and the blown steam of the train golden and rose, trailing and shimmering beyond the window.

January 1: Sun well up, losing red and paling into blinding gold, air fresh and cold, essence of snow melting in sun, checking baggage and wandering toward the sea in a strange city. It is Sunday morning, and we have not slept, but the coffee and the bacon and eggs sustain, and the longing for the sea. We walk arm in arm in the broad, pastel streets, down the Avenue de Victoire, past the pink casino with light green shutters, through the green park and formal gardens with little pink and fuschia flowers and spiky green palms and blinding white statues, and the sunlight like cream on the elaborate clean facades of the fresh-painted hotels with all the little black wrought-iron Steinberg balcony fringes. There is the sea, heaving blue against the roundly pebbled shore, and the white gulls planing and crying in the quiet air, like the breath from a glass of iced champagne. Everywhere little black-clad people walk along the sparkling Sunday morning pavement, sitting in the turquoise-painted deck chairs along the Promenade des Anglais and facing into the rising sun: painted bleached blondes pass by in high heels, black slacks, fur coats and sun glasses; old men in navy-blue berets amble stiffly along, smoking pipes, blinking behind dark glasses; someone has brought out a pet monkey, and a little crowd has gathered to watch the monkey jump for the lowest branches of the palm and swing by one long hairy black arm.

The promenade is broad, with wide white sidewalks and brilliant green palms. On the left, as we walk toward the steep humped hill which shuts off the view of the old harbor, there are small one-story restaurants, with bright plaid table cloths, and picture windows facing out on the sea. It is warm in the sun, even if the air is chill yet in the early morning, and a few people are sitting at the pastel wicker tables and chairs drinking coffee and reading the Sunday papers. Behind the pastel facades of the restaurants, the hills mount steeply, showing row upon row of pink and peach villas against the dark green of the foliage. We climb slowly the steep hill with the ruined stone turrets. As the road mounts, we look down on the right into the oblong blue of the old harbor, bordered by quais. The houses are crooked and pink, with peeling painted shutters and linen hanging out to dry. The sunlight turns the colors to pastel cream. The road mounts steeply, and in the gutter on the left, clear water gushes downhill from drainpipes.

As the hill grows steeper, we climb into dark green pines, watching the land fall away at the right, and the pink villas shining above the blinding blue curve of the bay. There are several branching paths that fork away from us up the hill. Below, in a shallow hollow, there is a graveyard neatly and closely packed with white marble monuments, like relics of a monumental chessboard: little white obelisks, marble vases, Greek arcades with a weeping marble woman, flat slabs, sarcophagi, a small white sphinx or two. We try to find a door to the cemetary, but it is surrounded by a high green-painted wooden wall, so we go on, up the road among the pines, climbing wide natural steps of earth braced with borders of white stone. The view of the sea breaks upon us, and toward Italy, the snow=capped peaks of the Alps rise proud and virginal, touched with the golden rose light of morning against the blue sky.

At the top of the hill there is a round pavilion, where two little men compete selling colored postcards and painted dolls with "Nice" embroidered on gaudy striped satin aprons. We walk to the stone railing, and look down at the vista of orange tile roofs spread out below. In the valleys the church bells are beginning, clear voices speaking a language of chapel spires, separate dings and dongs rising to mingle in the rare blue air around us.

Journal

26 March 1956 – 5 April 1956

March 26: monday morning: Paris

Eh bien! Quelle vie! I am here in Paris in a room at the Hotel Béarn just ready to move upstairs to a sunny attic room for 30 francs less a night; the people in the hotel are delightful and the croissons are moist & light and butter generous, so I shall stay, and consider myself lucky: scavenged a bit this morning for another cheaper place but they were all full for Easter holidays; it is a glorious blue day with all the freshness of the country and I skipped down the early morning streets feeling miraculously that I really belonged. It will be a fine stay. I can get along in my French; too. Remember Hotel de Valence: old woman was charming and although they were full, they have rooms for 400 francs.

Arrived in Paris early Saturday evening exhausted from sleepless holocaust night with Ted in London & thought at the end that the sweetly burbling Janet Drake with her big dark eyes and pointed white pixie face would drive me absolutely mad. Emmet;[n] in his sailor costume & cuteness appealed much less than the former night when he had acted like a man and read aloud part of his book on James Larkin; Irish labor leader. I just wanted to get off alone and wash and go to bed. It was twilight when we found a room for me at this Hotel Béarn & I felt absolutely deserted. Overcome by a disastrous impulse to run to Sassoon as formerly; I took myself in leash & washed my battered face, smeared with a purple bruise from Ted and my neck raw and wounded too, and decided to walk out toward Richard's and search for food on the way. Going downstairs, a nice-looking man in the telephone booth grinned at me, and I grinned back; well, after I got out & started walking (having stupidly left my map of Paris in Emmet's car) I realized the guy was following me. He overtook me and smiled again & I came right out & said "J'ai oublié mon plan de Paris, ainsi je suis un peu perdue." Well, that was all he needed; so we went back to the hotel & he got his map to loan me during my stay; eventually we ended up walking all along the Boulevard St. Germain & I had steak tartar & wine & meringue at a little brasserie with him. Two arty musicians came in to play while we ate, one with a violin & coronet of paper flowers; the other with a peculiar box that he ground like a coffee machine & tinny music came out. I decided to go to bed early & rest to be strong & see Sassoon in the morning. It was a big concession because I felt terribly alone.

The guy turned out to be, interestingly enough, the Paris correspondent for the newspaper Paese Sera in Rome: an Italian communist journalist; no less! Hence the olivetti which he loaned me for today. Well, in spite of the fact he spoke no English, we communicated magnificently, to my surprise; he is very cultured & we discussed communism in different countries (he is very idealistic & very much a humanist) and art: he admires Melville & Poe & TS Eliot (which he'd read in French: J Alfred Prufrock!) and I asked him about the French & Italian artists he wrote up for his paper. All most reassuring. Got courage from this & felt I could manage without Richard if necessary;

SUNDAY: I got up, still tired, and set out in the fresh morning air down the Rue du Bac past the Place des Invalides to Rue Duvivier, feeling chipper & quite gaie, preparing my opening speech.

I rang at No. 4 outside of which an old beggar woman was singing in a mournful monotone. The dark and suspicious concierge met me and blandly told me that Sassoon was not back nor would he be back probably until after Easter. I had been ready to bear a day or two alone, but this news shook me to the roots. I sat down in her livingroom and wrote an incoherent letter while the tears fell scalding and wet on the paper and her black poodle patted me with his paw and the radio blared: "Smile though your heart is breaking." I wrote and wrote, thinking that by some miracle he might walk in the door. But he had left no address, no messages, and my letters begging him to return in time were lying there blue and unread. I was really amazed at my situation; never before had a man gone off to leave me to cry after. Dried tears, patted poodle & asked where could find restaurant; wandered through fruit stalls in Champs du Mars through flowers & crowds bearing palm sprays (not like ours but all green small sprigs of leaves) and found large Brasserie where, I realized after entering, Sassoon had taken Jane & me to eat that first night. Ordered Assiette Anglaise & coffee (which came black & sour) and read Anouilh's <u>Antigone</u>, that magnificent part the chorus does about tragedy.

Gradually, amazingly, a calm stole over me. A feeling that I had as much right to take my time eating, to look around; to wander & sit in the sun in Paris as anyone; even more right. I felt downright happy when I ordered another cup of coffee with cream & it was much better. Paid bill & wandered off along Seine browsing in bookstalls & half hoping I'd meet Gary Haupt. Walked around Notre Dame to Marché aux Fleurs where hundreds of yellow, red & green birds chirped & skipped in cages: mille oiseau de toutes couleurs!

Then, inspired, I took my sketch book & squatted in the sun at the very end of the Ile de la Cité in a little green park of Henri 4 du Vert Galant & began to draw the vista through the Pont Neuf; it was a good composition with the arches of the bridge framing trees & another bridge, and I was aware of people standing all around me watching but I didn't look at them – just hummed & went on sketching. It was not very good, too unsure & messily shaded, but I think I will do line drawings from now on in the easy style of Matisse. Felt I knew that view though, through the fiber of my hand.

Back to hotel where I lay down exhausted. Giovanni came by to take me out to little bar to meet two of his friends: Lucio, a handsome young journalist from Rome, also Paris correspondent for Paese Sera, & his lovely blonde German mistress Margo who was exquisitely clad in a black tweed suit, black jersey with red & white monogram & red earrings. All four of us took the bus to Place Voltaire where we had supper: felt very thirsty so had juicy tomato salad & celeri, sardines & a fine pear cold as honey for dessert. Giovanni was very nice & told me how cultured he thought I was after a detailed discussion about De Chirico. To bed to feverish sleep, perhaps reaction to wild destructive London night which makes me so sad, now I think of it, because of Michael Boddy[n] coming in (I wouldn't have minded just Luke) and now all Cambridge will be duly informed that I am Ted's mistress or something equally absurd. He suggested we go to Jugoslavia; if only he knew me rightly! I foolishly did not give him time. I was so tired & so hungry. Such mistakes I make. Oh well, let them talk; I live in Whitstead & can ignore much.

Saturday morning: March 31

Gray today, and chilly; the first clouded sky since arrival a week ago; so much has happened; now am un peu fatiguée because I washed hair last night and it was almost two until it dried. Life has been a combination of fairy-tale coincidence and joie de vivre and shocks of beauty together with some hurtful self-questioning. I feel I could write and write if only I sat down alone for a few months and could let things come instead of always having such a short time; such moving about and problems with people. I have walked for miles and miles and seen much and wondered much.

Monday, March 26, continued: was walking along the Seine on the way to the American express when a good-looking but rather professional chap kept pace with me in the usual way, beside and slightly ahead, looking into my face and saying "charmante!" I never can look cold and as if I hadn't heard, so I just burst out laughing and this encouraged him so he fell in step. He was pale with a Slavic bone-structure (or what I call that: prominent forehead and diagonal emphatic cheekbones with deepset eyes) and diabolic green eyes which he evidently knew were diabolic. I had time and so walked with him along the quai looking over at the Ile de la Cité and started talking in French; he was Greek and his name was Dimitri and he had a great deal to say about "les grandes surfaces" of life while I argued with him that it was the little details and idiosyncrasies that gave it special meaning; he drew a sketch then in a few lines in my notebook of the slanty trunks of the trees against the wall of the quai with house roofs & windows: rather good and pleasantly lyrical; I remarked how the water of the Seine ran through our shadows as we sat at the brink and made a metaphor about our lives imposing a certain line and order on the flux of time; also, how the water running by the opposite bank glittered and shone greenly in the sun while directly below us it was brown and dirty, full of orange peels and sodden paper and stains of oil slick. I think he got increasingly disappointed that I was going to philosophize instead of flirt; and I felt increasingly sure that he was all pose; he spoke of his wife Zara who was killed in the war and I began to stop believing him; he sang a song in Greek and walked along with me to the American Express staring diabolically into the store windows and muttering about how in this world "Il faut être même sinistre!" But his having said "Allo dear" in English like a naughty little boy wanting to be patted made me feel he was very close to the gigolo and that professional slick disgusted me so I froze and was vague about my address when he asked me and left him at the Pam-Pam, which being an expensive Quartier, evidently served to scare him off. Ironically, when I first met him and he was tough and serious I toyed with the idea of sleeping with whomever took my fancy in the street in a kind of aesthetic fashion: there have been many handsome strong faces, probably some with sinewy minds. That kind of living for the mere delight of the moment, like eating an apple whole, is important, but there are ways and ways: the danger is that this can turn to mere hedonism and escape to blindness and irresponsibility, fear to link day to day, action to action. This must not be. I must be whole and learn to eat days like apples only after making as sure as possible that no plague therein will give me future indigestion. Oh foresight foresight.

I sat in the sun a bit and sketched from the right bank under the Pont Neuf a pleasant vista of bridge arches. A sweet little Jugoslavian boy and his two shy girl companions came to watch and while they hid behind my tree he asked if I would walk and let them show me Paris; I refused politely and later packed up and treked along the Seine to Avenue Diderot and left a note at Tony Gray's hotel: I felt I should let as many people as possible know where I was to compensate for missing Sassoon. Tony had not yet come in but at least I got the hotel right (I am becoming increasingly proud of my sense of direction here and getting almost instinctive about some places;) my feet were very tired from walking since morning so I crossed the river to the Jardin des Plantes and sat in the gathering dusk watching the children play in the avenues and listening to the goats baa in the wooden chalet-type pens; there was also a little white lamb standing splay-legged milking at his gray wooly mother. I was really weary when I got back to the hotel about 6 and lay down on the yellow bedspread to rest. The next thing I knew, I heard a loud knocking and my name called; I staggered up out of a deep dark fresh moist sleep and opened the door to find Tony and a short plumpish girl who turned out to be his sister Sally; gradually my head cleared and I realized it was the same evening and we all went out to supper at a rather stuffy place, all tall pale green walls and moulding and chandeliers with grumpy looking middle-aged men here and there, like a middle-class professional men's club. I was grateful for a good dinner and tried to be nice to Sally who was very serious and deadpan and who never walked because her feet hurt (looking at my paper-thin red ballerinas, she said somewhat resentfully: "I could never wear shoes like yours"). As if in chemical opposition to his dour sister who didn't drink wine, Tony was fearfully bright and game and witty: the kind of English chap who would be all daisy-fresh at eight in the morning and leap over tennisnets in immaculate white shorts his blond hair shining in the early sun saying "Tennis anyone" in a fearfully Oxford accent. I found him a bit tedious and yet let it ride because I thought he might just be fun as an escort, and he had a slender boyish kind of good looks which was pleasant enough. Came back after dinner, washed hair and to bed. It was good to have some human rapport, however limited and not to have to run the gauntlet of the Paris streets at night where men are always at the elbow.

Tuesday: March 27: Up betimes feeling fresh and gay and luxuriating in croissons and morning coffee; talked briefly with Giovanni at doorway; he is so dear and warm and friendly; no problems there, so pleasant. Crossed early morning Seine singing into the Tuileries which were just open and fresh, the black trees against the light beige ground and the white marble statues everywhere on the greens; the fountain at the sailing pool was shimmering in the light and I could see up the vista of geometrical lines of trees to the obleisk in the place de la Concorde to the Arc de Triomphe mistily beyond. My eye was caught right away by a quaint green citronnade stand which was just opening in among the trees, surrounded by bright orange umbrellas, so I rented a garden chair for 5 francs from a little wrinkled woman and began to sketch. I was doing the shading when I heard someone call "Sylvia" behind me and it was Tony and SAlly which really surprised me; I joined them for lemonade (sour) and a good little sponge cake at the stand and then decided to accompany them to the Eiffel Tower which I had ignored last time and caught myself looking forward to a lunch with them, they were really nice people and I was hungry for company.

We took a taxi at the Place because of Sally's feet and the Tour Eiffel was another tourist center: the great pyramid of angled girders rose over head and on its four legs it resembled and kind of mechanical Martian monster about to take lumbering steps across the Seine and walk off. It cost 200 francs to climb to the 2nd floor and we got together into the little car railway. The view was fine and after I got over my perennial jelly-terror of approaching the railing or cracks where one can see down into an infernal machine of girders I enjoyed the gray-green crooks of the Seine, recognized the spires of Notre Dame and the gray-brown smutch which was the Bois de Boulogne; the white domes of Sacre Coeur dominated all from the hill of Montmartre, like a Byzantine wedding cake. Directly below the people moved in black dots on the green geometry of the park and the red and yellow sunshades on the apartment windows looked like the inspiration for a Mondrian. We entered the restaurant to eat dinner and I was appalled at the posh formal service and ridiculous high prices; I felt very uncomfortable because I knew I couldn't afford to pay and would have to go without supper to make up for the extravagance which I didn't even enjoy. While Tony and Sally ate several courses and wine, I just had a rather meager cold chicken with salad and water and coffee. I felt rather angry and resolved never to get in a situation like that again and felt terribly sensible and economical; we parted at the bridge and I went off to the Avenue Montaigne and got a very cheap ticket to Anouilh's comedy "Ornifle" for the evening and felt extremely proud again at my independence and courage; just as I ate in the same restaurant my first day here as I did before with Sassoon, so I got a ticket to the very play in the theater where I had that ridiculous tantrum last winter about our seats not being side by side but one in front of the other which resulted in Sassoon's sweetly humoring me and turning in the tickets (now that I look back, I am appalled at my spoiled demanding behavior then: my greatest flaw is the smug satisfaction that I am intuitively right because I change and grow and then my new vision always seems right because it has increased insight; the process of enlightenment is, however, continuous, so I must realize that even my certainties at the moment will be chastened and altered and mellowed by time). Walked then up affluent Avenue to the Champs, crossed the Place de la Concorde and browsed in the expensive shopwindows on the Rue Royale by the Parthenon-imitation Eglise Madeleine, up the Rue de la Paix, glancing at sparkling diamonds, red delicate shoes and orange and smoky blue shoes and gold shoes (if I were wealthy, my idea of extravagance would be to have a closet full of colored shoes - - - just one or two styles: simple princess opera pump with tiny curved heel – in all the shades of the rainbow.) American Express again and the boring "Pas de lettres". Sat once more in Tuileries to finish sketch, then home to rest before theater. Dressed in black velvet and felt most chic in mackintosh, ironically, because of its swaggery cut; nonchalant, debonair, yet un peu triste because noone was there to chariot me. I walked fast along the dark deserted quais, amazed at the desertion by the Place; as I hurried along the Right Bank a lowslung black car passed and the driver turned to look; he evidently went round the block because he came back and oozed alongside while he begged me to come for a ride and I just walked faster; finally he got out and stopped, but I just kept on going; maybe he thought I was one of the more expensive Champs filles de joie? anyway he laughed when I said I was rushing to the theater & finally drove off:

I understood enough of the play to appreciate what was happening, but found Ornifle difficult often because of his fast river-current way of talking, and also his friend hard because of a vernacular accent. I also felt very much increasingly alone in the extreme right corner of the second balcony squeezed to the wall by several fat wheezy ugly women, aware that our balcony was mostly full of little groups of women and of all the couples in the orchestra. I walked out afterwards alone and feeling tragic as the crowds thinned, pairing up and off, and almost hoped that someone would accost me on the Champs and give me a sandwich, I was starving and a little faint from no supper. I talked aloud to myself and cried a little crossing the Place, blazing with lights and arush with deadly streams of cars; I gave up all idea of stopping on the Boulevard St. Germain for a snack and hurried down the Rue de Lille which I discovered was completely deserted, full of some kind of public arsenal-type buildings; a policeman was pacing his beat ahead and I hurried to keep near him until I got into the lighted hotel section; I cried and cursed Sassoon for leaving me thus open to jeopardy and missed him most that night; the moon was far off and sad over the dark cruel buildings and in my room I cried in black velvet on the yellow bedspread and wondered at my not having one to love; outside the roof shingles and chimney pots were misted magic and haunting in a blue wash of moonlight.

Wednesday: March 28: Lazed in bed this morning, weary from the late night and wrote a letter to mother which gave her the gay side; then pilgrimage without fruit to American express and indulged in real blast of hearty lunch at Pam-Pam to make up for my starvation & nobility yesterday: onion soup, rare chateaubriand steak, two glasses of red wine and apple tart. I felt much better; talked with rather boring man who lived in Montmartre & spoke English & claimed to know multitudes of languages & to have traveled partout: I find I am becoming much more practical and less impressionable; he left me his address and asked me to come see him (with friend) and promised that he could discuss all sorts of philosophy & literature; I nodded and said "Bien sûr" a few times until he finally left and I turned with joy to my apple tart, resolving never to take that invitation up; I am beginning to have a sense of what is questionable & what is not; when someone is vague about jobs and where money comes from and mentions painting or writing history books (this man was trying to prove something to contradict the encyclopedias about the discovery of India!) that is suspect: an attempt at coverup by arty arabesques. Probably Dmitri was a hairdresser & this man a waiter! Stopped by Seine in sun to sketch a harlequin-style kiosque which had taken my fancy near the Louvre: one of those round poster-stands in green with a mosque-like roof and colored pastel posters all around: talked with two dull Americans in army and a precocious little boy of fourteen named Bonalumi-Francis who was amazed that I wasn't married and having babies at my age and who told me to be careful because a man with a car was waiting until he left to come approach me; at last I had enough of this bright little chap and was glad when he left after telling me he would be happy to come to England if I paid his way! I was turning back to finish my little sketch of which I was fonder than any I'd done when I heard a voice behind me saying "Isn't that nice!" and whirled to see, of all people, blond blue-eyed solid Gary Haupt. I fell upon him with cries of joy, he seemed so honest and damn solid, and we crowed little exclamations about how we'd looked all over for each other; I'd just given up hope of meeting him that day, after endless walks along the Seine. I was so grateful for his simple presence & friendly escort, after wielding off men as dusk came. We had cognac on a windy corner with Joseph Shork & a friend of his, both of whom I disliked as dull heavy unintuitive plodding Americans on Fulbrights: no subtlety at all (and I don't think this is because Gary said Joe judged me superficial & flighty on the ship: without having even met me!!!) Then we walked down the Boulevard Raspail, had dinner (good salmon and buttered spinach at a very bad-service restaurant called Lutetia or something where the side benches were slippery leather that made it almost impossible to sit up without shooting under the table) and went to an absorbing if oversimplified surrealist movie in technicolor at the small Studio Montparnasse: "Rêves a Vendre": a sequence of dreams inspired by artists like Max Ernst, Man Ray, Ferdinand Léger, Calder and Marcel Duchamp: a mixture of droll (girl with the prefabricated heart sequence) and disturbing: blue man and ladders dissolving; smoking telephones and echo voices in red velvet baroque rooms. Fiery debate afterwards, by members of Film group; stayed a bit to watch & listen: where in America would there be such critical passion? Both mind and flame? I'm sure an American college audience would have gone out like contented cows, feeling comfortably avant garde without questions. Citron pressé in little modern bar nextdoor and métro home.

Thursday: March 29: Lovely elated day with Gary, very gay and light: walked to Ile de La Cité and sat on bench before the Palais de la Justice for hours in the gray chill air sketching the Tabac and café opposite: ironically, his sketch – light and whimsical and airy, and mine – heavy and structured in simple shaded geometric forms and designs: funny, but both reverted to deeper side of personality more outwardly suitable to the other; ate salad shell with cold salmon and mayonnaisse & ham & cheese & wine at Pam-Pam. Walked liltingly through Tuileries and bought the most lovely enormous brilliant-blue balloon from a brown wrinkled gypsy-woman in the park who reminded me of the one in Mary Poppins who sold balloons that had peoples names on them and took them flying through the air; There was only one blue one, and it was huge and round as the world; caught in a loose mesh of red string with little tri-color streamers and a long string; walked everywhere, along quias to Notre Dame and everybody looked and marveled and smiled; sat in park by Seine and watched children playing while eating icecream cones: they all looked up wide eyed and reached up and smiled and said "Ballon." Orange Pressé (real one with orange squeezed in front of us) at café & dinner at "Sérail" on Rue de la Harpe; where I dined so often and happily with Richard right next to our hotel with the blue velvet room the color of my balloon; grew increasingly sad and tearful through shishkebab and wine supper and felt rather sorry for myself; left Gary at hotel and felt: what more can I do to conquer all the places we've been and make them mine and not just ours? I'd tried two restaurants and the play, all symbolic: at least I've got my own sunny yellow room full of rosebuds: it is mine and I am as complete in it as could be without a man; happy as could be without my man. I am riding the horses one by one and breaking them in.

Friday: March 30:
A strange day passing through ecstasy unto certain sorrow and the raining of questions sad and lonely on the dark rooftops. Met Gary early & walked to Pont Royal where I met Tony, feeling very chic in my white pleated skirt and aqua sweater & red shoes & red & white polka dotted hairscarf; citronnade at kiosque and he was gay and quite sweet; a little more subdued with his sister gone; we took the metro to Pigalle and got out in the hot sun by the honkeytonk square and began climbing the little narrow roads to the top of Montmartre; the shops were dark stenchful holes and reeked of garlic and cheap tobacco. In the sun there was a magic of decay: scabbed pastel posters, leprous umber walls, flowers sprouting out of filth. Climbed Rue Vieuville & series of steeply angled steps to Place du Tertre which was chock full of tourists and bad bad artists in various stances doing charcoal portraits or muddy paintings of the domes of Sacre Coeur; Tony and I walked about and looked at paintings until a small man asked if he could cut my silouhette "comme un cadeau", so I stood in the middle of the square in the middle of Montmartre and gazed at the brilliant restaurants in the middle of a gathering crowd which ohed and ahed and which was just what the little man

wanted to attract customers: so I got a free silhouette and by this time Tony was putting his arm around my waist when we walked and I could feel that bristling barbed wit mellowing: we stood in front of Sacré Coeur in the sun watching the tourist busses grunt up the hill, full of deadpan people sheltered by sunproof-windproof-bulletproof-glass domes; inside the church it was cool and dark as a well with red patches of light from the windows: Tony described Chartres a bit and some rather gratifying sensitivity came out. Had exquisite lunch just off commercial square where they were serving mobs under the trees and playing violin-lilty tunes, where the man with picture frame and paper flowers around his head was yelling and doing stunts. We avoided all this in the shady grove of the peaceful "Auberge du Coucou" and had fine salade de tomate, delectable veau sautéed in mushrooms and buttery potatoes and bottle of iced white wine which sent us floating into the afternoon like birds, all airy and gay; Tony bought me a bunch of violets and was increasingly attentive and I mellowed to fondness. I left all thought of the American Express in the pale gold aura of wine and felt most beautiful and slightly damned; Tony mentioned the Rue du Bac métro stop and I thought: well, so he comes back to the hotel; I felt that the day was like a shimmering shell of pearliness and must be treated lightly like a soap-bubble, so floated to the hotel and Tony showed no signs of farewell; so up the steps to the room where it was cool and we washed and lay down, he had grown more beautiful and golden to me all afternoon and I was only wishful and happy for this time with him for he was growing more rare and gentle, so we lay together and it was good and kissed gently and it was good and his skin was smooth and taut and his body was lean and sweetly put together, so shirt by slip we undressed and embraced until we were quite naked and I began to want him; but when I went off to the bathroom for a few minutes he reflected and later froze when I came back and it was I think partly because he felt I was compex and he lived in England and did not want involvings, and I was sorry a little because I had come so close to having him there in the dusk and his body was so right and lovely and strong and golden and he dawned gentle and sweet: I imagine he used to be like this when he was young, or when he played the piano; Oxford I think has ruined him, with that snob brash conceit and consciousness of going with the Rothschild girl and the "toast of Oxford", Lady Tweedsmuir's daughter Ann. So he dressed and with the layers put on his decorum. We walked out in the blue dusk along the wet misty Seine and had tea in a modern bar on the quai where a mysterious woman in little high creamy leather boots; slacks and a brilliant red shirt with enormous sleeves came for supper with the dearest girl in costume & mantilla with an enormous teddy bear and Spanish doll; then the métro to the Champs Elysees where we saw Grace Kelley in Hitchcock's fine technicolor film/ "To Catch a Theif" which brought back Nice and the Riviera with bangs of color to mind: our winter vacation, Sassoon's and mine. Another horse. Then Tony and I walked together back down the Champs past the circle of lighted fountains in the Rond Point to the miraculous blaze of the Place which was illuminated for the first time, with the Crillon & Marine buildings framing the Eglise Madeleine and the shining splashing dolphin fountains and the horses galloping that Richard sent me on his lovely winter postcard, and the sheer white shaft of the obelisk with the eyes and birds and heiroglyphs. On along the Seine and to the hotel where I knew it was the end, and he kissed my hand sweetly like the faint touch of the violet petals and I said nobly and integrally: "It has been a lovely day," and left him. I am sure, with the gift of Englishmen, he will dismiss this as an "episode" which has no relation to the high society life. I do not think I would like his friends or his kind of Oxford; he is right, oddly enough, when he casually says he is a bitchy chap; he is all for appearances, what money can buy (ironically enough); and family name. I think I am almost lucky to remember him sweet and golden and honest, for he was dear and honest, although he will sheathe this day in the false decorum of his superficial ethic as he sheathed himself in shirt and tie. So it was goodbye. There is no more there.

And again I ask myself: why? I must be so careful, and am going back to Cambridge and that gossip. I shall not go to London to descend on Ted; he has not written; he can come to me, and call me Sylvia not Shirley. And I shall be chaste and subdued this term and mystify those gossipmongers by work and seriousness!

Thursday: April 5: Outside all morning the rain came down on the gray rooftops and I lay quiet and warm in the shaded room of greenish light dreaming and wondering on the workings of this machine infernale, how much is chance and accident, how much a combination of that working on the will and the will working back to hack out its own happenings and how much is the will attracting all events like iron filings to a magnet which some days is strong, some days weak. How many times in my dreams have I met my dark marauder on the stairs, at a turning of the street, waiting on my bright yellow bed, knocking at the door, sitting only in his coat and hat with a small smile on a park bench; already he has split into many men; even while we hope, the blind is drawn down and the people turned to shadows acting in a private room beyond our view. Decisions are being made as we sit here, isolated, with the foolish mistake about our mail, all the letters of death and rejection, or love and money gone flying home to England to mock and wait and leave us fumbling curious with the wormeaten questions. I must live in utter ignorance for a week; and last night, stopping to talk with Giovanni who had been waiting late with the poem in Italian which he translated then to French about the mounds of wheat and ice breaking, I realized – with what clarity, what fulness, – that I only want to go home now, to the home where I have hewn out my peace and my sanctuary: not America but my Whitstead, my gable and my garden: there I can rest and grow fresh as morning milk and find again my faith and innocence, that innocence which is faith, belief in the rightnesses of these encounters with other men and other monuments where one must take wrong turnings if only to find new ways; faugh, such nobility, such moralizing: try the concrete, name names.

Somehow last night it came over me with terror and a kind of deadness and despair that I did not want to go to Germany or to Italy with that kind bewildered and how lucky (ironic that, he comes to more and more fortune) boy beside me at the ballet: the ballet of Phèdre, my phèdre with her dark flame and that billowing cloak of scarlet which was blood offered and blood spilt: the blond and proud Hippolyte with his green-maned horses, the pink and white fay Aricie, the stylized Neptune with his pale face and trident, and all those blue-green waves: can I be good for a week? no acidity, or lemon looks for those laborious puns and endless family trees: oh my God, what is it what is it? Why does one not learn to love and live with the boring daily bread that is good for one, that is comfortable, convenient and available? like Brave New World. Ha. So one can suffer or become Shakespeare? Ironically, I suffer and do not become Shakespeare – and it is my life which is passing, my life which is smutched and battered and running, each heartbeat; each clocktick being a fatal subtraction from the total number I was allowed in the beginning: or, not being such a complete fatalist, from the variety of numbers I was allowed to work from: how fortunate that we are blind. And yet where is there to go? I would profit by a week alone, a week reading and writing: my God, at this moment I wonder if I could have gone to live with Ted, but that is London and no place to wash (oh who cares) and the Boddy might paunchily properly lurch up the stairs at any moment. And I do not know Ted enough to know how he talks, how he talks: one night when I return? I shall send the postcard of Rousseau's Snakecharmer with a question. One night is not enough. I must think much; perhaps he will not answer and that will be simpler. But now I am a vagabond: I cannot wait for Richard longer, it has been two weeks, and he must have felt my strong will; London is Ted or too expensive.

So I leave early tomorrow morning with Gordon for Munich; can I make it good, without cursing myself for living off him? He wanted it this way, with me as a friend, and I must remember how the night before we met so accidentally and luckily in the American Express that I was too sick of small dark sleazy men at my elbow to venture out for supper; and Giovanni came then with his consolation and banana and drawers of dates and warm milk to comfort; how kind he has been. I considered sleeping with him even, but yesterday was in a way glad Gordon came, because Giovanni and I are so tender and kind to each other now that it is good; strange, how he and Lucio both have wives and children, and now they live here and with mistresses. With Whitstead barred, life has now become a rather terrible smorgasbord of different capitals and men who go with them: London and Ted, Paris and the dark absence of Richard and comfort and conversation of Giovanni, and Rome and the journey with Gordon/ And now having coldly discussed finances all morning with Gordon and with growing coldness having weighed in a frenzy of chill a sudden temptation to tell him I wasn't going and discussed these things also over ham and eggs and red wine in a little cafe around the corner, too much has been done already to break away: I do want to see Venice and Florence and Rome even if only in five short days, for I shall know where and how I wish to return. How it cries inside me now, and the words of was it Verlaine sing over and over: "Il pleure sur les toits comme il pleure dans mon coeur." And I would rather be alone with my typewriter than with Gordon, and his stupid stammering French and inability to make himself understood here, his utter lack of rapport, of that intuitive sensing of mood, disgusts me, yes, does. I feel the waiter in the bar smiling, charging too much and asking Gordon if he wants milk; I grinned sidewise at him for that one; with Gordon I am much more a worse kind of self; yet quoi faire?

Quoi faire? Is it some dread lack which makes my alternatives so deadly? Some feeble dependence on men which makes me throw myself on their protection and care and tenderness? Ha, but I have been alone in Pairs for two weeks, and there are no girls here, so except for Gary (whom I scrupulously said goodbye to and even gave up Chartres, because it would have been a kind of sacrilege without Richard or alone, for Gary even with his avowed sensitivity is so plodding in his manner that it kills nightingales) and Tony, whom I scared with my need and volcanic will, I have gone about alone; (Giovanni was a discovery and mine and a kind of triumph: it has been fine with him, just warm and tender enough and all that good talk in French and his friends and the little Epicerie where he took me after my tears for wonderful crush of human warmth and communion, and a soupplate of good stew and potatoes and cheese and red wine in the little crowded place.) - - - except for those dates and times which had two enchanting days (balloon and Don Camillo and Snow White with Gary; Montmartre and silouhette and Sacre Coeur and delectable veal and white wine with Tony) I have fought and conquered a desolate city. I think of him ever; is it because he is vanished that the dark image haunts me? Remember that time dancing in Nice - - - his slight undisciplined body: he can't swim, he is weak in a certain sense, he will never play baseball or teach math: that orange juice and broiled chicken solidity is utterly lacking and it is what Gary has and Gordon has (in the story: Dark Marauder, there will be a great contrast between the delicate snail-and-wine taste of Richard and the plain steak-steak and potatoes-with-nothing-done-to-them taste of Gary). And so I have been alone here, really, and my room might be taken back by the vacationing student if I tried to stay, and Giovanni might become a little difficult; and Richard might never come, and it is cold and wet now.

Yes, all the auguries are for departure: the Paris air grows cold and I shiver always and my white lingerie slowly turns gray and there is no bathtub; all gathers and with cold edges and blunt corners urges me to go; the train and the view will be a kind of solace; if only if only I can be civil to Gordon: why not? there is all that mess and scorn between us, and no bitterness ever entirely vanishes between the rejector and the rejected. I paid my complete train-fare through from Paris to Rome in francs today and got that over; the plane ticket is formidable, and I shall pay part of that in England if he needs it. I feel used enough to having men pay for my food, and even hotels, and feel that Gordon chose to do this for my company, with the understanding it was to be merely friendly company; so that I am not in debt, except I shall try to rise above this heavy despair with my Richard deserting me and going and 3 weeks being long enough for a very dangerous woman or a few which he has found, and my not being really angry only sorrowful with those great dark tearbrimming eyes of reproach which I know I could not stand to look at if the position were reversed; at the ballet last night I saw us entertaining in a large room hung with chandeliers and he chucked a pretty little blonde pixie under the chin the way he did me that first time with an almost insulting appreciation and challenge; my God, if he would come today I would stay here with him. I see him now even, back in Paris, calmly reading my letters and thinking: poor hysterical wronged one, and living with his Swiss girl, or Spanish girl. Could he ever be faithful in the way I so desperately need? Ah, and could I ever be colossal enough to accept him if he weren't without becoming a martyr or, worse, deliberately offering myself up to other men as a sacrifice in retaliation and desperation, a dive to destruction? Perhaps this is all in the cards, those cards with just so many kings and queens and just so many choices!

And now the alternatives revolve in a fatal dance and with the mailing of my postcards mother will know I am going to Rome and Ted will know I want to see him if only for one night (oh, I just want to be with him: he is the only one who can walk high as Richard and for that I even submit to all the Boddy pigeyes and sniveling gossip and talk and even Jane and the chosen ones knowing; for that I even let him call me Shirley the wrong name and know he does not know how much I could rip past her and be tender and wise, for now I am become too easy too soon and he will not bother to discover); shall I go to Jugoslavia with him? Or will I curse myself for deserting Elly and Spain? I miss a good woman; how could I dare think Elly was promiscuous in her attraction of the easy dark kind of men, when in fact I give with more to the strong clean lovely kinds; Ted can break walls; I could telegraph him tonight if I could come home to London and live there till Whitstead: the danger would be of his visitors, and he will perhaps have some, of his talk: "I tell you she just came and camped in my bed"; I lust for him, and in my mind I am ripped to bits by the words he welds and wields: oh; God; there is so little time; tonight all must happen; before 7 when I meet Gordon: he just now is the safest way: I would conquer two other countries (and however much I want to linger in Italy; is it not better to see five days and come back hungry to stay longer, having foraged first under a man's protection, still off season, able to explore without pickups?) ah yes. If Richard would come back now: I could devour pride and go to his place and ask the concierge if there was word: he might be there, hiding. He might be coming tomorrow; there might be a message (all of which I shall find out about too late). I could stay a few days and go back to England from here.

APPENDIX 8

Journal Fragment

1 April 1956

April 1
    Program: to win friends & influence people
→ <u>Don't drink much</u> – (remember misfortunes w. Iko after St. John's party, Hamish – 2 dates, St. Botolph's party & London night); stay sober.
→ <u>Be chaste</u> and don't throw self at people (cf. David Buck, Mallory, Iko, Hamish, ted, Tony Gray) – in spite of rumor & M. Boddy, let no one verify this term the flaws of last!
→ <u>Be friendly & more subdued</u> – if necessary, smog of " mystery woman" – quiet, nice, slightly bewildered at colored scandals. Refuse ease of Sally Bowles act.
→ <u>Work on inner life – to enrich</u> – concentrate on work for Krook – writing (stories; poems, articles for <u>Monitor</u> – Sketches) – <u>French daily</u>.
→ <u>Don't blab too much</u> – listen more; sympathize & "understand" people –
→ <u>Keep troubles to self.</u>
→ Bear mean gossip & snubbing & pass beyond it – be nice & positive to all –
→ <u>don't criticize anybody</u> to anyone else – misquoting is like a telephone game.
→ Don't date either Gary or Hamish – be nice but <u>not too enthusiastic</u> to Keith et al.
Be stoic when necessary & <u>write</u> – you have seen a lot, felt deeply & your problems are universal enough to be made meaningful – WRITE –

APPENDIX 9

Journal Fragment

16 April 1956

April 16

Re Ted: you have accepted his being; you were desperate for this and you know what you must pay: utter vigilance in Cambridge (rumor will be legion, but there must be no proof; never drink, keep calm); loss of Richard and whistling void in guts when he leaves you with memory of his big iron violent virile body, incredible tendernesses & rich voice which makes poems & quirked people & music. Knowledge of his utter big luck & power & blast by it as he goes on, beyond – <u>the first</u> to keep on beyond – to hundreds of other women, other poems – "I can make more love the more I make love." If Richard's tenderness & virility & aesthetic rapport made you despair of going & finding one after him, you will <u>never</u> find a huge derrick-striding Ted with poems & richness – he makes you feel small, too-secure: he is not tender and has no love for you. Only a body – a girl-poet, an interlude – Consider yourself lucky to have been stabbed by him; <u>never complain</u> or <u>be bitter</u> or ask for more than normal human consideration as an integrated being. <u>Let him go</u>. Have the guts. Make him happy: cook, play, read, but don't loose others – work for Krook, Varsity & home – keep other cups & flagons full – never accuse or nag – let him run, reap, rip – and glory in the temporary sun of his ruthless force –

Journal

26 June 1956 – 6 March 1961

Café Franco-Oriental"
June 26 – Paris

11[a]

12[b]

12

14[b]
Miss Drake Proceeds to Supper

No novice
In those elaborate rituals
Which allay the malice
Of knotted table & crooked chair,
The new woman in the ward
Wears purple, steps carefully
Among her secret combinations of eggshells
And breakable humming-birds,
Footing it, sallow as a mouse,
Between each cabbage-rose
Slowly opening their furred petals
To devour and drag her down
Into the carpet's design.

With bird-quick eye cocked askew
She can see in the nick of time
How perilous needles grain the floorboards
And outwit their brambled plan;
Now through her ambushed air,
Adazzle with bright shards
Of broken glass,
She edges with wary breath,
Fending off jag and tooth,
Until, turning sideways,
She lifts one webbed foot after the other
Into the still, sultry weather"
Of the patient's dining room.

17[b]
June 27 –
Old black hunched woman with beautiful painted bluegreen eyes & elegant
bones looking at herself in mirror after narrow mirror in storefronts. –

[verso 17b]
Until bird-racketing dawn"
When her shrike-face

pecked open those locked lids,
to eat crown, palace, all
That all night had kept free her male.
And with her yellow beak
Lie and suck
The last red-berried blood drop
from his trap heart.

19[b]

Parcae

As those three indefatigable women knit black landscapes shuttle through
their heads

reflection of 3 fat French women knitting in lighted train compartment at
night – black landscape, strung & knotted telephone wires, pointed fir trees
– rattling & streaming through the reflections of their blind complacent
faces, knitting webs of fate, utterly indifferent – landscape spins out of
heads, lowered lids – bloodclots – loop, stab thread with needles –

White apparently indifferent to exterior time-flux world, constant reflections are spinning it out of their heads through their fingertips

23[a-b]

1956

Benidorm – August 4: Saturday
CONCERNING WAVES

The bay of Benidorm is striated with color: at the horizon-line the sea is
dark Prussian blue, in strong contrast to the pale, distant sky which appears
almost white against the dark band of water. The central stretch of color,
nearer shore, is a violent peacock-green, shading into yellower tones as the
water-depth becomes more shallow until, directy in shore, light brown sand
tinges the breaking waves to greenish amber.

Far out at sea, the dark blue water is constantly broken by the abrupt
chalk-lines of white caps. Under the glaring sheen of the sun, the waves
ripple in like blue watered-silk, their crests rising as they near shore, hanging
like amber glass shot through with shadows of vivid green which run along

under tip of the waves curving. Then, about five yards from shore, the wave crest breaks, on a white froth of foam which rumples shoreward on the translucent plane of the wave ahead. The white froth thins to a flattened net work of foam which dwindles to spots & vanishes as the wave gathers again to break on shore.

The long running crest of the incoming wave travels like molten glass in whose liquid bulk the fragmented colors of sand and sky blur and melt into each other: amber of furrowed sand is glassed by bright blue-green. The wave gathers, piles up on itself as it moves, toppling on the wet, hard-packed sand of the beach in a broth of clouded brown water bordered with white foam bubbles that wink and shine in the sun. A thin translucent sheet of water fans up the beach, slips back, and dwindles into the advance of the next wave, leaving momentarily in the wet sand, a glassed blue reflection of the sky.

The air is full of the sibilant rhythmic rush of waves sousing the shore: the continuous whisper of crests breaking, rank on rank, into foam is punctuated by the thudding lash of each wave as it strikes shore, bubbles seething, then goes shriveling back into the sea in a cloudy backwash of water thickened with grains of sand.

26[a]
Nimble through thickets of the blood
time's fox steals red.

August 13 – Monday
BENIDORM: Bait-Diggers

At the border of the sea, an old man and three little boys bent from the waist, facing inland and scrabbled in the sand with their hands. The old man, browned from the sun, wore a faded light blue workshirt. His gray pants, splashed wet from the waves, were rolled up above the knee and he wore a small dark blue beret on his head. The little boys bent and reached forward, scraping the sand back through their straddled legs like puppy dogs digging for a bone. Two of the boys wore short sleeved khaki shirts and shorts, while the smallest wore a white undershirt and brief green pants. As they bent and dug, waves broke at their heels and seethed up about their ankles in a broth of white foam.

26[b]

August 13: Benidorm – two girls playing with diving equipment in the waves: one girl, tan and short, full-figured in a white bathing suit splashed with gaudy red flowers, puts on the blue plastic goggle, the strap around the back of her white bathing cap, the periscope sticking up over her head like a blue insect's antennae. She ducks under the water, her back showing like the hump of a turtle, the periscope jutting up as she floats face down, arms extended. The second girl, pale, in a green bathing suit, walks along, water up to her waist, pulling her friend along by the hands, periscope bobbing in the wave like a sunken submarine.

Plastic bag: The black plastic carrying bag shone with a gloss of patent-leather in the sun. A dusting of beige sand clung to the side as if spattered from a paint brush. Along the top and bottom of the bag, which was cylindrically shaped, brass nailheads gleamed, spaced about two inches apart. A curve of the bag's watermelon-red lining showed above the yellow cover of the book inside it.

27[a]–28[b]
August 18 – Benidorm – 1956
The houses of Benidorm cluster along the top of a rocky headland jutting out into the bay. The rocks rise, wedge-shaped, with the slope descending inland, about a hundred yards above sea level; the grain of the rocks is horizontal, and in crevices of the jagged cliffs sprout clumps of dark grass. At the uppermost left of the promontory is an elaborate white railing, scrolled as lace, bordering the Castillo observation platform; green treetops show above the slanting roof of the first one-story house which starts the hill of houses, also wedge shaped, with the narrowest segment balancing the widest segment of the cliff, on the far left, jutting into the sea. The houses pile up on each other as the rocky cliffs slope to the level of the beach, giving the impression of a cubist cliff dwelling, the colors of the houses, built squarely and in oblongs, vary from stark white to a sandy beige which blends with the warm orange tones of the rocky cliffs. The windows are generally dark oblongs occasionally arched; the stones of the houses on the lowest part of the slope toward the beach are of an orange, sun-worn, pebbled texture, like the crumbling walls of an old fortress. Next to the first low white bungalow is the taller blank stucco side of a house with an orange tile roof, partly hidden behind a two story house with white plaster peeling to soiled gray patches; this house has a second floor porch with a white

railing and bright blue-painted borders around the window frame. The level of the rock cliffs drops a stage then, and green foliage shows between the weathered white house and the narrow, tall three story house next door which is topped by a reddish tile roof and rises higher, with foundations lower, than the house preceding it; this tall house appears to be part of the Hotel Planesia, which is attached by balcony terraces arched by white arcades over hanging the sea; people, dark, small specks in the distance, are sitting on the lowest level of the balcony. The blurred words "Hotel Planesia" are printed in faded black letters on the long windowless side of the building.

Below the buildings of the hotel, a staircase cut in rock zigzags down to the beach; waves break against the boulders at the foot of the cliff. The buildings appear to be rooted in the slopes of stone, to have grown organically like blanched beige rock crystals from the cliffs. On the rocks to the right of the hotel sprouts a single palm trees, fronds splayed open like a green feather duster, above which rises the raw new brick of unfinished apartment houses. The tall square sided clock tower juts above these houses, with the arched windows of the belfry and clock-face which can be seen from all over town. The clock tower is the highest point of the rising, thickening wedge of buildings, after which the rooves slope away, following the line of the hill. Next to the clock tower, lower down, is the fluted blue dome of the Castillo, sloping down, its line followed by orange tiled rooftops which flatten out and level off at the foot of the hill.

Looking at the hill into the afternoon sun, the houses and cliffs are all thrown into warm orangey beige shadow, a dark trapezoid composed of the wedge of rocks sloping inland, then, the wedge of houses with its narrowest point on the summit of rocks falling directly, with only a slight jagged slope outward, to the sea. The sun sheens the foaming waves which curve in to the beach below the castle with a blinding silver glitter that flickers and sparkles with the constant seethe of water pouring shoreward. Color of the sea blurs out in the sun's dazzle to a foaming drench of radiance, out of which rises the shaded cliff promontory of Castle Hill.

30[a–b]

August 26 – Sunday
Paris: Hotel des deux Continents

Corner by sink: on the left wall of the room, viewed from the bed, there is an oblong of wall-space above five feet long, ten feet high, bordered on the left by a window located in dead-center of the wall, and on the right by the corner of the room opposite the door. This wall-space is divided in several sections – a smaller oblong of plastered white is set in the lower right-hand corner of the oblong, forming part of the washbowl cubicle which juts off on the wall coming in at right angles. A radiator blocks off a smaller oblong in the lowest right hand corner of the white plaster oblong. The radiator is angular, with shiny cream-painted tubes, four deep into the room, seven long; on top of the radiator, a board shelf holds a bluish plastic bag, flat-bottomed with an arched curved top, and a pale pink bag to the far left, with shiny embroidered flowers on it and a drooping cloth handle of the same material.

A brush (and comb) of blue plastic with white nylon bristles are in the left forground of the self, in front of the pink bag; a plastic oblong bottle with round blue cap and rumpled white linoleum shaving kit with blue flowers are arranged along the foreground of the shelf to the right. In the corner, at the right of the radiator, a column of several pipes rises from floor to fan up and out toward the left along the ceiling. Two slender creamy-painted pipes rise directly from floor to ceiling; at the left, a large pipe, & then two smaller ones, rise up and bend at the ceiling & wall juncture to run along the ceiling molding & curve up to disappear in the ceiling plaster at the left. A foot of sallow-painted beige molding runs along the floor; the oblong of white plaster is bordered by a narrow strip of the same molding; the remainder of the wall space, shaped like an inverted L, is covered with faded yellow wallpaper on which a faint, delicate design of whitish leaves & flowers is superimposed.

31[a]
Mrs. Nellie Meehan & Clifford, Herbert (cousin)"
Vera Rhoda Hilda Albert Willy Dora Sutcliffe
"All the Dead Dears"
Mrs. Mehan – rich-flavored dialect story. set in Yorkshire (Wuthering Heights background) – of present vivid influence of ghosts of those dead on woman who <u>almost</u> has second-sight – Begin – "I saw an angel once" – "my sister Miriam" – tales of hanging, pneumonia death (implied murder) mad cousins, dead good one – war photo in hospital ward – dandy photo with straw Benjies & silver knobbed canes – "He's got his leg off. He was killed. He's dead and he's dead."

"That day absolutely shone with bright and funny conversation." – "right good do" – "numb as a tree" – "I just got a postcard from Kathleen – She's in the arctic <u>circle</u>."

"She married the one who's experimenting with cows down in South Africa." central tragic figure – Uncle W." – drama of Cathy & Heathcliffe – close – visitor goes – Mrs Meehan sees "presence" – dazzle, near couch – "Ay – you're looking for Minnie. I know. Well you won't find her here. She's gone down to live in todmorden."

31[b]
Luminous – bluish –
Charlotte – watercolor
magic city of glass town

---

poems & stories

Anne – ms – 4 1/2" x 3 5/8"
poems

Manuscript magazines
colored drawing   – wooden soldiers in action
                          – Branwell age 10

Apostle cupboard   – <u>Jane Eyre</u>
chap. 20   – Charlotte B.

---

blue, red, white   horsehair
flowered quilt   quilt red
Withens – scarf, tasseled –

---

blue book, leather
Sofa – Emily died – 19th Dec. 1848

<u>Haworth</u> – Bronte Home – old rectory
St. Michael & all angels' church –
Haworth – Rev. Patrick Brönte
perpetual curate

---

walls – pink fleur de lis design on
thin grey & white stripe – portraits
samplers – cane – top hat –
father's study on right of entrance

---

samplers –

Emily Jane Bronte's rosewood writing desk – colored sealing wax – red
green brown cream – Clarkes enigmatic & puzzle wafers used in sealing
letters & ungummed envelopes

32[a]
memorials – collected by Henry Houston Bonnell of Philadelphia

Mr. Nichols study

Charlotte's needlework – cross-stitch
design – berries on stems

bead serviette rings by brontes – glass & white beads –

charlottes wedding wreath –
white lace & white flowers –
honeysuckle – faded

as children – brontes wrote books in microscopic script

size 1 1/2 in x 2 1/8 in –
"The young man's
magazine" (1830)

pew-sittings –

Charlotte's room –
pencils sketches of eyes, lips –
classical heads
Morocco work case – reels of cotton & embroidery
over fire place
exquisite watercolors – charlotte
a squirrel – "Condu's" blue boy visionary

32[b]
Charlotte – tiny black satin slippers
Silvery, pink & green paisley shawl

Nursery – scribble drawings on wall

wooden oblong cradle
toys – discovered under floor boards

33[a-b]
Tuesday pm
October 9 – incredible massed color of Clare gardens: "sudden in a shaft of sunlight." All flowers incandescent: tall frilled red, yellow & white dahlias, lavendar & mauve starry asters (michaelmas daisies); little woman feeding gabbling hectic squadrons of ducks over queen's silver street bridge – airplane view of shiny green mallard heads, speckled brown ladies & queer pure white duck; crossed ragged green meadows before Queens – graceful cinnamon grazing horses; purple clouded skies behind Kings chapel towers, showing stark white; dappled green ivy shade of path to clare. – green grot of sunken garden; reedy pool; green sanctums of eden – huge willow slanting over mallard green still water, bird chirp & twitter; trees turning slow gold, duck quack, green tent of slender draped willow leaves," great copper beech tree by Clare; bird whistle; slow glide of punt & canoe; swans nibbling grass at bank; Glossy green-waxed dark leaves of ivy, rhododendron, prickle-edged holly, pine needles.

34[a]
October 21 – turning of sap in vein sheen – early morning Sunday – bells – walk along river after night rain – all hung with wet, dew, lush, juicy – squdge of mud, puddles shining with sun – grass blades by river; frosted with gauze of drops yellow willow leaves – slow drift of gray-green river – process of leaves across sunken cloud & treescape – sun's double eye – white light – all turning – season turning – leaves fall, birds descend – spiders sheen of web – glide & coast of leaves in water slip & quag of mud – raucous claptrap of rooks – reflected light on water – brim of river – dark knotted willow trunks frame light – dark leaves on light water sap green – quaver of cloud, finned delicate willow leaves – translucent, shining amber spider – wind quaver all that green tumult over – procession – ceremony & pomp of dead season – spider – black-flecked – fishermen – speckled yellow leaves – prickle of gorse & nettle – malice glint & play of light – rise & raucous creak of rooks – light sky black flecked – polish – blue flies – sheen & gleam of wing – veined radiance

34[b (blank)]

35[a]
Novel:

Every person I see again. Everything comes full circle. Tony – pale, blond, shrunken – seen at railway station – whole floating Paris day returns – the circle of despair closes upon itself. The springtime of horror, drowning, where three men menaced & no choice was worth making, but one choice of all must be made – the German train shuttling to Munich – "You would have liked me if you knew me earlier" – take, seize, drink – amputate sight of links – be blind & steep in present. Darkened room. Pale lithe bodies. Yellow wallpaper – rose bouquets – refusal – rapid running away – petering into tea, movie – knowledge someday the final thing will happen. I will see him from another life, nod in slightly lofty, slightly amused recognition from a world totally other a world where the bedding of a young blond faun is utterly irrelevant More, inconceivable. Unwished.

35[b]
Poem:
Wild hot fury – cold snow: Thick white moor – mist – lamps hanging. dim points – still: still: frozen leaves – bunched blackbird: rage – "one second more, the cat-hiss would come out." Awareness of stifling smothering fury – walk in white blank world – symbol of shutting off from normal clear vision – futile outburst. human limits versus grand marmoreal vast power of cold, snow, stars & blackness – vanished daisies: white in head, remembered from summer – she imposes them on dry barren broken stalks – vivid sense of opposition, polar crossing of season, climate – black stone fences – stark wild landscape – tawn cat, red coal fires, burning cheeks, cat under coal house – starlings at scraps of fat – frosted hedge – pose vast impersonal white world of Nature against small violent spark of will

36[a]
The mushroom's black underpleats

Novel: Gordon: even as mother shaped body, wants woman to shape soul – unmade, derivative, impotent – Paris, Munich, Italy – Rome & Venice – Fainting in ugliness of St. Peter's – destruction urge – to debase self – yet soul holds back – No one to admire – curse of a woman having sex & brain – to find a man who combines both: with flaming shaping will – will to destruction – hatred of faithlessness – Paris – Rome – acrid, sick taste – shrunk maleness

37[b]-39[b]
<u>Starfish</u>
3 classes echinoderms –
Sea stars/asteroidea
brittle stars/ophiuroidea
feather stars/unstalked crinoidea

free moving – live mouth downward
feather stars swim or crawl, live mostly attached to some object mouth upwards

<u>Asterias</u> – N. Atlantic coasts – Central body – radiating out into five tapering arms – flattened upper surface covered with leathery skin in which ar small lobed plates of carbonate of lime, many bearing prickles, together forming a jointed reticulate skeleton – multitudes of small pincerlike pedicellariae –

<u>echinoderma</u> – sea star of this type – can crawl over any surface, can squeeze supple body through incredibly narrow crevices – 6 in. per minute
common sea star of N.A. south of Cape Cod (<u>Asterias forbesi</u>) very destructive to mussels & oysters – favorite food. – In attacking oysters or like bivalves – sea star fixes the suckers of 1 or 2 arms to 1 valve, those of the opposite arm to the other. Then straighten rays. Oyster can stand a strong sudden pull, but not a continued pull & eventually opens its shell. Sea star then extrudes stomach through mouth, digests oyster & after finished meal withdraws stomach.

Sea stars begin to eat voraciously when very young. One less than 3/8 in. across ate over 50 young clams of half that length in 6 days. A sea star – sexually mature in less than a year, produces many thousands of young
Vary in shape: sharpley stellate – long tapering rays, pentagonal. With angles of pentagon produced into slender spikelike arms – to circular almost. Mostly stellate – normally 5 rays.
1/2 in. to 3 ft. across
1,500 known kinds: 300 genera
Mostly predacuous – feeding on molluscs, barnales, worms, crustaceans,

smaller creatures which they take into their stomachs – but many are scavengers, feeding on detritus or swallowing mud & digesting out of it the organic matter sold as curios – exotic sea stars. Large bony tubercles from Pacific & Indian Oceans. Common shore – living brittle stars – snake – tails – live among seaweeds, eelgrass, in chinks & crevices of rocks or corals, buried in mud, lying on sea bottom in deep water – sea star or starfish – asteroid "prickle-skinned" – echinoderma in Greek – hedgehog & sea urchin "hérisser" Fr. – to bristle

echinoderm – multicellular (different from coelen tera = hollow guts) – bilateral – secondary radial symmetry five sectors – rays – arms five: fundamental sacs, canals, tubes carry water through body – hydraulic apparatus

              mouth   podia

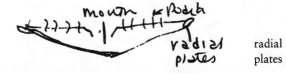

                                              radial
                                              plates

Geological history – free-floating – adapted to stationary life – radiation rose from mode of feeding – effect of gravity – fixed to sea-floor, mouth turned upward to food-bearing waters.

echinoderms – natural history – sluggish, frequently immobile – free forms shun light, hide or bear cloake of seaweed by day. Some – sea-stars light depths with glorious phosphoresence when stimulated

Crinoids & Pelmatozoa – have extracted millions of tons of lime from sea & built up huges masses of rock

sea-stars dont confine selves to carrion – attack living molluscs, oysters, mussels – terrible damage – smaller kinds eaten by bottom-fishes

Stelliformia – J H Linck
MacBride – Echinodermata – Camb. Nat. Hist. I (1906) on habits
spicular structure of skin – calate – crystalline carbonate of lime – in deeper layes of skin – minute spicules – beam & rafter work – grow together in small bones, plates, prickles – looks like net under microscope –
Pelmatozoa – stalk-animals

Eleutherozoa {stelliformia {asteroidea
Stelliformia – sea-stars – live as a rule with mouth down, from it radiate five
ciliated grooves – active search for & ingestion of animal food, alive or dead,
in large portions – asteroidea – crawl – tube feet – sea-star clings to object &
pulls itself along: suckers

self-division & regeneration break off portions of selves – under stimulus of
danger or to get out of difficulty – discarded portions can grow again
sea star – small arms with small body at one end – four little buds – comet
forms – confined to sea – depend on hydraulic system – constant interchange
between internal fluids & outer water through thin membrane – from tide-
mark down to 3 3/4 miles (3¾)

Between tidemarks – buried in moist sand – littoral or abyssal

40[a]
Whelans
Garage – white – green-double-doors – neat white picket gate separating
garbage & ash tins from the muddling paws of dogs. One door open, showing, on dirt floor, a bright, primary-colored tangle of childrens' toys: a red
fire truck with whitewalled tires, white steering wheel, white rails to hold on
to, a small green fronted toy truck with a red back, a red truck with grey
unloading box, an orange truck on its side, bent at a wasp waist – a red cart
with black rubber wheels – a dusty red tricycle. An orange handled junior-
size rake
Purple & green mottle tile roof. Shaped like a pyramid.

40[b]
August 9: Saturday: windy – speed boats on Connecticut white wakes cut
blue lawn, water – bright blue, twinkling! Sun: glint – green banks – fence of
trees
Skiers in invisible tow lines – curve & scallop of white shearing aside – birds,
swallows, martins ride & sun on the wind – sparse white cumulus – bleached
heads of rye – rye stubble – wallop & gaze of boats. Waving grass-seeded
heads – fountain heads of golden rod – lace plats of queen anne's lace
bright mustard fuzz – pollen – purple vetch bends nods inland from river
wind – rasp, cicada buzz – golden rod against blue water – green band of
trees, paler sky – crickets – dustcoated black sextons – yellow butterier than
the sun – prickle of bleached stubble – whisk heads

nip, shear, wallop, scallop
wallop & jolt of the upkicking wave

Midas' Country

41[a (blank)]

41[b]

42[a]^n
<u>Words</u>: December 1958:
souse   Audrey

broth   Maureen
dubious   Beverley
duckweed   Diana
abide

Names	(Loretta) Rock
	Winifred Root
Clarence Humberstone	Angela Rose
Sadie Hummel	Edith Rose
Floyd Hunkins	Mae Rose
Hunninghacker	Otto Rose
Hupfer	Quentin Rose
Ethel Hurry	Sadie Rose
Albert Lake	Nora Scully
Emment Lalley	Winona Scully
Francis Lalley	Una Shirley
Irene Lalley	Phyllis Shisler
Hazel Landry	Sadie Schneider
Ma digan	Jack Shockett
Ellen Mactwiggan	Betty Sisk
McQuilken	Jack Sisson
Louise Minard	Audrey Sisson
David Ogg	Betty Skerritt
Glenn Ogletree	Reggie Horton
Oikle	Diana Yates
Joan Oke	Nancy Teed
Minnie Nuzzy	Roy Skinner
Feener	Rita Skinner
Rose Quigley	Ada Sleeth
	Myra Sloper
	Smeedy
	Violet Sneed

42[b]″
Withens
Most people never get there, but stop in town for tea, pink frosted cakes, souvenir's & colored photographs of the place too far to talk to, visiting the Church of St. Michael & All Angels, the black stone rectory rooms of

memorabalia – wooden cradle, Charlotte's bridal crown of heirloom lace & honeysuckle, Emily's death couch, the small, luminous books & watercolors, the beaded napkin ring, the Apostle cupboard. They touched this, wore that, wrote here in a house redolent with ghosts. There are two ways to the stone house, both tiresome.

One, the public route from the town along green pastureland over stone stiles to the voluble white cataract that drops its long rag of water over rocks warped round, green-slimed, across a wooden footbridge to terrain of goatfoot-flattened grasses where a carriage road Ran a hundred years back in a time grand with the quick of their shaping tongues worn down to broken wall, old cellar hole, gate pillars leading from sheep turf to grouse country. The old carriage road's a sunk rut, the spring clear well & gurgle under grass too green to believe. The hulk of matted grey hair & a long skull to mark a sheepfold, a track worn, losing itself, but not lost.

The other – across the slow heave, hill on hill from any other direction across bog down to the middle of the world, green-slimed, boots squelchy – brown peat – earth untouched except by grouse foot – bluewhite spines of gorse, the burnt-sugar bracken – all eternity, wildness, loneliness – peat-colored water – the house – small, lasting – pebbles on roof, name scrawls on rock – inhospitable two trees on the lee side of the hill where the long winds come, piece the light in a stillness. The furious ghosts nowhere but in the heads of the visitors & the yellow-eyed shag sheep
House of love lasts as long as love in human mind – blue-spidling gorse

44[a-b]

Roger & Joan Stein
Friday –
⑥

St. Theresa of the Child Jesus baldaquin
baldachino – rich brocade, silk & gold
marble or stone canopy over altar or throne Canonisation & after anniversary of St. Thérèse passing to God – "an aviator arching overhead showered roses on the moving mass below . . . "
Sept. 30, 1925.
In Carfin, Scotland: "Roses streamed from Venetian masts outside & inside the Grotto itself. The Little Flower shrine was smothered in roses of every

hue. The village itself was adorned for the occasion, & her picture was proudly displayed outside well-nigh every door.

 Tobias viii, 9
"The Story of the springtime of a little White Flower"

Old St. Teresa – founded first house of Discalced (barefooted) Carmelite nuns in 1562, at Avila in Spain – Carmelite enclosure very strict – in the parlour a veil covers the grille. In addition to other penances the nuns abstain perpetually from flesh-meat, fast upon one meal a day from Sept. 14 til Easter, wear coarse garments, retire to rest on straw pallets about 11:30 pm & rise during greater part of year at 4:45
Hours of vocal prayer, two hours of mental prayer – proverbial gaiety –

"Oh, how I wish you would die, 'dear Mamma!' Astonished at being scolded for saying such a thing, she will answer: 'It is because I want you to go to Heaven, & you say that to get there we must die!" In her outbursts of affection for her Father, she wishes him also to die."

"Only one thing do I fear & that is to follow my own will. Accept then the offering I make of it, for I choose all that thou willest!"
St. Thérèse: during delirium
What fears, too, the devil inspired! Everything frightened me. The bed seemed to be surrounded by awful precipices, & nails in the wall would assume the ghastly appearance of huge, coal-black fingers, filling me with terror and at times making me cry out with fright. Once, whilst Papa stood looking at me in silence, the hat in his hand was suddenly transformed into some horrible shape & I showed such fear that he turned away sobbing.

Statue: Our lady of the smile – looks down on Thérèse –
Copy of Madonna by Bouchardon (1698–1762) for the Church of St. Sulpice in Paris:

Some asked if Our Lady had the Infant Jesus in her arms; others wished to know if Angels wer with her. These & further questions troubled & grieved me & I could only make one answer: 'Our Lady looked very beautiful; I saw her come towards me & smile."

"Yet I still feel the same daring confidence that one day I shall become a great saint. I am not trusting in my own merits, for I have none; but I trust in him who is Virtue & Holiness itself."

First Communion: Thérèse had disappeared like a drop of water lost in the immensity of the ocean; Jesus alone remained – He was the Master, the King. Had not Therese asked Him to take away the liberty which frightened her?

Imitation of Christ:

St. Teresa of Avila – is calle the Doctor of Mystical Theology because of her writings on the relations of the soul with God.

Padua: "venerated relic of St. Antony's tongue"

Loreto – 1291: Palestine passed completely into the hands of the Saracens, but, on May 10, the house where God became man & where the holy Family spent so many years was transported by angels to Tersato, in Illyria. Three years later, it was carried across the Adriatic to the province of Ancona, in Italy, where after further journeys it was set down finally in the middle of the road at Loreto in 1295. Such is the tradition & it has been accredited by many Popes & Saints & strengthened by miracles.

Catacombs – St. Cecelia's tomb –

45[a]
St. Thérèse: Santa Croce, Rome: the relics of the true Cross, together with two of the thorns & one of the Sacred Nails. –

For some time past I had offered myself to the Child Jesus, to be his little plaything; I told Him not to treat me like one of those precious toys which children only look at & dare not touch, but rather as a little ball of no value that could be thrown on the ground, tossed about, pierced, left in a corner, or pressed to His heart, just as it might please Him. In a word, all I desired was to amuse the Holy Child, to let Him play with me just as he felt inclined. "great spiritual aridity"

About this time" I began to have a preference for whatever was ugly & inconvenient, so much that I rejoiced when a pretty little water jug was taken from our cell & replaced by a big one, badly chipped all over . . .

Death of mother genevieve of St. Teresa

... " I received a very special grace. It was the first time I had assisted at a death bed ... Each of the Sisters hastened to claim something belonging to our beloved Mother, and you know the precious relic I treasure. During her agony I had noticed a tear glistening on her eyelash like a diamond, and that tear, the last of all those she had shed on earth, never fell; I saw it still shining as her body lay exposed in the choir. So when evening came I made bold to approach unseen, with a little piece of linen, and now I am the happy possessor of the last tear of a Saint."

St. Thérèse & the tear

Jesus treated me as a spoilt child for a longer time even than His more faithful spouses. After the influenza epidemic He came to me daily for several months, a privilege not shared by the Community

"All I want is a sign" –

45[b]–46[a]

"Scarcely had I laid my head on the pillow when I felt a hot stream rise to my lips, and thinking I was going to die, my heart almost broke with joy. I had already put out our lamp, so I mortified my curiosity till morning & went peacefully to sleep.

At five o'clock, the time for rising, I remembered immediately that I had some good news to learn, & going to the window I found, as I had expected, that our handkerchief was saturated with blood. What hope filled my heart!"

Oh, my God! from how much disquiet do we free ourselves by the vow of obedience!

On her deathbed:"

"Throughout my religious life the cold has caused me more physical pain than anything else – I have suffered from cold until I almost died of it."

One night she entreated the infirmarian to sprinkle her bed with Holy Water, saying: "The devil is beside me. I do not see him but I feel him; he torments me, holding me with a grip of iron that I may not find one crumb of comfort, & adding to my sufferings that I may be driven to despair ..."

Before the canonisation over 27 million souvenirs of the 'Little Flower' had been distributed. The demand for first class relics is unprecedented & is, of course, impossible to satisfy. Her Carfin shrine is happy to possess a piece of bone; also some of her hair, her Immaculate Conception rosary, an autograph prayer, a rose-petal, an artificial rose from her deathbed & various other secondary relics –

The remains of St. Therese were first exhumed . . . 1910 . . . as she foretold, nothing was found of her body but the bones, yet the palm-branch mentioned above was perfectly preserved & may be seen at the Carmel –

Certain extraordinary incidents – a lay sister who on kissing the feet of the servant of God was instantly cured of cerebral anemia – another nun was favored with a very strong perfume of violets while a third felt herself thrilled by a kiss bestowed on her by some invisible being. One sister perceived a bright light in the heavens & another saw a luminous crown which, rising from the earth, was soon lost in space . . .

supernatural cures of nuns & priests: tb, ulcers

"to believe oneself imperfect & others perfect – This is true happiness."

"The lowest place is the only spot on earth which is not open to envy. Here alone there is neither vanity nor affliction of spirit."

rubric: red heading, initial

"one fast-day . . . when our Reverend Mother ordered her some special food, I found her seasoning it with wormwood because it was too much to her taste."

. . . during her noviciate, one of our Sisters, when fastening the scapular for her, ran the large pin through her shoulder, & for hours she bore the pain with joy . . .

★ love will consume us only in the measure of our self-surrender ★

"God will do all I wish in Heaven, because I have never done my own will on earth . . ."

"The only thing that is all its own & is essential to its being is the stone: it possesses nothing beyond . . . "

46[b]
The juice went through him like a lightning bolt

———————

seasoning the beauties of this world with wormwood –

———————

Water Skiers
motion & verve against season's death

———————

dream – death & corpses in arms of love

———————

47[a]
Poems
Haworth & graves

———————

The Bull of Bendylaw – King & court: ceremony & rule – tapestry meadow, dasies, marigolds – playing card
King & queen –
Bull – Dionysiac force – inspiration
Male virility –
unbindable
Europa & bull
color: versus black bull

———————

Point Shirley, Revisited

Goatsucker night's black cockpit
cock chafers, moths
Nighthawks stomachs – moths grasshoppers, bugs, beetles, wasps, spider, ants, clover-leaf weevil, may beetles
eat on wing
Superstition – peasants: in all languages
Voice: Night jar: whirr – burr of a lathe
–perch: lengthwise – knots on limb
red eye: devil-bird in ceylon

<u>whiskered</u> bill
<u>mouth</u> enormous – net for insects,
Whippoor will – cavemouth, loud voice
Fear of darkness – those that move silently
<u>Nest</u> – rooftops & gravelly hills
<u>Puck</u> – disease in cattle
mischievous demon
<u>puck bird</u>

47[b]
gape thickly beset by strong bristles
moths & cock chafers
single burning note, vibration
silent flight, when disturbed, wings smite together
Night hawk, whippoor will – chuck will's widow
Sucking teats of goats – food –
injurious to calves – Puck bird
eggs on open bare spots
<u>enormous mouth, surprisingly wide gape</u>
net for capture of insects – stiff long bristles
whippoorwill, cave mouth, loud voice
<u>large eyes</u>

_____

Old world peasants – call about herds – believe birds subsist on stolen milk

52[a]″
white ceiling, waffle
round skylight
panelled wood
green leather seats – gold crest
① is this book obscene –
– <u>tendency</u> to deprave & corrupt persons who read it –
② whether defendants have established merits are so high that they out-
balance the obscenity & book is for public good –
– onus of proof on defendants
28 people in public court
consider <u>public</u>, not student of literature
person who knows nothing at all about literature or lawrence but buys book
for 3/6 – lunchtime break at factory, takes home to finish –

Jones – council on behalf of Crown – 'Keep your feet on ground' – don't get lost in higher realms of lit., sociology, ethics –

Two witnesses who made observations – (spectacles) Mrs. Bennett – 'a reader who is capable of understanding him could learn much of what his view is' –

Professor – 'impossible to understand any one book of L's without having read all' – This book a fundamental one in understand poet.

J: different picture to person with no knowledge or little learning – these consideration must apply –

53[a]-55[a]
Graham Hough – Christ's Coll. Camb.

Has studied L: & written book – one of most impt novelists of this cen & any cen. To assess lit merits of book – true & sincere representat – of aspect of life – peculiar & individual situation of char. – sexual rels of men & women – nature of proper marriage – great importance to us all.

(Lady C & lawful husband

Judge: a 'proper marriage' lady C & gamekeeper

nothing to indicate there was or would be a marriage – gamek had wife, Lord C. wouldn't divorce her)

H: not best of L's novels: abt. 5th

literary merit of pages not concerned w sex 'very high' – sexual sit. centre of book a great deal else as well – the rest not padding for sexual scenes – promiscuity hardly comes in question – very much condemned by Lawrence – a great deal of adulterous situations from Iliad on.

J: you are final judges

H: reason for repeated description of sexual scenes different, not repetitive v. impt. to show Lady C's development – entirely necessary – a bold experiment trying to study sex. situation more openly.

J: asked abt 4 letter words

No proper language to discuss sexual matters – either clinical or disgusting – secretive, morbid attitude. L tries to redeem normally obscene words.

J: be careful not to be led away by what some people have decided is real message & real thought of book. Is he using those words – coarse words – are those words part of general makeup of the book? not justified as being for pub good.

Miss Gardner: reader in Eng lit Oxford U, author,
among 5 or 6 greatest writers of this cen.

How far in your view are descriptions of sex relevant to meaning of book?

'core & heart of book's theme & meaning' was description of sexual intercourse

'a v. remarkable book, not wholly successful novel, some passages among greatest things he wrote.'

use of 4 letter words?

sexual act not shameful, word not shameful either.

Didn't think L. was able to redeem word & usage of word 'fuck' – talking abt. usage within book itself.

'certain aspects of mod soc. – degaded condition in which people live without beauty or joy – doesn't exempt any classes – relation bet. men & wom the fundamental thing wrong – the heart of this book. Society may thus be revivified.

–

J: Whether a person would be able to read into book what witnesses have said is in it.

<u>Mrs. Bennett</u> – fellow of Girton, author

L. greatest writer of fiction since Hardy. Genuineness of experience & purer writer has to express exp. – physical life impt. & is being neglected – people live poor & emasculated lives, living with half of themselves – deals with sex very seriously indeed – does <u>not</u> set promiscuous/intercourse/on a pedestal & adulterous. 'Adulterous' – a marriage can be broken when it is unfulfilled – book not against divorce – denied story is little more than padding – clearly interest w. social questions & class relation

Griffiths-Jones

Bennett – believes in marriage not in the legal sense

Judge: what is she talking about.

Bennett 'a sort of almost sacred book'

Jones: 'You said book shows author's view on marriage'

B – 'does make clear a union bet. two persons, who love one another of greatest importance' marriage shd be complete relation including physical, if it doesn't include physical rels, it should be terminated'

'clear distinction between affair & love relation with keeper'

J – when you (to jury) read book, were you 'capable of understanding?' what L's views of marriage is.

Jones: 'can you not bring book down from heights? You do not suggest that adulterous relationships show L's views of marriage –
J: 'lawful wedlock, madam'
'Is that not exactly what L. had done – ran off with friend's wife.' The whole book is about that subject is it not?

Lady Rebecca West – author of a no. of books.
L's rep. very high – discussed on high level throughout world – Lady C's Lover is full of sentences badly written. A man without formal education (not in home) – defect 'no sense of humor' a lot of pages ludicrous – still, has lit. merit – work of art – analysis of exp – life a serious matter, things beautiful –

Bishop (of Woolwich)
Ethics – clearly L. did not have a Christian valuation of sex – not ideal. trying to portray sex rel. as 'something essentially sacred.' – in a real sense as an 'act of holy communion'
Judge – is L trying to portray sex as something sacred?
effect of expurgation of 4-letter words wd suggest L was doing sth sordid – artistic integrity – not dealing with intercourse for itself –
Is book a valuable book in ethics?
Does stress real value of personal relations as such –
Bishop – not a treatise on marriage – concerned w. establishing a permanent spiritual relationship –
G-J. – a work of instruction? on the subject of ethics.
Bishop: No.
J: Does book portray life of immoral woman?
B: Not intended to serve immorality – Yes, a book Christians ought to read –

Professor Pinto – Prof at Nottingham
L. one of the greatest writers of 20th cen
Theme? a double theme – mechanization of humanity in industrial society – human happiness based on tenderness & affection. A high place in literary merit – a deeply moving story. A valuable work.

In some measure a moral tract?

Clergyman: 'book of moral purpose' – ethical & sociological merits.
'a study in compassion & human tenderness' – physical rel. dealt with

respect & honesty – nothing in it out of key or keeping. Part of Christian Tradition. God creator, man in creative relationship.

As a minister highest regard for marriage – book abt. couple with no regard for marriage?

No. Her marriage bonds all broke down. Not at liberty to throw over marriage bonds in order to get sexual satisfaction? That what this book is teaching?

Marriage had failed before this happened.

<u>Mr. Hoggart – lecturer of Leicester</u>

Exceptional lit. merit – best 20 novels in past 30 years. Not in any sense vicious, highly virtuous, if anything, puritanical. A moral book

Overwhelming impression – enormous reverence between human beings in love & physical relationship. Highly moral & not degrading of sex –

Judge – do you find any spark of affection till quite late in book? Or merely having sex & enjoying?

For you to say – you've read the book, you are the judge.

Young people? – a proper book –

Proper if they came to me to ask me – or asked parents – I wouldn't take responsibility on myself –

58[a]

THE INMATE

Monday: February 27, 1961 In Hospital

Still whole, I interest nobody. I am not among the cheerful smilers in plaster & bandages or the bubbling moaners behind the glass & pink wood partition. The sad, mustachioed doctor & his bright white starchy students pass me by. This is a religious establishment, great cleansings take place. Everybody has a secret. I watch them from my pillows, already exhausted. The fat girl in glasses walks by, testing her new leg, the noseless old woman, with her foot strung up in traction, the lady with the sour face, chest & arm in plaster, scratches herself inside with a stick 'My skin's ruckled up.' They'll cut her out Thursday. A helpful inmate in a red wool bathrobe brings the flowers back, sweet-lipped as children. All night they've been breathing in the hall dropping their pollens, daffodils, pink & red tulips, the hot purple & red eyed – anemones.

59[a]-63[a]

Potted plants for the veterans. Nobody complains or whines. In the black earphones hung on my silver bedstead a tiny voice nags me to listen. They won't unplug him. Immensely cheerful pink, blue & yellow birds distribute themselves among flowers, primarily pink, and simpering greenery on the white bed curtains. It is like an arbor when they close me in. Last night I got lost in the wet, black Sunday streets of Camden Town, walking resolutely in the wrong direction. I asked an old woman getting out of a car where the St. Pancras hospital was: she asked her old husband – he said: "It's a bit complicated. I better drive you there." I got into the back seat of the old comfortable car & burst into tears. 'I'd rather have a baby', I say, 'at least you've got something for it. 'That's what we all say', said the woman. The man angled the car through obscure, black glistening streets to the hospital. I stumbled through the rain, my bang in wet hanks plastered to my forehead. The Admissions office was shut – I walk down a long brilliantly-lit hall & a boy in brown takes me to Ward 1 in the elevator. The nurse asks me question & fills out a form. I want to answer more questions, I love questions. I feel a blissful slumping into boxes on forms. The lady next to me has a bandage under her neck – They found in a chest x-ray that her thyroid had grown into her lung & cut it out. Now, curtains drawn round her bed, an occupational therapist sounds to be hitting her: a-slap-a-slap-a-slap. All kinds of equipment is ferryied by – vacuum cleaners, stepladders, instruments for tipping up one end of the bed, a large aluminum box on wheels which is plugged into the wall – I think it is a hot-box for the steamed lunches. Last night I felt too sick for supper – had only a cup of Ovaltine, got into my night dress behind flowered curtains. A young, attractively lean Doctor 'Cabst' came round & asked me symptom questions. Put an exclamation after the observation that I might be pregnant again. Cold air blows down from the tall window on my head. The thyroid woman coughs dryly behind her curtain. A pretty young sociable woman named Rose came to chat with me last night, introduced me to a lively blackhaired lady in diaphanous pale blue nightgown named 'Bunny' who had 'been in Boston', another bright lady whose husband studied locusts in Africa – they both had malaria; he owns some zoo in South Devon to which he sent animals in pairs. Tried vacantly to read 'Paris Review.' A red & a white pill slowly dragged me into a fog. 'Lights out' at nine. The round globed ward lights switched to red – 8 red cutout circles in the twilight – light lingered everywhere. Goodnight, goodnight, bed-mates said, & reduced themselves to humps. I considered asking that my curtains be drawn, but then shut my eyes & found with surprising pleasure I had my own curtains which I could shut at will. Woken out of a shallow sleep at 5 by a bustle, creaking, running of water & clanking of buckets. At six, in the wan wet grey, the white lights came on – tea, temperatures, pulse. I washed, swabbed my privates with a blue antiseptic & urinated obligingly in a glass jar. Later they swabbed my nose to see 'if I was carrying any germs to infect wounds'. Breakfast about 7:30. Thin brown bread scraped penuriously with butter (or some substitute) so only a faint glaze testified to which side was the right side for the orange marmelade; tea, a shallow bowl of smoky saltless gruel, bacon & tomatoes (very good) & more tea – Bad, dreggy fusty coffee mid morning. Paperboy, chocolate & cigarette cart. Green graphs on polished aluminum clipboards hooked to the foot of each bed.

Tuesday: February 28. Today is the day. Amid the chatter & breakfasting off all the other patients I alone am quiet & without food. Yet I feel curiously less worried about losing my appendix than being electrocuted. The gently-spoken grey lady at my right "Duchess", or "Mrs Mac" goes home today. She goes to Harrow by ambulance, her frail form stooped now over a bowl of cornflakes in her white crocheted shawl. I feel slightly sick after <u>all</u> this waiting, but here where everyone is amiable with gracious smiles, it is impossible to indulge in mopes or self-pity, a very good thing. Last night a young nurse shaved me with exceedingly scratchy strokes, exposing that odd mole that grew on the left when I was pregnant. Today, after a sleeping pill, I woke when the nurse took my temperature & pulse. Had tea & buttered toast at 6:30. Then they took away my water & my milk. "Bunny", "Daisy", Jane, Rose. The goiter lady (her thyroid grew into her lung) on my left had a "pounding" yesterday – her bed raised at the foot & she pummelled "to loosen the phlegm" Daisy said interestedly. I too as the latest operative case, am of interest. Was I shaved? Will I have an enema? And so on. (Ted) came last night. Precisely one minute after 7.30 a crowd of shabby, short, sweet peering people was let into the ward – they fluxed in familiar directions, bringing a dark-coated handsome shape. Twice as tall as all of them. I felt as excited & infinitely happy as in the early days of our courtship. His face which I daily live with seemed the most kind & beautiful in the world. He brought an air letter from the New Yorker for me with a $100 contract for letting them have "first reading" of all my poems for a year! The date of the letter was that of our first meeting at the Botolph party 5 years ago. He brought steak sandwiches & apricot tarts & milk & fresh-squeezed orange juice – I felt afterwards that if I said "For him – he will be on the other side" – I could go through anything with courage – or at least reasonable fortitude.

Later – 10 am – now I'm really prepared for the slaughter – robed loosely in a pink & maroon striped surgical gown, a gauze turban & a strip of adhesive shuts off the sight of my wedding ring. The little nurse was snippy when I asked how long the operation took. Oblivion approaches. Now I'm close enough, I open my arms. I asked to have my flowered curtains left drawn – the privilege of a condemned prisoner – I don't want the curious gossipy well-meaning ladies peering for signs of fear, stupor or whatever. Evidently a lady went out on a trolley a few minutes back "Was she asleep?" "She looked asleep, she just lay there." Now they've given me the first injection – which will "dry my mouth, make me feel drunk & so I don't care what happens." A handsome lady anesthetist came in & told me about the details of that – my arm is swollen – right upper – a bee sting, red & hard to the touch. I feel a bubbly drowsiness take my heart & so shall only write in here after it's over – a letter from Ted reached me – my dear dear love.

Friday: March 3: Three days since my operation & I am myself again: the tough, gossipy curious enchanting entity I have not been for so long. The life here is made up of details. Petty pleasures & petty annoyances. Tuesday I was so drugged I knew nothing & nothing bothered me. Wednesday the drugs wore off & I felt sick & resentful of the lively health of the ward. Yesterday I felt tired & so-so. Today I threw of my fetters. – got up to wash & had my first laborious goat-shit, changed my hospital pink & red flapping jacket which left my bum bare to my frilly pink & white Victorian nightgown. They just wheeled one of the new women by on a stretcher – the muscular lime green porter loaded her on the trolley – the queer flat shape of a drugged body – the white turban, green blankets, eyes staring up, dumbly. The other night they say 'Thelma died.' I vaguely remember a lady in a yellow gown, youngish, wheeling the tea round. 'She died after her op." Outdoors it is sunny, smelling of wet sweet earth – A few stray airs filter in the windows. I remember luxuriating in these blowing airs on my first night when I lay wakeful after a day of sleep yet deeply drugged & invulnerable – it blew sweetly over the sleeping forms & stirred the curtains.

Annoyances & sorrows: The window above my bed was broken – cracked. First, before my op, a cold wet air laid itself on my head like a nasty poultice. Then, the day after my op, two men came to fix the window. My bed was wheeled out into mid-corridor. I felt unsettled, vulnerable. I was bumped. My side hurt. The fat girl in the wheelchair gave my dresser (locker) a great bump which jarred my bed. My side hurt. I slunk deeper into my pillows, exposed to strange peerers at the far end of the ward on all sides. I thought. 'Everybody going by bumps me,' I said to the nurse after an hour. 'I'd rather have the draft. I have to use the bedpan.' Chagrined, they had to wheel me back. When the workmen returned they were told to come back at one. They did come in visiting hours & move me out but Ted was there so I didnt care. Vacuuming They vacuum all day – little frizzy haired tarty fat lugubrious women mooching up the overnight dust – wooz – wooz. Then the bump & jingle of trolleys – bedpan trolleys, mouthwash trolleys, breakfast trolleys, tea trolleys, medicine trolleys. They thump on the floor & rattle. Then the typewriter hooknosed witch with the two crooked canes & green dressing-gown put out a huge black old-fashioned monster typewriter on the table in front of my bed. Bank-bonk-clatter-clatter. The worst curse – an unsteady typist. 'I'm not ready to go back to the office yet,' I said.

Snoring: the worst horror of all. I am next to the ward-snorer. The first night she came I was too drugged to hear her, but Wednesday morning a nurse laughingly remarked on it. That night I lay & tossed & ached till midnight: the stentorious roar echoed & magnified itself. The nurse with her flashlight said I couldn't have another sleeping pill so soon – she pulled the flowered curtain, woke the snorer up & turned her over, made me some hot ovaltine. Then the night sister came round with a second big blue pill which took me away in a warm bliss through all the petty bustle & noise from 5–10 am (Now the stretcher with its two green plastic pillows comes in again for the neighbor of the first woman in Bed 9. Green blankets. She looks just like the other woman – her eyes staring at the ceiling.) Last night I went to sleep before the old woman started to snore but woke with a start before 3 a.m. to hear her roaring. Got up to bathroom in a daze & grunted. Nothing happened. They finally made me some ovaltine & gave me two codeines which cut the sharp pang of my scar & the shooting gripes of wind in my bowels. I put the pillow over my head to shut out the noise & so woke at 7. Another peeve is that there are no bells to ring for the nurses – one has to rise on one elbow, – mine are pink & raw from hauling myself up – & shout 'Nurse' hoarsely. How a really sick person does, I don't know.

65[a–b], 66[b]–69[b]
Sunday: March 5: The fifth day after my op. I have been lazy about writing

in here – I feel fine now: an old soldier. Still with my stitches in & something to talk about. The stitches pull & twitch ("My mendings itch") but I demand codeine. Rose of the blue robe & white-haired "Granny" with the awful bloodshot crossed eyes, impressively black with iodine or some such when I came in – are going home today. Rose forgot her skirt so keeps her robe on – a symbol, that, of the desire to be "one of us". A dressed person, a person dressed for the street, is a bother here – not "one of us," a sort of masquerader. Rose wheels the trolley of flower vases about & distributes them – each glass vase or china pitcher is numbered with the Bed number of the patient on a bit of adhesive. The nurse just walked by with the square white cardboard spittoons. I shall have a story out of this, beginning "Tonight I deserve a blue light, I am one of them" – describing the shock of entering this queer highly rhythmical & ordered society as a stranger, an outsider, attuning oneself to the ward vibrations, undergoing the "initiation" – the real central common yet personal experience, & recovering in harmony. As soon as one is well, too well, one is excluded "unpopular" – the violet-gowned Miss Stapleton immediately to my left has relapsed. Her thyroid or goiter scar has healed, but she lies mouth open & eyes shut – her leg has swollen & hurts. She has phlebitis. She is going to a convalescent home after this. So is the lady with jaundice three beds down to my left next to Gran. She is bright yellow, has been 'opened' innumerable times & is going to Clacton-on-the Sea – to a convent convalescent home where the nuns bake their own bread & do up tasty dishes. 'The salt air does you good', I say. I face Helga's" pot of tulips & Charles' dying iris & daffodils. 'That yellow stuff's lasted well,' Daisy says of Miss Stapleton's bouquet. 'For-sigh-thia' drawls Maury with the pain-set face & tart tongue. She told me she'll never to, be able to move her arm, just her fingers. Now it is 1:40 pm Sunday afternoon. I have desperately washed, powdered my sallow bandaged body, combed my greasy hair – feel shoddily in need of a shampoo. Bunny & Joan are talking about the difference between "black Africans" & "white Afrikaans." The nurses are 'tidying' beds before visiting hours. To my own surprise I am allowed to go out & sit on a park bench in the sun with Ted & the Pooker" as I did yesterday all afternoon; I am immensely fond of all the nurses in their black & white pin striped dresses, white aprons & hats & black shoes & stockings. Their youth is the chief beauty about them – youth, absolute starched cleanliness & a comforting tidying-up & brow-smoothing air. The routine, even with the quite short nights' sleep (about 10–6, if lucky – swimming to it through Mrs. John's snores & clutching it through the nurse's morning bustle & glassy clatter) I feel more fresh

& rested than I have for months. I am above the 'sick level' of the place so I have an extra advantage – although I slightly cancel it by much bedside visiting & gossiping. I feel so fresh & peaceful now, in spite of a slight shiver at the thought of my stitches coming out – it is like a diverting holiday – my <u>first</u> since the baby was born almost a year ago: quite bracing. All morning talked to Jay Wynn across the way about her office & private life & nervous breakdown – cannot congratulate myself too much on this confidence because I blabbed about my own breakdown & mis-applied shock treatment. Shall outline her account after I come in tonight. Ted is actually having a rougher time than I – poor love sounded quite squashed yesterday 'How do you do it all? . . . The Pooker makes an astonishing amount of pots to wash . . . She wets a lot' & 'I seem to be eating mostly bread.' I felt needed & very happy & lucky. My life – as I compare it to those in the ward about me – is so fine – everything but money & a house – love & all.

A sunny day. Hot. The radiator at my back makes me sweat – I should have listed it among annoyances. The windows – the three bay windows on the far side of the ward are white & dazzling with sun. Dark green blinds, dulled moon-bulbs.

7:45 pm. twilight. Low voices, sleepy breathers. I was going to sleep till pill-time, but the sight of the old woman's hands clutching the shaped – bow-shaped, I suppose, pull-up bar on its curiously heavy iron prison chain stopped me. Those gnarled white roots of hands. Mrs. Fry was evidently run over by a car on some Friday or other – latest news is that she insisted on being moved to this hospital – nearer her home – from another, probably UCH.[n] She moans, yells, curses. 'You devil! You're trying to murder me' - - - over pills, or moving down in bed or something. 'Mother, mother - - - O how I've suffered'. She refuses medicine, calls the nurses constantly. I sat tonight (it's now 5 to 9) with the giggly RADA[n] girl – all short red hair, pink luminous baby-skin & even white teeth & giggles like a froth on champagne about the brain operation snorting horribly in her nose tubes & skull-sock. She told me Mrs. Fry's legs (both broken) were almost mended. Another story said they were just broken. The man who ran her over & his wife came tiptoeing in with flowers. 'How are you?' 'Very poorly, very poorly,' She says with relish.

Often, the nurses disappear. The old noseless lady of 82 with the broken leg in traction at the left-end of the row facing me yelled for a bedpan earlier

'Nurse' – her sock-face grotesquely leaning forward past the fat jolly dark Italian girl's. I gradually felt it devolve on me, bed by bed, to get a nurse. 'Nurse', the old lady yelled. I tried to cheer her up this morning by telling her a lady at <u>least</u> 10 years her senior with <u>two</u> broken legs was in the adjoining ward. 'God is Good' the old thing said. Immense cameraderie here. I am in an excellent position for "visiting round." The nurses are absolute angels.

<u>Monday</u>: March 6: 4:20 pm. In bed after an hour alone in the wan sun of the park reading the late poems of Pasternak – they excited me immensely – the free, lyric line & terse (though sometimes too fey) idiom. I felt: a new start can be made through these. This is the way back to the music. I wept to lose to my new tough prosiness. Tired after a ghastly night – the woman – Mrs. Fry – with the two white-root hands put on a huge scene – started calling for the police. 'Police, policeman, get me out of here' 'O how I suffer' theatrical wooing groans 'I'll call my doctor in in the morning to show how you leave me all night because of your whims' 'I'll tell your mummies on you.' The sister went in to her 'Why won't you take your medicine?' Evidently she had some pills to make her shit & shat all day & thinks they're trying to kill her like this. Some more cursing & I saw the nurse & sister in the lit office-cubicle gleefully preparing a hypodermic. Often she sounds manic – 'Ooo what are those around me? Walls walls walls . . . " "Those are windows,' the sister said firmly. 'What are those frocks on the chair?' 'Those are pillow-cases'. At about 3 I was woken by a crash & more wooing. She'd thrown a medicine glass down. Evidently on her first day here she hit a doctor with her pocket book.

My stitches pull & snick. I am tired.
– <u>Notes</u>: The pink 'bud-vases' of antiseptic over each bed our thermometers are kept in.
– The flower bowls on windowsills, the trolleys of valiant but dying flowers.
– The old lady's plastic flesh-coloured neck piece on her table like an extra head – peach – pink with air holes, white straps & silver studs & a lining of yellow sponge & pink flowered nightgown silk. Her bowl of fruit, CPSnow's 'New Men', stubborness – eats food out of tins her daughter brings
– Once last night the old lady Fry shouted 'You can laugh. I can laugh. He who laughs last laughs best.' I felt guilty as I had just smothered a snort in the pillow. But the nurse's laughed also.
– The sock-head nose-tube lady had water on the brain – snorkles & drools

dull eyed. Was a district-nurse, mannish, efficient – now 'she may go one way or the other – mental'.

Bed 1: Joan in a plaster cast from toe to bosom for 4 months knits dark green wool. Has a house on the sea in South Devon. Obvious brave front. Reads 'Horse & Hound'. Two sons 16 & 14. Sent to public school at 6 – 'The only thing.' Her entomologist husband, their life in Africa, studying locusts.

Bed 2: The ubiquitous popular Rose, born in Camden town & married at an early age to the boy round the corner, of Dutch descent & working at the same print factory for 15 years, with one son – is gone.

Bed 3: Mrs. Johns – the neckpiece lady – sits straight as a schoolmarm, reading. I guessed right about her – she thinks she's 'better' – keeps an utter schoolmarmish reserve which she broke for me yesterday. She is the wife of an elementary school headmaster, daughter of two country school teachers & grandaughter of school-teachers. Her daughter is a bossy gabby school teacher who – not surprisingly – divorced her husband in Africa before the birth of their first baby & she now lectures at the University of London – teaching teachers. She informed me, almost in tears, last night, that her daughter had looked at my books while I was out & said she had 'an intellectual next to her'. Said she felt 'so unfriendly' not talking, but she was always in pain, had a TB abscess in her spine. It was treated 'wrong' – as neuritis, with exercises – now very bad. She seems to stick to her trouble & has given her doctors & nurses a stiffneck resistance. Her night-snoring & sleeping all day is enough to make us all pitiless

I found out today who Mrs. Pfaffrath is – that elusive lady whose pool forms keep coming to our house. She is – or was – our dead landlady & a woman here knew her! I got round to talking to the prim trim North Irish Nelly in the middle bay-window as I dried my hair & found she once lived in our district. I asked if she knew Chalcot Square & she said 'I knew the landlady of Number 3'. She was married to a French wig-maker. Evidently there was a great demand for men's wigs after the war as lots of soldiers lost their hair & went bald for one reason or another.

Daisy is the real original. Wish I could overhear her stories. 'I could tell she's a Jew' she said triumphantly of wild Mrs. Fry. 'She said 'already'. That's what the Jews say.' 'I say already too, Jay put in gently, but that didn't deter Daisy: 'We're all like little animals' she said, 'waiting for dinner.'

The white-haired Jewess from Hackney in the lavender bed-sweater told me of her pale hard-working teacher daughter & her marvelous grandsons who are brilliant, one entering Oxford in geology. Impression of desperate grubbing study. She went to have a badly-fitted false leg improved Friday – has come back in because her other foot has 'gone bad' – a diabetic – my father's classic case – as the witchy Jewess in the green arsenic dressing-gown told me on my walk – she insisted on coming, but went right in.

Journal
June 1957 – June 1960

4[a]

London – June

queer lucid blue green sky – odd neon lights – blue-painted street lamps –
picadilly – Eros shooting earthward – water sliding down black pedestal,
wavering – steps – great neons: red coca-cola bullseye electric 'batteries' –
Piccadilly Circus – Soho: bars – brown wood, strutting pianos, singing –
langorous dead air – blonde tarts on corners, in doorways – "Le Macabre":
skeletons – innumerable private clubs – cruising cars, tall Virgo bobbies –
chez Auguste – vine leaves – wine bottles in great sweating buckets – flaming
salvers, bread sticks – odd modern apartments here & there – cubed glass
lavendar lights – great red double-decker busses moving

5[a]-7[b]

Ship-deck: 11 am – blowing, gusts, shadow on wooden decks of blown
steamer smoke. Red & blue thick steamer rugs blue swimming light. Radiant medium blue sea over lifeboats to right – red funnel riveted, back slanting – cold wind at back of neck – deck steward tilting down with white china
cups of bouillion & saltine biscuits. Clear blued shadows on white paint –
white spray waves cleaving aside from ship. Children playing tag, collecting
lady-bugs, red with black spots – sailor with scarred nose mopping edge of
deck with squeegee – Passengers – squat; ugly, bad pots: Jews, coarse – tan-
faced. Two bright negresses in gaudy colors: lime, tangerine, fuschia. sound:
motors, wind, whoo of funnels – red, white, blue – vivid – dazzle – tyranny
of present minute, present object: The Now and Here

---

vivid presence rules despotic over pale shadows of past & future

---

4 pm – Winter Garden: round & square white-linen clothed tables – people – wide-eyed freckled bony mother scolding & fratching at fat blond little girl in dutch cut; Jewish woman: plump, gray bob, pink lipstick: Brooklyn accent: "She was an exquisite person" "exquisite umbrella" – white jacketed waiters trays of white gilt-bordered cups, silver sugar bowls, gilt buttons – trays shoulder height. Flowers bordering frosted glass – red geraniums, pale unnatural lavendar hydrangeas – 4 o'clock gentility – round electric lights, like cream peppermint wafers – two mirror slatted columns – 4 portholes lit with light blue sky distinct from yellow electric glow – moment fills up – sudden "descent of angel": <u>brimming</u> – overflow – tears – violin strikes up – piano, drum – deep blue of sea – whole room tilts – fills porthole – dark blue half way up – white caps – deep interfusion – "Mountain Greenery"

Night on ship – windowless cabin, dark – artificial light through slats in door – no sense of day or night. Gleaming endless corridors, red & green arrows – boat-drill – life-savers – shuffle-board players – ship Newspaper & daily events card – throbbing – coffin-like bunks – straight narrow, tightly made beds – compact, but crowding – if one person opens a suitcase lid, everybody else has to get in bed – sense of waking deep in a coffin – early morning light on deck – cold, windy, overcast rows of empty deck chairs – blue & orange zig-zag patterns – deep-black-green waves directly under ship –

Woman at table – NY secretary to lawyers – envious, arriviste – 'But cabin class has so many more facilities.' Going abroad teaches you to be satisfied with where you live at home. Nothing in common with French if you don't know their language or share the same culture. Longing for "high-toned" "culture" – fancy – mucky-fine. Text-book man-catcher: "You must have a very responsible position." gross clerics – balsy crying over prunes – sudden sense of renewed creative gift: ability to "make of the moment something permanent" – air: threaded through with "Blue Room" – clatter of cups & dishes – Negresses in fruity tropical colors – tangerine, lime, watermelon pink –

---

words begin: interior monologue re-creating scene, re-arranging – speaking it – flower pellet unfolding in clear glass of the mind – bloom – into what? novel? <u>Make Diary</u> – catch each pellet & let it unfold in the storage aquarium of rare blooms – keep the creating creative <u>core</u> & integrity (not selling less for more than its worth) & no woman can have more – continuous social life kills or betrays inner world: to make it rare & strange

On bows – orange masts: 5 tons – black-blue sea – fierce wind plastering clothes to body, flipping whip streaks of hair – spray folding back from bow cleaving like white rich curd, blown thin rainbow in glass sheet of drops, growing from bow & arching back, to break, fragment & dissolve as spray fell, only to grow again, double, fray – as if ship were trailing rainbows, a wake of rainbows – glaring white paint – clear-cut – sense of the great whales moving, rising, shedding scuds of water from their great bulks and rising to view –

———————

blue & red, round & square table tops – "everybody in 'ospital" "Never fails to rain of a Sunday – drizzle – mean – low gray clouds, flat ugly sea –

———————

table characters: great stone-faced, red-knuckled, white-haired Scotsman – mammoth & silent eater – motherly huge talkative ribald Scotswoman "apple pie without the cheese": "I can stand canned berries, cherries, everything but canned apples." Loves Gordon McRae, Eroll Flynn. Likes movie: "all above love". Fish for dessert: kippers, herring, haddock.

—

Yorkshire woman: from near Hull: "looks darker than an Italian" – going to daughter in America who's having a baby – fat – diets, rather quiet, heavily lugubrious –

—

Black-haired secretary "to New York lawyers" – turning sour – pathetic effort to catch man: To impress balding married table-mate – "You must have a very responsible job". Social-climber in half-wistful, half-sour-grapes fashion: "cocktails in cabin-class – "more facilities" – dining in first class "formal" – gray little wardrobe – best dress, expensive, neat cut, low-back, but gray, gray fuzzy angora neck – Polish-Jew background – "culture" – "You can't have anything in common with French unless you speak their language or share their culture." Discrimination – travel in Italy, Venice, Rome. Waiter: "If you don't catch a man on this ship, you'll never catch one." Man: "Oh, she's got one. She's got me." Girl: (Resentment breaking out) Yeah, but he's well-married already. Elaborate sarcasm over ringing bitterness, lonely, lingering. Can't sleep: too cold, noise of fan, ventilator (didn't know how to turn it off) – sway of ship. Movie-vigil – "I was waiting for somebody, but I guess they're not coming." Saving seats.

Jolly balding cockney: short, black threads of hair plastered by hair-oil across bald spot – married – confiding – being sent by company to join ship in Bermuda – NY cruise – daughter married to American – going to have baby – kind man, frank – vaccination hurting – "fellows" in smokefilled cabin, exchanging stories, showing each other pictures – points out quartermasters going also to join ships – describes Jose Ferrer movie: "a lot of speaking, I like a lot of talking in a movie." Describes first, 2nd, 3rd butchers, baked bread, pie – great refrigerators

12[a–b]
Pine Cone: Placed on its circular base on the table, the dried-out pine cone, woody gray-brown in color, rose to a rounded summit like a hived anthill. When looked at from directly above, it's wooden petals flared, starting at the central and highest point with two tiny bent sticks not more than a third of an inch long and thinner than matchsticks. Two slightly larger brown-gray petals stuck out just below and square to these, forming a compass pointing N.S.E and W, set in a trefoil of larger petals, rising from the dark central nub of the cone and curving toward the middle, like the scooped lower half of a twig with pith removed, greyer and blunting at the tip. To the left, several petals were missing, so the next in the ruffle were a good deal larger and closer toward the base of the pine cone, while those on the right graded downward in a slow, regular increase of size after two frayed petals which showed a reddish yellow fiber where the gray woody surface peeled back. All the petals circling the centered trefoil fanned out, darkest at the base, shading through twist or warp to the whitish-gray tip, the whole cone forming a kind of stylized wooden rose of dull browny-gray petals, dead – stiff & brittle. Turning the pine cone in the hand and regarding it in profile, one sees the thin upper petals point skyward, gradually level out horizontal half way down, dark at the central stem and tipped with a whitish crescent, like a shallow saucer with a thorn-point base, and then, the lowest petals turn downward, spaced in a row, and the next row staggered beneath to form a fairly solid base of wooden frills.

26[b]–27[a]
Spaulding's Trailer:
Silver-gray trailer, set with window-length on clearing, door & two windows opening into pinegrove, floored with dry reddish pine needles. Trailer about 10 yards long, curving roof at either end – window oblong at either end: door, silver-gray, with square window curtained in white-dotted gauze

– green wooden steps – two, put up against door. Front side of trailer a garden of odds & ends: starting from left, under bedroom window – cardboard carton full of red & white-handled paintbrushes, cans of paint, dusty bottles of turp, scrub oak – sprout – yellow basket, plastic, full of mopheads – shovel, blue enamel tub, white dots – green & maroon rug & ash can, string & white wire-wooden table – covered with red earthenware pots, various sizes, green philodendron, green tea cups china, colander & baking pan full of red, purple, green beach plums, quahog shells, liquid soap. Under table: blue-sprigged pot, tinfoil, rubber plant, empty glass jug, green wastepaper basket with pink & yellow flowers, broom, pile of aluminium buckets, wicker basket of clothespins – under pine tre in front of door – geranium, red, in tin can covered with tin foil, pale yellow leaves, glass jug, green, with withered stalks. White china hen with 3 yellow chicks – large overturned waste basket, white, middle burned black on either end, scarred with red rust – plants – tin cans, red-leaves, philodendron. Wheel barrow of beach plums, rusty child's cart, beach plums in news paper – wash machine veiled with transparent paper, capped with canvas, wet mops, dishrag on pine tree, clothesline strung between trees – rusty-springed bedstead – 3 tin cans of plants in ice cube tray –

---

corn vases –

About two feet high – corn sheaf, vase, furled center of main corn stalk, corn-yellow grains, row of 3, corn on left, handle – husk, lined – deep green-yellow tip. Boy stood out on base – oval base about two inches high – frieze of leaves and flower buds. Boy – foot high – straw hat with corn leaf stuck in it, brown face, delicate features – black curly hair, pinky purple jacket open, yellow band around neck & front, yellow jersey with blue-stripes, pink kilt up about waist, falling to knees, brown bare feet on yellow green soil, right foot stepping out. Brown corked jug held in right hand, another fat brown corked jug under left arm, light blue mug in left hand, can stick little finger in it, background fan of leaves, corn flowers.

Girl – charming, smiling brown face, right arm bent, holding pink string of wicker basket, complete to tear in straw on her back, blue blouse & skirt with pink & yellow border, wide pink sash, yellow apron full of green-leaved-vegetables held up & to side in left sheathed knife hanging at right hip – green leaves scrolled about yellow-brown base – corn grains – pink outlined – inside of vase – pale turquoise: black hair parted in middle, down over right shoulder – pink scarf, fringe draped over head –

27[b or c]
Story: <u>The Great Big Nothing</u>
Gertrude Twiss New York secretary: point of view –
Scene: Queen Elizabeth, June crossing to America.
Mood: failure, misery, lemon-acid. She has saved & dreamed for Europe
trip. Quit job, bought expensive new wardrobe & gone. (grey, turquoise
colors). Lonely trip implied. Search for man. Failure. Sees seamy side of

everything. Europe "a great big nothing." Undermines & blackens everything she talks about: England – dark, crowded little parlors, Rome – the
nasty men. Main emotion: <u>envy</u> of all who have abundance of life –
    Characters at ship table, tourist class:
little balding jolly cockney, married.
Great motherly Irish woman
young married couple of <u>lovers</u>
Waiter's cruel, casual remark: "If you don't catch a man on this ship, you
never will."
Cabin class – dreams of grandeur – French doctor – glamor – intelligent –
love – all commodities she can't have – life: a great big nothing.
Statue of Liberty: irony: statue of own imprisonment in self, locks shut. "It's
not so much."
Everything coming into NYC anti-climax – Nothing but bitterness in self, so
she finds nothing of sweetness in outside world. Vicious circle.

41[a]
Mama McFague & The Corn Vase Girl
A House For Mama McFague
Spauldings: Myrtle & Lester: vivid character study. Work & sweat of Myrtle
to get up summer cabins – yet she never has a house – designs kitchens,
colors, slaves for money cleaning other people's summer places – working
for senile ladies – <u>too good</u>, too generous. Danger of heart attack, blood
pressure. Husband: sickly, bland, dependent & blithely impractical. Land in
pines. Quahog pile. Gets furniture from 2nd hand houses being demolished.
No house – lives in trailer in summer – hardships: love of flowers. Quahog
fritters. Beach plum jelly. Trailer flooded. <u>Guests</u> – locusts in harvest time.
Ratty kids. End of rope. Kid breaks one of McFague's statues. Now she can
bear to sell the other. Love of beauty. Girl broken. Legend. San Francisco
quake. Teddy Roosevelt. Down-payment on house.

41[b or c]
4a
4b Such collusion of mulish elements
2c As wore her broom straws to the nub.
4b She did not wear.
2c Hourly the moored clam & the crab
4b Lost in that welter
2c Of millstones, root & pith; the ebb

5a tide left their relics to clicker in the winds

Anger jolts like heartburn in the throat

97[a-c]
Trafalgar Square:" wooden benches, back to Nat. Gallery – hot June sun –
sparkling & sheen: lavendar-pink metalled neck of brown pigeon – bums
asleep under newspapers – round yellow-orange eye of pigeons, pink feet
– red & white checked flag flapping in blue sky over Canadian-pacific
clock – white & grey domes – back of black Lord Nelson on pillar – 9:30 am
– fountains begin – spurt – drift of water vapor slicking the green back of the
dolphins & mermaids
roar of traffics – red tops of great double decker busses moving to right,
black cabs – white highlights – sun high at left – front – green leaves in
granite oblong basins – gleam of brown metal desk lamps
traffic roar, squeal of brakes like high struck glass – guardian lions – white
light on metal flanks – dark squadrons of pigeons
derricks & cranes: skeletal building in background – cool clear lucid air –
drifted over by smoke, exhaust fumes, fountain spray – two wide fountain
basins, light from pool reflecting on underside – flap & flight of hundreds
of pigeons wheeling – woman in black passing – pigeons in basket, about
sandalled feet – statue of mermaids – limpid & flowing green

huge flapping wheel of pigeons round & round base of Nelsons pillar –
rainbow in spray – green water – white-shit on paving church spire – blue
clock face – gilt hands – pediment"

Letter

1 October 1957

Tuesday, October 1

Letter to a demon:
Last night I felt the sensation I have been reading about to no avail in James: the sick, soul-annihilating flux of fear in my blood switching its current to defiant fight. I could not sleep, although tired, and lay feeling my nerves shaved to pain & the groaning inner voice: oh, you can't teach, can't do anything. Can't write, can't think. And I lay under the negative icy flood of denial, thinking that voice was all my own, a part of me, and it must somehow conquer me & leave me with my worst visions: having had the chance to battle it & win day by day, and having failed.

I cannot ignore this murderous self: it is there. I smell it and feel it, but I will not give it my name. I shall shame it. When it says: you shall not sleep, you cannot teach, I shall go on anyway, knocking its nose in. It's biggest weapon is and has been the image of myself as a perfect success: in writing, teaching and living. As soon as I sniff non-success in the form of rejections, puzzled faces in class when I'm blurring a point, or a cold horror in personal relationships, I accuse myself of being a hypocrite, posing as better than I am, and being, at bottom lousy.

I am middling good. And I can live being middling good. I do not have advanced degrees, I do not have books published, I do not have teaching experience. I have a job teaching. I cannot rightly ask myself to be a better teacher than any of those teaching around me with degrees, books published and experience. I can only, from day to day, fight to be a better teacher than I was the day before. If, at the end of a year of hard work, partial failure, partial dogged communication of a poem or a story, I can say I am easier, more confident & a better teacher than I was the first day, I have done enough. I must face this image of myself as good for myself, and not freeze myself into a quivering jelly because I am not Mr. Fisher or Miss Dunn or any of the others.

I have a good self, that loves skies, hills, ideas, tasty meals, bright colors. My demon would murder this self by demanding it be a paragon, and saying it should run away if it is being anything less. I shall doggedly do my best and know it for that, no matter what other people say. I can learn to be a better teacher. But only by painful trial and error. Life is painful trial and error. I instinctively gave myself this job because I knew I needed the confidence it would give me as I needed food: it would be my first active facing of life & responsibility: something thousands of people face every day, with groans, maybe, or with dogged determination, or with joy. But they face it. I have this demon who wants me to run away screaming if I am going to be flawed, fallible. It wants me to think I'm so good I must be perfect. Or nothing. I am, on the contrary, something: a being who gets tired, has shyness to fight, has more trouble than most facing people easily. If I get through this year, kicking my demon down when it comes up, realising I'll be tired after a days work, and tired after correcting papers, and it's natural tiredness, not something to be ranted about in horror, I'll be able, piece by piece, to face the field of life, instead of running from it the minute it hurts.

The demon would humiliate me: throw me on my knees before the college president, my department chairman, everyone, crying: look at me, miserable, I can't do it. Talking about my fears to others feeds it. I shall show a calm front & fight it in the precincts of my own self, but never give it the social dignity of a public appearance, me running from it, and giving in to it. I'll work in my office roughly from 9 to 5 until I find myself doing better in class. In any case, I'll do something relaxing, different reading, etc. in the evenings. I'll keep myself intact, outside this job, this work. They can't ask more of me than my best, & only I know really where the limits on my best are. I have a choice: to flee from life and ruin myself forever because I can't be perfect right away, without pain & failure, and to face life on my own terms & "make the best of the job."

each day I shall record a dogged step ahead or a marking time in place. The material of reading is something I love. I must learn, slowly, how to best present it, managing class discussion: I must reject the grovelling image of the fearful beast in myself, which is an elaborate escape image, and face, force, days into line. I have an inner fight that won't be conquered by a motto or one night's resolution. My demon of negation will tempt me day by day, and I'll fight it, as something other than my essential self, which I am fighting to save: each day will have something to recommend it: whether the honest delight at watching the quick furred body of a squirrel, or sensing, deeply, the weather and color, or reading and thinking of something in a different light: a good explanation or 5 minutes in class to redeem a bad 45. Minute by minute to fight upward. Out from under that black cloud which would annihilate my whole being with its demand for perfection and measure, not of what I am, but of what I am not. I am what I am, and have written, lived and travelled: I have been worth what I have won, but must work to be worth more. I shall not be more by wishful thinking.

So: a stoic face. A position of irony, of double-vision. My job is serious, important, but nothing is more important than my life and my life in its fullest realized potential: jealousy, envy, desperate wishes to be someone else, someone already successful at teaching, is naive: Mr. Fisher, for all his student-love, has been left by his wife & children; Miss Williams,[n] for all her experience & knowledge, is irrevocably dull. Every one of these people, the divorced Schendler, the unmarried Johnson, has some flaw, some crack, and to be one of them would be to be flawed & cracked in another fashion. I'll shoulder my own crack, work on my James today, Hawthorne for next week & take life with gradual ease, dogged at first, but with more & more joy. My first victory was accepting this job, the second, coming up & plunging into it before my demon could say no, I wasn't good enough, the third, going to class after a night of no sleep & desperation, the fourth, facing my demon last night with Ted & spitting in its eye. I'll work hard on my planning, but work just as hard to build up a rich home life: to get writing again, to get my mind fertilized outside my job.

I shall not, carrion comfort, despair . . . etc.

No more knuckling under, groaning, moaning: one gets used to pain. This hurts. Not being perfect hurts. Having to bother about work in order to eat & have a house hurts. So what. It's about time. This is the month which ends a quarter of a century for me, lived under the shadow of fear: fear that I would fall short of some abstract perfection: I have often fought, fought &

won, not perfection, but an acceptance of myself as having a right to live on my own human, fallible terms.

Attitude is everything. No whining or fainting will get me out of this job & I'd not like to think what would happen to my integral self if it did. I've accepted my first check: I've signed on, and no little girl tactics are going to get me off, nor should they.

To the library. Finish James book, memorize my topics, maybe the squirrel story. Have fun. If I have fun, the class will have fun.

Come home tonight: read lawrence, or write, if possible. That will come too.

Vive le roi, le roi est mort, vive le roi.

Journal Fragment
5 November 1957

Tuesday night: November 5

Brief note: to self. Time to take myself in hand. I have been staggering about lugubrious, black, bleak, sick. Now to build into myself, to give myself backbone, however much I fail. If I get through this year, no matter how badly, it will be the biggest victory I've ever done. All my spoiled little girl selves cry to escape before my bad-teaching, ignorant somnolence is made drearily public among my old teachers and my new students. If I fainted, or paralysed myself, or pleaded gibberingly to Mr. Hill that I couldn't carry on, I'd probably escape all right: but how to face myself, to live after that? To write or be intelligent as a woman? It would be a worse trauma than this, although escape looks very sweet & plausible. This way, I can build up a dull, angry resentment & feel I'm going through with it & will deserve my freedom in June, for sacrificing a year of my life. 7 more months.

First of all? Keep quiet with Ted about worries. With him around, I am disastrously tempted to complain, to share fears and miseries. Misery loves company. But my fears are only magnified when reflected by him. So Mr. Fisher called tonight & is coming to sit in on my class Friday. Instead of complaining to Ted, feeling my tension grow, echoed in him, I am keeping quiet about it. I will make my test of self-control this week being quiet about it till its over. Ted's knowing can't help me in my responsibility. I've got to face it & prepare for it myself. My first day of Lawrence. Wednesday & Thursday to prepare for it. Keep rested. That's the main thing. Make up a couple of little lectures. Get class prepared.

The main thing is to get on top of this preparation. To figure how to start teaching them about style. For the first lesson, make up general lectures about Form of papers, organization, read from papers. Don't get exasperated. A calm front: start at <u>home</u>. Even with Ted I must learn to be very calm & happy: to let him have his time & not be selfish & spoil it. Maturity begins here, however bad I am. I must prepare lectures, however poor.

After this week, enjoy reading: make up ways to present symbol, style. Lectures for confidence. Don't look at year: from now till tomorrow. From then till the next day. Then next week. Then next week. Then, Thanksgiving, and a real chance at rehabilitation & work. I'll trudge on till then.

I <u>want</u> to enjoy this as much as I can. Which means I must work for preparation & not procrastinate in fear, and teach in sick fear. Confidence. It begins at home. In keeping Ted from knowing the worst. Then I won't know it myself. I'll be living with it. Rest, calm. Nothing will help if I get nervous & miserable & worry. It salves guilt to feel "at least I'm sick & miserable", that's payment for being a bad teacher. No. I'll try to brazen it out. To keep my outside contacts. Letters to Krook, Wendy. My being a bad teacher this year will only prove I can earn board & keep and not quit. I quit my waitress job; I wanted to quit my first babysitting job. I will not quit on this. I need somebody to slap me. It won't be Mr. Hill. It will be myself. Don't be spoiled, in dry accents. I contracted for this. I'll work to do my best, however bad, and not lose face.

Each week I'll make up some small new outpost to conquer: first I couldn't sleep without pills, now I can. First I couldn't see girls in my office without exhaustion, now I can. I can also write a letter, bake a good pie. Victories, however small. Now I'm going to be more ambitious: this week I won't share my worry about visiting with Ted, Nor my worries in general. I'll shut up and work. Confiding in him is my worst weakness. I feel he deserves to bear my pain and share it, but I must shoulder my aloneness somehow, and begin to be nobler. To work within my immediate job, demands & problems, and pretend that Ted is outside them, not drag him in at every moment. This is a beginning. To bear my Visitor alone.

Hospital Notes

HOSPITAL NOTES:"

Ethel D: 74: Memory worse on death of husband - - - wanders around house to get milk from icebox, putting it back under her bed, making days out of nights and nights out of days, thinking at times that she is in winter during the summer and vice versa. Unable to say how old she is. Daughters wanted to improve mother's condition. Diet? Piano lessons?

40 year old sewing machine salesman. Unusual symptom for him of depression. Tried to deal with it through active physical exercise at the Y, outdoor interests and, on occasion, prayer. Complains of absence of zip and drive which he formerly had in large quantities. Not selling as well as he used to. Job performed from 6–9 in evenings. Chronic eczema.

Ida M: 50: Jewish. Husband has ignored her for past 3 years. Only coming home late at night to sleep. Nervous, ill-tempered, impatient man. Constantly referring to her as a crazy deaf-mute. Against her going to any doctors. Will not get a divorce but tells her to. Dates present "sad" state of mind to marriage 12 years ago - - - followed courtship of over 10 years. Brought from Russia when a baby. Husband a cab driver.

Catherine B: 51: Intolerable behavior of husband. Extremely jealous and almost since time of marriage accused her of infidelity as well as having doubted the paternity at various times of various of their children. Extremely suspicious of wife - - - suspecting her every move and association. Things became quite intense about 4 years ago when he doubted paternity of certain of his children and demanded blood tests. Two times made gestures of killing wife. Husband constantly ranting and raving in very boisterous fashion, accusing her at the top of his lungs of infidelity.

Dominic R: Italian, West End. Mother & father first cousins. Two other children born paralyzed, blind, eventually died. Father a fisherman. Nervous about being knifed in the back. On guard duty in Korea began to read books on nervousness, seen in pamphlets advertised on subway. Crying jags.

25 year old twice-married once-divorced mother of three. "I hate my children". Fear of dark. Sleeps fully dressed.

Job: poultry company. Eviscerator of chickens. Loves job, really loves chickens, can eat them raw. Loves macaroni. Eats 1 lb dry weight at a time. Constantly asks mother for more food.

Sister Jean Marie: Catholic nun. Evaluated for noises in her ear. Gave up teaching position as principal at Academy. Feeling of head being big as though she were dizzy or faint. Noises sounded articulated but generally indistinguishable - - - few words heard. Rhythmic repetitions of Arizona or Amen. Also: angry woman's voice shouting high and a man's voice, pitched low but could not distinguish what they were saying. Other sensations - - - strumming of a low-pitched cello and other non-human voices.

Emily P: Invisible person in the house having sexual relations with her at night. Also with two sons and that she has heard various voices along with strange noises like there are many telephones rigged up in the house. Also complains of unpleasant odors emanating from her family. She is referred to in papers and on radio as being crazy - - - both talking about her in many indirect ways. Suspicious her family is attempting to poison her. Husband says wife has bought long knives and has threatened his death. He has buried the knives.

Laura D: Mother did not accept child's death. Withdrew literally and stopped talking. Has not recalled much of incidents surrounding illness, death and burial. Has "seen" and "talked" with daughter on occasions since. Occasions very real to patient. Child told her she was going to stay with God and patient should not cry. Two days ago "saw" child at a religious ceremony and fainted.

Laura R. Floridly tinted orange hair. Hat-check girl. Models in nude for photographer. Lesbian girlfriend.

Valborg M: Norwegian. Father: farmer & alcoholic in Minnesota.

Corinne H
Wesley B
Robert U
Mae W
Andrew A
Marcia L: Father, a man with no mouth.
Dorothy S: Nightmares: saw own head amputated but hanging on by skin.

Mannie L
Perry B
Arlene R

Mary M: dream: working at bedside of man resembling one of former patients who is middle-aged and has family and who was very friendly to her but no improperly so. In dream, while in bedroom, went to closet and looked into laundry bag and found five heads. Four were those of children whom she cannot identify. The fifth head was that of her mother as she appeared when patient was a child.

Engaged to a man with a glass eye. 4 years ago: neighbor's dog in back yard barked at night and not only noise, but population in town was increasing. Owing to efforts of her husband there are no longer any dogs in her town . . . unable to see insomnia as a result of tensions in herself and continues to blame it on dogs in the neighborhood. (I do feel I have a schizophrenic patient between my hands).

Ferrara: Fear of heart attack. Average day: 7:30 takes puppy out for a walk around the block. Goes and meets other fellows who may not be at work that day and they have a beer or two. Then returns home in mid-morning and watches TV shows. Wife may take children to beach for an outing but he stays home "because he is afraid something might happen." Foreman in Boston Molasses Factory.

Philip S: Feels guilty of father's death. Contractor: doorknobs and windows. Left father's business & set up on own. Father died while patient was at Country Club at a party.

Francis M: 39, epileptic. Unmarried cemetery worker. Chief complaint - - - wants to be able to make friends and go out with girls. Steady job at Cambridge cemetery, tending flowers. Very shy. Spends most of free time at home listening to records, or going to movies, feeling constantly alone.

Spero P: 34 years old. White, single elementary school principal. Fears asphyxia and death. Inability to maintain intense relationship with a girl when marriage is considered. Intensely absorbed in hatred of mother. Curses her as vain, inhuman, vicious, strict, stubborn, foul old woman who administered inhuman beatings upon him when young. Fear of own impotence. States he can excel at anything and can prove it to anyone. Can annihilate anyone in argument.

First husband lost at sea from private yacht.

Edward C: Episodic attacks in which he doesn't feel himself. During attacks feels sense of unreality. When he watches TV he feels he is the one who is creating everything. Once a hurricane came and when the hurricane was over he felt it was he who had created the hurricane and all the damage that was done.

3rd year Harvard student majoring in government. Member of Quill and Scroll. Very ambitious. Wants to go to law school and into politics and reach the highest peak in political fields.

Barbara H: Felt something moving in her stomach. Might turn to animal or be pregnant, and have puppies. Turn into mule or horse. Thought she was growing hair on face. 35, married, white.

John M: 44, has lived in Medford for "three centuries". Everything has to be perfect with

Philomena T. While making a cake found she'd left out one ingredient. Went crazy, pulling hair, banging fist, smashing hands against the wall.

Mary T: 67, married. Buttonhole-maker in factories.

Lillian J; 68 year old woman. Fascinating obsessional thought she's pregnant. Boyfriend (52) for last 30 years. Won't marry him. Sex play. Husband (first) died after 6 years marriage of TB. 11 room rooming house.

Martin R:
Edson F: Large plot going on. Raped in his sleep - - - "They put me to stud". Produces a number of documents to indicate his existence. Birth certificate. Poll tax papers and naturalization papers.

Leonard R.

William H: 66, retired railroad expressman. Never developed any real interest or any resources within himself. Only sustained perfect source of gratification his job: an extremely efficient hard-working ionist.

Charles L
Robert H
Lillian E
Mary B
Arthur B: older looking than 46. Absence of teeth and grossly wrinkled skin.
Minnie L: People on Tv talked crazy talk and seemed mixed up. Newspapers seemed different and foolish. Awful tightness in her chest "like a bear was squeezing her" and she dreamed about things she'd seen on the TV during day. Middle-aged with scraggly hair and a single prominent tooth in upper jaw.

John M.
Mary Ellen J.
Aurora L: Father meat-cutter, husband undertaker.

John M: Machinist. Newton Ball Bearing Co. Engineer New England City Ice Co. Exterminator. Mightmare: grain of sand rested on chest, would increase in size to that of a house: sensation of smothering, being crushed.

Frank S: Tonsils and adenoids: cloth over eyes, ether: Thought he was in rollers of a cottonmill; fought to be free.

"I feel guilty over my 'social malevolences'." Dates onset of illness from reading of The Rebel by Camus. Feels he has significantly hurt emotionally vulnerable people by threatening and distainful looks. In Germany felt desire to hurt or punish German people. Did this by threatening looks at passers-by. During this time felt personality more magnetic and powerful than that of most people.

Staircase: EW case: clerk runs for record, breaks head, internal injuries, dies. Electrician at Christmas: ladder falls in main lobby.

Secretary's Meeting:
Dr. Crawford in Skin? He's dead six or seven years. A patient said she had Dr. Crawford. Bick Avenue. "Oh I had BRECK." Appointment slips.

Smoke in sunlight. Oval table polished. Silver jewelry in Mexico. Portraits in sepia of Civil War vintage doctors. Bookcases with glass doors. Green blinds. Three windows. Red and green curtains. Pink slips: refers: benches and wood chairs. Clock in box of blond wood. Pale green walls. Four light fixtures. Lamp bowls.

Are you going to Amputation? Yellow and blue slips. Room dedicated in 1892. Daily statistics: Coming down without clinic stamp or date. Some aren't coming at all. Some aren't added correctly. Box by opticians window. Clinic, month, year. Blank out date. Stamp sheets ahead.

Red folder records sent through my mistake instead of to Balcony. Bright red square eliminated. Cant have 100% perfect with thousands of records coming through. Hold box records posted in referral book.

Send slip to record room. Some hold indefinately. 15 day treatment. Record room infuriated when you call for a record in hold box.

National Diabetes Week, November 19 & 20. 1% unsuspected diabetes. Booths. So there you are girls.

APPENDIX 15

Journal

1962

THE TYRERS: GEORGE, MARJORIE (50), NICOLA (16)"
First George comes bustling out at National Provincial Bank - - - he is the
manager. "My wife has been meaning to come to see you." Oh tell her to
come any afternoon after three, I say. Much, much later after no wife - - -
"My wife fell downstairs and hurt her leg, that's why she hasn't been up
before this, I didn't want you to think she was being rude." Well I hadn't
thought of it before that; then I did think of it. Almost immediately after 3
one afternoon the front bell rang and a woman - - - narrow, sharp, all in
browns I thought, kerchief, coat, boots, came in. Ted joined me for tea in the
red front room - - - only it wasn't red then yet, still had the old green &
orange rug and the bare wood window seat. Marjorie Tyrer talked. I
couldn't figure her last name. Was it Taylor? Tah-eyrer? Her anecdotes.
Finding rubber poncho or some off bit of value on the roadside & bringing it
to the police station. The moustached town constable saying she should
bring it to her nearest police stating. "This is my nearest." He peering, trying
to guess, then she revealing her identity, he sweeping a seat clean with a
pocket handkerchief - - - "Oh, do come in." Her wry, sarcastic, critical talk.
The Rector came to tea with his wife when he first came to town some 6
years ago. After George saying "Why didn't you tell me?" (he having been
dead silent all through tea). "Tell you what?" "That she was much the
ugliest woman?" George could hardly talk, he thought the Rector's wife so
ugly. Marjorie hadn't mentioned her looks to him, he always called her too
critical. Marjorie Irish, born in Athlone (province? town?). George a Devo-
nian, with 4 brothers & a queer sister named Sylvia - - - his father a man of
consequence. Marjorie's father a bank manager in Ireland.

New Year's Party - - - Saturday night before Sunday New Year's. Drinks. I still pregnant, within 17 days of Nicholas, immense in Chinese blue satin maternity top. A sense of In. Rang at the side door of the bank. Came up into diningroom - - - a tree hung with lights, plastic ribands, Christmas cards. Warmth, people standing round about. I recognized Doctor Webb, his blond, side-look, weak Cornish chin. His dark wife Joan my target. The Tyrer's daughter, 16 year-old Nicola home from Headington, the fashionable private school in Oxford Marjorie liked because of the wonderful parquet floor and curving entrance stair. The private school in Plymouth was all wrong - - - the playing field was miles from the school, and think of the girls catching cold on the drafty bus journey after playing out in the rain! Nicola pretty, with short auburn hair, clear skin, pale, fashionable, baby-faced. A striving to be with it sort. Bad at maths. Good at what? Notion of her going to University giving Ted idea of "saving" or educating her. Inviting her round to sample our books. A fine crowd of festivity and merriment. Marjorie's sister Ruth, a housekeeper in London and humorous grey-haired lady, and Nicola passing miraculously replenished snacks - - - a hump of hollowed bread filled with mustard and stuck with small hot sausages on picks. Pineapple, cheese, creamcheese and prunes, hot pasties. I drank an immense amount of sweet sherry. No lacunas in food or drink. A white-haired Danish architect turned British farmer, talked first to Ted, then, me. We were enchanted with him. I talked to Joan, short, dark, intelligent-seeming, about help, babies, her sister who turned from actress to nurse in London. Marjorie interrupting us, shifting us round. A Welsh mathematician from Dulwich College telling me of his navy days in California, Coos Bay, the girl he let off in a pine forest. When he went to re-find her, found her living in unimaginable squalor in a huge tent with immense family. The friend - - - Dick Wakeford, oddly mechanical pale fellow, who is scientific-farming his 100 acres in Bondleigh. His lively wife Betty (who never makes her beds before noon, Nicola reported to Marjorie, & has washmachine, spindryer, dishwasher, but no fridge!) She's the blonde one, I said later to Marjorie, trying to place people. Marjorie wrinkled her nose: Mouse, I'd say. A curious desperate sense of being locked in among these people, a cream, longing toward London, the big world. Why are we here? Ted & I very excited. Our first social event in North Tawton. Our last, so far. Also met short, dark Jewy looking Mrs. Young whose husband is head of the Devon Water Board - - - the impression she wears green eyeshadow. Came home almost 3 hours later to a pink, desperate Nancy, left alone with no radio or TV or work to do.

Later Nicola came over, very dressed for the occasion with a dark ribbon binding back her short auburn hair, black stockings, dark dress and rich brown-black scarf knit by grandmother. Her obvious bid for Ted's interest. He wanted to give her "Orlando". I groaned and gave her "The Catcher in the Rye". Ted's Biblical need to preach. She dutifully read this: thought Salinger's style "went on too long". Her absolute uncritical sense - - - recommended "Angelique and the Sultan". Ted later wrote her a letter at school analyzing "The Windhover". Her cutely theatrical account of listening to Ted's play (part of it) on the wireless, the romantic little-girl part "a part I'd love to play myself". I felt awfully old, wise, entrenched. But very inclined to pull up my stockings. Breathless over "Winnie the Pooh". I shall be in the future, omnipresent. A young girl's complete flowerlike involvement in self, beautifying, opening to advantage. This is the need I have, in my 30th year - - - to unclutch the sticky loving fingers of babies & treat myself to myself and my husband alone for a bit. To purge myself of sour milk, urinous nappies, bits of lint and the loving slovenliness of motherhood.

My tea at Tyrers. My stiffness with George vanishing. He came up from the bank for tea. I had wanted to talk & gossip with Marjorie & Nicola. Nicola in Bondleigh at Wakefords. While George was out, I talked with Marjorie about childbirth. She hadn't wanted children. Married George late. He wanted children. Went to war. Nicola "unexpected". Marjorie had her in Ireland. Had a nurse. Never woke at night. Fed her on bottle on return to England. During courtship George deluged her with cookbooks. "Have you read the one I gave you last week yet?" Her dislike of babies, cooking, housewifery. What I wondered did she like? She plays a lot of golf, loved living in London. They have accounts at Harrod's, Fortnum's. Couldn't tell what their livingroom had in it. Vague impression of stuffed comfortable sofa and wing chairs. A dun beige quality brooding over everything. I still don't know. Reproductions of an oriental. Pot ducks flying up wall. Probably very expensive. Must catalogue rugs, upholstery, next time. Talked of choosing private schools. Their tour for Nicola. Didn't want to turn out a queer person like George's sister Sylvia - - - she, if she came into the room, wouldn't say a word to me, had no social graces. A sense of silence about her - - - repressed horrors. I fascinated. She had stood behind Marjorie in a bus queue during the war with a strange man. Marjorie myopic, wondered if it was Sylvia? "Is that you, Sylvia?" Why yes, Marjorie, I was wondering when you'd notice me. The strange man her husband. One of George's brothers,

Marjorie told me later, committed suicide. In bad health, though young. Marjorie afraid of George doing same - - - he has had two heart attacks, lives under the shadow. Won't drive far. Gets giddy, depressed in bad weather.

Since - - - George has come over a great deal. His tender, nervous concern for Frieda, very sweet & genuine. "She'll fall." Waiting for her to climb down from windowseat. My initial awe melting. He calls for Marjorie - - - got Ted onto good radio just in time for play-broadcast of The Wound. George is a Hi-fi fan. His collection of records. Subscribes to The Gramophone. Our local electrician an expert. Everything, it turns out, thrives in North Tawton. We have a great clambering ariel. George's bright red cheeks. Marjorie brought out Mrs. VonHombeck's woven skirts and stoles - - - handsome, one rich red with pale silver-beige embroidery. Marjorie's stories of sharp retorts to the Rector (her refusal to volunteer to mind a local Old People's recreation room), to a Plymouth landlady who peered out the door every time someone came in ("I don't think a robber would be interested in anything of yours.") and so on.

Both came over last week after days in London. Got seats at "Beyond the Fringe" by way of Ruth's employer who is in ITV - - - raved over Jonathan Miller. Marjorie's story of getting the Right spring coat for 9 guineas. A drama. Their pub in Mayfair (or Kensington?) that has the thinnest of rare roast beef. They stay at the Ivanhoe. Nicola away at schools since very young. Her emergency appendectomy - - - Marjorie did not visit her (George had been ill). Took her oddly long legged bear Algy, a white-grey creature dressed in period suit I saw at Marjorie's. Lost Algy in hospital. Eventually he returned, but missing one arm. Even at 16 took Algy out of hotel during fire alarm. Have invited the lot of 3 to dinner this Sunday.

1962 Feb. 22: Knocked, or rather rang, the Tyrers bell after hearing George had a mild heart attack & the Tyrers wouldn't be coming to dinner. Met by Marjorie, very brisk and handsome - - - nursing seems to bring a fine self out. Brown pleasantly-waved hair, stockings, brown gracefully heeled but sensible shoes, a brown cashmere cardigan over a yellow blouse and brooch. I lingered in the pink and blue gleaming kitchen while she put tea things on a tray. George was in bed. He was to eat nothing but chicken and fish. We went into the parlor, with its big bay over the Square and the white and red of Bloggs garage. The sun poured in. I dragged myself to look round and put colors into words. Yes it was all brown and cream.

Shiney cream-colored wallpaper with a minute white embossed pattern. Brown, medium brown, window curtains. Two chairs in windowbay. A cream radiator under window, with newspaper on it. A great dull blue-eyed television set. The walls crammed with awful reproductions of Devon hills, a country gate, and a big reproduction of an Indonesian girl in muted tans, silvergreys and lilacs I thought looked familiar. George had bought it in London, & that was where I remembered it from. The trouble about my noticing had been that there was so much. The livingroom suite in a brown tone, with a pattern of dull yellow and pink flowers, probably roses. A green - - - unpleasant verdigris green rug with flowers patterned over it. And a bookcase from which the complete Rudyard Kipling leapt out, and all sorts of other dull old books in dated bindings, with the air of a second hand shop. A table with curios laid out, from Marjorie's mother - - - a Duke of Wellington conserve bowl, a French bud vase of glass, embossed with silver filigree, a smashed and mended oriental vase, all pink cherry blossom and green vines. And an incredible pottery alligator, upright, with green paws holding a purse, in a sunbonnet and long skirt, with brown glass eyes! Awful, but compelling. A primitive drollery. Then the mantel - - - tiny china children or angels on candlesticks, a minute Crown Derby teacup and saucer, lots of big Oriental pitchers. I had more biscuits & lots of tea. We talked of cooking (M. was making G. sweetbreads for supper; the family can't stand fat; M. had a pork casserole dish she always serves for company), the butcher (M's complaints about his fillet steak, her bringing back of cuts not tender or thick enough), banking (M's description of it as a competitive business - - - she has no entertaining because there is no other bank in town; the abusiveness of some customers; a bank manager has to know all sorts of intimate details to give loans etc.; she forgot to sign a cheque to the butcher). My very pleasant sense of warmth, hot tea, and being neatly dressed for a change. George called out from the bedroom to give me some sherry. I asked the name of the sherry it was so good: Harvey's Bristol Milk. And how to make tea, complaining my tea was so bad. Six o'clock struck twice, the church clock, and then the Square clock. I poked my head in at George - - - he very dear, tousled grey hair, red cheeks, propped up on pillows, like a young boy. Felt refreshed, enlivened, renewed. Very at home.

Feb.24: N. came for tea. I managed a girdle & stockings & heels and felt a new person. Set up the table in the playroom, with the westering sun, instead of the cold, darkening back kitchen. She in a charcoal gray cashmere twin-set, dark skirt, stockings, flats with gold buckles, furry dark peajacket, newly from hairdressers. A hard, catty, snippety nature. I sat & talked with her for a while. She talked completely of herself - - - what she said to Head-mistress, how she got her hair done, how she loved Bridget Bardot, how she wanted to reduce to have a nice shape (What's wrong with your shape, says Ted). Called Ted down. She talked on & on. The Seven Samurai "bored her". It was Ted's favorite film, but it bored him too. She will of course take anything from him & who doesn't love to have bright young youth listen to pontificatings. "Everybody is always saying I'm bumptious." The product of finishing school: finished. I took her up to see the baby - - - she couldn't care less, perfectly natural. Was dying to peer into other rooms with shut doors and upstairs - - - remembered house vaguely from Arundel's time. Talk of prefects privileges to shop in Oxford, her white mac & blue headscarf, told again how she listened to Ted's radio program, how an English teacher was a fan of his. Terribly critical of Lady Arundel, the midwife's poor son who "blushes whenever he meets her." Small wonder.

Sunday: Feb.24: I should have known it. My instincts were right. At 10:30 the doorbell rang. I should have answered it. I was in my slippers, without makeup, my hair down on all sides when Nicola came in. "I'm not too early?" Oh no, said Ted. He made her a cup of tea and she stood in the kitchen while I finished my coffee and Frieda her bacon. I had made the mistake of saying I'd be interested in seeing her poetry anthology at school. Ted & I ridiculed it gently. I kept wanting to get to work. Furious that Ted had invited anyone in. The morning gone, 11:30 by the time I gave her her book back and said I didn't think I needed to keep it - - - which would have involved in dropping it round before 10 tomorrow. Now I have a respite till April 4th in which I may get started on my book. She is shrewd, pushing, absolutely shameless. I shall ask Marjorie when the moment arrives to con-fine visits to afternoons. I <u>must</u> have my mornings in peace. Her incredible angling last night to get driven to the movies in Exeter (I want to see "Fanny", how should I get there?) It did not occur to Ted to offer to drive her; he suggested a taxi. I mentioned how we despised Maurice Chevalier, & how Ted in particular disliked musicals. On the assumption that I am as fascinating as T., I shall be ominipotent - - - chauffeur, entertainer, hostess, if the occasion arises. A charming ignorance as to any difference between us. Her models: Bridgette Bardot & Lolita. Telling.

Friday: March 2: Drawn in spite of myself to ring the Tyrers bell, having been to the bank at 5 minutes to 3 with two American checks and imagined the boys would be horrorstruck at having extra work before closing time. Then thought the T's might think it a snub if I went to town without Frieda & didn't ask how George was. These dim things in back of it. I rang the bell & Marjorie popped to the door in her brown cashmere, very neat and fine. Went up, feeling ponderous & clumpy in my suede jacket <u>and</u> big green cord coat. "I like your coat," Marjorie said, in a way that made me feel the opposite behind her words. We sat in the sunfilled front room. I could see, suddenly, that the wallpaper was a glossy embossed cream, and the ceiling an shiny embossed white, very newish. "I hope Nicola didn't bother you." I saw immediately that Nicola had retailed the whole of her two visits in a fashion which escapes me, because I consider our life so natural, but which I can construct from her usual critical malices ("Lady Arundell never looked smart when she came into North Tawton"). Talked of the wallpaper - - - they had had the Bank House redecorated at the expense of the bank when they came: a new kitchen and bath, as the former man had been a bachelor with an old mother who had someone do for her. The bank allowed 15s. for the parlor, 12/6 for the bedroom and 7/6 for the spareroom. "Well, if <u>that's</u> all they feel the Manager deserves." This is George's first managership. (Late?) Then a story about a darling boy in the Navy they knew who ended up marrying a terribly drab American girl with stringy hair to her shoulders. Why? She must have had money. <u>He</u> didn't have money. Two terribly drab children. I read this as a sort of allegory - - - the usual infuriating assumption American girls have lots and lots of money. Felt terribly sorry for this poor girl. Then the bell, just as Marjorie asked me with no feeling, and perfunctorily, to stay for tea. Betty Wakeford. She came bounding up in a suede jacket with glasses, a long Jewy nose and open grin, and fresh crimped high-fronted hairdo (done in Winkleigh that morning). "So sorry I didn't come to tea at your place yesterday." She had a pile of new books for Marjorie. A sense of their close relation. They talked of the Hunt Ball to be held in the Town Hall that night. Betty & Dick were going; and Hugh and Joan Webb; and the Chemist, Mr. Holcombe, and his wife. "Bulgy". Why? When strapless gowns came in she wore one and bulged all over it; Marjorie's eyes glinted cattily. Later it occurred to me that "Bulgy", whom I imagined as a drab fat, was probably the voluptuous blonde I've seen off & on in the Chemists: a good excuse for cattiness. Betty would "Twist", she'd seen how on the telly. I had the strong intuition Marjorie had peered into our life all she needed to make a judgment, had judged, and now our relation would be quite formal. Mine certainly will be. N. shall visit if she visits, not live here as she might. I later sobbed - - - for the poor heard-of

American girl, and for the flat malice of people I keep dreaming into friends.

Noticed, for the first time, a set of lustre jugs on top of M's sideboard. A raw copper lustre. With pink highlights, and a blue enameled band round the middle on which, badly-painted fruits and flowers. What fruits, what flowers? Next time must see. Asked how George was, but M. really said nothing. Turned out Betty had seen him in the morning ("I hope I didn't tire him out".) A sly sense of being just by that much shut out.

Friday: March 9: Met M. in Boyd's. "Do come up just for two minutes." I had Frieda in her soiled pale blue snowsuit jacket. A completely different atmosphere. Me? She? Carried Frieda up the steep steps. The wall paper in the lower half of the hall (or rather on the lower half of the hall wall up and downstairs) a pleasant pattern of a few wheat stalks in red, brown & black on white. Ruth, down from London, in a rust-colored shantung blouse, to the left of the fire, George, with his iron grey hair down in front looking handsome and raffish, with a silk, red handkerchief looped to counterfeit a bloom in his buttonhole. Very hot and snug. I had a glass of Bristol milk. Frieda stared. They brought out a straight child's wood chair with a brown-upholstered seat, and two fine antique teddybears - - - one huge, with a naive primitive expression, big glass eyes and fur that had been pale lavender, worn now to smoky grey, and a little purple and black bear. Frieda smiled. M. said Mr. Fursman was an admirer of her ("Have you seen her smile") Frieda pushed the little bear through the chair back and onto the floor. Threw down the big bear. Laughed charmingly. "Nicola is trying to imitate Ted" - - - a letter from N. with a "poem" brought out, about her trying to study and her brain being vacant.

Last, time, how Marjorie's glasses kept reflecting the light, in glittering oblongs, into my eyes. She was facing the bright bay window, and I could not look at her mouth, or an ear, but forced myself to try to pierce the glancing shields of light to the eyes behind them. Got a headache, continually deflected.

R. had seen a huge white owl in a toyshop in Gloucester road. Her grey tight hair. An Agatha Christie housefrau. We talked of the fine old toys. M. told of going to a shop down a row of teddybears with a friend. "Now that's the only one with the right expression." The saleslady, overhearing, delighted:

"That's just what I said when I was unpacking them - - - that's the only one with the right expression."

April 18: There have been many visits, back & forth. Now there is the astounding & relieving fact of imminent departure. George had a heart attack. He is being retired from the bank. They are moving to Richmond, Surrey, bag, baggage. And Nicola. Nicola is home from school on a month's easter holiday. She came yesterday afternoon. I was on the toilet on the landing in a tangle of my workman's overalls. Heard the professionally husky voice: Anybody home? Ted went down. I hauled myself together & flew down. She wore a dark peajacket, green blouse & gold heart locket. Very pale pink lips & white complexion. Auburn hair. Can I take Frieda for a walk? I stared, smiled, in my pleasant obtuse way which I so enjoy now that I am a scatty mother of almost 30. Walk? Walk? Isn't it the right time, she asked. I thought: she has been put up to it. O any day but today, I said. Frieda, as it happens, has been bitten by a crow. She is very upset. I have just been trying to get her to go to sleep. Nicola admitted that the weather - - - suddenly cold, grey & overcast - - - was not very good. I blithered on about the crow bite - - - how Ted had introduced Frieda to this big black baby crow in spite of my motherly forebodings, & how the crow had, indeed, snapped at her & drawn blood. I knew Frieda was pottering around upstairs in her bare bottom. Ted, very harrassed, went up to do his Baskin article[n] & put her away. He said later she had shat on the floor in the interval. I held & arranged the baby, nosing him idly like a bunch of white flowers. Saw George at the gate. Nicola was asking me what I was going to do that afternoon: could she help. I saw Marjorie more & more clearly behind this. O I am going to mow the lawn, I said vaguely. I don't quite see how help, there's only the one mower. I welcomed George. He looked very ruddy & tyrolean in a green felt hat, walking tweeds & a cane. We talked about the crow. I think he had come to see how Nicola was doing. She was very catty about her 80 year old grandmother whom she was to visit with her father the next day, he having asked for a bunch of daffodils to take. The old woman always talked business (so boring), thought she was older than she was and should therefore be respected, couldn't cook any more & insisted on serving terrible pastries. I felt very sorry for the old woman. George had never seen the property. So I led the two through the tennis court up onto the back hill of daffodils. Nicola was holding Nicholas, pale & blinking in his white bonnet & knitted blanket. She had no "feeling" for him as a baby, a person. She was doing something, learning to do something, like making a salmon kedgeree. She grew misty-eyed, even wet-eyed. Now she was going to miss North Tawton. O Nicola, I jokingly said, I thought you were very eager to leave this dull town. O no, not now, that it came to the point. George said, somehow deftly fitting it in, that maybe now we would "ask Nicola down." I was dumbfounded, but only smiled obtusely. What in God's name, I thought, would she find of interest in staying with us. Then of course, it came: a husband. Or at least an entry ticket into this literary London society. Ted had mentioned John Wain[n] was coming down & they'd seen him on television. Then that Marvin Kane[n] was down, doing a recording of me for the BBC. So Marjorie emerged behind Nicola's sudden helpfulness (very clever, too) and advance nostalgia for the town she couldn't till this moment, stand. Nicola left with George, a little defeated. The weather closed in and became very mean and cold. I got Frieda out, and the lawnmower.

Thurs. Apr.19: Nicola tripped in, in heels and a white silk scarf with large and fashionable black polka dots, to collect the large bunch of 40 daffodils I had arranged to give george for the trip to the grandmother. I asked if Marjorie would be home that afternoon. Yes. I felt called upon to do something. Nicola had remarked loudly and somehow meaningfully that she only had two more weeks in North Tawton. It occurred to me I was somehow intended to do something. Dinner, as I had once thought, seemed out of the question for 6, with Ted's family coming. So I stopped, after my shopping, to ask the three ladies, Ruth, Marjorie and Nicola, to tea on Saturday. I rang. Marjorie knocked from the upstairs bay window over the square. She was offish and a bit scatty. As if some thing had not come to pass. Her first remark was about trying to fit the furniture into the rooms of the new flat, hopelessly. I thought that if they had cut the price of their imitation old-fashioned Welsh dresser, refectory table & unsatisfactory wheelback chairs by two thirds, from the preposterous £150, we might have relieved her of some of her baggage. I sat for a minute in the sunny room, noticing the huge, ugly floorlamps, one of giant size, and both with frightful shades, frightful in pattern and color too. Almost immediately the bell rang. It was a Mr. Bateman, from Sampford Courtenay with an aged terrier named Tim, whose muzzle was grey (he was 12 years old) and who shook upsettingly, as if with palsy. Mr. Bateman was very stiff & dapper. A skyey blue chiffon neckerchief, cinnamon-colored check tweeds. We spoke perfunctorily of animals, after my crow account: of mynah birds, talking crows, & the like. I rose to leave just as Ruth melted into the room, stooped a bit effacingly, her grey hair tightly crimped from the hairdresser's in Exeter. Marjorie accompanied me downstairs. I made much of the coming arrival of Ted's relatives & the immense work they would involve.

Recollections: Ruth came to tea alone. Talk almost solely of her very fat girlhood in Athlone, and suspicious advances by monks and gay priests. Chucking her under the chin, asking to accompany her to horseraces, playing tennis etcetera. My reply, almost continually: I didn't know priests would do that. My, my. The incredible fixed reminiscences of a spinster. Her looking out at German bombers, realizing she was in a nightgown, & retreating in blushes from the window, and the ring of young men leaning from neighboring windows. Then the scone & Devon cream tea for Frieda & me at Tyrers: Frieda glowing & beautiful & good at table, everybody, Ruth especially, playing with her. She seizing on a few fuzzy animals that were conspicuously put out. Of a koala bear, Nicola said, it was bumpy & stiff. Marjorie chided: O you mustn't say that of something you are trying to sell. The odd ambiguity - - - they have given us large old bears, old baby pillowslips by the half dozen; then they bring out books at a shilling each, a fusty urine-yellow doll's tea-set. Their noses sharpen: that's twenty-five bob.

Recollections: My visit to Marjorie, in bed, with bronchitis. She grey & quenched. I brought back the christening gown of limerick lace from her grandmother's wedding dress she had loaned me, & showed her a little picture of Nicholas in the gown. I left Frieda in the livingroom with Ruth Pearson. Marjorie was drinking lemonade. She had that queer camouflaged look, of blending into obsequious grey-brown surroundings obsequiously and grey-brownly, so that I would be at an utter loss to describe the furnishings of the room, except to say my impression was of immense and depressed wardrobes, towering. George joined us. They looked at each other. Shall we tell Sylvia our news? I surmised it. Good or bad? Both, George had been "retired". They were leaving in 6 weeks for a flat that had miraculously & independently turned up in Richmond. I felt uncomfortably like bursting out laughing. I managed tears. My worries of N's increasing limpetlike cling in the next 3 years disappeared. I could be magnanimous.

Almost immediately, they gave me a price list of things they were going to sell. I was astounded. They were letting us have the favor of "first choice". The prices were very high. Trust a banker, I thought. He must think my grant installments are a life legacy. My first thought: what in God's name would I want of their stuff. There turned out to be, startlingly, an antique oak dropleaf table I coveted for Ted. We bought it for £25, which I felt wiped out any obligations to buy anything else. But bought also a handsome round, brass tray-table & a coal scuttled in brass like a shining embossed helmet, and a mirror. The brass & the table complete our livingroom. The table is a heavenly find. Then they loaded Frieda with old toys Nicola did not want. Showed others that were for sale. I smiled, admired, but said no more about them.

Ted went to tea after the scone & Devon cream tea. Came home at 7. After the harrowing visit of the Roses, those ghastly two girls. I very tired & faint, heard two voices. Flew down with the baby & materialized in the front door. Nicola & Ted standing at opposite sides of the path under the bare laburnum like kids back from the date, she posed & coy. I came out, sniffing the baby like a restorative. I just brought back some of daddy's records, she said. May I come over Friday and listen to your German linguaphone records? I have a better idea, I said, and rushed in and took out the records & booklet & thrust them into her hands. "This way you can study them to your heart's content all the rest of your vacation." She had asked Ted if the secretary in his "Secretary" poem was a real person. So hopes begin. For some time I seriously considered smashing our old & ridiculous box victrola with an axe. Then this need passed, & I grew a little wiser.

April 21: I had invited the three ladies to tea in George's absence, over Easter, visiting his mother: Ruth, Marjorie, Nicola. Only Marjorie & Nicola came. Ruth had a heavy cold & was sorry. Hilda and Vicky" had arrived earlier that morning, surprisingly, and in the heavy rain had helped me clean house. I had baked a big yellow sponge cake. We all sat in the livingroom for a bit, Nicola on the window seat talking to me, and Marjorie almost, but not quite, ignoring Hilda & Vicky. Obviously it was a shock to the Tyrers not to be our only & honored guests. Their self-centredness came out with a violence. Nicola told of the vacuum cleaner episode that morning: Mrs. Crocker had been cleaning under her bed when the vac stopped. They extracted a hairpin, but it still wouldn't go. They sent it to the Hockings for mending. The Hocking boy Roger came back with the machine and a pair of Nicola's black bikini pants, underpants, I presume, which had been extracted from it. Her idols: Brigitte Bardot and Lolita. The sun filled the playroom over tea. Hilda & Vicky & Marjorie & Nicola did not mix. I felt very partisan for the former, Marjorie left at quarter to six. Nicola putting on her stylish white makintosh. Marjorie had worn the usual buff or dun colored cashmere sweater with a pleasant buff & black-squared skirt. Nicola in a navyblue sweater. Her very thick legs.

April 24: A new & fearsome strategy on the Tyrers part. Nicola called up while we were embroiled with the curious blond Swedish lady journalist to ask if she could come and "read in our garden". I was aghast. It is one thing to ask to come around for a cup of tea, but to ask to come and lead a private life in our garden as if it were a public park is appalling. I was so fuming at the Swedish girl after Hilda & Vicky that I had a marvelous time saying how we had more company and were all sprawled out in the garden, so No. It was just as Ted said - - - if we get to know people too well here they will be using our garden as a place to come get a pleasant stroll & free tea. I had an intuitive fear the lot of them will come today & ask if they can have free run of the place as they are just about to leave & it "surely couldn't inconvenience us for two weeks." Later, Marjorie called. She wanted to tell Nicola to come home. Nicola is not with us, I said. Oh. This gave a new insight. Marjorie & Nicola had arranged, before Marjorie "took her nap" (as Nicola said she was doing when she phoned) that Nicola should come to our garden & read, and anticipated no refusal. I had a suspicion that Nicola had told her mother we wouldn't "let her come" in a rage & Marjorie had said: I'll settle them, I'll call & pretend I think you're there & get to the bottom of this. This is what I suspicioned. In any case, I had a beautiful chance to talk on about our fresh set of guests & Marjorie was forced to commiserate on my busyness. Now I can add the excuse of our having a lot of back work to do. To give the illusion of sweet loving charm while refusing. A marvelous art I must develop.

Anyhow, I vaguely said Nicola <u>had</u> called about coming, but we had company again (What, <u>still</u>!) and she had said something about going over to the Bennett's. She had actually said she would read in the Bennetts field. This new tack I think was accelerated by Ted's picture & the rave writeup by Toynbee in this Sunday's <u>Observer</u>.

May 1: Nicola came over to say goodbye, stocky & white & near to tears in a school blazer. She had been yelled at by her mother, about the loss of a button & more or less driven out. Ted sat out a bit, talking, while I cut the long grass of the garden border with scissors. Then Ted went in to his study, saying: Goodbye, be seeing you. Very huffily Nicola said: I don't know what you mean, I'm going back to school tomorrow, as if she expected us to extend some concrete invitation to back up the words. It's a manner of speaking, I said gently; we don't like to say goodbye. She sat with me, leafing through a copy of Vogue she had brought & giving me a little monologue on each page, talked of "almond"-toed shoes, and the new round toe (I said I thought it was the old round toe) and how she had bought a blue beret in Exeter, and how wonderful Brigitte Bardot was, she had started so many styles. The clock struck six, and she left. Ted says he saw them all exiting in best clothes from the Bank House the next morning, to accompany Nicola partway back to school & go on to Weston-super-Mer themselves for a few days.

May 6: Saw George coming up the back way. Took him into the front room, where he jounced Frieda on his lap (Hold daddy, she cried, wriggling to get down and over to Ted) and passed the time of day. Very natty in grey suit, red silk scarf in pocket and red tie, as if a leashed flamboyance could now show itself since he was free of Bank rules & respectability. He seemed lessened, deposed, slightly abashed by all his leisure.

May 7: The final farewell: dinner with Marjorie and Ruth at Burton Hall. I was feeling awful, with this crabby bacterial infection which made me want to rush out in agony to pee every few minutes, & felt I might dash home any minute. Marjorie all dolled up, new hairdo, new vibrant self full of stories about self, cutting Ruth off rudely every time she opened her mouth: obviously trying on a charming new nature in preparation for Richmond. Ruth's stammer bad. An indifferent dinner of steak & custard-fruit pudding. Marjorie in grey-and-white striped spring suit and lustre beads. Sat in lounge with old deaf woman. New bank manager had been at supper, but M. said not a word. Story of selling their Ireland house, the flautist in the other part, the stain on the mantel, the girl lost her engagement ring there, but later found it in her pocket. We left at 9 with a feeling of immense freedom. North Tawton, with the T's departure, an easier much more restful place.

THE MIDWIFE: WINIFRED DAVIES.
First met in Doctoer Webb's office last fall at my first checkup. A short, rotundish but not at all fat, capable grey-haired woman with a wise, moral face, in a blue uniform under a round-brimmed blue hat. I felt she would judge, kindly, but without great mercy. Her fine opportunities to visit me and observe the habits and domestic setup of the new arrivals. Very aware

that our being undefined "artists", with no provable or ostensible or obvious work, plus me being an American (the stereotype of pampered wealth), would prejudice a staid English countrywoman against me. Her first judgment in my favor came the first day in the office, when I told her I nursed the baby, Frieda, for 10 months and that Ted was my "home-help". There was some hope for us!

Nurse D. is by some odd linking I have yet to discover, the niece of Mrs. Hamilton. They are two pillars. They must know everything, or almost everything. Nurse D.'s visits invariably came when I most intuitively suspected them simply because I had been lax about house-work to get to my study. Nothing Ted could say could stop her - - - she would forge up the stairs, he preceding desperately to warn me, and I would see her smiling white head over his shoulder at the study door. I would be in my pink fluffy bathrobe (over my layers of maternity clothes, for warmth), and she would say "artist's outfit", go into the bedroom, find the bed unmade, and I would have hastily thrown a newspaper over the pink plastic pot of violently yellow urine I had not bothered to empty, on the principle that all housework wait till after noon. She obviously relished seeing how far and of what sort our house-decorating was - - - observed our bedroom Indian rug was "very like her own" (the ultimate approval). One morning she seemed all twinkly with news, could hardly wait to say "My son's schoolfriend is a fan of your husband's". By some incredible coincidence, Nurse D's only son, Garnett (a family name in the North) had a schoolfriend at the Merchant Tailor (Taylor?) School in London who had written Ted about his book and received an answer postmarked "North Tawton", whereupon he asked Garnett if he knew a Ted Hughes. We were "placed". I felt very pleased.

Nurse D.'s husband is the mystery. Was he killed in the war? Garnett is roughly 19, hers was a "war marriage". She has had to bring up the boy on her own. He was not very bright (news courtesy of Marjorie T.) and she had difficulty getting him in a good school. She raises Pekinese pedigree pups. Had one she doted on. She killed it by accidentally stepping on it. It used to go everywhere with her. A horrible story. As the baby approached in time, Nurse D.'s manner grew sweeter, gentler, more amiable. I felt very glad she would be my midwife, and lucky the baby came not on her day-off, and just before she took a "holiday" to tend her sick father at a hotel in South Tawton (a man over 80, with two pneumonia attacks, living with his wife while they had a house built).

Jan.17: The day of Nicholas' birth I woke with niggling cramps in the morning. Called Nurse D. as she had asked, but apologetically - - - the cramps seemed a small thing. She appeared early, made an X on my mountainous stomach in the place where she heard the baby's heart, said she would be home all afternoon. I felt very calm and excited and eager, but surprised the rhythm of the birth and the order of things was so different from my time with Frieda, when the waters woke me by breaking spectacularly at 1 a.m. April 1st and the labor pains were every 5 minutes within an hour, and the baby born at 5:45 at sunup. 4 hours and 45 minutes all told. All day the cramps kept up every half hour or so, fading and returning. I sat on a stool in a blank, limbo-mood, impatient for the real thing to begin. Did some baking. Then, the moment Frieda was in bed, the cramps started in earnest. I waited for about 2 hours till the rhythm was established and the pains really strong enough for me to think I wanted gas & the nurse. She had told me to call "as soon as you feel: I wish Nurse Davies were here".

Nurse D. arrive about 9 p.m. I heard her little blue car drive into the court, and Ted helped her carry up all the heavy equipment. Immediately she set up the gas cylinder on a chair by my bed - - - a black suitcase-like box with a red cylinder of gas & air set in it, and a tube and mask which she showed me how to use by pressing my index finger in a hole and breathing when the pains came. She put on a white apron and a white head-scarf and sat on the right of the bed, and Ted on the left, and I held the mask, and we started in to gossip. It was wonderfully pleasant. Each time a pain came I breathed into the mask, listening to them talk, Nurse. D. holding my hand till the pain was over. The room was warm, the red-lit Pifco purring, the night still and cold, the pink & white checked curtains drawn against it. I felt Nurse. D. liked us both, and I felt perfectly delighted with her. Instead of the mindless crawling about and beating my head against the wall as with the worst cramps with Frieda, I felt perfectly in possession of myself, able to do something for myself. The cramps surprised me, they were very strong and kept on and on.

Nurse D. came from Lancashire (I think, not Yorkshire), had a wonderful big family (7?), and her mother had lots of help. She had a fine childhood, she said, and a nanny. I forget most of the picture she painted now, alas. She has brothers and sisters scattered about - - - a brother who was headmaster of a wellknown boys' public school here and who is now head of one in Australia; a sister, I think, in Canada. She has about 10 dogs, 3 of which are allowed to take turns coming into the house. She gardens. She has an acre or two and wants to raise geese, then sell the geese & buy sheep, then sell the sheep & buy a cow.

The time went on, the cramps went on. She advised us about a man to mow the long grass-field. We talked of our hopes of cultivating the gardens and lawns at Court Green. Then she asked if I was ready to push. I wanted to be. But I wasnt. Finally, she looked and said I could, if I felt like it. I started to push, putting down the mask which I didn't feel to need now I could get to work. My stomach mountained huge ahead of me, and, superstitiously, I shut my eyes, so I would feel and see from the inside - - - a horror of seeing the baby before Ted told me it was normal. I pushed. "My you are a good pusher, the best pusher I've seen." I felt very proud. But after a while the nurse looked and told me I had better stop pushing for a bit - - - the baby's head had not descended far enough, the waters had not broken. I was dimly eager for the waters to break, grew worried as to why they had not, imagined the baby drowning up there. The minute I stopped pushing, the pains made themselves felt, awful, utterly twisting. At the same moment, I was aware that I seemed to be breathing only air in the mask, which I had taken up. The cylinder of gas had run out. There was no more. No more to be sent for, either, as the next day, Thursday, was the day Nurse.D. collected her next allotment. I felt very upset at this. Ted & Nurse D. held my feet. Then I lost sense of time. Nurse D. told Ted to call Dr. Webb and tell him to come, the waters had not broken, he would give me a shot. I had a tearing pain in my left side that dwarfed the labor pains. Told them, in a dazed slow voice utterly possessed by the pain and the sight, glimpsed between lids opened for a split second, of my still frighteningly huge stomach which did not seem to have altered during all the hours. Nurse D. looked very serious. Her face bent over me. Where? I knew she was worried. Ted called the Doctor. I felt Nurse D. do something, I think she broke the membrane herself. There was a great gush: Oh, oh, oh, I heard myself say, as the awful pressure released itself and water came out and wet my back. Earlier she had got 2 ounces of urine out of me, after I first complained of the pain. I felt a huge black circular weight, like the end of a cannon or crowbar, pressing forward between my legs. I had my eyes squeezed shut and felt this black force blotting out my brain and utterly possessing me. A horrible fear it would split me and burst through me, leaving me in bloody shreds, but I could not help myself, it was too big for me. "It's too big, too big," I heard myself say. "Breath easily, as if you were going to sleep," the nurse said. In a kind of vengeance, I dug my nails in her hand, as if this would save the terrible thing from tearing through me. I tried to breathe and not push, or let the thing push. But it did not diminish its pressure or go away.

Nurse D. gently unloosed my fingers. The black force grew imperceptibly. I felt panic-stricken - - - I had nothing to do with it, It controlled me. "I can't help it," I cried, or whispered, and then in three great bursts, the black thing hurtled itself out of me, one, two, three, dragging three shrieks after it: Oh, Oh, Oh. A great wall of water seemed to come with it. "Here he is!" I heard Ted say. It was over. I felt the great weight gone in a moment. I felt thin, like air, as if I would float away, and perfectly awake. I lifted my head and looked up. "Did he tear me to bits?" I felt I must be ripped and bloody from all that power breaking out of me. "Not a scratch," said Nurse D. I couldn't believe it. I lifted my head and saw my first son, Nicholas Farrar Hughes, blue and glistening on the bed a foot from me, in a pool of wet, with a cross, black frown and oddly low, angry brow, looking up at me, frown-wrinkles between his eyes and his blue scrotum and penis large and blue, as if carved on a totem. Ted was pulling back the wet sheets and Nurse D. mopping up the great amounts of water that had come with him.

Then the nurse wrapped the baby up and put him in my arms. Doctor Webb arrived. It had happened at 5 minutes to midnight. The clock struck 12. The baby squirmed and cried, warm in the crook of my arm. Doctor Webb put his fingers digging into my stomach and told me to cough. The afterbirth flew out into a pyrex bowl, which crimsoned with blood. It was whole. We had a son. I felt no surge of love. I wasn't sure I liked him. His head bothered me, the low brow. Later Doctor Webb told me his forehead had probably caught or crowned on my pelvic bone and kept him from coming. The baby weighed 9 pounds 11 ounces - - - that was why he had been so long. Frieda was only 7 pounds 4 ounces. I felt immensely proud. The nurse liked him. She tidied up after the Doctor left, changing the bed, piling up the dirty linen, sorting out the bloody things to be soaked in cold water and salt in the tub. Everything was beautiful and neat and calm. The baby washed and dressed in his carrycot, so silent I had Ted get up and make sure he was breathing. The nurse said goodnight. It felt like Christmas Eve, full of rightness & promise.

Jan.18: Nurse D appeared. We were touseled, half asleep. I had got up and washed and put on lipstick. I felt wonderful. She thought I had put on "war paint" before washing. I felt very proud of Nicholas, and fond. It had taken a night to be sure I liked him - - - his head shaped up beautifully - - - the skull plates had overlapped to get him through the boney door, and filled out, a handsome male head with a back brain-shelf. Dark, black-blue eyes, a furze of hair like a crewcut. The nurse did not completely bathe him - - - it was too cold. She washed him. Frieda was introduced to the "boy baby". She squirmed like a curious, agitated little animal. Nurse D's voice seemed to hypnotize her into obedience. She held the pins for the nurse, sat on the bed & held the baby with great pride. Then the nurse sat the baby in one arm and Frieda in the other. "Mother's two babies," she said. I felt her wisdom, her wonderful calm managing. That was the last day she came, & I missed her immensely. A 10 day misery of my milk waiting a week, the baby starving & crying all night, culminating in two nights of 103° milk fever followed, with me at war with the two substitute midwives & Doctor Webb. Then all readjusted, smoothed. The milk came flowing; penicillin cured my fever. Nurse D. returned to stretch the baby's foreskin - - - which has been a trauma for me, with Doctor Webb making "a surgical operation" of it, the baby howling and bleeding & me, wet with fever, almost fainting with tears on the chair, the nurse and doctor screening the baby from me with their bodies. Nurse D's return, hair freshly curled, fresh after her two weeks vigil over her sick father (sent to hospital the day before), smoothed things back to normal. Ended the grim parenthesis. Chairs and tables took their places, served once more.

May 16: Our second entering wedge. Is it that Mrs. D. disliked the Tyrers & waited till they were gone? At any rate, she invited us to tea to meet a Mrs. Macnamara on her own day off. We climbed the steep hill off the main street opposite the secondary modern school to where Mrs. D's new house sat spanking white overlooking the meadows that greenly undulated toward the purple domes of Dartmoor. A flashy blue car parked outside next to the nurse's discreet pale one. Her house all white walls, full of light, big windows overlooking a plateau of close-cropped green lawn and a rather bald display of flowers - - - heather, tulips, anemones. A great many Pekinese dogs yapping like fur mice from a wire enclosure. Mrs. Macnamara a handsome white-haired woman (descended from Irish farmers), with red lipstick and a feminine blue-figured blouse and silvery suit. Exuded wealth, wellbeing. Had come round originally to buy a Pekinese. Lived at Cadbury House beyond Crediton. Her husband, Mrs. D. said, was something in ITV, and lived in a flat in London till he was to retire, for Mrs. Macnamara couldn't bear going back to London. She had fallen in love with the house, which had

9 acres and was under repair. She had a lot of cats, one ginger one in shreds, pelt split, eye hanging out, from a fight, which she had to go home to swab. She had a doctor daughter in Washington state, married to a doctor, who was the "highest earning woman" in the state, according to a tax official. The daughter had two daughters of her own and an adopted child. She had three miscarriages before she had a baby, and lost her baby son, born a siamese twin with the other twin an embryo in his bowel. Insisted on knowing why his prognosis was only to live 8 hours, bundled up the dying baby & traveled 200 miles by train to where he could be operated on by a friend. Then nursed him ("he was quite blind, and deaf, and his hands could grip nothing, they just lay flat") although she knew he could die in three months, which he did. Ever since she has been impossible, behaved badly, her father won't let her into the house. Ironically, she was a child-specialist, called on all over to diagnose, prescribe. She had an adopted sister, adopted when she was 12 & had polio, and of the same age. Sisters devoted to each other.

We ate tea round a table, a yellow-frosted banana cake with cherries, very good currant buns, dainty tea-service. Kitchen in half walled-off area, red counters, big windows overlooking moors. Photographs of places framed in narrow black & hung on white walls. A silver-embroidered oriental screen in livingroom, an African violet, a little vase of early lilies-of-the-valley, a sunny windowseat, a handsome radio with all the foreign stations. Mrs. Davies in grey, with silver earrings. After Mrs. M. left, she showed us the garden in a high wind, then the upstairs, the stark white rooms, large built-in cupboards, Garnet's room with a beerbottle lamp & trophies from pubs, a set of literature in matched jackets. Her own room with framed photos of a fat shy boy and a pekinese, a gas ring by the bed, a telephone. Modern lavatory. Her wired kennel of Pekes, jumping, praying, the babies a fat beary grey, toddling endearingly. Saw just-hatched blackbirds in hedge, a luminous Martian green, pulsing like hearts. Arranged for luncheon at Mrs. Macnamara's in a fortnight.

MRS. HAMILTON AT CRISPENS.
A tall, imposing white-haired woman at the back door early on - - - a sense of her measuring, judging. Invited me to coffee with Frieda. She lives across the street at an angle to the right in a handsome white house with black trim, and a wattle fence protecting her garden beautifully groomed by a retired gardener. With her aged dachshund Pixie. She had dropped in on old Mrs. Arundel every day during her years alone here, and has been living in North

Tawton for about 25 years. During the war her daughter Camilla (from where I got the name for Dido in my novel) stayed with her: they had a victory garden at the back. Mrs. Hamilton an eminent woman, admirable. I like her more & more. She "would have been a doctor" if women had been educated in her day. As it is, her granddaughter (Camilla's daughter, I think) is studying medicine at Edinborough. Virginia (I think) had her 21st birthday this winter - - - Camilla made a sit-down luncheon for over 40 people. Virginia got hundreds of pounds, records, jewels etc. I was pleased to tell Mrs. Hamilton I had gone to Cambridge. That is the sort of thing that she would be pleased at. She seemed very hard of hearing at first, and I dreaded meeting her because I feel very reluctant to raise my voice - - - it makes everything one says seem rather fatuous because of the unnatural emphasis.

Mrs. H's interior: I came in the fall. The long livingroom with French windows out onto the screened lawn and flower border was jammed with flowers; bunches of huge chrysanthemums and dahlias arranged with no art in clumps of yellow, pink and tawny orange and red. Mrs. H. a marvel with Frieda. Not at all put off or silly as many grownups are. Let her go so far, gave her a box with a sixpence in it to shake. Frieda well behaved. A handsome Staffordshire (I think) pot dog on a side table - - - a wonderful red-orange and white. Pixie, like a patched sausage, dozed at the hearth. A coal fire perfectly banked, burned like something artificial - - - one could not imagine that it left ash or clinkers - - - it was so high & full, glowing rosily. A handsome brick fireplace: copper coal scuttle, a flat, plaited woodbasket, gleaming brass tongs & brush. Mrs. H. has a son too, in Brooke Bond Tea. She lived in India, her husband was a coffee planter. Her tiny immaculate pale blue Morris. The sense of grandeur and expansion behind her. Comfort & the happiness of knowing precisely what she wants and how to achieve it. Very sensible.

Then she came here: sat at tea in the front room and told us of the place before our time - - - the gardener who kept all the gardens going, the austerities of the old lady with her stone kitchen floors, no electricity or phone. Asked about Ted's writing. Very curious, but benignly so. Brought round a bunch of yellow mimosa when I had Nicholas.

Feb.6: Brought Nicholas to see Mrs. H. on his first day out. (Mrs. H. is dying to see Nicholas, said the midwife on her morning visit). Waited in cold wintry sun in front alcove, too timid to go in, for Mrs. H. to return from market. She <u>really</u> admired Nicholas. Made me take off his white cap so she could see the shape of his head and remarked at the back brain-bulge of it. Her pleasure at his maleness; asked if Frieda was jealous. When I said Ted seemed to be reluctant it was not another girl, she said: I suspect he's jealous for Frieda. Her queer, fine "listening" quality. Something N.T. for example does not at all have. I tried to notice colors, fabrics. Everything very very rich - - - deep blue velvet piled curtains, deep blue & white orientals, worn, elegant. A polished board floor. A bookcase containing, surprisingly, the <u>Lord of the Rings</u>, and, not surprisingly, all of Winston Churchills books on the war & the English peoples. A lot of old gardening and travel books. I must look closer some time to get the thin titles. Mrs. H. made good mugs of nescafe. "In the North," she said "we have a custom on the baby's first visit." She went into the kitchen and bustled about getting a paper bag with a match (for a good match), coal (to light the fire), salt for health, a sixpence for wealth, and an egg for I'm not sure what. Said she is flying to the Near East for two weeks with a friend.

Feb.21: Mrs. H. materialized outside my study this morning: source of a great Fratch between Ted & me - - - my sense of surprise invasion. This is my one symbolic sanctum. Stunned, I asked her in. Ted got a chair, & I & she both realized the awkwardness of it. She had come to say goodbye & see baby before her 2 weeks in Beirut, Rome etc. I took her to see Nicholas, not before her eyes had taken in the study in such detail as offered - - - "this was the boys' playroom" (which boys?). The sense that Mrs. H. wanted to see how we lived in the back rooms. She looked at my long unbraided hair as if to take it in, drink the last inch, and make a judgment. I very upset, angry. As if we could be observed, examined at any moment simply because we were to shy or polite to say Nay, or She's working, I'll get her down. Or please wait here. My anger at Ted being a man, not at Mrs. H., really.

May 12: Had not seen Mrs. Hamilton for three months. Ted met her in town & she suggested I come over this afternoon, Saturday. Stood at the door with the dressed-up baby & Frieda and rang and rang. No sound of Pixie barking. Felt cross and neatened for nothing; then I heard a bumping around upstairs, and knocked very loudly. Mrs. H. finally came to the door. Showed me around the garden first: a blaze of colors, little gravel paths, raised stone walls. One very pink cherry tree over a garden bench. A fire of wallflowers, red, yellow, pumpkin. I began to see the virtue of these common and popular garden creatures. An ornamental pool with a great orange carp. Begonias, peonies, lupins, lots of tulips, giant pansies. Immaculate weedless beds. We had tea. Frieda in a whiney spoilt mood. Carried about a glass ashtray with a provocative naughty look. Ran outside with a little table & put it on the grass. Mrs. H. had caught a chill in Italy. Had seen the pyramids. Loved Rhodes. She was to leave Monday for a fortnight at her daughter's. Admired Nicholas' head, no doubt but that he was a boy, she said. Frieda cried at the clock musical bell. Felt her competition with Nicholas for attention. Indoors, great bouquets of cherry blossom and tulips. Where was Pixie? She had died in Mrs. H.'s absence. A tone of muted grief. Advised me to dig up and burn my tulips, as from the symptoms I described they had fire-disease.

MR. & MRS. WATKINS
March 1: Thursday: My first visit to the Watkins, in the Court Green cottage on the corner, adjoining Rose Key's, and, on the front, the crippled Elsie's (Elsie Taylor, with the high black boot, humpback and the stuffed fox under glass in her parlor). I wanted to give some return to this crippled couple for their gift of three big, handsome chrysanthemums, one yellow and two mauve, and the pink potted primula they brought after I had Nicholas. So I made and sugared some one-egg cupcakes. Rang, with Frieda. The (I think) blind Mr. Watkins answered the door, and I told him who I was. I could not look into his white eyes. He led me into a fearful, dark parlor with dark brown veneered objects standing about and giving off the depressing smell of old people, varnish and stale upholstery. Led me through a door into a long room with a table and windows looking over (or rather up to) a little garden set on a level halfway up the house, with a well, between it and the house, of paving. "It's a pity, we've just had tea or you could have some." I sat down, with Frieda on my lap. She looked as if she were going to burst into tears - - - like a little animal frightened by the darkness and sad smells.

Mrs. Watkins came out, took the cakes. I saw she had a handsome fruit cake, with one quarter cut out, on the table, cleared of tea things. Green and red and brown fruit studded the bottom of the yellow slab sides, and it rose to a browned crown. There was also a jar of black currant jelly she had preserved herself. I made conversation.

The Watkins lived in London (Wimbledon) during the bombings. Their windows were out. Mrs. Watkins hugged her neighbor (a publican's wife) during the raids as they sat under the stairs. "If we had been killed, we would have died with out arms around each other." They stayed in London because of their son Lawrence who was in the forces. They thought if he was wounded or came home, they would be there for him, holding the home front. I hadn't the heart to ask where Lawrence was now, for fear he would be dead.

Then they moved to Broadwoodkelly (a few miles from North Tawton). The soil there was poor, nothing like the rich red soil here. They had to work the garden too hard, it was too much for them, ¾ of an acre, so they moved to this cottage. They were waiting for a decorator, a Mr. Delve, to paper their front room, so they did not know when they could come to tea (how are the two related?) Mr. Delve had to fix the wall. Something about a heavy mirror, now in their dining room, that had either been about to fall off the parlor wall, or was shoring up a faulty parlor wall. I couldn't tell. They go to the library in North Tawton for books, but only seldom. The stairs up to the library room are too much for <u>Mrs.</u> Watkins and Mr. Watkins is blind and couldn't read the titles if he went himself. "We're a couple of old crocks." They are Catholics, too. I left with Frieda, horribly eager to get out into the fresh air. The smell of age and crippling a real pain to me. Can't stand it.

Mrs. Watkins had taken my cakes carefully off the plate, washed and dried the plate, and handed it back to me. The bushy plants on tall stalks in the garden were, Mr. Watkins told me, "greens".

THE WEBBS: DOCTOR HUGH WEBB, JOAN WEBB. HOLLY & CLAIRE.
Met Doctor Webb very early after our move last fall in his surgery. A youngish, Cornish Doctor Hindley sort, but one imagines, a conservative. Tall, lean, blondish hair, blue eyes, and a habit of smiling a "shy" Perry Norton sort of smile to one side. The sense his eyes never look at you direct, but flake off to one side also. He has an older brother evidently who is head pediatrician for the whole Taunton area. This next week when I go in for my 7 week checkup and to have Nicholas vaccinated, I must do a notation of his clothes. An impression of rather pale, watery heather-tweeds. His very modern, clean surgery across the street and up from the ugly brick Devon Water Board building, Mrs. Hamilton's "Crispens", and adjoining two small cottages. White plaster with a garage. A surgically clean waitingroom with pale green walls, two long benches on either side, a curtained window and a table of magazines. His office filled by a desk, an acre of mangy looking patients'

files, then a little examining room warmed by a wall electric heater, with scales, a cot.

At the Tyrer's New Year's party walked into the room and saw Doctor Webb towering above the rest, rather glassy on (I think) whisky, which brought out a weak chin and watery eye. It was his wife I was after. Monopolized her: a short, dark girl with dark, soft eyes. A sister in London being a nurse who had been an actress. This sounded promising. The Webbs had lived in Nigeria, come back to England to send their children to good schools, lived in the lower part of town in an awful house with rats and damp. The old doctor whose partnership Hugh Webb had was to sell them his house subject to reasonable survey, but the place was evidently a wreck. They bought some land on the hill and built a modern house which I am dying to see. It is called "Mistle Mead" - - - Dr. Webb called home one day and named it - - - it has lots of mistle thrushes evidently. Joan has household help all day (according to Nancy she has trouble with help - - - bosses them too much or something and they leave her). But Mrs. Tyrer interrupted our corner talk just as we got started, to circulate the white-haired old Danish farmer Mr. Holm who drank bottles of pure whisky, according to George.

My next relation to Dr. Webb very stormy & angry - - - when I had the milk fever Ted called him up at midnight & asked him what to do. He said he'd be round with penicillin in the morning. Came, and I was very weak but perfectly normal in temperature, having sweated the fever out in one great bath at 4 a.m. Then there was the gruesome business of his stretching the baby's foreskin which had not been stretched properly by Nurse Davies or Nurse Skinner or the awful Okehampton Nurse whose name escapes me (who flew out of the house to the doctor the next morning after my reporting I'd had a 103 temperature again - - - "What! you take your own temperature!" - - - to report the room was an inferno at 60°, that I still hadn't put on the controversial bra which was supposed to be the source of all my ills etc.) The baby screaming for twenty minutes; I couldn't look, but stayed grimly in the room, wet and paper-wobbly holding on a chair. Blood over everything. I hated Dr. Webb for not seeing to the baby's foreskin before, having been perfectly prepared to accept the custom of not circumcising a baby. He upset in his way. The next day he sent word back via the Okehampton Nurse that I should "get up or go to hospital." It dawned on me he thought I was malingering. Ted & I readied a barrage for him when he came. "What? Don't you take you own temperatures here?" and so on. We cornered him so

654

he suddenly snatched up a letter on my bed table and blurted "May I read this?" Incredible. "Surely," I said. It was a letter to me asking to print some poems in an American paperback anthology. We thought afterwards it must have been a desperate attempt to get out of a corner & change the subject. My grudges vanished. An odd sidelight - - - a man in his surgery had a pain in his stomach. "What do you think you have?" Cancer of the kidney, was the reply. So Dr. Webb will cost the Health Service hundreds of pounds to have the tests to show there is no cancer of the kidney. Very odd. Does he ask patients to give their own diagnosis and have no alternative of his own? What if the man <u>did</u> have cancer of the kidney???

Dr. Webb belongs to a shooting syndicate at 6 pounds a year. They shoot at Ash Ridge Manor. Will they ever invite us socially? I would like to know the wife - - - she seems to give him trouble. Neurotic?

NANCY AXWORTHY & MISCELLANEOUS INTELLIGENCE
April 25: Nancy has not been to clean all this week. Her mother-in-law was sick again last Tuesday. Nancy's husband Walter had gone to a contest of Devon bellringers the previous weekend. Then his mother was taken. I met Nancy's friend, the humpbacked Elsie Taylor who lives in a tiny cottage with a stuffed fox at the bottom of our lane, and she said Nancy was sitting up all night and had to wash four of the old lady's sheets in one day as she was wetting the bed and vomiting. Then, as Ted & I were going in the early dusk to deliver our great weekly bouquet of daffodils to Jim, on Friday, Elsie came stumping out in her high, black orthopedic boot called "Mrs. Hughes, Mr. Hughes." Nancy's mother-in-law had died that afternoon, from a heart attack. I felt an immense relief, that I would not lose my invaluably helpful Nancy for her need to nurse a sick & malingering mother-in-law. So selfish am I. But the old lady was evidently a terrible patient, never doing what the doctor said, and Elsie herself said Walter said it was a mercy, if she had to go, that she didn't linger.

The funeral is to be at 2:30 this afternoon. Elsie stumped up yesterday morning to ask if she could buy four shillings worth of daffodils. Of course we said no, we could bring down a big bunch, we had been meaning to bring her a bunch. So last night we picked about 150 daffodils & I went down in the clear pink twilight & knocked. Elsie was not a home. But this morning the top half of her Dutch door was open & she was waiting. "How much am I in your debt?" Oh nothing, I said. She said she is going in a week to the

holiday for the disabled (who come from as far as Oxfordshire) to Westward
Ho! They come every year for two weeks. The Rotary Club takes them out
for lunch. They are very high up, in this big place, with a ballroom. She can
see the Isle of Lundy from her bed. I said to send the daffodils with our love.
Nancy, she said, will be up to see me tomorrow.

Nancy's husband Walter is a big heavy smiling blond man who works for
Jim Bennett. He went through a ceiling he was repairing and strained his
back. Marjorie Tyrer says when he came to repair their bathtub he broke a
scale by stepping on it. He is a bellringer, the number seven bell, a big one.
He is head of the North Tawton fire department (which has a drill every
Wednesday at 7), and teaches woodworking at the local school. I hope to
take woodworking this next fall.

CHARLIE POLLARD & The Beekeepers.
June 7: The midwife stopped up to see Ted at noon to remind him that the
Devon beekeepers were having a meeting at 6 at Charlie Pollard's. We were
interested in starting a hive, so dumped the babies in bed and jumped in the
car and dashed down the hill past the old factory to Mill Lane, a row of pale
orange stucco cottages on the Taw, which gets flooded whenever the river
rises. We drove into the dusty, ugly paved parking lot under the grey peaks
of the factory buildings, unused since 1928 and now only used for wool
storage. We felt very new & shy, I hugging my bare arms in the cool of the
evening for I had not thought to bring a sweater. We crossed a little bridge to
the yard where a group of miscellaneous Devonians were standing - - - an
assortment of shapeless men in brown speckled bulgy tweeds, Mr. Pollard in
white shirtsleeves, with his dark, nice brown eyes and oddly Jewy head, tan,
balding, dark-haired. I saw two women, one very large, tall, stout, in a
glistening aqua-blue raincoat, the other cadaverous as a librarian in a dun
raincoat. Mr. Pollard glided toward us & stood for a moment on the bridge-
end, talking. He indicated a pile of hives, like white and green blocks of
wood with little gables & said we could have one, if we would like to fix it
up. A small pale blue car pulled into the yard: the midwife. Her moony beam
came at us through the windscreen. Then the rector came pontificating
across the bridge & there was a silence that grew round him. He carried a
curious contraption - - - a dark felt hat with a screen box built on under it,
and cloth for a neckpiece under that. I thought the hat a clerical bee-keeping
hat, and that he must have made it for himself. Then I saw, on the grass, and
in hands, everybody was holding a bee-hat, some with netting of nylon, most

with box screening, some with khaki round hats, I felt barer & barer. People became concerned. Have you no hat? Have you no coat? Then a dry little woman came up, Mrs. Jenkins, the secretary of the society, with tired, short blond hair. "I have a boiler suit." She went to her car and came back with a small, white silk button-down smock, the sort pharmacist's assistants use. I put it on and buttoned it & felt more protected. Last year, said the midwife, Charlie's Pollard's bees were bad-tempered and made everybody run. Everyone seemed to be waiting for someone. But then we all slowly filed after Charlie Pollard to his beehives. We threaded our way through neatly weeded allotment gardens, one with bits of tinfoil and a fan of black and white feathers on a string, very decorative, to scare the birds, and twiggy leantos over the plants. Black-eyed sweetpea-like blooms: broadbeans, somebody said. The grey ugly backs of the factory. Then we came to a clearing, roughly scythed, with one hive, a double-brood hive, two layers. From this hive Charlie Pollard wanted to make three hives. I understood very little. The men gathered round the hive. Charlie Pollard started squirting smoke from a little funnel with a hand-bellows attached to it round the entry at the bottom of the hive. "Too much smoke," hissed the large blue-raincoated woman next to me. "What do you do if they sting?" I whispered, as the bees, now Charlie had lifted the top off the hive, were zinging out and dancing round as at the end of long elastics. (Charlie had produced a fashionable white straw Italian hat for me with a black nylon veil that collapsed perilously in to my face in the least wind. The rector had tucked it in to my collar, much to my surprise. "Bees always crawl up, never down," he said. I had drawn it down loose over my shoulders.) The woman said: "Stand behind me, I'll protect you." I did. (I had spoken to her husband earlier, a handsome, rather sarcastic man standing apart, silver-hair, a military blue eye. Plaid tie, checked shirt, plaid vest, all different. Tweedy suit, navy-blue beret. His wife, he had said, kept 12 hives & was the expert. The bees always stung him. His nose & lips, his wife later said.)

The men were lifting out rectangular yellow slides, crusted with bees, crawling, swarming. I felt prickles all over me, & itches. I had one pocket & was advised to keep my hands in this and not move. "See all the bees round the Rectors dark trousers!" whispered the woman. "They don't seem to like white." I was grateful for my white smock. The Rector was somehow an odd-man-out, referred to now and then by Charlie jestingly: "Eh, Rector?" "Maybe they want to join his church," one man, emboldened by the anonymity of the hats, suggested.

Noticed: a surround of tall white cow-parsley, pursy yellow gorse-bloom, an old Christmas tree, white hawthorn, strong-smelling.

The donning of the hats had been an odd ceremony. Their ugliness & anonymity very compelling, as if we were all party to a rite. They were brown or grey or faded green felt, mostly, but there was one white straw boater with a ribbon. All faces, shaded, became alike. Commerce became possible with complete strangers.

The men were lifting slides, Charlie Pollard squirting smoke, into another box. They were looking for queen cells - - - long, pendulous honeycolored cells from which the new queens would come. The blue-coated woman pointed them out. She was from British Guiana, had lived alone in the jungle for 18 years, lost £25 pounds on her first bees there - - - there had been no honey for them to eat. I was aware of bees buzzing and stalling before my face. The veil seemed hallucinatory. I could not see it for moments at a time. Then I became aware I was in a bone-stiff trance, intolerably tense, and shifted round to where I could see better. "Spirit of my dead father, protect me!" I arrogantly prayed. A dark, rather nice "unruly" looking man came up through the cut grasses. Everyone turned, murmured "O Mr. Jenner, we didn't think you were coming."

This, then, the awaited expert, the "government man" from Exeter. An hour late. He donned a white boiler suit and a very expert bee-hat - - - a vivid green dome, square black screen box for head, joined with yellow cloth at the corners, and a white neckpiece. The men muttered, told what had been done. They began looking for the old queen. Slide after slide was lifted, examined on both sides. To no avail. Myriads of crawling, creeping bees. As I understood it from my blue bee-lady, the first new queen out would kill the old ones, so the new queencells were moved to different hives. The old queen would be left in hers. But they couldn't find her. Usually the old queen swarmed before the new queen hatched. This was to prevent swarming. I heard words like "supersede", "queen excluder" (a slatted screen of metal only workers could crawl through). The rector slipped away unnoticed, then the midwife. "He used too much smoke" was the general criticism of Charlie Pollard. The queen hates smoke. She might have swarmed earlier. She might be hiding. She was not marked. It grew later. Eight. Eight-thirty. The hives were parceled up, queen excluders put on. An old beamy brown man wisely jutted a forefinger as we left: "She's in that one." The beekeepers clustered around Mr. Jenner with questions. The secretary sold chances for a bee-festival.

Friday: June 8: Ted & I drove down to Charlie Pollard's about 9 tonight to collect our hive. He was standing at the door of his cottage in Mill Lane, the corner one, in white shirtsleeves, collar open, showing dark chest-hairs & a white mail-knit undershirt. His pretty blonde wife smiled & waved. We went over the bridge to the shed, with its rotovator, orange, resting at the end. Talked of floods, fish, Ash Ridge: the Taw flooded his place over & over. He was wanting to move up, had an eye on the lodge at Ash Ridge, had hives up there. His father-in-law had been head gardener when they had six gardeners. Told of great heaters to dry hay artificially & turn it to meal: 2 thousand, 4 thousand the machines cost, were lying up there now, hardly used. He hadn't been able to get any more flood insurance once he had claimed. Had his rugs cleaned, but they were flat: you can live with them, I can't, he told the inspector. Had to have the upholstered sofa & chairs all redone at the bottom. Walked down the first step from the 2nd floor one night & put his foot in water. A big salmon inhabited his reach of the Taw. "To be honest with you," he said, over & over. "To be honest with you." Showed us his big barny black offices. A honey ripener with a beautiful sweet-smelling slow gold slosh of honey at the bottom. Loaned us a bee-book. We loaded with our creaky old wood hive. He said if we cleaned it an painted it over Whitsun, he'd order a swarm of docile bees. Had showed us his beautiful-red-gold Italian queen the day before, with her glossy green mark on the thorax, I think. He had made it. To see her the better. The bees were bad-tempered, though. She would lay a lot of docile bees. We said: Docile, be sure now, & drove home.

MAJOR AND MRS. BILLYEALD (Winkleigh)
Whitsun June 10: Met the Billyealds at Charlie Pollard's bee-meeting and were invited to tea. We found the house "Small as a postage stamp", on the Eggesford Road. "Eve Leary", the name of the compound in British Guiana (I think). A tiny, cramped brick house all on one floor like a holiday camp, with a glass grape arbor built all along the front overlooking a view of rolling green farmland to Dartmoor, and a kitchen built along the back. An impeccably mown lawn back and front. Beehives, painted pink and white, in a nettly enclosure at the bottom of the front lawn, with lots of big blue cornflowers ("they love those") and red and yellow broom "three and six a cutting") round about. And a new shed, one of those self-erectable ones with

a clean gravel floor, for bee equipment and watching. Infinitely fine vegetable garden - - - rows of thick, bushy strawberry plants, some with white flowers, some with embryonic green berries beginning: sweetpeas climbing sticks, rhubarb, a weed-grown asparagus patch (the only slovenly corner), Velocity cabbages, goosegog, round & lucent green & hairy, celery, broadbeans. The superbly weeded rows. Then a pile of hens in a battery, eggs collected by the Chumleigh man, not the Okehampton man (who was too fussy about washing the eggs). Seedlings set out in myriad tin cans.

Mrs. Bertha Billyeald an amazing & indomitable woman: white short hair, tall, keen blue eyes & pink cheeks. Quite greedy, though fattish, she ate lots of scones & cream & jam for tea. She cans (or bottles) about 200 weight of jam a year. And extracts her own honey. Secretary of the Conservatives in the country. At the end of the afternoon, she brought out her scrapbook of her life in British Guiana. An astounding document. Lots of pictures of waterfalls seen from the air in her three-seater plane; her black silk flying suit, like Amelia Earhart; her handsome pilot; close calls. Pictures of her with short hair, in pants, handsome herself, ordering a cowering black to move some dirt, on horseback, driving a locomotive which she & her engineer built, straightening the 7-mile railway tracks they made to help get the timber to the river. A succession of wood houses, grander & grander, as they made more & more money. They were at first too poor to buy meat; at the end the grant was sold for £180,000. I couldn't understand whether the Major was her first husband, or second. Or whether she & her father built the timber plantation, or she & her husband. At one point, she said she had no children but attended a Mother's Union meet as she had cared for a lot. And then, when she was showing me the pictures of children & weddings in the hall, she seemed to say "These are <u>his</u> children", meaning the Major's? Her father, George Manly, an amazing man of 89 in white linen jacket with that military blue eye who attributes his health to drinking a quart of rum a day all his life, said that when a jaguar was troubling them, she locked up all the dogs 7 resolved to shoot it. Heard a noise, a scratching, at the house window in the dark. Crept downstairs with rifle & outside: saw a dark shape fall from the window. That's a dog, she thought, that the jaguar has thrown out. I'll save it. She ran & embraced the dark object, which turned out to be the jaguar. It dashed off & hid in the chicken shed. She went over & shot into the shed, then did run. In the morning the natives found the jaguar in there, dead, shot through the lung. So she is a big woman. Very opinionated. Said that these women get multiple sclerosis from worrying over their husbands' bad health and not accepting what God has sent them!

Major Stanley Billyeald curiously the odd-man out. Always making jocular references to his wife's expertise (on bees) & domination: "She has her finger on my jugular." A man of action; can't stand still. His father was a drunkard journalist & pot-boiler. He started in the ranks of the calvalry himself & worked up to head of the C.I.D. in British Guiana. An immense admiration, sardonic, for lawyers: how they can make monkeys of truths & learned men. He writes all winter: reports. Can't talk standing still: walks round & round the lawn, with a sort of horse-rider's lurch. His blue eye, also, his clipped silver moustache. The old man, his father-in-law, a sort of elderly double of himself. Three things I'll tell you, he said: There is no sentiment in business. There is no honesty in politics. And self-interest makes the world go round. All right, I said. I give you those. Gave Ted a box of little Velocity cabbages in tins & a couple of bunches of very odd cylindrical green celery ("for soup").

George Manly, the old man, was according to his daughter all sorts of wonderful & odd things. He seemed drastically hungry for a listener. Brought out his photograph album with prize-winning photos he had taken: of an old hawker with white hair and wrinkled like Methuselah; a fat little native baby eating dirt; snow on a wire fence ("That's a bee-comb", some-one guessed, to his delight), hand-colored lily-pads like violent green saucers, and moonlight on the big waterfall (Kaieteur?), the highest in the world, in British Guiana. Bertha B. said something about his being a crack marksman, a world champion, & a trick entertainer on a party with the king & queen (which?)) He brought Ted to his bedroom at the end, to show him little boxes of jewelry he made from loose colored rhinestones & frames which he gave to friends; showed him his watercolors for doing photo-graphs, and his mother and father, an oval black and white portrait of a dark, oppressed little woman & bearded smiling patriarchal man (her par-ents were killed in the Mutiny; she was married at 14). He prided himself on making the baby smile. Pretended to eat Frieda's parsley & then gave it back, while she made her queer "shy" face, sliding her eyes to one side under her lids. Promised to tell a story of a cockroach. Gave me a sprig of "rose-mary for remembrance" as we left. Brought out a Captain Hornblower book, autographed to him from C.S. Forester, whose picture he had taken atop the big falls.

Elizabeth, a blond, quiet plump faced sweet-looking girl of 13 was home from boardingschool to stay with her grandparents. She brought out her toys, a dog, a doll, to amuse Frieda & played with her; later cuddled and cooed over the baby.

A big tea laid, scones, cream, cherry jelly; a chocolate cake with rich dark frosting; little cut sandwiches. Tea a bit awkward, drafty, in the tiny diningroom crammed with sideboards & tables. Two bedrooms, a bath & a tiny front room with a TV made up the interior of the house.

The old man, on showing his photos: "That's the girl who has two children in New Zealand, that's the one with the voice Bertha's going to visit this week, that's the boy that's dead, that's the mother of the lot . . . " and a photo of his wife, dead 25-years, with a paper in her lap showing headlines about Hitler.

MR. ELLIS (86): 16 Fore Street
July 4: Mr. Ellis, said the midwife, had a piano. It looked horrible she said, but was supposed to be in good tone. We walked round in the heat of the afternoon. Asked at a wrong door first. A smiling white-haired woman directed us to the next house in the street on the steep hill. She had a queer old zombie-dog, pink-grey flesh showing through shorn hair, at her door: it is not mine, it is a farmer's on the hill, it is an ancient sort of sheepdog like they used to use, and it comes to me for scraps. We rang. No answer. She had been listening and came down: I expect he can't hear, he is listening to the wireless. She pounded, went in: there are some young people to see you. A very old, crabbed white haired man, but somehow lively, met us. He had been sitting in front of a radio, had a tea tray with currant buns on the made-up bed in the sittingroom. Led us out back through a dark scabrous kitchen, did away with a bucket (urine?) and showed us a fusty old piano, the veneer peeling. We lifted, hopelessly, the keyboard cover. It was his wife's, who had died four years ago at the age of 74 or so. Hadn't been opened. We tried a few notes. Every other one stuck, motionless, and a substance, matted dust or the decay of the interior, seeped up between the keys.

Then he began to talk. Are those your writings in the window? I asked. I had seen some odd placards with large plain childlike writing about "the scandal of the century" and "would he have left his pram if he did not intend to stay?" and "Water Board" and "National Assistance Board". A kind of public plaint, indecipherable, written first in pencil, then over again on the same card in ink. One placard was upside down. These, evidently were his grievances. He had been robbed by his brother and sister of seven fields: property had been left to his brother and his heirs (that's me, isn't it, his heir?) and sold. A doctor in Wales had given him two injections a day, by nurses, and paralysed his left side, then said he had a stroke. His wife had died - - - they wouldn't take her into hospital because she was incurable. What had she died of - - - a broken heart? His son-in-law was a Freemason in Okehampton - - - the Freemasons were in power, they were robbing him, cheating him. The National Assistance were robbing him. He had written to the Queen. Somebody in a paper had said pink lustre cups were worth hundreds of pounds. He showed us fours saucers and three cups in pink lustre in his cupboard. The man had said he would be in the district & have a look & value them, but of course never came. His wife had fallen from the bed, it was like a butcher shop, and no one came. Her daughter did not come and broke her heart. He had to leave the door unlocked Thursday night for the nurse, and some one might steal the cups. He had china as well, a dinner set and a lovely teaset. There was a desk, with two polished brass candlesticks & a brass bell. Winston Churchill had fallen, and look at the treatment he had. Mr. Ellis fell, and was an hour picking himself up by himself. The flood of injustice went on, a great apocalyptic melding of perhaps slights or real small grievances. The police man walked down the other side of the street, nose in the air, and did not read his complaints in the window, which were there for all to see. We edged out, in distress, telling him to talk to the nurse, she was nice. Yes, the nurses are all good, he admitted, I have had a lot of them . . . And we went.

ROSE & PERCY KEY (68)[n]

Retired Londoners, our nearest neighbors, live in Number 4 Court Green cottages on the steep rocky slant of our driveway, looking into our high side hedge through the small front windows. The cottage joined to the Watkins' cottage on the corner, joined in turn to the tiny white cottage of humpbacked Elsie fronting the street. A wreck when they bought it: hadn't been lived in for 2 years, all muck & falling plaster. They worked it to comfort all themselves. A telly (on hire purchase, almost paid off), a small back garden under our thatched cottage and strawberry patch, hidden by a dense screen of holly and bush there, and by a wattle fence & homemade garage on the drive-side. Tiny rooms, bright, modernish. The typical British wallpaper - - - a pale beige embossed with faintly sheened white roses, the effect of cream scum patterns on weak tea. Starchy white curtains, good for peeking from behind. A stuffed, comfortable livingroom suite. A fireplace glowing with coal and wood block. Pictures of the three daughters in wedding dress - - - an album of the model daughter: hard-faced, black hair, a Jewy rapaciousness. In modeling school they stole an expensive sweater her mother bought. Two grandsons, one from each other daughter. All daughters live in London - - - Betty, Yvonne & the third. A side room full of gaudy satin materials the first day I came to visit, and a sewing machine on which Rose runs up mattress coverings for a firm in Okehampton in cerise and fuschia shiny stuff with lurid sprawling patterns. Percy "caretakes" a firm one day a month. Upstairs, a pink bathroom, floors all sealed with new lino, flounces and mirrors and chrome. A new cooker in the kitchen (the other hire purchase item), a cage of pistachio and pale-blue budgies creaking and whistling, up a step from the livingroom.

First encounter: Rose brought a tray of tea for us and the workmen the day we moved in. A lively youngish looking woman, brim full of gabble, seeming to listen not to you, but to another invisible person slightly to one side who is telling her something interesting and a bit similar, but much more compellingly. Her lightish brown hair, smooth face, plumping body. In her middle 50's? Percy seems 20 years older, very tall, spare, almost cadaverous. Wears a blue peajacket. A weathered, humorous wry face. Was a pub keeper in London. South London. Oddly sensitive about Frieda and the baby. Asks very right questions. Sings to Frieda. Eye running, losing weight, no appetite, depressed after Christmas. Mrs. Key caught Dr. Webb coming down from me one day. Got Percy a checkup. An Xray. He was coming out with others from their Xrays but, unlike them, had no chart. "Where's your chart, Perce?" Oh, the nurse said, he's to come back for another after lunch. Now he is in Hawksmoor Chest Hospital in the hills in Bovey Tracy for a fortnight. Rose's ignorance - - - why a 2-week checkup? Is it a checkup or a treatment. She says she will ask tomorrow when the Crawfords drive her out for a visit. My startlement: these people ask nothing, they just go to be treat' like mild cows.

Have been to church with Rose & Percy - - - the rector put me on to them. Percy the church-goer. Rose not so much. They go every few weeks, sit in the same pew in the middle on the left. Rose's series of smart hats. She could be in her late 30's. Other encounters - - - to tea with them with Ted & Frieda. A smart tea - - - hot herring on toast, a plate of fancy tea cakes, all sugar &

frosting. Frieda flushed from the fire, shy enough to be good. Everybody barking at her to stay away from the huge blue-glazed eye and gold buttons of the telly in the corner, the great fancy silent companion, she burying her head in tears in the armchair cushion at the sharp voices, for what reason? Looked through album of all daughters - - - bright, lively, pretty, with half-stewed, handsomeish dark husbands. The model daughter fancily posed before a traditional weddingcake. The sideboard & telly & threepiece suite take up every inch of space. The cramped, steamy cosy place. Then they came to tea with us. Percy much later. Rose dressed up but deprecating "Ooh, look at these stockings Sylvia", whipping up her skirt to reveal a shabbyish pair of thick stockings. "Percy said my suit had the seam open down the back when it came back from the cleaners, but no matter."

The last time Rose came to tea I had a big fancy sponge cake made with 6 eggs I had meant for the Tyrers on Sunday, but they didn't come, George had stayed in bed. I broached it for Rose. She made a praising remark. Gobbled it. Seemed very nervous and flighty. Talked on about pensions - - - Percy had been ill one year and hadn't paid it, now their pension was forever cut short (she got 29s. a week instead of the full 30s.) and they couldn't pay up the year ("Oh" said the nasty official "everybody would do that if we let them". And why not?) Shocking. How to get on on a pension. They rent their London house to one daughter. Can't buy much - - - not on hire purchase. It's all right to do that if you're young. After little more than half an hour, Rose jumped up to a knock at the back door. "That's Perce." A garbled excuse about going off with the Crawfords somewhere. The Crawfords (Morris' parents) very fancy, have, it seems, much money, a house on the hill, a brand-new car from their firm, all brothers and fathers and sons and cousins who make money by selling paper sacks they collect from farmers, god knows how. I resentful. "You didn't mind my coming?" Her slippery eyes. She repeats everything I say to the Crawfords. My repeating the rector's "We can see everything that goes on at Court Green" in innocence turning into a bad bedroom joke and getting repeated back to me by Sylvia Crawford.

Met Percy on the street in front of the butcher's, his watery eyes in the lean face set somewhere in space. Told me he'd have to go into hospital for tests. I dropped in on Rose with a plate of absolutely indigestible "Black Walnut flavored" cupcakes from a Betty Crocker mix Mrs. Tyrer had dug out of her closet in the kitchen ("George and I never eat cakes and pies") and which seemed suspiciously ancient, but thought the sugary stuff would appeal to Percy, who ate a pound of jelly babies a week. Rang once, twice. A suspicious delay. Rose came to the door still shaking with tears. Frieda ran down from our gate and came in with me. I found myself saying "Take it easy, love", heartening nothings. "I'm so lonely", Rose wailed. Percy had gone into hospital Sunday. It was last Tuesday. "I know I've got the telly and things to do, look, I've just done a big washing, but you get so used to having them around the house." She burst into fresh tears. I put my arms around her, gave her a hug. "I've hardly eaten anything today, look, I'm writing Perce a letter ... " She sniffed, showed a scrawled pencil message on the kitchen table. I ordered her to make tea, told her to come up for tea anytime. She wiped her face, peculiarly blanked out by her bare sorrows. Frieda fiddled with small ornaments, climbed the step in the kitchen & exclaimed over the birds. I left, in a hurry, to catch Marjorie Tyrer who was coming to tea after her London weekend.

Thursday: Feb. 15: Dropped by to see Rose and ask her if she could come to dinner this weekend. Had a lamb leg. Wanted to be kind, return the roast beef & gravy dinner she brought up when I had the baby a month ago, & the white knitted suit. Her vagueness. She retold the story of the Doctor & Percy's eye. Flew on: how Percy had called up on the phone, asked for a sweater - - - he sat out on the balcony, had a nice room with only one other man. She was going to get the sweater in Exeter Friday, the Crawfords were driving her to visit him Saturday. I asked her to dinner Sunday. She paused, looked vague, didn't know if she was going ("supposed to go") to dinner at Crawfords Sunday, couldn't afford to let them down, she depended on them for her rides to Percy (she drives, but not their own present car, it's too big). I told her a bit dryly that maybe she could find out & let me know. Aware of my impossibility as charitable worker - - take my bloody offer & be grateful. She spoke of Ted's driving her to Percy Tuesday. I a bit dubious - - - what had he said? How far was the hospital from Exeter? She looked miffed - - - I said Ted had a dentist appointment; when were the hospital hours. Two to four. Well, would that give him time to shop & do errands & go to the dentist? I knew perfectly well Ted planned to go fishing early in the day & had no doubt thought he could drop her in the environs of the hospital for the day. She said she had no way of getting there (it being an intricate route). Her flightiness. Ted said he had told her he would drop her at Newton Abbot where he had understood she could get a bus to the hospital. Her translation of this into his spending the day driving her & waiting for her. I told her to let us know if she could come to dinner, thinking she could well think about letting us down, too. My dislike for the elder Mrs. C. Her great gabby jeweled encrusted tartiness. R. a flighty, fickle gossipy lady with a good enough heart.

<u>Friday, Feb. 16</u>: A flying visit from Rose. Ted let her in and she came to the playroom where we were typing opposite each other in piles of sprawled paper over the dull pewter pot of steaming tea. "My isn't it lovely and warm." We urged her to have a cup of tea. She sat in the orange striped deck chair. "My isn't it hot." She was expecting a phone call from "the girls" (her daughters)? News: they asked for her permission to operate on Percy - - - her voice quavered. She couldn't see why, he was in no pain, if you operate like that it throws your system off some way, but "if it'll prolong his life". Ted pored hopelessly over maps of Exeter and Bovey Tracy, his day of fishing evaporating in face of the obvious impossibility of meeting Rose halfway. The prospect of Percy in hospital 6 weeks nudging us to sacrifice half a day - - - her kindnesses, our slowness. So he will take her to and from & forget the fishing. What is this "shadow" or "spot"? She visits him Saturday, has promised to find out all. Is it old scars, fresh scars? He is 68. She said she was going to Crawfords on Sunday, but said she'd come to us on Monday for noon dinner. I have utterly forgot to describe what she wore: must train myself better, from head to toe.

Feb.21: Popped in on Rose, with Frieda, to get my application for Family Allowance witnessed. She & her model daughter (Betty) down from London at dinner at 1. Betty a handsome, lean, hard-faced girl with black short hair, a racing-horse body, a sharp nose & chin. Came in to boss mother, tell her how to sign form. Rose Emma Key, Mrs. in parenthesis. Blue eyeshadow from train trip down. Percy operated on, to be operated on that night. Dropped by the next night, Feb. 22, for news - - - he had had part of his lung taken out, was resting comfortably. What was it? They didn't know (!), would find out Saturday when they went to visit him. They didn't want Rose to come visit him the first day. What was it? Betty: "Excuse me, I have a boil on my nose." The TV set blaring. Frieda cried, startled. Then fascinated. A closeup of a dumptruck emptying rocks. "Ohhh."

April 17: A terrible thumping on our door about 2 o'clock. Ted and Frieda and I were eating lunch in the kitchen. Do you suppose that's the mail? I asked, thinking Ted might have won some fabulous prize. My words were cut short by Rose's hysterical voice "Ted, Ted, come quick, I think Percy's had a stroke." We flung the door open, & there was Rose Key, wild-eyed, clutching her open blouse which showed her slip and gabbling. "I've called the doctor," she cried, turning to rush back to her cottage, Ted after her. I thought I would stay and wait, and then something in me said, now, you must see this, you have never seen a stroke or a dead person. So I went. Percy was in his chair in front of the television set, twitching in a fearsome way, utterly gone off, mumbling over what I thought must be his false teeth, his eyes twitching askew, and shaking as if pierced by weak electric shocks. Rose clutched Ted. I stared from the doorway. The doctor's car drew immediately up by the hedge at the bottom of the lane. He came very slowly and ceremoniuosly, head seriously lowered, to the door. Ready to meet death, I suppose. He said Thank you, and we melted back to the house. I have been waiting for this, I said. And Ted said he had, too. I was seized by dry retching at the thought of that horrible mumbling over false teeth. A disgust. Ted & I hugged each other. Frieda looked on peacefully from her lunch, her big blue eyes untroubled & clear. Later, we knocked. The elder Mrs. Crawford was there, & the shambling blond Morris. Rose said Percy was sleeping, and so he was, back to us on the couch. He had had five strokes that day. One more, the doctor said, and he would be gone. Ted went in later. Percy said Hello Ted, and asked after the babies.

He had been walking in the wind among our narcissi in his peajacket a few days before. He had a double rupture from coughing. The sense his morale, his spirit, had gone. That he had given in with this. Everybody, it seems, is going or dying in this cold mean spring.

April 22 Easter Sunday: Ted and I were picking daffodils in the early evening. Rose had been arguing with Percy, and I had discreetly let my picking lead me to the hedge overlooking the lane in front of their house. I heard Rose saying "You've got to take it easy, Perce," in a cross voice. Then she lowered it. Popped out & stood. Ted had sat Frieda & the baby & me in the daffodils to take pictures. "Sylvia" she yoohooed across. I did not answer immediately because Ted was taking the picture. "Sylvia!" "Just a minute Rose." Then she asked if she could buy a bunch of daffodils. Ted & I knew she knew we would not ask for money. Disliked her scrounging to get something out of us. We brought by a bunch. Percy was sitting up in the bed made up in the livingroom for him after his stroke like a toothless bird, beaming a cracked smile, his cheeks bright pink like a baby's. As we went in, a couple in Easter outfit came up, she with a pink hat and a bunch of red, purple and pink anemones, he moustached & serious. She all dovey bosom & coos. They had kept the Fountains pub. Now they lived in The Nest (we've come home to roost!), that white cute cottage opposite the Ring O' Bells. She told me almost immediately that she was a Catholic & set up the altar in the Town Hall after the Saturday night dances. This meant her staying up late. A young girl waiting for a ride home had come up once and said "Pardon me, but I can't help thinking What a transformation, first it is a dance hall, and then it is all neatened up into a church," or some such. "Hubby isn't Catholic, but Hubby waits up and helps me." How nice, I said, for hubbies to be so broadminded. Percy kept trying to say things in a vowelly mouthing which Rose translated for us. "You can't raise a nation on fish alone" was one of the sayings.

April 25: Stopped for a second to talk to Rose on my way up from bringing a load of daffodils to Elsie for the funeral of Nancy's mother-in-law this afternoon. We exchanged baby-information: how Nicholas had been crying the past two days and might be teething ("Babies are so forward nowadays," says Rose.) and how Percy had dressed himself and walked round to the back. Wasn't it wonderful. That's modern medicine, I said.

May 15: Heard a whooshing outside the gate as I came into the house with a load of clean laundry, and dashed to the big kitchen window to see who was trespassing. Old Percy, with fixed, mad blue eye and a rusty scythe, was attacking the "Japanese creeper" bambooey plant which had shot up green in the alley by the drive. I was outraged and scared. He had come over, beckoning in his sinister senile way, a few days ago with a bag of fusty jellybabies for Frieda which I immediately threw away, and warned me that this Japanese creeper was overtaking our field and we better cut it down. I told Ted Percy was cutting down the stalks & we flew out. Hey Percy, leave off that, Ted said. I stood disapproving behind him, wiping my hands on a towel. Percy smiled foolishly, mumbled. Thought I was doing you a favor, he says. The scythe clattered out of his shaking hand onto the gravel. He had left a green mesh of stalks, almost impossible to detach from the roots after his botched cutting. No sign of Rose. Had intuition she was hiding. She had come over a few days before to buy some daffodils for this Hubby-loving Catholic who'd been helping her round the house. I thought I'd let her pay for these in earnest, as it was a gift. Why should I supply free gifts for other people to give? Said a bob a dozen. She looked stunned. Is that too much for you? I asked dryly. It obviously was. She must have expected further largesse. I told her that was what we charged everyone & picked her 3 dozen for her 2 bob while she sat over a cup of tea & minded Frieda. It had been pouring all day & I wore my Wellingtons. Now she has invited me down for a cup of tea today (May 17), and I feel sick about going because Percy makes me sick. I won't bring Frieda, I think. Rose told Ted yesterday that Percy goes "funny", has his left arm & side hang loose. Says she hopes the doctor will say something about this when Percy goes for the post-operation checkup.

May 17: Rose had popped out the day before & asked me for tea. I gardened heavily up to the church clock's striking four. Went down in my brown work-pants. She all dressed up in a blue suit, freshly done dark brown hair (dyed?) and stockings riddled with runs. Raised her eyebrows at my wet knees. Percy not so bad, livelier, but his left hand goes dead and he seems always to be having turns. Saw she had four cups all ready, & herrings on toast, so ran up for Ted. His presence a relief. Rose mouthed about Percy's condition, very bad, she had to dress him, he took all her time. I had a revulsion at the cold herrings on cold toast, a feeling they took on a corruption from Percy. Discussing the cost of heating, admiring their new gas poker fixed in fireplace, we say Mrs. Crawford, resplendent in black furry cossack cap, dragging the sullen, shaved-bob Rebecca, age 3 in July, & exhibiting a flat silver ring and eating, as always and forever, a cellophane tube of colored sweets. I took this occasion to leave & attend to Nicholas (who was screaming on his back in the pram) and Frieda (crying upstairs). The Crawfords, Jack odd & sidelong & extinguished, came over, ostensibly to see Nicholas. Mrs. C. said she thought I looked like Sylvia C's baby Paula. I felt flattered. She thinks Ted looks just like her son Morris. Resemblances to loved one's the height of praise. Discussed Morris' new milk cow (cost about £75), the future of apples.

June 7: Well, Percy Key is dying. That is the verdict. Poor old Perce, says everybody. Rose comes up almost every day. "Te-ed" she calls in her hysterical, throbbing voice. And Ted comes, from the study, the tennis court, the orchard, wherever, to lift the dying man from his armchair to his bed. He is very quiet afterwards. He is a bag of bones, says Ted. I saw him in one "turn" or "do", lying back on the bed, toothless, all beakiness of nose and chin, eyes sunken as if they were not, shuddering and blinking in a fearful way. And all about the world is gold and green, dripping with laburnum and buttercups and the sweet stench of June. In the cottage the fire is on and it is a dark twilight. The midwife said Percy would go into a coma this weekend and then "anything could happen". The sleeping pills the doctor gives him don't work, says Rose. He is calling all night: Rose, Rose, Rose. It has happened so quickly. First Rose stopped the doctor in January when I had the baby for a look at Percy's running eye and a check on his weight-loss. Then he was in hospital for lung x-rays. Then in again for a big surgery for "something on the lung". Did they find him so far gone with cancer they sewed him up again? Then home, walking, improving, but oddly quenched in his brightness & his songs. I found a wrinkled white paper bag of dusty jellybabies in the car yesterday from Rose. Then his five strokes. Now his diminishing.

Everybody has so easily given him up. Rose looks younger & younger. Sylvia Crawford set her hair yesterday. She felt creepy about it, left baby Paula with me & came over in between rinses in her frilly apron, dark-haired, white-skinned, with her high, sweet child-voice. Percy looked terrible since she had seen him last, she said. She thought cancer went wild if it was exposed to the air. The general sentiment of townsfolk: doctors just experiment on you in hospital. One you're in, if you're old, you're a goner.

June 9: Met the Rector coming out of his house-building site across the road. He turned up the lane to Court Green with me. I could feel his professional gravity coming over him. He read the notice on Rose's door as I went on up, then went round back. "Sylvia!" I heard Rose hiss behind me, and turned. She was pantomiming the rector's arrival & making lemon-moues & rejecting motions with one hand, very chipper.

July 2: Percy Key is dead. He died just at midnight, Monday, June 25th, and was buried Friday, June 29th, at 2:30. I find this difficult to believe. It all began with his eye watering, and Rose calling in the doctor, just after the birth of Nicholas. I have written a long poem "Berck-Plage" about it. Very moved. Several terrible glimpses.

Ted had for some days stopped lifting Percy in and out of bed. He could not take his sleeping pills, or swallow. The doctor was starting to give him injections. Morphia? He was in pain when he was conscious. The nurse counted 45 seconds between one breath and another. I decided to see him, I must see him, so went with Ted and Frieda. Rose and the smiling Catholic woman were lying on deck chairs in the yard. Rose's white face crumpled the minute she tried to speak. "The nurse told us to sit out. There's no more we can do. Isn't it awful to see him like this?" See him if you like, she told me. I went in through the quiet kitchen with Ted. The livingroom was full, still, hot with some awful translation taking place. Percy lay back on a heap of white pillows in his striped pajamas, his face already passed from human-ity, the nose a spiralling fleshless beak in thin air, the chin fallen in a point from it, like an opposite pole, and the mouth like an inverted black heart stamped into the yellow flesh between, a great raucous breath coming and going there with great effort like an awful bird, caught, but about to depart. His eyes showed through partly open lids like dissolved soaps or a clotted pus. I was very sick at this and had a bad migraine over my left eye for the rest of the day. The end, even of so marginal a man, a horror.

When Ted & I drove out to Exeter to catch the London train the following morning, the stone house was still, dewy and peaceful, the curtains stirring in the dawn air. He is dead, I said. Or he will be dead when we get back. He had died that night, mother said over the phone, when I called her up the following evening.

Went down after his death, the next day, the 27th. Ted had been down in the morning, said Percy was still on the bed, very yellow, his jaw bound and a book, a big brown book, propping it till it stiffened properly. When I went down they had just brought the coffin & put him in. The livingroom where he had lain was in an upheaval - - - bed rolled from the wall, mattresses on the lawn, sheets and pillows washed & airing. He lay in the sewing room, or parlor, in a long coffin of orangey soap-colored oak with silver handles, the lid propped against the wall at his head with a silver scroll: Percy Key, Died June 25, 1962. The raw date a shock. A sheet covered the coffin. Rose lifted it. A pale white beaked face, as of paper, rose under the veil that covered the hole cut in the glued white cloth cover. The mouth looked glued, the face powdered. She quickly put down the sheet. I hugged her. She kissed me and burst into tears. The dark, rotund sister from London with purple eye-circles deplored: They have no hearse, they have only a cart.

Friday, the day of the funeral, hot and blue, with theatrical white clouds passing. Ted & I, dressed in hot blacks, passed the church, saw the bowler-hatted men coming out of the gate with a high, spider-wheeled black cart.

They are going to call for the corpse, we said; we left a grocery order. The awful feeling of great grins coming onto the face, unstoppable. A relief; this is the hostage for death, we are safe for the time-being. We strolled round the church in the bright heat, the pollarded green limes like green balls, the far hills red, just ploughed, and one stooked with newly glittering wheat. Debated whether to wait out, or go in. Elsie, with her stump-foot was going in. Then Grace, Jim's wife. We went in. Heard priest meeting corpse at gate, incantating, coming close. Hair-raising. We stood. The flowery casket, nodding and flirting its petals, led up the aisle. The handsome mourners in black down to gloves & handbag, Rose, three daughters including the marble-beautiful model, one husband, Mrs. Crawford & the Catholic, smiling, only not smiling, the smile in abeyance, suspended. I hardly heard a word of the service, Mr. Lane for once quenched by the grandeur of ceremony, a vessel, as it should be.

Then we followed the funeral party after the casket out the side door to the street going up the hill to the cemetary. Behind the high black cart, which had started up with the priest swaying in black and white at a decorous pace, the funeral cars - - - one car, a taxi, then Jack Crawford, looking green and scared, in his big new red car. We got in with him. "Well, old Perce always wanted to be buried in Devon." You could see he felt he was next. I felt tears come. Ted motioned me to look at the slow uplifted faces of children in the primary school yard, all seated on rest rugs, utterly without grief, only bland curiosity, turning after us. We got out at the cemetary gate, the day blazing. Followed the black backs of the women. Six bowler hats of the bearers left at the first yew bushes in the grass. The coffin on boards, words said, ashses to ashes - - - that is what remained, not glory, not heaven. The amazingly narrow coffin lowered into the narrow red earth opening, left. The women led round, in a kind of goodbye circle, Rose rapt and beautiful and frozen, the Catholic dropping a handfull of earth which clattered. A great impulse welled in me to cast earth also, but it seemed as if it might be indecent, hurrying Percy into oblivion. We left the open grave. An unfinished feeling. Is he to be left up there uncovered, all alone? Walked home over the back hill, gathering immense stalks of fuchsia foxgloves and swinging our jackets in the heat.

July 4: Saw Rose, in a borrowed black velours hat, letting herself into the house. She going to London, but will return in a week. She had been having her hair done, guilltily, a wave of tight curls. "I looked so awful." She had

NOTES

These notes include identifications of significant people and places mentioned in Sylvia Plath's journals, as well as explanations of textual variants. Introductory paragraphs describe the physical characteristics of each journal. Notes are grouped by the individual journals to which they apply and are keyed to the page numbers of the printed journals. The terms to be identified (retaining Plath's original spelling and punctuation) are presented in italic type. Following a colon, explanations appear in roman type. People and places are identified at their first mention in the journals. Whenever possible, full names and dates are supplied, along with the individual's relationship to Sylvia Plath. Women are generally identified by the name they used when Plath knew them. Maiden names are often supplied as middle names for married female contacts. Notes for Plath's classmates include their academic degrees in the current format preferred by the college or university from which they graduated. Some graduate degrees are also supplied. Notes for Plath's professors and colleagues include their highest academic rank at Smith College or Cambridge University. Descriptions of other contacts include their professions. Current locations of businesses appear in these notes. The following abbreviations are used: SP (Sylvia Plath) and TH (Ted Hughes).

SP started keeping a diary when she was eleven. Her eight early diaries and journals, written between 1944 and 1949, are in the Sylvia Plath Collection at the Lilly Library, Indiana University, Bloomington, Indiana. The collection also contains eight diaries and annotated calendars, written between January 1951 and July 1957, and two scrapbooks from high school and college.

JOURNAL July 1950 – July 1953

Autograph manuscript on lined paper bound in three-quarter red and black cloth ledger binding, gold-stamped on spine: LAW / NOTES / 6-L / COOP. *Pagination:* 432 numbered pages (pages 421–32 blank); 26.7 × 20.5 cm.

8   *Ilo*: Ilo Pill, an Estonian refugee; dated and corresponded with SP, 1950–1953.
– *(being raped.)*: this phrase is written in SP's autograph in a different ink.
9   *Bob*: Robert George Riedeman (1930–); B.A. 1952, M.S. 1955, University of New Hampshire; dated SP, 1949–1950.
– *Linden Street*: located in Wellesley, Massachusetts, near the railroad tracks.
10 *mother*: Aurelia Schober Plath (1906–1994); associate professor, College of Practical Arts and Letters, Boston University, 1942–1971; SP's mother.
– *farm*: Lookout Farm, South Natick, Massachusetts. SP worked at Lookout Farm, summer 1950.
15 *Eddie Cohen*: Edward M. Cohen (1928–); SP's correspondent from Chicago, Illinois. Cohen and SP corresponded from 1950 until 1954 and met during SP's spring vacations in 1951 and 1952.
17 *Peter*: Peter Aldrich; SP's neighbor from Wellesley, Massachusetts. C. Duane Aldrich and Elizabeth Cannon Aldrich lived across the street from the Plaths at 23 Elmwood Road with their nine children: Duane, Peter, Stephen, John, Mark, Elizabeth, Ann, Amy, and Sarah.
19 *Warren*: Warren Joseph Plath (1935–); educated at Phillips Exeter Academy, Exeter, New Hampshire; A.B. 1957, Harvard College; Fulbright student at the University of Bonn, 1957–1958; Ph.D. 1964, Harvard University; SP's brother.
22 *best story*: SP's 'Den of Lions' published in *Seventeen* 10 (May 1951), third-place winner in *Seventeen*'s short-story contest.
24 *Bill*: William Albert Gallup, Jr (1929–); B.A. 1951, Amherst College; dated SP in 1950.
– *Perry*: Charles Perry Norton (1932–); B.S. 1954, Yale College; M.D. 1957, Boston University School of Medicine; SP's friend from Wellesley, Massachusetts. SP dated Perry Norton in high school and later dated his older brother Richard Norton.
– *Amherst*: Amherst, Massachusetts. Amherst College and the University of Massachusetts are located in Amherst, Massachusetts.
25 *I cannot*: 'A̶n̶d̶ I cannot' appears in the original manuscript (line 8 of entry 32).

26 *enough heart-beat*: '~~And~~ enough heart-beat' appears in the original manuscript (line 30 of entry 32).

 – *And warmth enough . . .* : following this line (line 35 of entry 32), SP deleted the following stanza: 'For a dry, crisp / Flat, stale / Saltless tower ~~of~~ / For a limp wisp, / Sad, pale / Moon wet flower. / (And never you / Haunts my days. / I am dry and barren / And the river of voices / Of girls in the adjoining room / Smoothes the edges / Of my dismays. / To bed, and sleep, / And tearless creep / The formless gray hours, / No laughter and no sunlight / And no flowers.)'

28 *Anne Davidow*: Ann Davidow (1932–); SP's friend from Highland Park, Illinois. Ann Davidow withdrew from Smith College in January 1951 following her first semester.

 – *Guy*: Guy Wyman Wilbor (1932–); B.A. 1954, Amherst College; dated SP, 1950–1951.

 – *Austin*: Austin Walsh Kenefick, Jr (1932–); B.A. 1954, Amherst College; briefly dated SP in 1950.

29 *Pat*: Patricia Gibson O'Neil (1932–); B.A. 1954, Smith College; SP's friend from Wellesley, Massachusetts.

 – *Corby Johnson*: Corbet Stephens Johnson, Jr (1932–); B.A. 1953, Amherst College; briefly dated SP in 1950.

 – *Haven House*: residence of SP during her first two years at Smith College, 1950–1952. Haven House is located at 96 Elm Street, Northampton, Massachusetts.

30 *Grammy*: Aurelia Greenwood Schober (1887–1956); SP's maternal grandmother.

 – *Clem*: Clement Moore Henry; Warren Plath's roommate at Phillips Exeter Academy.

 – *Hump*: Robert Hills Humphrey; B.Arch. 1952, Rensselaer Polytechnic Institute; dated SP, 1950–1951.

 – *Tooky*: probably SP's classmate Lois Winslow Sisson (1931–); B.A. 1952, Smith College; M.A. 1958, University of Chicago; married Robert Webb Ames (divorced 1969).

32 *House Dance*: each student residence at Smith College hosted its own winter and spring dances in the 1950s.

34 *Hopkins House*: student residence at Smith College located on the west side of Haven House. Hopkins House was designed in 1861 by William Fenno Pratt in the Gothic Revival style.

36 *mental hospital on the hill in back of the college*: Northampton State Hospital, Northampton, Massachusetts, home to nearly 2,500 patients in the 1950s.

37 *Marcia*: Marcia Brown (1932–); B.A. 1954, Smith College; SP's friend and roommate at Haven House during her sophomore year.

40 *father*: Otto Emil Plath (1885–1940); German instructor and biology professor at Boston University, 1922–1940; SP's father.

43 *And you won't see him if he asks again*: SP originally ended entry 45 with the following sentences: 'But you will see him if he asks again. You are a girl.' SP erased these sentences and wrote: 'And you won't see him if he asks again.' Earlier in the paragraph SP originally wrote: 'You know that you will go out with him again if he asks.' She later changed 'will' to 'won't'. SP continued to see Bill after her first date.

44 *would no doubt be shallow*: SP wrote the following definitions at the top of page 81 in the original manuscript in reference to entry 47:
'shallow: low in frequency and amplitude
'deep: high in frequency and amplitude   *ⱮⱮⱮⱮⱮⱮⱮ* 81

46 *Mr. Crockett*: Wilbury A. Crockett (1913–1994); SP's English teacher at Wellesley High School (formerly Gamaliel Bradford High School), 1947–1950.

48 *Dick*: Richard Allen Norton (1929–   ); B.A. 1951, Yale College; M.D. 1957, Harvard University; dated SP, 1951–1953. Norton's parents Mildred Smith Norton (1905–   ) and William Bunnell Norton (1905–1990) were friends of Aurelia Plath.

50 *Lake Saltonstall*: Saltonstall Ridge and the west side of Lake Saltonstall are located in East Haven, Connecticut.

51 *Chem Lab*: Yale University's Sterling Chemistry Laboratory, Prospect Street, New Haven, Connecticut.

52 *younger brother*: David William Norton (1944–   ); youngest brother of Richard Allen Norton.

56 *the lady or the tiger*: reference to the short story 'The Lady, or The Tiger?' by Frank R. Stockton (1882).

– *experimental film*: art film *Un Chien Andalou*, directed by Luis Buñuel and Salvador Dalí in 1928.

62 *art studio*: located in the old Hillyer Art Building at Smith College; replaced by the Fine Arts Center in 1972.

– *Cohen*: H. George Cohen (1913–1980); art professor, Smith College, 1940–1978. Cohen taught basic design (Art 13) completed by SP, 1950–1951, and principles, methods and techniques of drawing and painting (Art 210) completed by SP, 1951–1952.

– *Botany*: general botany course (Botany 11) completed by SP, 1950–1951. The course was directed by Kenneth E. Wright (1902–1988); botany professor, Smith College, 1946–1967; SP's faculty adviser; SP's colleague, 1957–1958.

64 *Grampy*: Frank Schober (1880–1965); *maître d'hôtel* at Brookline Country Club; SP's maternal grandfather.

65 *Mrs. Koffka*: Elisabeth Ahlgrimm Koffka (1896–1994); history professor, Smith College, 1929–1961. Koffka taught general European history (History 11) completed by SP, 1950–1951.

66 *Cape*: Cape Cod, Massachusetts, a peninsula in eastern Massachusetts.

69 *Mayos*: Dr Frederic B. Mayo (1915–) and Anne Blodgett Mayo (1918–1990). During the summer of 1951, SP was a mother's helper at the Mayos' home in Swampscott, Massachusetts, where she took care of their three children: Frederic (1944–), Esther ('Pinny') (1947–), and Joanne (1949–).

70 *Marblehead*: Marblehead, Massachusetts, a coastal town north of Swampscott, Massachusetts.

78 *Blodgetts*: John Henry Blodgett (1881–1971) and Ruth Sargent Paine Blodgett (1890–1967), B.A. 1912, Smith College, and their children: Esther Blodgett Meyer (1916–), B.A. 1937, Smith College; Anne Blodgett Mayo (1918–1990); John H. Blodgett, Jr (Jack); and Donald W. Blodgett. Marcia Brown took care of Mrs Meyer's children who lived at their grandparents' home in Swampscott, Massachusetts, during the summer of 1951.

92 *Ann*: Elizabeth Ann Hunt (1930–); A.B. 1952, English, Radcliffe College.

98 *Frank and Louise, Dot and Joe*: SP's uncle Frank Richard Schober (1919–) married to Louise Bowman Schober (1920–), and SP's aunt Dorothy Schober Benotti (1911–1981) married to Joseph Benotti (1911–1996).

104 *Honor Board*: a student-faculty group that judged infringements of the academic honor system at Smith College. During the 1952–1953 academic year, SP served as secretary of Honor Board, under the direction of Helen Whitcomb Randall (1908–2000); English professor at Smith College, 1931-1973; dean of the college, 1948–1960; SP's colleague, 1957–1958.

– *Press Board*: SP wrote news releases about Smith College for local papers, including the *Springfield Daily News,* the *Springfield Union*, and the *Daily Hampshire Gazette*, as a Press Board correspondent, 1951–1954.

– *Smith Review*: a literary magazine of Smith College. During her junior and senior years, SP served on the editorial board of the *Smith Review.*

– *Belmont Hotel*: SP worked as a waitress at the Belmont, a hotel in West Harwich, Massachusetts, June 1952.

– *Alison*: Alison Vera Smith (1933–); SP's friend and Smith classmate from New York City. In June 1952, Alison Smith withdrew from Smith College to attend Johns Hopkins University.

108 *Princeton boy*: Philip Livingston Poe Brawner (1931–); B.A. 1953, Princeton University; dated SP in 1952. Brawner was vice-president of the American Whig-Cliosophic Society, Princeton's debating club, which also published the *Nassau Literary Magazine.*

– *College Fiction Contest*: SP's short story 'Sunday at the Mintons" won one of two first prizes ($500) in *Mademoiselle*'s national fiction contest and was published in *Mademoiselle* 35 (August 1952).

– *encouraging letter from a well-known publisher*: SP received a 26 June 1952 letter from Harold Strauss, editor-in-chief of Alfred A. Knopf, Inc.

114 *Polly*: Pauline LeClaire; B.S. 1956, social and behavioral sciences, University of Massachusetts; SP's roommate at the Belmont, June 1952.

- *Ray*: Ray C. Wunderlich, Jr (1929–   ); B.S. 1951, University of Florida; M.D. 1955, Columbia University; dated SP, 1952–1953.

- *Art Kramer*: Arthur Bennet Kramer (1927–   ); B.S. 1949, Yale College; M.A. 1951, LL.B., 1953, Yale University; dated SP, 1952–1953.

115 *Rodger*: Roger Bradford Decker (1931–1993); B.A. 1953, Princeton University; dated SP in 1952.

119 *Cantors*: Margaret Kiefer Cantor (1910–   ) and M. Michael Cantor (1906–   ). During the summer of 1952, SP was a mother's helper at the Cantors' summer home in Chatham, Massachusetts, where she took care of their children: Joan (1939–   ), Susana (1947–   ), and William Michael (1949–   ). A twenty-two-year-old cousin, Marvin Cantor, frequently visited.

124 *first story in print*: SP's short story 'And Summer Will Not Come Again', *Seventeen* 9 (August 1950).

- *Val Gendron*: American fiction writer Val Gendron (1913–   ), formerly Ruth C. Fantus.

125 *August 12*: SP dated Robert Shepard Cochran (1935–1956) during the summer of 1952. He was a senior at the Clark School in Hanover, New Hampshire, and a summer resident of Chatham, Massachusetts.

138 *Attila*: Attila A. Kassay, Hungarian; B.A. 1955, business administration, Northeastern University; dated SP in 1952.

141 *Jim McNealy*: James DuBois McNeely (1933–   ); B.A. 1954, B.Arch. 1960, Yale College; dated SP in 1952.

- *Mrs. Morrill*: SP studied watercolor painting with Mrs Morrill, summer 1949.

- *Sue Slye*: Susan Slye (1930–   ); B.A. 1952, Smith College; resident of Haven House with SP.

143 *Phy. Sci. 193*: SP completed the first semester of an interdepartmental course about the world of atoms (Physical Science 193), fall 1952, and audited the second half of the course, spring 1953. The course was directed by Kenneth Wayne Sherk (1907–1972); professor of chemistry, Smith College, 1935–1972; SP's colleague 1957–1958.

145 *Constantine*: Constantine Sidamon-Eristoff (1930–   ), American; Russian Orthodox (religion); B.S. 1952, Princeton University; dated SP, 1951–1952.

146 *John Hall*: John A. Hall; B.A. 1953, Williams College; dated SP in 1949.

- *Doctor Booth*: Dr Marion Frances Booth (1899–1963); college physician and professor of bacteriology and public health, Smith College, 1941–1961; SP's Smith psychiatrist, 1954–1955; SP's colleague, 1957–1958. SP served on Honor Board with Dr Booth, 1952–1953.

- *Miss Drew*: Elizabeth A. Drew (1887–1965); English professor, Smith College, 1946–1961; SP's colleague, 1957–1958. Drew taught a course on the literature of the nineteenth and twentieth centuries (English 211) completed by SP, 1951–1952, and modern poetry (English unit) completed by SP, 1952–1953.

146 *Francesca Raccioppi*: Dr Francesca M. Racioppi Benotti (1916–1998); the Plaths' family doctor who practiced in Wellesley, Massachusetts, under her maiden name Francesca M. Racioppi, M.D.

149 *Prouty*: American novelist Olive Higgins Prouty (1882–1974). SP received the Olive Higgins Prouty scholarship when she was a student at Smith College.

 – *Cal*: Carol Lynn Raybin (1932–   ); B.A. 1954, Smith College; friend of SP.

155 *Thanksgiving I met a man*: Perry Norton's classmate Myron Lotz (1932–   ); B.S. 1954, Yale College; Henry fellow, 1955–1956, Oxford University; M.D. 1958, Yale University; intern at Massachusetts General Hospital, Boston, 1958–1959; dated SP, 1952–1954.

 – *Saranac*: SP visited Richard Norton at Ray Brook, a sanatorium in Saranac, New York, where he was recovering from tuberculosis, 1952–1953.

157 *Haven, Albright, Wallace, Northrop, Gillett*: student houses at Smith College. Wallace House was razed in 1959.

 – *Browns*: Marcia Brown and her mother Carol Taylor Brown. During her junior year, Marcia Brown lived off campus with her mother at 211 Crescent Street, Northampton, Massachusetts.

 – *I moved to a new house*: SP was required to work one hour per day for part of her room and board at Lawrence House, where she lived from September 1952 until her graduation from Smith College in June 1955. SP's roommate junior year was Mary A. Bonneville (1931–   ); B.A. 1953, Smith College.

 – *Chaucer unit*: medieval literature taught by Howard Rollin Patch (1889–1963); English professor, Smith College, 1919–1957.

158 *Milton next term*: Milton (English 39) taught by Eleanor Terry Lincoln (1903–1994); English professor, Smith College, 1934–1968; SP's colleague, 1957–1958.

162 *Schubert*: Shubert Theater, 247 College Street, New Haven, Connecticut.

 – *Al Haverman*: SP attended Christmas vespers and the Haven House dance on 15 December 1951 with Richard Norton's friend Al Haverman.

171 *Rahar's*: Rahar's Inn, a bar and restaurant located at 7 Old South Street, Northampton, Massachusetts, in the 1950s.

 – *coffee shop*: the Coffee Shop, a restaurant located at 56 Green Street, Northampton, Massachusetts, in the 1950s.

172 *gordon*: Gordon Ames Lameyer (1930–1991); B.A. 1953, Amherst College; dated SP, 1953–1955; traveled with SP in Europe, April 1956. Gordon Lameyer was encouraged to date SP by his mother Helen Ames Lameyer (1894–1980), B.A. 1918, Smith College.

173 *McCurdy*: Philip Emerald McCurdy (1935–   ); A.B. 1956, Harvard College; SP's friend from Wellesley, Massachusetts.

174 *170*: entry 170 is followed by entry 180 in the original manuscript.

175 *Doctor Chrisman*: O. Donald Chrisman (1917–   ); a Northampton
orthopaedist who maintained private clinic hours at the Elizabeth Mason
Infirmary, Smith College.

176 *Look Park*: Look Memorial Park, Northampton, Massachusetts.

178 *junior phi bete*: SP was elected to Phi Beta Kappa, September 1953.

 – *sandy*: son of M. E. Lynn and Dr William Lynn, Richard Norton's physician at
Ray Brook. Sandy Lynn died in an accident on 3 March 1953.

180 *Auden*: English-born poet Wystan Hugh Auden (1907–1973); William Allan
Neilson Research Professor, Smith College, 1953.

185 *BU*: Boston University (Boston, Massachusetts).

 – *O'Connor*: Irish-born writer Michael John O'Donovan (1903–1966) who
published under the name Frank O'Connor. In 1953, O'Connor taught two
courses at the Harvard University Summer School: the twentieth-century novel
and the short story, an advanced composition course with limited enrollment.

186 *Hans*: Hans-Joachim Neupert; SP's correspondent from Grebenhain, Germany.
Neupert and SP corresponded from 1947 to 1952.

 – *Smith Quarterly article*: SP's article '*Smith Review* Revived' published in the
Smith Alumnae Quarterly 45 (Fall 1953).

187 *Miss Abels*: Cyrilly Abels (1904–1975); managing editor of *Mademoiselle*,
1947–1962. SP worked for Abels as guest managing editor of *Mademoiselle*,
June 1953. During her month in New York, SP dated United Nations
simultaneous interpreter Gary Kamirloff and Peruvian legal delegate José
Antonio La Vias. Carol LeVarn, SP, and many of the other guest editors suffered
from ptomaine poisoning on 17 June 1953.

JOURNAL 22 November 1955 – 18 April 1956

Typescript on white paper with autograph manuscript corrections, 38 numbered
leaves; 28 × 21.7 cm. Many of the entries in this journal are excerpts from letters
to Richard Sassoon.

191 *Excerpt from letter*: 'Excerpt from letter ~~to Sassoon~~.' appears in the original
typescript.

 – *at midnight, <u>when the moon makes blue lizard scales of roof shingles</u>*: 'Cf.
poem' written in SP's autograph in the margin opposite this line, possibly a
reference to an image in SP's poem 'Dialogue Over a Ouija Board'.

192 *sassoon*: Richard Laurence Sassoon (1934–   ); B.A. 1955, Yale College;
attended the Sorbonne, 1955–1956; dated SP, 1954–1956. Sassoon was born in
Paris, France, and raised in Tryon, North Carolina.

193 *Excerpt: December 11*: 'Excerpt: December 11 ~~Letter to Sassoon~~.' appears in
the original typescript.

194 *January 11*: '~~To Sassoon~~: January 11' appears in the original typescript.

194 *from letter january 15*: 'from letter ~~to Sassoon~~ january 15' appears in the
    original typescript.

195 *January 28*: '~~To Sassoon~~: January 28' appears in the original typescript.

197 *Win*: Winthrop Dickinson Means (1933–   ), American; A.B. 1955, Harvard
    College; Fulbright fellow, research student, Emmanuel College, Cambridge,
    1955–1956; Ph.D. 1960, geology, University of California, Berkeley; friend of
    SP.

  – *John*: John Nicholas Lythgoe (1934–   ), British; B.A. 1957, Ph.D. 1961,
    natural sciences, Trinity College, Cambridge; dated SP, 1955–1956.

  – *Chris*: Christopher Rene Levenson (1934–   ), British; B.A. 1957, English
    and modern languages, Downing College, Cambridge; dated SP,
    1955–1956.

198 *Nat*: Warren Plath's friend Nathaniel D. LaMar, Jr (1933–   ), American; A.B.
    1955, Harvard College; research student on a Henry fellowship at Pembroke
    College, Cambridge, 1955–1956; dated SP, 1955–1956.

  – *Mallory*: Joseph Mallory Wober (1936–   ), British; B.A. 1957, natural
    sciences, King's College, Cambridge; dated SP, 1955–1956.

  – *Iko*: Isaac Meshoulem (1934–   ), Israeli; B.A. 1957, M.A. 1961, economics
    and law, Pembroke College, Cambridge; dated SP, 1955–1956.

  – *Brian*: Brian Neal Howard Desmond Corkery (1933–   ), British; B.A. 1957,
    history, Pembroke College, Cambridge; dated SP, 1955–1956.

  – *Martin*: Martin Deckett (1931–   ), British; B.A. 1956, M.A. 1960,
    mathematics and economics, Pembroke College, Cambridge; dated SP in
    1955.

  – *David*: David Keith Rodney Buck (1933–1989), British; B.A. 1958, English,
    Christ's College, Cambridge; dated SP in 1955.

199 *Stephen Spender*: English writer Stephen Harold Spender (1909–1995).

  – *Jane*: Jane Lucille Baltzell (1935–   ), American; B.A. 1955, Brown
    University; B.A. 1957, Newnham College, Cambridge; Ph.D. 1965,
    University of California, Berkeley. Baltzell read English on a Marshall
    scholarship at Cambridge and was SP's housemate at Whitstead,
    1955–1956.

200 *bronze boy*: a copy of Andrea del Verrocchio's sculpture *Boy with Dolphin*
    stands in Newnham College gardens, a 1930 gift of Miss Fanner.

201 *Vence story*: SP's short story 'The Matisse Chapel', inspired by her January
    1956 trip to Vence, France, with Richard Sassoon. SP visited the Chapelle du
    Rosaire designed by Henri Matisse.

  – *Elly*: Elinor Linda Friedman (1934–   ), American; B.A. 1956, Smith College;
    SP's friend.

  – *Sue*: Susan Lynn Weller (1933–1990), American; B.A. 1955, Smith College;
    B.A. 1958, M.A. 1962, philosophy, politics, and economics, Somerville
    College, Oxford; SP's friend and fellow resident of Lawrence House.

202 *I was going mad night after night being a screaming whore in a yellow dress*: SP
played the part of Alice in the Cambridge Amateur Dramatics Club production
of Ben Jonson's *Bartholomew Fair*, winter 1955.

- *Dick Gilling*: Christopher Richard Gilling (1933–), British; B.A. 1956,
English, Trinity Hall, Cambridge; dated SP in 1955.

203 *Cambridge article and drawing*: SP's article 'Leaves from a Cambridge
Notebook' published in the *Christian Science Monitor* (5 March 1956 and
6 March 1956).

- *Redpath*: Robert Theodore Holmes Redpath (1913–1997); fellow of Trinity
College, Cambridge, and lecturer in English, 1951–1980.

- *Grove Lodge*: a house situated next to the Fitzwilliam Museum at Cambridge
University used for lectures in the 1950s.

205 *P.S.*: the entire postscript is written in SP's autograph.

206 *Hamish*: David Hamish Stewart (1933–), Canadian; B.A. 1956, English,
Queens' College, Cambridge; dated SP in 1956.

207 *Derek*: Derek William Strahan (1935–), British/North Ireland; B.A. 1956,
modern and medieval languages (French and Spanish), Queens' College,
Cambridge; dated SP in 1956.

- *Ira*: Ira O. Scott, Jr (1918–), American; instructor at Harvard University,
1953–1955; dated SP, summer 1954.

- *St. Botolph's*: Cambridge journal *Saint Botolph's Review*, edited by David
Ross. A party was held on 25 February 1956 to celebrate the launching of this
new literary journal.

- *Hunter*: Nancy Jean Hunter (1933–), American; B.A. 1955, Smith College;
SP's friend and roommate at Lawrence House, 1954–1955. During the summer
of 1954, SP and Hunter also sublet an apartment in Cambridge, Massachusetts,
with Kay Quinn and Joan Smith.

- *E. Lucas Meyers*: Elvis Lucas Myers (1930–), American; B.A. 1953,
University of the South; B.A. 1956, archaeology and anthropology, Downing
College, Cambridge; friend of Ted Hughes and contributor to *Saint Botolph's
Review*.

209 *Mr. Fisher*: Alfred Young Fisher (1902–1970); English professor, Smith College,
1937–1967; SP's colleague, 1957–1958. SP completed a special studies in
poetry writing with Fisher, 1954–1955.

- *Mr. Kazin*: Alfred Kazin (1915–1998); William Allan Neilson Research
Professor, Smith College, 1954–1955. Kazin taught short story writing (English
347) and the twentieth-century American novel (English 417) completed by SP,
1954–1955.

- *Mr. Gibian*: George Gibian (1924–); associate professor of English and
Russian literature, Smith College, 1951–1961; SP's thesis adviser, 1954–1955;
SP's colleague, 1957–1958. Gibian taught Tolstoy and Dostoevsky (Russian
literature 35b) completed by SP, spring 1954. SP's thesis *The Magic Mirror: A*

Study of the Double in Two of Dostoevsky's Novels was awarded the Marjorie Hope Nicolson Prize in 1955.

210 *Falcon's Yard*: Falcon Yard, an old inn yard reached from a city centre street called Petty Cury in Cambridge, England.

– *Bert*: Bertram Wyatt-Brown (1932–), American; B.A. 1953, University of the South; B.A. 1957, history, King's College, Cambridge; dated SP's housemate Jane Baltzell.

211 *Dan Huys*: Daniel Huws (1932–), British; B.A. 1955, Peterhouse, Cambridge; friend of Ted Hughes and contributor to *Saint Botolph's Review*. Huws lent Hughes his flat at 18 Rugby Street, London, 1955–1956.

– *Than Minton*: Nathaniel David Minton (1935–), British; B.A. 1956, M.A. 1975, natural sciences, Trinity College, Cambridge; friend of Ted Hughes and contributor to *Saint Botolph's Review*.

– *Weissbort*: Daniel Jack Weissbort (1935–), British; B.A. 1956, M.A. 1981, economics and history, Queens' College, Cambridge; friend of Ted Hughes and contributor to *Saint Botolph's Review*.

– *Ross*: David Andrews Ross (1935–), British; B.A. 1956, M.A. 1971, history, Peterhouse, Cambridge; friend of Ted Hughes and editor of *Saint Botolph's Review*.

– *Ted Hughes*: English poet Edward James Hughes (1930–1998); B.A. 1954, M.A. 1958, archaeology and anthropology, Pembroke College, Cambridge; SP's husband, 1956–1963.

215 *Varsity*: Cambridge weekly undergraduate newspaper. SP wrote articles for *Varsity*.

– *Philip Booth*: Philip E. Booth (1925–); assistant professor of English, Wellesley College, 1954–1961; married to Margaret Tillman Booth; nephew of Smith College physician Dr Marion Frances Booth.

216 *March 1*: '~~To Richard~~: March 1' appears in the original typescript.

218 *"Only listen to me this last once*: '~~My darling Richard~~. "Only listen to me this last once.' appears in the original typescript.

– *Being a woman*: 'Being a woman, ~~my darling one~~, it is like being crucified' appears in the original typescript.

219 *For, I am committed to you*: 'For, ~~my Richard~~, I am committed to you' appears in the original typescript.

– *I thought even*: 'I thought even, at the most desperate time, when I was so sick and could not sleep, but only lie and curse the flesh, ~~of Gordon~~ whom I was going to marry' appears in the original typescript.

– *I was thinking of the few times in my life*: 'I was thinking, ~~my darling~~, of the few times in my life' appears in the original typescript.

220 *Wertz*: Richard Wayne Wertz (1933–), American; B.A. 1955, Yale College; resident of Westminster College, Cambridge, 1955–1956; friend of Nancy Hunter; roommate of Richard Sassoon at Yale College; dated SP, 1955–1956.

224 *Ruth Beuscher*: SP's American psychiatrist Ruth Tiffany Barnhouse Beuscher (1923–1999). SP was Dr Beuscher's patient at McLean Hospital in 1953 and continued private therapy through 1959.

 – *Keith*: Robert Keith Middlemas (1935–), British; B.A. 1958, history, Pembroke College, Cambridge; friend of SP.

225 *Miss Burton*: Kathleen Marguerite Passmore Burton (1921–); lecturer in English, Newnham College, Cambridge,1949–1960; director of studies in English, 1952–1960; SP's director of studies and supervisor.

 – *Miss Welsford*: Enid Elder Hancock Welsford (1892–1981); director of studies in English, Newnham College, Cambridge, 1929–1952; author of *The Fool: His Social and Literary History* (London: Faber and Faber, 1935). SP attended Welsford's lectures on tragedy in 1955.

 – *Dr. Krook*: Dorothea Greenberg Krook (1920–1989); research fellow at Newnham College, Cambridge, and assistant lecturer in English, 1954–1958; SP's supervisor.

 – *Lou*: Louis Hollister Healy, Jr (1929–1992), American; B.S. 1951, engineering, Yale College; dated SP in 1954. Healy was SP's neighbor during the summer of 1954 when she was living in Cambridge, Massachusetts, and attending elementary German classes at the Harvard University Summer School.

 – *Gary*: Garry Eugene Haupt (1933–1979), American; B.A. 1955, Yale College; B.A. 1957, English, Pembroke College, Cambridge; dated SP in 1956.

226 *Miss Barrett*: Anne Judith Barrett (1930–); temporary assistant lecturer in French, Girton College, Cambridge, 1956–1957; SP's French tutor, 1955–1956.

229 *Manuscript club*: Wrexham Trust Association at Yale University.

 – *Willey*: Basil Willey (1897–1978); lecturer and King Edward VII Professor of English, Cambridge University, 1923–1964.

232 *Dr. Davy*: Brian William Davy (1914–1993); SP's Cambridge psychiatrist in 1956.

235 *Dreaming of being home in Winthrop*: the word 'poem' is written in SP's autograph in the fore-edge margin opposite this paragraph in the original typescript, possibly a reference to SP's poem 'Dream with Clam-Diggers'.

 – *April 18*: 'T̶o̶ ̶S̶a̶s̶s̶o̶o̶n̶: April 18' appears in the original typescript.

JOURNAL 15 July 1956

Typescript on white paper with autograph manuscript corrections, 5 numbered leaves; 27.7 × 21.5 cm.

239 *Benidorm*: a fishing village in eastern Spain on the Mediterranean Sea.

 – *strewn with a few odd crabs, star-fish and shells*: 'm̶i̶x̶e̶d̶ strewn with o̶c̶c̶a̶s̶i̶o̶n̶a̶l̶ a few odd crabs, star-fish and shells / squid.' appears in the original typescript.

240 *Alicante*: a Mediterranean port in southeastern Spain.

243 *We also had trouble with the petrol stove*: In the inner margin opposite this sentence, SP wrote the following calculation: 500 divided by 40 equals 12.

JOURNAL 22 July 1956 – 26 August 1956

Typescript with autograph manuscript corrections, 18 leaves, probably torn from a Challenge Triplicate Book; 24.7 × 18.1 cm. Each leaf is stamped with a number. Triplicate leaves with the same number are differentiated in these notes by [a], [b], and [c]. Leaf [a] is ruled paper and leaves [b] and [c] are blank paper. Many leaves are missing. SP used this copybook for her creative writing as well as journal writing. Many of the surviving journal entries are drafts for short stories and articles, including 'Sketchbook of a Spanish Summer'.

247 *Benidorm: July 22*: entry typed on leaves 4[b–c]–5[a] of the original copybook.
249 *book about how all the animals became*: TH's children's book *How the Whale Became* (London: Faber and Faber, 1963).
 – *Tomas Ortunio*: SP and TH rented a house at 59 Tomas Ortunio, Benidorm, Provincia de Alicante, Spain, after their brief stay with Señora Mangada.
250 *Benidorm: July 23 (continued)*: typed on leaf 10[a] of the original copybook. The first part of this entry is lacking.
251 *In the station*: SP's fictional entry is typed on leaves 20[a-c] of the original copybook. The draft fragment begins with the phrase 'grayed the sky and they switched trains at Irun.' The word 'omit' is written in SP's autograph in the inner margin at the top of leaf 20[a].
253 *Benidorm: August 14*: entry typed on leaves 70[b–c]–71[a–b] of the original copybook.
254 *Vox*: TH filled out an application to teach at Instituto Vox (Madrid, Spain).
255 *Ted finding ant-track*: 'Ants' is written in SP's autograph in the inner margin opposite this paragraph, possibly a reference to the ant imagery in SP's poem 'Spider'.
256 *Benidorm: August 17*: entry typed on leaves 76[b–c]–77[a] of the original copybook.
259 *Pinewood studios*: When TH met SP in 1956, he was a reader at Pinewood Studios Ltd, a British film studio chaired by J. Arthur Rank.
260 *Paris: August 26*: entry typed on leaf 83[b or c] of the original copybook. The word 'SPAIN' is printed in SP's autograph at the top of the leaf.
261 *Sketchbook of a Spanish Summer*: entry typed on leaves 92[b–c]–93[a] of the original copybook. SP's article 'Sketchbook of a Spanish Summer' was published with four of her drawings in the *Christian Science Monitor* (5 and 6 November 1956).

JOURNAL 3 January 1957 – 11 March 1957

Typescript on white paper with autograph manuscript corrections, 10 leaves; 27.8 × 21.5 cm.

267 *Cambridge: January 3: Walk to Granchester*: 'See last pages: Fish & chip shop' is written at the top of the first leaf in SP's autograph along with the phrase 'Cows & Chaucer' in the inner margin opposite the first paragraph describing SP's walk from Cambridge along the river Granta to nearby Grantchester, England.
269 *SRL*: New York weekly *Saturday Review of Literature*.
 – *Wendy*: Wendy Christie; friend of Dorothea Krook and SP from Cambridge, England.
270 *ML Rosenthal*: American poet and critic Macha Louis Rosenthal (1917–1996); poetry editor of the *Nation*, 1956–1961.
272 *giovanni*: Giovanni Perego; Paris correspondent of *Paese Sera;* dated SP, spring 1956.
274 *Mary Ellen Chase*: American writer Mary Ellen Chase (1887–1973); professor of English, Smith College, 1926–1955.
276 *Turned onto the Fen Causeway*: 'Fish & Chips' is written in SP's autograph next to this paragraph in the inner margin.

JOURNAL 15 July 1957 – 21 August 1957

Typescript on white paper with autograph manuscript corrections and underlining, 10 leaves; 27.8 × 21.4 cm.

283 *Dan Aaron*: Daniel Aaron (1912–   ); English professor, Smith College, 1939–1972; director of the freshman English course (English 11) taught by SP, 1957–1958.
 – *Sam Lawrence*: American publisher Seymour Lawrence (1926–1994).
286 *Spaulding*: Myrtle and Lester Spaulding; proprietors of Hidden Acres, a cottage colony on McKoy Road in Eastham, Massachusetts. SP and TH stayed in one of the Spauldings' cabins during the summer of 1957.
287 *Ted's rosy mother*: SP's mother-in-law Edith Farrar Hughes (1898–1969); married to William Henry Hughes (1894–1981).
 – *Sat Eve Post*: Philadelphia journal the *Saturday Evening Post*.
289 *Sassoons*: George Thornycroft Sassoon (1936–   ), British; B.A. 1958, natural sciences, King's College, Cambridge; son of English poet Siegfried Sassoon and distant cousin of SP's friend Richard Sassoon. In 1957, George Sassoon and his wife Stephanie Munro Sassoon (1938–   ) lived above SP and TH at 55 Eltisley Avenue, Cambridge, England.
 – *Miss Cohen*: Ruth Louisa Cohen (1906–1991); principal of Newnham College, Cambridge, 1954–1972.

289 *Miss Morris*: Irene Victoria Morris (1913–); lecturer in German, Newnham College, Cambridge, 1947–1966.

– *white goddess*: reference to *The White Goddess* by Robert Graves (1948).

290 *How we cling to these days of July: August is a September month*: SP changed 'mother' to 'month' in the original typescript.

291 *July 29: Monday*: the names next to this heading are written in SP's autograph.

292 *Get into novel deep enough so it will go on at the same time*: SP placed an exclamation mark in the inner margin against this sentence.

294 *Yesterday, the rejection of my poetry book*: SP's poetry collection 'Two Lovers and a Beachcomber' was rejected for the Yale Series of Younger Poets Award in 1957.

295 *A.C.Rich*: American poet Adrienne Cecile Rich (1929–).

– *Donald Hall*: American poet Donald Hall (1928–).

– *Mavis Gallant*: Canadian short story writer Mavis Gallant (1922–). SP read Gallant's short stories in the *New Yorker* and her novel *Green Water, Green Sky* (1959).

296 *Hamp*: SP's abbreviation for Northampton, Massachusetts.

JOURNAL 28 August 1957 – 14 October 1958

Autograph manuscript on lined paper half-bound in red cloth with maroon paper over boards, blind-stamped on back cover: C. Combridge Ltd. / Birmingham / C. B. 900. *Pagination:* iv,181,[3] numbered pages (pages 177–78 are lacking); 32.2 × 20 cm. *Provenance*: When this journal was sold to Smith College in 1981, it was wrapped in acid-free tissue paper and sealed in an envelope, with the following note written on the paper envelope (in TH's autograph): 'Sylvia Plath / Diary 1957–59 / Sealed 2^d Sept 1981 / in presence of / Ted Hughes / Not to be opened until 11^t February 2013 / WITNESSED BY: / R. L. Davids (signature) / Felix Pryor (signature)'. Unsealed by TH on 14 September 1998.

301 *(girl thought she wanted "sultry")*: '(girl / she thought she wanted "sultry")' appears in the original manuscript.

303 *Sibyl Moss*: the following names also appear in the original manuscript at the end of the first short story: 'Sibyl / Moss, Evi / Glidden, Milton / Greenough, Curt-Quandt / ~~Ward~~ Will / Geoffrey-Fleischmann'.

– *Evi Larkin*: 'Evi Larkin, ~~Lois~~ Jill Holly Ford, Julian Gascoigne, ~~Bradley~~ Chandler Whipple' appear in the original manuscript at the end of the second short story.

304 *Max Goldberg*: Maxwell Henry Goldberg (1907–); English professor, University of Massachusetts (Amherst campus), 1928–1930, 1933–1962; head of the English department in 1958 when TH taught at the university.

305 *Mr. Hill*: SP's colleague Charles Jarvis Hill (1904–1999); English professor,

Smith College, 1932–1966; acting chairman of the English department, fall 1957.

305 *Freeman's yellow house*: William H. Freeman (1884–1954) and Marion Saunders Freeman (1908–1998) lived at 8 Somerset Terrace, Winthrop, Massachusetts, with their children David (1932–) and Ruth (1933–). The Freemans were neighbors and friends of the Plath family.

309 *Mr. Petersson*: Robert Torsten Petersson (1918–); English professor, Smith College, 1952–1985; SP's colleague, 1957–1958.

– *James*: British writer James Guy Bramwell (1911–), who published under the pseudonym James Byrom. SP read Byrom's autobiography *The Unfinished Man* (1957).

– *Joan*: SP's British colleague Joan Maxwell Bramwell (1923–); English professor, Smith College, 1957–1992; married to British writer James Guy Bramwell.

– *Sally*: Sallie Harris Sears (1932–); instructor of English, Smith College, 1957–1961; SP's colleague, 1957–1958.

310 *Monas*: Sidney Monas (1924–); assistant professor of history, Smith College, 1957–1962; SP's colleague, 1957–1958.

– *Marlies*: Marlies Kallmann Danziger (1926–); assistant professor of English, Smith College, 1951–1958; SP's colleague, 1957–1958.

– *Leonard*: American fiction writer Leonard Michaels (1933–); friend of SP's Smith classmate Elinor Friedman.

– *Sage*: Sage Hall at Smith College with an auditorium seating 700 persons.

311 *McKee*: Minerva and John McKee; SP's neighbors. The McKees rented a second-floor apartment at 337 Elm Street, Northampton, Massachusetts.

– *Spofford*: Edward Washburn Spofford (1931–); classics instructor, Smith College, 1957–1961; SP's colleague, 1957–1958.

– *Ventura*: Dody Ventura is a character in SP's short story 'Stone Boy with Dolphin', along with Leonard, Mrs Guinea, Miss Minchell, and Hamish, among others.

– *Dido*: Dido Milroy Merwin; married to American poet William Stanley Merwin (1927–), separated in 1968 and divorced in 1978. Dido Merwin's maiden name was Diana Whalley. She was born in 1912 or 1914 in Gloucestershire, England, and died in 1990.

314 *Arvin*: Newton Arvin (1900–1963); English professor, Smith College, 1922–1960; SP's colleague, 1957–1958; resident of 45 Prospect Street, Northampton, Massachusetts. Arvin taught American fiction from 1830 to 1900 (English 321) at Smith College. SP completed this course as a student in 1954 and corrected papers for it as an instructor in 1958.

– *Oscar Williams*: American poet Oscar Williams (1900–1964); married to the American poet Gene Derwood (1909–1954). Williams mailed a sound recording of *The Poems of Gene Derwood* (Spoken Arts, 1955) to TH in 1958.

Williams also concluded his revised edition of *The Pocket Book of Modern Verse* (1958) with three poems by TH: 'The Martyrdom of Bishop Farrar', 'The Hag', and 'The Thought-Fox'.

316 *Mike*: Davenport Plumer III (1932–); B.A. 1955, Dartmouth College; married to SP's friend Marcia Brown (divorced 1969). Plumer adopted boy-girl twins and a younger son with Marcia Brown and fathered a daughter in a subsequent marriage.

317 *Bob Tucker*: TH's colleague Robert G. Tucker (1921–1982); English professor, University of Massachusetts (Amherst campus), 1951–1981; married to Jean Knorr Tucker.

– *Sid Kaplan*: TH's colleague Sidney Kaplan (1913–1993); English professor, University of Massachusetts (Amherst campus), 1946–1978; married to Emma Nogrady Kaplan (1911–), assistant reference librarian, Smith College, 1953–1977.

– *Leonard Baskin*: American sculptor and graphic artist Leonard Baskin (1922–2000); art professor, Smith College, 1953–1974; SP's colleague, 1957–1958; friend of TH and SP.

318 *Wendell*: Wendell Stacy Johnson (1927–1990); associate professor of English, Smith College, 1952–1962; SP's colleague, 1957–1958.

– *Alison*: D. Alison Gilbert (1931–); assistant professor of history, Smith College, 1958–1959; SP's colleague in 1958.

321 *Miss Van der Poel*: Priscilla Paine Van der Poel (1907–1994); art history professor, Smith College, 1934–1972. SP audited Van der Poel's course on modern art (Art 315) in 1958.

322 *Dunn*: Esther Cloudman Dunn (1891–1977); English professor, Smith College, 1922–1960; SP's colleague, 1957–1958. Dunn taught Shakespeare (English 36) completed by SP, 1954–1955.

– *Isabella Gardner*: American poet Isabella Gardner (1915–1981).

323 *Sultans*: SP's colleague Stanley Sultan (1928–); instructor of English, Smith College, 1955–1959; married to Florence Lehman Sultan (divorced 1964); father of James Lehman and Sonia Elizabeth.

– *Tuesday night: February 4th*: entries for 4 February 1958 (evening) through 28 February 1958 are written on pages 32–59 and 1–28 of the original manuscript (numbered simultaneously by SP).

326 *Paul Roche*: Donald Robert Paul Roche (1928–); instructor of English, Smith College, 1956–1958; SP's colleague, 1957–1958. Roche read from his unpublished reminiscences of Virginia Woolf, 'Portrait of Virginia', on 27 February 1958 and from his translation of *Oedipus the King* with TH and members of the Smith College faculty on 21 May 1958.

– *Clarissa*: Clarissa Tanner Roche (1931–); married to SP's colleague Paul Roche (divorced 1983); mother of Pandora, Martin, Vanessa, and Cordelia. Paul Roche was hired as an instructor at Smith College through the connections of Clarissa Roche's aunt Virginia Traphagen (1904–1968), B.A. 1926, Smith College.

326 *John Sweeney*: John Lincoln Sweeney (1906–1986); professor of English, Harvard University; sixth curator of the Woodberry Poetry Room at Harvard University; married to Celtic literature scholar Maíre Sweeney; brother of James Johnson Sweeney, former head of the Museum of Modern Art, N.Y., N.Y.

- *Pat Hecht*: Patricia Harris Hecht (1933–); married to SP's colleague Anthony Hecht (divorced 1961); mother of Jason and Adam.

327 *Olwyn*: Olwyn Marguerite Hughes (1928–); SP's sister-in-law.

- *Whelans*: Northampton police sergeant James J. Whalen (1916–1998) and Constance Linko Whalen (1928–). SP and TH rented a furnished third-floor apartment from the Whalens, who lived at 337 Elm Street, Northampton, Massachusetts, with their three children: David, Lawrence, and Sara.

328 *Buckleys*: On 6 October 1951, Mr and Mrs William F. Buckley hosted a supper dance at their home in Sharon, Connecticut, in honour of their daughter Maureen Lee Buckley (1933–1964); B.A. 1954, Smith College. Maureen Buckley invited all her housemates at Haven House to the party, including SP.

329 *Tony Hecht*: American poet Anthony Evan Hecht (1923–); assistant professor of English, Smith College, 1956–1962; SP's colleague, 1957–1958. SP interviewed Hecht for her article 'Poets on Campus' published in *Mademoiselle* 37 (August 1953).

- *Wheelwright*: Philip Ellis Wheelwright (1901–); William Allan Neilson Research Professor, Smith College, 1958. SP and TH attended Wheelwright's 10 February 1958 Neilson lecture 'Humanism and Symbolism'.

330 *Antoine*: TH's friend Antoine Michel Marie Tavera (1926–); B.A. 1953, M.A. 1957, Pembroke College, Cambridge; Licencié ès Lettres, 1948, Diplômé d'Etudes Supérieures, 1949, Agrégé de l'Université, 1955, Sorbonne; instructor in French, Mount Holyoke College, 1956–1958; resident of Dickinson House, South Hadley, Massachusetts.

331 *Miss Hornbeak*: Katherine Gee Hornbeak (1897–1985); English professor, Smith College, 1930–1962; SP's colleague, 1957–1958. SP and Hornbeak shared an office (room 59) in William Allan Neilson Library, Smith College.

333 *Van Voris*: William Hoover Van Voris (1923–); English professor, Smith College, 1957–1988; SP's colleague, 1957–1958.

334 *Barry Fudger*: Barry John Fudger (1934–1984), British; B.A. 1959, M.A. 1965, English, St John's College, Cambridge.

- *Ildiko Hayes*: Ildiko Patricia Hayes (1936–), British; B.A. 1958, English Newnham College, Cambridge.

- *Judy Linton*: Judith Anne Linton (1936–), British; B.A. 1957, M.A. 1965, English, Newnham College, Cambridge.

- *Dan Massey*: Daniel Raymond Massey (1933–1998), British; B.A. 1956, M.A.

1960, English, King's College, Cambridge; fellow actor with SP in the Cambridge Amateur Dramatics Club production of *Bartholomew Fair* in 1955.

334 *Ben Nash*: Benjamin Joliffe Nash (1935–), British; B.A. 1958, modern and medieval languages, King's College, Cambridge.

337 *Tony*: Anthony James Gray (1936–), British; M.A. 1956, New College, Oxford; toured Paris with SP, spring 1956.

339 *Sylvan*: Sylvan Schendler (1925–); assistant professor of English, Smith College, 1956–1967; SP's colleague, 1957–1958.

 – *Bill Scott*: William Taussig Scott (1916–1999); physics professor, Smith College, 1945–1962; SP's colleague, 1957–1958.

341 *March 1*: entries for 1 March 1958 through 6 April 1958 ('chocolate rabbit & ten tiny') are written on pages 60–90 and 1–31 in the original manuscript (numbered simultaneously by SP).

345 *millionairess*: Anna B. Eldon; resident of 345 Elm Street, Northampton, Massachusetts; SP's neighbor.

 – *Dave Clarke*: TH's colleague David Ridgley Clark (1920–); English professor, University of Massachusetts (Amherst campus), 1951–1985; married to Mary Matthieu Clark. SP attended a poetry reading by Clark, TH, and two other members of the English department on 4 March 1958 in the Norfolk Room of the student union at the university.

347 *Ann*: American writer Ann Birstein (1927–); second wife of Alfred Kazin, SP's creative writing instructor at Smith College.

351 *Miss Schnieders*: Marie Schnieders (1906–1973); German professor, Smith College, 1937–1971; 1954 class dean; SP's colleague, 1957–1958.

 – *Reinhart Lettau*: Reinhard Adolf Lettau (1929–1996); associate professor of German, Smith College, 1957–1967; SP's colleague, 1957–1958.

352 *Peter Viereck*: American poet Peter Robert Edwin Viereck (1916–); assistant professor of history, Smith College, 1947–1948; history professor, Mount Holyoke College, 1948–1987; since 1991, Russian history professor, Mount Holyoke College.

 – *George Abbe*: American poet George Bancroft Abbe (1911–). SP and TH attended Abbe's 17 March 1958 lecture 'The Poet as Novelist' at Smith College.

353 *Evelyn*: Evelyn Ann Masi (1927–); assistant professor of philosophy, Mount Holyoke College, 1956–1961.

 – *Miss Mill*: Anna Jean Mill (1892–1981); English professor, Mount Holyoke College, 1931–1966.

356 *Wrinch*: Dorothy Maud Wrinch (1894–1976); lecturer, research fellow, and visiting professor of physics, Smith College, 1941–1966.

362 *chocolate eggs, each wrapped*: Following this phrase, entries for 6 April 1958 through 11 May 1958 are written on pages 91–120 and 1–30 of the original manuscript (numbered simultaneously by SP).

365 *Al Conrad*: Alfred Haskell Conrad (1924–1970); associate professor of economics, Harvard University, 1954–1966; married to American poet Adrienne Cecile Rich.

367 *Pierson*: Carol Pierson (1932–   ); B.A. 1954, Smith College; SP's friend and fellow resident of Haven House, 1950–1952.

368 *Peter Davison*: American poet Peter Hubert Davison (1928–   ); assistant editor at Harcourt, Brace & Co., 1953–1955; assistant to the director at Harvard University Press, 1955–1956; editor at the Atlantic Monthly Press, 1956–1985; dated SP in 1955. Davison married SP's Smith housemate Jane Truslow in 1959 and fathered Edward Angus and Lesley Truslow.

375 *Spanish Gordon*: probably Manuel E. Durán (1925–   ); associate professor of Spanish, Smith College, 1953–1960; SP's colleague, 1957–1958.

376 *Lee Anderson*: American poet Lee Anderson (1896–1972). Anderson recorded SP reading her poems on 18 April 1958 in Springfield, Massachusetts, for the Archive of Recorded Poetry and Literature (Library of Congress).

378 *Kay*: J. Catherine Annis Gibian (1926–1993); married to SP's colleague George Gibian (divorced 1967); mother of Peter, Mark, Stephen, Gregory, and Lauren. 'Cay' was Mrs Gibian's nickname.

 – *Denis Johnston*: Irish playwright William Denis Johnston (1901–1984); English professor, Mount Holyoke College, 1950–1962; professor of theatre and speech, Smith College, 1960–1966. SP and TH saw Johnston's 2 May 1958 production of *Finnegans Wake* in the Chapin Auditorium of Mary E. Woolley Hall at Mount Holyoke College.

379 *Robert Lowell*: American poet Robert Traill Spence Lowell, Jr (1917–1977). SP and TH attended Lowell's 6 May 1958 poetry reading at the University of Massachusetts (Amherst campus). In 1959, SP audited writing of poetry (English 306), Lowell's creative writing course at Boston University where he was lecturer on English.

 – *Esther*: Esther Tane Baskin (1926–1973); married to SP's colleague Leonard Baskin; mother of Tobias Isaac Baskin; author of *Creatures of Darkness* (Boston: Little, Brown, 1962).

 – *Marie*: Marie Edith Borroff (1923–   ); associate professor of English, Smith College, 1948–1960; SP's colleague, 1957–1958.

380 *African students scholarships*: Smith College's Relief Committee collected donations in William Allan Neilson Library, 7–14 May 1958, for the African Medical Scholarship Trust Fund to aid victims of apartheid in South Africa.

381 *May 13*: entries for 13 May 1958 through 4 July 1958 are written on pages 121–50 and 1–30 of the original manuscript (numbered simultaneously by SP).

383 *John Lehmann*: English writer and editor Rudolph John Frederick Lehmann (1907–1987); founding editor of the *London Magazine*, 1953–1961.

384 *Aunt Alice*: TH's aunt Alice Thomas Farrar; married to Walter Farrar.

387 *Jean Stafford*: American writer Jean Stafford (1915–1979); first wife of American poet Robert Lowell (divorced 1948). Lowell dedicated *Lord Weary's Castle* (1946) 'To Jean'.

388 *Chris Denney*: Christine Kingsley Denny (1934–   ); teaching fellow in theatre, Smith College, 1956–1958; M.A. 1959, Smith College.

389 *Jackie*: Jacqueline Van Voris (1922–   ); married to SP's colleague William Van Voris; mother of Alice and Richard.

399 *Thursday: July 4*: SP's 3 July 1958 entry misdated 'July 4'.

404 *Cruikshank*: William H. Cruickshank, Jr (1925–   ); SP's Wellesley neighbor. William H. Cruickshank and Dorinda Pell Cruickshank lived next door to the Plath family at 24 Elmwood Road, Wellesley, Massachusetts, with their four children: Dorinda, Pell, Blair, and Cara.

405 *June 17*: SP's 17 July 1958 entry misdated 'June 17'.

 – *Rodman*: American poet and art critic Selden Rodman (1909–   ); father of Oriana Rodman with his third wife Maja Wojciechowska. Rodman's article on Leonard Baskin, 'A Writer as Collector', was published in *Art in America* 46 (summer 1958).

414 *Mrs. Yates*: Catherine C. Yates; resident of 333 Elm Street, Northampton, Massachusetts; SP's neighbor.

415 *Oesterreich*: SP read *Possession, Demoniacal and Other* by Traugott Konstantin Oesterreich (London: Kegan Paul, Trench, Trubner & Co., 1930).

 – *seive*: SP's pen and ink drawing follows her notes on demoniac possession and is embedded within this and the following sentence in the original manuscript. Two parallel lines begin this paragraph in the original.

420 *I must write – every morning, an*: following this phrase, pages 177–78 of the original journal are missing. The text up to 'Who else in the world could I live with' (14 September 1958 entry) is transcribed from an incomplete typescript supplied by the Sylvia Plath estate.

425 *Otto Emil / Glasby-Boole / Nettleton / Mrs. Whorley / Mrs. Groobey*: SP bracketed these five names.

JOURNAL 12 December 1958 – 15 November 1959

Typescript on verso of pink Smith College memorandum paper with autograph manuscript corrections, annotations, and drawings, 71 leaves; 27.8 × 21.8 cm. *Provenance:* When this journal was sold to Smith College in 1981, it was wrapped in acid-free tissue paper and sealed in an envelope, with the following note written on the paper envelope (in TH's autograph): 'SYLVIA PLATH / BEUTSCHER NOTES / Sealed 2nd Sept 1981 / in presence of Ted Hughes / Not to be opened until during / the lifetime of Aurelia Schober Plath and Warren Plath, S.P.'s / mother and brother. / WITNESSED BY: / R. L. Davids (signature) / Felix Pryor (signature)'. Unsealed by TH on 14 September 1998.

438 *Why don't I write a novel?*: after this question is written 'I have! August 22, 1961: THE BELL JAR' in SP's autograph.

442 *Gerta*: American poet Gerta Kennedy; editor at Houghton Mifflin Co.

– *Fassett's*: Stephen B. Fassett (1915–1980); married to Hungarian pianist Agatha Fassett; head of the Fassett Recording Studio (Boston, Massachusetts), where SP and TH recorded their poetry for the Woodberry Poetry Room at Harvard University.

– *Richard Gill*: Richard Thomas Gill (1927–   ); assistant professor and lecturer in economics at Harvard University and master of Leverett House, 1949–1971; married to Elizabeth Bjornson Gill.

444 *Jane Truslow*: Jane Auchincloss Truslow (1932–1981); B.A. 1955, Smith College; resident of Lawrence House with SP, 1952–1955. Truslow married SP's friend Peter Davison on 7 March 1959.

458 *Rosalind*: American writer Rosalind Baker Wilson (1923–   ); editor at Houghton Mifflin Co., 1949–1958, 1962–1964.

459 *Roger & Joan Stein*: Roger Breed Stein (1932–   ); graduate student at Harvard University, A.B. 1954, A. M. 1958, Ph.D. 1960; married to Joan Workman Stein (divorced 1976).

463 *Elizabeth Harkwicke*: American writer Elizabeth Bruce Hardwick (1916–   ); married to American poet Robert Lowell (divorced 1972).

– *Peter Brooks*: American poet Peter Brooks; married to ballet instructor Esther Brooks; friend of Robert Lowell.

465 *Wilbur*: American poet Richard Purdy Wilbur (1921–   ); English professor, Wesleyan University, 1957–1977. SP interviewed Wilbur for her article 'Poets on Campus' published in *Mademoiselle* 37 (August 1953).

– *Shirley*: Shirley Baldwin Norton (1931–1995); married to SP's friend Dr C. Perry Norton (divorced 1978); mother of John Christopher, Steven Arthur, Heidi, and David Allan.

468 *Joanne*: Joanne Colburn Norton (1932–   ); married to SP's friend Dr Richard Allen Norton.

– *Kunitz*: American poet Stanley Jasspon Kunitz (1905–   ); married to American artist Elise Asher (1914–   ).

469 *Ann Hopkins*: Ann Hopkins; resident of Cambridge, Massachusetts; summer resident of Martha's Vineyard; friend of Peter Davison and SP.

– *writing (which I somehow boggle at spelling)*: the word 'writing' was mistyped and corrected by SP in the original typescript.

470 *Arthur and Geraldine (Kohlenberger?)*: American writer Geraldine Warburg Kohlenberg; married to Arthur Kohlenberg; mother of Teresa and Andrew Max; later married to Dr Louis Zetzel.

– *Engel*: American novelist Monroe Engel (1921–   ); assistant professor of English and lecturer at Harvard University, 1955–1989. SP mentioned Engel's second novel *The Visions of Nicholas Solon* (1959).

475 *Ann Sexton*: American poet Anne Harvey Sexton (1928–1974). In 1959, Sexton audited Robert Lowell's poetry writing course at Boston University with SP and George Starbuck.

476 *Ingalls*: Daniel Henry Holmes Ingalls (1916–   ); assistant and associate professor, 1949–1956, Wales Professor of Sanskrit and chairman of the department of Sanskrit and Indian studies, Harvard University, 1956–1983; married to Phyllis Day Ingalls; father of Sarah, Rachel, and Daniel. SP worked part-time for Ingalls, spring 1959.

478 *Starbuck*: American poet George Edwin Starbuck (1931–1996); editor at Houghton Mifflin Co., 1958–1961; married Janice King, 25 April 1955 (divorced); father of Margaret Mary, Stephen George, and John Edward by his first wife Janice King.

483 *MK*: American writer Maxine Winokur Kumin (1925–   ).

  – *PJHH*: American poet Peter J. Henniker-Heaton; editor of the Home Forum page at the *Christian Science Monitor*, 1952–1963.

485 *Hitchen*: Rev. Herbert Hitchen (1894–1979); born in Norland, Yorkshire; pastor of the Unitarian Church of Northampton, Massachusetts, 1958–1966; collector of Irish literature.

  – *Max*: Rev. Max David Gaebler (1921–   ), minister of the First Unitarian Society of Madison, Wisconsin, 1952–1987; son of Hans Gaebler, who was a friend of Otto Plath.

489 *Frances Minturn Howard*: American poet and author Frances Minturn Hall Howard (1905–1995); great-granddaughter of Julia Ward Howe; married to Thomas Clark Howard.

492 *Dudley Fitts*: American poet, critic, and translator Dudley Fitts (1903–1968); English instructor at Phillips Academy, Andover, Massachusetts.

494 *John Holmes*: American poet John Albert Holmes (1904–1962); English professor, Tufts University, 1934–1962.

  – *Galway Kinnell*: American poet and translator Galway Kinnell (1927–   ).

497 *Emilie McLeod*: American author Emilie Warren McLeod (1926–1982); children's book editor at the Atlantic Monthly Press, 1956–1976, associate director, 1976–1982.

501 *September 16*: '22.P.' is written after this heading in an unidentified hand.

502 *Yaddo: Library*: SP's 24 September 1959 descriptions and drawings of the library at Yaddo are in her autograph.

507 *Mrs. A.*: Elizabeth Ames (1885–1977); executive director of Yaddo, 1923–1969.

  – *Miss Pardee*: Allena Pardee (d. 1947); tutor and governess of Christina Trask and Spencer Trask, Jr, until their death in 1888; companion to Katrina Trask until her death in 1922; first secretary of Yaddo.

510 *Jim Shannon*: James Shannon; buildings and grounds staff member at Yaddo.

511 *May Swenson*: American writer May Swenson (1919–1989); guest at Yaddo

from 2 November to 3 December 1959. SP read Swenson's second book of
poetry *A Cage of Spines* (1958), including 'By Morning', 'At Breakfast', and
'Almanac'.

515 *Gordon Binkerd*: American composer Gordon Ware Binkerd (1916–); music
professor, University of Illinois, 1949–1971; guest at Yaddo from 30 September
to 6 December 1959.

518 *Polly*: American poet Pauline Hanson (1910–); resident secretary of Yaddo,
1950–1975; acting director, fall 1959.

 – *Nicholas*: SP was pregnant with her daughter Frieda Rebecca Hughes (born
1 April 1960) when she wrote 'The Manor Garden'. SP's son Nicholas Farrar
Hughes was not born until 17 January 1962.

521 *M. Cowley*: American writer Malcolm Cowley (1898–1989); literary adviser at
Viking Press, 1948–1985. Cowley served on the board of Yaddo, 1958–1989.

522 *Howard*: American painter Howard Sand Rogovin (1927–); guest at Yaddo
from 2 July to 4 December 1959; served as assistant to the executive director of
Yaddo, September–December 1959.

525 *NOVEMBER 11*: entries for 11 November 1959 through 15 November 1959
are typed on white paper with three-hole punching.

526 *Ted's play*: TH's first verse play 'The House of Taurus' based upon *The Bacchae*
by Euripides.

527 *Monteith*: Charles Montgomery Monteith (1921–1995), editor and director of
Faber and Faber, 1953–1973, vice-chairman, 1974–1976, chairman, 1977–
1980; TH's editor.

APPENDIX I JOURNAL FRAGMENT 17 – 19 October 1951

Autograph manuscript on lined notebook paper, 4 leaves (6 pages); 27.9 × 21.4 cm.
SP wrote this entry while she was recovering from sinusitis at the Elizabeth Mason
Infirmary, Smith College. Another journal fragment, written by SP in March 1951,
is part of the Sylvia Plath Collection at the Lilly Library, Indiana University, in her
August 1949 – March 1951 diary, pages 32–35.

533 *HMS*: Harvard Medical School (Boston, Massachusetts).

534 *government*: introduction to politics (Government 11); *Religion*: introduction
to the study of religion (Religion 14); *art*: principles, methods and techniques of
drawing and painting (Art 210); *English lit course*: literature of the nineteenth
and twentieth centuries (English 211); *creative writing course*: practice in
various forms of writing (English 220), completed by SP, 1951–1952.

 – *two basal metabolism cases that came in for the morning*: 'two basal
metabolism cases / patients that came in for the morning' appears in the original
manuscript.

537 *Miss Gill*: Elizabeth Gill; nursing assistant at Smith College.

APPENDIX 2 BACK TO SCHOOL COMMANDMENTS

Autograph manuscript list on yellow paper, 1 leaf; 27.8 × 14 cm. SP probably
wrote this list in January 1953. *Annotated:* first three entries are crossed out;
next to commandments 1–8, SP wrote 'O.K.'; next to commandment 9, 'Well . . . /
I'm / trying'; next to *silence from Myron* in commandment 10, 'O.K.! / going / to /
Jr. / Prom!'; below the P.S., SP drew an arrow and wrote 'January 18: / I'll say!'

538 *Davis:* Robert Gorham Davis (1908–1998); English professor, Smith College,
    1943–1958. Davis taught studies in style and form (English 347), a creative
    writing course completed by SP, 1952–1953. SP also served on Honor Board
    with Davis, 1952–1953.

APPENDIX 3 JOURNAL FRAGMENTS 24 March 1953 – 9 April 1953

Typescripts, 3 leaves, torn from pocket notebooks. SP probably typed the 24 March
fragment in 1953; 15.5 × 9.6 cm, 21.5 × 13.9 cm, 12.5 × 6.2 cm.

539 *true Confession:* SP's short story 'I Lied for Love'.

APPENDIX 4 JOURNAL FRAGMENT 19 June 1953

Typescript on verso of yellow Street & Smith Publications memorandum paper, 1
leaf. 21.5 × 13.9 cm. Fragment from June 1953 when SP was guest managing editor
of *Mademoiselle* in New York. SP's annotated 1953 calendar is in the Sylvia Plath
Collection at the Lilly Library, Indiana University.

541 *All right, so the headlines blare the two of them are going to be killed:* Julius
    and Ethel Rosenberg were executed on 19 June 1953 by the United States
    government for conspiracy of espionage.

APPENDIX 5 LETTER June – July 1953

Typescript, 3 leaves; 27.8 × 21.5 cm. *Verso of leaves [2–3]:* typed drafts of 3 July
1953 letters to the director of graduate schools at Columbia University requesting
information about scholarships and graduate programs in education, journalism,
English, and psychology.

544 *Sally:* Sarah Schaffer (1933–); B.A. 1954, Smith College. During the summer
    of 1953, Sally Schaffer shared an apartment in Cambridge, Massachusetts, with
    SP's Smith classmates Jane Truslow and Marcia Brown.

APPENDIX 6 JOURNAL FRAGMENT 31 December 1955 – 1 January 1956

Typescript on lined paper with autograph manuscript corrections, 5 numbered leaves, torn from a two-hole notebook; 20.2 × 16 cm.

547 *New Year's Eve: 1956*: 'Nice: winter / Paris: spring vacation' is written in SP's autograph above the heading.

APPENDIX 7 JOURNAL 26 March 1956 – 5 April 1956

Typescript on lined paper with autograph manuscript corrections, 24 numbered leaves, torn from a two-hole notebook; 20.2 × 16 cm. SP visited TH at 18 Rugby Street in London at the beginning of her spring break.

552 *Emmet*: Emmet J. Larkin (1927–   ); B.A. 1950, New York University; M.A. 1951, Ph.D. 1957, Columbia University; graduate student at London School of Economics and Political Science, 1955–1956; author of *James Larkin: Irish Labour Leader, 1876–1947* (Boston: M.I.T. Press, 1965). In March 1956, Emmet Larkin gave SP and his British friend Janet Drake a ride to Paris.

554 *Boddy*: Michael George Boddy (1934–   ), British; B.A. 1956, M.A. 1960, English, Queens' College, Cambridge; friend of Daniel Huws.

APPENDIX 8 JOURNAL FRAGMENT 1 April 1956

Autograph manuscript on lined paper, 1 leaf, torn from a two-hole notebook; 20.2 × 16 cm. *Verso* (in SP's autograph): '2 × 550 = 1•100'

APPENDIX 9 JOURNAL FRAGMENT 16 April 1956

Autograph manuscript on lined paper, 1 leaf, torn from a two-hole notebook; 20.2 × 16 cm.

APPENDIX 10 JOURNAL 26 June 1956 – 6 March 1961

Autograph manuscript, 70 leaves, in blue paper wrappers; 21.3 × 13 cm. Each leaf is stamped with a number in black ink. Duplicate leaves with the same number are differentiated by [a] and [b] in these notes. Leaf [a] is ruled paper and leaf [b] is blank paper. Many leaves are missing. SP used this copybook to record descriptions, creative writing ideas, poems, reading notes, and drawings.
Printed cover: Challenge Duplicate Book, 100 leaves in duplicate (Feint Ref. 6565).
Inside front cover (in TH's autograph):

'Leave Benidorm   Arr.   ~~Alic~~ Valencia'
'" ~~Alicante~~ Valencia   arr   Barc.'
'" Barcelona   arr   Cerbère'

Inside front cover (in SP's autograph): 'NB – Ted – list of eccentrics at Cambridge'.

571 *Café Franco-Oriental*: SP's drawings from the Café Franco-Oriental are on leaf
10[b] of the original copybook.

574 *Into the still, sultry weather*: '~~And is come~~ / Into the still, sultry weather'
appears in the original copybook.
Until bird-racketing dawn: 'Until ~~sallow~~ bird-racketing dawn / When her
shrike-face / pecked open those locked lids, / (And ate) to eat crown, palace, all /
That all night had (kept) ~~safe~~ free her male (~~whole~~.) / And with her yellow beak /
Lie and suck / The last red-berried blood drop / from his trap ~~raw~~ heart.'
appears on the verso of leaf 17[b] of the original copybook, a draft of SP's poem
'The Shrike'.

579 *Mrs. Nellie Meehan & Clifford, Herbert (cousin)*: SP originally wrote 'Herbert
(brother)' in the original manuscript below which is the name 'Gabert'. A
fragment of lined paper filed with this copybook includes the following phrases
(in SP's autograph): '– Daffy: numb as a tree/ – I just got a postcard from
Kathleen – she's in The Arctic Circle –.' Some of these phrases appear in SP's
short story 'All the Dead Dears'.

580 *Uncle W*: TH's uncle Walter Farrar; brother of Edith Farrar Hughes.

582 *green tent of slender draped willow leaves*: 'green vault / tent of slender draped
willow leaves' appears in the original copybook.

587 *42[a]*: poem fragments are written on the verso of leaf 42[a] (in TH's autograph)
– 'A wind off Scout Rock / Wounds many a neck; / Any neck may lack /
Protection some old sock / Could provide well– / Pride prevents ~~what's ill~~ us all.
/ I mean, using a sock. / ~~Using of a sock, I mean,~~ / For swaddling the glottle. /
Inwardly, plying of the bottle, / Outwardly, from New York / ~~Come a scrap of
comfort~~ / Come / ~~Parks in New York~~ / ~~New York you walk~~ / ~~A long way from
New York~~ / ~~Warm with the fat of Xmas Pork~~ / ~~If,~~ / ~~Over the Atlantic~~ / ~~Where
waves are frantic~~ /~~And winds at their antics~~ / Over Atlantic / Waves frantic /
Winds at their antics / ~~Blow~~ / or ~~blow~~ flutter a little / Bit lighter; and what'll /
Swaddle your glottle. / Now ply the bottle.'

588 *42[b]*: SP's description of Top Withens is torn into thirds and glued onto
another sheet of paper with the word 'Howarth?' written on the inner margin
in SP's autograph.

591 *About this time*: this paragraph is bracketed and starred in the inner margin of
leaf 45[a].

592 <u>On her deathbed</u>: this paragraph is bracketed, starred, and the word 'COLD' is
printed in the inner margin of leaf 45[b].

595 *52[a]*: SP attended the second day of the obscenity trial for *Lady Chatterley's
Lover*, held on 27 October 1960 at the Old Bailey in London. Witnesses for
the defense included: Graham Goulden Hough, Dame Helen Louise Gardner,
Joan Bennett, Dame Rebecca West, John A. T. Robinson (bishop of
Woolwich), Vivian de Sola Pinto, Rev. Alfred Stephan Hopkinson, and
Richard Hoggart.

604 *Helga*: Helga Kobuszewski Huws (1931–), German; married to TH's
  Cambridge friend Daniel Huws.
  – *Pooker*: Frieda Rebecca Hughes (1960–), SP's and TH's daughter.
605 *UCH*: University College Hospital (London, England).
  – *RADA*: Royal Academy of Dramatic Art (London, England).

APPENDIX 11 JOURNAL June 1957 – June 1960

Autograph manuscript, 20 leaves, probably torn from a Challenge Triplicate Book;
20.8 × 13.8 cm. Each leaf is stamped with a number in blue ink. Triplicate leaves with
the same number are differentiated by [a], [b], [c] in these notes. Leaf [a] is ruled
paper and leaves [b] and [c] are blank paper. Many leaves are missing. The surviving
pages are torn into thirds and glued onto backing paper. SP used this copybook to
record descriptions, conversations, creative writing ideas, poems, and drawings.

616 *Trafalgar Square*: SP's description of Trafalgar Square was probably written in
  June 1960, but may have been written in June of 1961 or 1962.
617 *pediment*: verso of leaf 97[c] (in TH's autograph) – 'Frontal / Blandish / Blank
  (rob) / Blare / Blatter / Blatant / Fetor / Replica / Ampoule / Festerer / Fiat.'

APPENDIX 12 LETTER 1 October 1957

Typescript on white paper with autograph manuscript corrections, 4 numbered
pages; 21.5 × 14 cm.

620 *Miss Williams*: Edna Rees Williams (1899–1992); English professor, Smith
  College, 1930–1964; SP's colleague, 1957–1958. Williams taught freshman
  English (English 11) completed by SP, 1950–1951.

APPENDIX 13 JOURNAL FRAGMENT 5 November 1957

Typescript on white paper with autograph manuscript corrections, 2 numbered
leaves; 21.5 × 14 cm.

APPENDIX 14 HOSPITAL NOTES

Typescript on verso of pink Smith College memorandum paper, 5 numbered leaves;
27.8 × 21.8 cm. These case histories were typed in 1958 when SP worked at
Massachusetts General Hospital's adult psychiatric clinic.

624 *HOSPITAL NOTES*: '5.P.' is written after this heading in an unidentified hand.
  Surnames are omitted throughout this appendix by the editor.

Typescript on lined legal-size paper with autograph manuscript corrections, 34 pages (5 blank); 33 × 21.5 cm. SP's descriptions of her Devonshire neighbors were typed over a period of months. They are arranged thematically by the editor as SP did not indicate a specific order.

630 *NICOLA (16)*: SP typed the phrase 'on April 14, 1962.' above Nicola Tyrer's name and age. Presumably, Nicola Tyrer's sixteenth birthday was on 14 April 1962.

638 *Baskin article*: TH's introduction to *Leonard Baskin: Woodcuts and Wood-engravings* (London: RWS Galleries, 1962).

639 *John Wain*: English writer John Barrington Wain (1925–1994).

– *Marvin Kane*: American-born actor and author Marvin Kane (1929–). Kane interviewed SP in North Tawton on 10 April 1962 and again on 20 August 1962. *A World of Sound* was broadcast on 7 September 1962 by the BBC Home Service as part of a seven-programme series with the overall title *What Made You Stay?* The series was about Americans like Kane and SP who had decided to live in England. SP and Kane also read poems for the BBC Third Programme, 1960–1963.

641 *Hilda and Vicky*: TH's aunt Hilda A. Farrar (1908–); mother of TH's cousin Victoria Farrar (1938–).

663 *ROSE & PERCY KEY (68)*: '13.P.' is written after this heading in an unidentified hand.

SP and TH separated in October of 1962. In December 1962, SP moved to London with her children to a two-floor maisonette at 23 Fitzroy Road near Primrose Hill and Regent's Park. Heinemann published The Bell Jar *in London on 14 January 1963 under the pseudonym Victoria Lucas. SP committed suicide in her London apartment on 11 February 1963.*

An annotated daily calendar for 1962 (Letts Royal Office Tablet Diary, 1 January 1962 – 5 January 1963) is part of the Sylvia Plath Collection at Smith College along with letters, drafts of poems, and a final typescript of 'ARIEL and other poems by Sylvia Plath'.

I would like to thank the Hughes family, particularly Frieda and Nicholas Hughes, for giving me this opportunity to edit the journals of Sylvia Plath. It has been a labor of love. In addition, I would like to express my gratitude to Smith College, particularly Martin Antonetti, curator of rare books, and Sarah M. Pritchard who kindly gave me a seven-month leave of absence from my responsibilities in the Mortimer Rare Book Room to complete this project. I would also like to thank the chairman of Faber and Faber, Matthew Evans, as well as editors Jonathan Riley, Jane Feaver, Charles Boyle, designer Ron Costley, and publishing director Joanna Mackle for publishing the manuscript. In addition, I would like to thank editors LuAnn Walther and Diana Secker Larson at Anchor Books for their help with the American edition, along with publicity director Jennifer Marshall and production editor Barbara Richard.

A number of family, friends, and professional contacts of Sylvia Plath provided information reflected in these notes. In addition to Frieda Hughes, I would like to thank Warren Plath and his daughter Susan Plath Winston. I also appreciate the information received from Ruth Tiffany Barnhouse, Joan Maxwell Bramwell, Mr and Mrs M. Michael Cantor, Dr O. Donald Chrisman, Edward M. Cohen, Peter H. Davison, Dorothy Davy, Rev. Max D. Gaebler, Ruth Freeman Geissler, George Gibian, Anthony Hecht, Daniel Huws, Marvin Kane, Elinor Friedman Klein, Emmet J. Larkin, Ann Safford Mandel, Enid Epstein Mark, Dr Frederic B. Mayo, W.S. Merwin, Dr C. Perry Norton, Dr Richard A. Norton, Davenport Plumer III, Clarissa Roche, Marcia B. Stern, Stanley Sultan, and Constance L. Whalen.

A number of scholars contributed their insights and expertise as well. I would like to thank professors Lynda K. Bundtzen (Williams College), Frank H. Ellis (Smith College), Mary H. Laprade (Smith College), Richard Larschan (University of Massachusetts at Dartmouth), Sherry Marker (Smith College), Robin W. Peel (University of Plymouth), and Susan Van Dyne (Smith College).

My colleagues at Smith College contributed in so many ways to this publication. I would like to thank Susan Sanborn Barker and Barbara B. Blumenthal who carefully transcribed and proofed the original journals. I am indebted to the reference staff, particularly Robin Kinder, who answered the many general queries associated with this project. Specific information about alumnae and faculty at Smith College was gleaned from the college records by Mary Irwin and from the archives by Karen Eberhart and Nanci Young. I also appreciate the help of Sherrill Redmon and the entire staff of the Sophia Smith Collection, including Susan Boone, Maida Goodwin, Amy E. Hague, Margaret R. Jessup, Kathleen Banks Nutter, and Burd B. Schlessinger. Questions about specific disciplines were answered by librarians Rocco Piccinino, Jr (science), Barbara Polowy (art) and Marlene Wong (music). In addition, I would like to thank Christina M. Ryan and Naomi C. Sturtevant for their interlibrary loan services, college photographer Marlene Znoy, and student assistant Margaret S. Chilton.

Archivists, librarians, and curators at other institutions provided valuable information as well. I would particularly like to thank Dr Elisabeth Leedham-Green, deputy keeper at Cambridge University, Anne Thomson at Newnham College, and Philip Moss at Oxford University. Archivists at American universities who deserve special thanks include Brian A. Sullivan and David A. Ware at Harvard University; John S. Weeren at Princeton University; and Diane E. Kaplan, William R. Massa, Jr, Danelle Moon, and Christine Weideman at Yale University. Five-college colleagues who were especially helpful include Daria D'Arienzo (Amherst College), Patricia Albright (Mount Holyoke College), Linda Seidman and Ute Bargmann (University of Massachusetts, Amherst), I appreciate the generosity of Saundra Taylor, Rebecca Cape, and the entire staff of the Lilly Library at Indiana University during my visit to their Sylvia Plath Collection. Information was also kindly provided by Annie Armour (University of the South), Alison Brown (Northeastern University), Sylvia Kennick Brown (Williams College), Kim Ehritt (Middlebury College), Stephen Enniss (Emory University), Megan Flynn (Wellesley Free Library), Ronna Frick (Wellesley High School), Anna M. Grant (Bishop's University, Quebec), Gretchen Koerpel (Rensselaer Polytechnic Institute), Kathy Kraft (Radcliffe College), Lesley M. Leduc (Yaddo), Martha Magane (Eastham Library), Leigh Montgomery (*The Christian Science Monitor*), Anne M. Ostendarp and Amber L. Ruggles (Dartmouth University), William Roberts (University of California, Berkeley), R.C. Rybnikar (Babson College), Susan Searcy (University of Nevada, Reno), Jay Satterfield (University of Chicago), T. Michael Womack (Library of Congress), and Mylinda S. Woodward (University of New Hampshire). In addition, I appreciate the contributions of Peter Brooks, Robert Meeropol, Philip H. Ryder, and Peter K. Steinberg.

Finally, I would like to thank my friend, Janet Snow Ritchie, for copyediting my notes, my husband, Bohdan Kukil, for helping me with his humor and wit to maintain a healthy perspective during this project, my acupuncturist, Dr Jonathan S. Klate, for keeping me healthy, and Dianne Hunter, my English professor at Trinity College, who first introduced me to the powerful words of Sylvia Plath.

Karen Valuckas Kukil
July 28, 1999

INDEX

This is an index to *The Unabridged Journals of Sylvia Plath, 1950–1962*, including the appendices and notes. It does not include references to the introductory material. Significant people, places, and subjects are indexed. Whenever possible, correct spellings appear in the index. Proper names have been verified against library authority records. Maiden names are generally preferred for female classmates of Sylvia Plath. Nicknames and other identifiers are occasionally included in parentheses. Important artistic, cultural, literary, and musical influences are indexed. Literary works are listed by their published titles under individual authors, and include references to specific quotations mentioned by Plath. (Cross-references for quotations are supplied as needed.) Motion pictures appear by title. Famous people and subjects relevant to the study of American and British popular culture of the 1950s and early 1960s are included, as well as a few select images important to Sylvia Plath's work. Plath's poetry and prose are indexed by titles or first lines under Sylvia Plath (works) and include notes and plot summaries, drafts, and references to specific published and unpublished works. References to the process of writing fiction are grouped under Creative writing. A variety of subheadings are arranged under Sylvia Plath that refer to her physical appearance, personality, and health. The following abbreviations are used: SP (Sylvia Plath); TH (Ted Hughes); FL (first line).

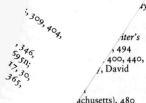